4944

D0908856

MASTERWORKS
OF
CHILDREN'S
LITERATURE

MASTERWORKS
OF
CHILDREN'S
LITERATURE

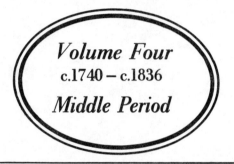

Volume Four
c.1740 – c.1836
Middle Period

EDITED BY *Robert Bator*

GENERAL EDITOR: *Jonathan Cott*

THE STONEHILL PUBLISHING COMPANY
IN ASSOCIATION WITH
CHELSEA HOUSE PUBLISHERS
NEW YORK

GENERAL EDITOR: Jonathan Cott
ADVISORY EDITOR: Robert G. Miner, Jr.
VOLUME EDITOR: Robert Bator
PROJECT DIRECTOR: Esther Mitgang
DESIGNER: Paul Bacon
EDITORIAL STAFF: Joy Johannessen, Philip Minges III, Claire Bottler
PRODUCTION: Coco Dupuy, Heather White, Sandra Su, Susan Lusk, Christopher Newton

First Printing
Printed and Bound in the United States of America
ISBN: 0-87754-378-X
LC: 79-89986

Chelsea House Publishers
    Harold Steinberg, Chairman and Publisher
    Andrew E. Norman, President
    Susan Lusk, Vice President
A Division of Chelsea House Educational Communications, Inc.,
133 Christopher Street, New York, NY 10014.

Contents

John Aikin and Anna Laetitia Aikin Barbauld:
    Evenings at Home (SELECTIONS) 1

Elizabeth Pinchard: *Dramatic Dialogues* (VOLUME I) 45

Maria Edgeworth: *The Parent's Assistant* (SELECTIONS) 109

Edward Augustus Kendall: *Keeper's Travels in Search of His Master* 189

Ann and Jane Taylor: *Rhymes for the Nursery* 227

William Roscoe: *The Butterfly's Ball*
    Catherine Ann Dorset: *The Peacock at Home* 261

Charles and Mary Lamb: *Mrs. Leicester's School* 279

"Arabella Argus": *The Juvenile Spectator* (VOLUME I) 331

Charles Lamb: *Prince Dorus* 425

Martha Butt Sherwood: *The History of Little Henry and His Bearer* 439

A Select Bibliography of Secondary Works 463

11

Evenings at Home, or, The Juvenile Budget Opened

By JOHN AIKIN and ANNA LAETITIA AIKIN BARBAULD

SELECTIONS

EVENINGS AT HOME,

OR, THE

JUVENILE BUDGET OPENED:

BY

DR. AIKIN AND MRS. BARBAULD.

FIFTEENTH EDITION,

THE WHOLE CAREFULLY REVISED, CORRECTED THROUGHOUT, AND NEWLY
ARRANGED BY

ARTHUR AIKIN, ESQ. F.L.S. &c., AND MISS AIKIN,

WITH SOME ADDITIONAL PIECES BY THE AUTHORS.

ILLUSTRATED WITH FINE ENGRAVINGS AFTER
HARVEY.

LONDON:

PRINTED FOR BALDWIN AND CRADOCK;

LONGMAN, REES, AND CO.; JOHN MURRAY; JOSEPH BOOKER; DARTON AND
HARVEY; HAMILTON, ADAMS, AND CO.; SMITH, ELDER, AND CO.;
AND SIMPKIN, MARSHALL, AND CO.

1836.

J OHN AIKIN *(1747–1822) was the brother of Anna Laetitia Aikin Barbauld, with whom he collaborated on* Evenings at Home— *"a collection of very pretty tales to awaken the growing mind to enquiry and the use of its reasoning powers, and to inspire it with sentiments of humanity, virtue and piety"* (Monthly Review, *November 1793). Originally written for Aikin's two youngest children, Lucy and Edmund, it contains "thirty-one evenings" of dialogues, tales, natural science, and poetry in six volumes (1792–1796) arranged, as John Aikin admits in the original preface, in a "promiscuous order" that the authors think "will prove more agreeable than a methodical arrangement." Mrs. Barbauld was responsible for fourteen of the original ninety-nine selections, about a half-volume of the original six.*

The Aikin-Barbauld compilation had its fifteenth edition in 1836 and was still in print in 1899. Individual selections were often anthologized. "Eyes and no Eyes" is the best-known tale. A masterful detective story, "The Trial," was reprinted by E. V. Lucas in Old Fashioned Tales *(1905). It was meant by Aikin to be a sequel to Richard Johnson's* Juvenile Trials *(1772). While pacifism permeates many of the selections, especially "Things by their Right Names," there is no sectarian evangelizing in* Evenings at Home. *The Edgeworths in* Practical Education *(1798) found it "the best book for children of seven to ten that has appeared."*

Too long to be reprinted in its entirety, Evenings at Home *is represented by selections from the fifteenth (1836) edition rearranged by Lucy and Arthur Aikin, children of John Aikin, who added one additional tale by Mrs. Barbauld. The text substantially agrees with the original edition. Some of the "evenings" have been omitted, and those that appear are not complete. Unless otherwise noted, the selections are by John Aikin.*

Introduction.

THE MANSION-HOUSE of the pleasant village of *Beechgrove* was inhabited by the family of FAIRBORNE, consisting of the master and mistress, and a numerous progeny of children of both sexes. Of these, part were educated at home under their parents' care, and part were sent out to school. The house was seldom unprovided with visiters, the intimate friends or relations of the owners, who were entertained with cheerfulness and hospitality, free from ceremony and parade. They formed, during their stay, part of the family; and were ready to concur with Mr. and Mrs. Fairborne in any little domestic plan for varying their amusements, and particularly for promoting the instruction and entertainment of the younger part of the household. As some of them were accustomed to writing, they would frequently produce a fable, a story, or dialogue, adapted to the age and understanding of the young people. It was always considered as a high favour when they would so employ themselves; and when the pieces were once read over, they were carefully deposited by Mrs. Fairborne in a box, of which she kept the key. None of these were allowed to be taken out again till all the children were assembled in the holidays. It was then made one of the evening amusements of the family to *rummage the budget,* as their phrase was. One of the least children was sent to the box, who putting in its little hand, drew out the paper that came next, and brought it into the parlour. This was then read distinctly by one of the older ones; and after it had undergone sufficient consideration, another little messenger was dispatched for a fresh supply; and so on, till as much time had been spent in this manner as the parents thought proper. Other children were admitted to these readings; and as the *Budget of Beechgrove Hall* became somewhat celebrated in the neighbourhood, its proprietors were at length urged to lay it open to the public. They were induced to comply; and thus, without further preface, begins the 'First Evening.'

First Evening

The Flying Fish.

[Mrs. Barbauld]

T HE FLYING FISH, says the fable, had originally no wings, but being of an ambitious and discontented temper, she repined at being always confined to the waters, and wished to soar in the air. "If I could fly like the birds," said she, "I should not only see more of the beauties of nature, but I should be able to escape from those fish which are continually pursuing me, and which render my life miserable." She therefore petitioned Jupiter for a pair of wings; and immediately she perceived her fins to expand. They suddenly grew to the length of her whole body, and became at the same time so strong as to do the office of a pinion. She was at first much pleased with her new powers, and looked with an air of disdain on all her former companions; but she soon perceived herself exposed to new dangers. When flying in the air, she was incessantly pursued by the Tropic Bird and the Albatross; and when for safety she dropped into the water, she was so fatigued with her flight, that she was less able than ever to escape from her old enemies the fish. Finding herself more unhappy than before, she now begged of Jupiter to recall his present; but Jupiter said to her, "When I gave you your wings, I well knew they would prove a curse; but your proud and restless disposition deserved this disappointment. Now, therefore, what you begged as a favour, keep as a punishment!"

Travellers' Wonders.

O NE WINTER'S EVENING as *Captain Compass* was sitting by the fireside with his children all around him, little Jack said to him, "Papa, pray tell us some stories about what you have seen in your voyages. I have been vastly entertained, whilst you were abroad, with Gulliver's Travels, and the adventures of Sinbad the Sailor; and I think, as you have gone round and round the world, you must have met with things as wonderful as they did."—"No, my dear," said the Captain, "I never met with Lilliputians or Brobdignagians, I assure you, nor ever saw the black loadstone mountain, or the valley of diamonds; but, to be sure, I have seen a great variety of people, and their different manners and ways of living; and if it will be any entertainment to you, I will tell you some curious particulars of what I observed."—"Pray do, Papa," cried Jack and all his brothers and sisters: so they drew close round him, and he began as follows:—

"Well then—I was once, about this time of the year, in a country where it was very cold, and the poor inhabitants had much ado to keep themselves from starving. They were clad partly in the skins of beasts, made smooth and soft by a particular art, but chiefly in garments made from the outward covering of a middle-sized quadruped, which they were so cruel as to strip off his back while he was alive. They dwelt in habitations, part of which was sunk underground. The materials were either stones, or earth hardened by fire; and so violent in that country were the storms of wind and rain, that many of them covered their roofs all over with stones. The walls of their houses had holes to let in the light: but to prevent the cold air and wet from coming in, they were covered by a sort of transparent stone, made artifically of melted sand or flints. As wood was rather scarce, I know not what they would have done for firing, had they not discovered in the bowels of the earth a very extraordinary kind of stone, which when put among burning wood, caught fire and flamed like a torch."

"Dear me," said Jack, "what a wonderful stone! I suppose it was somewhat like what we call fire-stones, that shine so when we rub them together."—"I don't think they would burn," replied the Captain; "besides, these are of a darker colour.

"Well—but their diet too was remarkable. Some of them ate fish that had been hung up in the smoke till they were quite dry and hard; and along with it they ate either the roots of plants, or a sort of coarse black cake made of powdered seeds. These were the poorer class; the richer had a whiter kind of cake, which they were fond of daubing over with a greasy matter that was the product of a large animal among them. This grease they used, too, in almost all their dishes, and, when fresh, it really was not unpalatable. They likewise devoured the flesh of many birds and beasts when they could get it; and ate the leaves and other parts of a variety of vegetables growing in the country, some absolutely raw, others variously prepared by the aid of fire. Another great article of food was the curd of milk, pressed into a hard mass and salted. This had so rank a smell, that persons of weak stomachs often could not bear to come near it. For drink, they made great use of the water in which certain dry leaves had been steeped. These leaves, I was told, came from a great distance. They had likewise a method of preparing a liquor of the seeds of a grass-like plant steeped in water with the addition of a bitter herb, and then set to work or ferment. I was prevailed upon to taste it, and thought it at first nauseous enough, but in time I liked it pretty well. When a large quantity of the ingredients is used, it becomes perfectly intoxicating. But what astonished me most, was their use of a liquor so excessively hot and pungent, that it seems like liquid fire. I once got a mouthful of it by mistake, taking it for water, which it resembles in appearance, but I thought it would instantly have taken away my breath. Indeed, people are not unfrequently killed by it; and yet many of them swallow it greedily whenever they can get it. This, too, is said to be prepared from the seeds above-mentioned, which are innocent and even salutary in their natural state, though made to yield such a pernicious juice. The strangest custom that I believe prevails in any nation I found here, which was, that some take a mighty pleasure in filling their mouths full of stinking smoke; and others, in thrusting a nasty powder up their nostrils."

"I should think it would choke them," said Jack. "It almost did me," answered his father, "only to stand by while they did it—but use, it is truly said, is second nature.

"I was glad enough to leave this cold climate; and about half a year after, I fell in with a people enjoying a delicious temperature of air, and a country full of beauty and verdure. The trees and shrubs were furnished with a great variety of fruits, which, with other vegetable products, constituted a large part of the food of the inhabitants. I particularly relished certain berries growing in bunches, some white and some red, of a very pleasant sourish taste, and so transparent, that one might see the seeds at their very centre. Here were whole fields full of extremely odoriferous flowers, which they told me were succeeded by pods bearing seeds, that afforded good nourishment to man and beast. A great variety of birds enlivened the groves and woods; among which I was entertained with one, that without any teaching spoke almost as articulately as a parrot, though indeed it was only the repetition of a single word. The people were tolerably gentle and civilized, and possessed many of the arts of life. Their dress was very various. Many were clad only in a thin cloth made of the long fibres of the stalk of a plant cultivated for the purpose, which they prepared by soaking in water, and then beating with large mallets. Others wore cloth woven from a sort of vegetable wool, growing in pods upon bushes. But the most singular material was a fine glossy stuff, used chiefly by the richer classes, which, as I was credibly informed, is manufactured out of the webs of caterpillars—a most wonderful circumstance, if we consider the immense number of caterpillars necessary to the production of so large a quantity of stuff as I saw used. This people are very fantastic in their dress, especially the women, whose apparel consists of a great number of articles impossible to be described, and strangely disguising the natural form of the body. In some instances they seem very cleanly; but in others, the Hottentots can scarce go beyond them; particularly in the management of their hair, which is all matted and stiffened with the fat of swine and other animals, mixed up with powders of various colours and ingredients. Like most Indian nations, they use feathers in their head-dress. One thing surprised me much, which was, that they bring up in their houses an animal of the tiger kind, with formidable teeth and claws, which, notwithstanding its natural ferocity, is played with and caressed by the most timid and delicate of their women."

"I am sure I would not play with it," said Jack. "Why, you might chance to get an ugly scratch if you did," said the Captain.

"The language of this nation seems very harsh and unintelligible to a foreigner, yet they converse among one another with great ease and quickness. One of the oddest customs is that which men use on saluting each other. Let the weather be what it will, they uncover their heads, and remain uncovered for some time, if they mean to be extraordinarily respectful."

"Why that's like pulling off our hats," said Jack.— "Ah, ah! papa," cried Betsy, "I have found you out. You have been telling us of our own country, and what is done at home, all this while!"—"But," said Jack, "we don't burn stones or eat grease and powdered seeds, or wear skins and caterpillars' webs, or play with tigers."—"No?" said the Captain— "pray what are coals but stones? and is not butter, grease; and corn, seeds; and leather, skins; and silk, the web of a kind of caterpillar? And may we not as well call a cat an animal of the tiger-kind, as a tiger an animal of the cat-kind? So, if you recollect what I have been describing, you will find, with Betsy's help, that all the other wonderful things I have told you of are matters familiar among ourselves. But I meant to show you, that a foreigner might easily represent everything as equally strange and wonderful among us as we could do with respect to his country; and also to make you sensible that we daily call a great many things by their names, without ever inquiring into their nature and properties; so that, in reality, it is only their names, and not the things themselves, with which we are acquainted."

Second Evening

The Price of Pleasure.

"I THINK I will take a ride," said the little *Lord Linger*, after breakfast; "bring me my boots, and let my horse be brought to the door."

The horse was saddled, and his lordship's spurs were putting on.

"No," said he, "I'll have my low chair and the ponies, and take a drive round the park."

The horse was led back, and the ponies were almost harnessed, when his lordship sent his valet to countermand them. He would walk into the corn field, and see how the new pointer hunted.

"After all," says he, "I think I will stay at home, and play a game or two at billiards."

He played half a game, but could not make a stroke to please himself. His tutor, who was present, now thought it a good opportunity to ask his lordship if he would read a little.

"Why—I think—I will; for I am tired of doing nothing. What shall we have?"

"Your lordship left off last time in one of the finest passages of the Æneid. Suppose we finish it?"

"Well—ay; but—no—I had rather go on with Hume's history. Or—suppose we do some geography?"

"With all my heart. The globes are upon the study table."

They went to the study; and the little lord, leaning upon his elbows, looked at the globe—then twirled it round two or three times—and then listened patiently while the tutor explained some of its parts and uses. But whilst he was in the midst of a problem, "Come," said his lordship, "now for a little Virgil."

The book was brought; and the pupil, with a good deal of help, got through twenty lines.

"Well," said he, ringing the bell, "I think we have done a good deal. Tom! bring my bow and arrows."

The fine London-made bow, in its green case, and the quiver with all its appurtenances, were brought, and his lordship went down to the place where the shooting butts were erected. He aimed a few shafts at the target, but not coming near it, he shot all the remainder at random, and then ordered out his horse.

He sauntered, with a servant at his heels, for a mile or two through the lanes, and came, just as the clock struck twelve, to a village green, close by which a school was kept. A door flew open, and out burst a shoal of boys, who, spreading over the green, with immoderate vociferation, instantly began a variety of sports. Some fell to marbles, some to trap-ball, some to leap-frog. In short, not one of the whole crew but was eagerly employed. Every thing was noise, motion, and pleasure. Lord Linger, riding slowly up, espied one of his tenant's sons, who had been formerly admitted as a playfellow of his, and called him from the throng.

"Jack," said he, "how do you like school?"

"O, pretty well, my lord."

"What—have you a good deal of play?"

"O no! We have only from twelve to two for playing and eating our dinners; and then an hour before supper."

"That is very little indeed!"

"But *we play heartily when we do play, and work when we work.* Good bye, my lord! It is my turn to go in at trap!"

So saying, Jack ran off.

"I wish I was a school-boy!" cried the little lord to himself.

Third Evening

Order and Disorder,—A Fairy Tale.

JULIET WAS A CLEVER, well-disposed girl, but apt to be heedless. She could learn her lessons very well, but commonly as much time was taken up in getting her things together as in doing what she was set about. If she was to work, there was generally the housewife to seek in one place, and the thread-papers in another. The scissors were left in her pocket upstairs, and the thimble was rolling about the floor. In writing, the copy-book was generally missing, the ink dried up, and the pens, new and old, all tumbled about the cupboard. The slate and slate-pencil were never found together. In making her exercises, the English dictionary always came to hand instead of the French grammar; and when she was to read a chapter, she usually got hold of Robinson Crusoe, or the World Displayed, instead of the Testament.

Juliet's mamma was almost tired of teaching her, so she sent her to make a visit to an old lady in the country, a very good woman, but rather strict with young folks. Here she was shut up in a room above stairs by herself after breakfast every day, till she had quite finished the tasks set her. This house was one of the very few that are still haunted by fairies. One of these, whose name was *Disorder*, took a pleasure in plaguing poor Juliet. She was a frightful figure to look at, being crooked and squint-eyed, with her hair hanging about her face, and her dress put on all awry, and full of rents and tatters. She prevailed on the old lady to let her set Juliet her tasks; so one morning she came up with a work-bag full of threads of silk of all sorts of colours, mixed and entangled together, and a flower very nicely worked to copy. It was a pansy, and the gradual melting of its hues into one another was imitated with great accuracy and beauty. "Here, Miss," said she, "my mistress has sent you a piece of work to do, and she insists upon having it done before you come down to dinner. You will find all the materials in this bag."

Juliet took the flower and the bag, and turned out all the silks upon the table. She slowly pulled out a red and a purple, and a blue and a yellow, and at length fixed upon one to begin working with. After taking two or three stitches, and looking at her model, she found another shade was wanted. This was to be hunted out from the bunch, and a long while it took her to find it. It was soon necessary to change it for another. Juliet saw that, in going on at this rate, it would take days instead of hours to work the flower, so she laid down the needle and fell a crying. After this had continued some time, she was startled at the sound of some[one] stamping on the floor; and taking her handkerchief from her eyes, she spied a diminutive female figure advancing towards her. She was as upright as an arrow, and had not so much as a hair out of its place, or the least article of her dress rumpled or discomposed. When she came up to Juliet, "My dear," said she, "I heard you crying, and knowing you to be a good girl in the main, I am come to your assistance. My name is *Order:* your mamma is well acquainted with me, though this is the first time you ever saw me; but I hope we shall know one another better for the future." She then jumped upon the table, and with a wand gave a tap upon the heap of entangled silk. Immediately the threads separated, and arranged themselves in a long row consisting of little skeins, in which all of the same colour were collected together, those approaching nearest in shade being placed next each other. This done, she disappeared. Juliet, as soon as her surprise was over, resumed her work, and found it go on with ease and pleasure. She finished the flower by dinner-time, and obtained great praise for the neatness of the execution.

The next day the ill-natured fairy came up, with a great book under her arm. "This," said she, "is my mistress's house-book, and she says you must draw out against dinner an exact account of what it has cost her last year in all the articles of house-keeping, including clothes, rent, taxes, wages, and the like. You must state separately the amount of every article, under the heads of baker, butcher, milliner, shoemaker, and so forth, taking special care not to miss a single thing entered down in the book. Here is a quire of paper, and a parcel of pens." So saying, with a malicious grin, she left her.

Juli[et] turned pale at the very thought of the task she had to perform. She opened the great book, and saw all the pages closely written, but in the most confused manner possible. Here was, "Paid Mr. Crusty for a week's bread and baking," so much. Then, "Paid Mr. Pinchtoe for shoes," so much. "Paid half a year's rent," so much. Then came a butcher's bill, succeeded by a milliner's, and that by a tallow-chandler's. "What shall I do?" cried poor Juliet—"where am I to begin, and how can I possibly pick out all these things? Was ever such a tedious, perplexing task? O that my good little creature were here again with her wand!"

She had but just uttered these words when the fairy Order stood before her. "Don't be startled, my dear," said she; "I knew your wish, and made haste to comply with it. Let me see your book." She turned over a few leaves, and then cried, "I see my cross-grained sister has played you a trick. She has brought you the *day-book* instead of the *ledger;* but I will set the matter to rights instantly." She vanished, and presently returned with another book, in which she showed Juliet every one of the articles required, standing at the tops of the pages, and all the particulars entered under them from the day-book; so that there was nothing for her to do but cast up the sums, and copy out the heads with their amount in single lines. As Juliet was a ready accountant, she was not long in finishing the business, and produced her account neatly written on one sheet of paper, at dinner.

The next day, Juliet's tormentor brought her up a large box full of letters stamped upon small bits of ivory, capitals and common letters of all sorts, but jumbled together promiscuously, as if they had been shaken in a bag. "Now, Miss," said she, "before you come down to dinner, you must exactly copy out this poem in these ivory letters, placing them line by line on the floor of your room."

Juliet thought at first that this task would be pretty sport enough; but when she set about it, she found such trouble in hunting out the letters she wanted, every one seeming to come to hand before the right one, that she proceeded very slowly; and the poem being a long one, it was plain that night would come before it was finished. Sitting down, and crying for her kind friend, was therefore her only resource.

Order was not far distant, for, indeed, she had been watching her proceedings all the while. She made herself visible, and giving a tap on the letters with her wand, they immediately arranged themselves alphabetically in little double heaps, the small in one, and the great in the other. After this operation, Juliet's task went on with such expedition, that she called up the old lady an hour before dinner, to be witness to its completion.

The good lady kissed her, and told her, that as she hoped she was now made fully sensible of the benefits of order, and the inconveniences of disorder, she would not confine her any longer to work by herself at set tasks, but she should come and sit with her. Juliet took such pains to please her, by doing everything with the greatest neatness and regularity, and reforming all her careless habits, that when she was sent back to her mother, the following presents were made her, constantly to remind her of the beauty and advantage of order.

A cabinet of English coins, in which all the gold and silver money of our kings was arranged in the order of their reigns.

A set of plaster casts of the Roman emperors.

A cabinet of beautiful shells, displayed according to the most approved system.

A very complete box of water-colours, and another of crayons, sorted in all the shades of the primary colours.

And a very nice housewife, with all the implements belonging to a sempstress, and a good store of the best needles in sizes.

Eighth Evening

Things by their Right Names.

[Mrs. Barbauld]

CHARLES.

PAPA, you grow very lazy. Last winter you used to tell us stories, and now you never tell us any; and we are all got round the fire quite ready to hear you. Pray, dear papa, let us have a very pretty one.

FATHER.

With all my heart—What shall it be?

CHARLES.

A bloody murder, papa!

FATHER.

A bloody murder! Well then—once upon a time, some men dressed all alike. . . .

CHARLES.

With black crapes over their faces?

FATHER.

No; they had steel caps on:—having crossed a dark heath, wound cautiously along the skirts of a deep forest. . . . .

CHARLES.

They were ill-looking fellows, I dare say?

FATHER.

I cannot say so; on the contrary, they were as tall, personable men as most one shall see:—leaving on their right hand an old ruined tower on the hill. . . .

CHARLES.

At midnight, just as the clock struck twelve; was it not, papa?

FATHER.

No, really; it was on a fine balmy summer's morning;—they moved forwards, one behind another. . .

CHARLES.

As still as death, creeping along under the hedges?

FATHER.

On the contrary—they walked remarkably upright; and so far from endeavouring to be hushed and still, they made a loud noise as they came along, with several sorts of instruments.

CHARLES.

But, papa, they would be found out immediately.

FATHER.

They did not seem to wish to conceal themselves: on the contrary, they gloried in what they were about. They moved forwards, I say, to a large plain, where stood a neat pretty village which they set on fire.

CHARLES.

Set a village on fire, wicked wretches!

FATHER.

And while it was burning they murdered—twenty thousand men.

CHARLES.

O fie! papa! You don't intend I should believe this; I thought all along you were making up a tale, as you often do; but you shall not catch me this time. What! they lay still, I suppose, and let these fellows cut their throats?

FATHER.

No, truly, they resisted as long as they could.

CHARLES.

How should these men kill twenty thousand people, pray?

FATHER.

Why not? the *murderers* were thirty thousand.

CHARLES.

O, now I have found you out! you mean a BATTLE.

FATHER.

Indeed I do. I do not know any *murders* half so bloody.

Thirteenth Evening

Tit for Tat,—A Tale.

A LAW there is of ancient fame,
  By Nature's self in every land implanted,
Lex Talionis is its Latin name;
  But if an English term be wanted,
Give your next neighbour but a pat,
He'll give you back as good, and tell
    you—*tit for tat*.

This *tit for tat*, it seems, not men alone,
But elephants, for legal justice own;

In proof of this a story I shall tell ye,
Imported from the famous town of
    Delhi.

A mighty elephant that swell'd the state
    Of Aurengzebe the Great,
  One day was taken by his driver,
  To drink and cool him in the river;
The driver on his neck was seated,
    And, as he rode along,
  By some acquaintance in the throng
With a ripe cocoa-nut was treated.

A cocoa-nut's a pretty fruit enough,
But guarded by a shell, both hard and
    tough.
    The fellow tried, and tried, and tried,
      Working and sweating,
      Pishing and fretting,
    To find out its inside,
And pick the kernel for his eating.

At length, quite out of patience grown,
"Who'll reach me up," he cries, "a stone
    To break this plaguy shell?
    But stay, I've here a solid bone
      May do perhaps as well."
So half in earnest, half in jest,
He bang'd it on the forehead of his
    beast.

An elephant, they say, has human
    feeling,
    And full as well as we he knows
    The difference between words and
      blows,
Between horse-play and civil dealing.
    Use him but well, he'll do his best,
And serve you faithfully and truly;
    But insults unprovoked he can't
      digest,
He studies o'er them, and repays them
    duly.

"To make my head an anvil, (thought
    the creature,)
Was never, certainly, the will of
    Nature;
    So, master mine! you may repent:"
Then, shaking his broad ears, away he
    went:
    The driver took him to the water,

    And thought no more about the
      matter;
But Elephant within his memory hid
    it;
He *felt* the wrong,—the other only *did*
    it.

A week or two elapsed, one market
    day
Again the beast and driver took
    their way;
Through rows of shops and booths
    they pass'd
With eatables and trinkets stored,
    Till to a gard'ner's stall they came at
    last.
Where cocoa-nuts lay piled upon the
    board,—
    "Ha!" thought the elephant, "'tis
    now my turn
To show this method of nut-breaking;
    My friend above will like to learn,
Though at the cost of a head-aching."

Then in his curling trunk he took a
    heap,
And waved it o'er his neck a sudden
    sweep,
    And on the hapless driver's sconce
      He laid a blow so hard and full,
    That crack'd the nuts at once,
      But with them crack'd his skull.

    Young folks, whene'er you feel
    inclined
To rompish sports and freedoms rough,
    Bear *tit for tat* in mind,
Nor give an elephant a cuff,
    To be repaid in kind.

On Wine and Spirits.

GEORGE AND HARRY, accompanied by their tutor, went one day to pay a visit to a neighbouring gentleman, their father's friend. They were very kindly received, and shown all about the gardens and pleasure-grounds; but nothing took their fancy so much as an extensive grapery, hung round with bunches of various kinds fully ripe, and almost too big for the vines to support. They were liberally treated with the fruit, and carried away some bunches to eat as they walked. During their return, as they were picking their grapes, George said to the Tutor, "A thought is just come into my head, Sir. Wine, you know, is called the juice of the grape; but wine is hot, and intoxicates people that drink much of it. Now we have had a good deal of grape-juice this morning, and yet I do not feel heated, nor does it seem at all to have got into our heads. What is the reason of this?"

TUTOR.

The reason is, that grape-juice is not wine, though wine is made from it.

GEORGE. Pray how is it made then?

TUTOR.

I will tell you; for it is a matter worth knowing. The juice pressed from the grapes, called *must*, is at first a sweet watery liquor, with a little tartness, but with no strength or spirit. After it has stood awhile, it begins to grow thick and muddy, it moves up and down, and throws scum and bubbles of air to the surface. This is called *working* or *fermenting*. It continues in this state for some time, more or less, according to the quantity of the juice and the temperature of the weather, and then gradually settles again, becoming clearer than at first. It has now lost its sweet flat taste, and acquired a briskness and pungency, with a heating and intoxicating property; that is, it has become *wine*. This natural process is called the *vinous fermentation,* and many liquors besides grape-juice are capable of undergoing it.

GEORGE.

I have heard of the working of beer and ale. Is that of the same kind?

TUTOR.

It is; and beer and ale may properly be called barley-wine; for you know they are clear, brisk, and intoxicating. In the same manner, cider is apple-wine, and mead is honey-wine; and you have heard of raisin and currant-wine, and a great many others.

HARRY.

Yes, there is elder-wine, and cowslip-wine, and orange-wine.

GEORGE.

Will everything of that sort make wine?

TUTOR.

All vegetable juices that are sweet are capable of fermenting, and of producing a liquor of a vinous nature; but if they have little sweetness, the liquor is proportionally weak and poor, and is apt to become sour or vapid.

HARRY.

But barley is not sweet.

TUTOR.

Barley as it comes from the ear is not; but before it is used for brewing, it is made into *malt*, and then it is sensibly sweet. You know what malt is?

HARRY.

I have seen heaps of it in the malt-house, but I do not know how it is made.

TUTOR.

Barley is made malt by putting it in heaps and wetting it, when it becomes hot, and swells, and would sprout out just as if it were sown, unless it were then dried in a kiln.

By this operation it acquires a sweet taste. You have drunk sweet-wort?

HARRY.

Yes.

TUTOR.

Well, this is made by steeping malt in hot water. The water extracts and dissolves all the sweet or sugary part of the malt. It then becomes like a naturally sweet juice.

GEORGE.

Would not sugar and water then make wine?

TUTOR.

It would; and the wines made in England of our common fruits and flowers have all a good deal of sugar in them. Cowslip flowers, for example, give little more than the flavour to the wine named from them, and it is the sugar added to them which properly makes the wine.

GEORGE.

But none of these wines are so good as grape wine?

TUTOR.

No. The grape, from the richness and abundance of its juice, is the fruit universally preferred for making wine, where it comes to perfection, which it seldom does in our climate, except by means of artificial heat.

GEORGE.

I suppose, then, grapes are finest in the hottest countries?

TUTOR.

Not so, neither; they are properly a fruit of the temperate zone, and do not grow well between the tropics. And in very hot countries it is scarcely possible to make wines of any kind to keep, for they ferment so strongly as to turn sour almost immediately.

GEORGE.

I think I have read of palm-wine on the coast of Guinea.

TUTOR.

Yes. A sweet juice flows abundantly from incisions in certain species of the palm, which ferments immediately, and makes a very pleasant sort of weak wine. But it must be drunk the same day it is made, for on the next it is as sour as vinegar.

GEORGE.

What is vinegar—is it not sour wine?

TUTOR.

Everything that makes wine will make vinegar also; and the stronger the wine the stronger the vinegar. The vinous fermentation must be first brought on, but it need not produce perfect wine, for when the intention is to make vinegar, the liquor is kept still warm, and it goes on without stopping to another kind of fermentation, called the *acetous*, the product of which is vinegar.

GEORGE.

I have heard of alegar. I suppose that is vinegar made of ale.

TUTOR.

It is—but as ale is not so strong as wine, the vinegar made from it is not so sharp or perfect. But housewives make good vinegar with sugar and water.

HARRY.

Will vinegar make people drunk if they take too much of it?

TUTOR.

No: the wine loses its intoxicating quality as well as its taste on turning to vinegar.

GEORGE.

What are spirituous liquors—have they not something to do with wine?

TUTOR.

Yes: they consist of the spirituous or intoxicating part of wine separated from the rest. You may remember that, on talking of distillation, I told you that it was the raising of a liquor in steam or vapour, and condensing it again; and that some liquors were more easily turned to vapour than others, and were therefore called more volatile or evaporable. Now, wine is a mixed or compound liquor, of which the greater part is water; but what heats and intoxicates is *vinous spirit*. This spirit, being much more volatile than water, on the application of a gentle heat, flies off in vapour, and may be collected by itself in distilling vessels;—and thus are made spirituous liquors.

GEORGE.

Will everything that you called wine yield spirits?

TUTOR.

Yes: everything that has undergone the vinous fermentation. Thus, in England a great deal of malt spirit is made from a kind of wort brought into fermentation, and then set directly to distil, without first making ale or beer of it. Gin is a spirituous liquor also got from corn, and flavoured with juniper berries. Even potatoes, carrots, and turnips may be made to afford spirits, by first fermenting their juices. In the West Indies, rum is distilled from the dregs of the sugar canes washed out by water and fermented. But brandy is distilled from the fermented juice of the grape, and is made in the wine countries.

GEORGE.

Is spirit of wine different from spirituous liquors?

TUTOR.

It is the strongest part of them got by distilling over again; for all these still contain a good deal of water, along with a pure spirit, which may be separated by a gentler heat than was used at first. But in order to procure this as strong and pure as possible, it must be distilled several times over, always leaving some of the watery part behind. When perfectly pure, it is the same, whatever spirituous liquor it is got from.

HARRY.

My mamma has little bottles of lavender water. What is that?

TUTOR.

It is a spirit of wine flavoured with lavender flowers; and it may in like manner be flavoured with many other fragrant things, since their odoriferous part is volatile, and will rise in vapour along with the spirit.

HARRY.

Will not spirit of wine burn violently?

GEORGE.

That it will, I can tell you: and so will rum and brandy; for you know it was set on fire when we made snap-dragon.

TUTOR.

All spirituous liquors are highly inflammable, and the more so the purer they are. One way of trying the purity of spirit is to see if it will burn all away without leaving any moisture behind. Then it is much lighter than water, and that affords another way of judging of its strength. A hollow ivory ball is set to swim in it; and the deeper it sinks down, the lighter, and therefore the more spirituous, is the liquor.

GEORGE.

I have heard much of the mischief done by spirituous liquors—pray what good do they do?

TUTOR.

The use and abuse of wine and spirits is a very copious subject; and there is scarcely any gift of human art, the general effects of which are more dubious. You know what wine is said to be given for in the Bible?

GEORGE.

To make glad the heart of man.

TUTOR.

Right. And nothing has such an immediate effect in inspiring vigour of body and mind as wine. It banishes sorrow and care, recruits from fatigue, enlivens the fancy, inflames the courage, and performs a hundred fine things, of which I could bring you abundant proof from the poets. The physicians, too, speak almost as much in its favour, both in diet and medicine. But its really good effects are only when used in moderation; and it unfortunately is one of those things which man can hardly be brought to use moderately. Excess in wine brings on effects the very contrary to its benefits. It stupifies and enfeebles the mind, and fills the body with incurable diseases. And this it does even when used without intoxication. But a drunken man loses for the time every distinction of a reasonable creature, and becomes worse than a brute beast. On this account Mahomet entirely forbade its use to his followers, and to this day it is not publicly drunk in any of the countries that receive the Mahometan religion.

HARRY.

Was not that right?

TUTOR.

I think not. If we were entirely to renounce every thing that may be misused, we should have scarce any enjoyments left; and it is a proper exercise of our strength of mind to use good things with moderation, when we have it in our power to do otherwise.

GEORGE.

But spirituous liquors are not good at all, are they?

TUTOR.

They have so little good and so much bad in them, that I confess I wish their common use could be abolished altogether. They are generally taken by the lowest class of people for the express purpose of intoxication; and they are much sooner prejudicial to the health than wine, and, indeed, when drunk unmixed are no better than slow poison.

GEORGE.

Spirit of wine is useful, though, for several things—is it not?

TUTOR.

Yes; and I would have all spirits kept in the hands of chemists and artists who know how to employ them usefully. Spirits of wine will dissolve many things that water will not. Apothecaries use them in drawing tinctures, and artists in preparing colours and making varnishes. They are likewise very powerful preservatives from corruption. You may have seen serpents and insects brought from abroad in phials full of spirits.

GEORGE.

I have.

HARRY.

And I know of another use of spirits.

TUTOR.

What is that?

HARRY.

To burn in lamps. My grand-mamma has a tea-kettle with a lamp under it to keep the water hot, and she burns spirits in it.

TUTOR.

So she does. Well—so much for the use of these liquors.

GEORGE.

But you have said nothing about ale and beer. Are they wholesome?

TUTOR.

Yes, in moderation. But they are sadly abused too, and rob many men of their health as well as their money and senses.

GEORGE.

Small beer does no harm however.

TUTOR.

No—and we will indulge in a good draught of it when we get home.

HARRY.

I like water better.

TUTOR.

Then drink it by all means. He that is satisfied with water has one want the less, and may defy thirst, in this country, at least.

Fourteenth Evening
Trial*

Of a complaint made against sundry Persons for breaking the Windows of DOROTHY CAREFUL, *Widow and dealer in Gingerbread.*

THE COURT BEING SEATED, there appeared in person the widow *Dorothy Careful,* to make a complaint against *Henry Luckless,* and other person or persons unknown, for break- ing three panes of glass, value ninepence, in the house of the said widow. Being directed to tell her case to the court, she made a curtsey, and began as follows:—

"Please your lordship, I was sitting at work by my fireside, between the hours of six and seven in the evening, just as it was growing dusk, and little Jack was spinning beside me, when all at once crack went the window, and down fell a little basket of cakes that was set up against it. I started up, and cried to Jack, 'Bless me, what's the matter?' So, says Jack, 'Somebody has thrown a stone and broke the window, and I dare say it is

---

* This was meant as a sequel of that very pleasing and ingenious little work, entitled *Juvenile Trials,* in which a Court of Justice is supposed to be instituted in a boarding-school, composed of the scholars themselves, for the purpose of trying offences committed at school.

some of the schoolboys.' With that I ran out of the house, and saw some boys making off as fast as they could go. So I ran after them as quick as my old legs would carry me; but I should never have come near them, if one had not happened to fall down. Him I caught and brought back to my house, when Jack knew him at once to be Master Harry Luckless. So I told him I would complain of him the next day; and I hope your worship will make him pay the damage, and I think he deserves a good whipping into the bargain, for injuring a poor widow woman."

The Judge having heard Mrs. Careful's story, desired her to sit down; and then calling up Master Luckless, asked him what he had to say for himself. Luckless appeared with his face a good deal scratched, and looking very ruefully. After making his bow, and sobbing two or three times, he said:—

"My lord, I am as innocent of this matter as any boy in the school, and I am sure I have suffered enough about it already. My lord, Billy Thompson and I were playing in the lane near Mrs. Careful's house, when we heard the window crash; and directly after she came running out towards us. Upon this Billy ran away, and I ran too, thinking I might bear the blame. But after running a little way, I stumbled over something that lay in the road, and before I could get up again she overtook me, and caught me by the hair, and began lugging and cuffing me. I told her it was not I that broke her window, but it did not signify; so she dragged me to the light, lugging and scratching me all the while, and then said she would inform against me; and that is all I know of the matter."

JUDGE.

I find, good woman, you were willing to revenge yourself, without waiting for the justice of this court.

WIDOW CAREFUL.

My lord, I confess I was put into a passion, and did not properly consider what I was doing.

JUDGE.

Well, where is Billy Thompson?

BILLY.

Here, my lord.

JUDGE.

You have heard what Harry Luckless says. Declare upon your honour whether he has spoken the truth.

BILLY.

My lord, I am sure neither he nor I had any concern in breaking the window. We were standing together at the time, and I ran on hearing the door open, for fear of being charged with it, and he followed. But what became of him I did not stay to see.

JUDGE.

So you let your friend shift for himself, and only thought of saving yourself. But did you see any other person about the house or in the lane?

BILLY.

My lord, I thought I heard somebody on the other side of the hedge, creeping along, a little before the window was broken, but I saw nobody.

JUDGE.

You hear, good woman, what is alleged in behalf of the person you have accused. Have you any other evidence against him?

WIDOW CAREFUL.

One might be sure that they would deny it, and tell lies for one another; but I hope I am not to be put off in that manner.

JUDGE.

I must tell you, mistress, that you give too much liberty to your tongue, and are guilty of as much injustice as that of which you complain. I should be sorry, indeed, if the young gentlemen of this school deserved the general character of liars. You will find among us, I hope, as just a sense of what is right and honourable, as among those who are older; and our worthy master certainly would not permit us to try offences in this manner, if he thought us capable of bearing false witness in each other's favour.

WIDOW CAREFUL.

I ask your lordship's pardon, I did not mean to offend: but it is a heavy loss for a poor woman, and though I did not catch the boy in the fact, he was the nearest when it was done.

JUDGE.

As this is no more than a suspicion, and he has the positive evidence of his school-fellow in his favour, it will be impossible to convict him, consistently with the rules of justice. Have you discovered any other circumstance that may point out the offender?

WIDOW CAREFUL.

My lord, next morning Jack found on the floor this top, which I suppose the window was broke with.

JUDGE.

Hand it up—Here, gentlemen of the Jury, please to examine it, and see if you can discover any thing of its owner.

JURYMAN.

Here is P. R. cut upon it.

ANOTHER.

Yes, and I am sure I remember Peter Riot's having just such a one.

ANOTHER.

So do I.

JUDGE.

Master Riot, is this your top?

RIOT.

I don't know, my lord, perhaps it may be mine; I have had a great many tops, and when I have done with them, I throw them away, and any body may pick them up that pleases. You see it has lost its peg.

JUDGE.

Very well, sir. Mrs. Careful, you may retire.

WIDOW CAREFUL.

And must I have no amends, my lord?

JUDGE.

Have patience. Leave every thing to the court. We shall do you all the justice in our power.

As soon as the widow was gone, the Judge rose from his seat, and with much solemnity thus addressed the assembly:—

"Gentlemen,—this business, I confess, gives me much dissatisfaction. A poor woman has been insulted and injured in her property, apparently without provocation; and though she has not been able to convict the offender, it cannot be doubted that she, as well as the world in general, will impute the crime to some of our society. Though I am in my own mind convinced that in her passion she charged an innocent person, yet the circumstance of the top is a strong suspicion, indeed almost a proof, that the perpetrator of this unmanly mischief was one of our body. The owner of the top has justly observed, that its having been his property is no certain proof against him. Since therefore, in the present defect of evidence, the whole school must remain burdened with the discredit of this action, and share in the guilt of it, I think fit, in the first place, to decree, that restitution shall be made to the sufferer out of the public chest; and next that a court of inquiry be instituted for the express purpose of searching thoroughly into this affair, with power to examine all persons upon honour who are thought likely to be able to throw light upon it. I hope, gentlemen, these measures meet with your concurrence?"

The whole court bowed to the judge, and expressed their entire satisfaction with his determination.

It was then ordered, that the public treasurer should go to the Widow Careful's house, and pay her the sum of one shilling, making at the same time a handsome apology in the name of the school. And six persons were taken by lot out of the jury to compose the court of inquiry, which was to sit in the evening.

The court then adjourned.

On the meeting of the court of inquiry, the first thing proposed by the President was, that the persons who usually played with Master Riot should be sent for. Accordingly Tom Frisk and Bob Loiter were summoned, when the President asked them upon their honour if they knew the top to have been Riot's. They said they did. They were then asked whether they remembered when Riot had it in his possession?

FRISK.

He had it the day before yesterday, and split a top of mine with it.

LOITER.

Yes, and then, as he was making a stroke at mine, the peg flew out.

PRESIDENT.

What did he then do with it?

FRISK.

He put it into his pocket, and said, as it was a strong top, he would have it mended.

PRESIDENT.

Then he did not throw it away, or give it to any body?

LOITER.

No; he pocketed it up, and we saw no more of it.

PRESIDENT.

Do you know of any quarrel he had with Widow Careful?

FRISK.

Yes; a day or two before, he went to her shop for some gingerbread; but, as he already owed her sixpence, she would not let him have any till he had paid his debts.

PRESIDENT.

How did he take the disappointment?

FRISK.

He said he would be revenged on her.

PRESIDENT.

Are you sure he used such words?

FRISK.

Yes; Loiter heard him as well as myself.

LOITER.

I did, Sir.

PRESIDENT.

Do either of you know any more of this affair?

BOTH. No, Sir.

PRESIDENT. You may go.

The president now observed that these witnesses had done a great deal in establishing proofs against Riot; for it was now pretty certain that no one but himself could have been in possession of the top at the time the crime was committed; and also it appeared that he had declared a malicious intention against the woman, which it was highly probable he would put into execution.—As the court were debating about the next step to be taken, they were acquainted that Jack, the widow's son, was waiting at the school-door for admission; and a person being sent out for him, Riot was found threatening the boy, and bidding him go home about his business. The boy, however, was conveyed safely into the room, when he thus addressed himself to the president:—

JACK.

Sir, and please your worship, as I was looking about this morning for sticks in the hedge over against our house, I found this buckle. So I thought to myself, sure this must belong to the rascal that broke our windows. So I have brought it to see if any body in the school would own it.

PRESIDENT.

On which side of the hedge did you find it?

JACK.

On the other side from our house, in the close.

PRESIDENT.

Let us see it. Gentlemen, this is so smart a buckle, that I am sure I remember it at once, and so I dare say you all do?

ALL.

It is Riot's.

PRESIDENT.

Has any body observed Riot's shoes to-day?

ONE BOY.

Yes, he has got them tied with strings.

PRESIDENT.

Very well, gentlemen; we have nothing more to do than to draw up an account of all the evidence we have heard, and lay it before his lordship. Jack, you may go home.

JACK.

Pray, Sir, let somebody go with me, for I am afraid of Riot, who has just been threatening me at the door.

PRESIDENT.

Master Bold will please to go along with the boy.

The minutes of the court were then drawn up, and the President took them to the

Judge's chamber. After the Judge had perused them, he ordered an indictment to be drawn up against Peter Riot, "for that he meanly, clandestinely, and with malice aforethought, had broken three panes in the window of Widow Careful, with a certain instrument called a top, whereby he had committed an atrocious injury on an innocent person, and had brought a disgrace upon the society to which he belonged." At the same time, he sent an officer to inform Master Riot that his trial would come on next morning.

Riot, who was with some of his gay companions, affected to treat the matter with great indifference, and even to make a jest of it. However, in the morning he thought it best to endeavour to make it up; and accordingly, when the court was assembled, he sent one of his friends with a shilling, saying that he would not trouble them with any further inquiries, but would pay the sum that had been issued out of the public stock. On the receipt of this message the Judge rose with much severity in his countenance; and observing, that by such a contemptuous behaviour towards the court the criminal had greatly added to his offence, he ordered two officers with their staves immediately to go and bring in Riot, and to use force if he should resist them. The culprit, thinking it best to submit, was presently led in between the two officers; when, being placed at the bar, the Judge thus addressed him:—

"I am sorry, Sir, that any member of this society can be so little sensible of the nature of a crime, and so little acquainted with the principles of a court of justice, as you have shown yourself to be, by the proposal you took the improper liberty of sending to us. If you meant it as a confession of your guilt, you certainly ought to have waited to receive from us the penalty we thought proper to inflict, and not to have imagined that an offer of the mere payment of damages would satisfy the claims of justice against you. If you had only broken the window by accident, and of your own accord offered restitution, nothing less than the full damages could have been accepted. But you now stand charged with having done this mischief, meanly, secretly, and maliciously, and thereby have added a great deal of criminal intention to the act. Can you then think that a court like this, designed to watch over the morals, as well as protect the properties of our community, can so slightly pass over such aggravated offences? You can claim no merit from confessing the crime, now that you know so much evidence will appear against you. And if you choose still to plead not guilty, you are at liberty to do it, and we will proceed immediately to the trial, without taking any advantage of the confession implied by your offer of payment."

Riot stood silent for some time, and then begged to be allowed to consult with his friends what was best for him to do. This was agreed to, and he was permitted to retire, though under guard of an officer. After a short absence, he returned with more humility in his looks, and said that he pleaded guilty, and threw himself on the mercy of the court. The Judge then made a speech of some length, for the purpose of convincing the prisoner as well as the bystanders of the enormity of the crime. He then pronounced the following sentence:—

"You, Peter Riot, are hereby sentenced to pay the sum of half-a-crown to the public treasury, as a satisfaction for the mischief you have done, and your attempt to conceal it. You are to repair to the house of Widow Careful, accompanied by such witnesses as we shall appoint, and there having first paid her the sum you owe her, you shall ask her pardon for the insult you offered her. You shall likewise, to-morrow, after school, stand up in your place, and before all the scholars ask pardon for the disgrace you have been the means of bringing upon the society; and in particular you shall apologize to Master Luckless, for the disagreeable circumstance you were the means of bringing him into. Till all this is complied with, you shall not presume to come into the play-ground, or join in any of the diversions of the school; and all persons are hereby admonished not to keep you company till this is done."

Riot was then dismissed to his room; and in the afternoon he was taken to the widow's, who was pleased to receive his submission graciously, and at the same time to apologize for her own improper treatment of Master Luckless, to whom she sent a present of a nice ball by way of amends.

Thus ended this important business.

Sixteenth Evening
On Presence of Mind.

M RS. F. ONE DAY having occasion to be blooded, sent for a surgeon. As soon as he entered the room, her young daughter, Eliza, started up, and was hastily going away, when her mother called her back.

MRS. F.

Eliza, do not go, I want you to stay by me.

ELIZA.

Dear mamma! I can never bear to see you blooded.

MRS. F.

Why not? what harm will it do you?

ELIZA.

O dear! I cannot look at blood. Besides, I cannot bear to see you hurt, mamma!

MRS. F.

Oh, if I can bear to feel it, surely you may to see it. But come—you *must* stay, and we will talk about it afterwards.

Eliza then, pale and trembling, stood by her mother and saw the whole operation. She could not help, however, turning her head away when the incision was made, and the first flow of blood made her start and shudder. When all was over, and the surgeon gone, Mrs. F. began.

Well, Eliza, what do you think of the mighty matter now? Would it not have been very foolish to have run away from it?

ELIZA.

O mamma! how frightened I was when he took out his lancet. Did it not hurt you a great deal?

MRS. F.

No, very little. And if it had, it was to do me good, you know.

ELIZA.

But why should I stay to see it? I could do you no good.

MRS. F.

Perhaps not; but it will do you good to be accustomed to such sights.

ELIZA.

Why, mamma?

MRS. F.

Because instances are every day happening in which it is our duty to assist fellow-creatures in circumstances of pain and distress; and if we were to indulge a reluctance to come near to them on those occasions, we should never acquire either the knowledge or the presence of mind necessary for the purpose.

ELIZA.

But if I had been told how to help people in such cases, could not I do it without being used to see them?

MRS. F.

No. We have all naturally a horror at every thing which is the cause of pain and danger to ourselves or others; and nothing but habit can give most of us the presence of mind necessary to enable us in such occurrences to employ our knowledge to the best advantage.

ELIZA.

What is *presence of mind,* mamma?

MRS. F.

It is that steady possession of ourselves in cases of alarm, that prevents us from being flurried and frightened. You have heard the expression of *having all our wits about us.* That is the effect of presence of mind, and a most inestimable quality it is, for without it we are full as likely to run into danger as to avoid it. Do you not remember hearing of your cousin Mary's cap taking fire from a candle?

ELIZA.

O yes—very well.

MRS. F.

Well—the maid, as soon as she saw it, set up a great scream, and ran out of the room; and Mary might have been burnt to death for any assistance she could give her.

ELIZA.

How foolish that was!

MRS. F.

Yes—the girl had not the least presence of mind, and the consequence was, depriving her of all recollection and making her entirely useless. But as soon as your aunt came up, she took the right method for preventing the mischief. The cap was too much on fire to be pulled off; so she whipped a quilt from the bed and flung it round Mary's head, and thus stifled the flame.

ELIZA.

Mary was a good deal scorched, though.

MRS. F.

Yes—but it was very well that it was no worse. If the maid, however, had acted with any sense at first, no harm would have been done, except burning the cap. I remember a much more fatal example of the want of presence of mind. The mistress of a family was awakened by flames bursting through the wainscot into her chamber. She flew to the stair case; and in her confusion, instead of going up stairs to call her children, who slept together in the nursery overhead, and who might all have escaped by the top of the house, she ran down, and with much danger made way through the fire, into the street. When she had got thither, the thought of her poor children rushed into her mind, but it was too late. The stairs had caught fire, so that nobody could get near them, and they were burned in their beds.

ELIZA.

What a sad thing!

MRS. F.

Sad indeed! Now, I will tell you of a different conduct. A lady was awakened by the crackling of fire, and saw it shining under her chamber-door. Her husband would have immediately opened the door, but she prevented him, since the smoke and flame would then have burst in upon them.

The children with a maid slept in a room opening out of theirs. She went and awakened them; and tying together the sheets and blankets, she sent down the maid from the window first, and then let down the children one by one to her. Last of all she descended herself. A few minutes after, the floor fell in, and all the house was in flames.

ELIZA.

What a happy escape!

MRS. F.

Yes—and with what cool recollection of mind it was managed! For mothers to love their children, and be willing to run any hazards for them, is common; but in weak minds that very love is apt to prevent exertions in the time of danger. I knew a lady who had a fine little boy sitting in her lap. He put a whole plum into his mouth, which slipped into his throat and choked him. The poor fellow turned black and struggled violently; and the mother was so frightened, that instead of putting her finger in his throat, and pulling out the plum, which might easily have been done, she laid him on the floor, and ran to call for assistance. But the maids who came up were as much flurried as she; and the child died before anything effectual was done to relieve him.

ELIZA.

How unhappy she must have been about it!

MRS. F.

Yes. It threw her into an illness which had liked to have cost her her life.

Another lady, seeing her little boy climb up a high ladder, set up a violent scream that frightened the child, so that he fell down and was much hurt; whereas, if she had possessed command enough over herself to speak to him gently, he might have got down safely.

ELIZA.

Dear mamma! what is that running down your arm?—O, it is blood!

MRS. F.

Yes—my arm bleeds again. I have stirred it too soon.

ELIZA.

Dear! What shall I do?

MRS. F.

Don't frighten yourself. I shall stop the blood by pressing on the orifice with my finger. In the mean time do you ring the bell.

> [Eliza *rings—a servant comes.*

MRS. F.

Betty, my arm bleeds. Can you tie it up again?

BETTY. I believe I can, madam.

> [*She takes off the bandage and puts on another.*

ELIZA.

I hope it is stopped now?

MRS. F.

It is. Betty has done it very well. You see she went about it with composure. This accident puts me in mind of another story which is very well worth hearing. A man once reaping in the field cut his arm dreadfully with his sickle, and divided an artery.

ELIZA.

What is that, mamma?

MRS. F.

It is one of the canals or pipes through which the blood from the heart runs like water in a pipe brought from a reservoir. When one of these is cut it bleeds very violently, and the only way to stop it is to make a pressure between the wounded place and the heart, in order to intercept the course of the blood towards it. Well—this poor man bled profusely; and the people about him, both men and women, were so stupified with fright, that some ran one way, some another, and some stood stock still. In short, he would have soon bled to death, had not a brisk stout-hearted wench, who came up, slipped off her garter, and bound it tight above the wound, by which means the bleeding was stopped till proper help could be procured.

ELIZA.

What a clever wench! But how did she know what to do?

MRS. F.

She had perhaps heard it, as you have done now; and so probably had some of the others, but they had not presence of mind enough to put it into practice. It is a much greater trial of courage, however, when the danger presses upon ourselves as well as others. Suppose a furious bull was to come upon you in the midst of a field. You could not possibly escape him by running, and attempting it would destroy your only chance of safety.

ELIZA.

What would that be?

MRS. F.

I have a story for that too. The mother of that Mr. Day, who wrote *Sandford and Merton*, was distinguished, as he also was, for courage and presence of mind. When a young woman, she was one day walking in the fields with a companion, when they perceived a bull coming to them, roaring and tossing about his head in the most tremendous manner.

ELIZA.

O, how I should have screamed!

MRS. F.

I dare say you would; and so did her companion. But she bid her walk away behind her as gently as she could, whilst she herself stopped short, and faced the bull, eyeing him with a determined countenance. The bull, when he had come near, stopped also, pawing the ground and roaring. Few animals will attack a man who steadily waits for him. In a while, she drew back some steps, still facing the bull. The bull followed. She stopped, and then he stopped. In this manner, she made good her retreat to the stile over which her companion had before got. She then turned and sprung over it; and got clear out of danger.

ELIZA.

That was bravely done, indeed! But I think very few women could have done as much.

MRS. F.

Such a degree of cool resolution, to be sure, is not common. But I have read of a lady in the East Indies who showed at least as much. She was sitting out of doors with a party of pleasure, when they were aware of a huge tiger that had crept through a hedge near them, and was just ready to make his fatal spring. They were struck with the utmost consternation; but she, with an umbrella in her hand, turned to the tiger, and suddenly spread it full in his face. This unusual assault so terrified the beast, that, taking a prodigious leap, he sprung over the fence, and plunged out of sight into the neighbouring thicket.

ELIZA.

Well—that was the boldest thing I ever heard of! But is it possible, mamma, to make one's self courageous?

MRS. F.

Courage, my dear, is of two kinds; one the gift of nature, the other of reason and habit. Men have naturally more courage than women; that is, they are less affected by danger; it makes a less impression upon them, and does not flutter their spirits so much. This is owing to the difference of their bodily constitution; and from the same cause some men and some women are more courageous than others. But the other kind of courage may in some measure be acquired by every one. Reason teaches us to face smaller dangers in order to avoid greater, and even to undergo the greatest when our duty requires it. Habit makes us less affected by particular dangers which have often come in our way. A sailor does not feel the danger of a storm so much as a landsman, but if he was mounted upon a spirited horse in a fox-chase he would probably be the most timorous man in company. The courage of women is chiefly tried in domestic dangers. They are attendants on the sick and dying; and they must qualify themselves to go through many scenes of terror in these situations, which would alarm the stoutest-hearted man who was not accustomed to them.

ELIZA.

I have heard that women generally bear pain and illness better than men.

MRS. F.

They do so, because they are more used to them, both in themselves and others.

ELIZA.

I think I should not be afraid again to see anybody blooded.

MRS. F.

I hope not. It was for that purpose I made you stand by me. And I would have you always force yourself to look on and give assistance in cases of this kind, however painful it may at first be to you, that you may as soon as possible gain that presence of mind which arises from habit.

ELIZA.

But would that make me like to be blooded myself?

MRS. F.

Not to *like* it, but to lose all foolish fears about it, and submit calmly to it when good for you. But I hope you have sense enough to do that already.

Seventeenth Evening

Phaeton Junior; or, The Gig Demolished.

Y<small>E</small> heroes of the upper form,
  Who long for whip and reins,
Come listen to a dismal tale,
  Set forth in dismal strains.

Young *Jehu* was a lad of fame,
  As all the school could tell;
At cricket, taw, and prison-bars
  He bore away the bell.

Now welcome Whitsuntide was come,
  And boys with merry hearts
Were gone to visit dear mamma,
  And eat her pies and tarts.

As soon as Jehu saw his sire,
  A boon! a boon! he cried;
O, if I am your darling boy,
  Let me not be denied.

My darling boy indeed thou art,
  The father wise replied;
So name the boon; I promise thee
  It shall not be denied.

Then give me, Sir, your long-lash'd
    whip,
  And give your gig and pair,
To drive alone to yonder town,
  And flourish through the fair.

The father shook his head; My son,
  You know not what you ask;
To drive a gig in crowded streets
  Is no such easy task.

The horses, full of rest and corn,
  Scarce I myself can guide;
And much I fear, if you attempt,
  Some mischief will betide.

Then think, dear boy, of something
    else,
  That's better worth your wishing;
A bow and quiver, bats and balls,
  A rod and lines for fishing.

But nothing could young Jehu please
  Except a touch at driving;
'Twas all in vain, his father found,
  To spend his breath in striving.

At least attend, rash boy! he cried,
  And follow good advice,
Or in a ditch both gig and you
  Will tumble in a trice.

Spare, spare the whip, hold hard the
    reins,
  The steeds go fast enough;
Keep in the middle beaten track,
  Nor cross the ruts so rough:

And when within the town you come,
  Be sure, with special care,
Drive clear of sign-posts, booths, and
    stalls,
  And monsters of the fair.

The youth scarce heard his father out,
  But roar'd—Bring out the whiskey!
With joy he view'd the rolling wheels,
  And prancing ponies frisky.

He seized the reins, and up he sprung,
  And waved the whistling lash;
Take care; take care! his father cried:
  But off he went slap-dash.

Who's this light spark? the horses
    thought,

We'll try your strength, young
   master;
So o'er the ragged turnpike-road
   Still faster ran and faster.

Young Jehu, tott'ring in his seat,
   Now wish'd to pull them in;
But pulling from so young a hand
   They valued not a pin.

A drove of grunting pigs before
   Now fill'd up half the way;
Dash through the midst the horses
   drove,
   And made a rueful day:

For some were trampled under foot,
   Some crush'd beneath the wheel;
Lord! how the drivers cursed and swore
   And how the pigs did squeal!

A farmer's wife, on old blind Ball,
   Went slowly on the road,
With butter, eggs, and cheese, and
   cream,
   In two large panniers stow'd.

Ere Ball could stride the rut, amain
   The gig came thund'ring on,
Crash went the panniers, and the dame
   And Ball lay overthrown.

Now through the town the mettled
   pair
   Ran rattling o'er the stones;
They drove the crowd from side to
   side,
   And shook poor Jehu's bones.

When lo! directly in their course,
   A monstrous form appear'd,—
A shaggy bear that stalk'd and roar'd
   On hinder legs uprear'd.

Sideways they started at the sight,
   And whisk'd the gig half round,

Then 'cross the crowded market-place
   They flew with furious bound.

First o'er a heap of crock'ryware
   The rapid car they whirl'd;
And jugs, and mugs, and pots, and
   pans,
   In fragments wide they hurl'd.

A booth stood near with tempting
   cakes
   And grocery richly fraught;
All Birmingham on t'other side
   The dazzled optics caught.

With active spring the nimble steeds
   Rush'd through the pass between,
And scarcely touch'd; the car behind
   Got through not quite so clean:

For while one wheel one stall engaged,
   Its fellow took the other;
Dire was the clash; down fell the
   booths,
   And made a dreadful pother.

Nuts, oranges, and gingerbread,
   And figs here roll'd around;
And scissars, knives, and thimbles
   there
   Bestrew'd the glitt'ring ground.

The fall of boards, the shouts and cries,
   Urged on the horses faster;
And as they flew, at ev'ry step,
   They caused some new disaster.

Here lay o'erturn'd, in woeful plight,
   A pedlar and his pack;
There, in a showman's broken box,
   All London went to wrack.

But now the fates decreed to stop
   The ruin of the day,
And make the gig and driver too
   A heavy reck'ning pay.

A ditch there lay both broad and deep,
  Where streams as black as Styx
From every quarter of the town
  Their muddy currents mix.

Down to its brink in heedless haste
  The frantic horses flew,
And in the midst, with sudden jerk,
  Their burden overthrew.

The prostrate gig with desp'rate force
  They soon pull'd out again,
And at their heels in ruin dire
  Dragg'd lumb'ring o'er the plain.

Here lay a wheel, the axle there,
  The body there remain'd,
Till, sever'd limb from limb, the car
  Nor name nor shape retain'd.

But Jehu must not be forgot,
  Left flound'ring in the flood,

With clothes all drench'd, and mouth
    and eyes
  Beplaster'd o'er with mud.

In piteous case he waded through
  And gain'd the slipp'ry side,
Where grinning crowds were gather'd
    round
  To mock his fallen pride.

They led him to a neighbouring pump
  To clear his dismal face,
Whence cold and heartless home he
    slunk,
  Involved in sore disgrace.

And many a bill for damage done
  His father had to pay.
Take warning, youthful drivers all!
  From Jehu's first essay.

Nineteenth Evening
The Female Choice,—A Tale.

A YOUNG GIRL, having fatigued herself one hot day with running about the garden, sat herself down in pleasant arbour, where she presently fell asleep. During her slumbers, two female figures presented themselves before her. One was loosely habited in a thin robe of pink with light green trimmings. Her sash of silver gauze flowed to the ground. Her fair hair fell in ringlets down her neck; and her head-dress consisted of artificial flowers interwoven with feathers. She held in one hand a ball-ticket, and the other a fancy-dress all covered with spangles and knots of gay riband. She advanced smiling to the girl, and with a familiar air thus addressed her:—

"My dearest Melissa, I am a kind genius, who have watched you from your birth, and have joyfully beheld all your beauties expand, till at length they have rendered you a companion worthy of me. See what I have brought you. This dress and this ticket will give you free access to all the ravishing delights of my palace. With me you will pass your days in a perpetual round of ever-varying amusements. Like the gay butterfly, you will have no other business than to flutter from flower to flower, and spread your charms before admiring spectators. No restraints, no toils, no dull tasks are to be found within my happy domains. All is pleasure, life, and good humour. Come, then, my dear! Let me put this dress on you, which will make you quite enchanting; and away, away, with me!"

Melissa felt a strong inclination to comply with the call of this inviting nymph; but first she thought it would be prudent at least to ask her name.

"My name," said she, "is DISSIPATION."

The other female then advanced. She was clothed in a close habit of brown stuff, simply relieved with white. She wore her smooth hair under a plain cap. Her whole person was perfectly neat and clean. Her look was serious, but satisfied; and her air was staid and compassed. She held in one hand a distaff; on the opposite arm hung a workbasket; and the girdle round her waist was garnished with scissors, knitting needles, reels, and other implements of female labour. A bunch of keys hung at her side. She thus accosted the sleeping girl:—

"Melissa, I am the genius who have ever been the friend and companion of your mother; and I now offer my protection to you. I have no allurements to tempt you with, like those of my gay rival. Instead of spending all your time in amusements, if you enter yourself of my train, you must rise early, and pass the long day in a variety of employments, some of them difficult, some laborious, and all requiring some exertion of body or mind. You must dress plainly, live mostly at home, and aim at being useful rather than shining. But in return I will ensure you content, even spirits, self-approbation, and the esteem of all who thoroughly know you. If these offers appear to your young mind less inviting than those of my rival, be assured, however, that they are more real. She has promised much more than she can ever make good. Perpetual pleasures are no more in the power of Dissipation, than of Vice or Folly to bestow. Her delights quickly pall, and are inevitably succeeded by languor and disgust. She appears to you under disguise, and what you see is not her real face. For myself, I shall never seem to you less amiable than I now do, but, on the contrary, you will like me better and better. If I look grave to you now, you will hear me sing at my work; and when work is over, I can dance too. But I have said enough. It is time for you to choose whom you will follow, and upon that choice all your happiness depends. If you would know my name, it is HOUSEWIFERY."

Melissa heard her with more attention than delight; and though overawed by her manner, she could not help turning again to take another look at the first speaker. She beheld her still offering her presents with so bewitching an air that she felt it scarcely possible to resist: when, by a lucky accident, the mask with which Dissipation's face was so artfully covered, fell off. As soon as Melissa beheld, instead of the smiling features of youth and cheerfulness, a countenance wan and ghastly with sickness, and soured by fretfulness, she turned away with horror, and gave her hand unreluctantly to her sober and sincere companion.

Twenty-fourth Evening
The Goldfinch and Linnet.

A GAUDY *Goldfinch*, pert and gay,
Hopping blythe from spray to spray,
Full of frolic, full of spring,
With head well plumed and burnish'd
    wing,

Spied a sober *Linnet* hen,
Sitting all alone,
And bow'd and chirp'd, and bow'd
    again;
And with familiar tone

He thus the dame address'd
As to her side he closely press'd:—
  "I hope, my dear, I don't intrude,
By breaking on your solitude?
But it has always been my passion
To forward pleasant conversation;
And I should be a stupid bird
To pass the fair without a word;
I, who have been for ever noted
To be the sex's most devoted.
Besides, a damsel unattended,
Left unnoticed and unfriended,
Appears (excuse me) so forlorn,
That I can scarce suppose,
To any she that e'er was born,
'Twould be the thing she chose.
How happy, then, I'm now at leisure
To wait upon a lady's pleasure;
And all this morn have nought to do
But pay my duty, love, to you.
  "What, silent!—Ah, those looks
    demure,
And eyes of languor make me sure
That in my random idle chatter
I quite mistook the matter!
It is not spleen or contemplation
That draws you to the cover;
But 'tis some tender assignation;
Well!—who's the favoured lover?
I met hard by, in quaker suit,
A youth sedately grave and mute;
And from the maxim, like to like,
Perhaps the *sober youth* might strike:
Yes, yes, 'tis he, I'll lay my life,
Who hopes to get you for his wife.
  "But come, my dear, I know you're
    wise,

Compare and judge, and use your
    eyes;
No female yet could e'er behold
The lustre of my red and gold,
My ivory bill and jetty crest,
But all was done, and I was blest.
Come, brighten up and act with spirit,
And take the fortune that you merit."

He ceased—*Linnetta* thus replied,
With cool contempt and decent
    pride:—
  " 'Tis pity, Sir, a youth so sweet,
In form and manners so complete,
Should do an humble maid the honour
To waste his precious time upon her.
A poor forsaken she, you know,
Can do no credit to a beau;
And worse would be the case
If meeting one whose faith was
    plighted,
He should incur the sad disgrace
Of being slighted.
  "Now, Sir, the *sober-suited youth*,
Whom you were pleased to mention,
To those small merits, sense and truth,
And generous love, has some
    pretension;
And then, to give him all his due,
He sings, Sir, full as well as you,
And sometimes can be silent too.
In short, my taste is so perverse,
And such my wayward fate,
That it would be my greatest curse
To have a *coxcomb* to my mate."
  This said, away she scuds,
And leaves *beau Goldfinch* in the suds.

Twenty-sixth Evening

Difference and Agreement; or, Sunday Morning.

IT WAS SUNDAY MORNING. All the bells were ringing for church, and the streets were filled with people moving in all directions.

Here, numbers of well-dressed persons, and a long train of charity children, were thronging in at the wide doors of a large handsome church. There, a smaller number, almost equally gay in dress, were entering an elegant meeting-house. Up one alley, a Roman Catholic congregation was turning into their retired chapel, every one crossing himself with a finger dipped in holy water as he went in. The opposite side of the street was covered with a train of Quakers, distinguished by their plain and neat attire and sedate aspect, who walked without ceremony into a room as plain as themselves, and took their seats, the men on one side, and the women on the other, in silence. A spacious building was filled with an overflowing crowd of Methodists, most of them meanly habited, but decent and serious in demeanour; while a small society of Baptists in the neighbourhood quietly occupied their humble place of assembly.

Presently the different services began. The church resounded with the solemn organ, and with the indistinct murmurs of a large body of people following the minister in responsive prayers. From the meeting were heard the slow psalm, and the single voice of the leader of their devotions. The Roman Catholic chapel was enlivened by strains of music, the tinkling of a small bell, and a perpetual change of service and ceremonial. A profound silence and unvarying look and posture announced the self-recollection and mental devotion of the Quakers.

Mr. *Ambrose* led his son *Edwin* round all these different assemblies as a spectator. *Edwin* viewed every thing with great attention, and was often impatient to inquire of his father the meaning of what he saw; but Mr. *Ambrose* would not suffer him to disturb any of the congregations even by a whisper. When they had gone through the whole, *Edwin* found a great number of questions to put to his father, who explained every thing to him in the best manner he could. At length says *Edwin*,

"But why cannot all these people agree to go to the same place, and worship God the same way?"

"And why should they agree?" (replied his father). "Do not you see that people differ in a hundred other things? Do they all dress alike, and eat and drink alike, and keep the same hours, and use the same diversions?"

"Ay—but those are things in which they have a right to do as they please."

"And they have a right, too, to worship God as they please. It is their own business, and concerns none but themselves."

"But has not God ordered particular ways of worshipping him?"

"He has directed the mind and spirit with which he is to be worshipped, but not the particular form and manner. That is left for every one to choose, according as suits his temper and opinions. All these people like their own way best, and why should they leave it for the choice of another? Religion is one of the things in which *mankind were made to differ*."

The several congregations now began to be dismissed, and the street was again overspread with persons of all the different sects, going promiscuously to their respective homes. It chanced that a poor man fell down in the street in a fit of apoplexy, and lay for dead. His wife and children stood round him crying and lamenting in the bitterest distress. The beholders immediately flocked round, and, with looks and expressions of the warmest compassion, gave their help. A churchman raised the man from the ground, by lifting him under the arms, while a Dissenter held his head, and wiped his face with his handkerchief. A Roman Catholic lady took out her smelling-bottle, and assiduously applied it to his nose. A [m]ethodist ran for a doctor. A Quaker supported and comforted the woman. and a Baptist took care of the children.

Edwin and his father were among the spectators. "Here," said Mr. *Ambrose,* "is a thing in *which mankind were made to agree."*

On Emblems.

PRAY, PAPA (said *Cecilia*), what is an *emblem?* I have met with the word in my lesson to-day, and I do not quite understand it.

An emblem, my dear (replied he), is a visible image of an invisible thing.

CECILIA.

A visible image of—I can hardly comprehend—

PAPA.

Well, I will explain it more at length. There are certain notions that we form in our minds without the help of our eyes or any of our senses. Thus, Virtue, Vice, Honour, Disgrace, Time, Death, and the like, are not sensible objects, but ideas of the under-standing.

CECILIA.

Yes—We cannot feel them or see them, but we can think about them.

PAPA.

True. Now it sometimes happens that we wish to represent one of these in a visible form; that is, to offer something to the sight that shall raise a similar notion in the minds of the beholders. In order to do this, we must take some action or circumstance belonging to it, capable of being expressed by painting or sculpture, and this is called a *type* or *emblem.*

CECILIA.

But how can this be done?

PAPA.

I will tell you by an example. You know the Sessions-house where trials are held. It would be easy to write over the door in order to distinguish it, "This is the Sessions-house;" but it is a more ingenious and elegant way of pointing it out, to place upon the building a figure representing the purpose for which it was erected, namely, to distribute *justice.* For this end the notion of justice is to be *personified,* that is, changed from an idea of the understanding into one of the sight. A human figure is therefore made, distinguished by tokens which bear a relation to the character of that virtue. Justice carefully *weighs* both sides of a cause; she is therefore represented as holding a *pair of scales.* It is her office to *punish* crimes; she therefore bears a *sword.* This is then an *emblematical figure,* and the sword and scales are *emblems.*

CECILIA.

I understand this very well. But why is she blindfolded?

PAPA.

To denote her impartiality—that she decides only from the merits of the case, and not from a view of the parties.

CECILIA.

How can she weigh any thing, though, when her eyes are blinded?

PAPA.

Well objected. These are two inconsistent emblems; each proper in itself, but when used together, making a contradictory action. An artist of judgment will therefore drop one of them; and accordingly the best modern figures of Justice have the balance and sword, without the bandage over the eyes.

CECILIA.

Is there not the same fault in making Cupid blindfolded, and yet putting a bow and arrow into his hands?

PAPA.

There is. It is a gross absurdity, and not countenanced by the ancient descriptions of Cupid, who is represented as the surest of all archers.

CECILIA.

I have a figure of *Death* in my fable-book. I suppose that is emblematical?

PAPA.

Certainly, or you could not know that it meant Death. How is he represented?

CECILIA.

He is nothing but bones, and he holds a scythe in one hand, and an hour-glass in the other.

PAPA.

Well—how do you interpret these emblems?

CECILIA.

I suppose he is all bones, because nothing but bones are left after a dead body has lain long in the grave.

PAPA.

True. This, however, is not so properly an emblem, as the real and visible effect of death. But the scythe?

CECILIA.

Is not that because death mows down every thing?

PAPA.

It is. No instrument could so properly represent the wide-wasting sway of death, which sweeps down the race of animals like flowers falling under the hands of the mower. It is a simile used in the Scriptures.

CECILIA.

The hour-glass, I suppose, is to show people their time is come.

PAPA.

Right. In the hour-glass that Death holds, all the sand is run out from the upper to the lower part. Have you never observed upon a monument an old figure, with wings, and a scythe, and with his head bald all but a single lock before?

CECILIA.

O yes;—and I have been told it is *Time*.

PAPA.

Well—and what do you make of it? Why is he old?

CECILIA.

O! because time has lasted a long while.

PAPA.

And why has he wings?

CECILIA.

Because time is swift, and flies away.

PAPA.

What does his scythe mean?

CECILIA.

I suppose that is because he destroys and cuts down every thing, like Death.

PAPA.

True. I think, however, a weapon rather slower in operation, as a pick-axe, would have been more suitable to the gradual action of time. But what is his single lock of hair for?

CECILIA.

I have been thinking, and cannot make it out.

PAPA.

I thought that would puzzle you. It relates to time as giving *opportunity* for doing anything. It is to be seized as it presents itself, or it will escape, and cannot be recovered. Thus the proverb says, "Take time by the forelock." Well—now you understand what emblems are.

CECILIA.

Yes, I think I do. I suppose the painted sugar loaves over the grocer's shop, and the mortar over the apothecary's, are emblems too?

PAPA.

Not so properly. They are only the pictures of things which are themselves the objects of sight, as the real sugar-loaf in the shop of the grocer, and the real mortar in that of the apothecary. However, an implement belonging to a particular rank or profession is commonly used as an emblem to point out the man exercising that rank or profession. Thus a crown is considered as an emblem of a king; a sword or spear, of a soldier; an anchor, of a sailor; and the like.

CECILIA.

I remember Captain Heartwell, when he came to see us, had the figure of an anchor on all his buttons.

PAPA.

He had. That was the emblem or badge of his belonging to the navy.

CECILIA.

But you told me that an emblem was a visible sign of an invisible thing; yet a sea-captain is not an invisible thing.

PAPA.

He is not invisible as a man, but his profession is invisible.

CECILIA.

I do not well understand that.

PAPA.

Profession is a *quality*, belonging equally to a number of individuals, however different they may be in external form and appearance. It may be added or taken away without any visible change. Thus, if Captain Heartwell were to give up his commission, he would appear to you the same man as before. It is plain, therefore, that what in that case he had lost, namely, his profession, was a thing invisible. It is one of those ideas of the understanding which I before mentioned to you, as different from a sensible idea.

CECILIA.

I comprehend it now.

PAPA.

I have got here a few emblematical pictures. Suppose you try whether you can find out their meaning.

CECILIA.

O yes—I shall like that very well.

PAPA.

Here is a man standing on the summit of a steep cliff, and going to ascend a ladder which he has planted against a cloud.

CECILIA.

Let me see!—that must be *Ambition,* I think.

PAPA.

How do you explain it?

CECILIA.

He is got very high already, but he wants to be still higher; so he ventures up the ladder, though it is only supported by a cloud, and hangs over a precipice.

PAPA.

Very right. Here is now another man, hoodwinked, who is crossing a raging torrent upon stepping-stones.

CECILIA.

Then he will certainly fall in. I suppose he is one that runs into danger without considering whither he is going?

PAPA.

Yes; and you may call him *Fool-hardiness.* Do you see this hand coming out of a black cloud, and putting an extinguisher upon a lamp?

CECILIA.

I do. If that lamp be the lamp of life, the hand that extinguishes it must be *Death.*

PAPA.

Very just. Here is an old half-ruined building, supported by props; and the figure of Time is sawing through one of the props.

CECILIA.

That must be *Old Age,* surely.

PAPA.

It is. The next is a man leaning upon a breaking crutch.

CECILIA.

I don't well know what to make of that.

PAPA.

It is intended for *Instability;* however, it might also stand for *False Confidence.* Here is a man poring over a sun-dial with a candle in his hand.

CECILIA.

I am at a loss for that, too.

PAPA.

Consider—a sun-dial is only made to tell the hour by the light of the sun.

CECILIA.

Then this man must know nothing about it.

PAPA.

True; and his name is therefore *Ignorance.* Here is a walking-stick, the lower part of which is set in the water, and it appears crooked. What does that denote?

CECILIA.

Is the stick really crooked?

PAPA.

No; but it is the property of water to give that appearance.

CECILIA.

Then it must signify *Deception.*

PAPA.

It does. I dare say you will at once know this fellow who is running as fast as his legs will carry him, and looking back at his shadow.

CECILIA.

He must be *Fear* or *Terror,* I fancy.

PAPA.

Yes; you may call him which you please. But who is this sower, that scatters seeds in the ground?

CECILIA.

Let me consider. I think there is a parable in the Bible about seed sown, and it therefore signifies something like *Instruction.*

PAPA.

True; but it may also represent *Hope,* for no one would sow without hoping to reap the fruit. What do you think of this candle held before a mirror, in which its figure is exactly reflected?

CECILIA.

I do not know what it means.

PAPA.

It represents *Truth;* the essence of which consists in the fidelity with which objects are received and reflected back by our minds. The object is here a luminous one, to show the clearness and brightness of Truth. Here is next an upright column, the perfect straightness of which is shown by a plumb-line hanging from its summit, and exactly parallel to the side of the column.

CECILIA.

I suppose that must represent *Uprightness.*

PAPA.

Yes—or in other words, *Rectitude.* The strength and stability of the pillar alone denote the security produced by this virtue. You see here a woman disentangling and reeling off a very perplexed skein of thread.

CECILIA.

She must have a great deal of patience.

PAPA.

True. She is *Patience* herself. The brooding hen, sitting beside her, is another emblem of the same quality that aids the interpretation. Who do you think this pleasing female is, that looks with such kindness upon the drooping plant she is watering?

CECILIA.

That must be *Charity,* I believe.

PAPA.

It is; or you may call her *Benignity,* which is nearly the same thing. Here is a lady

sitting demurely, with one finger on her lip, while she holds a bridle in her other hand.
CECILIA.

The finger on the lip I suppose denotes Silence. The bridle must mean confinement. I should almost fancy her to be a School-mistress.
PAPA.

Ha! ha! I hope, indeed, many school-mistresses are endued with her spirit, for she is *Prudence* or *Discretion*. Well—we are now got to the end of our pictures, and upon the whole you have interpreted them very prettily.
CECILIA.

But I have one question to ask you, papa. In these pictures and others that I have seen of the same sort, almost all the *good* qualities are represented in the form of *women*. What is the reason of that?
PAPA.

It is certainly a compliment, my dear, either to your sex's person or mind. The inventor either chose the figure of a female to clothe each agreeable quality in, because he thought that the most agreeable form, and therefore best suited it; or he meant to imply that the female character is really the most virtuous and amiable. I rather believe that the first was his intention, but I shall not object to your taking it in the light of the second.
CECILIA.

But is it true—is it true?
PAPA.

Why, I can give you very good authority for the preference of the female sex in a moral view. One Ledyard, a great traveller, who had walked through almost all the countries of Europe, and at last died in an expedition to explore the internal parts of Africa, gave a most decisive and pleasing testimony in favour of the superior character of women, whether savage or civilized. I was so much pleased with it, that I put great part of it into verse; and if it will not make you vain, I will give you a copy of my lines.
CECILIA.

O, pray do!
PAPA.

Here they are. Read them.

LEDYARD'S PRAISE OF WOMEN.

Through many a land and clime a ranger,
  With toilsome steps, I've held my way,
A lonely, unprotected stranger,
  To all the stranger's ills a prey.

While steering thus my course precarious,
  My fortune still had been to find
Men's hearts and dispositions various,
  But gentle Woman ever kind.

Alive to ev'ry tender feeling,
  To deeds of mercy ever prone,

The wounds of pain and sorrow healing
  With soft compassion's sweetest tone.

No proud delay, no dark suspicion,
  Stints the free bounty of their heart;
They turn not from the sad petition,
  But cheerful aid at once impart.

Form'd in benevolence of nature,
  Obliging, modest, gay, and mild,
Woman's the same endearing creature
  In courtly town and savage wild.

When parch'd with thirst, with hunger wasted,
  Her friendly hand refreshment gave,
How sweet the coarsest food has tasted!
  What cordial in the simple wave!

Her courteous looks, her words caressing,
  Shed comfort on the fainting soul:
Woman's the stranger's general blessing,
  From sultry India to the Pole.

Twenty-seventh Evening

Generous Revenge.

At THE PERIOD when the republic of Genoa was divided between the factions of the nobles and the people, *Uberto*, a man of low origin, but of an elevated mind and superior talents, and enriched by commerce, having raised himself to be the head of a popular party, maintained for a considerable time a democratic form of government.

The nobles at length uniting all their efforts, succeeded in subverting this state of things, and regained their former supremacy. They used their victory with considerable rigour; and in particular having imprisoned *Uberto*, proceeded against him as a traitor, and thought they displayed sufficient lenity in passing a sentence upon him of perpetual banishment, and the confiscation of all his property. *Adorno*, who was then possessed of the first magistracy, a man haughty in temper, and proud of ancient nobility, though otherwise not void of generous sentiments, in pronouncing this sentence on *Uberto*, aggravated its severity by the insolent terms in which he conveyed it. "You (said he) — you, the son of a base mechanic, who have dared to trample upon the nobles of Genoa— you, by their clemency, are only doomed to shrink again into the nothingness whence you sprung."

Uberto received his condemnation with respectful submission to the court; yet stung by the manner in which it was expressed, he could not forbear saying to *Adorno*, "that perhaps he might hereafter find cause to repent the language he had used to a man capable of sentiments as elevated as his own." He then made his obeisance and retired; and after taking leave of his friends, embarked in a vessel bound for Naples, and quitted his native country without a tear.

He collected some debts due to him in the Neapolitan dominions, and with the wreck of his fortune went to settle on one of the islands in the Archipelago belonging to the state of Venice. Here his industry and capacity in mercantile pursuits raised him in a course of years to greater wealth than he had possessed in his most prosperous days at Genoa; and his reputation for honour and generosity equalled his fortune.

Among other places which he frequently visited as a merchant, was the city of Tunis, at that time in friendship with the Venetians, though hostile to most of the other Italian states, and especially to Genoa. As *Uberto* was on a visit to one of the first men of that place at his country house, he saw a young Christian slave at work in irons, whose appearance excited his attention. The youth seemed oppressed with labour, to which his delicate frame had not been accustomed, and while he leaned at intervals upon the instrument with which he was working, a sigh burst from his full heart, and a tear stole down his cheek. *Uberto* eyed him with tender compassion, and addressed him in Italian. The youth eagerly caught the sounds of his native tongue, and replying to his inquiries, informed him he was a Genoese. "And what is your name, young man?" said *Uberto*. "You need not be afraid of confessing to *me* your birth and condition."

"Alas!" (he answered) "I fear my captors already suspect enough to demand a large ransom. My father is indeed one of the first men in Genoa. His name is *Adorno*, and I am his only son." "*Adorno!*" *Uberto* checked himself from uttering more aloud, but to himself he cried, "Thank Heaven! then I shall be nobly revenged."

He took leave of the youth, and immediately went to inquire after the corsair captain who claimed a right in young *Adorno*, and having found him, demanded the price of his ransom. He learned that he was considered as a captive of value, and that less than two thousand crowns would not be accepted. *Uberto* paid the sum; and causing his servant to follow him with a horse and a complete suit of handsome apparel, he returned to the youth, who was working as before, and told him he was free. With his own hands he took off his fetters, and helped him to change his dress, and mount on horseback. The youth was tempted to think it all a dream, and the flutter of emotion almost deprived him of the power of returning thanks to his generous benefactor. He was soon, however, convinced of the reality of his good fortune, by sharing the lodging and table of *Uberto*.

After a stay of some days at Tunis to despatch the remainder of his business, *Uberto* departed homewards accompanied by young *Adorno*, who by his pleasing manners had highly ingratiated himself with him. *Uberto* kept him some time at his house, treating him with all the respect and affection he could have shown for the son of his dearest friend. At length, having a safe opportunity of sending him to Genoa, he gave him a faithful servant for a conductor, fitted him out with every convenience, slipped a purse of gold into one hand, and a letter into the other, and thus addressed him:

"My dear youth, I could with much pleasure detain you longer in my humble mansion, but I feel your impatience to revisit your friends, and I am sensible that it would be cruelty to deprive them longer than necessary of the joy they will receive in recovering you. Deign to accept this provision for your voyage, and deliver this letter to your father. *He* probably may recollect somewhat of me, though you are too young to do so. Farewell! I shall not soon forget you, and I hope you will not forget me." *Adorno* poured out the effusions of a grateful and affectionate heart, and they parted with mutual tears and embraces.

The young man had a prosperous voyage home; and the transport with which he was again beheld by his almost heart-broken parents may more easily be conceived than described. After learning that he had been a captive in Tunis (for it was supposed that the ship in which he sailed had foundered at sea), "And to whom," said old *Adorno*, "am I indebted for the inestimable benefit of restoring you to my arms?"—"This letter," said his son, "will inform you." He opened it, and read as follows:

"That son of a vile mechanic, who told you that one day you might repent the scorn with which you treated him, has the satisfaction of seeing his prediction accomplished. For know, proud noble! that the deliverer of your only son from slavery is

"*The banished Uberto.*"

Adorno dropped the letter and covered his face with his hand, while his son was displaying in the warmest language of gratitude the virtues of *Uberto*, and the truly paternal kindness he had experienced from him. As the debt could not be cancelled,

Adorno resolved if possible to repay it. He made such powerful intercessions with the other nobles, that the sentence pronounced on *Uberto* was reversed, and full permission given him to return to Genoa. In apprising him of this event, *Adorno* expressed his sense of the obligations he lay under to him, acknowledged the genuine nobleness of his character, and requested his friendship. *Uberto* returned to his country, and closed his days in peace, with the universal esteem of his fellow-citizens.

Epilogue.

AND now, so many *Evenings* past,
Our *Budget*'s fairly out at last;
Exhausted all its various store,
Nor like to be replenish'd more.
Then, youthful friends, farewell! my heart
Shall speak a blessing as we part.
　　May Wisdom's seeds in every mind
Fit soil and careful culture find;
Each generous plant with vigour shoot,
And kindly ripen into fruit!
Hope of the world, the *rising race*,
May Heaven with fostering love embrace,
And turning to a whiter page,
Commence with them a *better age!*
An age of light and joy, which we,
Alas! in promise only see.

J. A.

12

Dramatic Dialogues
By ELIZABETH PINCHARD

VOLUME ONE

FRONTISPIECE.

P. 154.

Laura offering Relief to Ruth Saunders.

DRAMATIC DIALOGUES,

FOR THE

USE

OF

YOUNG PERSONS.

BY THE AUTHOR OF

THE BLIND CHILD.

" True Critics enquire, Does the Work relate to the Interests
of Mankind?—Is its Object useful, and its End moral?—
Will it inform the Understanding, and amend the Heart?"
ESSAY ON SOLITUDE, BY M. ZIMMERMANN.

LONDON:

PRINTED FOR E. NEWBERY, THE CORNER OF ST.
PAUL'S CHURCH-YARD.

M,DCC,XCII.

[*Entered at Stationer's Hall.*]

Eᴌɪᴢᴀʙᴇᴛʜ ᴘɪɴᴄʜᴀʀᴅ *illustrates the changing attitudes of the later eighteenth century. Reared on a whole cult of sentiment born of an anti-Hobbesian ethic, eighteenth-century adults had been telling children to do good in order to feel good. There was not only a man of feeling but a child of feeling. The 1780s and 1790s witnessed a counterreaction to affected sentimentality. The principal aim of Elizabeth Pinchard's* The Blind Child . . . by a Lady *(1791) was "*. . . *to repress that excessive softness of heart which too frequently involves its possessor in a train of evils, and which is by no means true* sensibility—*that exquisite gift of heaven." Emily, who does not run away from suffering, is praised by a surgeon. She also cares for Helen, a nine-year-old blind child whom Mrs. Trimmer (in* The Guardian of Education*) felt could have been more cheerful. There were ten editions of this affecting tale by 1814.*

The Two Cousins, A Moral Story for the Use of Young Persons, in which is exemplified the Necessity of Moderation and Justice to the Attainment of Happiness *(1794) was printed by Elizabeth Newbery. Pinchard contrasts the city with the country child, as did Thomas Day. Mrs. Leyster, a widow, lives near the industrious poor in the village of Fair Lawn, where her daughter Constatio outshines her urban cousin.*

In Dramatic Dialogues *(I, 1792) the play "Sensibility" shows again how false sensibility disables one from action. Isabella fears touching her wounded parrot, but Cecilia, the child of true sensibility, has no such squeamishness. The second volume of* Dramatic Dialogues *(also 1792) contained the following plays: "Charles the First, an Historical Drama," "The Little Country Visitor," "Prince Henry," "The Distrest Family," and "The Village Wedding." Unlike Madame de Genlis' twenty-four plays in four volumes* (Theatre of Education *in English, 1781), Pinchard's plays were not meant to be performed but were rather closet dramas to "captivate" children.*

There were other dramas for children, such as Little Dramas for Young People on Subjects taken from English History *by Mrs. B. Hoole, later Mrs. Hofland (1810), and* Dramas for Children: Imitated from the French of L. F. Jauffret *(1809). But the true popularizer of drama for children in England was Hannah More's* Sacred Dramas *(1782), which went into nineteen editions. A facsimile edition was published in 1973:* Sacred Dramas: chiefly intended for young persons: the subjects taken from the Bible *(Bern, Switzerland: Herbert Lang).*

The first volume of Dramatic Dialogues *is reprinted from a first edition in the Austrian Collection of the Regenstein Library of the University of Chicago.*

Volume One

Preface.

To PUBLISH A WORK with the Title borne by this, may, perhaps, by some, be thought presumption, when it is recollected that Madame de Genlis has already occupied the Dramatic line, in a manner to be imitated by few, and, probably, to be equalled by none.—But a comparison of this work with the Theatre of Education, of that great Author, would be unfair as to execution, and unjust as to design.—The Writer of this work does not, like Madame de Genlis, intend her Dramatic Dialogues to be performed; well aware that the length of the Scenes, in some places, and the simplicity of the Plot in all, would render them flat and heavy in representation. The motives by which she was induced to throw her Stories into Dialogue, were a belief that young people are easily captivated and interested by this manner of writing, and the convenience of avoiding the *"said she,"* and *"replied she,"* which becomes so fatiguing in a narration of any length, and which she was so often obliged to break in her last work.

This short explanation the Authoress thought due to herself, lest she should be suspected of endeavouring to imitate one of the first Authors the Age has produced.

If these simple Dialogues should be considered as an additional barrier against the encroachments of error, and an additional support to the efforts of Virtue, the Writer will be most happy; and she trusts them, tho' not without fear, yet not without hope, to the candour of a generous Public, who at least will give her credit for purity of intention.

The Misfortunes of Anger.

A DRAMA.
IN TWO PARTS.

CHARACTERS.

MRS. SELWYN,	— GOVERNESS TO JULIET.
PAULINA,	— HER COUSIN.
MARY,	— HER MAID.
JULIET,	
FANNY,	— A LITTLE GIRL.

"Our Passions gone, and Reason in her Throne,
"We wonder at the Mischief we have done."—WALLER.

SCENE, A PARLOUR.

Mary enters, lifts up a tambour frame which appears to have
been thrown down, picks up the spangles, silks, &c.—She speaks.

So MISS JULIET has been here, I see!—What put her into a rage with her tambour, I wonder?—Oh! I see, this rose-bud does not look well, so down it went, I'll warrant it, and here lie the spangles and twist thrown all over the floor. For my part, I wonder the frame was not all broke to smash, it would have been like her.—Ah! here comes Miss Paulina! There's a young lady, marry, I wish our's was like her, but no hope of that!

Enter Paulina, *(with a book.)*

PAULINA.

Mary, have you seen my cousin?

MARY.

No, Miss, not since breakfast.

PAULINA.

I left her here at her tambour frame—She said she would work while I read to her.

MARY.

Aye, Miss, but something has gone wrong since that.—*Here* I found the frame, and there lay the silks—Truly, I'm glad I was not here, they'd ha' been thrown at my head.

PAULINA.

Perhaps she is gone to her own room, I'll seek her; if she comes here in the mean time, Mary, tell her I am up stairs.

MARY.

Yes, Miss, to be sure I will.—(*Paulina goes out.*)—Ah! by my truth, there's some pleasure in doing any thing for you, one does not get pinched and called names!—So here's the Governess, yawning as usual, but just up.

Enter Mrs. Selwyn.

(*She speaks in a slow, dull manner, and yawns often.*)

MRS. SELWYN.

Well, Mary!—Where's Miss Juliet?

MARY.

I don't know, Ma'am, not I, she is in one of her passions to-day; every thing goes wrong with her; she was ready to fight with the looking-glass, while I dressed her this morning, and I don't know how many pinches I got for not being quick enough to please her.

MRS. SELWYN.

She's a strange girl, I can't help laughing at her sometimes.

MARY.

Laughing, Tis no laughing matter, ma'am, I can tell you that, and it only makes her worse.

MRS. SELWYN.

She fatigues me so! I really cannot stay with her long at a time.

MARY, (*aside.*)

No, truly, you take care not to have too much trouble!

Mrs. Selwyn draws a chair indolently, and takes out her work.

MRS. SELWYN.

Well, Mary, go and tell her to come to me, I want her to read.

MARY.

Lord, ma'am, I'm quite afraid to go, she won't mind me.

MRS. SELWYN, (*yawning.*)

And she'll fatigue me sadly too, well, never mind, she'll come bye-and-bye.

Enter Fanny, (*crying.*)

MARY.

What's the matter with you, Fanny, what are you crying for?

FANNY.

Miss Juliet!—Miss Juliet!—Oh dear.

MRS. SELWYN.

Child, don't make so much noise, what has Miss Juliet done to you?

FANNY.

Why, ma'am, an please you, she met me in the garden, about half an hour agone, I was a coming up, ma'am, to beg a little milk for my little sister, for mother is very bad, and so she said as how——

MRS. SELWYN. Don't talk so fast, let's hear what Miss Juliet did.

FANNY.

Yes, ma'am, and so, ma'am; if you please, I met Miss Juliet; and so she asked me what I wanted, and so I told, and so she——

MRS. SELWYN.

Grant me patience! How many more *so's?*

MARY.

Don't make such a long story, Fanny, tell us, at once, what made you cry.

FANNY.

Yes, I'm a going, so miss asked me to play wi' she, for she said his honour was gone out and Madam Selwyn wa'nt up, and Master Charles was gone to school, and Miss Paulina was up stairs, and she did not know what to do wi' herself.

MRS. SELWYN.

So, there's all the family disposed of.—Well, child, what then?

FANNY.

Then we went up stairs, ma'am, and miss shewed me her doll, and we played, but at last,—Oh dear, oh dear!

MRS. SELWYN.

I never heard such a girl in my life.—What happened then?

FANNY.

Why, miss beat me, yes, she did, ever so hard, and scratch'd me.

MRS. SELWYN.

What, all at once, without any cause?

FANNY.

Yes, ma'am, 'cause I let the doll fall.

MRS. SELWYN, *(laughing.)*

What nonsense!—Go away, child, take your milk, and bid the cook give you some broth.

FANNY.

Yes, ma'am, thank you ma'am. *(Aside.)* —But I wo'nt come here any more to be beat about so. *(Mary and Fanny go out.)*

Enter Juliet, *(with her doll.)*

JULIET.

Where's Fanny Wood?

MRS. SELWYN.

Gone home, miss, do you think any body will stay where you are, to be beat and scratched?

JULIET.

I don't care. What business had she to throw down my doll?

MRS. SELWYN.

Do you think she did it on purpose?

JULIET.

I don't know.—Let her take more care then.

MRS. SELWYN.

Has she spoil'd it?

JULIET. No.

MRS. SELWYN.

Well then, what was there to be in such a rage about?—Come and read.

JULIET.

Not till I have dressed my doll.

MRS. SELWYN.

Well,—make haste then.— *(A pause, Mrs. Selwyn works but slowly and idly, Juliet dresses her doll, at last, she stamps her foot, and says:—*

You tiresome creature, won't you be dress'd?

MRS. SELWYN.

My stars, Miss Juliet, how you make one start.—What is the matter now?

JULIET.

Why, my nasty doll is such a torment.

MRS. SELWYN.

Very pretty, to quarrel with a bit of painted wood!—Oh! you silly child!—Come, leave your doll, and let me hear you read.

JULIET.

I tell you I won't.

MRS. SELWYN.

Oh! you are a sweet little girl, so mild and so obliging; how everybody loves you.

JULIET, (crying.)

Let me alone then!

MRS. SELWYN.

Pretty creature!—What a sweet face!—Look how your doll stares at you!

JULIET, (Rising in a passion, and throwing her doll across the room.)

I wish the doll was a thousand miles off, a little provoking creature!— (Mrs. Selwyn laughs.) —I won't be laugh'd at, that I won't.

MRS. SELWYN.

How will you help it?—Leave off crying directly, or I will shut you up for two hours. — (Another pause, Juliet still cries, but by degrees becomes quiet, after some time she calls.) —Mary!—Mary!

MRS. SELWYN.

What now, miss?

JULIET.

I want Mary.— (calls) —Mary, I say!

Enter Mary.

MARY.

Mercy, miss, I came as soon as ever I heard you.

JULIET.

You are always so slow.—Take down my goldfinch, and fetch me some seed and water.

MARY.

Yes, miss. (She reaches the bird down, then goes out, and returns with some water and seed.)

JULIET.

Come my pretty, let your mistress feed you, I love you very much.— (She feeds it.)

MRS. SELWYN.

Yes, you love it vastly just now, but sometimes you are ready to wring its neck, when it does not eat to please you.

MARY, (aside.)

One would think Mrs. Selwyn liked to see her in a passion, she delights so in teazing her!

JULIET, (feeding the bird.) Oh, you little torment, you won't eat out of my hand!

MRS. SELWYN.

There, I told you so, now, miss, you had better beat the bird, or throw it across the room, as you did your doll.

JULIET.

So I will, if I please.

MRS. SELWYN.

Do, I would advise you!

MARY.

Dear ma'am, how *can* you?

JULIET.

Come, eat then.—You *won't!*—You nasty, little obstinate, ungrateful creature,—I'll teach you to teaze me, I will.— (*She snatches the bird out of the cage in a passion, gives it a squeeze, then looks at it, and bursts into tears.*) —Oh! Heaven, I have killed my bird!—

MARY.

Oh, dear, miss, I hope not.

JULIET.

Look at it, Mary, pray try if you can fetch it to life!—Oh my poor bird.—Is it dead, Mary?——

MARY.

Yes, miss, you have killed it.

JULIET.

I!—*I have killed it!*—I that loved it so!—Oh! how unhappy I am!

MARY.

Don't cry so, miss, you was not so much to blame now.

Enter Paulina.

PAULINA.

Dear Juliet, what's the matter?

JULIET, (*throws herself into Paulina's arms.*)

Oh! cousin, why did you leave me?—I am never so naughty when you are with me.

PAULINA.

My dear, I have been seeking you, at last I heard you was playing with Fanny Wood, so then I sat down to write to mama.—But what has happened?--

MRS. SELWYN.

Oh! Miss Juliet has been in one of her usual furies.—I must dress.—I am tired out with her.—Mary will tell you, Miss Paulina. (*She goes out.*)

MARY, (*muttering.*)

And 'tis as much your fault as her's this time, I must say, teaze, teaze, for ever.

PAULINA.

Mary, what is the matter?

MARY.

Shall I tell, miss?

JULIET.

Oh! my cousin will hate me.

PAULINA. *I* hate you, my dear, no, I shall pity you.

MARY.

Why, miss, my young lady was feeding her bird, and hurt it some-how, and 'tis dead.

JULIET.

No, Paulina, that is not all; I was angry with my poor bird, I gave it a sudden squeeze, and killed it.

PAULINA.

My dear cousin, you almost redeem your faults by this openness of heart.—How I pity you, how much you must feel on this occasion!

JULIET, (weeping, but with gentleness.)

But you, who are so good, how much you must detest me!

MARY.

To tell you the truth, Miss Paulina, my young lady was not so much to blame as she is sometimes. Mrs. Selwyn did teaze her sadly, that she did, to be sure.

JULIET.

But that was not my bird's fault!—Ah, my poor bird, he will never eat out of my hand again!—How could I be so cruel as to hurt a little creature who loved me so dearly.

PAULINA.

Leave us, Mary. (Mary goes out.)

PAULINA, JULIET.

PAULINA.

Do not distress yourself so much, my dear Juliet.

JULIET.

Do I not deserve to be distressed?

PAULINA.

You have certainly been wrong.

JULIET.

Ah! You do not know half how naughty I have been: I pinched Mary, I beat Fanny Wood!—What is it makes me so wicked, Paulina? I always know when I am so, and I am unhappy; then I fret, and do wrong again.

PAULINA.

I can easily conceive all that, you are greatly to be pitied.

JULIET.

But you are the only person (except my father) who ever speaks to me as if I had common sense!—Mary shrugs up her shoulders and leaves me as soon as she can.— Mrs. Selwyn laughs at me and treats me like a baby. It was but just now she bade me "look how my doll stared at me!" And that put me into such a passion, that I threw my doll across the room.

PAULINA.

Certainly Mrs. Selwyn does not treat you properly, but that does not justify you. You are now, my dear, more than twelve years old; at that age, though children, we are no longer babies, but you do not seek to improve yourself. You read, indeed, because you love reading, but not with a steady view to your own improvement, and almost all the remainder of your time is spent in dressing your doll and playing with Fanny Wood, who is too ignorant to be a proper companion for you; thus you tempt others to treat you like a baby.—I do not offend you?

JULIET.

No, no,—I like to hear you because you speak to me gently, and I feel what you say.

Pray, dear Paulina, tell me what I must do to be like you.

PAULINA.

My dear Juliet, I wish you a better example;—if you were with us, mama would soon teach you to be all your friends could wish.—But Juliet, with the understanding nature has given you, you may do much for yourself. In the words of a very great author I will tell you that

> ———— "There is no soul
> More able to direct you than yourself,
> If with the sap of Reason you would quench,
> Or but allay the Fire of Passion!"————

Read more, and reflect.—Whenever you find yourself getting angry, leave the cause of your displeasure, take a book which amuses you, and read till you find yourself calm and easy. Struggle with your violent passions, and think to what dreadful consequences they will lead if you indulge them.

JULIET.

Consequences!

PAULINA.

Yes, my dear cousin, I know not to what an excess they may transport you in time, if they are not now opposed.—My mother told me, the other day, she had just read the history of a man, who, when a boy, squeezed his squirrel to death as you did your bird, and when he grew up, after various crimes, being angry with his wife, his child, who was in her arms, happened to cry while he was speaking, and, in a fit of passion, he laid his hand on it, and strangled it in a moment!

JULIET.

Oh! Heaven, how shocking; do you think it *possible*, Paulina, do you think it *possible* I should ever do so?

PAULINA.

It is impossible to say to what extravagance passion may lead!—But yesterday you would have detested the idea of injuring your bird—and are we not told in the Bible, that when the Prophet foretold to Hazael* the miseries he would bring on his country, and the cruelties of which he would be guilty, he exclaimed, "Is thy servant a *dog* that he should do this *great* thing?"—And yet when he gave way to his passions, he exactly verified the Prophet's words.

JULIET.

Oh, Paulina! you terrify me extremely—I will indeed try to be good—I will not beat Fanny, nor pinch Charles any more.

PAULINA.

I wish you may not.—It is time for us to dress, your father will be at home presently, and I hear Charles is just come from school. (*They go out.*)

END OF THE FIRST PART.

---

* See 8th Chapter of the 2d Book of Kings.

Part The Second.

*Juliet enters from the garden, she draws a chair,
sits down, and leans her head on her hand.*

JULIET.

I HAVE a sad head-ach, it always comes when I cry so much.—How true is what
Paulina said just now, that I make myself wretched by indulging my passions!—Why
did nobody ever tell me so before?— (*She takes a picture from her bosom and kisses it.*)
—Oh, my dear mother!—You died too early to form, by your example, the daughter
you loved so tenderly!—Wretched girl!—Why do I ever, for a moment, forget the
character which my father drew of my mother when he gave me this picture.—"Be
like your mother, my Juliet; she was mild and gentle to all, she was beloved by every
one who knew her! her dying wish was, that you might be virtuous!—My child, be
worthy of your mother!—Yes, those were exactly his words. Ah! how little do I fulfil
her wishes!—I, who ill-treat the servant to whose care she intrusted my infancy--Who
abuse a poor child whose situation should make me pity her!—I whom every body hates!
—Torn by contrary feelings!—Capable of knowing when I do wrong, yet yielding to the
next temptation.——In spite of my faults, am I not to be pitied?

Enter Mary.

MARY.

Miss, my master bade me tell you he is going to Mr. Richley's, and shall be back in less
than an hour.

JULIET.

Very well.

MARY.

What is the matter, miss, you are crying?

JULIET.

I have reason to cry.

MARY.

I am sure, miss, I don't know any young lady who might be happier.—You have the
best of fathers.

JULIET.

Ah! that is true.

MARY.

And here you have a fine house, where you are, as one may say, mistress, and a carriage,
and every earthly thing you can wish.—Only think of the poor children down in the
village: the little Wood's, whose mother is so sick, and who are half starved!

JULIET.

Alas, yes!—And I have ill-treated poor Fanny!—My dear Mary, do go down to the
village and give her this shilling; I will beg papa, presently, to send our apothecary to
her mother.

MARY.

Oh, miss, what a pity you are not always good, how every body would love you.

JULIET.

I hope they will in future.

Enter Paulina.

PAULINA.

Juliet, what are you going to do?

JULIET.

I am going to read to Mrs. Selwyn, in her own room, and afterwards Charles and I are going to play.

PAULINA.

Very well, then I will finish my letter to mama.

JULIET.

Do so.—I shall not stay long with Mrs. Selwyn.—Let me know, Mary, when my father comes in.

MARY.

Yes, miss. (*Juliet goes out.*)

PAULINA, MARY.

MARY.

Miss Juliet seems very unhappy to-day.

PAULINA.

Yes, she has naturally a strong sense of what is right; she feels that she is wrong, and of course is unhappy.

MARY.

I cannot help loving her, though she is sometimes so much out of the way. She was a sweet child before she grew so passionate, and she has a great deal of good about her still. How my poor lady would have grieved had she lived to see her so head-strong!

PAULINA.

Had it pleased Heaven to spare Mrs. Beecher, Juliet would probably have been a very different character; she has an admirable understanding, but she is ill educated.

MARY.

That's true, indeed, miss. I take the liberty of speaking to you, because you know how I love all this family, and that I have lived in it long enough to know something about it.

PAULINA.

Yes, Mary, you may speak to me without fear; I know your attachment to your late lady and all that belonged to her.

MARY.

Ah, miss, I wish my young lady lived with you, you are so mild and so sensible, and my lady your mother is so fine a character———

PAULINA.

I have reason to glory in my mother.—May I be one day like her.

MARY.

You will, miss, nay, you *are* already; truly I hear of you from all parts.—But I know you don't wish to be praised.—What I was going to say, is this:—Nobody hears us?—No.—Indeed, Miss Paulina, Mrs. Selwyn is not fit to have the care of my young lady.

PAULINA.

It is true indeed.

MARY.

She sets her no example but laziness, and she teazes her out of her wits;—if you had but heard her this morning——

PAULINA.

I see it with pain. She has no command over my cousin, because she puts herself on a level with her by mean teazing and raillery;—a passionate temper was never mended by irritation.——By the way, I don't much like this scheme of playing with Charles; Juliet and he always quarrel, and I am afraid he will overthrow all her good resolutions. I mean to speak to my uncle, to-night, about Mrs. Selwyn, not to blame or censure her, but merely to say I think she does not exactly follow the right method of managing my cousin's temper.

MARY.

Truly I think not.

PAULINA.

I intend to ask my uncle to let Juliet return with me, I know mama wishes it.

MARY.

I wish he may, miss, with all my heart.

PAULINA.

Well, I will go and write my letter.

(*She is going, when Juliet rushes in apparently much terrified.*)

JULIET.

Oh Paulina!—Mary!—Help, help!

MARY.

Oh dear, miss, what's the matter?

JULIET.

My brother!—help—help him!—go to him.

(*Mary runs out, Juliet sinks down with her head against a chair, Paulina goes to her.*)

PAULINA.

Cousin!—My dear Juliet, what is the matter?—Oh, Heaven! she is fainting!—What shall I do, shall I run to Charles?—No, I cannot leave this dear girl.—Juliet, revive, smell to my salts.— (*Juliet recovering, rises on her knees, and clings round Paulina.*)

JULIET.

Oh, Paulina! Send for some help.—Run to my father.—My father!—Good Heaven! he will hate me for ever.—I shall be banished his sight; plead for me Paulina!—Wretched girl!—What will become of me!

PAULINA.

For pity's sake tell me what you have done?

JULIET.

What have I done?—I know not!—Perhaps I have killed my brother!

PAULINA, (*shudders and shrinks back.*)

Unhappy girl!

JULIET.

Oh! well may you shudder, well may you look at me with horror!—You who warned me; how dare I clasp my arms round you.—Those hands, which, (how can I live to tell

it) perhaps have murdered my brother. (*She faints.*)

PAULINA.

With what terror do I hear her, (*she leans over her.*) Wretched victim of ungovern'd passion!—Revive, fear not my reproaches!—Ah, thou art already too miserable!

Enter Mary.

MARY.

Ah, miss, what shall we do?—I have sent for a surgeon.

PAULINA.

How is he hurt?

MARY.

Alas! I know not how much, the knife has struck him near the eye.

PAULINA.

The knife!

MARY.

Yes, they were at play and quarrelled, Miss Juliet had a knife in her hand, which she threw at him.

PAULINA.

How dreadful!—let us run to him!—Yet, Juliet! But why should I seek to revive her! —Unhappy creature, she wakes but to woe!—Perhaps he may be blinded!—I stiffen with horror!—Ah, I hear the surgeon; follow me, Mary! (*They run out.*)

(JULIET, *alone and recovering.*)

Paulina, where am I!—You will not speak!—What have I done!—Ah I remember—too, too well I remember!—(*She raises herself*)—They are gone!—They leave me!—to die alone!—Alas I deserve it!—Am I worthy that one creature should pity me!—Yet the torments I endure!—Can they atone for my crime?—Never, never!—Dreadful idea!—must I suffer thro' life the anguish I feel at this moment?—Thro' *life*—what terrible fears crowd upon me!—(*she kneels.*) Oh God of *mercy!* hear me, pity me!—Ah He is a God of *justice!*—Can he forgive *me* who have murdered my Brother?—What a wretch am I!———

Enter Mary.

MARY.

Miss Juliet, are you better?

JULIET.

Yes, Mary.—Have you seen———

MARY.

Your brother?—yes, Miss.

JULIET.

Ah, you weep!

MARY.

Truly yes, I am frightened to death.

JULIET.

I am the unhappy cause.—I dread to hear—I dare not ask.

MARY.

The surgeon is with him; I could not stay any longer to see him suffer so.

JULIET. Suffer!

MARY.

Yes, the surgeon is obliged to hurt him, to find if the wound is—I cannot speak it!

JULIET.

Mortal you would say?—How is it that *I* have courage to pronounce that horrible word? —Ah, I gather courage from the excess of my despair.

MARY.

Oh my poor master, what will he say!

JULIET.

Do not distract me!—Pity for a moment the pangs I suffer!—Leave me, Mary, leave me, I implore you!—Go, learn if there is any hope! (*Mary goes out.*)

JULIET.

I have lost every-thing!—My father will drive me from him for ever—I shall quit every-thing I love!—My friends, my relations will blush when my name is mentioned— Never more shall I revisit these scenes, so dear to my infancy!—Let me not recall the years I have past—years of innocence and happiness!—Go where I will, I shall be pointed at and hated.—Even the picture of my mother, which used in all my distresses to console me, I can never see again.—I should fancy it reproached me.—And all this misery I have incurred by one moment of passion!—Oh God, if thou should'st this once deign to save me, never, never, will I be guilty again!

Enter Paulina, (*running.*)

PAULINA.

Juliet!—my dear cousin!—be comforted.

JULIET.

Ah! what then!—What!—may I, dare I hope!

PAULINA.

Yes—the surgeon says he is in no danger.

JULIET, (*throwing herself into her arms.*)

Oh my best Paulina!

PAULINA, (*embracing her with tears.*)

I ran to you the instant I heard it.

JULIET.

I have not deserved your goodness.

PAULINA.

Ah Juliet!—if the knife had gone ever so little on one side, Charles would have been killed, or on the other, and he would have been blinded for ever.

JULIET.

Oh merciful, Almighty God!—from what misery has thy providence preserved me!—even now I cannot behold myself without horror.—Have I deserved the mercy I have met with?—No!—tho' innocent in intention, my action was guilty.—I could not wish to hurt my brother, yet took the means to do so!—Detested passion!—Oh Paulina, I am cured for ever!

PAULINA.

I dare hope so!—The lessons of this day have been striking.—They shew how one step in evil leads to another.—Aweful and horrid might have been the event, but as it has proved, we will hope this instruction has been directed by Providence, to warn you of your danger!

JULIET.

It has done it completely.—But Paulina, where is my father?

PAULINA.

I hear him now in the hall.

JULIET.

Oh Paulina, I dare not see him.

PAULINA.

I will go to him, and I hope, return with your pardon.

JULIET.

My best friend—let actions speak my gratitude; deign but to counsel and direct me, henceforth I will be guided by you alone. (*Paulina goes out.*)

Enter Mrs. Selwyn *and* Mary.

MARY.

Well, Miss Juliet, make yourself easy, all goes well.

JULIET.

Thank God!

MRS. SELWYN.

You have had good fortune, Miss, I can tell you.

JULIET.

Good fortune, Ma'am! I dare to consider it as the act of Divine Providence, if not to save *me*, yet to preserve my father from misery.

MRS. SELWYN.

You improve, Miss, your language is really fine.

JULIET.

Misfortunes correct the heart, and strong feelings excite strong expression.—I hope I shall improve.

MRS. SELWYN.

You astonish me!—you who but this morning were dressing your doll, to be making *wise* remarks, is indeed surprising!

JULIET.

I am not a fool, tho' I have acted like one.

MARY.

No, no, they an't very wise that take you for a fool. I have often heard you talk to my master as sensible as any-body in the world.

MRS. SELWYN.

Miss Juliet never indulged me with any of her sensible conversation.

MARY.

Truly no, because you treated her like a baby.

MRS. SELWYN.

You take great liberties.

MARY.

I beg your pardon, Ma'am, but I have often told you you did not know my young lady so well as I did.

MRS. SELWYN.

The more sense she has, the more shame for her to behave as she has done.

JULIET.

Too true indeed!—my conscience tells me I have not the excuse of folly.—But I have suffer'd passion to over-run and darken all my good qualities. This one hour has driven it from my heart. I am no longer a foolish child.

Enter Paulina.

PAULINA.

Come, my dearest Juliet.—Charles is with your father, he knows all, he forgives you, he calls for you.

JULIET.

I owe every-thing to you!

PAULINA.

I have more good news for you—one word.

(*Mrs. Selwyn and Mary retire to the back of the Scene.*) You go home with me— you are to stay with us as long as you please!

JULIET.

Delightful!—

PAULINA.

Your father dismisses Mrs. Selwyn.

JULIET.

Ah I am sorry!—She is poor, and she has taught me many things.

PAULINA.

My good cousin, how I love that gratitude!—your father will allow her a pension, we have settled all that since I left you.

JULIET.

Oh my best cousin!—how much do I owe you.

PAULINA.

I am overpaid if you are happy.

JULIET.

To be so I must be good.—That will be the work of your hands!—How will you be loved by your friends, by your mother, by Heaven itself!—yes that *will* repay you.

PAULINA.

Let us go, my uncle expects us. *Scene closes.*

Sensibility.

A DRAMA.
IN TWO PARTS.

CHARACTERS.

MRS. MELVILLE,
MRS. RIVERS,
CECILIA, — DAUGHTER OF MRS. RIVERS.
ISABELLA, — DAUGHTER OF MRS. MELVILLE.
MARTHA, — MRS. MELVILLE'S MAID.

——Exclamations, tender tones, fond tears,
And all the graceful drap'ry Pity wears,
These are not Pity's self, they but express
Her inward suff'rings, by her pictured dress;
And these fair marks, reluctant I relate,
These lovely symbols may be counterfeit.
SENSIBILITY.—MISS MOORE.

SCENE, A DRESSING-ROOM, AT MRS. MELVILLE'S.

(A Table standing with Work, and Books.)
Enter Mrs. Rivers, Cecilia, and Martha.

MARTHA.

PRAY, MA'AM, walk in, I will let my mistress know you are here, she is walking in the garden with Miss Melville.—Won't you please to sit?

(She places chairs, they sit down.)

MRS. RIVERS.

Thank you, Martha, don't hurry your mistress. *(Martha goes out.)*

CECILIA.

This is a pretty room, mama.

MRS. RIVERS.

Very much so, I see it again with great pleasure.

CECILIA.

It is some time, I think, since you were here.

MRS. RIVERS.

Yes, near two years. Mrs. Melville has been gone so long on business of her late husband's to an estate he had in Jamaica.

CECILIA.

How glad you will be to see her again! What a delightful day we shall spend!

MRS. RIVERS.

It will indeed give me great pleasure.

CECILIA.

But her daughter!—Oh, mama, what joy to her to see her mother again after an absence of two years!—I should envy her, if I had not passed those two years with the best of mothers.

MRS. RIVERS.

She has indeed probably lost much by so long an absence from her who is so well able to instruct her.

CECILIA.

Undoubtedly!—Ah, whose instructions can teach the heart so soon as those of a mother, whose reproofs proceed from affection, whose praises are the greatest glory of a child!

MRS. RIVERS.

It is true,—a child must be obstinate indeed, who refuses to listen to the instructions of a fond mother.—Mrs. Melville is entitled to her daughter's best affections, not only by the goodness of her heart and understanding, but by the sacrifices she has made for her sake.—When Mr. Melville died, he left his large estate in Jamaica to his little girl: on enquiry, her mother found that the estate had been, and still was, ill managed by the steward; in short, that nothing but the presence of some person interested in its improvement could render it half so valuable as it had been supposed.—She determined, therefore, to overcome her dread of the sea, which all her life had been extreme; to leave her friends, her sister, even her child, in England, and undertake the voyage herself.—This she has done; has restored the estate to the most flourishing condition, and is now returned to enjoy the reward of her labours.

CECILIA.

What a charming character!—(*A short pause.*) I like this room very much, 'tis so pleasant and quiet— (*She rises and walks about*) —Mama, may I look at this book?

MRS. RIVERS.

If you please, as it is lying open to every-one's inspection, it cannot be improper, but it is impertinent and ill-bred to look even into *printed* books, which are placed out of immediate view.

CECILIA.

"The Beauties of Sterne!"—It has Miss Melville's name in it.—I do not know this book, Mama.

MRS. RIVERS.

No, my dear, tho' it has great merit in point of writing and sentiment, it is not exactly the book I should chuse for you at present. In my opinion it recommends too much the enervating mind of Sensibility, to which I so greatly object.—But here come Mrs. Melville and Isabella.

Enter Mrs. Melville *and* Isabella.

MRS. MELVILLE.

My dear friend, how much I rejoice to see you!

MRS. RIVERS.

The pleasure is mutual, believe me!—It is so long since we met, I began to fear we should meet no more!—This is, I believe, Miss Melville, but so grown I should hardly have known her!

MRS. MELVILLE.

Not more than Miss Rivers.—I must have these young people acquainted.

(*Mrs. Melville introduces Cecilia and Isabella to each other, they curtsy, and seem to talk apart.*)

MRS. RIVERS. I hope they will be so, nothing can give me more pleasure.

MRS. MELVILLE.

But I forget to beg your pardon for keeping you waiting, I had strolled beyond the garden into the field, and Martha could not find me.—She has shewn you into a litter'd room.

MRS. RIVERS.

No apology is necessary, I have long known and loved this room.

MRS. MELVILLE.

It is my daughter's now, I gave it up to her the day after my return, and she has already brought hither her books and work—so that she has the confusion to answer for— (*smiling.*)

MRS. RIVERS.

It is a becoming confusion, I like to see books and work about in a young person's apartment.

ISABELLA.

Mine would have been in better order, mama, if you had not called me away suddenly.—Besides I hardly know where I am, or what I do at present.

MRS. RIVERS.

I dare say, my dear, you have hardly yet recovered, if I may so express myself, the happiness of seeing your mother!

ISABELLA.

No indeed, Ma'am!—The extreme joy almost overcame me. It may well be called *recovery*, for such delight is really suffering! (*Mrs. Rivers looks at her with some surprise.*)

MRS. MELVILLE.

Mine was, and still is, exquisite!—To return once more to my friends, to my sister, to my daughter, is happiness so great as wholly to repay me all I have suffered in my absence from them!

MRS. RIVERS.

No doubt, every sacrifice we make of pleasure to duty will, sooner or later, be repaid; even the conviction of having done so carries with it a comfort to the heart superior to all the advantages to be derived from a deviation from virtue.

MRS. MELVILLE.

You say true. It was with extreme regret that I prepared to quit England, and to leave my daughter; but the assurance that my departure was necessary to her future welfare, the dread of endangering her health, then extremely delicate, by taking her with me, and the conviction that I left her in proper care, conspired to determine me, and I am now repaid.

ISABELLA.

But, mama, I should have been *so* afraid of the sea and storms!

MRS. MELVILLE.

Go, you are a silly child, to form such a terrible idea of dangers, which are principally imaginary.—But, my dear Mrs. Rivers, will you go with me to my greenhouse?—I have some curious West-India plants.

MRS. RIVERS.

With all my heart.—Children, will you stay here, or go with us?

MRS. MELVILLE.

Oh, they shall remain here.—They will become better acquainted in our absence.
(*Mrs. Rivers and Mrs. Melville go out.*)

CECILIA, ISABELLA.

ISABELLA.

Let us sit down, my dear Miss Rivers. (*They sit.*)—What pleasure I hope to derive from your acquaintance!

CECILIA.

My mother I am sure will be happy in my forming an intimacy with you, she has so high an opinion of Mrs. Melville!

ISABELLA.

It will give me infinite pleasure.—Suffer me to say I already feel I shall love you extremely, I am already attached to you.—Dear Cecilia, may I believe the impression is mutual!

CECILIA.

I have no doubt, on a farther acquaintance, my gratitude for your kindness will ripen into real regard.

ISABELLA.

You are very good!—(*She assumes a melancholy air.*)—Hitherto I have been very unfortunate in my friendships!

CECILIA, (*with a smile.*)

You are very young to complain of that.

ISABELLA, (*earnestly.*)

Alas yes!—The misfortune of too great *sensibility* is mine.—You can have no idea what I have suffered—what I do at this moment suffer!

CECILIA.

You alarm and distress me.—What at your age can have happened to make you so uneasy?

ISABELLA, (*shedding tears.*)

Alas, my dear Cecilia, amidst all my joy for the return of my mother, I endure severe regret, *bitter anguish* I might call it.

CECILIA.

Good Heaven! on what account.

ISABELLA, *(embracing her.)*

Amiable girl!—I see you sympathize with me.

CECILIA.

I do indeed, but surely you would not have told me so much without intending to explain yourself.

ISABELLA.

No, my *sweet friend.**—From your tenderness I expect the only consolation of which my situation is capable.—How will your kind and gentle nature pity me when you hear the loss I have sustained!

CECILIA.

What can it be, when your mother is still with you?

ISABELLA.

At the seat of my aunt, where I have been during my mother's absence, I contracted a *strong* and *ardent* attachment to a young lady about your age.—I even think you resemble her,—you have the same softness of complexion, the same sweet smile!

CECILIA, *(embracing her.)*

Ah, my dear Isabella, I will spare you the relation.—I guess too easily what you have suffered!—It is true I have never formed any friendship out of my own family, but I can conceive what its feelings must be.—And have you really lost, for ever, a tie so tender?

ISABELLA.

Not, I hope, *for ever.*

CECILIA.

How!—I have misunderstood you.—I believe you meant to have said she was dead.

ISABELLA.

Oh no!—I should hardly be able to survive so great a misfortune.—Is it not enough to be separated from her?

CECILIA.

You fear you shall, perhaps, meet her no more!

ISABELLA.

No.—She is to spend the greatest part of the summer with me.

CECILIA.

I do not understand—what then do you lament?

ISABELLA.

What?—Surely her absence at present!

CECILIA.

What the absence of a few months do you regret so deeply!—I profess you surprise me!

ISABELLA, *(a little disconcerted.)*

But I have been so accustomed to see her every day, she is so charming—and my misfortune is too great sensibility!

CECILIA.

Can sensibility become a misfortune and a torment?—I have been taught to consider it as the source of goodness and delight.—True, indeed, we may be sometimes severely pained by the impossibility of relieving those whom we pity, by the illness of friends,

---

* The inflated and strong language Isabella uses, is one symptom of False Sensibility.—To apply violent terms on common occasions is equally absurd and unnatural.

and various other circumstances, but at the same time an active wish to do good warms and chears the heart, and when we stifle our anguish and carefully attend the sick-bed of those we love, do we not feel such comfort as half repays us for the sorrow we endure in seeing them suffer!

ISABELLA.

But unfortunately I feel so much, I can do very little to relieve the pain of those I love; my presence of mind forsakes me, and I become unable to assist them.

CECILIA.

But pardon me for saying that it is a sort of weakness against which we ought to struggle, our feeling becomes useless, worse than useless; it *disables* us if it does not *prompt* us to action. We might as well not feel for the unhappy, as not seek to relieve them!

ISABELLA.

I sympathise with them, but my spirits are so weak I can do little more.

CECILIA.

I protest I do not understand you.

Enter Martha.

MARTHA.

Oh, dear Miss Melville, a sad thing has happened!

ISABELLA.

Oh Heavens! what? You alarm me beyond expression!

MARTHA.

Don't be too much frightened, miss, 'tis well it's no worse, but you will be vexed?——

ISABELLA.

I entreat you to tell me what has happened at once.

MARTHA.

Why, miss, your pretty parrot has hurt himself sadly.

ISABELLA.

Ah! my poor parrot, what has he done?

MARTHA.

Miss, he was standing upon his perch, when a great dog followed the baker into the kitchen, Poll was frightened, and flew to the window, dash'd himself against a pane of glass, broke it, and cut himself very much with the pieces.

ISABELLA, (*in tears.*)

Oh! what shall I do, what shall I do!

CECILIA.

My dear Isabella, don't distress yourself so,—I dare say he will soon be well again,—let us go and see if we can do any thing for him.

ISABELLA.

Oh! I cannot bear to see him.

MARTHA.

Dear miss, he will soon be well, but somebody should put something to the cut.

ISABELLA.

Martha, will you?

MARTHA.

I would with all my heart, Miss, but I burned my hand so yesterday I cannot hold him, and our silly cook is afraid of his biting her.

ISABELLA.

Will Thomas?

MARTHA.

Thomas is not at home, Miss.

CECILIA.

Dear Isabella, I will do it—'tis true I shall be sorry to see the poor creature in pain, but I cannot bear the idea of not assisting him.

ISABELLA.

You are extremely good!

CECILIA.

Poor thing! he is suffering all this time. Come, my dear, let us go to him.

ISABELLA.

Oh, I cannot see him.

CECILIA.

Not see him!

MARTHA.

Dear Miss, the poor thing knows you, and he will be quiet if you are by.

ISABELLA.

Oh, but indeed it will make me ill.

CECILIA.

Pooh, pooh, a run in the garden will soon make you well again!

ISABELLA.

What spirits you have!

CECILIA.

To be sure—that is natural at my age—what have *I* to be melancholy about?

ISABELLA.

You are very happy!

CECILIA.

You have as much cause to be happy as I have; but come along. (*They go out.*)

MARTHA.

That's a charming young lady!—How she runs along, and how chearful she looks!— What ails Miss Isabella, I wonder; she always looks sorrowful, and sighs, and walks so slowly, I see that already.—Truly, that is unnatural at her age.

Enter Mrs. Rivers, Mrs Melville.

MRS. MELVILLE.

Martha, where are the young ladies?

MARTHA.

Marry, Ma'am, they are gone to see the poor Parrot; he has hurt himself, and they are gone to help him.

MRS. MELVILLE.

Very well, they are well employed. (*Martha goes out.*)

MRS. MELVILLE, MRS. RIVERS.

MRS. MELVILLE.

My dear friend, I am so charmed to see you, and so anxious to talk with you, that I fear I shall quite fatigue you with *prate!*

MRS. RIVERS.

Not at all; assure yourself I am too much interested in all which concerns you, and am indeed eager to have an unrestrained conversation with you.

MRS. MELVILLE.

I am equally eager; and as the first subject to a fond mother is her child, we will talk of ours. I am not quite satisfied with Isabella.

MRS. RIVERS.

How so?—She appears gentle and sensible!

MRS. MELVILLE.

Yes, she has many good qualities, but I see with pain that one of the most amiable she carries to an excess which makes me wish she possessed it not: it gives her so much pain, and will thro' life be so often a source of distress to her, that I could almost wish to suppress it entirely.

MRS. RIVERS.

Pray tell me what it is—you really alarm me!

MRS. MELVILLE.

Sensibility.

MRS. RIVERS.

I am amazed!

MRS. MELVILLE.

I once hardly could have believed I should wish a child of mine to want Sensibility, but I see in Isabella how much it tends to increase the unavoidable distresses of human life, even to *create* them where they are not; so that I really think had I another child to educate, I should labour as much as possible to suppress this pleasing, but unhappy quality.

MRS. RIVERS.

I must repeat, you amaze me!—What! Sensibility!—The first and best gift of Heaven— would you rob your child of *that?*—Not only is it the sweetest grace of youth, but the principal source of its virtues.—Can you conceive any great or good action which has ever been performed by a person wanting Sensibility? Did you ever hear of any really great character who wanted this endowment? Have I then a right to rob my child of that which alone can lead to exalted virtue, and to the train of delight by which it is accompanied?—How sweetly, as well as truly, says a certain charming Authoress,

> "Cold and inert the mental powers would lie,
> Without this quick'ning spark of Deity.
> To draw the rich materials from the mine,
> To bid the mass of intellect refine;
> To melt the firm, to animate the cold,
> And Heav'n's own impress stamp on Nature's gold;
> To give immortal *Mind* its *firmest* tone,
> Oh Sensibility!—is all thine own!"

MRS. MELVILLE.

I agree with you fully, my dear friend, as to the *graces* and *charms* of Sensibility; but allow me to differ from you a moment. Was not *Cato* a great character, yet had he sensibility who did not shed a tear over the body of his son, just slain in battle?

MRS. RIVERS.

Undoubtedly yes.—First we ought to consider the education which was given to the Romans.—We ought to recollect that their country was the chief object of their love, and that they were taught to despise all considerations which interfered with their duty to that.—Thus when Cato saw the dead body of his son, he did not weep, because *true* Sensibility exalted his mind to the height of patriotism, which made him willingly yield his son a victim to Rome.—He wished also to encourage the sinking Romans, by making their lives less valuable in their eyes, when he, to whom they looked for example, could so chearfully part with that life which was dearer to him than his own.—What but Sensibility could have awakened this high sense of duty, and heroic resolution?

MRS. MELVILLE.

But that is exactly what I complain of. Sensibility, at least the sensibility I am used to see, *enervates* and *weakens* the mind; it destroys this heroic resolution, this preference of duty to indulgence.

MRS. RIVERS.

"The Sensibility you are used to see," these words explain to me your meaning.

MRS. MELVILLE.

You think then there are two kinds of Sensibility?

MRS. RIVERS.

Undoubtedly.—Or rather I should say that which is commonly dignified with that charming name, is unworthy of it; and if you will allow me to say so, by what I have seen of Miss Melville's, that is the Sensibility she possesses, though perhaps mixed and blended with the true mind. Let us refer again to the delightful Authoress I have already quoted, whose every line contains meaning and reason.

> " 'Tis not to mourn because a Sparrow dies,
> To rave in artificial extasies!"

I would have Sensibility a *spring* of *Action*. I would have it directed to a generous, firm line of Conduct. In short, it should be *Principle refined and pointed*. I would have young people taught to treat every creature with mercy and kindness, but I would not have them waste their tenderness and affection on a set of Animals. I would have them anxious to relieve every thing in distress, but I would not have them

> Boast quick rapture trembling in their eye,
> If from the Spider's web they save a Fly.

Far would I be from wishing them to have the word *Sensibility* continually in their mouths, tho' I would never for an instant have it quit their hearts. It ought to *animate*, not *deject* them; to *strengthen*, not *enervate* their minds.

MRS. MELVILLE.

You are perfectly right, my dear friend, but how shall we teach young people to draw the line?

MRS. RIVERS.

By not suffering them to pass it, without reprehension; by not praising them for *feeling*, by not allowing them to exaggerate their *language*, which leads to that hateful exaggeration of Sentiment I so much dislike.—Accustomed to express themselves strongly, to say they *"love,"* they *"detest"*—they are in *"anguish,"* in *"extasy,"* they strive to make their feelings correspond with their words: if they succeed, their imaginations become inflamed and delusive; if they do not, they are perpetually affected and unnatural.—Let them ask themselves, whether they really *feel* what they *express*, when they say they *love* or *hate* any-thing; let them first consider whether it is worth *loving* or *hating*, and then whether they really *do* love or hate it: they will then not be so easily deceived *themselves*, which, I believe, generally is the case before they seek to deceive *others*.

MRS. MELVILLE.

I am sure you are right, and I shall earnestly press this knowledge of *herself* on Isabella.

MRS. RIVERS.

I have always done so with Cecilia; and I wish young people would consider how much more amiable, simple unaffected manners are, than that pompous pretence of feeling and tenderness of which some are so fond.

Enter Martha.

MARTHA.

The dinner is ready, Ma'am.

MRS. MELVILLE.

Very well, we are coming. (*They go out.*)

END OF THE FIRST PART.

Part The Second.

Enter Cecilia and Isabella.

ISABELLA.

T HIS ROOM IS COOLER than the dining parlour.

CECILIA.

It is remarkably pleasant and quiet.

ISABELLA, (*sighing.*)

Come let us sit, I am wretchedly out of spirits.

CECILIA.

I saw with great concern that you appeared out of spirits at dinner, and that your mama looked uneasy at it.—What is the matter, are you not well?

ISABELLA.

Yes, well—that is tolerably well—but the sight of my poor Parrot this morning has made me quite unhappy.

CECILIA.

But, my dear, you ought not to suffer it to do so!

ISABELLA.

Bless me! can I feel as I please?

CECILIA.

In a great measure.

ISABELLA.

I am glad you think so.—Then you are never unhappy I suppose, for I believe nobody would chuse to be so!

CECILIA.

Pardon me.—There are cases in which we must *feel* unhappy, whether we struggle against it or not: but do you not think much of our unhappiness depends on our indulging melancholy, or striving against it?

ISABELLA.

Perhaps it may, but why will you not allow the present to be one of the cases you mention?

CECILIA.

I cannot think it of consequence enough. It is true I pity the poor bird, and if I were attached to him, as I dare say you are, I should be extremely concerned, but still as my concern would do him no good, and as I had done all I could to relieve him, I should strive against it, and make myself easy.

ISABELLA.

But *I* cannot—it makes me unhappy.

CECILIA.

That is what it ought not to do.

ISABELLA.

Do you make no allowance for the difference of dispositions?

CECILIA.

Yes,—but I also believe we can greatly correct and alter our own.

ISABELLA.

And you think *I* need this correction?

CECILIA.

You are not angry with me!

ISABELLA.

No—but

CECILIA.

Nay, that is unfair—we were speaking generally—you asked my sentiments, or I should not have given them; if I have offended you, I sincerely beg your pardon.

ISABELLA.

No, no, you have not offended me—yet I will own much less than what you have said would have offended me in some people; but you speak so sensibly, and with so much goodness, I love to hear you tho' it is to blame me.

CECILIA.

I did not mean to *blame you:* I could not think of taking that liberty.—Let us drop the subject.

ISABELLA.

No, no, we will not drop it.—I shall think you are angry, if you do not tell me all you think.

CECILIA.

What would you have me tell you?

ISABELLA.

Whether I really, in your opinion, require the correction you talk of?

CECILIA.

I have not a right, on so short an acquaintance, to decide.

ISABELLA.

You will not tell me—but I beg of you to be sincere!

CECILIA.

Well then remember you have no right to be offended.—I *do* think you suffer your feelings to govern you too much.

ISABELLA.

Well I will not dispute the word *suffer*, since you say I might correct it, but tell me how?

CECILIA.

Are *you* convinced the correction is necessary?

ISABELLA.

Perhaps not entirely.

CECILIA.

Permit me to ask you a few questions.

ISABELLA.

With all my heart.

CECILIA.

Suppose your mother, or any of your friends, were ill, what would you do?

ISABELLA.

I should be very much grieved!

CECILIA.

Of course—but should you attend to them yourself, or how should you act?

ISABELLA.

I should wish to attend them, but I fear I should be too unhappy!

CECILIA.

If you were yourself ill, how should you expect your mother to act?

ISABELLA.

Oh I know very well she would attend me constantly!

CECILIA.

Well, do you not believe she would feel a great deal?

ISABELLA.

Oh yes, I am sure of it!

CECILIA.

Should you not be very much distress'd, if, instead of attending you, she disturbed you by continual sighs and tears, and rendered herself so incapable of assisting as to be obliged to leave you to the care of servants?

ISABELLA.

Certainly!

CECILIA.

The inference is so obvious, I will leave you to draw it for yourself.—Only let me hint, if every-body felt as you say *you* do, and acted in consequence, what would become of those who are sick, or in danger?

ISABELLA.

You are certainly right—but how am I to conquer this excessive feeling?

CECILIA.

Simply by not indulging it.—Perhaps your mind will sometimes turn itself from a suffering object; but do not heed it.—*Force* it to act.—Do not say "I *cannot*"— but *try.*— *Think* you can, and you will be able.

ISABELLA. Do you think so?

CECILIA.

I am even sure of it.—I will give you an instance: I am myself extremely afraid of *Fire!* and used to tell my mama I believed, if my bed were on fire, I should be burnt for want of resolution to move. She took a great deal of pains to reason me out of this belief, which she foresaw might be so dangerous.—Last summer, when we were at my aunt's, I was one evening in my own room, which joins the nursery, where her little girl was sleeping, the nursery maid was just gone down stairs, I smelt fire, and running into the nursery, saw that the cat had jumped on a table where the maid had placed a candle, and had beat the candle into the cradle where the baby was—the quilt was in a blaze!

ISABELLA. Oh mercy!—what did you do!

CECILIA.

My first impulse was to run for help, but struck with the idea that the infant would be burnt or stifled before help could arrive, I said to myself "Oh mama, let me now re-member your lessons!"—I flew to the cradle, snatched up a small carpet, and threw it into the cradle; it extinguished the flame: I then seized the child, and ran with her down stairs.—You may suppose that my mother and aunt thought me distracted; but when I explained to them what had happened, I thought my aunt would never cease thanking and praising me.—She told me I had saved her from despair and distraction; that her child should be taught to love me as a second mother.—In short, I cannot repeat to you half she said, or describe the painful delight I felt in her gratitude and joy.

ISABELLA.

But did you not suffer from the fright?

CECILIA.

A little.—I felt sick and faint; mama gave me some drops, and I cried a good deal; after which I was quite well, and never can think myself grateful enough to Heaven, for giving me courage to rescue the poor infant!

ISABELLA.

Well, I *admire* you!—but I fear I should never be able to *imitate* you!

CECILIA.

Only give me your promise that you will try, and I am sure you will be able.

Enter Mrs. Melville *and* Mrs. Rivers.

MRS. RIVERS.

So, my dear girls, you have run away from us!—Indeed the dining parlour is so warm, that we were glad to quit it also.

ISABELLA.

It is very warm indeed, ma'am.

CECILIA, (*to Mrs. Melville.*)

I am afraid you are not well, ma'am?

MRS. MELVILLE.

Not very well indeed.

ISABELLA.

Oh, mama, what is the matter?

MRS. RIVERS.

Are you faint?—Sit down.

(She places a chair, and Mrs. Melville sits down.)

ISABELLA.

Speak to me, mama!—Oh, what shall I do!

CECILIA.

My dear, you alarm your mama; she will be better presently; I will fetch some water.

(She runs out. Mrs. Rivers gives her salts to Mrs. Melville, who becomes more and more faint. Isabella runs about distractedly, and crying.)

MRS. RIVERS.

My dear Isabella, don't be so frighten'd! Open the window, and bathe your mother's forehead with this Hungary water.

ISABELLA. Oh I cannot, indeed I cannot, I am so frighten'd!

MRS. RIVERS.

Silly girl, how can you be such a coward!

(Cecilia returns with water. Martha comes in; they sprinkle Mrs. Melville with water. Cecilia supports her. Isabella continues crying.)

MRS. RIVERS.

Isabella, I am quite ashamed of you—how can you be so childish!

ISABELLA.

Oh, mama is dying, I am sure.

MRS. RIVERS.

Dying!—what nonsense!—she is even now recovering.—My dear friend, are you better?

MRS. MELVILLE.

Yes, I am better, I thank you.—My eyes are still dim.—Who is this supporting me?—My dear Isabella!—Dear child, do not be alarmed, I am better!

(Isabella advances. Cecilia makes signs to her to come forward.)

MARTHA.

Dear ma'am, we are all frighten'd, Miss Isabella is as bad as you almost!

MRS. MELVILLE, *(leaning her head on Cecilia.)*

Don't be frighted, my love; I am better indeed.—I ought to be well, when you are so attentive to me.—Ah! what happiness for a mother to be supported in the arms of her child.—I feel your tears on my face, speak to me Isabella.

ISABELLA, *(falling on her knees before her mother, and kissing her hands)*

Ah mama, I am here!

MRS. MELVILLE.

Who then is this?—Cecilia!—It is to you then that I am obliged for assistance! *(A short pause, during which Isabella appears much confused.)*—Thank you, my dear.—I am subject to these attacks in warm weather, but I am now well.

MRS. RIVERS.

My dear Mrs. Melville, had you not better go to your own room?

MRS. MELVILLE.

I will presently; you and Cecilia will have the goodness to assist me.

ISABELLA.

Ah mama, why do you not say, Isabella will assist me?

MRS. MELVILLE.

We naturally look for help towards those from whom we have received it.

ISABELLA.

Ah mama, it is true indeed I have not been so happy as to be of use to you, but can you believe I did not wish it?

MRS. MELVILLE.

We can only judge of the heart by the actions it produces.

CECILIA, *(eagerly.)*

Dear ma'am, if you could have seen Isabella's distress, her alarm—she is incapable.—Oh can you believe your child could neglect you!

MRS. MELVILLE.

Generous girl! how I love that amiable warmth.

ISABELLA. Mother, my dearest mother, forgive me!

MRS. MELVILLE.

If you are conscious of no offence, why ask forgiveness?

ISABELLA.

Can I think myself innocent, when you are displeased with me?

MRS. RIVERS.

How amiable is that sentiment! It must procure your pardon.—My dear friend, believe me, Isabella suffered exceedingly; her distress alone caused that appearance of neglect you condemn.

MRS. MELVILLE.

If too much feeling, or too little, cause the same effect, ought they not to be equally condemned?

MRS. RIVERS.

If not *equally*, *both* ought to be.—But this is not a time to argue.—You will increase your indisposition by talking, and at least Isabella cannot feel *your* displeasure *too* much.—Forgive her, I beg of you!

CECILIA.

Dearest madam, forgive Isabella.—Look at her; can you see her distress, and not pity her?—Her constitution is slight; the alarm was too much for her.—Her extreme affection for you was the cause of it.

MRS. MELVILLE.

Rise, my dear girl, I forgive the apparent slight!

ISABELLA.

Oh believe, believe, it could not proceed from my heart!

MRS. MELVILLE, *(embracing her.)*

Let us speak of it no more, but correct and suppress in future, I beg of you, that excess of feeling, which renders you incapable of doing your duty.—Come, my dear friend, you will have the goodness to go with me into my own room.—I will lie down awhile.

ISABELLA.

Mama, will you not suffer me to assist you?

MRS. MELVILLE.

If I do not, my dear, it is not because I am still angry with you; but because I do not need your attendance: in less than an hour I dare say I shall be well enough to meet you at the tea-table.—This faintness has only been owing to the heat; I have felt it all day.

ISABELLA.

And yet you have not complained.

MRS. MELVILLE.

No, since complaining could not cool the air, and consequently could not relieve my faintness.—Stay here, my child, with Cecilia, and both of you recover yourselves before I return.

(Mrs. Melville, Mrs. Rivers, and Martha, go out.)

CECILIA, ISABELLA.

(Isabella sits down, and leans her head on her hand.)

CECILIA.

My dear, will you take a little hartshorn and water?

ISABELLA. No, thank you.

CECILIA.

Be easy, my dear girl, since your mama is quite reconciled to you!

ISABELLA.

Ah Cecilia, if I had but recollected, your kind and wise counsels, I should not have incurred her displeasure!

CECILIA.

In future, you will, I doubt not, act otherwise.

ISABELLA.

I hope so!—Never let me again incur a pang so severe as that I felt when my mother spoke of the sweetness of being assisted by her child, when I had not been of the least service to her.—And again, when she said "You and Cecilia will assist me"—as if I were not there! as if, alas, but too justly, I were a useless, helpless being!

CECILIA.

Let us drop these unpleasant ideas, and hope that the consequence will be a fixed resolution on your part to encourage fortitude and activity, and to repress enervating and excessive feeling.

ISABELLA.

It shall indeed; and still, dear Cecilia, counsel and advise me. Be as sincere as I have hitherto found you; be my monitor, my adviser, and my *advocate*.—Dear girl, (embracing her) how can I ever enough thank you for those generous tears you shed, when pleading for me to my mother!—My heart, at least, has for once elected a real friend!

CECILIA.

I hope so, but the same facility with which I was exalted to that character, might expose you to much deceit and treachery.—You see I use the privilige you give me.

ISABELLA.

Do so always, and assist me if you can, to root up my idle prejudices altogether, and to renounce, for ever, the exaggerated expressions and unnatural sentiments of that which you have convinced me is false SENSIBILITY. *Scene closes.*

The Little Trifler.

A DRAMA.
IN THREE PARTS.

CHARACTERS.

MRS. MILDMAY,
SOPHIA, ⎫
EUDOCIA, ⎬ HER DAUGHTERS.
LAURA, ⎭
MRS. CECIL, GOVERNESS TO THE MISS MILDMAYS.
RUTH SAUNDERS, A POOR WOMAN.
SALLY.

The Story of Melanthon affords a striking Lesson on the value of Time, which was, that whenever he made an Appointment, he always expected not only the Hour, but the Minute, should be fixed; that the Day might not run out in the Idleness of Suspense.—JOHNSON.

SCENE, A ROOM WITH BOOK-CASES, FRAMES, A HARPSICHORD, GLOBES, &c.

Enter Mrs. Cecil, Sophia, and Eudocia.

SOPHIA.

I FEEL SO CHEARFUL this fine morning, that I hope I shall get through my employments comfortably before we go for our ride.

EUDOCIA.

Yes, and the sun is so enlivening, we shall enjoy our airing of all things.

MRS. CECIL.

To do that, you must all of you perform your tasks well.—As to Miss Mildmay, I need not remind her, she is always ready.

SOPHIA.

You are always too good to me, my dear governess.

EUDOCIA.

Not better than you deserve, Sophia, we are all ready to allow that.

MRS. CECIL.

Yes, yes, the praise of candour and affection belongs to you equally.—But we lose time.—Where is Miss Laura?—Idling, I dare say. I never shall succeed in my endeavors to teach that child the value of those minutes she wastes so abominably!—Nothing but a concurrence of circumstances will make her aware of the necessity there is, if we would go through our duties properly, of being punctual. 'Tis past nine, she must know it, and yet she is not here.—Do, Miss Eudocia, ring the bell. *(Eudocia rings the bell, they draw a small table, and sit down to work.)*

Enter Sally.

MRS. CECIL.

Sally, pray tell Miss Laura 'tis past nine; I want her here.

SALLY. Yes, ma'am. *(She goes out.)*

EUDOCIA.

Don't you think Sally a very good girl, ma'am?

MRS. CECIL.

Yes, I do indeed. Your mama has had her in her service six years, all that time she has behaved unexceptionably. She was very young when she came hither, and had before been tolerably educated; therefore I do not object to your talking to her sometimes, though I strictly forbid your doing so to the other servants.

SOPHIA.

We are perfectly convinced of the propriety of that. Indeed I cannot conceive how any one can wish it, their language is so unpleasant; and can one expect either pleasure or improvement from those who have had no education.

MRS. CECIL.

Those must have a very bad taste who do.

Laura *runs in.*

LAURA.

Dear ma'am, is it nine o'clock?

MRS. CECIL.

Yes, a full quarter after; what have you been doing?

LAURA.

Why, ma'am, I asked after breakfast what it was o'clock, and they said it wanted a quarter of nine, so I thought I would set one of my drawers in order, but I did not begin directly, and I fancy that made me so late.

MRS. CECIL.

Yes, most likely—your drawers generally require more than a quarter of an hour to set them to rights, and even of that quarter it seems you trifled away part. If you would but consider whether it is possible to do what you undertake in the time you can spare to it, you would not be so often behind your time.—And how have you left your cloaths now?

LAURA.

Oh, ma'am, when Sally called me, I *push'd* them all into the drawer as well as I could.

EUDOCIA, *(laughing.)*

Push'd them!—yes, your things are generally pretty well *push'd*, as you call it!

LAURA.

You have nothing to do with that.

MRS. CECIL.

Come, come, leaving off talking, and get to work—but remember I *will* have your drawer set to rights before you go out.

LAURA.

Oh I shall have plenty of time to do that.

MRS. CECIL.

Aye!—that is exactly your way!—You always have plenty of time in *idea*, and none in *reality*; of course you are always *unpunctual*.

LAURA.

If I am, it is not a *great* fault.

SOPHIA.

Fye Laura!

MRS. CECIL.

Is it not a great fault?—There I differ from you.—It leads to very unpleasant consequences at least—often to very bad ones. In the first place, you trifle away a great deal of time: for instance, your sisters have been at work some minutes; of course their tasks will be done sooner, and they will have the more time for other employments.—It is a chance if you are ready to go out with your mama: you have all your work to do; to read French, and to put your drawers in order.

LAURA.

Well, all that is *my* loss!

MRS. CECIL.

Your accent and manner are a little impertinent, but I will pass that over, as I wish, if possible, to convince you by reasoning.—Suppose then, when you are older, you should appoint a friend to meet you at any place, and because you forget, or over stay your time, she is disappointed, and has her trouble for nothing—That will be *her* loss, I think!

LAURA.

Yes, but it would not be of much consequence.

MRS. CECIL.

You are very slow to be convinced!—Suppose her business is of consequence, and cannot be delayed!

LAURA.

Oh but I should know that, and should be sure to be there!

MRS. CECIL.

Very well! if you can all at once break thro' a settled habit, you have greater command of yourself than I give you credit for.—You will see, and we shall learn, if you do not regret the many moments you have lost in idle trifling.—When do you mean to begin work?

(Laura takes several pieces of work out of her bag.)

MRS. CECIL.

Why do you take out so much at once? you cannot do it all!

LAURA.

Which should I do, ma'am?

MRS. CECIL.

This is what you left on Saturday, on promise to do it to-day; and this is your task for this morning, which I *will* have done.

LAURA.

But there is so much!

MRS. CECIL.

Not so much as I have given your sisters!

LAURA.

But they are older!

MRS. CECIL.

Yes, and somewhat more industrious: there is not too much for you; so no more disputing, but begin.

(Laura sits down by Sophia. After a short pause, she yawns; then leans on Sophia's chair, and whispers to her. Sophia makes no answer.)

LAURA, *(in a low voice.)*

Now *pray* do, Sophia!—You cannot think how much I shall be obliged to you.

SOPHIA.

Have done, Laura!

LAURA.

Hush, don't speak so loud!

SOPHIA.

I do not chuse to whisper!

MRS. CECIL.

Pray what are you doing, Miss Laura? Attend to your work, I beg of you; you are like all idle people, fond of disturbing others.

(A short pause, during which they work. When Mrs. Cecil is not observing her, Laura wraps her work round her thread papers like a doll, and jogs Eudocia.)

LAURA.

Eudocia, look, look, I say, is not it droll?

(Eudocia looks up; tries to stifle a laugh, but cannot. Mrs. Cecil looks towards them. Laura snatches up her work.)

MRS. CECIL. How now, young ladies?

EUDOCIA.

My stars, Laura, you are so ridiculous, you make me laugh!

LAURA, *(laughing.)*

I!—'Twas the thread-papers!

MRS. CECIL.

Oh to be sure!—Have done, I charge you.—*(Another pause, then Laura whispers Sophia.)*

SOPHIA.

Do pray be quiet, Laura, you are very teazing.

MRS. CECIL.

What is all this about?—Miss Mildmay, what is she saying?

SOPHIA.

Asking me, ma'am, to tell her something I have refused to let her know twenty times already.

MRS. CECIL.

She is very impertinent.—I shall remove you, Miss Laura, if you torment your sister so.

LAURA.

Because it is so cross, ma'am, it cannot be a secret, only she chuses to make it one on purpose to teaze me.

MRS. CECIL.

That is *very* likely!—But no more of this.

LAURA.

Dear ma'am, it's something so very odd.

MRS. CECIL.

Hold your peace!

EUDOCIA.

What does she want to know, Sophia?

LAURA.

I want to know what——

MRS. CECIL.

I insist on your not speaking.—You have all the faults of a Trifler, curious, impertinent, chattering.—I wish you could see how disagreeable you make yourself.

EUDOCIA.

Here comes mama.

Enter Mrs. Mildmay.

(They rise.—The girls run and embrace their mother.)

MRS. MILDMAY.

Sit still, Mrs. Cecil.—My dear girls, how are you?

ALL.

Quite well, mama, thank ye—are you well?

MRS. MILDMAY.

Yes; tho' a little late this morning.

MRS. CECIL.

You sat late last night, ma'am.

MRS. MILDMAY.

Yes, the pleasure of seeing my son detained me later than usual.—How do your pupils behave, Mrs. Cecil?

MRS. CECIL.

Vastly well, ma'am, except a little——

MRS. MILDMAY.

Laura, I suppose—you are conscious, I see!—I too have a complaint to make.

LAURA.

Dear mama!

MRS. MILDMAY.

Yes, I have indeed, but sit down to your works.

LAURA.

Should I sit, mama, while you are speaking to me?

MRS. CECIL.

No, my dear, I shall excuse as much of your work as you would have done in the time.

MRS. MILDMAY.

As much as she *might* have done, my dear Mrs. Cecil; what she *would* have done is, I fancy, rather doubtful.

MRS. CECIL.

Yes, indeed, ma'am.

MRS. MILDMAY, *(sits down; Laura stands before her.)*

You look a little alarm'd, Laura, but I am not very angry with you, since I believe your fault proceeded as usual from want of thought.—Yesterday, at church, my dear, you behaved very ill.—In the first place, while we stood up, I saw your eyes wandering all over the church: in the next place, while we were sitting, you whisper'd to Eudocia, jogged her elbow, and tried to make her laugh.—Now, my dear, I beg you to consider how very improper all this is.—Do you know for what purpose we go to church?

LAURA.

Yes, mama, surely, to pray to God.

MRS. MILDMAY.

Well then, can you think such behaviour proper?

LAURA.

But it was not during the prayers.

MRS. MILDMAY.

True, but part was during the psalms, which are intended as immediate addresses to our Creator, of both praise and prayer; therefore we *stand* to shew our reverence and attention.—When we were sitting, it was to hear the lessons read; that is, selected parts of the holy scripture, the immediate word of God, and the rule by which we are to direct our life.—Even if the service had not been begun, or had been ended, to talk and laugh would have been highly improper.—It unfits the mind for serious duties, and implies a lightness and thoughtlessness, which ought not to be indulged or allowed in a place sacred to our maker.—Our Saviour shewed his disapprobation of any thing which might disturb the tranquility and decency of the holy place, by driving from the Temple (the place of worship) at Jerusalem those whom human laws allowed to transact business there, saying, "It is written, my house shall be called the house of prayer, but ye have made it a den of thieves."—I am sure if you were in the King's presence, you would not be so ill-bred as to laugh and whisper, when he was speaking to you, or allowing another to do so; how much less then, when God speaks to you by his scriptures, ought you to behave irreverently?

LAURA.

I am fully convinced, mama, I am much obliged to you for taking the trouble of instructing me; and, I assure you, I will never behave so again.

EUDOCIA.

I thank you also, mama, for I never saw this matter so clearly before.—I knew it was wrong to talk at church, but sometimes I have forgotten it; now I think nothing will ever tempt me to do so again.

MRS. MILDMAY.

I am always happy, my children, to be of service to you, and while I see you willing to be convinced and to amend, I am over-paid for any trouble I can be at in instructing you.—Laura, return to your work.—At one o'clock, you will all be ready to go out; I shall not wait a minute for any-body, unless Mrs. Cecil can give me a good reason for the delay. Sophia, your brother will take you in his phæton; our cold provisions are all packed up.—I hope to hear a good account of you all: remember, that if you would enjoy the ride, and the sight of the gardens we are to visit, you must behave well.—Good-bye.— Mrs. Cecil, a good morning to you.—I hope you will like our ride.

MRS. CECIL.

Yes, ma'am, I have no doubt of it; a good morning to you.   *(Mrs. Mildmay goes out.)*

LAURA.

Now, Mrs. Cecil, how much will you allow me, to leave of my work?

EUDOCIA.

That is Laura's first concern!

LAURA.

So it would be yours, if you had as much to do as I have.

EUDOCIA.

I *had* as much at first.

LAURA.

But mama has not been talking to you.

EUDOCIA.

No, because I behaved better yesterday than you did.

SOPHIA.

Eudocia, when my mother is satisfied with the atonement for a fault, it does not become us to mention it reproachfully.

LAURA.

Thank ye, Sophia, you seldom take my part, and Eudocia deserves a *good lecture* this time, however!

EUDOCIA.

Then you think I do not *often* deserve one?

MRS. CECIL.

However that may be, you certainly *do* now.—Have done disputing, Eudocia, that is your principal fault; you have been wrong all the way now; you had, as your sister observed, no right, nor was it kind, to resume a subject your mama had done with; and to answer so sharply and so often, shews an inclination to quarrel, very unpleasant and improper.

EUDOCIA, *(after a short pause.)*

It is very true, I have been wrong. Laura, I beg your pardon.

LAURA.

Oh my dear, how good you are!—I am not angry!

SOPHIA.

How sweetly was that said!—How amiable is candour!

MRS. CECIL.

Yes, indeed, I am pleased with Eudocia!

LAURA.

Well, nothing affects me like hearing any one say in that honest way, "I was wrong, I beg your pardon."—I never can help crying, and I feel so sorry, and so humble, and so pleased with them.—But in spite of all that, I never can prevail on myself to ask pardon; I feel so ashamed, and so afraid of being laughed at!

MRS. CECIL.

That is *false* shame.—No shame is just, but the shame of a bad or improper action; and as to being laughed at, the person who *can* laugh at another for doing as she ought, must be unable to taste the sweetness of virtue, and the *exaltation* of *humility*.—But go on with your work, Laura: I shall allow you to leave off, when you have done so much, (*measuring her work.*) —You have been sadly idle. Eudocia, you may now read: bring that little book of manuscripts your mama gave you on Saturday.

EUDOCIA.

Yes, ma'am.— (*She sits down by Mrs. Cecil; takes a small book, and reads.*) "Come ye who love to see what is beautiful—come who wish to enjoy what is sublime—come and I will direct your eyes to the bright Moon, which rides triumphantly on the bosom of Heaven. Is she not beautiful, when breaking thro' the black clouds which surround her, she diffuses splendour around!—Is she not sublime when sinking beneath the sable veil, she just tinges with lucid silver its unequal edges!—Again she swells above the heavy vapour, and shines in perfect beauty.—So rises from the false imputations of malicious slander, the undiminished lustre of true virtue. The machinations of evil men, the unavoidable concurrence of accident, may awhile overspread the beauty of a good name with heavy clouds, but its splendour shall return, and its enemies shall fly before it like the broken and disjointed track, which flies from the face of the Moon.—Comfort yourselves, then, ye sons of men: despair not, because darkness, or even the shadow of death, surrounds you.—Time shall make manifest the beauty of goodness, and its soft lustre shall diffuse a sweet and calm satisfaction into the bosoms of all who believed it."

SOPHIA.

That is very pretty.

MRS. CECIL.

The imitation of Mrs. Barbauld's hymn, "Come, and I will shew you what is beautiful" —at the beginning of this little piece, is obvious; but though inferior to that charming production, it is not without merit.—Read one more, Miss Eudocia.

Eudocia *reads.*

How swiftly does imagination wing her flight!—Ere an instant has rolled over our head she conveys us to the most distant quarter of the globe; she represents to our mind the most remote events!—Time and distance fade before her, and her way is as unmarked as it is swift. We set out with one idea, and without being sensible of the progressive change, we find ourselves meditating another.—Imagination then is like a voyager who, embarking on an immense river, is lulled by the sound of the rippling water into a soft repose: he awakes and finds himself in another country; the trees, the flowers, the whole face of nature is changed: perhaps he has in his slumber passed from the most gloomy scenes to the most enlivened, but he shudders in reflecting that he has probably also passed a tremendous fall, or a lurking quicksand!—In like manner the mind, wrapt in contemplation, may perhaps touch on the confines of some forbidden idea, some false principle, or scheme of guilt.—Happy those who pass them without harm; who do not indulge in such imaginations, but, if they perceive them, start aside, and direct their course to a more desireable climate."

MRS. CECIL.

Very well—that is sufficient.—Maintenant, Mademoiselle Laure, apportez moi votre Telemaque.*

LAURA.

Oui, Madame.**— (*She rises, looks in the book-case, then says*) Oh dear, it is not here, 'tis up stairs!

MRS. CECIL.

How came it up stairs?

LAURA.

Mama desired to hear me read while she dress'd yesterday, and afterwards I took the book into my own room, and forgot to bring it down.

MRS. CECIL.

Well, make haste and fetch it; there is so much time lost!

LAURA.

Oh I shall be back in a minute.

(*She runs out.*)

MRS. CECIL.

What a careless child!

(*Laura returns with the book; she sits down and reads.*)

"Narbal me regardoit avec étonnement, et il crut appercevoir en moi je ne scai quoi de heureux qui vient des dons du Ciel, et qui n'est point dans le commun des hommes: il etoit naturellement sincère et genereux; il fut touché de mon malheur, et me parla avec une confiance, que les Dieux lui inspirèrent pour me fauver d'un grand peril, &c. &c.

MRS. CECIL.

That is well read; now Miss Mildmay you will translate it.

(*Laura returns to her work; Sophia takes the book.*)

"Narbal regarded me with astonishment, and believed he perceived in me a certain expression of goodness, which is the gift of Heaven, and is not common among men. He was naturally sincere and generous; he was touched with my misfortunes, and he spoke to me with a confidence which the Gods inspired, to save me from imminent danger.—Telemachus, said he to me, I neither do nor can doubt that which you tell me. The softness and virtue painted on your countenance will not suffer me to suspect you; I even feel that the Gods whom I have always served love you, and decree that I shall regard you as my son. I will give you salutary counsels, and in return I only demand that you shall be secret.—Fear not, said I to him, that I shall find any difficulty in concealing those things which you confide to me. Though young, I am old in the habit of never revealing my

---

* Now, Miss Laura, bring me your Telemachus.
** Yes, ma'am.

own secrets, and still less the secrets of others. How have you been able, said he, in such extreme youth, to accustom yourself to secresy: I shall be delighted to know by what means you have acquired that quality, which is the foundation of the wisest conduct, and without which all talents are useless? When Ulysses, I replied, departed for the siege of Troy, he took me on his knees, holding me in his arms, (as I have been told) and after he had kissed me tenderly, he used these words, tho' I could not understand them. Oh! my son, may the Gods never suffer me to see thee again; rather let the fatal scissars cut the thread of thy days ere it be half formed, as the reaper cuts down with his sickle a tender flower as it begins to open; may my enemies dash thee in pieces before the eyes of thy mother and myself, if thou art doomed one day to be corrupted and to abandon virtue! —Oh! my friends, continued he, I leave to you a son so dear: take care of his infancy. If you love me, banish from him pernicious flattery; teach him how to conquer his passions, that he may be like a tender plant which men often bend in order to make it grow up-right: above all, forget nothing which may render him just, benevolent, sincere, and faithful in keeping a secret: whoever is capable of lying, does not deserve to live; and whoever knows not how to be silent, is unworthy to govern. I repeat these words exactly, because care was taken to recount them to me frequently, and that they sunk into the bottom of my heart."

MRS. CECIL.

Very well rendered indeed.

SOPHIA.

This is a charming passage!—One sees in the first part of it, how agreeable to all men is a candid open countenance, which can only be preserved by retaining Truth in the heart.

MRS. CECIL.

Yes, and the latter part is an excellent lesson.—When you are disposed to teaze your sisters out of a secret, Laura, recollect this passage, and learn the necessity of a prudent reserve.

LAURA.

But Ulysses said, "whoever could not be silent was unworthy to *govern*," my sisters are not going to *govern*.

MRS. CECIL.

I never saw a young lady more ingenious at finding *objections*. These words were addressed to a young prince, therefore the word *govern* is used, but secresy is a quality equally necessary in all situations, besides, you may probably some time or other *govern* a *family*, though not a *kingdom*, and believe me, you would find yourself very ill qualified to do that if you told your servants, your neighbours, and whoever would hear you, all the concerns of your household, and every thing which came to your knowledge.— Have you done work, young ladies?—'Tis past twelve.

SOPHIA.

I have.

EUDOCIA.

And I.

LAURA.

I have a little bit.

MRS. CECIL.

You must have been very idle, for I gave you very little.—You must dress, and set your drawer in order, so make haste.

(Sophia and Eudocia rise, fold their work, and put it away.)

Enter Mrs. Mildmay.

MRS. MILDMAY.

Laura, what's the reason your poor squirrel has not been cleaned and fed?—I heard him very restless, looked at him, and found he had nothing to eat or drink.

LAURA.

Oh dear, mama, on Saturday I had not time, yesterday I could not do it, and this morning, before breakfast, I had so much to do.

MRS. CECIL.

I told you then not to trifle so much time away, in putting on your cloaths. In the midst of dressing, you took a fancy of reading two old letters, which you found in one of your drawers, then in spite of my remonstrances you entirely new dressed your doll, and had only time to take half a turn in the garden, though your sisters and I walked a considerable time.

MRS. MILDMAY.

That is always the way. You will take improper times to do things. You have no regularity, no idea how much time it will take to accomplish such and such things.—When you had the squirrel, it was on promise to take care of it yourself; you shall not go out till he is fed.

LAURA.

But, mama, I have not quite done work, I must put my drawer in order, and dress myself, I shall not be ready.—Mayn't Sally clean my squirrel's cage?

MRS. MILDMAY.

No, she shall not.—'Tis your own fault if you are not ready, and I will not indulge you in such idle ways.—Let me hear what you have done since breakfast?

LAURA.

Mama, I began putting my drawer to rights, which I had not time to finish: I have read French, and hemmed all this muslin.

MRS. MILDMAY.

And you, Eudocia.

EUDOCIA.

Mama, I made part of a paper-box, and wrote my journal in my pocket-book, before school hour; and since I have read, and worked this pattern of my frock.

MRS. MILDMAY.

There, Laura, and all that in exactly the same time you have had!

LAURA.

Indeed, mama, I will manage better another time!

MRS. MILDMAY.

Very well; at present, however, you must do all you have to do.

SOPHIA.

Mrs. Cecil, shall we dress?

MRS. CECIL.

Yes, if you please.

MRS. MILDMAY.

I am dressed, therefore, Mrs. Cecil, I will take care that Laura finishes her employments while you dress.

MRS. CECIL.

Thank you, ma'am.

LAURA.

Dear Mrs. Cecil, excuse me this bit of work!

MRS. MILDMAY.

No, Mrs. Cecil, I beg you will not!

MRS. CECIL.

Indeed, ma'am, I am not at all disposed to do so, unless you should desire it.

(Mrs. Cecil, Sophia, and Eudocia, go out. Mrs. Mildmay reads.—A pause.)

LAURA.

Mama, I have done work.

MRS. MILDMAY.

Very well; go then, and do all you have undertaken, and, if you are ready, you shall go with me.

LAURA.

Mama, tell me what's o'clock?

MRS. MILDMAY.

Half past twelve.

LAURA.

And you go at one.—Well, I think, I shall be ready.

MRS. MILDMAY.

I think you will not.   *(They go out.)*

END OF THE FIRST PART.

Part The Second.

Enter Mrs. Mildmay, meeting Mrs. Cecil, Sophia, and Eudocia.

MRS. MILDMAY.

W ELL, Mrs. Cecil, are you ready? Where's Laura?

MRS. CECIL.

Not ready, ma'am.

MRS. MILDMAY.

Then I shall not wait; she deserves to be left behind, and 'tis now ten minutes past one.

SOPHIA.

Mama, she will be ready in five minutes.

MRS. MILDMAY.

No matter, it is already past the time I had fixed; we are to be at home by five, and we shall have barely time to see the gardens.—It is her own fault: let us go.

EUDOCIA.

Oh I am very sorry indeed Laura will not go!

Enter Sally.

SALLY.

Ma'am, Miss Laura begs you will be good enough to wait ten minutes; she will be dressed in that time.

MRS. MILDMAY.

No, I will not; I have said I will not, and she knows I always keep my word. Come, Mrs. Cecil, come children. Sally, tell Laura to confine herself to this room and the garden, while we are gone; I will not have her running about among the servants.—Lay the cloth for her here.

(They go out.)

SALLY.

I am very sorry for poor Miss Laura, she will be so vexed!—But she is always past her time.—To-day, truly, she has been chattering to me instead of dressing, though she knew her mama would not wait. "Oh I have plenty of time, it is not near one!"—that is her way.—Oh here she comes.

(Laura runs in.)

LAURA.

Sally, do you know where my gloves are?—I am ready now!

SALLY.

Ah miss!

LAURA.

What?—Bless me!—Sure mama is not gone!

SALLY.

Indeed, miss, I am sorry to say she is.

LAURA.

You jest, I am sure!

SALLY.

No, truly miss, I should not take that liberty. Your mama would not wait a minute longer; both Miss Mildmay and Miss Eudocia tried to prevail on her, but she said you knew she never broke her word.

LAURA, *(with tears in her eyes.)*

You may go, Sally.

SALLY.

Miss, your mama ordered me to tell you, she desired you to stay in this room.

LAURA.

Very well.

(Sally goes out. Laura draws a chair, throws herself into it; rises again, and walks impatiently about the room.)

LAURA.

It is too bad, I declare!—To go without me; and to order me to stay in this room.— What is the reason of that, I wonder.—And George is gone with them. He goes away tomorrow.—This last day, which I thought to have spent so pleasantly, to be so disappointed. —'Tis very cross in mama, I am sure.— *(She wipes her eyes.)* I am always to blame: "Laura did this"—"Laura did that"—Laura is always wrong.—— (*She pauses.*) After all, I certainly might have been ready.—How did I *dare* say, mama was *cross*.—What! mama, who is always so kind, so indulgent, so equal in her sweetness of temper!—It was very wrong in me.—dear mama, though you cannot hear me, I ask your pardon.—Well, what shall I do while they are gone?—How tedious the time is.— (*A pause.*) Lord bless me, I wish I might walk in the garden.—Perhaps mama said I might: I will enquire.— (*She goes to the door, and calls*) Sally!—Sally!   (*Sally comes in.*)

SALLY.

Did you call, miss?

LAURA.

Yes.—Did mama say I might walk in the garden?

SALLY.

Yes, miss; I thought I had told you, this room and the garden.—My mistress said, you should not run about among the servants.

LAURA.

Oh that was the reason!—I am glad I know that.—Apropos, I wish I could find out this mighty secret of Sophia's.—Sally, do you know it?

SALLY.

What, miss?

LAURA.

Why, I'll tell you. About a month ago, mama gave Sophia two guineas, and told her to buy whatever she liked best with it. She gave one to Eudocia, and one to me. Eudocia bought a small writing desk; and I bought a squirrel's cage, and some flower seeds for my garden: but Sophia said she would wait awhile, and consider before she bought. Well, yesterday it came into my head that she had not bought any thing; and I asked her what she should purchase with her two guineas.—She coloured a little, and said, "Oh something I shall like."—Mrs. Cecil smiled, and I have never been able to get a more direct answer from Sophia.—Now, Sally, do you know what she means to buy?

SALLY.

Dear miss, is it likely I should know?

LAURA.

No, but you *might* nevertheless.

SALLY.

And if I did, what advantage would it be to you to be told?

LAURA.

Oh then you *do* know!—Ah ha!—Come, my dear Sally, tell me, I pray you!

SALLY.

I did not say I knew, miss.

LAURA. Oh, but I am sure of it.—Pray tell me.

SALLY.

Fye, miss!—Consider, if I did know, your sister must have told me in confidence; and do you think I would betray her?—Oh no, my good mistress has taught me better!

LAURA.

Well, you know, however; so she has determined on something, that is one step gained. —I shall soon guess what!

SALLY.

But, Miss Laura, who told you I knew?

LAURA.

Who?—yourself!

SALLY.

I!—that I could not!—I said *if,* but it was only supposing!

LAURA.

What then you don't know!

SALLY, *(laughing.)*

That you should really fancy Miss Mildmay had told me!—Surely she would have told you first!

LAURA.

No, no, she would not.

SALLY.

Why, miss?

LAURA.

Because she thinks I should tell.

SALLY.

Then you believe she thinks I would not?

LAURA.

I suppose so!

SALLY.

You pay me a great compliment, miss; which I will try to deserve.

LAURA.

Well, I cannot tell whether you know or not, but I have not told you all.—Mrs. Cecil and Sophia have risen half an hour earlier than common this last fortnight, and I wish I knew what for; I never could find out how they had employed themselves.

SALLY.

Well, miss, if I might venture to speak, I should say it was not worth taking so much trouble to know.

LAURA. If I think it is, that's enough.—I do not ask your advice.

SALLY.

I beg your pardon, miss.

LAURA.

You may go.   *(Sally goes out.)*

LAURA.

Let me consider!—What, can Sophia want to purchase books?—She has plenty, and mama is always buying for her.—A box of colours.—She has one.—New music—perhaps—but why make a secret of it?—Ah!—a locket of mama's hair! That must be it!—I dare say it is very pretty, and she means to surprise us with it, I suppose!—But then what have Mrs. Cecil and Sophia been doing in the morning?—Oh, perhaps, they are painting a *device* for it.—Yes, yes, that is it!

Enter Sally.

SALLY.

Miss, there is a woman below stairs, in great distress; she is very poor, and she begs to see you.

LAURA.

Well, shew her up; I will speak to her here.

SALLY.

Yes, miss.

(Sally goes out.)

LAURA.

What shall I be able to do for her, I have but half a crown, but I can speak to mama.
Enter Sally, *and* Ruth Saunders.

SALLY.

That is Miss Laura.

LAURA.

Come in, good woman.
(Sally goes out.—Ruth curtsies, and comes a little forward.)

LAURA.

What can I do for you?

RUTH.

Miss, I came to beg some relief from my lady, but your servants tell me she is not at home, so I made bold to ask leave to speak to you, miss.

LAURA.

Very well; what can I do to serve you?

RUTH.

Alas aday, my young lady, I am grievous poor; I am a widow, with three children, the eldest of 'em is out at service, but the two little ones are too young to go out: my old mother lives with us; she is helpless, and you may think, miss, I find it hard to keep so many with the work of my own hands.—In the summer, I work in the fields: in the winter, I spin; and my children help me as well as they can. For two years, that my husband has been dead, we have done pretty well, 'till this last winter.

LAURA.

What happened then?

RUTH.

Alas, miss! in the autumn, I was so unhappy as to get an ague, which hindered my working a great deal; my children could do but little; they began to get dirty and ragged; it cut me to the heart to see them so, and not be able to help them!—To compleat my misfortune, a dog got into my little garden, and killed my two hens, whose eggs used to furnish us with a sure penny. Things went from bad to worse; I was fain to run in debt to my landlord, and tho' now the summer is coming on, and I am better, I hope I should be able to pay him; the cruel man declares he will seize for rent to-morrow morning.

LAURA.

What is *seizing for rent?*

RUTH.

Ah, miss! he will take all our little cloaths and furniture, and the very beds we lye on, my poor old mother's and all, to sell them, and pay himself.

LAURA.

Can he be so cruel?—Is he poor?

RUTH.

No, miss, he has four hundred pounds a year, and only himself and his wife to keep.—

What will become of my poor children, and my mother!—At seventy years old; must she be turned out to starve?

LAURA, *(eagerly.)*

No, no, she shall not—be easy—I promise you, she shall not.—Poor, good woman, how I pity you—but what do you owe this unfeeling wretch?

RUTH.

Oh, good young lady, a great deal!

LAURA.

But how much?

RUTH.

Thirty shillings, for half a year's rent.

LAURA.

Oh how unfortunate I am!—If I had not spent my guinea, I should have had almost enough; and perhaps he would have waited awhile.

RUTH.

Ah, miss, you are very good!—but don't think I came here to beg my lady to pay for me; no, indeed, miss, I only thought if she would speak to my landlord, he would may-be wait a little; and indeed I hope I shall pay him every farthing.

LAURA.

I am sure mama will do that, and perhaps more. I will speak to her for you, good woman; make yourself easy, I will do all I can for you.

RUTH.

Thank you a thousand times, good young lady; we shall all pray for, and bless you. I have often seen your two sisters walking with Madam Cecil, and I have thought when Miss Mildmay looked so kindly on my poor little girls, while they opened the gate for her, and said with her sweet voice, "Poor children, there's a penny for you."—I have thought, if she did but know how wretched we were, she would speak to my lady for us; but I had not the heart to tell her, 'till now; things getting so bad, I thought I would try at least.

LAURA.

You did very right.—Call again at six o'clock; I will see you, and before that I will speak to mama, you may depend on it.—In the mean time, I will give you this half crown; I have no more.

RUTH.

No, miss, I thank you, I will not rob you; you will do all for me in speaking to your mama.—She is so good, she deserves to have good children, and she is rewarded!

LAURA.

But I insist on your taking this money; I wish it was more.

RUTH.

It does not become me to refuse your favors.

LAURA.

Take it, buy something with it for your mother.—Good woman, I love you for being so kind to her! *(She calls)* Sally!
                                                                    (Enter Sally.)
Take this good woman with you, and give her something to eat; mama will not object to that.

SALLY.

No, miss, I am sure.

LAURA.

And when she comes again, let me know.—A good day to you.—Oh, tell me your name?

RUTH.

Ruth Saunders, miss.

LAURA.

Very well, I shall remember.

RUTH.

Your servant, miss, a thousand thanks.   *(Sally and Ruth go out.)*

LAURA.

Well, I shall not regret being left at home, since it has been the cause of my seeing this poor woman.   *(Sally comes in.)*

Do you know that woman, Sally?

SALLY.

Yes, miss, I have seen her often; she is very poor.

LAURA.

So I hear—but why I wonder did she never come hither before?

SALLY.

Ah, miss! 'tis very hard to beg; people who have been used to keep themselves by their own industry, are ashamed and afraid to ask relief.

LAURA.

Ashamed, perhaps; but why *afraid?*

SALLY.

Because, miss, so many gentlefolks are cross and hard-hearted; and one says—"Where did you learn all that history," and another says, "Ah, a sad story, if it is true!"

LAURA.

But that is abominable; if we don't chuse to give, we need not *insult* the poor creature who begs from us.

SALLY.

Very true, miss, but too many don't think of that; they forget that a beggar has any feeling. I once saw a poor man colour like scarlet, and his eyes sparkle with anger, at a gentleman, who said he was an impostor; but, poor wretch, he recollected himself, put his hand on his bosom, sighed and passed on.—I gave him a trifle; he bowed, and I saw the tears in his eyes; he did not speak.—Poor creature, truly he was cut to the heart.

LAURA.

You are a good girl, Sally—but tell me what you know of this poor woman?

SALLY.

Why, miss, she lives in a little cottage just at the end of the village, and keeps it very neat, when she is well; she has two pretty children, and her mother (a good old woman) lives with her: the old woman is lame, but has all her senses, and when dame Saunders was so ill, the poor old woman used to cry, and the little girls, thinking to comfort her, said, "Don't cry grandmother, I will feed you, and put on your clean cap for you."

LAURA.

Poor little dears!—how did you know this, Sally?

SALLY.

Oh I heard them one day, miss; when I was walking by the house, I saw the poor woman standing at the door; she look'd sickly, so I asked her a few questions, and found the ague was off that day, and she was crept to the door for a little air.

LAURA.

And when was this?

SALLY.

About a month ago, miss.

LAURA.

And why did you not tell mama?

SALLY.

I did, miss, and my mistress ordered cook to send her some broth twice or three times, and Miss Sophia sent her a shilling.

LAURA.

I never heard of that.

SALLY.

No, miss, because Miss Sophia never tells the good she does.

LAURA.

That is right, but I wonder I don't hear of it.—Indeed, I never see any poor people; they don't come here, I fancy?

SALLY.

No, miss, your governess and sisters find them out when they walk of a morning before breakfast.

LAURA.

That may be, for I don't know how, I seldom have time to walk of a morning. Well, I will walk in the garden, and then learn my grammar-task; then, for once, I shall be beforehand.—Afterwards I will dine.—You will lay the cloth, Sally.

SALLY.

Yes, miss. *(Laura goes out.)*

SALLY, *(putting the room in order.)*

Miss Laura is very good; she has an excellent heart, but she is so light-headed and careless; 'tis a great pity, and I hope she will break herself of it in time; no doubt she will, for she has very good sense. Well, this room will do now. *(She goes out.)*

END OF THE SECOND PART.

Part The Third.

Mrs. Mildmay, Mrs. Cecil, Sophia, Eudocia, taking off their Cloaks and Hats, which they give to Sally.

MRS. MILDMAY.

WHERE IS LAURA, Sally?

SALLY.

Ma'am, she is walking in the garden.

MRS. MILDMAY.

Has she dined?

SALLY.

Yes, ma'am.

MRS. MILDMAY.

Well, call her hither directly.   *(Sally goes out.)*

MRS. CECIL.

We have had a delightful day indeed.

SOPHIA.

Very charming; and our little hasty dinner I enjoyed wonderfully.

MRS. MILDMAY.

I never ate with better appetite in my life, than in the snug little cottage George found out for us.

EUDOCIA.

I only wished for Laura.

SOPHIA.

That indeed was only wanting to make our party complete.

Enter Laura.

LAURA.

Oh, mama, are you returned; I did not expect you quite so soon.

MRS. MILDMAY.

'Tis past five; but, Laura, your brother has not ordered his phaeton from the door, having prevailed on me to suffer you to take a little ride with him.

LAURA.

And may I go, mama?

MRS. MILDMAY.

Yes, if you have behaved well since we have been gone.

LAURA.

Yes indeed, mama, I have only been in this room and the garden, and I have learned my grammar-task.

MRS. MILDMAY.

Well, go then.

LAURA.

Yes, mama, thank you! thank you!—

(She runs a few steps; then returns, and whispers to Sophia.)

SOPHIA.

Pshaw, nonsense!

LAURA.

Aye, but I have indeed.

MRS. MILDMAY.

Come, come, Laura, get your hat, and be gone; your brother waits.

LAURA.

Yes, mama—Good bye—Good bye, Mrs. Cecil, Sophia, Eudocia, your most obedient.

(She runs out.)

MRS. MILDMAY.

What did she say to you, Sophia?

SOPHIA.

That she had discovered my secret, mama.

MRS. MILDMAY.

What does she mean?

SOPHIA.

You know, mama, how I have disposed of the two guineas you were so good as to give me, and Laura has been teazing me since yesterday to know what I mean to buy: I refused to tell her, and she fancies she has guess'd it.

MRS. MILDMAY.

Silly child, how light her head is!

SOPHIA.

But perhaps she really knows.—She may have learned from Sally, who bought my materials, and even assisted in the work.

MRS. CECIL.

No, I believe Sally is perfectly faithful.

MRS. MILDMAY.

I believe so too.—We will ask her presently, if Laura has been questioning her.—But why did you so much object to Laura's knowing it, my dear?

SOPHIA.

Because, mama, Laura can no more keep a secret, than she can let any one else keep it in peace, and I know she would have told every-body she had met with; which, for many reasons, I wish'd to avoid.

MRS. MILDMAY.

It is very true, that those who are extremely curious, are generally unable to keep a secret, because it gratifies their self-importance, to shew that *they* know more than *others,* and because they hope to obtain new secrets, in return for those they tell: not considering, that a wise person will never place confidence in one who has abused the same trust from another.

MRS. CECIL.

There is nothing, I think, on which young people ought to be more scrupulous than on the subject of Confidence.—Let them not be over-fond of seeking a trust, which generally brings with it anxiety and care; but if by any accident, or any necessity, they find themselves in possession of a secret, they ought, with extreme delicacy and caution, to preserve a trust so sacred.

MRS. MILDMAY.

Most surely.—And the limits of Confidence are very strict.—It is not *only* what our friends say, prefaced by "*I beg you will not tell this,*" which we ought to consider as *confided* to us. Every thing which we can suppose they would not *wish* revealed, we ought to consider as told in confidence. Having once confided in a person, we do not say every minute, "*don't mention that.*"—We suppose their own prudence will teach them what ought to be kept secret; and *every thing* is told in confidence which passes between friends, either relating to their situations, sentiments, or opinions; often, indeed, when referring to these circumstances in others.

EUDOCIA.

Mama, I have heard people say, that we ought not to tell to one friend what another has told us.

MRS. MILDMAY.

Certainly not. The person who confides in *you* may not have an equally good opinion of your friend, or circumstances may render it very improper to entrust *her*. *You* may not be able to judge of these circumstances; therefore you ought to be as reserved to her as to the rest of the world: besides, *she* also might have a *friend*, to whom she might not scruple to tell the secret; that friend another, and so on without any bound.

EUDOCIA.

I see that very clearly.—But suppose I should know the person who entrusts me is also very intimate with my friend, and loves her, might I not then talk about the affair with her?

MRS. MILDMAY.

No, not without leave from the person who entrusts you; if she chuses to tell this third person, she *can*; if not, you may be sure she has some reason against it. I lately read a story exactly in point.—When Gen. Monk projected the Restoration of Charles the IId, he maintained the strictest reserve on the subject, even to his friends.—He sent, however, for his brother, Dr. Monk, intending to confide his plan to him, and even giving him some hints respecting it.—When Dr. Monk arrived, while waiting for admission to the General, he entered into conversation with the General's Chaplain, in whom he knew he confided, and talked with him on the plan.—When he was admitted to his brother, the General asked him, if he had mentioned the subject to any one?—"To nobody," said the Doctor, "but to your Chaplain, whom I know you trust."—The General immediately changed countenance, dropped the discourse, and soon after sent his brother away; not chusing to trust a man who had talked on a subject of so much consequence to another, even tho' he would himself have trusted him*. A proof of his wisdom; for surely Dr. Monk had evidently shewed a want of delicacy in his sentiments, which rendered him unfit to have the care of a plan so important!

SOPHIA.

I admire the General's conduct extremely.

MRS. CECIL.

He was undoubtedly right. The faculty of keeping a secret is highly necessary, yet rarely possessed. I made Laura remark that admirable passage in Telemachus to-day, because I remember the effect it had on myself.† Always fond of reading, Telemachus fell early into my hands: I was not above eight years old when that passage struck me; I reflected on it, and it has influenced my conduct ever since. Such indeed has been the constant advantage I have derived from books.—My mother died young; and my father, encumbered with the care of a family, left us in great measure to educate ourselves. I was naturally very passionate, very idle, fond of beginning every thing, and ending nothing; but with a constant fondness for reading, which in the end supplied to me the place of

---

* See Hume's History of England.

† This is absolutely fact, of a child well known to the Author.

an instructor.—The same author, I have always loved so much, says in another place*, "Heureux ceux qui se divertissent en s'intruisant, et qui se plaisent à cultiver leur ésprit par les sciences! En quelque endroit que la fortune ennemie les jette, ils portent toujours avec eux dequoi s'entretenir. Et l'ennui, qui devore les autres hommes au milieu même des delices, est inconnu à ceux qui savent s'occuper par quelque lecture. Heureux ceux qui aiment à lire."—When I saw any very amiable character represented in my books, I considered whether I *had* or *wanted* the qualities I admired so much. This was often a most unpleasant task, but I obliged myself to persevere in the enquiry; and having decided, tried to act accordingly.—When I read of any disagreeable character, and my heart told me I had its faults, I did not drive the conviction from me, but tried to correct myself.

MRS. MILDMAY.

An admirable example, and well worthy of being followed by those young people whose parents are either dead, or so engaged in business, as not to be able to attend to them: such young people would do well to observe the convictions of their own heart, and reason, and follow them, not refuse to listen to them.

EUDOCIA.

I have often heard people say, it is of no use to *read* without *reflection*; but I never quite understood what was meant by reflection before. However, we are very happy in having a mother and governess so well able to instruct us.

MRS. MILDMAY.

Very true, you have great advantages; but that does not render reflection less necessary to you: without it, our precepts will be soon forgotten; and when you come to act for yourself, you will look round for those rules by which indeed you have been guided, but which you have neglected to implant in your heart; and missing them, you will no more know how to act in the world, than a man to find his way thro' a wood, which he had often seen at a distance, but whose particular situation he had neglected to mark.

Enter Sally.

SALLY.

Pray, ma'am, is Miss Laura here?

MRS. MILDMAY.

No, Sally, she is gone out with her brother.—Why; do you want her?

SALLY.

Ma'am, there is a poor woman below, who came while you were out: she saw Miss Laura, who desired her to call again at six o'clock.—It is six o'clock now.

MRS. MILDMAY.

Yes, but Laura has surely forgotten the appointment!—Idle child!—she will never learn to be punctual.—Where is the woman? I will see her.

SALLY.

She is down stairs, ma'am. It is Dame Saunders.

---

* "Happy those who are amused by Instruction, and take delight in cultivating their minds by Science. Into whatever situation unkind Fortune may cast them, they carry always with them the means of conversation. And that fatiguing Idleness, which devours so many, even in the midst of Pleasure, is unknown to them who know how to employ themselves in reading.— Happy those who love to read!"

SOPHIA.

Indeed!—then perhaps—but she knew nothing of it; so Laura could not learn from her.

MRS. MILDMAY.

What? Is it the woman for whom your gift was intended?

SOPHIA.

Yes, mama.

MRS. MILDMAY.

Sally, did Laura question you about the purchase Miss Mildmay meant to make with her two guineas?

SALLY.

Yes, ma'am, but I told her nothing; indeed, she does not know that I know any thing about it.

MRS. MILDMAY.

That is right.—Come with me, Sophia; we will talk to the poor woman.

(Mrs. Mildmay, Sophia, and Sally, go out.)

MRS. CECIL, EUDOCIA.

MRS. CECIL.

How shameful for Laura to have neglected an appointment; on which, probably, the peace and happiness of this poor woman depended!—And to have been surpassed by her servant in faithfulness and secresy!—All her faults proceed from carelessness, inattention, and want of punctuality.—Great vices, as well as great virtues, are rare; but it is those errors, which seem at first trifling, but which grow upon us by degrees, of which we ought principally to beware.

EUDOCIA.

But, Mrs. Cecil, Laura is so young.

MRS. CECIL.

Yes, she is young; but, with the advantages she has, she ought to know better: however, she has a good heart, and understanding; and, I hope, she will correct herself.

EUDOCIA.

Oh yes, I hope so!

(A short pause, then)

Enter Sophia.

SOPHIA.

Oh, Mrs. Cecil, mama has rendered this poor woman *so* happy!—She has been in the greatest distress about her rent: mama has given her money to·pay it, and money to buy food and cloaths. I have desired her to wait, while Sally fetches down the box I design for her.—Will you go with me, and give it to her?

MRS. CECIL.

With all my heart.

EUDOCIA.

Pray, sister, let me go also.

SOPHIA.

My dear, I should be happy to do so; but I wish very much you would be kind enough to stay in this room. Laura will be at home in a few minutes; if she finds no one here, she will follow us; and mama is determined to punish her, for neglecting this poor woman, by leaving her in doubt whether she has been here or not.

EUDOCIA.

Very well—I will call with you, then, to-morrow.

SOPHIA.

If you please; you oblige me extremely by this compliance.—Only think, Laura had promised Ruth Saunders to represent her situation to mama, and to give her the answer at six o'clock. She forgot all that—but she gave her all the money she had; and Ruth said, behaved so kindly to her, as to make her quite happy.

MRS. CECIL.

How capable she is of behaving well, if she does but think!

(Mrs. Cecil, and Sophia, go out.)

EUDOCIA.

It is very true, indeed, that a habit of carelessness injures one extremely.—Laura this morning could not believe she should ever neglect an appointment of consequence.—Oh here she comes!

Enter Laura.

LAURA.

So, Eudocia!—Where are mama and Mrs. Cecil; and Sophia, I don't see her either?—We have had a charming ride! My brother was very good to take me out, and he has been telling me such delightful things about the sights in London; he promises to ask mama to let me go next autumn, and see them.—Shall you not wish me to go, Eudocia?

EUDOCIA.

To be sure; why do you think I would not?

LAURA.

Oh, because you looked so grave.

EUDOCIA.

Did I look grave?

LAURA.

Yes, I think so.—Have you drank tea?

EUDOCIA.

No; of course we should wait for my brother.

LAURA, *(in a jesting tone.)*

And for *me*, I hope you think I am of consequence enough to be waited for!

EUDOCIA, *(smiling.)*

What do *you* think?

LAURA.

Ah you sly girl!—I know what you mean: 'tis true, mama did not think so this morning.

EUDOCIA.

I assure you, we all wished for you.

LAURA.

Oh I don't doubt it at all. I shall be more punctual another time; for tho' I liked my ride, it did not make amends for losing so much pleasure.—And George must go to-morrow: he says it will be a month before he comes again.—How good he is; how I love him!

EUDOCIA.

How we all love him!—He is so attentive to us all!—Oh here comes Sophia.

Enter Sophia.

EUDOCIA.

Sophia, what are you come already?

SOPHIA.

Yes, I have been extremely delighted!

EUDOCIA.

Was she pleased?

SOPHIA.

Oh you never saw any thing so happy!

LAURA.

So! so!—More secrets!—Ah ha, Sophia!—I have found out the *last* however!—Another time, I hope, you will trust *me!*

SOPHIA.

Not the sooner because I find you curious, and prying into what I wish to hide from you.

LAURA.

Well, but my little Sophia, my dear sweet Sophia, don't be angry; you know I could not help guessing!

SOPHIA.

You guess'd, did you?

LAURA.

Yes, I guess'd: well, Sophia, is it very beautiful?

SOPHIA.

Oh, very beautiful, if one did but know what you meant.

LAURA.

You don't then, I suppose?—Is the *device* handsome?

SOPHIA.

The *device!*—What nonsense!

LAURA.

What, then; I suppose you will not own you have purchased a locket, with mama's hair?

SOPHIA.

You have a fine guess, indeed!

LAURA.

A true one, I fancy?

SOPHIA.

For once, you are entirely mistaken.

LAURA.

What can it be then!—Now, Sophia, do tell me.

SOPHIA.

Perhaps.

LAURA.

Oh do, pray do; indeed I will not tell.

SOPHIA.

I wish I had more reason to trust your promises; however, 'tis no longer a secret, so, if you wish it, I will tell you.

LAURA.

Oh yes, yes, make haste, Sophia, make haste!

SOPHIA.

You must know then, that, during the winter, I observed two pretty little girls, in the village, almost without cloaths; I pitied them very much, and wished I could relieve them. I began by saving all I could out of my allowance, and had already some shillings in advance, when mama gave me the two guineas: with her leave, I laid it out entirely in cloaths for the two little girls, and their mother, of whose distress I heard sad accounts.— Mrs. Cecil, Sally, and I, have been hard at work in making these cloaths, whenever we could find time, and all is now finished.

LAURA.

So, then, Sally knew!

SOPHIA.

Yes.

LAURA.

She would not tell!

SOPHIA.

What, you tried to make her?

LAURA.

I asked her—a little.

SOPHIA.

Fye, Laura!—You must have supposed she knew in confidence, if she knew at all! Only think what a shame, that your servant should know better how to act with respect to secresy than you.

LAURA.

Well, that is true; but, Sophia, who are these little girls?

SOPHIA.

Their mother's name is Ruth Saunders.

LAURA.

Ruth Saunders!—Oh goodness!—Is it six o'clock?

SOPHIA.

Six!—'tis almost seven!

LAURA.

Oh, where is mama!—Let me see her directly!—Where is Sally?

SOPHIA.

What is the matter?

EUDOCIA.

Dear Laura.

SOPHIA, *(aside to her.)*

Hush.—What's the matter, Laura?

LAURA.

Oh, don't ask me!—I am ashamed of myself; tell me where is mama.

SOPHIA.

Mama is busy; you cannot see her.

LAURA.

Oh, I must, I must!—Sally! Sally.   *(She runs to ring the bell.)*

SOPHIA.

Oh, Eudocia, how I feel for her!

EUDOCIA.

I can hardly bear to see her so unhappy.

SOPHIA.

Mama has commanded silence!

LAURA.

Sally! Sally!—why don't you come.

(Sally runs in.)

SALLY.

Miss!—Bless me, what's the matter?

LAURA.

Sally, has Ruth Saunders been here?

SALLY.

Yes, miss.

LAURA.

Without seeing me!—What must she think of me!—It is almost dark too!—I shall not be able to see her to-night, and to-morrow!—Oh, poor creature, how unhappy she is.—But if I can see mama, it may not be yet too late!—Dear Sophia, if you have any love for me, ask mama to let me see her!—I have something of great consequence to say.

SOPHIA.

Indeed, my dear girl, it grieves me to refuse you, but mama has forbidden me to interrupt her.

LAURA.

How can you be so unkind!—Indeed it is very cruel, and you seem not to feel for me.

SOPHIA.

Believe me, my dear, I feel for you very much.

LAURA.

Why then will you not intercede for me?

SOPHIA.

I have told you already, that mama

LAURA.

Oh mama would hear me, if she knew—but how we lose time!—It will be dark, and I shall be too late.—Eudocia will *you* ask mama to let me see her?

EUDOCIA.

I hear her coming.

LAURA.

Oh then I may still succeed!

Enter Mrs. Mildmay, *and* Mrs. Cecil.

LAURA, *(running to Mrs. Mildmay.)*

Mama, dear mama, will you have the goodness to hear me!

MRS. MILDMAY.

What would you say?—Why this extreme agitation?

LAURA.

Oh mama, while you were gone, a poor woman came hither: she wanted relief from you; I saw her, I promised to intercede for her, and give her the answer at six o'clock.—

Her landlord has threaten'd to take all her goods for rent to-morrow morning. She hopes I shall prevail on you to plead for her to him. Dearest mama, will you grant me this favour? Indeed she deserves your goodness!

MRS. MILDMAY.

How do you know that?

LAURA.

Because, mama, she told me all her story: she has been sick; she has two children, and an old mother.

MRS. MILDMAY.

But, Laura, it is easy to say all that; nay, it may be true, and yet she may be idle and undeserving. You know I never exert myself but in favour of worthy objects. I have now no time to enquire, 'tis past seven, and very near dark; can I learn the truth of this story to-night?

LAURA.

But, mama, to-morrow will be too late.

MRS. MILDMAY.

Why then, did you not tell me the story sooner?

LAURA.

I intended to do so, as soon as you came home, mama, but——

MRS. MILDMAY.

But you forgot it!—Is it not so?—You chose the pleasure of a ride, rather than the gratifying these poor people.—Thus you have lost, from your carelessness and unpunctuality, an opportunity of doing a good action, of making a whole family happy, and of increasing my love for you!

LAURA.

Oh, mama, I have been sadly to blame indeed, but I assure you this shall be the last time. Only hear me this once!—try what you can do for this poor woman; Sally knows her, nay Sophia knows her: enquire of them!—Punish me as you please, but do not punish her for my fault!

MRS. MILDMAY.

Only imagine this poor creature's disappointment, when told you were not at home. Think of her distress: she had then lost her only hope!—See her returning to her cottage, where she had left her mother and children anxious for the success of her petition; hear her with tears say, "Ah my children we must be ruined; the person who promised us assistance has forgotten us!—She is gone out; she has not mentioned us to her mother, and tomorrow we shall be turned out to starve!"

LAURA, *(throwing herself at her mother's feet.)*

Oh, mama, I implore you to save me from being the cause of this misery!—Indeed, I am cured for ever of my folly; I will never be trifling, inconsiderate, and unpunctual again!

MRS. MILDMAY, *(raising her.)*

Promises of amendment do not prove any thing, yet I must hope this lesson will reach your heart!—If I were as inconsiderate as you, all the sad consequences I have described to you would be realized, and even all I can do will hardly efface from the mind of this poor woman the anguish she suffered when told you were gone out, and had not mentioned her to me.

LAURA.

Then, mama, you will be good enough to assist her?

MRS. MILDMAY.

Certainly; your breach of promise can be no reason why I should fail in my duty: but if I had waited till I heard the story from you, it would really have been too late for me to do any thing in it, as I could not have learned all I wanted to know at this time.

LAURA.

Had you then heard it before?

MRS. MILDMAY.

Yes; Sally, not finding you, came to me. I saw the poor woman; heard her story, and having had reason before to believe it, I relieved her. Sophia has given her a box of cloaths; and she is gone home perfectly happy.

LAURA.

Oh, mama, how good you are to every body!—Indeed, you may believe, I will profit by this lesson. I can never again run such a risk of making any one miserable.

MRS. CECIL.

You must then break yourself of the habit of trifling; for you see now, as I told you this morning, it cannot be dismissed at once, whenever it is of consequence it should be!

LAURA.

Oh, it is true, indeed!—even, at least, when I came home, if I had not trifled away the time, by asking Sophia impertinent questions, I should have found it less impossible to serve this poor woman!—dear Sophia, I will never teaze you again.

SOPHIA.

Believe me, it hurt me extremely, to keep the truth from you, when I saw you so distressed; but mama had commanded me not to tell you.

EUDOCIA.

As to me, I was on the point of telling.

LAURA.

Mama, do you forgive me?

MRS. MILDMAY.

I forgive you, hoping you will correct yourself, and that you now see the fault, you thought so trifling, is really of serious consequence: but altho' I am no longer *displeased*, I shall inflict a punishment in addition to that which you have already suffered. I shall not permit you to have any share in the farther assistance we mean to give this poor woman; nor to call on her with your sisters for a full fortnight; if, in that time, I see any instance of unpunctuality in your conduct, I shall extend the time as long as I think proper.—So you will lose the pleasure of seeing her happiness, and the joy of her old mother and children, for the gift Sophia has made them!

LAURA.

Oh, mama, this is indeed a punishment—but I deserve it!—However, I hope—I am sure I shall see her at the end of the *fortnight!*

MRS. MILDMAY.

I hope you will.—But 'tis late.—Let us go down stairs to tea.—And let this occurrence teach us all never to forget our promises, or let any gratification tempt us to neglect our positive engagements.

FINIS.

The Parent's Assistant
By MARIA EDGEWORTH

SELECTIONS

LAZY LAWRENCE.

Page 30.

Painted by W. Harvey_Engraved by F. Bacon.

THE PARENT'S ASSISTANT

BY

MARIA EDGEWORTH.

VOL. I.

Painted by W. Harvey_Engraved by F. Bacon.

M ARIA EDGEWORTH *(1767–1849) is the one eighteenth-century author whose work for children was regularly reprinted through the middle of the twentieth century.* The Parent's Assistant *(the title of which Maria neither picked nor approved) was in print as late as 1948. Some would say Edgeworth is the only Georgian writer whose stories deserve to be preserved for twentieth-century children.*

The Parent's Assistant *first appeared in three volumes in 1796. An 1800 edition in six volumes added eight new stories and reserved three others for* Early Lessons, *the collective title of three books for younger children (Harry and Lucy, Rosamond, and Frank) totaling ten volumes, with four more volumes added to conclude the series in 1825.* Early Lessons *was a continuation by Maria Edgeworth of the Harry and Lucy stories that her father and step-mother (Honora Sneyd Edgeworth) began in 1778. It was meant for her six-year-old half-brother William, while* The Parent's Assistant *was for children from ten to about thirteen. The less successful* Moral Tales for Young People *(5 vols., 1801) was geared to the adolescent reader.*

To Maria Edgeworth's work for children should be added Practical Education *(2 vols., 1798), a collection of knowledgeable essays on the education of children, which she wrote with her father, Richard Lovell Edgeworth. Among her successful adult novels were* Castle Rackrent *(1800) and* Patronage *(1814).*

Some critics of Edgeworth deplore her lack of description in stories for children and her rather obvious class consciousness, in contrast to someone like Thomas Day. One nineteenth-century writer, Julian Hawthorne, bitterly scored Edgeworth's "prim and narrow moral code." Testifying that he was raised on her stories, he declared them ". . . the most persistently malignant of all sources of error in the design of children's literature." But Edgeworth's use of dramatic incident and action keep her tales from dullness, even if her ethics seem smug today. Perhaps having had a large brood of siblings at Edgeworthstown in Ireland helped Maria enliven her characters, even the overly heroic "Simple Susan," whom Scott liked so much.

Marilyn Butler, in Maria Edgeworth: A Literary Biography *(Oxford: Clarendon Press, 1972), blames Thomas Day for discouraging Maria's publications. Radical in other ways, Day had a sexist dislike of "female authorship" and cheered the fact that Maria's first try at a children's book, a translation of Madame de Genlis'* Adèle et Théodore, *was aborted when another translation beat it to press. Only after Day's death did Maria Edgeworth have a chance to prove that her stories for children should be published.*

The following selections from The Parent's Assistant *are reprinted from a three-volume edition published in London in 1840. The complete contents of that edition are: Volume I— "Lazy Lawrence," "Tarlton," "The False Key," "The Birth-day Present," "Simple Susan"; Volume II— "The Bracelets," "Little Merchants," "Old Poz," "The Mimic," "Mademoiselle Panache;" Volume III— "The Basket Woman," "The White Pigeon," "The Orphans," "Waste Not, Want Not," "Forgive and Forget," "Barring Out," "Eton Montem."*

Volume One

Lazy Lawrence.

I N THE PLEASANT VALLEY of Ashton there lived an elderly woman of the name of Preston: she had a small neat cottage, and there was not a weed to be seen in her garden. It was upon her garden that she chiefly depended for support: it consisted of strawberry-beds, and one small border for flowers. The pinks and roses she tied up in nice nosegays, and sent either to Clifton or Bristol to be sold; as to her strawberries, she did not send them to market, because it was the custom for numbers of people to come from Clifton, in the summer-time, to eat strawberries and cream at the gardens in Ashton.

Now the widow Preston was so obliging, active, and good-humoured, that every one who came to see her was pleased. She lived happily in this manner for several years; but, alas! one autumn she fell sick, and, during her illness, every thing went wrong; her garden was neglected, her cow died, and all the money which she had saved was spent in paying for medicines. The winter passed away, while she was so weak that she could earn but little by her work; and when the summer came her rent was called for, and the rent was not ready in her little'purse as usual. She begged a few months' delay, and they were granted to her; but at the end of that time there was no resource but to sell her horse Lightfoot. Now Lightfoot, though perhaps he had seen his best days, was a very great favourite; in his youth he had always carried the dame to market behind her husband; and it was now her little son Jem's turn to ride him. It was Jem's business to feed Light-foot, and to take care of him; a charge which he never neglected, for, besides being a very good-natured, he was a very industrious boy.

"It will go near to break my Jem's heart," said dame Preston to herself, as she sat one evening beside the fire, stirring the embers, and considering how she had best open the matter to her son, who stood opposite to her, eating a dry crust of bread very heartily for supper.

"Jem," said the old woman, "what, art hungry?"

"That I am, brave and hungry!"

"Aye! no wonder, you've been brave hard at work—Eh?"

"Brave hard! I wish it was not so dark, mother, that you might just step out and see the great bed I've dug; I know you'd say it was no bad day's work—and, oh mother! I've good news; Farmer Truck will give us the giant strawberries, and I'm to go for 'em to-morrow morning, and I'll be back afore breakfast!"

"Bless the boy! how he talks!—Four mile there, and four mile back again, afore breakfast!"

"Aye, upon Lightfoot, you know, mother, very easily, mayn't I?"

"Aye, child!"

"Why do you sigh, mother?"

"Finish thy supper, child."

"I've done!" cried Jem, swallowing the last mouthful hastily, as if he thought he had been too long at supper—"and now for the great needle. I must see and mend Lightfoot's bridle afore I go to bed."—To work he set, by the light of the fire; and the dame having once more stirred it, began again with, "Jem, dear, does he go lame at all now?"—"What, Lightfoot! Oh la, no, not he!—never was so well of his lameness in all his life—he's growing quite young again, I think; and then he's so fat he can hardly wag." "Bless him—that's right—we must see, Jem, and keep him fat."

"For what, mother?"

"For Monday fortnight at the fair. He's to be ——— sold!"

"Lightfoot!" cried Jem, and let the bridle fall from his hand; and "*will* mother sell Lightfoot?"

"*Will!* no: but I *must*, Jem."

"Must; who says you *must?* why *must* you, mother?"

"I must, I say, child—Why, must not I pay my debts honestly—and must not I pay my rent; and was not it called for long and long ago; and have not I had time; and did not I promise to pay it for certain Monday fortnight, and am not I two guineas short, and where am I to get two guineas? So what signifies talking, child?" said the widow, leaning her head upon her arm, "Lightfoot must go."

Jem was silent for a few minutes.—"Two guineas; that's a great, great deal. If I worked, and worked, and worked ever so hard, I could no ways earn two guineas *afore* Monday fortnight—could I, mother?"

"Lord help thee, no; not an' work thyself to death."

"But I could earn something, though, I say," cried Jem proudly; "and I *will* earn *something*—if it be ever so little it will be *something*—and I shall do my very best; so I will."

"That I'm sure of, my child," said his mother, drawing him towards her, and kissing him; "you were always a good industrious lad, *that* I will say afore your face or behind your back;—but it won't do now—Lightfoot *must* go."

Jem turned away, struggling to hide his tears, and went to bed without saying a word more. But he knew that crying would do no good: so he presently wiped his eyes, and lay awake, considering what he could possibly do to save the horse. "If I get ever so little," he still said to himself, "it will be *something;* and who knows but landlord might then wait a bit longer? and we might make it all up in time; for a penny a day might come to two guineas in time."

But how to get the first penny was the question. Then he recollected that one day when he had been sent to Clifton to sell some flowers, he had seen an old woman with a board beside her covered with various sparkling stones, which people stopped to look at as they passed, and he remembered that some people bought the stones; one paid two-pence, another three-pence, and another six-pence for them; and Jem heard her say that she got them amongst the neighbouring rocks: so he thought that if he tried he might find some too, and sell them as she had done.

Early in the morning he wakened full of his schemes, jumped up, dressed himself, and, having given one look at poor Lightfoot in his stable, set off to Clifton in search of the old woman, to inquire where she found her sparkling stones. But it was too early in the morning, the old woman was not at her seat; so he turned back again disappointed. He did not waste his time waiting for her, but saddled and bridled Lightfoot, and went to farmer Truck's for the giant strawberries. A great part of the morning was spent in putting them into the ground; and as soon as that was finished, he set out again in quest of the old woman, whom, to his great joy, he spied sitting at her corner of the street with her board before her. But this old woman was deaf and cross; and when at last Jem made her hear his questions, he could get no answer from her, but that she found the fossils where he would never find any more. "But can't I look where you looked?" "Look away, nobody hinders you," replied the old woman; and these were the only words she would say. Jem was not, however, a boy to be easily discouraged; he went to the rocks and walked slowly along, looking at all the stones as he passed. Presently he came to a place where a number of men were at work loosening some large rocks, and one amongst the workmen was stooping down looking for something very eagerly; Jem ran up, and asked if he could help him. "Yes," said the man, "you can; I've just dropped, amongst this heap of rubbish, a fine piece of crystal that I got to-day." "What kind of a looking thing is it?" said Jem. "White, and like glass," said the man, and went on working whilst Jem looked very carefully over the heap of rubbish for a great while. "Come," said the man, "it's gone for ever; don't trouble yourself any more, my boy." "It's no trouble; I'll look a little longer; we'll not give it up so soon," said Jem; and, after he had looked a little longer, he found the piece of crystal. "Thank'e," said the man, "you are a fine industrious little fellow." Jem, encouraged by the tone of voice in which the man spoke this, ventured to ask him the same questions which he asked the old woman. "One good turn deserves another," said the man; "we are going to dinner just now, and shall leave off work—wait for me here, and I'll make it worth your while."

Jem waited; and, as he was very attentively observing how the workmen went on with their work, he heard somebody near him give a great yawn, and turning round, he saw stretched upon grass beside the river, a boy about his own age, who he knew very well went in the village of Ashton by the name of Lazy Lawrence; a name which he most justly deserved, for he never did any thing from morning to night; he neither worked nor played, but sauntered and lounged about restless and yawning. His father was an alehouse-keeper, and, being generally drunk, could take no care of his son; so that Lazy Lawrence grew every day worse and worse. However, some of the neighbours said that he was a good-natured poor fellow enough, and would never do any one harm but himself; whilst others, who were wiser, often shook their heads, and told him that idleness was the root of all evil.

"What Lawrence!" cried Jem to him, when he saw him lying upon the grass—"what, are you asleep?" "Not quite." "Are you awake?" "Not quite." "What are you doing there?" "Nothing." "What are you thinking of?" "Nothing." "What makes you lie there?" "I don't know—because I can't find any body to play with me to-day—Will you come and play?" "No, I can't; I'm busy." "Busy!" cried Lawrence, stretching himself, "you are always busy—I would not be you for the world, to have so much to do always." "And I," said Jem, laughing, "would not be you for the world, to have nothing to do." So they parted, for the workman just then called Jem to follow him. He took him home to his own house, and showed him a parcel of fossils which he had gathered, he said, on purpose to sell, but had never had time yet to sort them. He set about it, however, now; and having picked out those which he judged the be the best, he put them into a small basket, and gave them to Jem to sell, upon condition that he should bring him half of what he got. Jem, pleased to be employed, was ready to agree to what the man proposed, provided his mother had no objection to it. When he went home to dinner, he told his mother his scheme; and she smiled and said he might do as he pleased, for she was not afraid of his being from home. "You are not an idle boy," said she, "so there is little danger of your getting into any mischief."

Accordingly Jem that evening took his stand, with his little basket, upon the bank of the river, just at the place where people land from a ferry-boat, and where the walk turns to the wells, where numbers of people perpetually pass to drink the waters. He chose his place well, and waited almost all evening, offering his fossils with great assiduity to every passenger: but not one person bought any. "Holloa!" cried some sailors, who had just rowed a boat to land, "bear a hand here, will you, my little fellow, and carry these parcels for us into yonder house." Jem ran down immediately for the parcels, and did what he was asked to do so quickly, and with so much good will, that the master of the boat took notice of him, and when he was going away, stopped to ask him what he had got in his little basket: and when he saw that they were fossils, he immediately told Jem to follow him, for that he was going to carry some shells he had brought from abroad to a lady in the neighbourhood who was making a grotto. "She will very likely buy your stones into the bargain; come along, my lad; we can but try."

The lady lived but a very little way off, so that they were soon at her house. She was alone in her parlour, and was sorting a bundle of feathers of different colours: they lay on a sheet of pasteboard upon a window-seat, and it happened that as the sailor was bustling round the table to show off his shells, he knocked down the sheet of pasteboard, and scattered all the feathers.

The lady looked very sorry, which Jem observing, he took the opportunity whilst she was busy looking over the sailor's bag of shells, to gather together all the feathers, and sort them according to their different colours, as he had seen them sorted when he first came into the room.

"Where is the little boy you brought with you? I thought I saw him here just now." "And here I am, ma'am," cried Jem, creeping from under the table with some few remaining feathers which he had picked from the carpet; "I thought," added he, pointing to the others, "I had better be doing something than standing idle, ma'am." She smiled, and, pleased with his activity and simplicity, began to ask him several questions; such as, who he was, where he lived, what employment he had, and how much a-day he earned by gathering fossils. "This is the first day I ever tried," said Jem; "I never sold any yet, and if you don't buy 'em now, ma'am, I'm afraid nobody else will, for I've asked every body else." "Come then," said the lady, laughing, "if that is the case, I think I had better buy them all." So emptying all the fossils out of his basket, she put half a crown into it. Jem's eyes sparkled with joy. "Oh, thank you ma'am," said he, "I will be sure to bring you as many more to-morrow." "Yes, but I don't promise you," said she, "to give you half a crown to-morrow." "But, perhaps, though you don't promise it, you will." "No," said the lady, "do not deceive yourself; I assure you that I will not. *That*, instead of encouraging you to be industrious, would teach you to be idle." Jem did not quite understand what she meant by this, but answered, "I'm sure I don't wish to be idle; what I want is to earn something every day, if I knew how: I'm sure I don't wish to be idle. If you knew all, you'd know I do not." "How do you mean, *If I knew all?*" "Why, I mean if you knew about Lightfoot." "Who's Lightfoot?" "Why, mammy's horse," added Jem, looking out of the window; "I must make haste home and feed him afore it gets dark; he'll wonder what's gone with me." "Let him wonder a few minutes longer," said the lady, "and tell me the rest of your story." "I've no story, ma'am, to tell, but as how mammy says he must go to the fair Monday fortnight to be sold, if she can't get the two guineas for her rent; and I should be main sorry to part with him, for I love him and he loves me; so I'll work for him, I will, all I can: to be sure, as mammy says, I have no chance, such a little fellow as I am, of earning two guineas afore Monday fortnight." "But are you in earnest willing to work?" said the lady; "you know there is a great deal of difference between picking up a few stones, and working steadily every day, and all day long." "But," said Jem, "I would work every day, and all day long." "Then," said the lady, "I will give you work. Come here to-morrow morning, and my gardener will set you to weed the shrubberies, and I will pay you six-pence a-day. Remember you must be at the gates by six o'clock." Jem bowed, thanked her, and went away. It was late in the evening, and he was impatient to get home to feed Lightfoot; yet he recollected that he had promised the man who had trusted him to sell the fossils, that he would bring him half of what he got for them; so he thought that he had better go to him directly: and away he went, running along by the water-side about a quarter of a mile, till he came to the man's house. He was just come home from work, and was surprised when Jem showed him the half-crown, saying, "Look what I got for the stones; you are to have half, you know." "No," said the man, when he had heard his story, "I shall not take half of that; it was given to you. I expected but a shilling at the most, and the half of that is but six-pence, and that I'll take.—Wife! give the lad two shillings, and take this half-crown." So his wife opened an old glove, and took out two shillings; and the man, as she opened the glove, put in his fingers, and took out a little silver penny.—"There, he shall have that into the bargain for his honesty—Honesty is the best policy—There's a lucky penny for you, that I've kept ever since I can remember." "Don't you ever go to part with it, do ye hear?" cried the woman. "Let him do what he will with it, wife," said the man. "But," argued the wife, "another penny would do just as well to buy gingerbread, and that's what it will go for." "No, that it shall not, I promise you," said Jem; and so he ran away home, fed Lightfoot, stroked him, went to bed, jumped up at five o'clock in the morning, and went singing to work as gay as a lark.

Four days he worked, "every day and all day long;" and the lady every evening, when she came out to walk in the garden, looked at his work. At last she said to her gardener, "This little boy works very hard." "Never had so good a little boy about the grounds," said the gardener; "he's always at his work, let me come by when I will, and he has got twice as much done as another would do; yes, twice as much, ma'am; for look here—he began at this here rose bush, and now he's got to where you stand, ma'am; and here is the day's work that t'other boy, and he's three years older too, did to-day—I say, measure Jem's fairly, and it's twice as much, I'm sure." "Well," said the lady to her gardener, "show me how much is a fair good day's work for a boy of his age." "Come at six and go at six; why, about this much, ma'am," said the gardener, marking off a piece of the border with his spade. "Then, little boy," said the lady, "so much shall be your task every day; the gardener will mark it off for you; and when you've done, the rest of the day you may do what you please." Jem was extremely glad of this; and the next day he had finished his task by four o'clock, so that he had all the rest of the evening to himself. Jem was as fond of play as any little boy could be, and when he was at it, played with all the eagerness and gaiety imaginable: so as soon as he had finished his task, fed Lightfoot, and put by the six-pence he had earned that day, he ran to the play-ground in the village, where he found a party of boys playing, and amongst them Lazy Lawrence, who indeed was not playing, but lounging upon a gate with his thumb in his mouth. The rest were playing at cricket. Jem joined them, and was the merriest and most active amongst them; till, at last, when quite out of breath with running, he was obliged to give up to rest himself, and sat down upon the stile, close to the gate on which Lazy Lawrence was swinging. "And why don't you play, Lawrence?" said he. "I'm tired," said Lawrence. "Tired of what?" "I don't know well what tires me: grandmother says I'm ill, and I must take something—I don't know what ails me." "Oh, pugh! take a good race, one, two, three, and away, and you'll find yourself as well as ever. Come, run—one, two, three, and away." "Ah, no, I can't run indeed," said he, hanging back heavily; "you know I can play all day long if I like it, so I don't mind play as you do, who have only one hour for it." "So much the worse for you. Come now, I'm quite fresh again, will you have one game at ball? do." "No, I tell you, I can't; I'm as tired as if I had been working all day long as hard as a horse." "Ten times more," said Jem, "for I have been working all day long as hard as a horse, and yet you see I'm not a bit tired: only a little out of breath just now." "That's very odd," said Lawrence, and yawned, for want of some better answer; then taking out a handful of halfpence— "See what I have got from father to-day, because I asked him just at the right time, when he had drunk a glass or two; then I can get anything I want out of him—see! a penny, two-pence, three-pence, four-pence—there's eight-pence in all; would not you be happy if you had *eight-pence?*" "Why, I don't know," said Jem laughing, "for you don't seem happy, and you have *eight-pence*." "That does not signify though—I'm sure you only say that because you envy me—you don't know what it is to have eight-pence—you never had more than two-pence or three-pence at a time in all your life." Jem smiled. "Oh, as to that," said he, "you are mistaken, for I have at this very time more than two-pence, three-pence, or eight-pence either; I have—let me see—stones, two shillings; then five days' work, that's five six-pences, that's two shillings and six-pence, it makes in all four shillings and six-pence, and my silver penny, is four and seven-pence. Four and seven-pence!" "You have not," said Lawrence, roused so as absolutely to stand upright, "four and seven-pence! have you? Show it me, and then I'll believe you." "Follow me then," cried Jem, "and I will soon make you believe me; come." "Is it far?" said Lawrence, following, half-running, half-hobbling, till he came to the stable where Jem showed him his treasure. "And how did you come by it? honestly?" "Honestly! to be sure I did; I earned it all." "Bless me, earned it! well, I've a great mind to work; but then it's such hot weather; besides, grandmother says I'm not strong enough yet for hard work; and, besides, I know how to coax daddy out of money when I want it, so I need not work—But four and seven-pence! let's see, what will you do with it all?" "That's a secret," said Jem, looking great. "I can guess. I know what I'd do with it if it was mine. First, I'd buy pocketsful of gingerbread; then I'd buy ever so many apples and nuts: don't you love nuts? I'd buy nuts enough to last me from this time to Christmas, and I'd make little Newton crack 'em for me; for that's the worst of nuts, there's the trouble of cracking 'em." "Well, you never deserve to have a nut." "But you'll give me some of yours," said Lawrence in a fawning tone, for he thought it easier to coax than to work—"you'll give me some of your good things, won't you?" "I shall not have any of those good things," said Jem. "Then what will you do with all your money?"—"Oh, I know very well what to do with it; but, as I told you, that's a secret, and I sha'n't tell it any body—Come now, let's go back and play—their game's up, I dare say."—Lawrence went back with him full of curiosity, and out of humour with himself and his eight-pence. "If I had four and seven-pence," said he to himself, "I certainly should be happy."

The next day, as usual, Jem jumped up before six o'clock and went to his work, whilst Lazy Lawrence sauntered about without knowing what to do with himself. In the course of two days he laid out six-pence of his money in apples and gingerbread, and as long as these lasted he found himself well received by his companions; but at length the third day he spent his last halfpenny, and when it was gone, unfortunately some nuts tempted him very much, but he had no money to pay for them; so he ran home to coax his father, as he called it. When he got home he heard his father talking very loud, and at first he thought he was drunk; but when he opened the kitchen-door, he saw that he was not drunk, but angry.

"You lazy dog!" cried he, turning suddenly upon Lawrence, and gave him such a violent box on the ear as made the light flash from his eyes; "you lazy dog! see what you've done for me—look!—look, look, I say!" Lawrence looked as soon as he came to the use of his senses, and with fear, amazement, and remorse, beheld at least a dozen bottles burst, and the fine Worcestershire cider streaming over the floor. "Now, did not I order you three days ago to carry these bottles to the cellar; and did not I charge you to wire the corks? answer me, you lazy rascal; did not I?" "Yes," said Lawrence, scratching his head. "And why was it not done? I ask you," cried his father with renewed anger, as another bottle burst at the moment. "What do you stand there for, you lazy brat? why don't you move, I say? No, no," catching hold of him, "I believe you can't move; but I'll make you." And he shook him till Lawrence was so giddy he could not stand. "What had you to think of? what had you to do all day long, that you could not carry my cider, my Worcestershire cider, to the cellar when I bid you? But go, you'll never be good for any thing, you are such a lazy rascal—get out of my sight!" So saying, he pushed him out of the house-door, and Lawrence sneaked off, seeing that this was no time to make his petition for half-pence.

The next day he saw the nuts again, and, wishing for them more than ever, went home in hopes that his father, as he said to himself, would be in a better humour. But the cider was still fresh in his recollection, and the moment Lawrence began to whisper the word "halfpenny" in his ear, his father swore with a loud oath, "I will not give you a halfpenny, no, not a farthing, for a month to come; if you want money, go work for it; I've had enough of your laziness—Go work!" At these terrible words Lawrence burst into tears, and going to the side of a ditch, sat down and cried for an hour; and when he had cried till he could cry no more, he exerted himself so far as to empty his pockets, to see whether there might not happen to be one halfpenny left; and to his great joy, in the farthest corner of his pocket one halfpenny was found. With this he proceeded to the fruit-woman's stall. She was busy weighing out some plums, so he was obliged to wait; and, whilst he was waiting, he heard some people near him talking and laughing very loud. The fruit-woman's stall was at the gate of an inn-yard; and peeping through the gate in this yard, Lawrence saw a postilion and stable-boy about his own size playing at pitch-farthing. He stood by watching them for a few minutes. "I began but with one halfpenny," cried the stable-boy with an oath, "and now I've got two-pence!" added he, jingling the halfpence in his waistcoat-pocket, Lawrence was moved at the sound, and said to himself, "If I begin with one halfpenny, I may end like him with having two-pence; and it is easier to play at pitch-farthing than to work."

So he stepped forward, presenting his halfpenny, offering to toss up with the stable-boy, who, after looking him full in the face, accepted the proposal, and threw his halfpenny into the air. "Head or tail?" cried he. "Head," replied Lawrence, and it came up head. He seized the penny, surprised at his own success, and would have gone instantly to have laid it out in nuts; but the stable-boy stopped him, and tempted him to throw again. This time he lost; he threw again and won; and so he went on, sometimes losing, but most frequently winning, till half the morning was gone. At last, however, he chanced to win twice running, and, finding himself master of three halfpence, said he would play no more. The stable-boy, grumbling, swore he would have his revenge another time, and Lawrence went and bought the nuts. "It is a good thing," said he to himself, "to play at pitch-farthing: the next time I want a half-penny, I'll not ask my father for it, nor go to work neither." Satisfied with this resolution, he sat down to crack his nuts at his leisure, upon the horse-block in the inn-yard. Here, whilst he ate, he overheard the conversation of the stable-boys and postilions. At first their shocking oaths and loud wrangling frightened and shocked him; for Lawrence, though a *lazy*, had not yet learned to be a *wicked* boy. But, by degrees, he was accustomed to their swearing and quarrelling, and took a delight and interest in their disputes and battles. As this was an amusement which he could enjoy without any sort of exertion on his part, he soon grew so fond of it, that every day he returned to the stable-yard, and the horse-block became his constant seat. Here he found some relief from the insupportable fatigue of doing nothing; and here hour after hour, with his elbows on his knees, and his head on his hands, he sat the spectator of wickedness.

Gaming, cheating, and lying, soon become familiar to him; and, to complete his ruin, he formed a sudden and close intimacy with the stable-boy with whom he had first begun to game—a very bad boy. The consequences of this intimacy we shall presently see. But it is now time to inquire what little Jem has been doing all this while.

One day, after he had finished his task, the gardener asked him to stay a little while, to help him to carry some geranium pots into the hall. Jem, always active and obliging, readily stayed from play, and was carrying a heavy flower-pot, when his mistress crossed the hall. "What a terrible litter," said she, "you are a-making here—why don't you wipe your shoes upon the mat?" Jem turned round to look for the mat, but he saw none. "Oh!" said the lady, recollecting herself, "I can't blame you, for there is no mat." "No, ma'am," said the gardener, "nor I don't know when, if ever, the man will bring home those mats you bespoke, ma'am." "I am very sorry to hear that," said the lady: "I wish we could find somebody who would do them, if he can't—I should not care what sort of mats they were, so that one could wipe one's feet on them." Jem, as he was sweeping away the litter, when he heard these last words, said to himself, "Perhaps I could make a mat." And all the way home, as he trudged along whistling, he was thinking over a scheme for making mats, which, however bold it may appear, he did not despair of executing, with patience and industry. Many were the difficulties which his *"prophetic eye"* foresaw, but he felt within himself that spirit, which spurs men on to great enterprises, and makes them "trample on impossibilities."

He recollected, in the first place, that he had seen Lazy Lawrence, whilst he lounged upon the gate, twist a bit of heath into different shapes; and he thought that if he could find some way of plaiting heath firmly together, it would make a very pretty green, soft mat, which would do very well for one to wipe one's shoes on. About a mile from his mother's house, on the common which Jem rode over when he went to farmer Truck's for the giant strawberries, he remembered to have seen a great quantity of this heath; and as it was now only six o'clock in the evening, he knew that he should have time to feed Lightfoot, stroke him, go to the common, return, and make one trial of his skill before he went to bed.

Lightfoot carried him swiftly to the common, and there Jem gathered as much of the heath as he thought he should want. But, what toil, what time, what pains did it cost him, before he could make any thing like a mat! Twenty times he was ready to throw aside the heath, and give up his project, from impatience of repeated disappointments. But still he persevered. Nothing *truly great* can be accomplished without toil and time. Two hours he worked before he went to bed. All his play-hours the next day he spent at his mat; which, in all, made five hours of fruitless attempts. The sixth day, however, repaid him for the labours of the other five; he conquered his grand difficulty of fastening the heath substantially together, and at length completely finished a mat, which far surpassed his most sanguine expectations. He was extremely happy— sung, danced round it—whistled—looked at it again and again, and could hardly leave off looking at it when it was time to go to bed. He laid it by his bed-side, that he might see it the moment he awoke in the morning.

And now came the grand pleasure of carrying it to his mistress. She looked full as much surprised as he expected, when she saw it, and when she heard who made it. After having duly admired it, she asked him how much he expected for his mat. "Expect! —Nothing, ma'am," said Jem, "I meant to give it you if you'd have it; I did not mean to sell it. I made it at my play-hours, and I was very happy making it; and I'm very glad too that you like it; and if you please to keep it, ma'am—that's all." "But that's not all," said the lady. "Spend your time no more in weeding my garden, you can employ yourself much better; you shall have the reward of your ingenuity as well as of your industry. Make as many more such mats as you can, and I will take care and dispose of them for you." "Thank'e, ma'am," said Jem, making his best bow, for he thought by the lady's looks that she meant to do him a favour, though he repeated to himself, "Dispose of them; what does that mean?"

The next day he went to work to make more mats, and he soon learned to make them so well and quickly, that he was surprised at his own success. In every one he made he found less difficulty, so that instead of making two, he could soon make four, in a day. In a fortnight he made eighteen. It was Saturday night when he finished, and he carried, in three journeys, his eighteen mats to his mistress's house; piled them all up in the hall, and stood, with his hat off, with a look of proud humility, beside the pile, waiting for his mistress's appearance. Presently a folding door, at one end of the hall, opened, and he saw his mistress, with a great many gentlemen and ladies rising from several tables.

"Oh! there is my little boy, and his mats," cried the lady; and, followed by all the rest of the company, she came into the hall. Jem modestly retired whilst they looked at his mats; but in a minute or two his mistress beckoned to him, and, when he came into the middle of the circle, he saw that his pile of mats had disappeared. "Well," said the lady, smiling, "what do you see that makes you look so surprised?" "That all my mats are gone," said Jem; "but you are very welcome." "Are we?" said the lady; "well, take up your hat, and go home then, for you see that it is getting late, and you know, 'Lightfoot will wonder what's become of you.' " Jem turned round to take up his hat which he had left on the floor.

But how his countenance changed! the hat was heavy with shillings. Every one who had taken a mat had put in two shillings; so that for the eighteen mats he had got thirty-six shillings. "Thirty-six shillings!" said the lady; "five and seven-pence I think you told me you had earned already—how much does that make? I must add, I believe, one other six-pence to make out your two guineas." "Two guineas!" exclaimed Jem, now quite conquering his bashfulness, for at the moment he forgot where he was, and saw nobody that was by: "Two guineas!" cried he, clapping his hands together—"Oh Lightfoot! oh mother!" Then, recollecting himself, he saw his mistress, whom he now looked up to quite as a friend. "Will *you* thank them all," said he, scarcely daring to glance his eye round upon the company, "will *you* thank 'em, for you know I don't know how to thank 'em *rightly*." Every body thought, however, that they had been thanked *rightly*.

"Now we won't keep you any longer—only," said his mistress, "I have one thing to ask you, that I may be by when you show your treasure to your mother." "Come, then," said Jem, "come with me now." "Not now," said the lady laughing, "but I will come to Ashton to-morrow evening; perhaps your mother can find me a few strawberries."

"That she will," said Jem; "I'll search the garden myself." He now went home, but felt it a great restraint to wait till to-morrow evening before he told his mother. To console himself he flew to the stable; "Lightfoot, you're not to be sold to-morrow! poor fellow," said he, patting him, and then could not refrain from counting out his money. Whilst he was intent upon this, Jem was startled by a noise at the door; somebody was trying to pull up the latch. It opened, and there came in Lazy Lawrence, with a boy in a red jacket, who had a cock under his arm. They started when they got into the middle of the stable, and when they saw Jem, who had been at first hidden by the horse.

"We—we—we came," stammered Lazy Lawrence—"I mean, I came to—to—to—" "To ask you," continued the stable-boy in a bold tone, "whether you will go with us to the cock-fight on Monday? See, I've a fine cock here, and Lawrence told me you were a great friend of his, so I came."

Lawrence now attempted to say something in praise of the pleasures of cock-fighting, and in recommendation of his new companion. But Jem looked at the stable-boy with dislike and a sort of dread; then turning his eyes upon the cock with a look of compassion, said in a low voice to Lawrence, "Shall you like to stand by and see its eyes pecked out?" "I don't know," said Lawrence, "as to that; but they say a cock-fight's a fine sight, and it's no more cruel in me to go than another; and a great many go; and I've nothing else to do, so I shall go." "But I have something else to do," said Jem laughing, "so I shall not go." "But," continued Lawrence, "you know Monday is the great Bristol fair, and one must be merry then, of all days in the year." "One day in the year, sure there's no harm in being merry," said the stable-boy. "I hope not," said Jem; "for I know, for my part, I am merry every day in the year." "That's very odd," said Lawrence; "but I know, for my part, I would not for all the world miss going to the fair, for at least it will be something to talk of for half a year after. Come; you'll go, won't you?" "No," said Jem, still looking as if he did not like to talk before the ill-looking stranger. "Then what will you do with all your money?" "I'll tell you about that another time," whispered Jem; "and don't you go to see that cock's eyes pecked out; it won't make you merry, I'm sure." "If I had any thing else to divert me—" said

Lawrence, hesitating and yawning. "Come," cried the stable-boy, seizing his stretching arm, "come along," cried he; and, pulling him away from Jem, upon whom he cast a look of extreme contempt, "leave him alone, he's not the sort." "What a fool you are!" said he to Lawrence, the moment he got him out of the stable, "you might have known he would not go—else we should soon have trimmed him out of his four and seven-pence. But how came you to talk of four and seven-pence; I saw in the manger a hat full of silver." "Indeed!" exclaimed Lawrence. "Yes, indeed—but why did you stammer so when we first got in? you had like to have blown us all up." "I was so ashamed," said Lawrence, hanging down his head. "Ashamed! but you must not talk of shame now you are in for it, and I sha'n't let you off: you owe us half a crown, recollect, and I must be paid to-night; so see and get the money some how or other." After a considerable pause he added, "I'll answer for it he'd never miss half a crown out of all that silver." "But to steal," said Lawrence, drawing back with horror—"I never thought I should come to that—and from poor Jem too—the money that he has worked so hard for too." "But it is not stealing; we don't mean to steal; only to borrow it: and, if we win, as we certainly shall, at the cock-fight, pay it back again, and he'll never know any thing of the matter; and what harm will it do him? Besides, what signifies talking? you can't go to the cock-fight, or the fair either, if you don't; and I tell ye, we don't mean to steal it; we'll pay it again on Monday night." Lawrence made no reply, and they parted without his coming to any determination.

Here let us pause in our story—we are almost afraid to go on—the rest is very shock-ing—our little readers will shudder as they read. But it is better that they should know the truth, and see what the idle boy came to at last.

In the dead of the night Lawrence heard somebody tap at the window. He knew well who it was, for this was the signal agreed upon between him and his wicked companion. He trembled at the thoughts of what he was about to do, and lay quite still, with his head under the bed-clothes, till he heard the second tap. Then he got up, dressed himself, and opened his window. It was almost even with the ground. His companion said to him in a hollow voice, "Are you ready?" He made no answer, but got out of the window and followed. When he got to the stable a black cloud was just passing over the moon, and it was quite dark. "Where are you?" whispered Lawrence, groping about, "where are you? Speak to me." "I am here; give me your hand." Lawrence stretched out his hand. "Is that your hand?" said the wicked boy, as Lawrence laid hold of him; "how cold it felt!" "Let us go back," said Lawrence; "it is time yet." "It is no time to go back," replied the other, opening the door; "you've gone too far now to go back;" and he pushed Lawrence into the stable. "Have you found it? take care of the horse—have you done? what are you about? make haste, I hear a noise," said the stable-boy, who watched at the door. "I am feeling for the half crown, but I can't find it." "Bring all together." He brought Jem's broken flower-pot, with all the money in it, to the door.

The black cloud was now passed over the moon, and the light shone full upon them. "What do we stand here for?" said the stable-boy, snatching the flower-pot out of Lawrence's trembling hands, and pulling him away from the door. "Surely," cried Lawrence, "you won't take all! You said you'd only take half a crown, and pay it back on Monday—you said you'd only take half a crown!" "Hold your tongue!" replied the other, walking on, deaf to all remonstrances—"if I am to be hanged ever, it sha'n't be for half a crown." Lawrence's blood ran cold in his veins, and he felt as if all his hair stood on end. Not another word passed. His accomplice carried off the money, and Lawrence crept, with all the horrors of guilt upon him, to his restless bed. All night he was starting from frightful dreams; or else, broad awake, he lay listening to every small noise, unable to stir, and scarcely daring to breathe—tormented by that most dreadful of all kinds of fear, that fear which is the constant companion of an evil conscience. He thought the morning would never come; but when it was day, when he heard the birds sing, and saw every thing look cheerful as usual, he felt still more miserable. It was Sunday morning, and the bell rang for church. All the children of the village, dressed in their Sunday clothes, innocent and gay, and little Jem, the best and gayest amongst them, went flocking by his door to church. "Well, Lawrence," said Jem, pulling his coat as he passed, and saw Lawrence leaning against his father's door, "what makes you look so black?" "I," said Lawrence, starting, "why do you say that I look black?" "Nay, then," said Jem, "you look white enough now, if that will please you; for you're turned as pale as death." "Pale!" replied Lawrence, not knowing what he said; and turned abruptly away, for he dared not stand another look of Jem's; conscious that guilt was written in his face, he shunned every eye. He would now have given the world to have thrown off the load of guilt which lay upon his mind; he longed to follow Jem, to fall upon his knees, and confess all: dreading the moment when Jem should discover his loss, Lawrence dared not stay at home; and not knowing what to do, or where to go, he mechanically went to his old haunt at the stable-yard, and lurked thereabouts all day, with his accomplice, who tried in vain to quiet his fears and raise his spirits, by talking of the next day's cock-fight. It was agreed, that as soon as the dusk of the evening came on, they should go together into a certain lonely field, and there divide their booty.

In the mean time, Jem, when he returned from church, was very full of business, preparing for the reception of his mistress, of whose intended visit he had informed his mother; and whilst she was arranging the kitchen and their little parlour, he ran to search the strawberry beds. "Why, my Jem, how merry you are to-day!" said his mother, when he came in with the strawberries, and was jumping about the room playfully. "Now keep those spirits of yours, Jem, till you want 'em, and don't let it come upon you all at once. Have it in mind that to-morrow's fair-day, and Lightfoot must go. I bid farmer Truck call for him to-night; he said he'd take him along with his own, and he'll be here just now—and then I know how it will be with you, Jem!" "So do I!" cried Jem, swallowing his secret with great difficulty, and then turning head over heels four times running. A carriage passed the window and stopped at the door. Jem ran out; it was his mistress. She came in smiling, and soon made the old woman smile too, by praising the neatness of every thing in the house. But we shall pass over, however important they were deemed at the time, the praises of the strawberries, and of "my grandmother's china plate." Another knock was heard at the door. "Run, Jem," said his mother, "I hope it's our milk-woman with cream for the lady."—No; it was farmer Truck come for Lightfoot. The old woman's countenance fell. "Fetch him out, dear," said she, turning to her son; but Jem was gone; he flew out to the stable the moment he saw the flap of farmer Truck's great-coat.—"Sit ye down, farmer," said the old woman, after they had waited about five minutes in expectation of Jem's return. "You'd best sit down, if the lady will give you leave; for he'll not hurry himself back again. My boy's a fool, madam, about that there horse." Trying to laugh, she added, "I knew how Lightfoot and he would be loath enough to part—he won't bring him out till the last minute; so do sit ye down, neighbour." The farmer had scarcely sat down, when Jem, with a pale wild countenance, came back. "What's the matter?" said his mistress. "God bless the boy!" said his mother, looking at him quite frightened, whilst he tried to speak, but could not. She went up to him, and then leaning his head against her, he cried, "It's gone!—it's all gone!" and bursting into tears, he sobbed as if his little heart would break. "What's gone, love?" said his mother. "My two guineas—Lightfoot's two guineas. I went to fetch 'em to give you, mammy! but the broken flower-pot that I put them in, and all's gone! —quite gone!" repeated he, checking his sobs. "I saw them safe last night, and was showing 'em to Lightfoot; and I was so glad to think I had earned them all myself; and I thought how surprised you'd look, and how glad you'd be, and how you'd kiss me, and all!"

His mother listened to him with the greatest surprise, whilst his mistress stood in silence, looking first at the old woman, and then at Jem, with a penetrating eye, as if she suspected the truth of his story, and was afraid of becoming the dupe of her own compassion. "This is a very strange thing!" said she gravely. "How came you to leave all your money in a broken flower-pot in the stable? How came you not to give it to your mother to take care of?" "Why, don't you remember," said Jem, looking up in the midst of his tears; "why, don't you remember you your own self bid me not to tell her about it till you were by." "And did you not tell her?" "Nay, ask mammy," said Jem a little offended; and when afterwards the lady went on questioning him in a severe manner, as if she did not believe him, he at last made no answer. "Oh, Jem, Jem! why don't you speak to the lady?" said his mother. "I have spoke, and spoke the truth," said Jem, proudly, "and she did not believe me."

Still the lady, who had lived too long in the world to be without suspicion, maintained a cold manner, and determined to await the event without interfering, saying only, that she hoped the money would be found; and advised Jem to have done crying. "I have done," said Jem, "I shall cry no more." And as he had the greatest command over himself, he actually did not shed another tear, not even when the farmer got up to go, saying he could wait no longer. Jem silently went to bring out Lightfoot. The lady now took her seat where she could see all that passed at the open parlour window. The old woman stood at the door, and several idle people of the village, who had gathered round the lady's carriage, examining it, turned about to listen. In a minute or two Jem appeared, with a steady countenance, leading Lightfoot; and, when he came up, without saying a word put the bridle into farmer Truck's hand. "He *has been* a good horse," said the farmer. "He *is* a good horse!" cried Jem, and threw his arm over Lightfoot's neck, hiding his own face as he leaned upon him.

At this instant a party of milk-women went by; and one of them having set down her pail, came behind Jem, and gave him a pretty smart blow upon the back. He looked up. "And don't you know me?" said she. "I forget," said Jem; "I think I have seen your face before, but I forget." "Do you so? and you'll tell me just now," said she, half-opening her hand, "that you forgot who gave you this, and who charged you not to part with it, too." Here she quite opened her large hand, and on the palm of it appeared Jem's silver penny. "Where?" exclaimed Jem, seizing it, "oh where did you find it? and have you—oh tell me, have you got the rest of my money?" "I don't know nothing of your money—I don't know what you would be at," said the milk-woman. "But where, pray tell me, where did you find this?" "With them that you gave it to, I suppose," said the milk-woman, turning away suddenly to take up her milk-pail. But now Jem's mistress called to her through the window, begging her to stop, and joining in his entreaties to know how she came by the silver penny.

"Why, madam," said she, taking up the corner of her apron, "I came by it in an odd way, too—You must know my Betty is sick, so I come with the milk myself, though it's not what I'm used to; for my Betty—you know my Betty," said she, turning round to the old woman, "my Betty serves you, and she's a tight and stirring lassy, ma'am, I can assure—" "Yes, I don't doubt it," said the lady, impatiently; "but about the silver penny?" "Why, that's true; as I was coming along all alone, for the rest came a round, and I came a short cut across the field—No, you can't see it, madam, where you stand—but if you were here—" "I see it—I know it," said Jem, out of breath with anxiety. "Well—well—I rested my pail upon the stile, and sets me down a while, and there comes out of the hedge—I don't know well how, for they startled me, so I'd like to have thrown down my milk—two boys, one about the size of he," said she, pointing to Jem, "and one a matter taller, but ill-looking like, so I did not think to stir to make way for them, and they were like in a desperate hurry: so, without waiting for the stile, one of 'em pulled at the gate, and when it would not open (for it was tied with a pretty stout cord), one of 'em whips out with his knife and cuts it——

"Now have you a knife about you, sir?" continued the milk-woman to the farmer. He gave her his knife.

"Here now, ma'am, just sticking as it were here, between the blade and the haft, was the silver penny. He took no notice, but when he opened it, out it falls; still he takes no heed, but cuts the cord, as I said before, and through the gate they went, and out of sight in half a minute. I picks up the penny, for my heart misgave me that it was the very one husband had had a long time, and had given against my voice to *he*," pointing to Jem; "and I charged him not to part with it; and, ma'am, when I looked, I knew it by the mark, so I thought I should show it to *he*," again pointing to Jem, "and let him give it back to those it belongs to." "It belongs to me," said Jem; "I never gave it to any body—but—but—" "But," cried the farmer, "those boys have robbed him—it is they who have all his money." "Oh, which way did they go?" cried Jem, "I'll run after them."

"No, no," said the lady, calling to her servant; and she desired him to take his horse and ride after them. "Aye," added farmer Truck, "do you take the road, and I'll take the field way, and I'll be bound we'll have 'em presently."

Whilst they were gone in pursuit of the thieves, the lady, who was now thoroughly convinced of Jem's truth, desired her coachman would produce what she had ordered him to bring with him that evening. Out of the boot of the carriage the coachman immediately produced a new saddle and bridle.

How Jem's eyes sparkled when the saddle was thrown upon Lightfoot's back! "Put it on your horse yourself, Jem," said the lady—"it is yours."

Confused reports of Lightfoot's splendid accoutrements, of the pursuit of the thieves, and of the fine and generous lady, who was standing at Dame Preston's window, quickly spread through the village, and drew every body from their houses. They crowded round Jem to hear the story. The children especially, who were all fond of him, expressed the strongest indignation against the thieves. Every eye was on the stretch; and now some, who had run down the lane, came back shouting, "Here they are! they've got the thieves!"

The footman on horseback carried one boy before him; and the farmer, striding along, dragged another. The latter had on a red jacket, which little Jem immediately recollected, and scarcely dared lift his eyes to look at the boy on horseback. "Astonishing!" said he to himself, "it must be—yet surely it can't be Lawrence!" The footman rode as fast as the people would let him. The boy's hat was slouched, and his head hung down, so that nobody could see his face.

At this instant there was a disturbance in the crowd. A man who was half drunk pushed his way forwards, swearing that nobody should stop him; that he had a right to see; and he *would* see. And so he did; for, forcing through all resistance, he staggered up to the footman just as he was lifting down the boy he had carried before him. "I *will* —I tell you, I *will* see the thief!" cried the drunken man, pushing up the boy's hat. It was his own son. "Lawrence!" exclaimed the wretched father. The shock sobered him at once, and he hid his face in his hands.

There was an awful silence. Lawrence fell on his knees, and, in a voice that could scarcely be heard, made a full confession of all the circumstances of his guilt. "Such a young creature so wicked! What could put such wickedness into your head?" "Bad company," said Lawrence. "And how came you—what brought you into bad company?" "I don't know—except it was idleness." While this was saying, the farmer was emptying Lazy Lawrence's pockets; and when the money appeared, all his former companions in the village looked at each other with astonishment and terror. Their parents grasped their little hands closer, and cried, "Thanks to heaven! he is not my son—how often, when he was little, we used, as he lounged about, to tell him that idleness was the root of all evil."

As for the hardened wretch, his accomplice, every one was impatient to have him sent to gaol. He had put on a bold, insolent countenance, till he heard Lawrence's confession; till the money was found upon him; and he heard the milk-woman declare, that she would swear to the silver penny which he had dropped. Then he turned pale, and betrayed the strongest signs of fear. "We must take him before the justice," said the farmer, "and he'll be lodged in Bristol gaol." "Oh!" said Jem, springing forward when Lawrence's hands were going to be tied, "let him go—won't you—can't you, let him go?" "Yes, madam, for mercy's sake," said Jem's mother to the lady, "think what a disgrace to his family to be sent to gaol!" His father stood by wringing his hands in an agony of despair. "It's all my fault," cried he: "I brought him up in *idleness*." "But he'll never be idle any more;" said Jem; "won't you speak for him, ma'am?" "Don't ask the lady to speak for him," said the farmer; "it's better he should go to Bridewell now, than to the gallows by-and-by."

Nothing more was said, for every body felt the truth of the farmer's speech. Lawrence was sent to Bridewell for a month, and the stable-boy was transported to Botany Bay.

During Lawrence's confinement, Jem often visited him, and carried him such little presents as he could afford to give; and Jem could afford to be *generous*, because he was *industrious*. Lawrence's heart was touched by his kindness, and his example struck him so forcibly, that, when his confinement was ended, he resolved to set immediately to work; and, to the astonishment of all who knew him, soon became remarkable for industry; he was found early and late at his work, established a new character, and for ever lost the name of *Lazy Lawrence*.

The Birth-day Present.

"MAMMA," said Rosamond, after a long silence, "do you know what I have been thinking of all this time?"

"No, my dear.—What?"

"Why, mamma, about my cousin Bell's birth-day; do you know what day it is?"

"No, I don't remember."

"Dear mother! don't you remember it's the 22d of December? and her birth-day is the day after to-morrow. Don't you recollect now? But you never remember about birthdays, mamma: that was just what I was thinking of, that you never remember my sister Laura's birth-day, or—or—or *mine*, mamma."

"What do you mean, my dear? I remember your birth-day perfectly well."

"Indeed! but you never *keep* it though."

"What do you mean by keeping your birth-day?"

"Oh, mamma, you know very well—as Bell's birth-day is kept. In the first place there is a great dinner."

"And can Bell eat more upon her birth-day than upon any other day?"

"No: nor should I mind about the dinner, except the mince pies. But Bell has a great many nice things; I don't mean nice eatable things; but nice new playthings given to her always on her birth-day: and every body drinks her health, and she's so happy!"

"But stay, Rosamond, how you jumble things together! Is it every body's drinking her health that makes her so happy, or the new playthings, or the nice mince pies? I can easily believe that she is happy whilst she is eating a mince pie, or whilst she is playing; but how does every body's drinking her health at dinner make her happy?"

Rosamond paused, and then said she did not know. "But," added she, "the *nice new* playthings, mother!"

"But why the nice new playthings? Do you like them only because they are *new*?"

"Not *only*—I do not like playthings *only* because they are new, but Bell *does*, I believe —for that puts me in mind—Do you know, mother, she had a great drawer full of *old* playthings that she never used, and she said that they were good for nothing because they were *old*; but I thought many of them were good for a great deal more than the new ones. Now you shall be judge, mamma; I'll tell you all that was in the drawer."

"Nay, Rosamond, thank you, not just now; I have not time to listen to you."

"Well, then, mamma, the day after to-morrow I can show you the drawer; I want you to be judge very much, because I am sure I was in the right. And, mother," added Rosamond, stopping her as she was going out of the room, "will you—not now, but when you've time—will you tell me why you never keep my birth-day—why you never make any difference between that day and any other day?"

"And will you, Rosamond—not now, but when you have time to think about it—tell me why I should make any difference between your birth-day and any other day?"

Rosamond thought—but she could not find out any reason: besides, she suddenly recollected, that she had not time to think any longer, for there was a certain workbasket to be finished, which she was making for her cousin Bell, as a present upon her birth-day. The work was at a stand for want of some filigree paper, and as her mother was going out she asked her to take her with her that she might buy some. Her sister Laura went with them.

"Sister," said Rosamond, as they were walking along, "what have you done with your half-guinea?"

"I have it in my pocket."

"Dear! you will keep it for ever in your pocket: you know my godmother, when she gave it to you, said you would keep it longer than I should keep mine; and I know what she thought by her look at the time. I heard her say something to my mother."

"Yes," said Laura, smiling, "she whispered so loud, that I could not help hearing her too: she said I was a little miser."

"But did not you hear her say that I was very *generous?* and she'll see that she was not mistaken. I hope she'll be by when I give my basket to Bell—won't it be beautiful? —there is to be a wreath of myrtle, you know, round the handle, and a frost ground, and then the medallions——"

"Stay," interrupted her sister; for Rosamond, anticipating the glories of her work-basket, talked and walked so fast, that she had passed, without perceiving it, the shop where the filigree paper was to be bought. They turned back. Now it happened that the shop was the corner house of a street, and one of the windows looked out into a narrow lane: a coach full of ladies stopped at the door just before they went in, so that no one had time immediately to think of Rosamond and her filigree paper, and she went to the window, where she saw her sister Laura was looking earnestly at something that was passing in the lane.

Opposite to the window, at the door of a poor-looking house, there was sitting a little girl weaving lace. Her bobbins moved as quick as lightning, and she never once looked up from her work.

"Is not she very industrious?" said Laura: "and very honest too," added she in a minute afterwards; for just then a baker with a basket of rolls on his head passed, and by accident one of the rolls fell close to the little girl: she took it up eagerly, looked at it as if she was very hungry, then put aside her work, and ran after the baker to return it to him.

Whilst she was gone, a footman in a livery laced with silver, who belonged to the coach that stood at the shop-door, as he was lounging with one of his companions, chanced to spy the weaving-pillow, which she had left upon a stone before the door. To divert himself (for idle people do mischief often to divert themselves) he took up the pillow, and entangled all the bobbins. The little girl came back out of breath to her work; but what was her surprise and sorrow to find it spoiled: she twisted and untwisted, placed and replaced the bobbins, while the footman stood laughing at her distress. She got up gently, and was retiring into the house, when the silver-laced footman stopped her, saying insolently, "Sit still, child."

"I must go to my mother, sir," said the child; "besides you have spoiled all my lace— I can't stay."

"Can't you," said the brutal footman, snatching her weaving pillow again, "I'll teach you to complain of me." And he broke off, one after another, all the bobbins, put them into his pocket, rolled her weaving pillow down the dirty lane, then jumped up behind his mistress's coach, and was out of sight in an instant.

"Poor girl!" exclaimed Rosamond, no longer able to restrain her indignation at this injustice: "Poor little girl!"

At this instant her mother said to Rosamond—"Come now, my dear, if you want this filigree paper, buy it."

"Yes, madam," said Rosamond; and the idea of what her godmother and her cousin Bell would think of her generosity rushed again upon her imagination. All her feelings of pity were immediately suppressed. Satisfied with bestowing another exclamation upon the *"Poor little girl!"* she went to spend her half-guinea upon her filigree basket. In the mean time, she that was called *"the little miser,"* beckoned to the poor girl, and opening the window said, pointing to the cushion, "Is it quite spoiled?"

"Quite, quite spoiled! and I can't, nor mother neither, buy another; and I can't do any thing else for my bread." A few, but very few, tears fell as she said this.

"How much would another cost?" said Laura.

"Oh a great—*great* deal!"

"More than that?" said Laura, holding up her half-guinea.

"Oh, no."

"Then you can buy another with that," said Laura, dropping the half-guinea into her hand, and she shut the window before the child could find words to thank her; but not before she saw a look of joy and gratitude, which gave Laura more pleasure probably than all the praise which could have been bestowed upon her generosity.

Late on the morning of her cousin's birthday, Rosamond finished her work-basket. The carriage was at the door—Laura came running to call her; her father's voice was heard at the same instant; so she was obliged to go down with her basket but half wrapped up in silver paper, a circumstance at which she was a good deal disconcerted: for the pleasure of surprising Bell would be utterly lost, if one bit of the filigree should peep out before the proper time. As the carriage went on, Rosamond pulled the paper to one side and to the other, and by each of the four corners.

"It will never do, my dear," said her father, who had been watching her operations, "I am afraid you will never make a sheet of paper cover a box which is twice as large as itself."

"It is not a box, father," said Rosamond, a little peevishly: "it's a basket."

"Let us look at this basket," said he, taking it out of her unwilling hands; for she knew of what frail materials it was made, and she dreaded its coming to pieces under her father's examination.

He took hold of the handle rather roughly, and starting off the coach-seat, she cried—

"O sir! father! sir! you will spoil it indeed!" said she, with increased vehemence, when, after drawing aside the veil of silver-paper, she saw him grasp the myrtle-wreathed handle.

"Indeed, sir, you will spoil the poor handle!"

"But what is the use of *the poor handle*," said her father, "if we are not to take hold of it? And pray," continued he, turning the basket round with his finger and thumb, rather in a disrespectful manner—"pray is this the thing you have been about all this week? I have seen you all this week dabbling with paste and rags; I could not conceive what you were about—Is this the thing?"

"Yes, sir. You think then that I have wasted my time, because the basket is of no use: but then it is for a present for my cousin Bell."

"Your cousin Bell will be very much obliged to you for a present that is of no use: you had better have given her the purple jar."*

"Oh, father! I thought that you had forgotten that—it was two years ago: I'm not so silly now. But Bell will like the basket, I know, though it is of no use."

"Then you think Bell sillier *now* than you were two years ago. Well, perhaps that is true; but how comes it, Rosamond, now that you are so wise, that you are so fond of such a silly person?"

"*I*, father?" said Rosamond, hesitating; "I don't think I am *very* fond of her."

"I did not say *very* fond."

"Well, but I don't think I am at all fond of her."

"But you have spent a whole week in making this thing for her."

"Yes, and all my half-guinea besides."

"Yet you know her to be silly, and you are not fond of her at all; and you say you know this thing will be of no use to her."

"But it is her birth-day, sir; and I am sure she will *expect* something, and every body else will give her something."

"Then your reason for giving is because she expects you to give her something. And will you, or can you, or should you, always give, merely because others *expect*, or because somebody else gives?"

"Always!—no, not always."

"Oh, only on birth-days."

Rosamond laughing, "Now you are making a joke of me, papa, I see; but I thought you liked that people should be generous—my godmother said that she did."

"So do I, full as well as your godmother; but we have not yet quite settled what it is to be generous."

"Why, is it not generous to make presents?" said Rosamond.

"That is a question which it would take up a great deal of time to answer. But, for instance, to make a present of a thing that you know can be of no use, to a person you neither love nor esteem, because it is her birth-day, and because every body gives her something, and because she expects something, and because your godmother says she likes that people should be generous, seems to me, my dear Rosamond, to be, since I must say it, rather more like folly than generosity."

Rosamond looked down upon the basket, and was silent.

"Then I am a fool! am I?" said she, looking up at last.

"Because you have made *one* mistake? No. If you have sense enough to see your own mistakes, and can afterwards avoid them, you will never be a fool."

Here the carriage stopped, and Rosamond recollected that the basket was uncovered.

Now we must observe, that Rosamond's father had not been too severe upon Bell, when he called her a silly girl. From her infancy she had been humoured; and at eight years old she had the misfortune to be a spoiled child: she was idle, fretful, and selfish, so that nothing could make her happy. On her birth-day she expected, however, to be perfectly happy. Every body in the house tried to please her, and they succeeded so well, that between breakfast and dinner she had only six fits of crying. The cause of five of these fits no one could discover; but the last, and most lamentable, was occasioned

---

* See Early Lessons.

by a disappointment about a worked muslin frock, and accordingly at dressing-time her maid brought it to her, exclaiming—"See here, miss! what your mamma has sent you on your birth-day—Here's a frock fit for a queen—if it had but lace round the cuffs."

"And why has it not lace round the cuffs?—mamma said it should."

"Yes, but mistress was disappointed about the lace; it is not come home."

"Not come home, indeed! and didn't they know it was my birth-day? But then I say I won't wear it without the lace—I can't wear it without the lace—and I won't."

The lace, however, could not be had; and Bell at length submitted to let the frock be put on. "Come, Miss Bell, dry your eyes," said the maid who *educated* her; "dry your eyes, and I'll tell you something that will please you."

"What, then?" said the child, pouting and sobbing.

"Why——but you must not say that I told you."

"No—but if I am asked?"

"Why, if you are asked, you must tell the truth to be sure. So I'll hold my tongue, miss."

"Nay, tell me though, and I'll never tell if I am asked."

"Well, then," said the maid, "your cousin Rosamond is come, and has brought you the most *beautifullest* thing you ever saw in your life; but you are not to know any thing about it till after dinner, because she wants to surprise you; and mistress has put it into her wardrobe till after dinner."

"Till after dinner!" repeated Bell, impatiently; "I can't wait till then, I must see it this minute."

The maid refused her several times, till Bell burst into another fit of crying, and the maid fearing that her mistress would be angry with *her*, if Bell's eyes were red at dinner-time, consented to show her the basket.

"How pretty!—But let me have it in my own hands," said Bell, as the maid held the basket up out of her reach.

"Oh, no, you must not touch it; for if you should spoil it what would become of me?"

"Become of you, indeed!" exclaimed the spoiled child, who never considered any thing but her own immediate gratification—"Become of *you*, indeed!—what signifies that—I shan't spoil it; and I will have it in my own hands. If you don't hold it down for me directly, I'll tell that you showed it to me."

"Then you won't snatch it?"

"No, no, I won't indeed," said Bell; but she had learned from her maid a total disregard of truth. She snatched the basket the moment it was within her reach; a struggle ensued, in which the handle and lid were torn off, and one of the medallions crushed inwards, before the little fury returned to her senses. Calmed at this sight, the next question was, how she could conceal the mischief which she had done. After many attempts, the handle and lid were replaced, the basket was put exactly in the same spot in which it had stood before, and the maid charged the child "*to look as if nothing was the matter.*"

We hope that both children and parents will here pause for a moment to reflect. The habits of tyranny, meanness, and falsehood, which children acquire from living with bad servants, are scarcely ever conquered in the whole course of their future lives.

After shutting up the basket they left the room, and in the adjoining passage they found a poor girl waiting with a small parcel in her hand.

"What's your business?" said the maid.

"I have brought home the lace, madam, that was bespoke for the young lady."

"Oh, you have, have you, at last?" said Bell; "and pray why didn't you bring it sooner?"

The girl was going to answer, but the maid interrupted her, saying, "Come, come, none of your idle excuses; you are a little, idle, good-for-nothing thing, to disappoint Miss Bell upon her birth-day. But now you have brought it, let us look at it." The little girl gave the lace without reply, and the maid desired her to go about her business, and not to expect to be paid; for that her mistress could not see any body, *because* she was in a room full of company.

"May I call again, madam, this afternoon?" said the child, timidly.

"Lord bless my stars!" replied the maid, "what makes people so poor, I *wonders!* I wish mistress would buy her lace at the warehouse, as I told her, and not of these folks. Call again! yes, to be sure—I believe you'd call, call, call, twenty times for two-pence."

However ungraciously the permission to call again was granted, it was received with gratitude: the little girl departed with a cheerful countenance; and Bell teased her maid till she got her to sew the long-wished-for lace upon her cuffs.

Unfortunate Bell! All dinner-time passed, and people were so hungry, so busy, or so stupid, that not an eye observed her favourite piece of finery; till at length she was no longer able to conceal her impatience, and, turning to Laura, who sat next to her, she said—"You have no lace upon your cuffs; look how beautiful mine is!—Is not it? Don't you wish your mamma could afford to give you some like it? But you can't get any if she would, for this was made on purpose for me on my birth-day, and nobody can get a bit more any where, if they would give the world for it."

"But cannot the person who made it," said Laura, "make any more like it?"

"No, no, no!" cried Bell; for she had already learned, either from her maid or her mother, the mean pride, which values things, not for being really pretty or useful, but for being such as nobody else can procure.

"Nobody can get any like it, I say," repeated Bell; "nobody in all London can make it but one person, and that person will never make a bit for any body but me, I am sure —mamma won't let her, if I ask her not."

"Very well," said Laura coolly, "I do not want any of it; you need not be so violent: I assure you that I don't want any of it."

"Yes, but you do though," said Bell, more angrily.

"No, indeed," said Laura, smiling.

"You do in the bottom of your heart; but you say you don't to plague me, I know," cried Bell, swelling with disappointed vanity. "It is pretty for all that, and it cost a great deal of money too, and nobody shall have any like it, if they cried their eyes out."

Laura received this sentence in silence. Rosamond smiled. And at her smile, the ill-suppressed rage of the spoiled child burst forth into the seventh and loudest fit of crying which had been heard upon her birth-day.

"What's the matter, my pet?" cried her mother; "come to me, and tell me what's the matter."

Bell ran roaring to her mother; but no otherwise explaining the cause of her sorrow than by tearing the fine lace, with frantic gestures, from her cuffs, and throwing the fragments into her mother's lap.

"Oh! the lace, child! are you mad?" said her mother, catching hold of both her hands—"Your beautiful lace, my dear love—do you know how much it cost?"

"I don't care how much it cost—it is not beautiful, and I'll have none of it," replied Bell, sobbing—"for it is not beautiful."

"But it is beautiful," retorted her mother; "I chose the pattern myself. Who has put it into your head, child, to dislike it? Was it Nancy?" "No, not Nancy, but *them*, mamma," said Bell, pointing to Laura and Rosamond.

"Oh, fie! don't point," said her mother, putting down her stubborn finger; nor say *them*, like Nancy; I am sure you misunderstood. Miss Laura, I am sure, did not mean any such thing."

"No, madam; and I did not say any such thing, that I recollect," said Laura, gently.

"Oh no, indeed!" cried Rosamond, warmly rising in her sister's defence. But no defence or explanation was to be heard, for every body had now gathered round Bell, to dry her tears, and to comfort her for the mischief she had done to her own cuffs.

They succeeded so well, that in about a quarter of an hour the young lady's eyes, and the reddened arches over her eyebrows, came to their natural colour; and the business being thus happily hushed up, the mother, as a reward to her daughter for her good humour, begged that Rosamond would now be so good as to produce "her charming present."

Rosamond, followed by all the company, amongst whom, to her great joy was her godmother, proceeded to the dressing-room.

"Now, I am sure," thought she, "Bell will be surprised, and my godmother will see she was right about about my generosity."

The doors of the wardrobe were opened with due ceremony, and the filigree basket appeared in all its glory.

"Well, this is a charming present indeed!" said the godmother, who was one of the company; "*my* Rosamond knows how to make presents." And as she spoke she took hold of the basket, to lift it down to the admiring audience. Scarcely had she touched it, when lo! the myrtle wreath, the medallions, all dropped—the basket fell to the ground, and only the handle remained in her hand.

All eyes were fixed upon the wreck. Exclamations of sorrow were heard in various tones; and "Who can have done this?" was all that Rosamond could say. Bell stood in sullen silence, in which she obstinately persevered in the midst of the inquiries which were made about the disaster. At length the servants were summoned, and amongst them Nancy, miss Bell's maid and governess: she affected much surprise, when she saw what had befallen the basket, and declared that she knew nothing of the matter, but that she had seen her mistress in the morning put it quite safe into the wardrobe; and that, for her part, she had never touched it, or thought of touching it, in her born days. "Nor miss Bell neither, ma'am, I can answer for her; for she never knew of its being there, because I never so much as mentioned it to her, that there was such a thing in the house, because I knew Miss Rosamond wanted to surprise her with the secret—so I never mentioned a sentence of it—Did I miss Bell?"

Bell, putting on the deceitful look which her maid had taught her, answered boldly, *No;* but she had hold of Rosamond's hand, and at the instant she uttered this falsehood she squeezed it terribly.

"Why do you squeeze my hand so?" said Rosamond, in a low voice; "what are you afraid of?"

"Afraid of!" cried Bell, turning angrily; "I'm not afraid of any thing—I've nothing to be afraid about."

"Nay, I did not say you had," whispered Rosamond; "but only if you did by accident —You know what I mean—I should not be angry if you did—Only say so."

"I say I did not!" cried Bell furiously; "Mamma! Mamma! Nancy! my cousin Rosamond won't believe me! that's very hard—it's very rude! and I won't bear it—I won't."

"Don't be angry, love—don't;" said the maid.

"Nobody suspects you, darling;" said her mother.——"But she has too much sensibility. ——Don't cry, love, nobody suspected you."

"But you know," continued she, turning to the maid, "somebody must have done this, and I must know how it was done; miss Rosamond's charming present must not be spoiled in this way in my house, without my taking proper notice of it.——I assure you I am very angry about it, Rosamond."

Rosamond did not rejoice in her anger, and had nearly made a sad mistake, by speaking loud her thoughts—"*I was very foolish*——" she began, and stopped.

"Ma'am," cried the maid suddenly, "I'll venture to say I know who did it."

"Who?" said every one eagerly.

"Who?" said Bell, trembling.

"Why, miss, don't you recollect that little girl with the lace, that we saw peeping about in the passage: I'm sure she must have done it, for here she was by herself half an hour or more, and not another creature has been in mistress's dressing-room to my certain knowledge, since morning. Those sort of people have so much curiosity, I'm sure she must have been meddling with it," added the maid.

"Oh yes, that's the thing," said the mistress, decidedly.——"Well, miss Rosamond, for your comfort, she shall never come into my house again."

"O, that would not comfort me at all," said Rosamond; "besides, we are not sure that she did it; and if——" A single knock at the door was heard at this instant; it was the little girl who came to be paid for her lace.

"Call her in," said the lady of the house; "let us see her directly."

The maid, who was afraid that the girl's innocence would appear if she were produced, hesitated; but upon her mistress's repeating her commands, she was forced to obey.

The child came in with a look of simplicity, but when she saw the room full of company she was a little abashed. Rosamond and Laura looked at her and at one another with surprise; for it was the same little girl whom they had seen weaving lace.

"Is not it she?" whispered Rosamond to her sister.

"Yes, it is; but hush," said Laura, "she does not know us. Don't say a word; let us hear what she will say." Laura got behind the rest of the company as she spoke, so that the little girl could not see her.

"Vastly well!" said Bell's mother; "I am waiting to see how long you will have the assurance to stand there with that innocent look. Did you ever see that basket before?"

"Yes, ma'am," said the girl.

"*Yes, ma'am,*" cried the maid, "and what else do you know about it? You had better confess it at once, and mistress perhaps will say no more about it."

"Yes, do confess it," added Bell earnestly.

"Confess what, madam?" said the little girl; "I never touched the basket, madam."

"You never *touched* it; but you confess," interrupted Bell's mother, "that you *did see* it before. And pray how came you to see it? you must have opened my wardrobe."

"No, indeed, ma'am," said the little girl; "but I was waiting in the passage, ma'am, and this door was partly open; and," looking at the maid, "you know I could not help seeing it."

"Why, how could you see it through the doors of my wardrobe?" rejoined the lady.

The maid, frightened, pulled the little girl by the sleeve.

"Answer me," said the lady; "where did you see this basket?"

Another stronger pull.

"I saw it, madam, in her hands," looking at the maid; "and——"

"Well, and what became of it afterwards?"

"Ma'am," hesitating, "miss pulled, and by accident——I believe, I saw, ma'am—— miss, you know what I saw."

"I do not know—I do not know: and if I did, you had no business there—and mamma won't believe you, I am sure."

But every body else did, and their eyes were fixed upon Bell in a manner which made her feel rather ashamed.

"What do you all look at me so for? Why do you all look so? And am I to be shamed upon my birth-day?" cried she, bursting into a roar of passion; "and all for this nasty thing!" added she, pushing away the remains of the basket, and looking angrily at Rosamond.

"Bell! Bell! oh fie! fie! now I *am* ashamed of you—that's quite rude to your cousin," said her mother, who was more shocked at her daughter's want of politeness than at her falsehood. "Take her away, Nancy, till she has done crying," added she to the maid, who accordingly carried off her pupil.

Rosamond, during this scene, especially at the moment when her present was pushed away with such disdain, had been making reflections upon the nature of true generosity. A smile from her father, who stood by a silent spectator of the catastrophe of the filigree basket, gave rise to these reflections; nor were they entirely dissipated by the condolence of the rest of the company, nor even by the praises of her godmother, who to console her said—"Well, my dear Rosamond, I admire your generous spirit. You know I prophesied that your half-guinea would be gone the soonest—Did I not, Laura?" said she, appealing in a sarcastic tone to where she thought Laura was. "Where is Laura? I don't see her."

Laura came forward.

"You are too *prudent* to throw away your money like your sister: your half-guinea, I'll answer for it, is snug in your pocket—Is it not?"

"No, madam," answered she in a low voice. But low as the voice was, the poor little lace-girl heard it; and now, for the first time, fixing her eyes upon Laura, recollected her benefactress.

"Oh, that's the young lady!" she exclaimed, in a tone of joyful gratitude—"the good!— good young lady, who gave me the half-guinea, and would not stay to be thanked for it—but I *will* thank her now."

"The half-guinea, Laura!" said her godmother—— "What is all this?"

"I'll tell you, madam, if you please," said the little girl.

It was not in expectation of being praised for it, that Laura had been generous, and therefore every body was really touched with the history of the weaving-pillow; and whilst they praised felt a certain degree of respect, which is not always felt by those who pour forth eulogiums. *Respect* is not an improper word, even applied to a child of Laura's age; for let their age or situation be what it may, they command respect who deserve it.

"Ah, madam!" said Rosamond to her godmother, "now you see—you see she is *not* a little miser; I'm sure that's better than wasting half-a-guinea upon a filigree basket—Is it not, ma'am?" said she, with an eagerness which showed that she had forgotten all her own misfortunes in sympathy with her sister. "This is being *really generous*, father, is it not?"

"Yes, Rosamond," said her father, and he kissed her—"this *is* being really generous. It is not only by giving away money that we can show generosity,—it is by giving up to others any thing that we like ourselves: and therefore," added he, smiling, "it is really generous of you to give to your sister the thing you like best of all others."

"The thing I like the best of all others, father!" said Rosamond, half pleased, half vexed: "what is that I wonder? You don't mean *praise*, do you, sir?"

"Nay, you must decide that, Rosamond."

"Why, sir," said she, ingenuously, "perhaps it was ONCE the thing I liked best; but the pleasure I have just felt makes me like something else better."

Volume Two

Old Poz.

LUCY, DAUGHTER TO THE JUSTICE.
MRS. BUSTLE, LANDLADY OF THE SARACEN'S HEAD.

JUSTICE HEADSTRONG.
OLD MAN.
WILLIAM, A SERVANT.

SCENE I.

*The house of Justice Headstrong—a hall. Lucy watering some myrtles—
a servant behind the scenes is heard to say—*

I TELL YOU my master is not up—you can't see him; so go about your business, I say.

LUCY.

Whom are you speaking to, William? Who's that?

WILLIAM.

Only an old man, miss, with a complaint for my master.

LUCY.

Oh, then don't send him away—don't send him away.

WILLIAM.

But master has not had his chocolate, ma'am. He won't see anybody ever before he drinks his chocolate, you know, ma'am.

LUCY.

But let the old man then come in here—perhaps he can wait a little while—call him.

(Exit Servant.)

(Lucy sings, and goes on watering her myrtles—the servant shows in the Old Man.)

WILLIAM.

You can't see my master this hour, but miss will let you stay here.

LUCY *(aside)*.

Poor old man, how he trembles as he walks! *(Aloud.)* Sit down, sit down, my father will see you soon; pray sit down.

(He hesitates, she pushes a chair towards him.)

LUCY.

Pray sit down.

(He sits down.)

OLD MAN.

You are very good, miss; very good.

(Lucy goes to her myrtles again.)

LUCY.

Ah! I'm afraid this poor myrtle is quite dead—quite dead.

(The Old Man sighs, and she turns round.)

LUCY *(aside)*.

I wonder what can make him sigh so!— *(Aloud.)* My father won't make you wait long.

OLD MAN.

O ma'am, as long as he pleases—I'm in no haste—no haste: it's only a small matter.

LUCY.

But does a small matter make you sigh so?

OLD MAN.

Ah, miss; because, though it is a small matter in itself, it is not a small matter to me *(sighing again)*; it was my all, and I've lost it.

LUCY.

What do you mean? What have you lost?

OLD MAN.

Why, miss—but I won't trouble you about it.

LUCY.

But it won't trouble me at all—I mean, I wish to hear it—so tell it me.

OLD MAN.

Why, miss, I slept last night at the inn here in town—the Saracen's Head——

LUCY *(interrupts him)*.

Hark, there is my father coming down stairs; follow me—you may tell me your story as we go along.

OLD MAN.

I slept at the Saracen's Head, miss, and——

(Exit talking.)

SCENE II.

Justice Headstrong's Study.

(He appears in his night-gown and cap, with his gouty foot upon a stool—a table and chocolate beside him—Lucy is leaning on the arm of his chair.)

JUSTICE.

Well, well, my darling, presently—I'll see him presently.

LUCY.

Whilst you are drinking your chocolate, papa?

JUSTICE.

No, no, no—I never see anybody till I have done my chocolate, darling. (*He tastes his chocolate.*) There's no sugar in this, child.

LUCY.

Yes, indeed, papa.

JUSTICE.

No, child—there's *no* sugar, I tell you—that's poz!

LUCY.

Oh, but, papa, I assure you I put in two lumps myself.

JUSTICE.

There's *no* sugar, I say—why will you contradict me, child, for ever?—There's no sugar, I say.

(Lucy leans over him playfully, and with his tea-spoon pulls out two lumps of sugar.)

LUCY.

What's this, papa?

JUSTICE.

Pshaw! pshaw! pshaw! it is not melted, child—it is the same as no sugar. Oh, my foot, girl! my foot—you kill me—go, go, I'm busy—I've business to do. Go and send William to me; do you hear, love?

LUCY.

And the old man, papa?

JUSTICE.

What old man? I tell you what, I've been plagued ever since I was awake, and before I was awake, about that old man. If he can't wait, let him go about his business—don't you know, child, I never see any body till I've drank my chocolate; and I never will, if it was a duke, that's poz! Why, it has but just struck twelve; if he can't wait, he can go about his business, can't he?

LUCY.

O sir, he *can* wait. It was not he who was impatient: (*she comes back playfully*) it was only I, papa; don't be angry.

JUSTICE.

Well—well, well (*finishing his cup of chocolate, and pushing the dish away*) ; and at any rate there was not sugar enough—send William, send William, child, and I'll finish my own business, and then—

(*Exit Lucy dancing, "And then!—and then!"*)

JUSTICE, (*alone.*)

Oh this foot of mine! (*twinges*)—oh this foot! Aye, if Dr. Sparerib could cure one of the gout, then, indeed, I should think something of him—but, as to my leaving off my bottle of port, it's nonsense, it's all nonsense, I can't do it—I can't, and I won't for all the Dr. Spareribs in Christendom, that's poz!

Enter William.

JUSTICE.

William—oh! aye—hey—what answer, pray, did you bring from the Saracen's Head?—Did you see Mrs. Bustle herself, as I bid you?

WILLIAM.

Yes, sir, I saw the landlady herself—she said she would come up immediately, sir.

JUSTICE.

Ah, that's well—immediately?

WILLIAM.

Yes, sir, and I hear her voice below now.

JUSTICE.

O show her up, show Mrs. Bustle in.

Enter Mrs. Bustle, *the landlady of the Saracen's Head.*

LANDLADY.

Good-morrow to your worship!—I'm glad to see your worship look so purely—I came up with all speed (*taking breath*) . Our pie is in the oven—that was what you sent for me about, I take it.

JUSTICE.

True—true; sit down, good Mrs. Bustle, pray——

LANDLADY.

O your worship's always very good (*settling her apron*) ; I came up just as I was, only threw my shawl over me—I thought your worship would excuse—I'm quite, as it were, rejoiced to see your worship look so purely, and to find you up so hearty—

JUSTICE.

O, I'm very hearty (*coughing*), always hearty and thankful for it—I hope to see many Christmas doings yet, Mrs. Bustle—and so our pie is in the oven, I think you say?

LANDLADY.

In the oven, it is—I put it in with my own hands, and, if we have but good luck in the baking, it will be as pretty a goose-pie,—though I say it that should not say it,—as pretty a goose-pie as ever your worship set your eye upon.

JUSTICE.

Will you take a glass of any thing this morning, Mrs. Bustle?—I have some nice usquebaugh.

LANDLADY.

O no, your worship!—I thank your worship, though, as much as if I took it; but I just took my luncheon before I came up, or, more proper, *my sandwich,* I should say, for the fashion's sake, to be sure. A *luncheon* won't go down with nobody now-a-day *(laughs)* —I expect hostler and boots will be calling for their sandwiches just now *(laughs again)* —I'm sure I beg your worship's pardon for mentioning a *luncheon*.

JUSTICE.

O Mrs. Bustle, the word's a good word, for it means a good thing, ha! ha! ha! *(pulls out his watch)* —but, pray, is it luncheon time? Why, it's past one, I declare, and I thought I was up in remarkably good time, too.

LANDLADY.

Well, and to be sure, so it was remarkably good time for *your worship;* but folks in our way must be up by times, you know—I've been up and about these seven hours!

JUSTICE. *(stretching.)*

Seven hours!

LANDLADY.

Aye, indeed, eight I might say, for I'm an early little body, though I say it that should not say it—I *am* an early little body.

JUSTICE.

An early little body, as you say, Mrs. Bustle: so I shall have my goose-pie for dinner, hey?

LANDLADY.

For dinner, as sure as the clock strikes four; but I mustn't stay prating, for it may be spoiling if I'm away—so I must wish your worship a good morning. *(She curtsies.)*

JUSTICE.

No ceremony, no ceremony, good Mrs. Bustle; your servant.

Enter William, *to take away the chocolate—the Landlady is putting on her shawl.*

JUSTICE.

You may let that man know, William, that I have despatched my *own* business, and I am at leisure for his now— *(taking a pinch of snuff)* —hum—pray, William! *(Justice leans back gravely)* what sort of a looking fellow is he, pray?

WILLIAM.

Most like a sort of a travelling man, in my opinion, sir,—or something that way I take it.

(At these words, the Landlady turns round inquisitively, and delays, that she may listen whilst she is putting on and pinning her shawl.)

JUSTICE.

Hum—a sort of a travelling man—hum—lay my books out open at the title Vagrant; and, William, tell the cook that Mrs. Bustle promises me the goose-pie for dinner—four o'clock, do you hear? And show the old man in now.

(The Landlady looks eagerly towards the door as it opens, and exclaims—)

LANDLADY.

My old gentleman, as I hope to breathe!

Enter the Old Man.

(Lucy follows the Old Man on tip-toe—the Justice leans back, and looks consequential— the Landlady sets her arms a-kimbo; the Old Man starts as he sees her.)

JUSTICE.

What stops you, friend? Come forward, if you please.

LANDLADY. *(advancing.)*

So, sir! is it you, sir? Aye, you little looked, I warrant ye, to meet me here with his worship; but there you reckoned without your host—out of the frying-pan into the fire.

JUSTICE.

What is all this? What is this?

LANDLADY. (*running on.*)

None of your flummery stuff will go down with his worship no more than with me, I give ye warning—so you may go further and fare worse; and spare your breath to cool your porridge.

JUSTICE. (*waves his hand with dignity.*)

Mrs. Bustle, good Mrs. Bustle, remember where you are—silence! silence!—Come forward, sir, and let me hear what you have to say.

(The Old Man comes forward.)

JUSTICE.

Who, and what may you be, friend? and what is your business with me?

LANDLADY.

Sir, if your worship will give me leave— (*Justice makes a sign to her to be silent.*)

OLD MAN.

Please your worship, I am an old soldier.

LANDLADY. (*interrupting.*)

An old hypocrite, say.

JUSTICE.

Mrs. Bustle, pray—I desire—let the man speak.

OLD MAN.

For these two years past—ever since, please your worship—I wasn't able to work any longer,—for in my youth I *did* work as well as the best of them.

LANDLADY. (*eager to interrupt.*)

You work—you—

JUSTICE.

Let him finish his story, I say.

LUCY.

Aye, do, do, papa, speak for him. Pray, Mrs. Bustle——

LANDLADY. (*turning suddenly round to Lucy.*)

Miss!—A good morrow to you, ma'am—I humbly beg your apologies for not seeing you sooner, miss Lucy.

(Justice nods to the Old Man, who goes on.)

OLD MAN.

But, please your worship, it pleased God to take away the use of my left arm, and since that I have never been able to work.

LANDLADY.

Flummery! flummery!

JUSTICE. (*angrily.*)

Mrs. Bustle, I have desired silence, and I will have it, that's poz! You shall have your turn presently.

OLD MAN.

For these two years past—for why should I be ashamed to tell the truth—I have lived upon charity, and I scraped together a guinea and a half, and upwards; and I was travelling with it to my grandson, in the north, with him to end my days—but (*sighing*) —

JUSTICE.

But what? Proceed, pray, to the point.

OLD MAN.

But last night I slept here in town, please your worship, at the Saracen's Head.

LANDLADY. (*in a rage.*)

At the Saracen's Head! Yes, forsooth, none such ever slept at the Saracen's Head afore, or ever shall after, as long as my name's Bustle, and the Saracen's Head is the Saracen's Head.

JUSTICE.

Again! again!—Mrs. Landlady, this is downright—I have said you should speak presently —he *shall* speak first, since I've said it, that's poz! Speak on, friend: you slept last night at the Saracen's Head.

OLD MAN.

Yes, please your worship, and I accuse nobody; but at night I had my little money safe, and in the morning it was gone.

LANDLADY.

Gone! gone indeed in my house! and this is the way I'm to be treated! is it so? I couldn't but speak, please your worship, to such an inhuman-like, out-o'-the-way, scandalous charge, if King George, and all the Royal Family, were sitting in your worship's chair, besides you, to silence me. (*Turning to the Old Man.*) And this is your gratitude, forsooth! Didn't you tell me, that any hole in my house was good enough for you, you wheedling hypocrite? and my thanks is to call me and mine a pack of thieves.

OLD MAN.

O no, no, no, *no*—a pack of thieves by no means!

LANDLADY.

Aye, I thought when *I* came to speak we should have you upon your marrow-bones in—

JUSTICE (*imperiously.*)

Silence! five times have I commanded silence, and five times in vain; and I won't command any thing five times in vain, *that's poz!*

LANDLADY. (*in a pet, aside.*)

Old Poz!—(*Aloud.*) Then, your worship, I don't see any business I have to be waiting here—the folks will want me at home. (*Returning and whispering.*) Shall I send the goose-pie up, your worship, if it's ready?

JUSTICE. (*with magnanimity.*)

I care not for the goose-pie, Mrs. Bustle—do not talk to me of goose-pies—this is no place to talk of pies.

LANDLADY.

O, for that matter, your worship knows best to be sure.

(*Exit Landlady, angry.*)

SCENE III.

Justice Headstrong, Old Man, and Lucy.

LUCY.

Ah, now I'm glad he can speak—now tell papa; and you need not be afraid to speak to him, for he is very good-natured—don't contradict him though, because he told *me* not.

JUSTICE.

O darling, *you* shall contradict me as often as you please—only not before I've drank my chocolate, child—hey! Go on, my good friend; you see what it is to live in Old England, where, thank Heaven, the poorest of his Majesty's subjects may have justice, and speak his mind before the first man in the land. Now speak on, and you hear she tells you you need not be afraid of me. Speak on.

OLD MAN.

I thank your worship, I'm sure.

JUSTICE.

Thank me! for what, sir? I won't be thanked for doing justice, sir; so—but explain this matter. You lost your money, hey, at the Saracen's Head—you had it safe last night, hey?—and you missed it this morning? Are you sure you had it safe at night?

OLD MAN.

O, please your worship, quite sure, for I took it out and looked at it just before I said my prayers.

JUSTICE.

You did—did ye so—hum! pray, my good friend, where might you put your money when you went to bed?

OLD MAN.

Please your worship, where I always put it—always—in my tobacco-box.

JUSTICE.

Your tobacco-box! I never heard of such a thing—to make a *strong box* of a tobacco-box —ha! ha! ha!—hum—and you say the box and all was gone in the morning.

OLD MAN.

No, please your worship, no, not the box, the box was never stirred from the place where I put it. They left me the box.

JUSTICE.

Tut, tut, tut, man!—took the money and left the box; I'll never believe *that;* I'll never believe that any one could be such a fool. Tut, tut! the thing's impossible: it's well you are not upon oath.

OLD MAN.

If I was, please your worship, I should say the same, for it is the truth.

JUSTICE.

Don't tell me, don't tell me; I say the thing is impossible.

OLD MAN.

Please your worship, here's the box.

JUSTICE. (*goes on without looking at it.*)

Nonsense! nonsense! it's no such thing, it's no such thing, I say—no man would take the money, and leave the tobacco-box, I won't believe it—nothing shall make me believe it ever—that's poz.

LUCY. (*takes the box, and holds it up before her father's eyes.*) You did not see the box, did you, papa?

JUSTICE.

Yes, yes, yes, child—nonsense! it's all a lie from beginning to end. A man who tells one lie will tell a hundred—all a lie!—all a lie!

OLD MAN.

If your worship would give me leave—

JUSTICE.

Sir—it does not signify—it does not signify; I've said it, I've said it, and that's enough to convince me; and I'll tell you more, if my Lord Chief Justice of England told it to me, I would not believe it—that's poz!

LUCY. *(still playing with the box.)*

But how comes the box here, I wonder?

JUSTICE.

Pshaw! pshaw! pshaw! darling;—go to your dolls, darling, and don't be positive—go to your dolls, and don't talk of what you don't understand. What can you understand, I want to know, of the law?

LUCY.

No, papa, I didn't mean about the law; but about the box: because, if the man had taken it, how could it be here, you know, papa?

JUSTICE.

Hey, hey, what? Why, what I say is this, that I don't dispute that that box, that you hold in your hands, is a box; nay, for aught I know, it may be a tobacco-box—but it's clear to me, that if they left the box they did not take the money—and how do you dare, sir, to come before Justice Headstrong with a lie in your mouth?—recollect yourself, I'll give you time to recollect yourself.   *(A pause.)*

JUSTICE.

Well, sir, and what do you say now about the box?

OLD MAN.

Please your worship, with submission, I *can* say nothing but what I said before.

JUSTICE.

What, contradict me again, after I gave ye time to recollect yourself—I've done with ye, I have done: contradict me as often as you please, but you cannot impose upon me; I defy you to impose upon me!

OLD MAN.

Impose!

JUSTICE.

I know the law—I know the law! and I'll make you know it, too—one hour, I'll give you to recollect yourself, and if you don't give up this idle story,—I'll—I'll commit you as a vagrant—that's poz!—go, go, for the present. William, take him into the servant's hall, do you hear?—What, take the money, and leave the box!—I'll never believe it, that's poz!

(Lucy speaks to the Old Man as he is going off.)

LUCY.

Don't be frightened! don't be frightened—I mean, if you tell the truth, never be frightened.

OLD MAN.

If I tell the truth— *(turning up his eyes.)*

(Old Man is still held back by Lucy.)

LUCY.

One moment—answer me one question—because of something that just came into my head. Was the box shut fast when you left it?

OLD MAN.

No, miss, no!—open; it was open, for I could not find the lid in the dark—my candle went out.—*If* I tell the truth—oh!

(*Exit.*)

SCENE IV.

Justice's Study—the Justice is writing.

OLD MAN.

Well! I shall have but few days more misery in this world!

JUSTICE. (*looks up.*)

Why! why—why then, why will you be so positive to persist in a lie? Take the money and leave the box! obstinate blockhead! Here William (*showing the committal*), take this old gentleman to Holdfast, the constable, and give him this warrant.

Enter Lucy, *running, out of breath.*

LUCY.

I've found it! I've found it! I've found it! Here, old man, here's your money—here it is all—a guinea and a half, and a shilling and a sixpence,—just as he said, papa.

Enter Landlady.

LANDLADY.

O la! your worship, did you ever hear the like?

JUSTICE.

I've heard nothing, yet, that I can understand. First, have you secured the thief, I say?

LUCY. (*makes signs to the Landlady to be silent.*)

Yes, yes, yes! we have him safe—we have him prisoner. Shall he come in, papa?

JUSTICE.

Yes, child, by all means; and now I shall hear what possessed him to leave the box—I don't understand—there's something deep in all this,—I don't understand it. Now I do desire, Mrs. Landlady, nobody may speak a single word, whilst I am cross-examining the thief.

(*Landlady puts her finger upon her lips—Every body looks eagerly towards the door.*)

Re-enter Lucy, *with a huge wicker cage in her hand, containing a magpie—the* Justice *drops the committal out of his hand.*

JUSTICE.

Hey! what, Mrs. Landlady! the old magpie! hey!

LANDLADY.

Aye, your worship, my old magpie—who'd have thought it—Miss was very clever; it was she caught the thief. Miss was very clever.

OLD MAN.

Very good! very good!

JUSTICE.

Aye, darling! her father's own child! How was it, child?—Caught the thief *with the mainour,* hey! Tell us all—I will hear all—that's poz!

LUCY.

O, then, first I must tell you how I came to suspect Mr. Magpie. Do you remember, papa, that day last summer, that I went with you to the bowling-green of the Saracen's Head?

LANDLADY.

O, of all days in the year—but I ask pardon, miss.

LUCY.

Well, that day I heard my uncle and another gentleman telling stories of magpies hiding money; and they laid a wager about this old magpie—and they tried him—they put a shilling upon the table, and he ran away with it, and hid it—so I thought that he might do so again, you know, this time.

JUSTICE.

Right, right; it's a pity, child, you are not upon the bench; ha! ha! ha!

LUCY.

And when I went to his old hiding-place, there it was—but you see, papa, he did not take the box.

JUSTICE.

No, no, no! because the thief was a magpie—no *man* would have taken the money, and left the box. You see I was right—no *man* would have left the box, hey?

LUCY.

Certainly not, I suppose; but I'm so very glad, old man, that you have gotten your money.

JUSTICE.

Well, then, child, here, take my purse, and add that to it. We were a little too hasty with the committal—hey?

LANDLADY.

Aye, and I fear I was so, too; but when one is touched about the credit of one's house, one's apt to speak warmly.

OLD MAN.

O, I'm the happiest old man alive! You are all convinced I told you no lies. Say no more —say no more—I am the happiest man! Miss, you have made me the happiest man alive! Bless you for it!

LANDLADY.

Well, now, I'll tell you what—I know what I think—you must keep that there magpie, and make a show of him, and I warrant he'll bring you many an honest penny—for it's a *true story*, and folks will like to hear it, I hopes—

JUSTICE. (*eagerly.*)

And, friend, do you hear, you'll dine here to-day—you'll dine here; we have some excellent ale—I will have you drink my health, that's poz!—hey, you'll drink my health, won't you, hey?

OLD MAN. (*bows.*)

O, and the young lady's, if you please.

JUSTICE.

Aye, aye, drink her health—she deserves it—aye, drink my darling's health.

LANDLADY.

And, please your worship, it's the right time, I believe, to speak of the goose-pie now; and a charming pie it is, and it's on the table.

WILLIAM.

And Mr. Smack, the curate, and 'squire Solid, and the doctor, sir, are come, and dinner is upon the table.

JUSTICE.

Then let us say no more—but do justice immediately to the goose-pie—and, darling, put me in mind to tell this story after dinner.

(*After they go out, the Justice stops.*)

"Tell this story"—I don't know whether it tells well for me—but I'll never be positive any more—*that's poz.*

[FINIS]

Volume Three

The Orphans.

NEAR THE RUINS of the castle of Rossmore, in Ireland, is a small cabin, in which there once lived a widow, and her four children. As long as she was able to work she was very industrious, and was accounted the best spinner in the parish, but she overworked herself at last, and fell ill, so that she could not sit at her wheel as she used to do, and was obliged to give it up to her eldest daughter, Mary.

Mary was at this time about twelve years old. One evening she was sitting at the foot of her mother's bed, spinning, and her little brother and sisters were gathered round the fire, eating their potatoes and milk for supper.

"Bless them, the poor young creatures!" said the widow; who, as she lay on the bed, which she knew must be her death-bed, was thinking of what would become of her children after she was gone. Mary stopped her wheel, for she was afraid that the noise of it had wakened her mother, and would hinder her from going to sleep again.

"No need to stop the wheel, Mary dear, for me," said her mother, "I was not asleep; nor is it *that* which keeps me from sleep. But don't over-work yourself, Mary."

"O, no fear of that," replied Mary; "I'm strong and hearty."

"So was I once," said her mother.

"And so will you be again, I hope," said Mary, "when the fine weather comes again."

"The fine weather will never come again to me," said her mother; " 'tis a folly, Mary, to hope for that—but what I hope is, that you'll find some friend—some help—orphans as you'll soon all of you be. And one thing comforts my heart, even as I *am* lying here, that not a soul in the wide world I am leaving has to complain of me. Though poor, I have lived honest, and I have brought you up to be the same, Mary; and I am sure the little ones will take after you; for you'll be good to them—as good to them as you can."

Here the children, who had finished eating their suppers, came round the bed, to listen to what their mother was saying. She was tired of speaking, for she was very weak; but she shook their little hands, as they laid them on the bed; and joining them all together, she said—"Bless you, dears—Bless you—love, and help one another all you can—good night—good by."

Mary took the children away to their bed, for she saw that their mother was too ill to say more; but Mary did not herself know how ill she was. Her mother never spoke rightly afterwards, but talked in a confused way about some debts, and one in particular, which she owed to a school-mistress for Mary's schooling; and then she charged Mary to go and pay it, because she was not able to *go in* with it. At the end of the week she was dead and buried; and the orphans were left alone in their cabin.

The two youngest girls, Peggy and Nancy, were six and seven years old; Edmund was not yet nine, but he was a stout grown healthy boy, and well disposed to work. He had been used to bring home turf from the bog on his back, to lead cart-horses, and often to go on errands for gentlemen's families, who paid him sixpence or a shilling according to the distance which he went: so that Edmund, by some or other of these little employments, was, as he said, likely enough to earn his bread; and he told Mary, to have a good heart, for that he should every year grow able to do more and more, and that he should never forget his mother's words, when she last gave him her blessing, and joined their hands all together.

As for Peggy and Nancy, it was little that they could do; but they were good children: and Mary, when she considered that so much depended upon her, was resolved to exert herself to the utmost. Her first care was to pay those debts which her mother had mentioned to her, for which she left money done up carefully in separate papers. When all these were paid away, there was not enough left to pay both the rent of the cabin, and a year's schooling for herself and sisters, which was due to the school-mistress in a neighbouring village.

Mary was in hopes that the rent would not be called for immediately; but in this she was disappointed. Mr. Harvey, the gentleman on whose estate she lived, was in England, and, in his absence, all was managed by a Mr. Hopkins, an agent, who was a *hard man.** The driver came to Mary about a week after her mother's death, and told her that the rent must be brought in the next day, and that she must leave the cabin, for a new tenant was coming into it; that she was too young to have a house to herself, and that the only thing she had to do was, to get some neighbour to take her and her brother and sisters in, for charity's sake.

The driver finished by hinting, that she would not be so hardly used, if she had not brought upon herself the ill-will of miss Alice, the agent's daughter. Mary, it is true, had refused to give miss Alice a goat, upon which she had set her fancy; but this was the only offence of which she had been guilty, and, at the time she refused it, her mother wanted the goat's milk, which was the only thing she then liked to drink.

---

* A hard-hearted man.

Mary went immediately to Mr. Hopkins, the agent, to pay her rent; and she begged of him to let her stay another year in her cabin; but this he refused. It was now the 25th of September, and he said that the new tenant must come in on the 29th; so that she must quit it directly. Mary could not bear the thoughts of begging any of the neighbours to take her and her brother and sisters in *for charity's sake*, for the neighbours were all poor enough themselves: so she bethought herself, that she might find shelter in the ruins of the old castle of Rossmore, where she and her brother, in better times, had often played at hide-and-seek. The kitchen, and two other rooms near it, were yet covered-in tolerably well; and a little thatch, she thought, would make them comfortable through the winter. The agent consented to let her and her brother and sisters go in there, upon her paying him half a guinea, in hand, and promising to pay the same yearly.

Into these lodgings the orphans now removed, taking with them two bedsteads, a stool, chair, and a table, a sort of press, which contained what little clothes they had, and a chest, in which they had two hundred of meal. The chest was carried for them by some of the charitable neighbours, who likewise added to their scanty stock of potatoes and turf, what would make it last through the winter.

These children were well thought of and pitied, because their mother was known to have been all her life honest and industrious. "Sure," says one of the neighbours, "we can do no less than give a helping hand to the poor orphans, that are so ready to help themselves." So one helped to thatch the room in which they were to sleep, and another took their cow to graze upon his bit of land, on condition of having half the milk; and one and all said, they should be welcome to take share of their potatoes and buttermilk, if they should find their own ever fall short.

The half-guinea which Mr. Hopkins, the agent, required for letting Mary into the castle, was part of what she had to pay to the school-mistress, to whom above a guinea was due. Mary went to her, and took her goat along with her, and offered it in part of payment of the debt, as she had no more money left; but the school-mistress would not receive the goat. She said that she could afford to wait for her money till Mary was able to pay it; that she knew her to be an honest, industrious little girl, and she would trust her with more than a guinea. Mary thanked her; and she was glad to take the goat home again, as she was very fond of it.

Now being settled in their house, they went every day regularly to work: Mary spun nine cuts a-day, besides doing all that was to be done in the house; Edmund got fourpence a-day by his work, and Peggy and Anne earned twopence a-piece at the paper-mills near Navan, where they were employed to sort rags, and to cut them into small pieces.

When they had done work one day, Anne went to the master of the paper-mill, and asked him if she might have two sheets of large white paper, which were lying on the press; she offered a penny for the paper, but the master would not take anything from her, but gave her the paper, when he found that she wanted it to make a garland for her mother's grave. Anne and Peggy cut out the garland, and Mary, when it was finished, went along with them and Edmund to put it up: it was just a month after their mother's death.*

It happened that, at the time the orphans were putting up this garland, two young

---

* Garlands are usually put on the graves of *young* people; these children, perhaps, did not know this.

ladies, who were returning home after their evening walk, stopped at the gate of the church-yard, to look at the red light which the setting sun cast upon the window of the church. As the ladies were standing at the gate, they heard a voice near them crying— "O mother! mother! Are you gone for ever?" They could not see any one; so they walked softly round to the other side of the church, and there they saw Mary kneeling beside a grave, on which her brother and sisters were hanging their white garlands.

The children all stood still when they saw the two ladies passing near them; but Mary did not know anybody was passing, for her face was hid in her hands.

Isabella and Caroline (so these ladies were called) would not disturb the poor children, but they stopped in the village to inquire about them. It was at the house of the school-mistress that they stopped, and she gave them a good account of these orphans; she particularly commended Mary's honesty, in having immediately paid all her mother's debts to the utmost farthing, as far as her money would go; she told the ladies how Mary had been turned out of her house, and how she had offered her goat, of which she was very fond, to discharge a debt due for her schooling; and, in short, the school-mistress, who had known Mary for several years, spoke so well of her, that these ladies resolved that they would go to the old castle of Rossmore, to see her, the next day.

When they went there they found the room in which the children lived as clean and neat as such a ruined place could be made. Edmund was out working with a farmer, Mary was spinning, and her little sisters were measuring out some bog-berries, of which they had gathered a basketfull, for sale. Isabella, after telling Mary what an excellent character she had heard of her, inquired what it was she most wanted; and Mary said, that she had just worked up all her flax, and she was most in want of more flax for her wheel.

Isabella promised that she would send her a fresh supply of flax, and Caroline bought the bog-berries from the little girls, and gave them money enough to buy a pound of coarse cotton for knitting, as Mary said that she could teach them how to knit.

The supply of flax, which Isabella sent the next day, was of great service to Mary, as it kept her in employment for above a month: and when she sold the yarn which she had spun with it, she had money enough to buy some warm flannel, for winter wear. Besides spinning well, she had learned, at school, to do plain-work tolerably neatly, and Isabella and Caroline employed her to work for them, by which she earned a great deal more than she could by spinning. At her leisure hours she taught her sisters to read and write; and Edmund, with part of the money which he earned by his work out of doors, paid a schoolmaster for teaching him a little arithmetic. When the winter nights came on, he used to light his rush candles for Mary to work by. He had gathered and stripped a good provision of rushes in the month of August, and a neighbour gave them grease to dip them in.

One evening, just as he had lighted his candle, a footman came in, who was sent by Isabella with some plain-work to Mary. This servant was an Englishman, and he was but newly come over to Ireland. The rush candles caught his attention, for he had never seen any of them before, as he came from a part of England where they were not used.*

---

* See White's "Natural History of Selborne," page 198, quarto edition. This eloquent, well-informed, and benevolent writer, thought that no subject of rural economy, which could be of general utility, was beneath his notice. We cannot forbear quoting from him the following passage:—

"The proper species of rush for *our* purpose seems to be the *juncus effusus*, or common soft rush, which is to be found in moist pastures, by the sides of streams, and under hedges. The

Edmund, who was ready to oblige, and proud that his candles were noticed, showed the Englishman how they were made, and gave him a bundle of rushes. The servant was pleased with his good-nature in this trifling instance, and remembered it long after it was forgotten by Edmund.

Whenever his master wanted to send a messenger anywhere, Gilbert (for that was the servant's name) always employed his little friend Edmund, whom, upon further acquaintance, he liked better and better. He found that Edmund was both quick and exact in executing commissions. One day, after he had waited a great while at a gentleman's house for an answer to a letter, he was so impatient to get home, that he ran off without it. When he was questioned by Gilbert why he did not bring an answer, he did not attempt to make any excuse: he did not say "*There was no answer, please your honour,*" or, "*They bid me not wait,*" &c., but he told exactly the truth; and though Gilbert scolded him for being so impatient as not to wait, yet his telling him the truth was more to the boy's advantage than any excuse he could have made. After this he always believed when he said, "*There was no answer,*" or "*They bid me not wait,*" for Gilbert knew that he would not tell a lie to save himself from being scolded.

The orphans continued to assist one another in their work, according to their strength and abilities; and they went on in this manner for three years; and with what Mary got

---

rushes are in the best condition in the height of summer, but may be gathered so as to serve the purpose well, quite on to autumn. It would be needless to add, that the largest and longest are best. Decayed labourers, women, and children, make it their business to procure and prepare them. As soon as they are cut they must be flung into water, and kept there; for otherwise they will dry and shrink, and the peel will not run. At first a person would find it no easy matter to divest a rush of its peel or rind, so as to leave one regular, narrow, even rib from top to bottom, that may support the pith: but this, like other feats, soon becomes familiar, even to children; and we have seen an old woman, stone blind, performing this business with great despatch, and seldom failing to strip them with the nicest regularity. When the *junci* are thus far prepared, they must lay out on the grass to be bleached, and take the dew for some nights, and afterwards be dried in the sun. Some address is required in dipping these rushes in the scalding fat or grease; but this knack is also to be attained by practice.—A pound of common grease may be procured for fourpence, and about six pounds of grease will dip a pound of rushes, and one pound of rushes may be bought for one shilling: so that a pound of rushes, medicated and ready for use, will cost three shillings. If men that keep bees will mix a little wax with the grease, it will give it a consistency, and render it more cleanly, and make the rushes burn longer. Mutton suet would have the same effect.

"A good rush, which measured in length two feet four inches, being minuted, burnt only three minutes short of an hour. In a pound of dry rushes, avoirdupois, which I caused to be weighed and numbered, we found upwards of one thousand six hundred individuals. Now, suppose each of these burns, one with another, only half an hour, then a poor man will purchase eight hundred hours of light, a time exceeding thirty-three entire days, for three shillings. According to this account, each rush, before dipping, costs $\frac{1}{33}$ of a farthing, and $\frac{1}{11}$ afterwards. Thus, a poor family will enjoy five hours and a half of comfortable light for a farthing. An experienced old housekeeper assures me, that one pound and a half of rushes completely supply his family the year round, since working people burn no candles in the long days, because they rise and go to bed by daylight.

"Little farmers use rushes much in the short days, both morning and evening, in the dairy and kitchen; but the very poor, who are always the worst economists, and therefore must continue very poor, buy a halfpenny candle every evening, which, in their blowing, open rooms, does not burn much more than two hours. Thus they have only two hours' light for their money, instead of eleven."

If Mr. White had taken the trouble of extending his calculations, he would have found that the seemingly trifling article of economy which he recommends, would save to the nation a sum equal to the produce of a burdensome tax.

by her spinning and plain-work, and Edmund by leading cart-horses, going on errands, &c., and with little Peggy and Anne's earnings, the family contrived to live comfortably. Isabella and Caroline often visited them, and sometimes gave them clothes, and sometimes flax or cotton for their spinning and knitting; and these children did not *expect* that because the ladies did something for them, they should do every thing: they did not grow idle or wasteful.

When Edmund was about twelve years old, his friend Gilbert sent for him one day, and told him that his master had given him leave to have a boy in the house to assist him, and that his master told him he might choose one in the neighbourhood. Several were anxious to get into such a place, but Gilbert said that he preferred Edmund before them all, because he knew him to be an industrious, honest, good-natured lad, who always told the truth. So Edmund went into service at *the vicarage*, and his master was the father of Isabella and Caroline. He found his new way of life very pleasant, for he was well fed, well clothed, and well treated; and he every day learned more of his business, in which at first he was rather awkward. He was mindful to do all that Mr. Gilbert required of him; and he was so obliging to all his fellow-servants, that they could not help liking him; but there was one thing, which was at first rather disagreeable to him: he was obliged to wear shoes and stockings, and they hurt his feet. Besides this, when he waited at dinner, he made such a noise in walking, that his fellow-servants laughed at him. He told his sister Mary of this distress; and she made for him, after many trials, a pair of cloth shoes, with soles of plaited hemp.* In these he could walk without making the least noise; and as these shoes could not be worn out of doors, he was always sure to change them before he went out of doors; and consequently he had always clean shoes to wear in the house. It was soon remarked by the men-servants, that he had left off clumping so heavily; and it was observed by the maids, that he never dirtied the stairs or passages with his shoes. When he was praised for these things, he said it was his sister Mary who should be thanked, and not he; and he showed the shoes which she had made for him.

Isabella's maid bespoke a pair immediately, and sent Mary a pretty piece of calico for the outside. The last-maker made a last for her, and over this Mary sewed the calico vamps tight. Her brother advised her to try plaited packthread instead of hemp for the soles; and she found that this looked more neat than the hemp soles, and was likely to last longer. She plaited the packthread together in stands of about half an inch thick; and these were sewed firmly together at the bottom of the shoe. When they were finished, they fitted well, and the maid showed them to her mistress. Isabella and Caroline were so well pleased with Mary's ingenuity and kindness to her brother, that they bespoke from her two dozen of these shoes, and gave her three yards of coloured fustian to make them of, and galoon for the binding. When the shoes were completed, Isabella and Caroline disposed of them for her amongst their acquaintance, and got three shillings a pair for them. The young ladies, as soon as they had collected the money, walked to the old castle, where they found every thing neat and clean as usual. They had great pleasure in giving to this industrious girl the reward of her ingenuity, which she received with some surprise and more gratitude. They advised her to continue the shoe-making trade, as they found the shoes were liked, and they knew that they could have a sale for them at the *Repository* in Dublin.

---

* The author has seen a pair of shoes, such as are here described, made in a few hours.

Mary, encouraged by these kind friends, went on with her little manufacture with increased activity. Peggy and Anne plaited the packthread, and pasted the vamps and the lining together ready for her. Edmund was allowed to come home for an hour every morning, provided he was back again before eight o'clock. It was summer-time, and he got up early, because he liked to go home to see his sisters, and he took his share in the manufactory. It was his business to hammer the soles flat: and as soon as he came home every morning, he performed his task with so much cheerfulness, and sung so merrily at his work, that the hour of his arrival was always an hour of joy to the family.

Mary had presently employment enough upon her hands. Orders came to her for shoes from many families in the neighbourhood, and she could not get them finished fast enough. She, however, in the midst of her hurry, found time to make a very pretty pair with neat roses as a present for her school-mistress, who, now that she saw her pupil in a good state of business, consented to receive the amount of her old debt. Several of the children, who went to her school, were delighted with the sight of Mary's present, and went to the little manufactory at Rossmore castle, to find out how these shoes were made. Some went from curiosity, others from idleness; but when they saw how happy the little shoemakers seemed whilst busy at work, they longed to take some share in what was going forward. One begged Mary to let her plait some packthread for the soles; another helped Peggy and Anne to paste in the linings; and all who could get employment were pleased, for the idle ones were shoved out of the way. It became a custom with the children of the village, to resort to the old castle at their play-hours: and it was surprising to see how much was done by ten or twelve of them, each doing but a little at a time.

One morning Edmund and the little manufacturers were assembled very early, and they were busy at their work, all sitting round the meal-chest, which served them for a table.

"My hands must be washed," said George, a little boy who came running in; I ran so fast that I might be in time to go to work along with you all, that I tumbled down, and look how I have dirtied my hands. Most haste worse speed. My hands must be washed before I can do any thing."

Whilst George was washing his hands, two other little children who had just finished their morning's work, came to him to beg that he would blow some soap-bubbles for them, and they were all three eagerly blowing bubbles, and watching them mount into the air, when suddenly they were startled by a noise as loud as thunder: they were in a sort of outer court of the castle, next to the room in which all their companions were at work, and they ran precipitately into the room, exclaiming, "Did you hear that noise?"

"I thought I heard a clap of thunder," said Mary: "but why do you look so frightened?"

As she finished speaking, another and a louder noise, and the walls round about them shook. The children turned pale, and stood motionless; but Edmund threw down his hammer, and ran out to see what was the matter. Mary followed him, and they saw that a great chimney of the old ruins at the farthest side of the castle had fallen down, and this was the cause of the prodigious noise.

The part of the castle in which they lived seemed, as Edmund said, to be perfectly safe; but the children of the village were terrified, and thinking that the whole would come tumbling down directly, they ran to their homes as fast as they could. Edmund, who was a courageous lad, and proud of showing his courage, laughed at their cowardice; but Mary, who was very prudent, persuaded her brother to ask an experienced mason, who was building at his master's, to come and give his opinion whether their part of the castle was safe to live in or not. The mason came, and gave it as his opinion that the rooms they inhabited might last through the winter, but that no part of the ruins could stand another year. Mary was sorry to leave a place of which she had grown fond, poor as it was, having lived in it in peace and content ever since her mother's death, which was now nearly four years; but she determined to look out for some place to live in; and she had now money enough to pay the rent of a comfortable cabin. Without losing any time she went to a village that was at the end of the avenue leading to *the vicarage*, for she wished to get a lodging in this village, because it was so near to her brother, and to the ladies who had been so kind to her; she found that there was one newly-built house in this village unoccupied; it belonged to Mr. Harvey, her landlord, who was still in England; it was slated and neatly fitted up within side; but the rent of it was six guineas a year, and this was far above what Mary could afford to pay; three guineas a year she thought was the highest rent for which she could venture to engage; besides, she heard that several proposals had been made to Mr. Harvey for this house; and she knew that Mr. Hopkins, the agent, was not her friend, therefore she despaired of getting it. There was no other to be had in this village. Her brother was still more vexed than she was, that she could not find a place near him. He offered to give a guinea yearly towards the rent out of his wages; and Mr. Gilbert spoke about it for him to the steward, and inquired whether amongst any of those who had given in proposals, there might not be one who would be content with a part of the house, and who would join with Mary in paying the rent. None could be found but a woman who was a great scold, and a man who was famous for going to law about every trifle with his neighbours. Mary did not choose to have any thing to do with these people; she did not like to speak either to miss Isabella or Caroline about it, because she was not of an encroaching temper; and when they had done so much for her, she would have been ashamed to beg for more. She returned home to the old castle, mortified that she had no good news to tell Anne and Peggy, who she knew expected to hear, that she had found a nice house for them in the village near their brother.

"Bad news for you, Peggy," cried she, as soon as she got home.

"And bad news for you, Mary," replied her sisters, who looked very sorrowful.

"What's the matter?"

"Your poor goat is dead," replied Peggy; "there she is yonder lying under the great cornerstone; you can just see her leg. We cannot lift the stone from off her, it is so heavy. Betsy (*one of the neighbour's girls*) says she remembers, when she came to us to work early this morning, she saw the goat rubbing itself, and butting with its horns against the old tottering chimney."

"Many's the time," said Mary, "that I have driven the poor thing away from that place; I was always afraid she would shake that great ugly stone down upon her at last."

The goat, who had long been the favourite of Mary and her sisters, was lamented by them all. When Edmund came, he helped them to move the great stone from off the poor animal, who was crushed so as to be a terrible sight. As they were moving away this stone, in order to bury the goat, Anne found an odd looking piece of money, which seemed neither like a halfpenny, nor a shilling, nor a guinea.

"Here are more, a great many more of them," cried Peggy; and upon searching amongst the rubbish, they discovered a small iron pot, which seemed as if it had been filled with these coins, as a vast number of them were found about the spot where it fell. On examining these coins, Edmund thought that several of them looked like gold, and the girls exclaimed with great joy—"O Mary! Mary! this is come to us just in right time—now you can pay for the slated house. Never was any thing so lucky!"

But Mary, though nothing could have pleased her better than to have been able to pay for the house, observed, that they could not honestly touch any of this treasure, as it belonged to the owner of the castle. Edmund agreed with her, that they ought to carry it all immediately to Mr. Hopkins, the agent. Peggy and Anne were convinced by what Mary said, and they begged to go along with her and their brother, to take the coins to Mr. Hopkins. In their way they stopped at the vicarage, to show the treasure to Mr. Gilbert, who took it to the young ladies, Isabella and Caroline, and told them how it had been found.

It is not only by their superior riches, but it is yet more by their superior knowledge, that persons in the higher ranks of life may assist those in a lower condition.

Isabella, who had some knowledge of chemistry, discovered, by touching the coins with *aqua regia* (the only acid which affects gold), that several of them were of gold, and consequently of great value. Caroline also found out, that many of the coins were very valuable as curiosities. She recollected her father having shown to her the prints of the coins at the end of each king's rein, in Rapin's History of England; and upon comparing these impressions with the coins found by the orphans, she perceived that many of them were of the reign of Henry the Seventh.

People who are fond of collecting coins set a great value on these, as they are very scarce. Isabella and Caroline, knowing something of the character of Mr. Hopkins, the agent, had the precaution to count the coins, and to mark each of them with a cross, so small that it was scarcely visible to the naked eye, though it was easily to be seen through by a magnifying glass. They also begged their father, who was well acquainted with Mr. Harvey, the gentleman to whom Rossmore castle belonged, to write to him, and tell him how well these orphans had behaved about the treasure which they had found. The value of the coins was estimated at about thirty or forty guineas.

A few days after the fall of the chimney at Rossmore castle, as Mary and her sisters were sitting at their work, there came hobbling in an old woman, leaning on a crab-stick, that seemed to have been newly cut; she had a broken tobacco-pipe in her mouth; her head was wrapped up in two large red and blue handkerchiefs, with their corners hanging far down over the back of her neck, no shoes on her broad feet, nor stockings on her many-coloured legs; her petticoat was jagged at the bottom, and the skirt of her gown turned up over her shoulders, to serve instead of her cloak, which she had sold for whiskey. This old woman was well known amongst the country people by the name of *Goody Grope:** because she had, for many years, been in the habit of groping in old castles, and in moats,† and at the bottom of a round tower‡ in the neighbourhood, in search of treasure. In her youth she had heard some one talking, in a whisper, of an old prophecy, found in a bog, which said that, "before many St. Patrick's days should come about, there would be found a treasure under ground, by one within twenty miles round."

---

* *Goody* is not a word used in Ireland, *Collyogh* is the Irish appellation of an old woman: but as *Collyogh* might sound strangely to English ears, we have translated it by the word Goody.

† What are in Ireland called moats, are, in England, called Danish mounts, or barrows.

‡ Near Kells, in Ireland, there is a round tower, which was in imminent danger of being pulled down by an old woman's rooting at its foundation, in hopes of finding treasure.

This prophecy made a deep impression upon her; she also dreamed of it three times; and as the dream, she thought, was a sure token that the prophecy was to come true, she, from that time forwards, gave up her spinning-wheel and her knitting, and could think of nothing but hunting for the treasure, that was to be found by one *"within twenty miles round."*—Year after year St. Patrick's day came about, without her ever finding a farthing by all her groping; and as she was always idle, she grew poorer and poorer; besides, to comfort herself for her disappointments, and to give her spirits for fresh searches, she took to drinking: she sold all she had by degrees; but still she fancied, that the lucky day would come sooner or later, *that would pay for all.*

Goody Grope, however, reached her sixtieth year, without ever seeing this lucky day; and now, in her old age, she was a beggar, without a house to shelter her, a bed to lie on, or food to put into her mouth, but what she begged from the charity of those who had trusted more than she had to industry, and less to *luck*.

"Ah! Mary, honey! give me a potatoe, and a sup of something, for the love o' mercy; for not a bit have I had all day, except half a glass of whiskey, and a half-pennyworth of tobacco!"

Mary immediately set before her some milk, and picked a good potatoe out of the bowl for her; she was sorry to see such an old woman in such a wretched condition. Goody Grope said she would rather have spirits of some kind or other than milk; but Mary had no spirits to give her: so she sat herself down close to the fire, and after she had sighed and groaned, and smoked for some time, she said to Mary—

"Well, and what have you done with the treasure you had the luck to find?"

Mary told her, that she carried it to Mr. Hopkins, the agent.

"That's not what I would have done in your place," replied the old woman. "When good luck came to you, what a shame to turn your back upon it! But it is idle talking of what's done—that's past——but I'll try my luck in this here castle before next St. Patrick's day comes about: I was told it was more than twenty miles from our bog, or I would have been here long ago: but better late than never."

Mary was much alarmed, and not without reason, at this speech: for she knew that if Goody Grope once set to work at the foundation of the old castle of Rossmore, she would soon bring it all down. It was in vain to talk to Goody Grope of the danger of burying herself under the ruins, or of the improbability of her meeting with another pot of gold coins. She set her elbow upon her knees, and stopping her ears with her hands, bid Mary and her sisters not to waste their breath advising their elders; for that, let them say what they would, she would fall to work the next morning; *"barring** you'll make it worth my while to let it alone."

"And what will make it worth your while to let it alone?" said Mary, who saw that she must either get into a quarrel or give up her habitation, or comply with the conditions of this provoking old woman.

Half-a-crown, Goody Grope said, was the least she could be content to take.

Mary paid the half-crown, and was in hopes she had got rid for ever of her tormentor: but she was mistaken; for scarcely was the week at an end, before the old woman appeared before her again, and repeated her threats of falling to work the next morning, unless she had something given her to buy tobacco.

---

* Unless.

The next day, and the next, and the next, Goody Grope came on the same errand; and poor Mary, who could ill afford to supply her constantly with halfpence, at last exclaimed—"I am sure the finding of this treasure has not been any good-luck to us, but quite the contrary; and I wish we never had found it."

Mary did not yet know how much she was to suffer on account of this unfortunate pot of gold coins. Mr. Hopkins, the agent, imagined that no one knew of the discovery of this treasure but himself and these poor children, so, not being as honest as they were, he resolved to keep it for his own use. He was surprised, some weeks afterwards, to receive a letter from his employer, Mr. Harvey, demanding from him the coins which had been discovered at Rossmore castle. Hopkins had sold the gold coins, and some of the others; but he flattered himself that the children, and the young ladies to whom he now found they had been shown, could not tell whether what they had seen were gold or not; and he was not in the least apprehensive that those of Henry the Seventh's reign would be reclaimed from him, as he thought they had escaped attention. So he sent over the silver coins, and others of little value, and apologized for his not having mentioned them before, by saying, that he considered them as mere rubbish.

Mr. Harvey, in reply, observed that he could not consider as rubbish the gold coins which were amongst them when they were discovered; and he inquired why these gold coins, and those of the reign of Henry the Seventh, were not now sent to him.

Mr. Hopkins denied that he had ever received any such; but he was thunderstruck when Mr. Harvey, in reply to this falsehood, sent him a list of the coins which the orphans had deposited with him, and exact drawings of those that were missing. He informed him, that this list and these drawings came from two ladies, who had seen the coins in question.

Mr. Hopkins thought, that he had no means of escape but by boldly persisting in falsehood. He replied, that it was very likely such coins had been found at Rossmore castle, and that the ladies alluded to had probably seen them; but he positively declared, that they never came to his hands; that he had restored all that were deposited with him; and that as to the others, he supposed they must have been taken out of the pot by the children, or by Edmund or Mary in their way from the ladies' house to his.

The orphans were shocked and astonished when they heard, from Isabella and Caroline, the charge that was made against them; they looked at one another in silence for some moments; then Peggy exclaimed—"*Sure!* Mr. Hopkins has forgotten himself strangely!—Does he not remember Edmund's counting the things to him upon the great table in his hall, and we all standing by?—I remember it as well as if it was this instant."

"And so do I," cried Anne. "And don't you recollect, Mary, your picking out the gold ones, and telling Mr. Hopkins that they were gold; and he said you knew nothing of the matter; and I was going to tell him that Miss Isabella had tried them, and knew that they were gold; but just then there came in some tenants to pay their rent, and he pushed us out, and twitched from my hand the piece of gold, which I had taken up to show him the bright spot, which Miss Isabella had cleaned by the stuff that she had poured on it? I believe he was afraid I should steal it, he twitched it from my hand in such a hurry.—Do, Edmund, do, Mary—let us go to him, and put him in mind of all this."

"I'll go to him no more," said Edmund, sturdily. "He is a bad man—I'll never go to him again.—Mary, don't be cast down—we have no need to be cast down—we are honest."

"True," said Mary; "but is not it a hard case that we, who have lived, as my mother did all her life before us, in peace and honesty with all the world, should now have our good name taken from us, when——" Mary's voice faltered and stopped.

"It can't be taken from us," cried Edmund, "poor orphans though we are, and he a rich gentleman, as he calls himself. Let him say and do what he will, he can't hurt our good name."

Edmund was mistaken, alas! and Mary had but too much reason for her fears. The affair was a great deal talked of; and the agent spared no pains to have the story told his own way. The orphans, conscious of their own innocence, took no pains about the matter; and the consequence was, that all who knew them well, had no doubt of their honesty; but many who knew nothing of them, concluded that the agent must be in the right and the children in the wrong. The buzz of scandal went on for some time without reaching their ears, because they lived very retiredly: but one day, when Mary went to sell some stockings of Peggy's knitting, at the neighbouring fair, the man to whom she sold them bid her write her name on the back of a note, and exclaimed on seeing it—"Ho! ho! mistress: I'd not have had any dealings with you had I known your name sooner:—Where's the gold that you found at Rossmore castle?"

It was in vain that Mary related the fact; she saw that she gained no belief, as her character was not known to this man, or to any of those who were present. She left the fair as soon as she could; and though she struggled against it, she felt very melancholy. Still she exerted herself every day at her little manufacture; and she endeavoured to console herself by reflecting, that she had two friends left, who would not give up her character, and who continued steadily to protect her and her sisters.

Isabella and Caroline every where asserted their belief in the integrity of the orphans; but to prove it was, in this instance, out of their power. Mr. Hopkins, the agent, and his friends, constantly repeated, that the gold coins were taken away in coming from their house to his; and these ladies were blamed by many people for continuing to countenance those that were, with great reason, suspected to be thieves. The orphans were in a worse condition than ever when the winter came on, and their benefactresses left the country, to spend some months in Dublin. The old castle, it was true, was likely to last through the winter, as the mason said; but though the want of a comfortable house to live in was, a little while ago, the uppermost thing in Mary's thoughts, now it was not so.

One night, as Mary was going to bed, she heard some one knocking hard at the door: —"Mary, are you up?—let us in,"—cried a voice, which she knew to be the voice of Betsy Green, the post-master's daughter, who lived in the village near them.

She let Betsy in, and asked what she could want at such a time of night.

"Give me sixpence, and I'll tell you," said Betsy: "but waken Anne and Peggy.—— Here's a letter just come by the post for you, and I stepped over to you with it, because I guessed you'd be glad to have it, seeing it is your brother's hand-writing."

Peggy and Anne were soon roused when they heard that there was a letter from Edmund. It was by one of his rush candles that Mary read it; and the letter was as follows:—

"Dear Mary, Nancy, and little Peg,—

"Joy! joy!—I always said the truth would come out at last; and that he could not take our good name from us.—But I will not tell you how it all came about till we meet, which will be next week, as we (I mean master and mistress, and the young ladies,

—Bless them! and Mr. Gilbert and I) are coming down to the vicarage to keep the Christmas: and a happy Christmas 'tis likely to be for honest folks: as for they that are not honest, it is not for them to expect to be happy, at Christmas, or at any other time.—You shall know all when we meet: so, till then fare ye well, dear Mary, Nancy, and little Peg. Your joyful and affectionate brother,

"EDMUND."

To comprehend why Edmund was joyful, our readers must be informed of certain things which happened after Isabella and Caroline went to Dublin. One morning they went with their father and mother to see the magnificent library of a nobleman, who took generous and polite pleasure in thus sharing the advantages of his wealth and station with all who had any pretensions to science or literature. Knowing that the gentleman, who was now come to see his library, was skilled in antiquities, the nobleman opened a drawer of medals, to ask his opinion concerning the age of some coins, which he had lately purchased at a high price. They were the very same which the orphans had found at Rossmore castle. Isabella and Caroline knew them again instantly; and as the cross which Isabella had made on each of them was still visible through a magnifying glass, there could be no possibility of doubt.

The nobleman, who was much interested both by the story of these orphans, and the manner in which it was told to him, sent immediately for the person from whom he had purchased the coins. He was a Jew broker. At first he refused to tell from whom he got them, because he had bought them, he said, under a promise of secrecy. Being further pressed, he acknowledged that it was made a condition in his bargain, that he should not sell them to any one in Ireland; but that he had been tempted by the high price Lord ———— had offered.

At last, when the Jew was informed that the coins were stolen, and that he would be proceeded against as a receiver of stolen goods, if he did not confess the whole truth, he declared that he had purchased them from a gentleman, whom he had never seen before or since; but he added that he could swear to his person, if he saw him again.

Now Mr. Hopkins, the agent, was at this time in Dublin, and Caroline's father posted the Jew, the next day, in the back parlour of a banker's house, with whom Mr. Hopkins had, on this day, appointed to settle some accounts. Mr. Hopkins came—the Jew knew him—swore that he was the man who had sold the coins to him; and thus the guilt of the agent, and the innocence of the orphans, were completely proved.

A full account of all that happened was sent to England to Mr. Harvey, their landlord; and a few posts afterwards, there came a letter from him containing a dismissal of the dishonest agent, and a reward for the honest and industrious orphans. Mr. Harvey desired that Mary and her sisters might have the slated house, rent free, from this time forward, under the care of the ladies Isabella and Caroline, as long as Mary or her sisters should carry on in it any useful business. This was the joyful news which Edmund had to tell his sisters.

All the neighbours shared in their joy; and the day of their removal from the ruins of Rossmore castle to their new house was the happiest of the Christmas holidays. They were not envied for their prosperity: because every body saw that it was the reward of their good conduct; every body except Goody Grope: she exclaimed, as she wrung her hands with violent expressions of sorrow—"Bad luck to me! bad luck to me; Why didn't I go sooner to that there castle? It is all luck, all luck in this world; but I never had no luck. Think of the luck of these *childer*, that have found a pot of gold, and such great grand friends, and a slated house, and all: and here am I, with scarce a rag to cover me and not a potatoe to put into my mouth! I, that have been looking under ground all my days for treasure, not to have a half-penny at the last, to buy me tobacco."

"That is the very reason that you have not a half-penny," said Betsy: "here Mary has been working hard, and so have her two little sisters and her brother, for these five years past; and they have made money for themselves by their own industry—and friends too—not by luck, but by ————"

"Phoo! phoo!" interrupted Goody Grope; "don't be prating; don't I know, as well as you do, that they found a pot of gold, by *good luck;* and is not that the cause why they are going to live in the slated house now?"

"No," replied the postmaster's daughter; "this house is given to them *as a reward*—that was the word in the letter, for I saw it; Edmund showed it to me, and will show it to any one that wants to see. This house was given to them '*as a reward for their honesty.*' "

The Basket-Woman.

Toute leur étude étoit de se complaire et de s'entr'aider.
PAUL ET VIRGINIE

Their whole study was how to please and to help one another.

AT THE FOOT of a steep, slippery, white hill, near Dunstable in Bedfordshire, called Chalk Hill, there is a hut, or rather a hovel, which travellers could scarcely suppose could be inhabited, if they did not see the smoke rising from its peaked roof. An old woman lives in this hovel, and with her a little boy and girl, the children of a beggar, who died and left these orphans perishing with hunger; they thought themselves very happy the first time the good old woman took them into her hut, bid them warm themselves at her small fire, and gave them a crust of mouldy bread to eat: she had not much to give; but what she had she gave with good-will. She was very kind to these poor children, and worked hard at her spinning-wheel, and at her knitting, to support herself and them. She earned money also in another way: she used to follow all the carriages as they went up Chalk Hill; and when the horses stopped to take breath, or to rest themselves, she put stones behind the carriage-wheels, to prevent them from rolling backwards down the steep slippery hill.

The little boy and girl loved to stand beside the good-natured old woman's spinning-wheel, when she was spinning, and to talk to her. At these times she taught them something, which she said she hoped they would remember all their lives; she explained to them what is meant by telling the truth, and what it is to be honest; she taught them to dislike idleness, and to wish that they could be useful.

One evening, as they were standing beside her, the little boy said to her, "Grandmother," for that was the name by which she liked that these children should call her—"Grandmother, how often you are forced to get up from your spinning-wheel, and to follow the chaises and coaches up that steep hill, to put stones under the wheels, to hinder them from rolling back! The people who are in the carriages give you a half-penny or penny for doing this, don't they?" "Yes, child." "But it is very hard work for you to go up and down that hill; you often say that you are tired, and then you know that you cannot spin all that time; now if we might go up the hill, and put the stones behind the wheels, you could sit still at your work; and would not the people give us the half-pence? and could not we bring them all to you? Do, pray, dear grandmother, try us for one day—To-morrow will you?" "Yes," said the old woman, "I will try what you can do; but I must go up the hill along with you for the first two or three times, for fear you should get yourselves hurt." So, the next day the little boy and girl went with their grandmother, as they used to call her, up the steep hill; and she showed the boy how to prevent the wheels from rolling back, by putting stones behind them; and she said, "This is called scotching the wheels;" and she took off the boy's hat, and gave it to the little girl, to hold up to the carriage windows, ready for the half-pence. When she thought that the children knew how to manage for themselves, she left them and returned to her spinning-wheel. A great many carriages happened to go by this day, and the little girl received a great many half-pence: she carried them all in her brother's hat to her grandmother, in the evening; and the old woman smiled, and thanked the children; she said that they had been useful to her, and that her spinning had gone on finely, because she had been able to sit still at her wheel all day—"But, Paul, my boy," said she, "what is the matter with your hand?"

"Only a pinch, only one pinch that I got, as I was putting a stone behind the wheel of a chaise: it does not hurt me much, grandmother, and I've thought of a good thing for to-morrow; I shall never be hurt again, if you will only be so good as to give me the old handle of the broken crutch, grandmother, and the block of wood that lies in the chimney-corner, and that is of no use; I'll make it of some use, if I may have it." "Take it then, dear," said the old woman; "and you'll find the handle of the broken crutch under my bed."

Paul went to work immediately, and fastened one end of the pole into the block of wood, so as to make something like a dry rubbing-brush. "Look, grandmother, look at my *scotcher:* I call this thing my *scotcher,*" said Paul, "because I shall always scotch the wheels with it: I shall never pinch my fingers again; my hands, you see, will be safe at the end of this long stick; and, sister Anne, you need not be at the trouble of carrying any more stones after me up the hill; we shall never want stones any more, my scotcher will do without anything else, I hope. I wish it was morning, and that a carriage would come, that I might run up the hill, and try my scotcher." "And I wish that as many chaises may go by to-morrow as there did to-day, and that we may bring you as many half-pence too, grandmother," said the little girl. "So do I, my dear Anne," said the old woman; "for I mean that you and your brother shall have all the money that you get to-morrow; you may buy some gingerbread for yourselves, or some of those ripe plums that you saw at the fruit-stall, the other day, which is just going into Dunstable. I told you then that I could not afford to buy such things for you; but now, that you can earn half-pence for yourselves, children, it is fair that you should taste a ripe plum and a bit of gingerbread for once in your lives and away, dears."

"We'll bring some of the gingerbread home to her, sha'n't we, brother?" whispered little Anne. The morning came, but no carriages were heard, though Paul and his sister had risen at five o'clock, that they might be sure to be ready for early travellers. Paul kept his scotcher poised upon his shoulder, and watched eagerly at his station at the bottom of the hill: he did not wait long before a carriage came. He followed it up the hill: and the instant the postillion called to him, and bid him stop the wheels, he put his scotcher behind them, and found that it answered the purpose perfectly well. Many carriages went by this day; and Paul and Anne received a great many half-pence from the travellers. When it grew dusk in the evening, Anne said to her brother—"I don't think any more carriages will come by to-day; let us count the half-pence, and carry them home now to grandmother."

"No, not yet," answered Paul; "let them alone—let them lie still in the hole where I have put them: I dare say more carriages will come by before it is quite dark, and then we shall have more half-pence." Paul had taken the half-pence out of his hat, and he had put them into a hole in the high bank by the road side; and Anne said that she would not meddle with them, and that she would wait till her brother liked to count them; and Paul said, "if you will stay and watch here, I will go and gather some black-berries for you in the hedge in yonder field: stand you here-abouts half-way up the hill; and the moment you see any carriage coming along the road, run as fast as you can, and call me."

Anne waited a long time, or what she thought a long time; and she saw no carriage: and she trailed her brother's scotcher up and down till she was tired; then she stood still and looked again: and she saw no carriage; so she went sorrowfully into the field, and to the hedge where her brother was gathering blackberries, and she said, "Paul, I'm sadly tired: *sadly tired!*" said she; "and my eyes are quite strained with looking for chaises; no more chaises will come to-night; and your scotcher is lying there of no use upon the ground. Have not I waited long enough for to-day, Paul?" "O no," said Paul; "here are some blackberries for you; you had better wait a little bit longer; perhaps a carriage might go by whilst you are standing here talking to me." Anne, who was of a very obliging temper, and who liked to do what she was asked to do, went back to the place where the scotcher lay; and scarcely had she reached the spot, when she heard the noise of a carriage. She ran to call her brother; and, to their great joy, they now saw four chaises coming towards them. Paul, as soon as they went up the hill, followed with his scotcher; first he scotched the wheels of one carriage, then of another; and Anne was so much de-lighted with observing how well the scotcher stopped the wheels, and how much better it was than stones, that she forgot to go and hold her brother's hat to the travellers for half-pence, till she was roused by the voice of a little rosy girl, who was looking out of the window of one of the chaises. "Come close to the chaise-door," said the little girl; "here are some half-pence for you."

Anne held the hat; and she afterward went on to the other carriages; money was thrown to her from each of them: and when they had all gotten safely to the top of the hill, she and her brother sat down upon a large stone by the roadside to count their treasure. First they began by counting what was in the hat—"One, two, three, four, half-pence."

"But O brother, look at this!" exclaimed Anne; "this is not the same as the other half-pence."

"No, indeed, it is not," cried Paul; "it is no half-penny; it is a guinea, a bright golden guinea!" "Is it?" said Anne, who had never seen a guinea in her life before, and who did not know its value; "and will it do as well as a half-penny to buy gingerbread? I'll run to the fruit-stall, and ask the woman, shall I?"

"No, no," said Paul, "you need not ask any woman or any body but me; I can tell you all about it as well as any body in the whole world."

"The whole world! O Paul, you forget! not so well as my grandmother."

"Why, not so well as my grandmother, perhaps; but, Anne, I can tell you, that you must not talk yourself, Anne; but you must listen to me quietly, or else you won't understand what I am going to tell you; for I can assure you, that I don't think I quite understood it myself, Anne, the first time my grandmother told it to me, though I stood stock still, listening my best."

Prepared by this speech to hear something very difficult to be understood, Anne looked very grave; and her brother explained to her, that, with a guinea, she might buy two hundred and fifty-two times as many plums as she could get for a penny.

"Why, Paul, you know the fruit-woman said she would give us a dozen plums for a penny. Now for this little guinea would she give us two hundred and fifty-two dozen?"

"If she has so many, and if we like to have so many, to be sure she will," said Paul; "but I think we should not like to have two hundred and fifty-two dozen of plums; we could not eat such a number."

"But we could give some of them to my grandmother," said Anne.

"But still there would be too many for her and for us too," said Paul; "and when we had eaten the plums, there would be an end of all the pleasure; but now I'll tell you what I am thinking of, Anne, that we might buy something for my grandmother that would be very useful to her indeed with this guinea; something that would last a great while."

"What, brother? what sort of thing?"

"Something that she said she wanted very much last winter, when she was so ill of the rheumatism; something that she said yesterday, when you were making her bed, she wished she might be able to buy before next winter."

"I know! I know what you mean," said Anne, "a blanket; O, yes, Paul, that will be much better than plums; do let us buy a blanket for her; how glad she will be to see it; I will make her bed with the new blanket, and then bring her to look at it. But, Paul, how shall we buy a blanket? Where are blankets to be got?"

"Leave that to me, I'll manage that—I know where blankets can be got; I saw one hanging out of a shop the day I went last to Dunstable."

"You have seen a great many things at Dunstable, brother."

"Yes, a great many; but I never saw any thing there, or any where else, that I wished for half so much as I did for the blanket for my grandmother. Do you remember how she used to shiver with the cold last winter? I'll buy the blanket to-morrow, I'm going to Dunstable with her spinning."

"And you'll bring the blanket to me, and I shall make the bed very neatly, that will be all right! all happy!" said Anne, clapping her hands.

"But stay! hush! don't clap your hands so, Anne; it will not be all happy, I'm afraid," said Paul, and his countenance changed, and he looked very grave—"it will not be all right, I'm afraid, for there is one thing we have neither of us thought of, but that we ought to think about. We cannot buy the blanket, I'm afraid."

"Why, Paul? why?"

"Because I don't think this guinea is honestly ours."

"Nay, brother, but I'm sure it is honestly ours; it was given to us, and grandmother said all that was given to us to-day was to be our own."

"But who gave it to you, Anne?"

"Some of the people in those chaises, Paul; I don't know which of them, but I dare say it was the little rosy girl."

"No," said Paul, "for when she called you to the chaise-door, she said, 'Here's some half-pence for you.' Now, if she gave you the guinea, she must have given it to you by mistake."

"Well, but perhaps some of the people in the other chaises gave it to me, and did not give it to me by mistake, Paul. There was a gentleman reading in one of the chaises, and a lady, who looked very good-naturedly at me, and then the gentleman put down his book, and put his head out of the window, and looked at your scotcher, brother, and he asked me if that was your own making: and when I said yes, and that I was your sister, he smiled at me, and put his hand into his waistcoat pocket, and threw a handful of half-pence into the hat, and I dare say he gave us the guinea along with them, because he liked your scotcher so much."

"Why," said Paul, "that might be, to be sure; but I wish I was quite certain of it."

"Then, as we are not quite certain, had not we best go and ask my grandmother what she thinks about it?"

Paul thought this was excellent advice; and he was not a silly boy, who did not like to follow good advice; he went with his sister directly to his grandmother, showed her the guinea, and told her how they came by it.

"My dear honest children," said she, "I am very glad you told me all this; I am very glad that you did not buy either the plums or the blanket with this guinea; I'm sure it is not honestly ours; those who threw it to you gave it by mistake, I warrant; and what I would have you do, is, to get to Dunstable, and try, if you can, at either of the inns, to find out the person who gave it to you. It is now so late in the evening, that perhaps the travellers will sleep at Dunstable, instead of going on the next stage; and it is likely, that whosoever gave you the guinea, instead of a halfpenny, has found out his mistake by this time. All you can do, is to go and inquire for the gentleman who was reading in the chaise."

"O!" interrupted Paul, "I know a good way of finding him out; I remember it was a dark green chaise with red wheels: and I remember I read the innkeeper's name upon the chaise, '*John Nelson.*' (I am much obliged to you for teaching me to read, grand-mother.) You told me yesterday, grandmother, that the names written upon chaises are the names of the innkeepers to whom they belong. I read the name of the innkeeper upon that chaise: it was John Nelson. So Anne and I will go to both the inns in Dun-stable, and try to find out this chaise—John Nelson's. Come, Anne, let us set out before it gets quite dark."

Anne and her brother passed with great courage the tempting stall, that was covered with gingerbread and ripe plums, and pursued their way steadily through the streets of Dunstable; but Paul, when he came to the shop where he had seen the blankets, stopped for a moment and said, "It is a great pity, Anne, that the guinea is not ours; however, we are doing what is honest, and that is a comfort.——Here, we must go through this gateway, into the inn-yard: we are come to the Dun Cow."

"Cow," said Anne; "I see no cow."

"Look up, and you'll see the cow over your head," said Paul—"the sign—the picture.

Come, never mind looking at it now: I want to find out the green chaise that has John Nelson's name upon it."

Paul pushed forward, through a crowded passage, till he got into the inn-yard—there was a great noise and bustle; the hostlers were carrying in luggage; the postillions were rubbing down their horses, or rolling the chaises into the coach-house.

"What now? What business have you here, pray?" said a waiter, who almost ran over Paul, as he was crossing the yard in a great hurry, to get some empty bottles from the bottle-rack. "You've no business here, crowding up the yard; walk off, young gentleman, if you please."

"Pray give me leave, sir," said Paul, "to stay a few minutes, to look amongst these chaises for one dark green chaise with red wheels, that has Mr. John Nelson's name written upon it."

"What's that he says about a dark green chaise?" said one of the postillions.

"What should such a one as he is know about chaises?" interrupted the hasty waiter, as he was going to turn Paul out of the yard; but the hostler caught hold of his arm, and said, "May be the child *has* some business here; let's know what he has to say for himself."

The waiter was at this instant luckily obliged to leave them to attend the bell; and Paul told his business to the hostler, who, as soon as he saw the guinea and heard the story, shook Paul by the hand, and said, "Stand steady, my honest lad; I'll find the chaise for you, if it's to be found here; but John Nelson's chaises almost always drive to the Black Bull."

After some difficulty the green chaise with John Nelson's name upon it, and the postillion who drove the chaise, were found; and the postillion told Paul, that he was just going into the parlour to the gentleman he had driven, to be paid, and that he would carry the guinea with him.

"No," said Paul, "we should like to give it back ourselves."

"Yes," said the hostler, "that they have a right to do."

The postillion made no reply, but looked vexed, and went on towards the house, desiring the children would wait in the passage till his return.

In the passage there was standing a decent, clean, good-natured looking woman, with two huge straw baskets on each side of her. One of the baskets stood a little in the way of the entrance. A man who was pushing his way in, and carried in his hand a string of dead larks hung to a pole, impatient at being stopped, kicked down the straw basket, and all its contents were thrown out: bright straw hats, and boxes, and slippers, were all thrown in disorder upon the dirty ground.

"Oh, they will be trampled upon! they will be all spoiled!" exclaimed the woman to whom they belonged.

"We'll help you to pick them up, if you will let us," cried Paul and Anne; and they immediately ran to her assistance.

When the things were all safe in the basket again, the children expressed a great desire to know how such beautiful things could be made of straw; but the woman had not time to answer them, before the postillion came out of the parlour, and with him a gentleman's servant, who came to Paul, and clapping him upon the back, said, "So my little chap, I gave you a guinea for a half-penny, I hear; and I understand you've brought it back again—that's right—give me hold of it."

"No, brother," said Anne; "this is not the gentleman that was reading."

"Pooh, child, I came in Mr. Nelson's green chaise. Here's the postillion can tell you so. I and my master came in that chaise. It was my master that was reading, as you say: and it was he that threw the money out to you; he is going to bed; he is tired, and can't see you himself: he desires that you'll give me the guinea."

Paul was too honest himself to suspect that this man was telling him a falsehood; and he now readily produced his bright guinea, and delivered it into the servant's hands.

"Here's sixpence a-piece for you, children," said he, "and good night to you." He pushed them towards the door; but the basket-woman whispered to them as they went out, "Wait in the street till I come to you."

"Pray, Mrs. Landlady," cried this gentleman's servant, addressing himself to the land-lady, who just then came out of a room where some company were at supper, "Pray, Mrs. Landlady, please to let me have some roasted larks for my supper. You are famous for larks at Dunstable; and I make it a rule to taste the best of every thing, wherever I go; and, waiter, let me have a bottle of claret—Do you hear?"

"Larks and claret for his supper!" said the basket-woman to herself, as she looked at him from head to foot. The postillion was still waiting, as if to speak to him; and she observed them afterwards whispering and laughing together. "*No bad hit*" was a sentence which the servant pronounced several times.

Now it occurred to the basket-woman, that this man had cheated the children out of the guinea to pay for the larks and claret; and she thought that perhaps she could discover the truth. She waited quietly in the passage.

"Waiter!—Joe! Joe!" cried the landlady, "why don't you carry in the sweetmeat puffs and the tarts here to the company in the best parlour?"

"Coming, ma'am," answered the waiter; and with a large dish of tarts and puffs the waiter came from the bar; the landlady threw open the door of the best parlour, to let him in; and the basket-woman had now a full view of a large cheerful company; and amongst them several children sitting round a supper table.

"Aye," whispered the landlady, as the door closed after the waiter and the tarts, "there are customers enough, I warrant, for you in that room if you had but the luck to be called in. Pray what would you have the conscience, I wonder now, to charge me for these here half dozen little mats, to put under my dishes?"

"A trifle, ma'am," said the basket-woman: she let the landlady have the mats cheap: and the landlady then declared she would step in, and see if the company in the best parlour had done supper—"When they come to their wine," added she, "I'll speak a good word for you, and get you called in afore the children are sent to bed."

The landlady, after the usual speech of "*I hope the supper and every thing is to your liking, ladies and gentlemen*," began with, "If any of the young gentlemen or ladies would have a *cur'osity* to see any of our famous Dunstable straw-work, there's a decent body without would, I dare to say, be proud to show them her pincushion-boxes, and her baskets and slippers, and her other *cur'osities*."

The eyes of the children all turned towards their mother; their mother smiled, and im-mediately their father called in the basket-woman, and desired her to produce her *curiosities*.

The children gathered round her large pannier as it opened; but they did not touch any of her things.

"O papa!" cried a little rosy girl, "here are a pair of straw slippers, that would just fit you, I think; but would not straw shoes wear out very soon? and would not they let in the wet?"

"Yes, my dear," said her father, "but these slippers are meant————" "for powdering slippers, miss," interrupted the basket-woman.

"To wear when people are powdering their hair," continued the gentleman, "that they may not spoil their other shoes."

"And will you buy them, papa?"

"No, I cannot indulge myself," said her father, "in buying them now; I must make amends," said he, laughing, "for my carelessness; and as I threw away a guinea to-day, I must endeavour to save six-pence at least."

"Ah, the guinea that you threw by mistake into the little girl's hat, as we were coming up Chalk Hill. Mamma, I wonder that the little girl did not take notice of it's being a guinea, and that she did not run after the chaise to give it back again. I should think, if she had been an honest girl, she would have returned it."

"Miss!—Ma'am!—sir!" said the basket-woman, "if it would not be impertinent, may I speak a word?—A little boy and girl have just been here inquiring for a gentleman, who gave them a guinea, instead of a half-penny, by mistake; and, not five minutes ago, I saw the boy give the guinea to a gentleman's servant, who is there without, and who said his master desired it should be returned to him."

"There must be some mistake, or some trick in this," said the gentleman: "are the children gone?—I must see them—Send after them."

"I'll go for them myself," said the good-natured basket-woman; "I bid them wait in the street yonder; for my mind misgave me, that the man who spoke so short to them was a cheat—with his larks and his claret."

Paul and Anne were speedily summoned, and brought back by their friend the basket-woman; and Anne, the moment she saw the gentleman, knew that he was the very person who smiled upon her, who admired her brother's scotcher, and who threw a handful of half-pence into the hat; but she could not be certain, she said, that she received the guinea from him; she only thought it was most likely that she did.

"But I can be certain whether the guinea you returned be mine or no," said the gentleman; "I marked the guinea: it was a light one; the only light guinea I had, which I put in my waistcoat-pocket this morning."

He rang the bell, and desired the waiter to let the gentleman, who was in the room opposite to him, know that he wished to see him.

"The gentleman in the white parlour, sir, do you mean?"

"I mean the master of the servant who received a guinea from this child."

"He is a Mr. Pembroke, sir," said the waiter.

Mr. Pembroke came, and as soon as he heard what had happened, he desired the waiter to show him to the room where his servant was at supper.

The dishonest servant, who was supping upon larks and claret, knew nothing of what was going on; but his knife and fork dropped from his hand, and he overturned a bumper of claret, as he started up from table, in great surprise and terror, when his master came in with a face of indignation, and demanded "*The guinea*—the *guinea, sir!* that you got from this child—that guinea which you said I ordered you to ask for from this child."

The servant, confounded and half intoxicated, could only stammer out that he had more guineas than one about him, and that he really did not know which it was. He pulled his money out, and spread it upon the table with trembling hands—the marked guinea appeared—his master instantly turned him out of his service with strong expressions of contempt.

"And now, my little honest girl," said the gentleman who had admired her brother's scotcher, turning to Anne, "and now tell me who you are, and what you and your brother want or wish for most in the world."

In the same moment, Anne and Paul exclaimed, "The thing we wish for the most in the world is a blanket for our grandmother."

"She is not our grandmother in reality, I believe, sir," said Paul; "but she is just as good to us, and taught me to read, and taught Anne to knit, and taught us both that we should be honest—so she has—and I wish she had a new blanket before next winter, to keep her from the cold and the rheumatism. She had the rheumatism sadly, last winter, sir; and there is a blanket in this street, that would be just the thing for her."

"She shall have it then; and," continued the gentleman, "I will do something more for you—Do you like to be employed, or to be idle, best?"

"We like to have something to do always if we could, sir," said Paul; "but we are forced to be idle sometimes, because grandmother has not always things for us to do, that we *can* do well."

"Should you like to learn how to make such baskets as these?" said the gentleman, pointing to one of the Dunstable straw-baskets.

"O, very much!" said Paul.

"Very much!" said Anne.

"Then I should like to teach you how to make them," said the basket-woman; "for I'm sure of one thing, that you'd behave honestly to me."

The gentleman put a guinea into the good-natured basket-woman's hand, and told her that he knew she could not afford to teach them her trade for nothing.—"I shall come through Dunstable again in a few months," added he: "and I hope to see that you and your scholars are going on well. If I find that they are, I will do something more for you."

"But," said Anne, "we must tell all this to grandmother, and ask her about it; and I'm afraid—though I'm very happy—that it is getting very late, and that we should not stay here any longer."

"It is a fine moonlight-night," said the basket-woman; "and it is not far; I'll walk with you, and see you safe home myself."

The gentleman detained them a few minutes longer, till a messenger, whom he had dispatched to purchase the much-wished-for blanket, returned.

"Your grandmother will sleep well under this good blanket, I hope," said the gentleman, as he gave it into Paul's opened arms; "it has been obtained for her by the honesty of her adopted children."

Waste Not, Want Not; or, Two Strings to Your Bow.

MR. GRESHAM, a Bristol merchant, who had, by honourable industry and economy, accumulated a considerable fortune, retired from business to a new house which he had built upon the Downs, near Clifton. Mr. Gresham, however, did not imagine, that a new house alone could make him happy: he did not purpose to live in idleness and extravagance, for such a life would have been equally incompatible with his habits and his principles. He was fond of children, and as he had no sons, he determined to adopt one of his relations. He had two nephews, and he invited both of them to his house, that he might have an opportunity of judging of their dispositions, and of the habits which they had acquired.

Hal and Benjamin, Mr. Gresham's nephews, were about ten years old; they had been educated very differently; Hal was the son of the elder branch of the family; his father was a gentleman, who spent rather more than he could afford; and Hal, from the example of the servants in his father's family, with whom he had passed the first years of his childhood, learned to waste more of every thing than he used. He had been told, that "gentlemen should be above being careful and saving:" and he had unfortunately imbibed a notion, that extravagance is the sign of a generous, and economy of an avaricious, disposition.

Benjamin,* on the contrary, had been taught habits of care and foresight: his father had but a very small fortune, and was anxious that his son should early learn, that economy ensures independence, and sometimes puts it in the power of those who are not very rich to be very generous.

The morning after these two boys arrived at their uncle's, they were eager to see all the rooms in the house. Mr. Gresham accompanied them, and attended to their remarks and exclamations.

"O! what an excellent motto!" exclaimed Ben, when he read the following words, which were written in large characters over the chimney-piece, in his uncle's spacious kitchen:—

WASTE NOT, WANT NOT.

"Waste not, want not!" repeated his cousin Hal, in rather a contemptuous tone; "I think it looks stingy to servants; and no gentleman's servants, cooks especially, would like to have such a mean motto always staring them in the face."

Ben, who was not so conversant as his cousin in the ways of cooks and gentlemen's servants, made no reply to these observations.

Mr. Gresham was called away whilst his nephews were looking at the other rooms in the house. Some time afterwards he heard their voices in the hall.

"Boys," said he, "what are you doing there?"

"Nothing, sir," said Hal; "you were called away from us; and we did not know which way to go."

"And have you nothing to do?" said Mr. Gresham.

"No, sir, nothing," answered Hal, in a careless tone, like one who was well content with the state of habitual idleness.

"No, sir, nothing!" replied Ben, in a voice of lamentation.

"Come," said Mr. Gresham, "if you have nothing to do, lads, will you unpack these two parcels for me?"

The two parcels were exactly alike, both of them well tied up with good whip-cord—

---

* Benjamin, so called from Dr. Benjamin Franklin.

Ben took his parcel to a table, and, after breaking off the sealing-wax, began carefully to examine the knot, and then to untie it. Hal stood still, exactly in the spot where the parcel was put into his hands, and tried first at one corner, and then at another, to pull the string off by force: "I wish these people wouldn't tie up their parcels so tight, as if they were never to be undone," cried he, as he tugged at the cord; and he pulled the knot closer instead of loosening it.

"Ben! why how did ye get yours undone, man?—what's in your parcel?—I wonder what is in mine. I wish I could get this string off—I must cut it."

"O no," said Ben, who now had undone the last knot of his parcel, and who drew out the length of string with exultation, "don't cut it, Hal—look what a nice cord this is, and your's is the same; it's a pity to cut it; *'Waste not, want not!'* you know."

"Pooh!" said Hal, "what signifies a bit of pack-thread?"

"It is whip-cord," said Ben.

"Well, whip-cord! what signifies a bit of whip-cord! you can get a bit of whip-cord twice as long as that for two-pence; and who cares for two-pence! Not I, for one! so here it goes," cried Hal, drawing out his knife; and he cut the cord, precipitately, in sundry places.

"Lads! have you undone the parcels for me?" said Mr. Gresham, opening the parlour door as he spoke.

"Yes, sir," cried Hal; and he dragged off his half cut, half entangled string—"here's the parcel."

"And here's my parcel, uncle; and here's the string," said Ben.

"You may keep the string for your pains," said Mr. Gresham.

"Thank you, sir," said Ben: "what an excellent whip-cord it is!"

"And you, Hal," continued Mr. Gresham—"you may keep your string too, if it will be of any use to you."

"It will be of no use to me, thank you, sir," said Hal.

"No, I am afraid not, if this be it," said his uncle, taking up the jagged, knotted remains of Hal's cord.

A few days after this, Mr. Gresham gave to each of his nephews a new top.

"But how's this?" said Hal; "these tops have no strings; what shall we do for strings?"

"I have a string that will do very well for mine," said Ben; and he pulled out of his pocket the fine long, smooth string, which had tied up the parcel. With this he soon set up his top, which spun admirably well.

"O, how I wish that I had but a string!" said Hal: "what shall I do for a string? I'll tell you what: I can use the string that goes round my hat."

"But then," said Ben, "what will you do for a hat-band?"

"I'll manage to do without one," said Hal: and he took the string off his hat for his top. It soon was worn through; and he split his top by driving the peg too tightly into it. His cousin, Ben, let him set up his the next day; but Hal was not more fortunate or more careful when he meddled with other people's things than when he managed his own. He had scarcely played half an hour before he split it, by driving in the peg too violently.

Ben bore this misfortune with good-humour—"Come," said he, "it can't be helped! but give me the string, because *that* may still be of use for something else."

It happened some time afterwards, that a lady, who had been intimately acquainted with Hal's mother at Bath, that is to say, who had frequently met her at the card-table during the winter, now arrived at Clifton. She was informed by his mother that Hal was at Mr. Gresham's; and her sons, who were *friends* of his, came to see him, and invited him to spend the next day with them.

Hal joyfully accepted the invitation. He was always glad to go out to dine, because it gave him something to do, something to think of, or, at least, something to say. Besides this, he had been educated to think it was a fine thing to visit fine people; and lady Diana Sweepstakes (for that was the name of his mother's acquaintance) was a very fine lady; and her two sons intended to be very *great* gentlemen.

He was in a prodigious hurry when these young gentlemen knocked at his uncle's door the next day; but just as he got to the hall-door little Patty called to him from the top of the stairs, and told him that he had dropped his pocket-handkerchief.

"Pick it up, then, and bring it to me, quick, can't you, child," cried Hal, "for lady Di.'s sons are waiting for me?"

Little Patty did not know anything about lady Di.'s sons; but as she was very good-natured, and saw that her cousin Hal was, for some reason or other, in a desperate hurry, she ran down stairs as fast as she possibly could towards the landing-place, where the handkerchief lay:—but alas! before she reached the handkerchief, she fell, rolling down a whole flight of stairs; and, when her fall was at last stopped by the landing-place, she did not cry, but she writhed, as if she was in great pain.

"Where are you hurt, my love?" said Mr. Gresham, who came instantly, on hearing the noise of some one falling down stairs.

"Where are you hurt, my dear?"

"Here, papa," said the little girl, touching her ancle, which she had decently covered with her gown: "I believe I am hurt here, but not much," added she, trying to rise; "only it hurts me when I move."

"I'll carry you, don't move then," said her father: and he took her up in his arms.

"My shoe, I've lost one of my shoes," said she. Ben looked for it upon the stairs, and he found it sticking in a loop of whip-cord, which was entangled round one of the balusters. When this cord was drawn forth, it appeared that it was the very same jagged, entangled piece which Hal had pulled off his parcel. He had diverted himself with running up and down stairs, whipping the balusters with it, as he thought he could convert it to no better use; and with his usual carelessness, he at last left it hanging just where he happened to throw it when the dinner-bell rang. Poor little Patty's ancle was terribly sprained, and Hal reproached himself for his folly, and would have reproached himself longer, perhaps, if lady Di. Sweepstakes' sons had not hurried him away.

In the evening, Patty could not run about as she used to do; but she sat upon the sofa, and she said that, "she did not feel the pain of her ancle so *much*, whilst Ben was so good as to play at *jack-straws* with her."

"That's right, Ben; never be ashamed of being good-natured to those who are younger and weaker than yourself," said his uncle, smiling at seeing him produce his whip-cord, to indulge his little cousin with a game at her favourite cat's-cradle. "I shall not think you one bit less manly, because I see you playing at cat's-cradle with a little child of six years old."

Hal, however, was not precisely of his uncle's opinion; for when he returned in the evening and saw Ben playing with his little cousin, he could not help smiling contemptuously, and asked if he had been playing at cat's-cradle all night. In a heedless manner he made some enquiries after Patty's sprained ancle, and then he ran on to tell all the news he had heard at lady Diana Sweepstakes'—news which he thought would make him appear a person of vast importance.

"Do you know, uncle—Do you know, Ben," said he—"there's to be the most *famous* doings that ever were heard of upon the Downs here the first day of next month, which will be in a fortnight, thank my stars; I wish the fortnight was over; I shall think of nothing else, I know, till that happy day comes!"

Mr. Gresham inquired why the first of September was to be so much happier than any other day in the year.

"Why," replied Hal, "lady Diana Sweepstakes, you know, is a *famous* rider, and archer, and *all that*—"

"Very likely," said Mr. Gresham, soberly—"but what then?"

"Dear uncle!" cried Hal, "but you shall hear. There's to be a race upon the Downs the first of September, and after the race there's to be an archery meeting for the ladies, and lady Diana Sweepstakes is to be one of *them*. And after the ladies have done shooting—now, Ben, comes the best part of it! we boys are to have our turn, and lady Di. is to give a prize to the best marksman amongst us, of a very handsome bow and arrow! Do you know I've been practising already, and I'll show you to-morrow, as soon as it comes home, the *famous* bow and arrow that lady Diana has given me: but, perhaps," added he, with a scornful laugh, "you like a cat's-cradle better than a bow and arrow."

Ben made no reply to this taunt at the moment; but the next day, when Hal's new bow and arrow came home, he convinced him, that he knew how to use it very well.

"Ben," said his uncle, "you seem to be a good marksman, though you have not boasted of yourself. I'll give you a bow and arrow; and perhaps, if you practise, you may make yourself an archer before the first of September; and, in the mean time, you will not wish the fortnight to be over, for you will have something to do."

"O sir," interrupted Hal, "but if you mean that Ben should put in for the prize, he must have a uniform."

"Why *must* he?" said Mr. Gresham.

"Why, sir, because every body has—I mean every body that's any body;—and lady Diana was talking about the uniform all dinner time, and it's settled all about it except the buttons; the young Sweepstakes are to get theirs made first for patterns; they are to be white, faced with green; and they'll look very handsome, I'm sure; and I shall write to mamma to-night, as lady Diana bid me, about mine; and I shall tell her, to be sure to answer my letter, without fail, by return of the post; and then, if mamma makes no objection, which I know she won't, because she never thinks much about expense, and *all that*—then I shall bespeak my uniform, and get it made by the same tailor that makes for lady Diana and the young Sweepstakes."

"Mercy upon us!" said Mr. Gresham, who was almost stunned by the rapid vociferation with which this long speech about a uniform was pronounced.

"I don't pretend to understand these things," added he, with an air of simplicity, "but we will inquire, Ben, into the necessity of the case; and if it is necessary—or if you think it necessary, that you should have a uniform—why—I'll give you one."

"*You*, uncle!—Will you, *indeed*?" exclaimed Hal, with amazement painted in his countenance. "Well, that's the last thing in the world I should have expected!—You are not at all the sort of person I should have thought would care about a uniform; and now I should have supposed, you'd have thought it extravagant to have a coat on purpose only for one day; and I'm sure lady Diana Sweepstakes thought as I do: for when I told her that motto over your kitchen chimney, WASTE NOT, WANT NOT, she laughed, and said, that I had better not talk to you about uniforms, and that my mother was the proper person to write to about my uniform; but I'll tell lady Diana, uncle, how good you are, and how much she was mistaken."

"Take care how you do that," said Mr. Gresham; "for perhaps the lady was not mistaken."

"Nay, did not you say, just now, you would give poor Ben a uniform?"

"I said, I would, if he thought it necessary to have one."

"O, I'll answer for it, he'll think it necessary," said Hal, laughing, "because it is necessary."

"Allow him, at least, to judge for himself," said Mr. Gresham.

"My dear uncle, but I assure you," said Hal, earnestly, "there's no judging about the matter, because really, upon my word, lady Diana said distinctly, that her sons were to have uniforms, white faced with green, and a green and white cockade in their hats."

"May be so," said Mr. Gresham, still with the same look of calm simplicity; "put on your hats, boys, and come with me. I know a gentleman, whose sons are to be at this archery meeting; and we will inquire into all the particulars from him. Then, after we have seen him (it is not eleven o'clock yet), we shall have time enough to walk on to Bristol, and choose the cloth for Ben's uniform, if it is necessary."

"I cannot tell what to make of all he says," whispered Hal, as he reached down his hat; "do you think, Ben, he means to give you this uniform, or not?"

"I think," said Ben, "that he means to give me one, if it is necessary; or, as he said, if I think it is necessary."

"And that, to be sure, you will; won't you? or else you'll be a great fool, I know, after all I've told you. How can any one in the world know so much about the matter as I, who have dined with lady Diana Sweepstakes but yesterday, and heard all about it, from beginning to end? and as for this gentleman that we are going to, I'm sure, if he knows anything about the matter, he'll say exactly the same as I do."

"We shall hear," said Ben, with a degree of composure, which Hal could by no means comprehend, when a uniform was in question.

The gentleman upon whom Mr. Gresham called, had three sons, who were all to be at this archery meeting; and they unanimously assured him, in the presence of Hal and Ben, that they had never thought of buying uniforms for this grand occasion; and that, amongst the number of their acquaintance, they knew of but three boys, whose friends intended to be at such *an unnecessary* expense. Hal stood amazed—"Such are the varieties of opinion upon all the grand affairs of life," said Mr. Gresham, looking at his nephews —"What amongst one set of people you hear asserted to be absolutely necessary, you will hear, from another set of people, is quite unnecessary. All that can be done, my dear boys, in these difficult cases, is to judge for yourselves, which opinions, and which people, are the most reasonable."

Hal, who had been more accustomed to think of what was fashionable than of what was reasonable, without at all considering the good sense of what his uncle said to him, replied, with childish petulance, "Indeed, sir, I don't know what other people think; I only know what lady Diana Sweepstakes said."

The name of lady Diana Sweepstakes, Hal thought, must impress all present with respect; he was highly astonished, when, as he looked round, he saw a smile of contempt upon every one's countenance; and he was yet further bewildered when he heard her spoken of as a very silly, extravagant, ridiculous woman, whose opinion no prudent person would ask upon any subject, and whose example was to be shunned, instead of being imitated.

"Aye, my dear Hal," said his uncle, smiling at his look of amazement, "these are some of the things that young people must learn from experience. All the world do not agree in opinion about characters: you will hear the same person admired in one company, and blamed in another; so that we must still come round to the same point, *Judge for yourself.*"

Hal's thoughts were, however, at present, too full of the uniform to allow his judgment to act with perfect impartiality. As soon as their visit was over, and all the time they walked down the hill from Prince's-buildings, towards Bristol, he continued to repeat nearly the same arguments, which he had formerly used, respecting necessity, the uniform, and lady Diana Sweepstakes.

To all this Mr. Gresham made no reply; and longer had the young gentlemen expatiated upon the subject, which had so strongly seized upon his imagination, had not his senses been forcibly assailed at this instant by the delicious odours and tempting sight of certain cakes and jellies in a pastry-cook's shop.

"O uncle," said he, as his uncle was going to turn the corner to pursue the road to Bristol, "look at those jellies!" pointing to a confectioner's shop; "I must buy some of those good things; for I have got some halfpence in my pocket."

"Your having halfpence in your pocket is an excellent reason for eating," said Mr. Gresham, smiling.

"But I really am hungry," said Hal; "you know, uncle, it is a good while since breakfast."

His uncle, who was desirous to see his nephews act without restraint, that he might judge of their characters, bid them do as they pleased.

"Come, then, Ben, if you've any halfpence in your pocket."

"I'm not hungry," said Ben.

"I suppose *that* means, that you've no halfpence," said Hal, laughing, with the look of superiority, which he had been taught to think *the rich* might assume towards those who were convicted either of poverty or economy.

"Waste not, want not," said Ben to himself. Contrary to his cousin's surmise, he happened to have two pennyworth of halfpence actually in his pocket.

At the very moment Hal stepped into the pastry-cook's shop, a poor industrious man, with a wooden leg, who usually sweeps the dirty corner of the walk which turns at this spot to the Wells, held his hat to Ben, who, after glancing his eye at the petitioner's well-worn broom, instantly produced his two-pence. "I wish I had more halfpence for you, my good man," said he; "but I've only two-pence."

Hal came out of Mr. Millar's, the confectioner's shop, with a hatful of cakes in his hand.

Mr. Millar's dog was sitting on the flags before the door; and he looked up, with a wistful, begging eye, at Hal, who was eating a queen-cake.

Hal, who was wasteful even in his good-nature, threw a whole queen-cake to the dog, who swallowed it for a single mouthful.

"There goes two-pence in the form of a queen-cake," said Mr. Gresham.

Hal next offered some of his cakes to his uncle and cousin; but they thanked him, and refused to eat any, because, they said, they were not hungry; so he ate and ate, as he walked along, till at last he stopped, and said, "This bun tastes so bad after the queen-cakes, I can't bear it!" and he was going to fling it from him into the river.

"Oh, it is a pity to waste that good bun; we may be glad of it yet," said Ben; "give it to me, rather than throw it away."

"Why, I thought you said you were not hungry," said Hal.

"True, I am not hungry now; but that is no reason why I should never be hungry again."

"Well, there is the cake for you; take it, for it has made me sick; and I don't care what becomes of it."

Ben folded the refuse bit of his cousin's bun in a piece of paper, and put it into his pocket.

"I'm beginning to be exceedingly tired, or sick, or something," said Hal, "and as there is a stand of coaches somewhere hereabouts, had we not better take a coach, instead of walking all the way to Bristol?"

"For a stout archer?" said Mr. Gresham; "you are more easily tired than one might have expected. However, with all my heart; let us take a coach; for Ben asked me to show him the cathedral yesterday, and I believe I should find it rather too much for me to walk so far, though I am not sick with eating good things."

"*The cathedral!*" said Hal, after he had been seated in the coach about a quarter of an hour, and had somewhat recovered from his sickness. "The cathedral! Why, are we only going to Bristol to see the cathedral? I thought we came out to see about a uniform."

There was a dulness and melancholy kind of stupidity in Hal's countenance, as he pronounced these words like one wakening from a dream, which made both his uncle and cousin burst out a laughing.

"Why," said Hal, who was now piqued, "I'm sure you *did* say, uncle, you would go to Mr. * * *'s, to choose the cloth for the uniform."

"Very true: and so I will," said Mr. Gresham; "but we need not make a whole morning's work, need we, of looking at a piece of cloth? Cannot we see a uniform and a cathedral both in one morning?"

They went first to the cathedral. Hal's head was too full of the uniform to take any notice of the painted window, which immediately caught Ben's unembarrassed attention. He looked at the large stained figures on the Gothic window; and he observed their coloured shadows on the floor and walls.

Mr. Gresham, who perceived that he was eager on all subjects to gain information, took this opportunity of telling him several things about the lost art of painting on glass, Gothic arches, &c., which Hal thought extremely tiresome.

"Come! come! we shall be late, indeed," said Hal; "surely you've looked long enough, Ben, at this blue and red window."

"I'm only thinking about these coloured shadows," said Ben.

"I can show you, when we go home, Ben," said his uncle, "an entertaining paper on such shadows."*

"Hark!" cried Ben, "did you hear that noise?"

They all listened, and heard a bird singing in the cathedral.

"It's our old robin, sir," said the lad, who had opened the cathedral door for them.

"Yes," said Mr. Gresham, "there he is, boys—look—perched upon the organ; he often sits there, and sings whilst the organ is playing." "And," continued the lad who showed the cathedral, "he has lived here this many winters;† they say he is fifteen years old; and he is so tame, poor fellow, that if I had a bit of bread he'd come down and feed in my hand."

"I've a bit of bun here," cried Ben, joyfully, producing the remains of the bun which Hal but an hour before would have thrown away. "Pray let us see the poor robin eat out of your hand."

The lad crumbled the bun, and called to the robin, who fluttered and chirped, and seemed rejoiced at the sight of the bread; but yet he did not come down from his pinnacle on the organ.

"He is afraid of *us*," said Ben; "he is not used to eat before strangers, I suppose."

"Ah, no, sir," said the young man, with a deep sigh, "that is not the thing: he is used enough to eat afore company; time was, he'd have come down for me, before ever so many fine folks, and have eat his crumbs out of my hand, at my first call; but, poor fellow, it's not his fault now: he does not know me now, sir, since my accident, because of this great black patch."

The young man put his hand to his right eye, which was covered with a huge black patch.

Ben asked what *accident* he meant; and the lad told him that, a few weeks ago, he had lost the sight of his eye by the stroke of a stone, which reached him as he was passing under the rocks of Clifton, unluckily, when the workmen were blasting.

"I don't mind so much for myself, sir," said the lad; "but I can't work so well now, as I used to do before my accident, for my old mother, who has had *a stroke* of the palsy; and I've a many little brothers and sisters, not well able yet to get their own livelihood, though they be willing as willing can be."

"Where does your mother live?" said Mr. Gresham.

"Hard by, sir, just close to the church here: it was *her* that always had the showing of it to strangers, till she lost the use of her poor limbs."

"Shall we, may we, uncle, go that way?—This is the house: is it not?" said Ben, when they went out of the cathedral.

They went into the house: it was rather a hovel than a house; but, poor as it was, it was as neat as misery could make it.

The old woman was sitting up in her wretched bed, winding worsted; four meagre, ill-clothed, pale children were all busy, some of them sticking pins in paper for the pin-maker, and others sorting rags for the paper-maker.

"What a horrid place it is!" said Hal, sighing; "I did not know there were such shock-

---

* Vide Priestley's History on Vision, chapter on coloured shadows.
† This is true.

ing places in the world. I've often seen terrible-looking, tumble-down places, as we drove through the town in mama's carriage; but then I did not know who lived in them; and I never saw the inside of any of them. It is very dreadful, indeed, to think that people are forced to live in this way. I wish mamma would send me some more pocket-money, that I might do something for them. I had half-a-crown; but," continued he, feeling in his pockets, "I'm afraid I spent the last shilling of it this morning, upon those cakes that made me sick. I wish I had my shilling now, I'd give it to *these poor people.*"

Ben, though he was all this time silent, was as sorry as his talkative cousin for all these poor people. But there was some difference between the sorrow of these two boys.

Hal, after he was again seated in the hackney-coach, and had rattled through the busy streets of Bristol for a few minutes, quite forgot the spectacle of misery which he had seen: and the gay shops in Wine-street, and the idea of his green and white uniform, wholly occupied his imagination.

"Now for our uniforms!" cried he, as he jumped eagerly out of the coach, when his uncle stopped at the woollen-draper's door.

"Uncle," said Ben, stopping Mr. Gresham before he got out of the carriage, "I don't think a uniform is at all necessary for me. I'm very much obliged to you; but I would rather not have one. I have a very good coat; and I think it would be waste."

"Well, let me get out of the carriage, and we will see about it," said Mr. Gresham; "perhaps the sight of the beautiful green and white cloth, and the epaulettes (have you ever considered the epaulettes?) may tempt you to change your mind."

"O no," said Ben, laughing; "I shall not change my mind."

The green cloth, and the white cloth, and the epaulettes, were produced, to Hal's infinite satisfaction. His uncle took up a pen, and calculated for a few minutes; then, showing the back of the letter, upon which he was writing, to his nephews, "Cast up these sums, boys," said he, "and tell me whether I am right."

"Ben, do you do it," said Hal, a little embarrassed: "I am not quick at figures."

Ben *was*, and he went over his uncle's calculation very expeditiously.

"It is right, is it?" said Mr. Gresham.

"Yes, sir, quite right."

"Then by this calculation, I find I could for less than half the money your uniforms would cost purchase for each of you boys a warm great-coat, which you will want, I have a notion, this winter upon the Downs."

"O sir," said Hal, with an alarmed look; "but it is not winter *yet;* it is not cold weather yet. We sha'n't want great-coats *yet.*"

"Don't you remember how cold we were, Hal, the day before yesterday, in that sharp wind, when we were flying our kite upon the Downs?—and winter will come, though it is not come yet—I am sure, I should like to have a good warm great-coat very much."

Mr. Gresham took six guineas out of his purse; and he placed three of them before Hal, and three before Ben.

"Young gentlemen," said he, "I believe your uniforms would come to about three guineas a-piece. Now I will lay out this money for you just as you please: Hal, what say you?"

"Why, sir," said Hal, "a great-coat is a good thing, to be sure; and then, after the great-coat, as you said it would only cost half as much as the uniform, there would be some money to spare, would not there?"

"Yes, my dear, about five-and-twenty shillings."

"Five-and-twenty shillings! I could buy and do a great many things, to be sure, with five-and-twenty shillings; but then, *the thing is*, I must go without the uniform, if I have the great-coat."

"Certainly," said his uncle.

"Ah!" said Hal, sighing as he looked at the epaulettes, "uncle, if you would not be displeased, if I choose the uniform——"

"I shall not be displeased at your choosing whatever you like best," said Mr. Gresham.

"Well, then, thank you, sir, I think I had better have the uniform, because if I have not the uniform now directly, it will be of no use to me, as the archery meeting is the week after next, you know; and as to the great-coat, perhaps, between this time and the *very* cold weather, which, perhaps, won't be till Christmas, papa will buy a great-coat for me; and I'll ask mamma to give me some pocket-money to give away, and she will perhaps."

To all this conclusive conditional reasoning, which depended upon *perhaps*, three times repeated, Mr. Gresham made no reply; but he immediately bought the uniform for Hal, and desired that it should be sent to lady Diana Sweepstakes' sons' tailor, to be made up. The measure of Hal's happiness was now complete.

"And how am I to lay out the three guineas for you, Ben?" said Mr. Gresham; "speak, what do you wish for first?"

"A great-coat, uncle, if you please."

Mr. Gresham bought the coat; and after it was paid for, five-and-twenty shillings of Ben's three guineas remained.

"What's next, my boy?" said his uncle.

"Arrows, uncle, if you please: three arrows."

"My dear, I promised you a bow and arrows."

"No, uncle, you only said a bow."

"Well, I meant a bow and arrows. I'm glad you are so exact, however. It is better to claim less than more than what is promised. The three arrows you shall have. But go on; how shall I dispose of these five-and-twenty shillings for you?"

"In clothes, if you will be so good, uncle, for that poor boy, who has the great black patch on his eye."

"I always believed," said Mr. Gresham, shaking hands with Ben, "that economy and generosity were the best friends, instead of being enemies, as some silly, extravagant people would have us think them. Choose the poor blind boy's coat, my dear nephew, and pay for it. There's no occasion for my praising you about the matter; your best reward is in your own mind, child; and you want no other, or I'm mistaken. Now jump into the coach, boys, and let's be off. We shall be late, I'm afraid," continued he, as the coach drove on; "but I must let you stop, Ben, with your goods, at the poor boy's door."

When they came to the house, Mr. Gresham opened the coach door, and Ben jumped out with his parcel under his arm.

"Stay, stay! you must take me with you," said his pleased uncle; "I like to see people made happy, as well as you do."

"And so do I too!" said Hal; "let me come with you. I almost wish my uniform was not gone to the tailor's, so I do."

And when he saw the look of delight and gratitude with which the poor boy received the clothes which Ben gave him; and when he heard the mother and children thank him, Hal sighed, and said, "Well, I hope mamma will give me some more pocket-money soon."

Upon his return home, however, the sight of the *famous* bow and arrow which lady Diana Sweepstakes had sent him, recalled to his imagination all the joys of his green and white uniform; and he no longer wished that it had not been sent to the tailor's.

"But I don't understand, cousin Hal," said little Patty, "why you call this bow a *famous* bow: you say *famous* very often; and I don't know exactly what it means—a *famous* uniform—*famous* doings—I remember you said there are to be *famous* doings the first of September upon the Downs—What does *famous* mean?"

"O, why *famous* means——Now don't you know what *famous* means?——It means ——It is a word that people say——It is the fashion to say it——It means—it means *famous.*"

Patty laughed and said, "*This* does not explain it to me."

"No," said Hal, "nor can it be explained: if you don't understand it, that's not my fault: every body but little children, I suppose, understands it; but there's no explaining *those sort* of words, if you don't *take them* at once. There's to be *famous* doings upon the Downs the first of September; that is, grand, fine.—In short, what does it signify talking any longer, Patty, about the matter?—Give me my bow; for I must go out upon the Downs, and practise."

Ben accompanied him with the bow and the three arrows which his uncle had now given to him; and every day these two boys went out upon the Downs, and practised shooting with indefatigable perseverance. Where equal pains are taken, success is usually found to be pretty nearly equal. Our two archers, by constant practice, became expert marksmen; and before the day of trial they were so exactly matched in point of dexterity, that it was scarcely possible to decide which was superior.

The long-expected first of September at length arrived. "What sort of day is it?" was the first question that was asked by Hal and Ben, the moment that they awakened.

The sun shone bright; but there was a sharp and high wind.

"Ha!" said Ben, "I shall be glad of my good great-coat to-day; for I've a notion it will be rather cold upon the Downs, especially when we are standing still, as we must, whilst all the people are shooting."

"O, never mind! I don't think I shall feel it cold at all," said Hal, as he dressed himself in his new white and green uniform: and he viewed himself with much complacency.

"Good morning to you, uncle; how do you do?" said he, in a voice of exultation, when he entered the breakfast-room.

How do you do? seemed rather to mean, How do [you] like me in my uniform?

And his uncle's cool "Very well, I thank you, Hal," disappointed him, as it seemed only to say, Your uniform makes no difference in my opinion of you.

Even little Patty went on eating her breakfast much as usual, and talked of the pleasure of walking with her father to the Downs, and of all the little things which interested her; so that Hal's epaulettes were not the principal object in any one's imagination but his own.

"Papa," said Patty, "as we go up the hill where there is so much red mud, I must take care to pick my way nicely; and I must hold up my frock, as you desired me; and perhaps you will be so good, if I am not troublesome, to lift me over the very bad place where there are no stepping-stones. My ancle is entirely well, and I'm glad of that, or else I should not be able to walk so far as the Downs. How good you were to me, Ben, when I was in pain, the day I sprained my ancle! you played at jack-straws, and at cat's-cradle with me—O, that puts me in mind—Here are your gloves, which I asked you that night to let me mend. I've been a great while about them, but are not they very neatly mended, papa?—look at the sewing."

"I am not a very good judge of sewing, my dear little girl," said Mr. Gresham, examining the work with a close and scrupulous eye; "but in my opinion, here is one stitch that is rather too long; the white teeth are not quite even."

"O papa, I'll take out that long tooth in a minute," said Patty, laughing; "I did not think that you would have observed it so soon."

"I would not have you trust to my blindness," said her father, stroking her head fondly: "I observe every thing. I observe, for instance, that you are a grateful little girl, and that you are glad to be of use to those who have been kind to you; and for this I forgive you the long stitch."

"But it's out, it's out, papa," said Patty; "and the next time your gloves want mending, Ben, I'll mend them better."

"They are very nice, I think," said Ben, drawing them on; "and I am much obliged to you; I was just wishing I had a pair of gloves to keep my fingers warm to-day, for I never can shoot well when my hands are numbed. Look, Hal—you know how ragged these gloves were; you said they were good for nothing but to throw away; now look, there's not a hole in them," said he, spreading his fingers.

"Now, is it not very extraordinary," said Hal to himself, "that they should go on so long talking about an old pair of gloves, without scarcely saying a word about my new uniform? Well, the young Sweepstakes and lady Diana will talk enough about it; that's one comfort."

"Is not it time to think of setting out, sir?" said Hal to his uncle; "the company, you know, are to meet at the Ostrich at twelve, and the race to begin at one, and lady Diana's horses, I know, were ordered to be at the door at ten."

Mr. Stephen, the butler, here interrupted the hurrying young gentleman in his calculations—"There's a poor lad, sir, below, with a great black patch on his right eye, who is come from Bristol, and wants to speak a word with the young gentlemen, if you please. I told him, they were just going out with you, but he says he won't detain them above half a minute."

"Show him up, show him up," said Mr. Gresham.

"But I suppose," said Hal, with a sigh, "that Stephen mistook, when he said the young *gentlemen;* he only wants to see Ben, I dare say; I'm sure he has no reason to want to see me."

"Here he comes—O Ben, he is dressed in the new coat you gave him," whispered Hal, who was really a good-natured boy, though extravagant. "How much better he looks than he did in the ragged coat! Ah! he looked at you first, Ben;—and well he may!"

The boy bowed without any cringing servility, but with an open, decent freedom in his manner, which expressed that he had been obliged, but that he knew his young benefactor was not thinking of the obligation. He made as little distinction as possible between his bows to the two cousins.

"As I was sent with a message, by the clerk of our parish to Redland Chapel, out on the Downs, to-day, sir," said he to Mr. Gresham, "knowing your house lay in my way, my mother, sir, bid me call, and make bold to offer the young gentlemen two little worsted balls that she had worked for them," continued the lad, pulling out of his pocket two worsted balls worked in green and orange-coloured stripes: "they are but poor things, sir, she bid me say, to look at; but considering she had but one hand to work with, and *that* her left hand, you'll not despise 'em, we hopes."

He held the balls to Ben and Hal.—"They are both alike, gentlemen," said he; "if you'll be pleased to take 'em, they are better than they look, for they bound higher than your head; I cut the cork round for the inside myself, which was all I could do."

"They are nice balls, indeed; we are much obliged to you," said the boys, as they received them, and they proved them immediately. The balls struck the floor with a delightful sound, and rebounded higher than Mr. Gresham's head. Little Patty clapped her hands joyfully: but now a thundering double rap at the door was heard.

"The master Sweepstakes, sir," said Stephen, "are come for master Hal; they say, that all the young gentlemen who have archery uniforms are to walk together in a body, I think they say, sir; and they are to parade along the Well-Walk, they desired me to say, sir, with a drum and fife, and so up the hill by Prince's Place, and all to go upon the Downs together, to the place of meeting. I am not sure I'm right, sir, for both the young gentlemen spoke at once, and the wind is very high at the street door, so that I could not well make out all they said; but I believe this is the sense of it."

"Yes, yes," said Hal, eagerly, "it's all right; I know that is just what was settled the day I dined at lady Diana's; and lady Diana and a great party of gentlemen are to ride ——"

"Well, that is nothing to the purpose," interrupted Mr. Gresham. "Don't keep the master Sweepstakes waiting; decide—do you choose to go with them, or with us?"

"Sir—uncle—sir, you know, since all the *uniforms* agreed to go together—"

"Off with you then, Mr. Uniform, if you mean to go," said Mr. Gresham.

Hal ran down stairs in such a hurry that he forgot his bow and arrows.—Ben discovered this when he went to fetch his own; and the lad from Bristol, who had been ordered by Mr. Gresham to eat his breakfast before he proceeded to Redland Chapel, heard Ben talking about his cousin's bow and arrows.

"I know," said Ben, "he will be sorry not to have his bow with him, because here are the green knots tied to it, to match his cockade; and he said that the boys were all to carry their bows as part of the show."

"If you'll give me leave, sir," said the poor Bristol lad, "I shall have plenty of time; and I'll run down to the Well-Walk after the young gentleman, and take him his bow and arrows."

"Will you? I shall be much obliged to you," said Ben; and away went the boy with the bow that was ornamented with green ribands.

The public walk leading to the Wells was full of company. The windows of all the houses in St. Vincent's parade were crowded with well-dressed ladies, who were looking out in expectation of the archery procession. Parties of gentlemen and ladies, and a motley crowd of spectators, were seen moving backwards and forwards under the rocks, on the opposite side of the water. A barge, with coloured streamers flying, was waiting to take up a party, who were going upon the water. The bargemen rested upon their oars, and gazed with broad faces of curiosity on the busy scene that appeared upon the public walk.

The archers and archeresses were now drawn up on the flags under the semi-circular piazza just before Mrs. Yearsley's library. A little band of children, who had been mustered by lady Diana Sweepstakes' *spirited exertions,* closed the procession. They were now all in readiness. The drummer only waited for her ladyship's signal; and the archers' corps only waited for her ladyship's word of command to march.

"Where are your bow and arrows, my little man?" said her ladyship to Hal, as she reviewed her Lillyputian regiment. "You can't march, man, without your arms!"

Hal had despatched a messenger for his forgotten bow, but the messenger returned not; he looked from side to side in great distress—"O, there's my bow coming, I declare!" cried he—"look, I see the bow and the ribands; look now, between the trees, Charles Sweepstakes, on the Hot-well-Walk; it is coming!"

"But you've kept us all waiting a confounded time," said his impatient friend.

"It is that good-natured poor fellow from Bristol, I protest, that has brought it to me; I'm sure I don't deserve it from him," said Hal to himself, when he saw the lad with the black patch on his eye running quite out of breath towards him with his bow and arrows.

"Fall back, my good friend, fall back," said the military lady, as soon as he had delivered the bow to Hal: "I mean stand out of the way, for your great patch cuts no figure amongst us. Don't follow so close, now, as if you belonged to us, pray."

The poor boy had no ambition to partake the triumph; he *fell back* as soon as he understood the meaning of the lady's words. The drum beat, the fife played, the archers marched, the spectators admired. Hal stepped proudly, and felt as if the eyes of the whole universe were upon his epaulettes, or upon the facings of his uniform; whilst all the time he was considered only as part of a show. The walk appeared much shorter than usual; and he was extremely sorry, that lady Diana, when they were half way up the hill leading to Prince's Place, mounted her horse, because the road was dirty, and all the gentlemen and ladies, who accompanied her, followed her example, "We can leave the children to walk, you know," said she to the gentleman who helped her to mount her horse. "I must call to some of them, though, and leave orders where they are to *join.*"

She beckoned: and Hal, who was foremost, and proud to show his alacrity, ran on to receive her ladyship's orders. Now, as we have before observed, it was a sharp and windy day; and though lady Diana Sweepstakes was actually speaking to him, and looking at him, he could not prevent his nose from wanting to be blowed: he pulled out his handkerchief, and out rolled the new ball, which had been given to him just before he left home, and which, according to his usual careless habit, he had stuffed into his pocket in a hurry. "O, my new ball!" cried he, as he ran after it. As he stooped to pick it up, he let go his hat, which he had hitherto held on with anxious care; for the hat, though it had a fine green and white cockade, had no band or string round it. The string, as we may recollect, our wasteful hero had used in spinning his top. The hat was too large for his head without this band; a sudden gust of wind blew it off—lady Diana's horse started, and reared. She was a *famous* horsewoman, and sat him to the admiration of all beholders; but there was a puddle of red clay and water in this spot, and her ladyship's uniform-habit was a sufferer by the accident.

"Careless brat!" said she, "Why can't he keep his hat upon his head?"

In the mean time, the wind blew the hat down the hill, and Hal ran after it, amidst the laughter of his kind friends, the young Sweepstakes, and the rest of the little regiment. The hat was lodged, at length, upon a bank. Hal pursued it: he thought this bank was hard, but, alas! the moment he set his foot upon it, the foot sank. He tried to draw it back, his other foot slipped, and he fell prostrate, in his green and white uniform, into the treacherous bed of red mud. His companions, who had halted upon the top of the hill, stood laughing spectators of his misfortune.

It happened that the poor boy with the black patch upon his eye, who had been ordered by lady Diana to *"fall back"* and to *"keep at a distance,"* was now coming up the hill; and the moment he saw our fallen hero, he hastened to his assistance. He dragged poor Hal, who was a deplorable spectacle, out of the red mud; the obliging mistress of a lodging-house, as soon as she understood that the young gentleman was nephew to Mr. Gresham, to whom she had formerly let her house, received Hal, covered as he was with dirt.

The poor Bristol lad hastened to Mr. Gresham's for clean stockings and shoes for Hal. He was unwilling to give up his uniform; it was rubbed and rubbed, and a spot here and there was washed out; and he kept continually repeating—"When it's dry it will all brush off: when it's dry it will all brush off, won't it?" But soon the fear of being too late at the archery-meeting began to balance the dread of appearing in his stained habiliments: and he now as anxiously repeated, whilst the woman held the wet coat to the fire, "O, I shall be too late; indeed I shall be too late; make haste; it will never dry; hold it nearer—nearer to the fire: I shall lose my turn to shoot; O, give me the coat; I don't mind how it is, if I can but get it on."

Holding it nearer and nearer to the fire dried it quickly, to be sure, but it shrank it also so that it was no easy matter to get the coat on again.

However, Hal, who did not see the red splashes, which, in spite of all the operations, were too visible upon his shoulders and upon the skirts of his white coat behind, was pretty well satisfied to observe, that there was not one spot upon the facings. "Nobody," said he, "will take notice of my coat behind, I dare say. I think it looks as smart almost as ever!" and under this persuasion our young archer resumed his bow—his bow with green ribands now no more! and he pursued his way to the Downs.

All his companions were far out of sight. "I suppose," said he to his friend with the black patch—"I suppose my uncle and Ben had left home before you went for the shoes and stockings for me?"

"O yes, sir; the butler said they had been gone to the Downs a matter of a good half hour or more."

Hal trudged on as fast as he possibly could. When he got on the Downs, he saw numbers of carriages, and crowds of people, all going towards the place of meeting, at the Ostrich. He pressed forwards; he was at first so much afraid of being late, that he did not take notice of the mirth his motley appearance excited in all beholders. At length he reached the appointed spot. There was a great crowd of people: in the midst, he heard lady Diana's loud voice betting upon some one who was just going to shoot at the mark.

"So then the shooting is begun, is it?" said Hal. "O, let me in; pray let me into the circle! I'm one of the archers—I am, indeed; don't you see my green and white uniform?"

"Your red and white uniform, you mean," said the man to whom he addressed himself: and the people, as they opened a passage for him, could not refrain from laughing at the mixture of dirt and finery which it exhibited. In vain, when he got into the midst of the formidable circle, he looked to his friends, the young Sweepstakes, for their countenance and support: they were amongst the most unmerciful of the laughers. Lady Diana also seemed more to enjoy than to pity his confusion.

"Why could you not keep your hat upon your head, man?" said she, in her masculine tone. "You have been almost the ruin of my poor uniform-habit; but I've escaped better than you have. Don't stand there in the middle of the circle, or you'll have an arrow in your eyes just now, I've a notion."

Hal looked round in search of better friends—"O, where's my uncle?—where's Ben," said he. He was in such confusion, that, amongst the number of faces, he could scarcely distinguish one from another; but he felt somebody at this moment pull his elbow, and, to his great relief, he heard the friendly voice, and saw the good-natured face, of his cousin Ben.

"Come back; come behind these people," said Ben; "and put on my great-coat; here it is for you."

Right glad was Hal to cover his disgraced uniform with the rough great-coat, which he had formerly despised. He pulled the stained, drooping cockade out of his unfortunate hat; and he was now sufficiently recovered from his vexation to give an intelligible account of his accident to his uncle and Patty, who anxiously inquired what had detained him so long, and what had been the matter. In the midst of the history of his disaster, he was just proving to Patty that his taking the hat-band to spin his top had nothing to do with his misfortune; and he was at the same time endeavouring to refute his uncle's opinion, that the waste of the whip-cord, that tied the parcel, was the original cause of all his evils, when he was summoned to try his skill with his *famous* bow.

"My hands are numbed, I can scarcely feel," said he, rubbing them, and blowing upon the ends of his fingers.

"Come, come," cried young Sweepstakes, "I'm within one inch of the mark; who'll go nearer, I shall like to see. Shoot away, Hal; but first, understand our laws: we settled them before you came on the green. You are to have three shots, with your own bow and your own arrows; and nobody's to borrow or lend under pretence of other bows being better or worse, or under any pretence. Do you hear, Hal?"

This young gentleman had good reasons for being so strict in these laws, as he had observed that none of his companions had such an excellent bow as he had provided for himself. Some of the boys had forgotten to bring more than one arrow with them, and by his cunning regulation, that each person should shoot with his own arrows, many had lost one or two of their shots.

"You are a lucky fellow; you have your three arrows," said young Sweepstakes. "Come, we can't wait whilst you rub your fingers, man—shoot away."

Hal was rather surprised at the asperity with which his friend spoke. He little knew how easily acquaintances, who call themselves friends, can change when their interest comes in the slightest degree in competition with their friendship. Hurried by his impatient rival, and with his hands so much benumbed that he could scarcely feel how to fix the arrow in the string, he drew the bow. The arrow was within a quarter of an inch of master Sweepstakes' mark, which was the nearest that had yet been hit. Hal seized his second arrow—"If I have any luck," said he———But just as he pronounced the word *luck*, and as he bent his bow, the string broke in two, and the bow fell from his hands.

"There, it's all over with you," cried master Sweepstakes, with a triumphant laugh.

"Here's my bow for him and welcome," said Ben.

"No, no, sir; that is not fair; that's against the regulation. You may shoot with your own bow, if you choose it, or you may not, just as you think proper; but you must not lend it, sir."

It was now Ben's turn to make his trial. His first arrow was not successful. His second was exactly as near as Hal's first.

"You have but one more," said master Sweepstakes: "now for it!"

Ben, before he ventured his last arrow, prudently examined the string of his bow; and as he pulled it to try its strength, it cracked.

Master Sweepstakes clapped his hands with loud exultations, and insulting laughter. But his laughter ceased, when our provident hero calmly drew from his pocket an excellent piece of whip-cord.

"The everlasting whip-cord, I declare!" exclaimed Hal, when he saw that it was the very same that had tied up the parcel.

"Yes," said Ben, as he fastened it to his bow, "I put it into my pocket to-day, on purpose, because I thought I might happen to want it."

He drew his bow the third and last time.

"O, papa," cried little Patty, as his arrow hit the mark, "it's the nearest; is not it the nearest?"

Master Sweepstakes, with anxiety, examined the hit. There could be no doubt. Ben was victorious! The bow, the prize bow, was now delivered to him; and Hal, as he looked at the whip-cord, exclaimed, "How *lucky* this whip-cord has been to you, Ben!"

"It is *lucky*, perhaps you mean, that he took care of it," said Mr. Gresham.

"Aye," said Hal, "very true; he might well say, 'Waste not, want not;' it is a good thing to have two strings to one's bow."

Keeper's Travels
in Search of His Master

By EDWARD AUGUSTUS KENDALL

FRONTISPIECE.

KEEPER'S TRAVELS

IN SEARCH OF

His Master.

Ah me ! One moment from thy sight,
That thus my truant eye should stray !

Langhorne.

Philadelphia :

PUBLISHED BY JOHNSON & WARNER,
No. 147, MARKET STREET.

::::::::::
1808.

Edward augustus kendall *(1776–1842) seems to have majored in the juvenile animal story. Besides* Keeper's Travels in Search of His Master *(1798)—his most popular work— he penned* The Crested Wren *(1799),* The Sparrow *(1798),* The Canary Bird *(1799), and* The Swallow *(1800). His more conventional work for children includes* Lessons of Virtue; or, the Book of Happiness *(1801) and* Adventures of Musul; or, The Three Gifts with Other Tales *(1800), printed by Elizabeth Newbery, as were his earlier animal stories.*

The idea for the first-person account of the animal goes back at least to 1751 with Francis Coventry's The History of Pompey the Little; or, The Life and Adventures of a Lapdog. *If Coventry's book was a "canine Gil Blas,"* Keeper's Travels *is its juvenile counterpart which demonstrates that "the more I see of man, the more I like my dog." When a spaniel fawns, the reader is asked to forgive it one of man's vices. Keeper is surprised by occasional human benevolence. The dog even claims that sensibility makes him superior to other animals. All the adventures (being shot or almost hanged) stem from a "single moment of negligence." The moral purpose obtrudes somewhat, but this gave the book its original seal of approval:*

> *The story affords many occasions for the exertion of sensibility; suggests some pertinent criticisms, inculcates strongly the necessity and propriety of tenderness to animals, and impresses on every ductile heart sentiments of gratitude.—The termination is happy. Keeper is found in his peregrinations, caressed by the very lady who afterwards gives her hand to his master. This is poetical justice; and it leaves the heart satisfied that fidelity of attachment, even in brutes, is seldom left altogether unrewarded. (*Lady's Monthly Museum, *1798)*

All the world loves a happy ending. There were five editions by 1809, plus American editions, and the book remained in print until 1879. Keeper's Travels *was popular because, as Mary F. Thwaite (in* From Primer to Pleasure in Reading*) puts it, "Keeper is not a talking animal, but a real dog, one who behaves according to his nature."*

The same cannot be said of Kendall's bird stories, where the picaresque tale in the mouths of birds becomes bathos. The Crested Wren *ends with this pathetic plea: "May I hope that you will grant my other request? Will you guard my golden head from harm? At least, will you refrain from harming it yourself, if we should happen to meet?"*

At least Kendall avoided the excesses of S. J.'s The Life and Adventures of a Fly *(ca. 1789), a first-person account of the life of a fly from its birth at a grocers in Westminster. Besides falling into cisterns and being attacked by spiders, the fly meets benevolent children (girls) and mean children (boys) before penning his autobiography, which he leaves to a friendly writer in the inevitable garret.*

At the very beginning of the nineteenth century a reviewer of The Life and Adventures of a Fly *lamented that "in this book as in so many others of modern date, humanity towards animals is carried to an extreme." Children, it was noted, should not be branded murderers for killing flies. Ironically, the critic who found the animal tale had suddenly gone too far was none other than Sarah Kirby Trimmer, whose* Fabulous Histories *(1786) launched the animal tale for children.*

Keeper's Travels *is reprinted from an American edition (Philadelphia: Johnson and Warner, 1808) from the University of Illinois Library, Urbana, Illinois.*

DEDICATION TO
WILLIAM WEBB KENDALL:

Infans in brachia, &c. &c.

As the field-marshal of Russia is in his cradle the less turbulent character of Patron of Letters may not be prematurely offered to you. You will hereafter learn the use of reading in general: you will find it to be the support of all happiness, and the consolation of all misfortune: but the most extensive benefit that it confers upon mankind is, its continual effort to soften and ennoble the heart, which our intercourse with the world perpetually tends to petrify and debase. Youth, unless its early years have been deplorably abused, is alive to all the feelings of virtue: but,

> "Versed in the commerce of deceit,
> How soon the heart forgets to beat!"
>   LOGAN.

It is the muses' province, then, whether by history, by fable, by song, by admonition, or by reproof, it is the muses' province, to rouse and recall the genuine feelings of nature, which are those of goodness and of truth.

Perpetually employed in the pursuit of some fancied good, we are apt to rush forward careless what we tread upon—what we bruise, crush, and destroy. Hence it is evident that, we are daily prompted to treat with contempt the enjoyments, the comforts, and even the lives of others. This contempt easily introduces us to the perpetration of actual insult, outrage, and oppression.

The **penal statutes* are practical essays on morality, that seem to have succeeded in convincing us that these offences, when offered to mankind, are heinous in the extreme;—for they contain that persuasive argument, a threat of punishment.—But he who murders a sparrow, may assure himself that it is not his virtue that prevents him from murdering a man, when occasion may present itself; his forbearance will be the result of no other sentiment than Fear.

Many exertions are not making to obtain our compassion for the various animals for whom, in common with ourselves, the rain descends, and the sun shines: and I doubt not a rapid alteration of the opinions of mankind will reward these endeavours‡: but I cannot help anticipating the·time, when men shall acknowledge the Rights, instead of bestowing their compassion upon the creatures, whom, with themselves, God made, and made to be happy! If any part of their condition is to be compassionated,—it is that they are liable to the tyranny of man.

To this tyranny, because humble, and because affectionate—for their humility teaches them submission, and their affection, forgiveness—to this tyranny dogs are

---

* The laws under which murder, theft, &c. are punished.
‡ Among these I recommend to you, "An essay on Humanity to Animals:" by Thomas Young, A. M. Fellow of T[r]inity College, Cambridge.—In what is afterwards said, no allusion to that work is intended.—"Pity's Gift: a selection from the writings of Mr. Pratt," I could also wish you to read.

particularly exposed: yet these creatures possess virtues that deserve our esteem, a s[ua]vity of deportment that wins our love, and talents that demand our respect. One of these is the subject of the following pages. You will see some cherish, and some ill-treat him—I know which part you will wish to have acted—and I am happy that you cannot fail of frequent opportunities of displaying it.—Do not, however, be too confident in your untried virtue; that your heart condemns evil in others is no proof that you will not practise it yourself.—It would be shocking indeed, if you could be pleased with wickedness in speculation: but the commission is a different thing. I persuade myself, nevertheless, that frequent emotions of your heart, to reiterate which is the great business of books, will influence your conduct.

You will, probably, hereafter, be better acquainted with Keeper; but it is not to you, alone, I address this book; not for him alone I plead, nor for the race of Dogs only, but for the whole breathing world! I shall be fortunate if I contribute to the happiness of any one of those whom I am proud to call my fellow creatures.

I am yours, very affectionately,
THE AUTHOR.

April, 1798.

CHAPTER I

The Dilemma.

Keeper followed his master not only faithfully, but with care: yet it happened that being at a town in Gloucestershire, on the market day, he was so attentive to half a dozen fowls that were in a basket, standing for sale, that his master was out of sight before our dog could persuade himself to leave the favourite objects of allurement. Recovering himself, at length, he ran with haste and anxiety: but unable to discover the way his master had gone, and prevented by the multitude of people from seeing any person at a distance, the poor thing stood despairingly, looking round to no purpose, and sometimes running every way, in vain. He went back to the fowls where he had first forgotten his duty: he hastened from shamble to shamble, whither he had been with his master, in the course of the day, hoping to find him there again. His misery increased every moment. Accustomed to regard his master as the only source of his happiness; to receive from him his food, and his comforts; to know no pleasure but his smiles, nor any evil but his anger; he stood, now, forlorn, stripped, helpless, and unprotected. The market people at length dispersed; and, as the street became more open, he frequently fancied that he saw the object of his search among the distant passengers: and he spent the greater part of the day in fruitless sallies, to overtake the different persons who bore any resemblance to him, with whom were all his hopes.

It was twilight when, weary and oppressed, both with anxiety, and with hunger, he visited, for the sixth time, the inn at which they had put up, on their entrance of the town. Had they been used to frequent this place, or its neighbourhood, not only our wanderer would have readily found his way to his home-stead; but the hostler would, in all probability, recognising the attendant of a customer, have provided for his wants, and restored him to his owner: but the travellers had never visited the place before. They had journeyed this road for the first time, and their home was in Cambridgeshire; whither the master, after a search as anxious, made with an affection as sincere, and of which it need not be said, that it was equally unsuccessful with that we have described, had now directed his course, frequently looking back for his companion, and pleasing himself with the hope that he should soon be overtaken by him.

Keeper entered the inn with the most disconsolate deportment. He hastened to the apartment in which his master had been accommodated. Disappointed still, he visited the stable where the horses had been lodged; and the kitchen where the servant had refreshed. Here, still unable to discover his master, yet surrounded by towns-men and labourers, [who] were regaling themselves before a large fire, he gave way to little expressions of his sorrow. He uttered those mournful plainings that want no words to render them intelligible: that universal language which is every where understood, by the inhabitant of every region, and by all orders of beings. For nature has so finely attuned the ears of all her creatures, that the sounds of misfortune, and of sorrow, never fail to win attention; and with such skill has she set the notes, that they cannot be misconceived.

This unquietness and solicitude, naturally drew the eyes of the company upon him; and every one inquired whose dog it might be? One thought he had seen him in the market-place, and was certain he did not belong to any of the towns-people. A second *did* think him very like a dog that belonged to a neighbour of his; and really he should have thought it the same, only that the animal he spoke of, died three years before, of old age. Another was almost positive that it belonged to the 'squire: but the hostler contradicted this vehemently. It was no more like any dog of the 'squire's he said, than it was like his grand-mother. The other grew more certain from this contradiction. He particularized the dog he alluded to; and now the whole party joined against him—declaring that he could know nothing of dogs, or he would never have said any such thing. They were all agreed that the breed was quite different. Irritated by this reflection on his knowledge, the disputant thought it impossible to recede from his error. Would his opponents have acknowledged that his opinion was not wrong, as a sportsman, or that the breed was the same in the two dogs, he would willingly have given up the contest: but, as this was not to be granted him, he grew more obstinate than ever, and offered a wager—which has been called *a fool's argument,*—on the question: this was readily excepted, and stakes settled. During this debate each had by turns made Keeper welcome to their hearth, and a partaker of their meal. Relieved from the faintness of hunger, and cheered by the warmth of the fire, Keeper fell asleep, expecting the return of his master. The evening thus passed away as comfortably as his anxiety would permit; and during the night he was sheltered in a warm stable, where the hostler secured him, in order that he might be ready in the morning to determine the wager.

CHAPTER II

The Escape.

KEEPER SLEPT, and recovered himself from the fatigues of the day: but when light began to peep through the crevices of the stable, he rose to seek again the master he had lost. Unable, however, to leave, what was now his prison, he whined a considerable time; 'till he became sleepy again, and, for a short period, forgot his troubles. He would not have been so well satisfied with his lodgment, had it not happened to be the same in which his master's horses had been baited; and on this account he considered himself as, in some degree, at home.

He had not lain many minutes before he was awakened by the opening of the door. He immediately rushed, barking furiously, to repel the intrusion; and the boy, who had attempted to enter, and who was unacquainted with the reasons for the detention of his foe, immediately fled.

Keeper was now at liberty, and he instantly ran into the house, visiting every chamber-door. This search was like his former, unsuccessful; he quitted the inn, unobserved by the hostler; and took the road by which he had the day before, entered the town with his master.

He ran hastily along, without stopping to notice any thing, resolved to seek the house of a friend of his master, on whom they had called during their journey. This was considerably out of the direct homeward way, but here he hoped to find his master; and if he should not, still it was to him the *only* road: because the utmost of his knowledge, correct and surprising as it was, could only help to trace back the very steps he had trodden before.

He had travelled two hours without experiencing any thing that deserves to be recorded, when he entered a large town. He had indeed, received two or three lashes from waggoners and coachmen, unprovoked and without other motives than that the men had whips in their hands, and the dog was unable to avoid or resist their cruelty. Such temptations to the exercise of power, are seldom neglected by the low and ignorant; and there are these in every rank of life. Those who have neither wit nor knowledge, do *mischief* that they may be thought capable of doing *something;* and those to whom no respect is paid, because none is due, love to *insult*, that they may fancy themselves mighty. He had scarcely gone twenty feet into *Tetbury*, when a rabble of idle children began to hoot the forlorn stranger. Dismayed by their noise, he ran forward, and might have escaped their persecution, had not the common inclination to trouble the troubled, induced a band of butchers, and other tradesmen, to join in the hunt. These with a refinement, peculiar to reasoning animals, knew how to render even *virtue* subservient to *evil;* making use therefore of the *obedience* of their dogs they urged them, also to unite in the horrors of the scene.

Keeper found his pursuers gaining upon him, when, seeing a door open, he fled into the house, and tacitly claimed the protection of the place. It may be observed of dogs, that they always regard houses as their sanctuaries; that, when fatigued, lost or in danger, they constantly seek in these for rest and consolation; and that, while other animals shun man and his abodes, dogs seem to place their hopes and their confidence in both.

CHAPTER III

The Refuge.

KEEPER HAD NOW ESCAPED the malice of his tormentors, and lay trembling in the passage of the house; there they might not follow him; for it was occupied by an opulent inhabitant, who would of course resent their intrusion, and whom they dared not offend. Thus the power of the rich acting on the *interests* of the poor, it restrains their vices with energy, and persistency, that no police nor statutes can maintain.

Alarmed by the noise in the streets, the old lady of the house came to enquire the cause. The troop of vagabonds had dispersed; but she found Keeper covered with dirt, and terrified by his danger; and she learned from the servants, the causes of his condition. She encouraged the fugitive, and she offered him food. The first he received with gratitude; but the second, his fright, and his weariness, prevented him from accepting. He was washed from the filth that had been thrown upon him. The lady led him to her own fire, and in an hour he recovered his spirits, his strength, and his beauty. He was invigorated with food, and with caresses; and he acknowledged the blessings by the language of his eyes, and the cheerfulness of his demeanour. Yet, well as he was treated, he did not forget the journey he was about, nor the object of his toil: but he dreaded to leave the house; he heard his pursuers in his fancy; and he started from his dreams to escape them. It was near dinner time, when his protector's daughter, with her children, came to visit her; and Keeper was naturally introduced as a subject of novelty and commiseration. The children soon became familiar with him. They gave him pieces of cake to secure his friendship; and there was beside, something in his nature that made him particularly tender to children: with them he assumed a gentleness that did not always belong to his character. For though never intentionally violent and constantly good-natured, his play was, sometimes, boisterous and rude. This, on such occasions, he laid entirely aside: so that if he had before won protection and succour, by his misfortunes, he might now have secured them by his disposition and his beauty.

Dinner being ended, Keeper followed the children into the garden; where there was a small piece of water, then frozen over, on which his little company were very desirous he should walk, that they might see if he understood scating.

CHAPTER IV

The Accident.

KEEPER WAS PRESENTLY heard scratching at the parlour door; but his importunities were for some moments neglected. He then whined and barked with violence, and with an expression of agony that roused the attention of the company, who opened the door to be released from the noise of his intreaties. This was no sooner done than he rushed from it, panting for breath, and barking earnestly. Finding that he was not followed, he returned again, still restless, and almost frantic. It was some moments before it was recollected, that dogs never behave in that manner without *some* cause; that, though they are not always competent to judge of the extent of the danger they apprehend, their vigilance may be relied on as unremitting; and their warnings regarded as useful: and that the sympathetic sensibility of their nature, enables them to distinguish, owing to their intimacy with man, between his welfare and his disasters. Calling therefore to mind that the children were in the garden, the whole company now followed Keeper, who ran and returned, several times, before they could reach the spot, where, to their horror, they beheld only one of the three children, and this stood crying. The dog ran upon the ice, the middle of which was broken. The poor distressed creature scratched the margin of the crack, and whined in violent agitation. The only gentleman of the party leaped into the water. The mother of the child fainted. The servants being alarmed, assisted in the search, which was long, and could not be prosecuted without breaking the remaining ice. The *apparatus* of the Humane Society was not to be had: but a surgeon in the town understood the means of recovery recommended by that institution.—An institution that will give to the memory of HAWES, a monument which *time* shall enlarge and adorn, while he corrodes the statue of brass, and moulders away the pillars of marble.—Fortunately the surgeon arrived at the moment when one of the bodies was found. The other also was soon after discovered. The delay which had attended the search, rendered the restoration of life difficult. It was, however, accomplished. Keeper lay by the side of the bed, during the process and the children being left warmly covered, he returned with the rest of the company, in an agony of joy, to the parlour. Joy was, indeed, in every countenance: and it was an affecting situation, could Keeper have felt it, to be at least the second cause, and means made use of, to give pleasure so excessive to a circle thus numerous. The mother shed tears while she caressed the preserver of her children; and all were desirous to shew their affection for a creature that had done so much service. The old lady imputed the circumstance of Keeper's visit to a special Providence, for the Protection of her grand-children; and the vicar, who had benevolently assisted, said, he thought it could not be deemed an improper or low application of the text, if he applied to this event, the promise that has been made *that, the gift of even a Cup of Cold Water, bestowed for kindness' sake and charity's shall not lose its reward!* "We see" added he, "we see that no creature is so low, nor so weak, but it may do us infinite service—the *mouse* released a lion *from* confinement, as our friend Æsop has recorded. And if, therefore, this were the only motive we should, *for our own sakes,* behave well to every thing— I say, *this* consideration ought to influence us, *even* if we forget that none but *fools,* and cowards, can find any gratification in hurting what is *weaker than themselves;* if we forget that none but the *cruel,* would unnecessarily injure *any thing;* if we for- get that none but the *wicked* would dare to insult any of the creatures of GOD."

> "Who in *his* sovereign *wisdom,* made them *all!*"
>
> COWPER.

"And be sure," continued he, addressing himself to the child who had not fallen into the water, "be sure, my dear, you never pretend to think the smallness or triflingness of the creature, beast, bird, fish, insect, or reptile, any excuse of your crime: for remember

> "————————the *meanest* things that are,
> Are *free* to *live* and to *enjoy* that life,
> As God was *free* to form them at the first!"
>
> COWPER.

Every indulgence was heaped upon Keeper; and many plans were laid down for his future happiness: but Keeper left them only the merit of intention: for, late at night, perceiving the street quiet, and summoning courage to depart, he left the house, un- observed, and continued his journey.

CHAPTER V

The Blunderbuss.

THE NIGHT WAS DARK, yet he pursued the track, which, by the wonderful sagacity common to his species, he was enabled to recognize. He went as fast as his strength would permit; but this was much exceeded by his impatience. He passed alone and unmolested the greater part of the night. He was sometimes overtaken and met by mail- coaches; and terrified by their lamps. He passed inns where the sleepy helpers brought out harnessed horses to be changed, and in these inns he would gladly have sought a place of rest and shelter from the coldness of the air: but the ardour with which he sought his master would not suffer delay: and day-break discovered him to the early labourer, still pressing onward with swift and even pace.

He was interrupted during a few minutes, by a hare, that crossed his path; in pursuit of whom he traversed several acres of crisp and frost-whitened wheat. Having driven puss into a thorny thicket, whither he found it difficult to follow her, he gave up the chase, and returned with the haste of a truant to the road of his journey. Though this frolic had wasted a small portion of his time, and contributed to weary his feet, yet was it on the whole, very beneficial to him. The violence of the exertion had warmed his frozen limbs, and he returned with renewed vigour to his path.

He was now descending a hill, and he ran down with all the speed he could, for he recollected that in the bottom was a small inn, where his master had stopped, and he would fain persuade himself that there he should find him again. This hope cheered his bosom; and he felt a glow of pleasure to which he had long been a stranger. He delighted himself; and it would have been an unthankful office to have destroyed his expectations:

> "Pursue, poor imp, th' imaginary charm,
> Indulge gay hope, and fancy's pleasing fire:
> Fancy and hope, too soon shall of themselves expire!"
>
> BEATTIE.

The sign post appeared in view, and every nerve was strained to reach the goal of his hopes. A traveller on horseback was at the door; and he thought that he resembled his master. The traveller looked toward him; and he wondered that he was not greeted, returning wanderer as he was, with some token of affection and of joy. He feared that his master took no notice of him because he was angry; and he prepared to prostrate himself at his feet, and implore his forgiveness. He reached the house, and he approached the horseman only to discover his mistake, and to destroy his hopes; and in the moment of his disappointment, the man who was watering the horse, threw what remained in the pail, upon him. This was a trifling misfortune; but in his present distress, it affected him; and he thought himself the object of general persecution.

He went on, while the man laughed to see him wet and shivering. The water presently froze in his hair; and increased his coldness and his misery. He travelled four miles farther and entered a town wherein the mail stopped. The dangers of the night being at an end, the guard, as usual, discharged the contents of his piece. In performing this mighty feat, it is usual, also, to do some mischief, *if possible*. Keeper's sorrowful appearance attracted the eyes of the hero, at this unfortunate moment: he levelled a blunderbuss at our unsuspecting and plodding traveller, and, in an instant some small-shot were lodged near his shoulder, while a ball grazed his back, but happily passed over without inflicting a severer wound. Keeper did not immediately feel the shot. He winced from the smart which the ball presently occasioned. He was scared, too, by the report of the gun, and the shouts of his enemies; and he fled precipitately from the inhospitable place.

CHAPTER VI

[Ruminations.]

Where shall he rest secure from harms?
BEATTIE.

THE EXTREME TERROR with which Keeper hurried through the town, prevented him from feeling the extent of the injury he had received. Gaining, at last, the open and unfrequented road, his fears began to abate; and with them the rapidity of his steps. The blood whence had hitherto flowed unperceived, now began to mat his hair in congealed and frozen clots; and his stiffening joints soon rendered motion difficult and painful. His wounds were pierced by the keen air; and he limped along, slowly, and in torture.

His sufferings increased his weariness, and overcome by their acuteness, he lay down under a hay-rick, and folded up his legs, curling his body round to protect himself from the blast. He would have slept, but the anguish he endured, denied him even a short respite from his sorrows. He lay pondering his condition: and if he *anticipated* no evils *to come*, the same ignorance of future events, which men sometimes inconsiderately envy, shut from him the *hope of deliverance*, from those he already experienced. He did not espy *death* in the gloomy rear of his disasters making night hideous: but he thought himself confined *for ever* to his *present* bleak and unsheltered abode. He dreaded no *mortification* in his wounds, nor no *fever* in his pulse; but neither had any prospect of *relief* from the excruciating pang that *now* oppressed him. He despaired of seeing again the master of his heart. He believed that *his* presence would remove *all* evils: for he remembered his *kindness* with enthusiasm, and his *capacities* with admiration: and when you have blended *benevolence* with power, you have made a *divinity*.

These ruminations were disturbed by the noise of men and terriers, who were in pursuit of rats across the farm yard; and who discovering Keeper, immediately turned a portion of their fury against *him*. Keeper was roused by their approach, and hastily gained the road, where he limped along with all the expedition he could use until he found himself delivered from his new danger. Hard and calamitous as this intrusion on the repose of the weary, and the couch of the wounded, may appear, it was, in truth, a fortunate circumstance. For had he lain any time exposed to the intenseness of the frost, his limbs would, in all probability have become so completely numbed that he could not have risen again; and being besides deprived of his usual quantum of internal heat, by fatigue and hunger, the severity of the approaching night must have put an end to his existence, But "forced into *action* thus, in self-defence," he preserved, for the present, the use of his muscles; and proceeded, with infinite labour, on his way. The tardiness of his pace, nevertheless suffered his powers of motion to diminish every moment; and his condition conspired with the frigid atmosphere to bring on a drowsiness, to which he was repeatedly inclined to give way and which must, inevitably, have been a fatal one.

While thus dragging his miserable body, he could not help regarding *men* (the beings from whom he had received so many injuries) as monsters, whose whole occupation was to render every thing around them miserable. He was ready to ask,

> "Then what is man? And what man seeing this,
> And having human feelings, does not blush
> And hang his head, to own himself a man?"
>
> COWPER.

He knew some exceptions. Had he not been well treated by some even in his present pilgrimage, he had been led to suppose that all the kindness he had ever received from strangers, had been bestowed upon him because, in his *master's* presence, they *dared not* use him ill: for of the goodness, skill, and strength, which he attributed to his master, he was inclined to believe that the generality of the race possessed only the two latter, and that they used these for no purpose but to destroy. Fortunately, however, for the human character, an individual was at hand to rescue it from this universal stigma.

The apothecary of the next village was trotting homeward, and the hooves of his horse rung upon the frozen ground. Keeper looked back and dreaded a new tormenter. The apothecary, in the mean time, had watched the slow pace of the maimed and solitary traveller. On near approach, he was so moved at the appearance of the poor disconsolate beast, that after walking by his side a few paces, and perceiving that he was lame, owing to a recent wound, he alighted in order to administer whatever comfort his benevolence and knowledge could afford. Keeper at first retreated; for a *man* and that a *stranger* seemed to him, at this juncture, sufficient cause of alarm. The soothing voice with which he was invited, soon overcame, notwithstanding, the fears he had entertained; and led by the credulousness of sincerity, he advanced towards the hand that offered to cherish him. On coming close, he was farther encouraged by the countenance of the compassionate way-farer. For nature has kindly proivded all animals with instant perceptions of good and evil; and these perceptions are, perhaps, most strong and certain in infants and animals, because they are unprejudiced: while those of men are confused by accidental circumstances: dress, general reputation, and a thousand others.

The good man found that nothing could be done for Keeper's relief in their present situation. It was useless to apply any balsam or ointment, while the wounds were covered with coagulated blood, mingled with hair. He was much at a loss, how to get the dog to his own home: both because he doubted if he would follow him; and because he could not bear to see him walk in so much pain, with his hurts open to the evening frost. He tied his handkerchief over the part that was injured; at which operation Keeper complained loudly; because, like some wiser creatures, he did not comprehend the utility of the temporary and seeming evil. He was soon, however, reconciled to the bandage, and felt its benefits.

While the young surgeon was considering whether he should try to carry Keeper on his horse, the errand-cart over took him. To the driver he committed the care of his *protege*, who placed him in a basket of straw. In this comfortable nest he indulged his propensity to sleep, with safety; and was thus carried to the house of his benefactor.

CHAPTER VII

Caroline.

KEEPER DID NOT LIKE to be disturbed in his slumbers, and forced from the warm bed in which he had ridden. Much less was he pleased with the useful operations which succeeded this hardship. His shoulder was bathed with warm milk and water; and the hair cut away from the *cicatrices* which began to bleed afresh. In performing this essential and charitable office, the apothecary, who, till then, could not conjecture how the wounds had been occasioned discovered that several shot were lodged in a manner that endangered the future use of the limb. A task more important therefore remained; that of extracting these shot; and it was unfortunately, of a nature that would render resistance on Keeper's part, as certain as troublesome.

Keeper repented that he had surrendered himself into the hands of one, who, as he thought was like the rest of mankind, devising every method of torturing him. He knew not that the pain he was made to suffer, was the means of his future preservation and comfort.

During the time in which the apothecary was thus employed, a neighbour came in to pass an hour in conversation, it being then dark evening, and he assisted the painful kindness of the operation. They bound Keeper, and secured his mouth so that he could neither resist nor resent the excruciating torment which they were obliged to inflict. Keeper, suffered considerable agony, and by turns meditated vengeance on his tormentors, or submitted with patience to what he thought their *cruel* purpose.

Released, at length, he no longer remembered his resentment; but received their caresses with joy and gratitude. Ointments were now applied that cooled the throbbing sores. Bandages secured rest to the too much irritated parts; and he was lain near the fire to enjoy again his slumbers, and his repose.

It was not, it should be told, wholly to the surgeon and his friend, that Keeper owed all these attentions, nor was it these alone who witnessed and pitied his sufferings. It was Caroline who spread the lint with salve. It was Caroline who sewed the bandage; and who folded it again and again to insure his comfort. It was Caroline who laid flannel for a mattrass; and who gave him the little milk, and bread and butter, which he could find appetite to take. These *traits* of loveliness did not pass unnoticed or unrewarded by a gentleman who had entered the room during her exertions.

This gentleman happened to have passed through the town in which the disaster happened, at the moment in which the blunderbuss was fired. He saw Keeper run away but he did not then certainly know that he was wounded, his attention having been engrossed by an accident which the same act of wantonness had caused; and which had occasioned his present visit to the benevolent apothecary.

CHAPTER VIII

The Post Chaise.

THE GUARD HAD FIRED his blunderbuss at Keeper, at the instant when a chaise and four was passing rapidly through the high-street. The horses took fright, and dashed the carriage against the cross in the middle of the town. The violence of the concussion overturned it: and it was dragged by the horses, whose fright had increased, while the postillions were thrown, and great part of the harness and wheels broken. The gentleman who now called on our apothecary, being a magistrate, instantly ordered the guard into custody: and, the horses being stopped, hastened to inquire if any injury was sustained by the travellers.

On coming near he discovered that it was the carriage of an old and intimate friend. He found that this gentleman was only slightly bruised; but that his son, who was with him, had received several cuts and contusions, and was taken almost senseless to a surgeon in the town: whence, his wounds having been dressed, he was removed to the house of the magistrate, their original destination. He now requested his medical friend to accompany him on a visit to the unfortunate young gentleman. They left Caroline and their neighbour attending Keeper: They found a strong inclination to fever in the patient, whom the apothecary left, after a long visit promising to call in the morning.

Keeper's illness was increased by his anxiety for his master. His spirits were always dejected; and even the kindness, and the care, of the fair Caroline, failed to infuse his heart with permanent pleasure. His fellow sufferer, Henry Walwyn, lay for a considerable time in very imminent danger. It was three weeks before he was able to walk in the air. When he did, his friend introduced him to the house of the apothecary. He was desirous to see Keeper, who had shared the misfortunes of the day with him and the benefactors also, who had now almost recovered him from the baneful effects of them.

It will be supposed that great part of the conversation turned upon the accident they had encountered; upon the misfortunes of Keeper; and the relief which had been administered to him. "I am acquainted with a gentleman," said the magistrate, "who says he would always form his opinion of a man's character by his behaviour to dogs; and though the rule might sometimes misguide him, especially if too hastily applied, I am of opinion that it would, in general, be a very just criterion."

"People sometimes behave ill to dogs," rejoined the apothecary, "not through settled dislike, or uniform ill-nature, but merely in the moments of petulence and impatience."

"Your discrimination," answered the magistrate, fully directs your decision: for the man you describe is, more or less, a *petulant* man, though not of a settled bad disposition.—I say *bad disposition*, because, adopting my friend's maxim, I cannot think that there can be much that is worthy esteem in the character of a man who can ill use a creature so affectionate, and so faithful. I would risque no hopes of happiness with him: I should expect nothing from his feeling, his generosity, nor his gratitude. He must be "dead to nature and her charities."

"I agree with you, entirely;" said the elder Mr. Walwyn, "and if their assiduities are sometimes aukward and their caresses troublesome, yet, surely,

> "————nothing can come amiss
> That simpleness and duty tender!"

SHAKSPEARE.

CHAPTER IX

Dogs.

KEEPER WAS NOW so far recovered, that his life was no longer in danger; nor was there any reason to doubt his soon having the full use of the leg that had been injured: but he had not yet obtained strength sufficient to attempt the escape from his present abode which he certainly meditated. Kindly as he was used, and it was impossible he could receive more kindness any where, he had not forgot the master who had formerly cherished him, and whom he had lost through his own negligence and inattention. He began to entertain a better opinion of mankind than he had lately been induced to form: but still, of all the race, he loved none so dearly as his master; and, next to him, his family.

The conversation happened one day to bring on this subject. Caroline was much grieved to hear it the general opinion that Keeper would leave her as soon as he was well. She urged the well known gratitude of the species, in contradiction of an idea which she thought at once disgraceful to Keeper's character, and her attentions.

The magistrate said, he hoped the lady would forgive him, if he differed as to the inference to be drawn from the prevailing sentiment of gratitude: for to him it seemed, that this very feeling would lead the dog to seek again his original owner. The magistrate here enlarged on the virtues of dogs in general, and their characteristics.

"The understanding of dogs," he said, "surpasses that of all other animals, except man and the elephant."

"Are not apes and monkeys very sensible?"

"They are reckoned among the most stupid of quadrupeds;" answered the magistrate, "the appearance of understanding in them, is entirely in consequence of the resemblance which their form bears to that of man: but this similarity is, in fact, a convincing proof of their total want of capacity. Because, if they possessed this, in addition to the advantages of exterior conformation, they would never be surpassed by the dog, and the elephant, and even the horse; whose shape and organization differs so widely from ours."

"To what then is the superiority of dogs to be attributed?"

"Their sensibility. This makes them susceptible of affection, and capable of attachment. Nature has given them this disposition, which is improved by a constant society with man."

"That the qualifications of dogs," said the apothecary, "depends materially on their education, is evident from the extreme similarity of the habits and manners of different individuals. They are even silent or noisy, according to the company they are used to keep."

"Very true," said Walwyn, "the shepherd's dog who is all day long upon silent and solitary downs, scarcely ever barks; while ladies' lap-dogs—I beg Caroline's pardon—but, as she has no lap-dog, she will, perhaps, excuse my saying that, from some cause or other, lap-dogs are incessantly yelping."

"I dislike small dogs very much on that account;" said Caroline, "and I think larger dogs are not only more silent but better natured."

"They certainly are," said the magistrate, "and in this particular, the mastiff surpasses all the rest of the species, perhaps. He has so much temperance and judgment, that in performing the duty of a watch-dog, he will permit a stranger to come into the yard, or place which he is appointed to guard; and will go peaceably along with him through every part of it, so long as he touches nothing: but the moment he attempts to meddle with any of the goods, *or endeavours to leave the place* he informs him, first by gentle growling, or if that is ineffectual, by harsher means, that he must neither do mischief nor go away. He never uses violence unless resisted; and he will, even in this case, seize the person, throw him down, and hold him there for hours, without biting."

"Will all mastiffs behave thus?"

"Perhaps not: but this is their general character."

"The mastiff is peculiar to England, I believe?"

"Entirely so: it is called the *English dog*, by foreign naturalists."

"How many species of dogs are there?"

"To answer you as a Zoologist, I should say, twenty-three: the varieties of the wolf, the hyæna, the jackal, and the fox being included in that number; but I know that you rather intended to ask how many varieties there are of what are *commonly* called dogs?"

"I beg your pardon: I spoke incorrectly: I thank you for setting me right. Pray do you recollect the number of varieties?"

"It is perhaps, impossible to reckon exactly! They are almost without end. Thirty-five, however, with some sub-varieties, are described, as belonging to that species of dogs, if I recollect right, the species which is called the "Faithful Dog.""

"The dog then is *naturally* cruel?"

"He is; but his ferocious nature is conquered by gentleness. He is not therefore a mere machine, but acts from sentiment and reflection."

"It has been charged on the spaniel that man learned to fawn and be servile in imitation of that creature."

"A witty writer, in a periodical paper, the 'Mirror' of the 'World,' I think, entirely changes the accusation. After praising, being obliged at last, to admit that they do fawn and flatter, and sometimes, even the unworthy; he says, in extenuation, "we ought to look with great lenience on this fault, in an animal, who, after six thousand years intimacy with *man*, has learned but *one* of his vices."

CHAPTER X

The Hermit and his Dog.

On another occasion, a similar conversation brought to the recollection of the company a beautiful little tale by Pratt; and, at their request, Walwyn read it, as follows:

In life's fair morn, I knew an aged Seer,
Who sad and lonely pass'd his joyless year;
Betray'd, heart-broken, from the world he ran,

And shunn'd, oh dire extreme! the face of man;
Humbly he rear'd his hut within the wood,
Hermit's his vest, a hermit's was his food.
Nich'd in some corner of the gelid cave,
Where chilling drops the rugged rock-stone lave;
Hour after hour, the melancholy sage,
Drop after drop to reckon, would engage
The ling'ring day: and, trickling as they fell,
A tear went with them to the narrow well,
Then, thus he moraliz'd, as slow it pass'd:
"This brings me nearer Lucia than the last!
And this, now streaming from the eye," said he,
"Oh, my lov'd child! will bring me nearer thee!"
When first he roam'd, his Dog, with anxious care
His wand'rings watch'd, as emulous to share.
In vain the faithful brute was bid to go;
In vain the sorrower sought a lonely woe;
The hermit paus'd—the attendant dog was near;
Slept at his feet, and caught the falling tear:
Uprose the hermit, up the dog would rise;
And every way to win a master tries.
"Then be it so: come, faithful fool. He said."
One pat encouraged, and they sought the shade.
An unfrequented thicket soon they found;
And both repos'd upon the leafy ground:
Mellifluous murm'ring told the fountains nigh;
Fountains that well a pilgrims, drink supply;
And thence, by many a labyrinth is led,
Where every tree bestow'd a nightly bed.
Skill'd in the chace, the faithful creature brought
Whate'er at noon, or moonlight course he caught:
But the sage lent his sympathy to all;
Nor saw, unwept, his dumb associates fall,
He was, in sooth, the gentlest of his kind;
And, though a hermit, had a social mind:
"And why," said he, "must man subsist by prey?
Why stop yon melting music on the spray?
Why, when assail'd by hounds and hunters' cry,
Must half the harmless race in terrors die?
Why must we work of innocence the woe?
Still shall this bosom throb, those eyes o'erflow?
A heart, too tender, here, from man retires:
A heart that aches, if but a wren expires!"
Thus liv'd the master good, the servant true,
'Till to its God the master's spirit flew.
Beside a fount, which daily water gave,

Stooping to drink, the hermit found a grave.
All in the running stream his garments spread;
And dark damp verdure ill conceal'd his head.
The faithful servant, from that fatal day,
Watch'd the lov'd course, and hourly pin'd away;
His head upon his master's cheek was found;
While the obstructed water mourn'd around!

CHAPTER XI

The Departure.

IT WAS ON THE MORNING after Walwyn had read this little poem, that Keeper, fresh from the repose of the night, and invited by the brightness of the landscape, determined to proceed on his pilgrimage to the house of his master's friend. He left the gate before the family had risen; and ran with a light heart, while the ground, covered with hoar frost, reflected, in ten thousand spangles, the brilliance of the rising sun.

He had not advanced many paces before he fancied himself called by Caroline. He looked back: he stopped; and his spirits forsook him. The hope of seeing his master could scarcely support him under the affliction of leaving Caroline: she who had rescued him from misery: who had warmed and fed him: who had nursed and cherished him! He was not called; yet he determined to return once more, to the doors that had been opened to his sufferings; that had shut out persecution, at the moment when it seemed to follow him with hasty and unrelenting step. He returned, and loitered in the yard till Caroline appeared. He hastened to meet her with extacy. He prostrated himself. He wished to be forgiven the intention of leaving her: he licked her hand; and he paid homage without flattery: for it was the homage of affection, and of gratitude.

His behaviour was so extravagant that Caroline imagined something extraordinary had happened; but she did not guess that the little fugitive had attempted to leave her. He ran to the farthest extremity of the yard; he returned, and tearing round her, bounded again to a considerable distance; lessening, however the extent of his sallies at every repetition; and again rushed upon her to express his joy at beholding her again.

He remained the whole of that day unable to conquer his reluctance to leave Caroline, and the Apothecary: the night however was passed in making resolutions for the morning; and agreeably with these, no sooner were the doors open, than Keeper set forward on his journey.

The morning was fine, like that of the day preceding. Keeper was tolerably strong, though he had not wholly recovered his former activity; and the weather prompted that speed which best suited the impatience of his wishes. His progress was pleasant and uninterrupted, except in a single instance. Four or five oxen were grazing on the side of the road, and Keeper was obliged to pass them. He looked about for a by-way, that might enable him to avoid them. It was in vain: summoning, therefore, all his fortitude, he crept, cowering, slouching his ears, and hanging his tail, for they had already left the

herd, and menaced his approach. The humility with which he advanced did not reconcile his opponents. They rushed furiously toward him. They lowered their heads as
in the act of butting. Keeper was now surrounded. Death seemed inevitable. The poor
unoffending Keeper was to be the victim of their fury, and the sport of their tyrannous
strength. In this moment of danger, bewildered, and almost terrified to stupefaction;
encompassed on every side, and on the point of surrendering without hope, and without
capability of resistance, Keeper, as the last effort, made a desperate *sortie;* passing under
one of his most determined assailants, and receiving a slight graze from the horns of
another, he leaped on a frozen pool, hoping to cross it, and thus escape his pursuers.
Unfortunately, the ice was too slight to bear him. He sunk half way into the water,
and was much hurt by the edges of the ice that surrounded him, in his struggles to
escape. Hither the oxen followed him. Invigorated now by apprehension, he ploughed
up the ice before him; for every piece on which he rested, instantly gave way; and with
excessive pain and difficulty reached the opposite bank. This was so steep that his
efforts to scale it, terminated only in as many falls upon the broken ice and water; and
two or three of the oxen who had been impeded by the ice, came round to wait his
landing. In this dilemma, he worked his way to another edge of the pool, and, leaping
over a gate, gained an extensive meadow. He had not time to felicitate himself on his
deliverance, before he perceived other cattle coming toward him, with threatening
gestures, stamping the ground, and lifting their tails in the attitude of rage. Keeper
ran: but he presently found himself meeting one who was driving furiously at him. He
stood still, gazing on the foaming beast: the beast also stood still. He perceived a gap
which led to an adjoining field, and which was stopped up with a thin hurdle, and dead
bushes. He made toward this, and creeping through it in a moment, fancied himself safe.
The beast had pursued him close, and almost at the very instant in which Keeper passed,
ran his horns between the bars of [the] hurdle. The whole barrier gave way before the fury
of the enraged animal; who tossed the hurdle furiously into the air; and tore, with the
rest of the herd, in pursuit of Keeper. A path crossed this field which Keeper immediately
gained, and fled onward where a few soldiers were walking to the town. The soldiers
alarmed at the sudden approach of the cattle, in this angry mood, immediately ran
away, which conduct only increased their danger. They were even foolish enough to beat
the drums they had with them. Keeper fled to them for succour, and by so doing made
them sharers in his danger; and they by their behaviour, drew more completely on him,
and themselves, the anger of the common enemy. In this dangerous situation, which
they met so ignorantly, or imprudently, it can scarcely be thought that any thing could
have saved them, had not a gentleman coming the other way, perceiving their predica-
ment, called out to them to stand still, to face the oxen, and to cease the noise of the
drum. This was no sooner done than the cattle stopped. Then, wheeling round, they
sped to some distance, and again advanced, as if determined to attack. In a few seconds
they wheeled again, and at the end of every evolution they were nearer the terrified
passengers than before.

The gentleman now coming up, directed the party to pretend to meet the oxen. This
behaviour together with scaring them, by waving their hats, sticks, and other such actions,
soon enabled them to quit the field in safety.

The gentleman cautioned the soldiers that, if a similar accident at any time befel them,
the most dangerous conduct possible is, to run hastily away. "I was once," said he,

"somewhat in your situation. I found that whenever I turned my back, the animals galloped toward me; and I escaped by walking backward, slowly; and repeatedly menacing with my stick. The beasts frequently advanced, but were checked by my movements. These I practised until I had reached a gate; when, springing hastily, I secured myself from danger."

The travellers parted. Keeper gained the road by a circuitous course, which brought him into it at some distance from the scene of his first alarm.

CHAPTER XII
[*Thieves.*]

Keeper was very sore from the difficulties of his adventure; but his spirits were elated by the success of his efforts. He travelled with persisting quickness, although he soon became oppressed by fatigue, by hunger, and by thirst. He was many times disappointed by the appearance, of water which he found to be covered with ice; and this he could only lick: for he had not judgment enough to dream of breaking the surface.

Night-fall came on: it increased the coldness of the air and it involved him in darkness. Still, however, he continued plodding "his weary way."

Midnight passed while he was yet many miles from the house of his master's friend. He was scarcely able to go on; but he knew that he was approaching the place of his destination; and the thought encouraged him to exert all his power and his perseverance. A clock struck three, and though he knew not the meaning of the sound, he recollected to have heard it at the house whither he was bent. His heart leaped for joy; and he presently entered the yard-gate, the way he had been used to go in with the horses. No creature was to be seen, nor any noise to be heard, save the rustling of the horses at their mangers. After scratching at one or two of the doors without obtaining admittance, he lay down under a crib, upon some hay that had fallen from it, first walking round, and smelling his intended couch. Here, cold and damp, as it was, for night was at work, encrusting every blade, and pipe of straw, with frozen dew, yet here, cold and damp, as it was, Keeper lay in luxury; and rested from his fatigues and his dangers for more than two hours. He was awakened by footsteps, and whispering voices; and immediately sprung towards the sound, barking vehemently. Two men who were opening the granary door, threw stones at him, to intimidate his watchfulness, but this only increased his fury, and confirmed his suspicions. People were now heard in the house opening the windows. The theives therefore fled with precipitation. The master of the house saw one of them climbing over the paling, and immediately dispatched the groom, who was most completely dressed, in pursuit of /the robbers. The master was surprised to find himself roused by a dog whose voice he did not know, while his own dogs were silent, and not to be found. Immediately on seeing Keeper, he recollected him to be the dog of his friend; and received him with the same cordiality which Keeper, on his part, evinced at their meeting. He found that nothing had been carried away: but that it was certainly intended that the granary should have been pillaged; and he attributed the preservation of his property wholly to Keeper's vigilance. On this account, as well as because it was the dog of a very intimate friend, he paid him particular attention. He brought him into the house, and gave him food, of which Keeper stood much in need. In the mean time the groom returned, saying, that he was not able "to track the villains;" and with him came the yard dogs, whom he pretended to have found straggling, at some distance. He wished to persuade his master that the dogs had been decoyed away, in order to prevent the family from being apprized of the robbery. With respect to the motive, he was correct: of the rest, the truth was that [he] himself had muzzled the dogs, and lodged them in a barn at some distance from the premises.

Keeper had a particular aversion to any tinkling or clanking noise; and this was one of the few things that never failed to irritate him. The gentleman at whose house he now was, hoping of seeing his master, had several children, and among them, a son of about sixteen or seventeen years of age, whose name was Frederic. On the evening of the day on which Keeper arrived, the young 'squire was visited by a friend not quite so old as himself, who had lately engaged in military life. This young gentleman accidentally discovering Keeper's infirmity, found great entertainment in provoking him to bark at, and attack the fire-tongs, which he snapped incessantly, for this purpose, close to Keeper's head. Although this game was rather too noisy to afford much pleasure to the rest of the company; it might have gone on with considerable spirit, had not the soldier, with martial intrepidity, ventured to increase the exasperation 'till Keeper burst furiously upon him. The hero was no sooner attacked in his turn, than dropping the violence of offence, he sprang backward, with a violent shriek, almost over his chair. Recovered from this alarm, which ended without mischief, he again applied the tongs to Keeper's annoyance; and, at length, stooped his head, and put his own nose in Keeper's way, who instantly snapped at it, and pierced his upper lip. This kind of hurt usually causes an involuntary and instantaneous starting of tears, which flowing pretty freely on this occasion, while the blood trickled from the lip and forgot its usual office: "to blush and beautify the face." The son of Mars certainly did not look quite so brave as at the beginning of the fight: yet, it is to be remembered, to his honour, that he bore no malice to the victor. On the contrary, he sustained the fortune of war with becoming equanimity. In compliment, however, to the wounded knight, the master of the house thought proper to order Keeper out of the room, though neither he, nor any one else, blamed the part which Keeper had acted.

It was directed that Keeper should be tied up in the stable, that he might be preserved for his own master; where he slept comfortably 'till morning introduced a scene of new disasters.

CHAPTER XIII

The Sparrow-Hawk.

FREDERIC CAME by eight o'clock to visit the stranger. He had scarcely entered the stable when he observed some drops of blood, and scattered feathers, which he instantly knew to have belonged to a sparrow-hawk, that he kept tame, and of which he was exceedingly fond. He flew to be convinced of the loss of his bird, and finding the cage empty, immediately charged Keeper with the crime of killing and eating his hawk.

The first person he met, was the groom; and to him he related the story of Keeper's atrocious crime. The groom, it may be suspected, was glad of an opportunity of vengeance on the vigilant and faithful Keeper. He expressed much concern at his young master's loss, and inveighed against the author of it in the bitterest terms. Frederic vowed to be avenged of the murderer of his bird; in which design the groom encouraged him, and strongly recommended that he should be immediately hung at the stable door.

Frederic was mightily pleased with this project; he forgot that he should in so doing commit the very crime for which, as he idly fancied, a love of goodness, and abhorrence of cruelty, prompted him to punish Keeper. He forgot that Keeper could have no other motive for killing the hawk than the gratification of his own wants, an excuse which himself certainly could not plead.

The truth is, that it was not a love of goodness, but of power, that prompted the "little tyrant" to this act of authority. The offence was a mere pretext for this deed of *pretended* justice, but of *real* barbarity. Accordingly it was not sufficient that the life of the dog should pay for the life of the hawk. He adopted the proposal of hanging Keeper, but the summary and unceremonious manner suggested by the groom did not meet his approbation. He amused himself with planning the *etiquette* to be observed on the occasion, and ordered the culprit into close confinement, while he went to collect his brothers, his sisters, and his neighbours, to be witnesses of the sight.

His father happened to be gone on a short journey this morning, so that no interruption was to be apprehended from him: and his mother saw nothing but mystery and eagerness in the faces of the children, whom she supposed to be engaged in some great, but she did not think criminal, exploit.

The spectators being assembled with a mixture of expectation, and terror in their countenances, the prisoner was conveyed, with much formality, to a part of the garden, where the remaining feathers of the hawk were deposited. Matters were now prepared to hang Keeper over the grave; who much to the discomfiture of the starched faces that were met on this solemn occasion, was so indecorous as to play with a piece of stick, and sometimes with the rope that was fastened round his neck during the whole of the ceremony.

Having exhausted their ingenuity in inventing schemes for prolonging their wicked pleasure, the fatal moment at length arrived that was to put an end to Keeper's existence. To separate him for ever from the master whom he had sought so ardently and loved so dearly; to destroy those hopes for which he had suffered so many hardships; and to take away that life which Caroline had cherished so tenderly!

The cord was now drawn, and the unconscious victim of infantine barbarity suspended from a bough.

CHAPTER XIV

The Epitaph.

A VOICE NOW CALLED their attention, and their father was seen hastening up the walk. He commanded that Keeper should be released; but their confusion was so great that he came to the spot before his orders were obeyed, and instantly replaced Keeper on his feet.

He reprimanded them severely, and enquired the cause of so extraordinary an act of cruelty, which was, beside, an unpardonable insult to his friend, the owner of the dog.

The charge of killing the hawk was brought forward. This however, their father would not admit as any excuse. He next asked, who had suggested the idea of hanging the dog on this account? On hearing that the groom was the author of the detestable plan, he immediately dismissed him from his service; and having now some proofs of his being concerned in the intended robbery, caused him to be sent to gaol.

One of the servants came running with a wing, and part of the head of the hawk, which he had found in the cat's habitation. This discovery entirely freed Keeper from the charge. Particularly as dogs seldom or never eat the animals they kill; while cats almost always make a feast of their spoil.

Frederic remained in extreme disgrace: from which he was at length released, sincerely regretting that he had ever intended any thing so unbecoming his general good disposition, and understanding. Convinced that Keeper was wholly innocent of his bird's destruction, he only regretted its loss. He erected a monument to its memory whereon he inscribed the following verses. His father was so well pleased with the composition, that he became reconciled with him on the occasion; and, beside, bestowed rewards on him, as incitements to the future exercise of his abilities.

EPITAPH

On a tame Sparrow-Hawk.

LET not the stranger passing by,
Behold this grave with scornful eye;
Nor blameful deem the lowly shrine;
Nor undeserv'd the mournful line!

What tho', had Nature held her sway*,
Weak innocence had been his prey;
And tuneful victims daily bled:—
Still shall the muse lament him dead!

O thou, who, when the rosy spring
Her store of sweet delights doth bring,
Doth love so well the flow'ry way.
Where woodland wild notes hymn
    the day.

E'en thou forgive!—For who shall stand
'Gainst Nature's absolute command?
His means of *life*, by fate they bleed;
And the *decree* absolves the *deed!*

E'en thou forgive!—not hawks alone
With others lives maintain their own;
To feed the linnet, *nations* die!
And why unpitied falls the *fly?*

Ah thoughtful stranger, turn thine eyes
Where proud Augusta's† fanes arise;
Where sculpture lends her hand to
    trace
The laurell'd murd'rer's blood-stain'd
    face!

Him, born to feel his brother's woe;
Him, born at other's joy to glow;
To wipe affliction's tearful eye;
And bid the wretched cease to sigh;

Ah, me! mad conquest fir'd his soul!
For kindred lips he drugg'd the bowl!
He play'd the dark assassin's part——
And liv'd—to wound each virtuous heart!

* Had he continued in a natural, or wild state.　　† A Roman name for London.

If Man thus far mistakes his way,
And makes whom born to *love* his
    prey,
Hawks are but satires on our kind!
They act the part by heav'n design'd.

O blame not then this lowly shrine!
Nor scorn the mourner's feeble line!
Profane not this, his honour'd bed:
But, with the Muse lament the dead!

CHAPTER XV

The Rabbit-Warren.

IN THE MEAN TIME, Keeper took the first opportunity, after his fortunate release, to leave a house where he had, though greatly against the master's wish, received so much ill-treatment. Unable to discover his master, and having visited every place in which he could expect to find him, nearer than his own house, he now began his route thither, determined to let nothing delay his progress if he could possibly avoid it. He kept this resolution pretty regularly: yet he could not help running after sparrows, now and then; and he was much at a loss to account for their disappearance at his approach.

He continued travelling during several days; sometimes relieved from hunger, by finding a bone in his way through villages; and from fatigue, by resting under hedges, and on sunny banks. Sometimes fed: but, for the most part, oppressed by want and weariness.

At length his incessant exertion brought him as far as an extensive waste that lay on lofty hills. Huge blocks of stone peeped out in various parts; and the whole was scantily supplied with herbage. Here Keeper saw whole families of Rabbits racing in every direction, and he ran an hundred different ways in pursuit of them, as the old groups suddenly disappeared, and new ones became visible. Presently none were to be seen: and, while Keeper wondered at the change, a kite hovered over the place, and alarmed the whole long-eared neighbourhood. Keeper too had contributed to their consternation: and he, not distracted, now, by the variety of his game, pursued one of the grey fugitives into its burrow. He was soon impeded by the straightness of the path, and he spent a considerable time in scratching his way. The earth, though now frozen, was extremely light, and sandy: so that, when he had dug away the uppermost part, he soon covered himself with dirt: but this was all he *could* do. Meanwhile, the rabbits endured all the horrors of a siege: 'till Keeper recollecting his master, raised* it, and continued his progress.

While Keeper was running in many a serpentine direction, through alleys fenced by *ling* and withered *fern*, in his way to the high-road, the keeper of the warren, who happened to be at that time on the spot, observed our intruder, and immediately fired upon him. Keeper escaped unhurt, and ran impetuously along until he reached the road, and was lost to the gunner. Having been wounded when he last heard a similar noise, he made no doubt but he was, again, equally injured; and it was not before he had passed several hours, without feeling pain, that he recovered his spirits and his peace.

---

* Abandoned, gave it up.

CHAPTER XVI

The Forge.

OUR HONEST TRAVELLER now drew near the home he panted for: panted for, because it contained the long lost friend whom he so diligently sought. His little heart beat high with expectation: his eager feet redoubled their speed; and he was absorbed in the recollection of his master's kindnesses.

Happy would it have been for Keeper had he remembered his admonitions also: for, at that unlucky moment, an unmanaged horse galloped past him, which a man was endeavouring to lead to a neighbouring forge to be roughshod. A precaution very necessary, as the frost still continued. Keeper could not forbear assailing his heels: by which imprudence our hero received a kick that laid him in the dust. Stunned by the blow, he was insensible to any thing, until, waking to sorrow and repentance, he found himself, fastened by a cord, in a corner of a blacksmith's shop; to the door of which dismal region of noise and flames he had so rashly followed the animal that bruised him. To this confinement the sons of Vulcan had condemned him; in order as they said, "to see if they could not have some sport with the young cur, yet!" Several days passed, however, without affording them leisure either to hang, or to worry the captive. Neither the *tin kettle* nor the halter were yet ready. The poor creature would probably have been rescued from both by the arm of famine, had he not picked up the parings of the horse's hoofs that happened to lay near him: this, with the snow that fell through the crazy roof of his prison, was the whole of his miserable subsistence.

Ah! thought the sagacious, the guileless, but impetuous Keeper, why did I quit the path of duty? Why did I forget my kind master who has so often warned me from the fault that has brought me hither? Thus, in mournful plainings did he waste the tedious days of captivity and sorrow, 'till one propitious morning brought him a deliverer.

The young gentleman, who released Keeper, was the only son of the 'squire of the village, wherein the accident happened. He had come with his father's groom to give directions respecting a *pony* of his own, that was, on that day, to have his first shoes. He was about nine years of age, of a good natured and generous disposition, and was just come home for the holidays.

"Why should not that poor animal be set at liberty?" He asked, as he cast his eye upon the miserable, shivering, half-starved Keeper.

"You shall have him for a crown," rejoined the Blacksmith.

"I have not so much *in my pocket:*" said the young 'squire: "but, at home, I have a *crown piece*, given me this morning, by my grandmamma, to buy a twelfth-cake with: I had a guinea: but I gave it to kill the *French* with! I will run home and fetch my *crown piece!*"

He was out of sight in a moment, and soon returned with the *crown piece* and his knife; that he might have the pleasure of releasing Keeper himself. The difference between this conduct, and that of Frederic, in the preceding chapter, will strike every reader: and to which of the two the attribute of merit belongs; to which the applause of the good, and the gratification of the heart, appertains, will be equally obvious.

Having accomplished this undertaking, he immediately carried Keeper home, in his arms, to his papa, who commended his son's humanity; and these commendations, with those of his own heart, more than repaid him for the loss of his twelfth-cake.

Keeper, from his good manners, and good temper, soon became a universal favourite in the family; and was the perfect *idol* of his new master, insomuch that could the faithful dog have ever forgot the object of his journey, it would have been in this abode of indulgence and of rest. On the contrary, however, the same sentiment of gratitude that endeared this, his recent deliverer, perpetuated the recollection and esteem of him to whom he owed earlier, and, perhaps, greater, obligations. Consequently, therefore, he waited with anxiety for the first opportunity that might offer itself, to renew his researches. Meanwhile, the vigilance with which his young master preserved his prize, seemed to preclude all possibility of escape.

Among the methods which he used in order to detain Keeper, he tied him unto a four-wheel waggon, a Christmas-gift, whenever he went out. Considering this and other contrivances of the same nature, it is not to be wondered that, notwithstanding the caresses bestowed upon him, Keeper passed his time very unhappily, despairing of his liberty. At length, however, *black-monday* arrived; and his kind persecutor was obliged to leave him, and set off, with a sorrowful countenance for school. He departed, after having kissed Keeper many times, and enjoining the family to be sure to take care of him till his return.

He was no sooner gone than, maugre these instructions, Keeper found no difficulty in getting away; resolved, once more, to seek his master with undeviating feet.

CHAPTER XVII

The Fall of Snow.

THE WEATHER WAS not so fine as in the former part of his journey. It was gloomy, and intensely cold, and, at length, a heavy fall of snow succeeded. When it first began to descend, Keeper amused himself with chasing the flakes, which he mistook for feathers. Having caught one in his mouth, he felt in every part of it with his tongue, to discover his prize. A little time convinced him that it was metamorphosed into water; and, now, his coat was covered with the snow, which, melting, rendered his skin wet, and his whole condition deplorable. Keeper continued on, nevertheless, 'till, toward evening, finding that his legs sunk, almost entirely, at every step, while his back was loaded with the frozen water and being, beside, exceedingly fatigued, he sheltered himself in a hollow tree: where, having shaken as much of the wet from him, as possible, he lay down, and slept soundly 'till day-light. In the mean time, the descent of snow had been so immense that by the aperture, which he had entered, was wholly blocked up. This had kept him warmer than he would otherwise have been: but it now made him a prisoner, like Shakspeare's *Ariel*, in the trunk of a knotty oak. He scratched the blockade, and it easily admitted his paws: but, though a tolerably good miner, his abilities on this occasion availed him nothing: for the snow, by which he was enclosed, extended in one continued sheet, and lay, two or three feet thick, upon the ground. Despairing of deliverance, he turned round, and, to his joy, discovered light, in an oblique direction, at the upper part of the tree. This was, indeed, the *only* source from which light had been received into his cage: but he had not hitherto perceived it. He climbed hastily, and with ease, to this day-star of liberty. He exulted in its beams; and ascended toward it without apprehending any new difficulty. He did not know that though it could cheer and console his confinement, it could not insure his happiness in emancipation. There is, it must be allowed, a common error on this subject: for the splendid luminary of freedom is supposed, by many people, to have more power than it really has. He gained the open air, and was, at first, disappointed to find that the gate-way was not even with the ground. He looked about during some moments, with a melancholy face, at the unvaried but dazzling landscape—then, forgetting its soft contexture, he leaped from the tree, and was instantly buried up to the head in snow; the vast body of which, though not firm enough to support him, and so unstable as to drift with every wind, yet yielded but little to his endeavours to extricate himself. When on the tree, he had perceived a road marked out by the passing of one or two carriages: but, in his present low situation, this disappeared by enchantment, as it seemed to him. Nothing presented itself to his view, but one wide prospect of insipid and chilling whiteness. No sunny spot enlivened the distant view to console the weary and desponding traveller, but, in miserable snowy perspective,

> "Hills peep'd o'er hills, and alps on alps arose!"
>
> GOLDSMITH.

Gusts of wind frequently agitated the powdery expanse, and scattered its frozen particles on Keeper's defenceless head. It was his solace, in the midst of these troubles, that he had not incurred *this*, like his *last*, disaster, by any fault of his own; but, now, solace and trouble, pain, and pleasure, were approaching to an end. He howled piteously; and the blast bore his groans over the solitary waste. His murmurs became fainter, and less incessant. His body grew stiff; and the last remaining warmth of life was about to leave him. Even the recollection of his master became indistinct and lifeless, as the view before him had been: but now his eyes were closed. One look, one short and little look, he wished for; and his wildered fancy cheered his expiring moments with the form, and features of his master, he fancied that this friend of his life was endeavouring to rescue him from his misery. He thought that his warm hand was on his neck. He thought that he dug away the perishing snow. The idea became still less distinct: he even thought himself relieved from his misery. He fancied himself in the arms of his master. He was happy. He was insensible.

CHAPTER XVIII

The Peasant.

ATTRACTED BY KEEPER'S HOWLING, a peasant, who was going home to dinner, had waded through the snow, and taken him in his arms. It was this reality that had been distorted, by Keeper's imagination, into a vision of his master.

The peasant thought Keeper dead: yet he resolved to carry him home, and try what the little warmth his cottage afforded would do for his recovery. He wrapped him up in a sack, and bore him to his hovel that barely sheltered him and his family from the winds and the rains.

There the good woman fanned away the embers from a part of the hearth, and laid Keeper on the warm tiles. She rubbed him, and she lessened her little store of dried gorse or furz, to raise a fire that might reinvigorate him. Toward evening, Keeper began to recover, or, as he fancied, to awake. His senses returning by degrees, he looked round for his master, and barked at the strangers whom he saw. Unacquainted with his motives, they thought this an ungrateful return for their kindness, and therefore turned him out of doors. He, wondering what had befallen him since he fell asleep in the snow, recollected the cottage to be in his way home, and anticipated a speedy restoration to his master, whom he still thought he had seen in the day, but again missed in a most unaccountable manner.

It was moon-light, when, about ten o'clock, the gates of his master were before his eyes. He ran toward them in rapture, and creeping under rushed in an agony of joy to the kitchen door. Scratching violently, it was opened, and he ran round the kitchen, using every gesture, and tone of voice, by which he could express his pleasure. He was somewhat disappointed to find the servants strangers to him; while *they* began to be alarmed at his entrance. The women screamed, and the men prepared to attack Keeper with broomsticks. He, eluding their aim, darted into the inner part of the house, to visit the parlour. There the noise of the servants had spread the consternation, when Keeper terrified the whole company by his appearance.

What might have been his fate had it not been for a gentleman who quieted the agitation of the party, cannot be determined. He assured them that no danger was to be apprehended from the dog, who only seemed to be in high spirits, on some account or other, notwithstanding his starved condition. The conclusion of this remark was so well justified by Keeper's appearance, that all were desirous to see him well fed; and Keeper revelled in luxury during the whole evening: anxious, nevertheless, that his master was not to be seen. He whined at the door, and the indulgent gentleman having opened it, he searched the whole house over, hoping to find his master; but, disappointed, he returned again to the parlour, and scratching at the door was again admitted.

Every creature in the house was as strange to Keeper, as he was strange to them. The furniture, also, was new to him.

Since Keeper had parted from his master, that gentleman having sold his house advantageously, had removed to a more splendid habitation, at some distance from his former abode. Thus the reader is apprized of those circumstances that rendered Keeper still at a loss for his master, although he had arrived at, what he considered, his master's house.

Keeper's behaviour led the new comers to guess with tolerable correctness, the occasion of his visit. All were of opinion that the dog had lost his master, and the gentleman who had befriended him advised that it should be enquired if he had belonged to the former owner of the place. This was only a visitor, however; and though his advice was graciously received, it was totally disregarded.

CHAPTER XIX

Courage.

I T MAY BE FREQUENTLY OBSERVED, of animals, and of dogs chiefly, because with that class we are most intimately acquainted, that they are alarmed at objects which can do them no injury; sometimes small and insignificant; and, not unseldom, inanimate. Keeper had lain quietly before the fire while much conversation passed respecting him. He was not asleep, but had remained fixed in profound rumination on his disappointed hopes, his perilous journey, and his future expectations, when, turning his head toward the door, which some noise had occasioned him to think was about to be opened, and, possibly, by his master, his eye was attracted by a something, black as to colour, and shapeless, or indefinite with respect to its *contour* or outline. For as the subject of his attention lay in deep shade under a chair, its colour and its form mingled with the darkness that surrounded it; and owing to this indistinctness, it might, probably, assume a hundred different appearances, changing and succeeding with the conjectures of Keeper's imagination. After looking at it very attentively during some minutes he concluded that, whatever it might be, both his duty and his inclination called upon him to repel the intruder. Something was yet wanting to equip him for the adventure: this was resolution or courage: and let not the brave be too hasty to cast the reproach of cowardice on his delay. The policy of nations has given birth to so many false opinions respecting courage, that the task of undeceiving the world on that subject, by pursuing it through all its sophistic complications, were, perhaps, one of the most arduous and unsuccessful in which the philosopher could engage; and it is, certainly infinitely beyond the scope of the humble narrator of Keeper's travels: yet it may not be difficult, and, obviously, not irrelevant, to call to mind that the most valiant are afraid of danger to which they are unused, of the nature of which they can form no precise idea, and of which the consequences are *evidently* fatal. The soldier advances to the scymitar and the musquet, because to these he is accustomed, and because he has hitherto escaped their fury: but he flies from the scythe and the fork which the peasant can oppose to him. The most valorous chieftain would be terrified at the appearance of a monster in the field of battle: his useless spear, his armour, and his shield, would but incumber his retreat. It is related of Marshal Turenne, whose name has been ever, and justly, coupled with "daring do" and bravery, that being in the King's tent, when a famous stone-eater was boasting his exploits, and his capacities, the impostor told his Majesty that, if he pleased, he would "swallow that gentleman" (the Marshal) "whole, armour, and all!" The Marshal no sooner heard this extravagant proposal than he fled to his marque in the utmost dismay; and it was with difficulty that the King persuaded him, even on the next day, to venture from the security of his hiding place. This was not cowardice: it was credulity. If the Marshal believed, as plainly he did, that it was possible to the knave to eat him and his armour, his consequent behaviour was but timely prudence, and the result of the rational wish of self-preservation: for what would his sword and his valour have availed against an enemy who could destroy his opposer at a bite.

Courage* is, in truth, that venturous disposition of the mind which we applaud as brave and wise, or stigmatize as rash and fool-hardy, as it happens to succeed in its enterprize, or accord with our own opinions of the occasion of its exertion.

Keeper was not, then, cowardly: had the thing that alarmed him been a cat, a rat, or a bird; nay had a dozen thieves forced their passage into the room, he would have rushed on them with as much dauntless intrepidity as would equal a soldier's *own* story of his battles: but he was frightened agreeably with what has been said, because he could not comprehend the occasion of his terror. Determined at last, to examine the dreadful something that lay under the chair, he left the hearth, and approached with cautious steps. When he had arrived within a certain distance without ascertaining what the terrific appearance might be, he retreated a few steps, and again advanced, in another *radius*, toward the centre of attraction. Still, however, he kept at an awful distance, and, barking, sat down to watch its continuance, and its conduct. His behaviour had gained the observation of the company, and they regarded his motions with curiosity. As they were entirely ignorant of the matter that had drawn Keeper's notice, they were presently anxious to discover what was concealed under the chair, to which he pointed. Some were afraid of danger; and some were desirous to witness the various antics that Keeper played on the occasion, so that a few moments passed before the latent wonder was sought for. Keeper, being set on, began a furious attack: but did not advance many paces nearer his foe than before. He contented himself with loud threatenings of his wrath, and vauntings of his prowess. He tried the right hand and the left to no purpose; and again sat down to watch and to bark. The inquisitiveness of the spectators demanded an explanation: grasping therefore a candle in one hand, and the poker in the other, one of the party marched toward the *arcanum.* Dazzled by the flame, which he held close to his nose, he did not perceive that the poker was approaching Keeper's ribs. Keeper no sooner felt the burn than, turning, he came between the feet of the *illuminato:* the dog was trod upon: the man was bit: both roared out, and were presently struggling together, with the extinguished candle, and the fiery poker. The lookers-on caught the alarm; one over-turned the table, in his escape; and the room was deserted amid the stench of expiring tapers, and the shrieks of frightened females.

CHAPTER XX

The Discovery.

Ne let hobgoblins, names whose sense we see not,
Fray us with things that be not.

SPENSER.

T HE PARTY having rallied their spirits, returned to the scene of their disasters; when a cautious search having been made, by the whole troop in grand muster, some few standing boldly in the van, others peeping over the shoulders of these venturous souls;

---

* It is to be understood, that the passive quality, which we call *fortitude*, is not here spoken of.

some with their hands on the chairs, prepared to hurl them on the *giant* that lay squeezed under the stool; and one or two at the half-opened door, ready to make their escape, when the mystery should be revealed. The group being stationed somewhat in this manner, and cautious search having been made, there was discovered.—*a black hearth brush!!!*

Most were ready to censure Keeper's timidity forgetful of their own share in the farce that had been acted: but Keeper's friend reminded them of this, and then excused every one alike. Keeper, whose burns still tingled, now became the object of consideration; and turpentine being applied, he was materially relieved. The bite he had given was found to be of no importance; and his provocation was acknowledged.

The whole matter was afterwards the subject of mirthful recollection. Keeper only retained a woeful countenance: he still felt pain; and he still missed his master.

CHAPTER XXI

The Post.

T HE GENTLEMAN who had interfered in Keeper's behalf was a particularly good-natured man, and Keeper was his favourite again, in the morning. He gave Keeper sweet tea at breakfast, with which he was prodigiously delighted. Satiety will follow every enjoyment; and Keeper had drank enough of the tea sweet as it was. His friend then added milk and sugar; and the new temptation induced Keeper to take a new draught: its novelty abated, and he retired from this also. Made still more rich, and more sweet, he again indulged in a repetition of the debauch, until stupid from repletion, he lay down by the door, to cool and recover himself.

The conversation at breakfast, was chiefly engrossed by the accident of the evening preceding. Enquiries how each other had rested after the fright, were reciprocally made. The unfortunate gentleman who had *fallen* in the fray was the particular object of concern: and he, happily suffered nothing from his misfortune.

It was asked what could possibly have made the dog afraid of the broom? and the reply insensibly led the dialogue into a discussion on the nature of Fear; respecting which it was generally agreed that the object feared, is either something of known malignity and power; or which from its novelty and obscurity is totally *unknown* to us, and of which we are unable to form any regular notions. "It is astonishing," said Keeper's friend, "it is astonishing with what quickness and facility the imagination gives shapes and meanings to appearances and sounds that are, in themselves, indistinct: and it is equally observable that the moment the reality is discovered, the deception ceases. I remember that, passing along a road on a night that was nearly dark, I saw a something of a whitish colour on my way side. The foot-path was considerably above the level of the road; and the top of this object was beneath my feet. In the space of two minutes, I fancied that it assumed several different forms: at first I thought it a man, who, as I imagined, endeavoured to crouch close under the bank on which I stood: a moment after it seemed a pig: and in another, a calf. I confess to you that I was alarmed: not that I thought it supernatural. I think that my fear was wholly founded on the appre-hension of a robber: but this fear was considerably augmented from the fancied metamorphoses which the object seemed to undergo. In this situation it seemed to wear another shape; entirely fanciful and extravagant; it seemed to me something like a seal, an amphibious creature, of which the large round head was nearest to me. What strange ideas might have succeeded, had I suffered the delusion to continue, I cannot tell. I call them ideas: because the images were in my own brain, not in the object I looked at. Having spoken to it without receiving an answer, I determined to touch it. I acknowledge that I did this with some trepidation. I stood as far off as I could, and, stretching out my arm, directed my stick, with the extremity of which I touched the terrible thing that alarmed me. I cannot recite this circumstance without feeling a reiteration of the surprize I then experienced from finding that, at the very instant I touched the object, it was plainly and obviously a *post!* I did not need the aid of light or minute examination: but merely touching it, and with a stick, I clearly knew it to be a *post!* One remark immediately presents itself. Had men, at all times, examined any appearance that alarmed them, we never should have heard of centaurs, witches, ghosts, and fairies: as this, however, unfortunately, has not been done, it remains for us, observing how naturally such errors may be made, to disregard, as fabulous, every story respecting them.

CHAPTER XXII

The Passion of Fear.

DURING THE RECITAL of this little incident the whole company had been absorbed in the most profound attention: and though the *denouement* of the story produced a laugh, it may be questioned if the hearers were not disappointed of a pleasure they expected from hearing some marvellous event. And, beside, each was vexed with himself because the gratification of starting a conjecture which should be found to be true, was denied him. The most consoling thing now was to laugh at the story-teller, for his unreasonable apprehension. This was rendered incomplete: for he joined in the laugh, and then there was nobody to be laughed at.

Having wiped their eyes therefore, and discovered that their tea was cold, the conversation took a more sedate turn, and nearly became a philosophical discussion.

"I found," said the *post-seer*, "that what had appeared to me a large protuberant head was the top of the post, which was painted white, while the rest, that seemed to recede, was grey. Every one will therefore see why the white part, though not, in fact, nearer than the grey, should appear to me to be so, he will readily understand also why this portion should seem to be larger than the other: for none can have failed to notice, though not particularly conversant with the theory of colours, that those which are light produce the effect of projection, while the dark retire: an observation on which the whole art of painting *primarily* depends. To give this idea a more familiar exposition, —It must have been remarked that a person dressed in white, appears larger than when habited in black."

"There is another matter to be noticed," continued he, "I mean that strong conviction which the sense of feeling bestows. You will find naturalists agreed that without it, sight would be of little use. You saw the dog frightened at a broom; it is supposed

that animals have very imperfect ideas of the size of objects, because they have no arms
nor fingers to ascertain the dimensions of what they see. I should enter upon quite a
new subject, were I to discuss this matter fully: returning, therefore, to the point in
question, we may venture to affirm that had every appearance which may have frightened
the observer, through the medium of the eyes, been exposed to the test of feeling—
had it been touched with the toe, or with a stick—we should never have heard of
spirits or ghosts. I know that an idea has gone abroad that these gentry cannot be
felt—though, rather inconsistently, we are sometimes told of *cold* hands. Now, I will
allow that, to give some foundation to this stupid assertion, some attempts, and not
many, have been made to feel the pretty creatures. In reply to this, I shall recur to
what I have said of colours, owing to which, and other circumstances, we are frequently
deceived, in the gloom of night, as to the *nearness* of the object we see. Were a blind
man to receive his sight, he would, for some time, be puzzled in this respect, even at
noon-day. Now then it may happen that when some venturous hand has been stretched
forth as far as the owner thought necessary to touch the apparition, the poor innocent
lamp-post, or mile-stone, has been, unfortunately, placed, time immemorial, some dozen
yards farther off. From what I have said it will appear that, in proportion to our
ignorance we are liable to these alarms, and that, knowledge can remove these dreadful
evils from our minds: consequently, no other recommendation is necessary to make
young people very desirous of obtaining it. I say *knowledge*, because, for example, we
know that there are fixed rules in the economy of nature, agreeably with which a mile-
stone may be made to appear more or less distant, while, in fact, it remains in the
same place.

CHAPTER XXIII

Keeper's Master.

DURING THE PERIOD that had elapsed between Keeper's departure from Caroline, and
the occurrence of the circumstances, recorded in the latter chapters, the magistrate had
happened to mention the story of Keeper's misfortune, with that of Mr. Walwyn, in
the hearing of a gentleman who was acquainted with his master, and who knew that
he had lost his dog.

The magistrate accompanied the subject with many and warm praises of Caroline's
kindness of Keeper; and the gentleman with whom this conversation occurred reported
the whole to Keeper's master, who immediately paid a visit to the magistrate, wishing to
be farther informed of the matter. The magistrate related to him that, much to Caroline's
regret, the dog had left her. Keeper's master was certain from the description that it
was his dog, and felt grateful for the hospitality that had been shewn to him. He
accompanied the magistrate to the apothecary's house, to return his thanks, and, if possible, to get some clue by which the wanderer might be found.

Caroline said, that, beside lamenting the loss of the dog, it had concerned her that
he left the house before he was thoroughly recovered; but she was now doubly grieved
to find that he had not discovered the master, his fidelity to whom had withdrawn him
from her.

Keeper was the principal topic of animadversion during the whole visit: his absence was lamented; his return desired; and his merits extolled. The capacities of the whole race were descanted on, both as to their natural and acquired habits and endowments. With respect to the first it was mentioned, as remarkable, that so great an intimacy subsists between vultures and dogs in their wild state that they not only assemble together without contention to devour the dead carcasses of animals in America, from Nova-Scotia, to Terra del Fuego; but actually nurse their young in the same place. The Providence of the Creator, it was said, is very visible in causing this harmony between these rapacious creatures: for as it seems to have been intended that they should unite in ridding the earth of putrescent animal bodies that might otherwise infect the air, it was essential that the uniformity of the design should not be destroyed by dissensions between themselves. To render them fit for this useful office, they are exposed to the cravings of an almost insatiable appetite; and that *species* of the *genus* called the *wolf*, in which this want appears to rage with most violence, is said to seek relief from the pain of extreme hunger by swallowing earth and stones.

"We have no wolves in England, I believe?"

"They were extirpated before the end of the thirteenth century: prior to that period they were numerous in some of the counties. Sir Ewin Cameron of Locheil, is mentioned as the destroyer of the last in Scotland, in Lochaber, during the year 1680; and the last in Ireland was killed so lately, as 1710. They are to be found in all the quarters of the world, as high as the *arctic circle*."

"Although" said Keeper's Master, "wolves, foxes, hyænas, and jackals are joined by *naturalists* in the same *genus* on account of the similar conformation of their teeth, they bear little resemblance to each other in their manners. The jackal, indeed, when taken young, acquires the same affectionate disposition; and is by some late authors supposed to be the original stock of all our various kinds of dogs; and of the hyæna it may be observed, that one of the authors alluded to (Mr. Pennant) separates that *species*, making it a separate *genus*."

Of their social habits, and useful qualities, the substance of what was said, may be found in Mr. Cowper's "Task:" where, condemning cruelty to animals in general, he goes on to speak of dogs in particular.

'Superior as we are they yet depend
Not more on human help, than we on theirs.
Their strength, or speed, or vigilance were given
In aid of our defects. In some are found
Such teachable and apprehensive parts,
That man's attainments in his own concerns,
Match'd with th' expertness of the brutes in theirs,
Are oft-times vanquish'd and thrown far behind.
Some shew that nice sagacity of smell,
And read with such discernment, in the port
And figure of the man, his secret aim,
That oft we owe our safety to a skill
We could not teach, and must despair to learn.
But learn we might, if not too proud to stoop

To quadruped instructors, many a good
And useful quality, and virtue too,
Rarely exemplified among ourselves:
Affection never to be wean'd, or chanj'd
By any change of fortune: proof alike
Against unkindness, absence, and neglect:
Fidelity, that neither bribe nor threat
Can move nor warp: and gratitude for small
And trivial favours, lasting as the life,
And glist'ning even in the dying eye!'

CHAPTER XXIV

The Poem.

KEEPER'S MASTER was much charmed with Caroline: and having heard from her the story of the dog's introduction to her care, together with his behaviour on the morning before his departure, he wrote the following lines, and addressed them to Caroline, as an attempt to describe the feelings of his dog; some part, however, may be suspected to have been, mingled at least, with those of the master.

Cold and dark was the night, and poor Keeper was weary;
All smarting his wounds, and his journey was dreary;
The bleak blast blew o'er him, while shiv'ring, cried he:
"Ah! who will have pity, have pity on me!"

"A poor little wand'rer, afflicted I roam,
In search of my master, and master's lov'd home!
Ah! might I from pain and from trouble go free!—
But no one has pity, has pity on me!"

"Thee, lord of mine heart, could mine eyes once discover,
My pilgrimage ended, no longer a rover;
Oh how blest and how happy thy Keeper would be:
For *thou* would'st have pity, have pity on me!"

"But here while I travel, so hungry and weary,
All smarting my wounds, and my way cold and dreary,
O when shall my heart from its anguish be free:
For no one has pity, has pity on me!"

"While thus he lamented, his every joint paining,
Sweet Caroline heard, and she sooth'd all his plaining:
Then, grateful, he cried: "I from anguish am free
For Caroline had pity, had pity on me!"

"To thee who, so kindly, hast succour'd my woes,
My warm beating breast with true gratitude glows:
Yet still I must leave thee, my master to see!"
And *still* thou must have pity, have pity on me!"

"Yes, forgive me, sweet Caroline, if, thy bosom leaving,
After long time thy bounty and goodness receiving,
I depart, the dear lord of *my* bosom to see,
Tho' thou hast had pity, had pity on me!"

"Yet on thee, sweetest Caroline, wherever I wander,
On thee, evermore, shall my faithful heart ponder;
And still shall my wishes crave blessings for thee:
For thou didst take pity, take pity on me!"

"And if the dear lord of thy bosom's own choosing,
Thou should'st ever, like me, be in danger of losing:
If ever thou sigh'st its lov'd master to see,
May some friendly soother have pity on thee;"

"But from sorrow like this still may heav'n preserve thee!
May'st thou never lose hold of the hand that deserves thee!
Yet should'st thou—some saint, such as thou wast to me,
Shall Caroline have pity, have pity on thee!"

CHAPTER XXV

The Conclusion.

THE GENTLEMAN who had interfered in Keeper's behalf had finished his visit; and after his departure no notice was taken of his suggestion that, a message should be sent to enquire if the former owner of the house had lost his dog: While Keeper, finding that his master did not appear, became spiritless, and pined daily. At length, a villager having seen Keeper, positively assured the family that the dog belonged to the 'squire who lived there before; and was charged with the office of carrying the information. As Keeper could not be persuaded to follow him, he carried word to the master of Keeper's arrival. His master immediately came; and Keeper was standing at the door when he saw him at a distance. He ran towards him, half frantic with delight. He endeavoured to jump upon the horse, to reach him: but, not succeeding, his master alighted, and a scene of mutual gratulation took place. The mad and extravagant behaviour by which Keeper evinced his joy, can scarcely be described; while the master, on his part, felt, and displayed tokens of the most lively and sincere pleasure, at the restoration of an animal whose virtues he loved and whose loss he had deplored.

He led Keeper to Caroline: when the pleasure of both on seeing one another again, seemed to realize the master's poem. Between the apothecary too, and Keeper, much friendly intercourse took place; and the magistrate had his share of the honours of the meeting.

Some compliments passed between Caroline and the master, respecting *who* should now possess Keeper? These polite dissensions were not, however, of long duration. Whether it was to accommodate Keeper, who really disliked to part with Caroline; or from what other motive, it is not our province to enquire; but so it happened, Caroline and his master were married, and Keeper abided with both.

He has lived since happily and at ease. Here ended his troubles. If the recital of them has afforded any entertainment: If it has given pleasure, to a tearful, or a smiling countenance, the dog has not *journeyed*, nor the historian *written*, in vain: and if, in the contemplation of the morality occasionally inculcated, it shall be observed that, the whole narrative exhibits a series of misfortunes that were incurred by one single act of negligence: if it stamp on the memory of any reader this important lesson: one error, one dereliction from the path of right; one moment's inattention to, or abandonment of virtue, though trivial and harmless in itself, may expose us to the whole train of vices and sorrows: if such a lesson have been taught, and if it have been deeply impressed, the book will not be thought the less amusing, because it is instructive!

THE END.

Rhymes for the Nursery

By ANN and JANE TAYLOR

Moore del. et sculp.

THE DUNCE of a KITTEN

Published by Harvey & Darton.

RHYMES

FOR

THE NURSERY.

BY THE

Authors of " Original Poems."

TWENTY-SEVENTH EDITION.

———

LONDON:
PRINTED FOR DARTON AND HARVEY,
GRACECHURCH STREET.
———
1835.

Six MEMBERS *of the Taylor family were engaged in book publication. Besides the father, Isaac, and the mother, Ann Martin Taylor, there were the sons Isaac and Jefferys and the daughters Ann (1782–1866) and Jane (1783–1824).* Original Poems, for Infant Minds *(2 vols., 1804–1805) was written when Ann was only twenty-two and Jane twenty-one. Besides their poetry, it included verses by both Isaac Taylors, Bernard Barton (a family friend), plus thirty-four poems by Adelaide O'Keeffe (1776–1855), someone they had never met. Having "written to order," Ann explained, "we had no control over the getting out of the volumes and should have been better pleased if contributions from other hands had been omitted." Despite the publisher's caprice, within less than a year the first five editions were issued and, eventually, French, German, and Russian translations. The book is still available.*

Rhymes for the Nursery *(1806) also had many editions—twenty-seven by 1835. There were eighty-one poems in all, none more famous than "Twinkle, Twinkle, Little Star," which Lewis Carroll twisted into "Twinkle, Twinkle, Little Bat" several generations later.*

Clearly the Taylor sisters had cornered the market on poetry for children in the early nineteenth century. For example, their Hymns for Infant Minds *(1810) had sixty editions by 1890. After 1812—the year Ann married Joseph Gilbert—the Taylor sisters published separately. In 1883 a collected edition of forty-one Taylor verses (*Little Ann and Other Poems*) appeared.*

Darton claims that before Original Poems—*and outside of Isaac Watts—it was nearly true that there were no original poems printed for children. Among the few were John Marchant's* Puerilia *(1751) and* Lusus Juveniles; or, Youth's Recreation *(1753), but the latter hardly seems adapted to children, especially selections like "Decoy Ducks; or, the Pleasure of a Brothel." Nathaniel Cotton's* Vision in Verse, for the Entertainment and Instruction of Younger Minds *went through many editions and has been reprinted (3rd ed., London, 1752) as part of a series of reprints in facsimile from the Osborne Collection of Early Children's Books (Bern, Switzerland: Herbert Lang, 1973).*

Rhymes for the Nursery *is reprinted from the twenty-seventh edition (London: Darton, Harvey and Darton, 1835). Attribution of the poems, designated by the initials A. T. and J. T. after each poem, is based on Christina Duff Stewart,* The Taylors of Ongar: An Analytical Bio-Bibliography *(New York: Garland Publishing, 1975), I, 97.*

The Cow.

Thank you, pretty cow, that made
Pleasant milk, to soak my bread;
Ev'ry day, and ev'ry night,
Warm, and fresh, and sweet, and
  white.

Do not chew the hemlock rank,
Growing on the weedy bank;
But the yellow cowslips eat,
They will make it very sweet.

Where the purple violet grows,
Where the bubbling water flows,
Where the grass is fresh and fine,
Pretty cow, go there and dine.   [A. T.]

Good Night.

Baby, baby, lay your head,
On your pretty cradle bed;
Shut your eye-peeps, now the day
And the light are gone away;
All the clothes are tuck'd in tight;
Little baby dear, good night.

Yes, my darling, well I know
How the bitter wind doth blow;
And the winter's snow and rain,
Patter on the window-pane;
But they cannot come in here,
To my little baby dear:

For the curtains warm, are spread
Round about her cradle bed;
And her little night-cap hides
Ev'ry breath of air besides;
So, till morning shineth bright,
Little baby dear, good night.   [A. T.]

Getting up.

Baby, baby, ope your eye,
For the sun is in the sky,
And he's peeping once again
Through the frosty window-pane;
Little baby, do not keep
Any longer fast asleep.

There now, sit in mother's lap,
That she may untie your cap,
For the little strings have got
Twisted into *such* a knot;
Ah! for shame,—you've been at play
With the bobbin, as you lay.

There it comes, now let us see
Where your petticoats can be:
O! they're in the window-seat,
Folded very smooth and neat:
When my baby older grows,
She shall double up her clothes.

Now one pretty little kiss,
For dressing you so nice as this,
And, before we go down stairs,
Don't forget to say your pray'rs;
For 'tis God who loves to keep
Little babies while they sleep.   [A. T.]

Mamma and the Baby.

What a little thing am I!
  Hardly higher than the table;
I can eat, and play, and cry,
  But to work I am not able.

Nothing in the world I know,
  But mamma will try and show me;
Sweet mamma, I love her so,
  She's so very kind unto me.

And she sets me on her knee
  Very often, for some kisses:
O! how good I'll try to be,
  For such a dear mamma as this is!
[A. T.]

The Sparrows.

Hop about, pretty sparrows, and
    pick up the hay,
  And the twigs, and the wool, and
    the moss;
Indeed, I'll stand far enough out of
    your way,
  Don't fly from the window so cross.

I don't mean to catch you, you dear
    little Dick,
  And fasten you up in a cage;
To hop all day long on a straight bit
    of stick,
  Or to flutter about in a rage.

I only just want to stand by you and
    see
  How you gather the twigs for your
    house;
Or sit at the foot of the jenneting tree,
  While you twitter a song in the
    boughs.

O! dear, if you'd eat a crumb out of
    my hand,
  How happy and glad should I be;
Then come, pretty bird, while I quietly
    stand
  At the foot of the jenneting tree.
[A. T.]

Good Mamma.

Love, come and sit upon my knee,
And give me kisses, one, two, three,

And tell me whether you love me,
My baby.

For this I'm sure, that I love you,
And many, many things I do,
And all day long I sit and sew
For baby.

And then at night I lay awake,
Thinking of things that I can make,
And trouble that I mean to take
For baby.

And when you're good and do not cry,
Nor into wicked passions fly,
You can't think how papa and I
Love baby.

But if my little girl should grow
To be a naughty child, I know
'Twould grieve mamma to serve her
    so,
My baby.

And when you saw me pale and thin,
By grieving for my baby's sin,
I think you'd wish that you had been
A better baby. [A. T.]

Learning to go alone.

Come, my darling, come away,
Take a pretty walk to-day;
Run along and never fear,
I'll take care of baby dear;
Up and down with little feet,
That's the way to walk, my sweet.

Now it is so very near,
Soon she'll get to mother dear.
There she comes along at last,
Here's my finger, hold it fast;
Now one pretty little kiss,
After such a walk as this.
[A. T.]

The little Girl that beat her Sister.

Go, go, my naughty girl, and kiss
　　Your little sister dear;
I must not have such things as this,
　　Nor noisy quarrels here.

What! little children scold and fight,
　　That ought to be so mild;
O! Mary, 'tis a shocking sight
　　To see an angry child.

I can't imagine, for my part,
　　The reason of your folly,
As if she did you any hurt,
　　By playing with your dolly.

See, how the little tears do run
　　Fast from her wat'ry eye;
Come, my sweet innocent, have done,
　　'Twill do no good to cry.

Go, Mary, wipe her tears away,
　　And make it up with kisses;
And never turn a pretty play,
　　To such a pet as this is.   [A. T.]

The little Girl to her Dolly.

There, go to sleep, dolly, in own
　　mother's lap;
I've put on your night-gown and neat
　　little cap;
So sleep, pretty baby, and shut up
　　your eye,
Bye, bye, little Dolly, lie still, and bye
　　bye.

I'll lay my clean handkerchief over
　　your head,

And then make believe that my lap is
　　your bed;
So hush, little dear, and be sure you
　　don't cry:
Bye bye, little dolly, lie still, and bye
　　bye.

There, now it is morning, and time to
　　get up,
And I'll crumb you a mess, in my doll's
　　china cup;
So wake, little baby, and open your
　　eye,
For I think it high time to have done
　　with bye bye.   [A. T.]

The Star.

Twinkle, twinkle, little star,
How I wonder what you are!
Up above the world so high,
Like a diamond in the sky.

When the blazing sun is gone,
When he nothing shines upon,
Then you show your little light,
Twinkle, twinkle, all the night.

Then the trav'ller in the dark,
Thanks you for your tiny spark:
He could not see which way to go,
If you did not twinkle so.

In the dark blue sky you keep,
And often through my curtains peep,
For you never shut your eye,
'Till the sun is in the sky.

As your bright and tiny spark,
Lights the trav'ller in the dark,—
Though I know not what you are,
Twinkle, twinkle, little star.   [J. T.]

Come and play in the Garden.

Little sister, come away,
And let us in the garden play,
For it is a pleasant day.

On the grass-plat let us sit,
Or, if you please, we'll play a bit,
And run about all over it.

But the fruit we will not pick,
For that would be a naughty trick,
And, very likely, make us sick.

Nor will we pluck the pretty flow'rs,
That grow about the beds and bow'rs,
Because, you know, they are not ours.

We'll pluck the daisies, white and red,
Because mamma has often said,
That we may gather them instead.

And much I hope we always may
Our very dear mamma obey,
And mind whatever she may say. [J. T.]

About learning to read.

Here's a pretty gay book, full of
verses to sing,
But Lucy can't read it—O, what a sad
thing!
And such funny stories—and pictures
too—look!
I am glad I can read such a beautiful
book.

But come, little Lucy, then what do
you say?
Shall I begin teaching you pretty
great A?
And then all the letters that stand in
a row,

That you may be able to read it, you
know?

A great many children have no good
mamma,
To teach them to read, and poor
children they are;
But Lucy shall learn all her letters to
tell,
And I hope, by and by, she will read
very well. [J. T.]

No Breakfast for Growler.

No, naughty Growler, get away,
You shall not have a bit;
Now when I speak, how dare you stay:
I can't spare any, Sir, I say,
And so you need not sit.

Poor Growler! do not make him go,
But recollect, before,
That he has never serv'd you so,
For you have giv'n him many a blow,
That patiently he bore.

Poor Growler! if he could but speak,
He'd tell, (as well he might,)
How he would bear with many a freak,
And wag his tail, and look so meek,
And neither bark nor bite.

Upon his back he lets you ride,
And drive about the yard,
And now, while sitting by your side,
To have a bit of bread denied
Is really very hard.

And all your little tricks he'll bear,
And never seem to mind,
And yet you say you cannot spare
One bit of breakfast for his share,
Altho' he is so kind! [J. T.]

Poor Children.

WHEN I go in the meadows, or
walk in the street,
Very often a many poor children I
meet,
With no shoes or stockings to cover
their feet.

Their clothes are all ragged, and let
in the cold,
And they have very little to eat, I am
told:
O dear! 'tis a pitiful sight to behold.

And then, what is worse, very often
they are
Quite naughty and wicked--I never
can bear,
To hear how they quarrel together and
swear.

For often they use naughty words in
their play;
And I might have been quite as
wicked as they,
Had I not been taught better, I've
heard mamma say.

O, how very thankful I always should
be,
That I have kind parents to watch
over me,
Who teach me from wickedness ever
to flee!

And as mamma tells me, I certainly
should
Mind all that is taught me, and be
very good,
For if those poor children knew better
--they would.   [J. T.]

Learning to draw.

COME, here is a slate, and a pencil,
and string,
So now sit you down, dear, and draw
pretty thing;
A man, and a cow, and a horse, and
a tree,
And when you have finish'd, pray
show them to me.

What! cannot you do it? Shall I show
you how?
Come, give me your pencil, I'll draw
you a cow.
You've made the poor creature look
very forlorn!
She has but three legs, dear, and only
one horn.

Now look, I have drawn you a beautiful cow,
And see, here's a dicky-bird perch'd on
a bough,
And here are some more, flying down
from above:
There now, is not that very pretty, my
love.

O yes, very pretty! now make me some
more,
A house with a gate, and a window,
and door,
And a little boy flying his kite with a
string:
O, thank you, mamma, now I'll draw
pretty thing.   [J. T.]

What Clothes are made of.

COME here to papa, and I'll tell my
dear boy,

(For I think he would never have
  guess'd,)
How many poor animals we must
  employ,
Before little Charles can be drest.

The pretty sheep gives you the wool
  from his sides,
  To make you a jacket to use;
And the dog or the seal must be
  stripp'd of their hides,
  To give you a couple of shoes.

And then the grey rabbit contributes
  his share:
  He helps to provide you a hat;
For this must be made of his delicate
  hair,
  And so you may thank him for that.

And many poor animals suffer besides,
  And each of them gives us a share,
Pull off their warm clothing, or give
  us their hides,
  That we may have plenty to wear.

Then as the poor creatures are suffer'd
  to give
  So much for the comfort of man,
I think 'tis but right, that, as long as
  they live,
  We should do all for *them* that we
  can.   [J. T.]

Little Girls must not fret.

W HAT is it that makes little Harriet
  cry?
Come, then, let mamma wipe the tear
  from her eye:
There—lay down your head on my
  bosom—that's right,
And now tell mamma what's the matter to-night.

What! baby is sleepy and tired with
  play?
Come, Betty, make haste, then, and
  fetch her away;
But do not be fretful, my darling,
  because
Mamma cannot love little girls that
  are cross.

She shall soon go to bed and forget it
  all there.
Ah! here's her sweet smile come again,
  I declare;
That's right, for I thought you quite
  naughty before:
Good night, my dear girl, but don't
  fret any more.   [J. T.]

Charles and Animals.

T HE cow has a horn, and the fish
  has a gill;
The horse has a hoof, and the duck
  has a bill;
The bird has a wing, that on high he
  may sail;
And the lion a mane, and the monkey
  a tail;
And they swim, or they fly, or they
  walk, or they eat,
With fin, or with wing, or with bill,
  or with feet.
And Charles has two hands, with five
  fingers to each,
On purpose to hold with, to work,
  and to reach;
No birds, beasts, or fishes, for work
  or for play,
Have any thing half so convenient
  as they;
But if he don't use them, and *keep*
  them in use,
He'd better have had but two legs,
  like a goose.   [J. T.]

Breakfast and Puss.

Here's my baby's bread and milk,
For her lip as soft as silk;
Here's the basin clean and neat,
Here's the spoon, of silver sweet,
Here's the stool, and here's the chair,
For my little lady fair.

No, you must not spill it out,
And drop the bread and milk about;
But let it stand before you flat,
And pray remember pussy cat:
Poor old pussy cat, that purrs
All so patiently for hers.

True, she runs about the house,
Catching, now and then, a mouse;
But, though she thinks it very nice,
That only makes a *tiny* slice,
So don't forget that you should stop,
And leave poor puss a little drop. [A. T.]

The Flower and the Lady, about getting up.

Pretty flower, tell me why
  All your leaves do open wide,
Every morning, when on high
  The noble sun begins to ride.

This is why, my lady fair,
  If you would the reason know,
For betimes the pleasant air
  Very cheerfully doth blow.

And the birds on every tree
  Sing a merry, merry tune,
And the busy honey bee
  Comes to suck my sugar soon.

This is all the reason why
  I my little leaves undo;

Lady, lady, wake and try
  If I have not told you true.   [A. T.]

The Baby's Dance.

Dance, little baby, dance up high,
Never mind, baby, mother is by;
Crow and caper, caper and crow,
There, little baby, there you go;
Up to the ceiling, down to the ground,
Backwards and forwards, round and
    round;
Then dance, little baby, and mother
    shall sing,
With the merry gay coral, ding, ding-
    a-ding, ding.   [A. T.]

For a little Girl that did not like to be washed.

What! cry when I wash you, not
    love to be clean!
There, go and be dirty, unfit to be
    seen:
And till you leave off, and I see you
    have smil'd,
I'll not take the trouble to wash such
    a child.

Suppose I should leave you now, just
    as you are,
Do you think you'd deserve a sweet
    kiss from papa,
Or to sit on his knee, and learn pretty
    great A,
With fingers that have not been wash'd
    all the day?

Ay, look at your fingers, you see it is
    so,
Did you ever behold such a black little
    row?

And for *once* you may look at yourself
   in the glass:
There's a face, to belong to a good
   little lass!
Come, come then, I see you're beginning to clear,
You won't be so foolish again, will you,
   dear?   [A. T.]

The Cut.

Well, what's the matter? there's a
   face!
   What, has it cut a vein?
And is it quite a shocking place?
   Come, let us look again.

I see it bleeds, but never mind
   That tiny little drop;
I don't believe you'll ever find
   That crying makes it stop.

'Tis sad indeed to cry at pain,
   For any but a baby;
If *that* should chance to cut a vein,
   We should not wonder, may be.

But such a man as you should try
   To bear a little sorrow:
So run along, and wipe your eye,
   'Twill all be well to-morrow.   [A. T.]

The little Girl that could not read.

I don't know my letters, and what
   shall I do?
For I've got a nice book, but I can't
   read it through;
O dear, how I wish that my letters I
   knew!

I think I had better begin them to-day,
For 'tis like a dunce to be always at
   play:
Mamma, will you teach little baby
   great A?

And then, B and C, as they stand in
   the row,
One after another, as far as they go,
For then I can read my new story,
   you know.

So pray, mamma, teach me at once,
   and you'll see,
What a very good child little baby will
   be,
To try and remember her A, B, C, D.
         [A. T.]

Questions and Answers.

Who show'd the little ant the way
   Her narrow hole to bore?
And spend the pleasant summer day,
   In laying up her store?

The sparrow builds her clever nest,
   Of wool, and hay, and moss;
Who told her how to weave it best,
   And lay the twigs across?

Who taught the busy bee to fly
   Among the sweetest flow'rs,
And lay his store of honey by,
   To eat in winter hours.

'Twas God who show'd them all the
   way,
   And gave their little skill,
And teaches children, if they pray,
   To do his holy will.   [A. T.]

Playing with Fire.

I've seen a little girl, mamma,
That had got such a dreadful scar,
All down her arms, and neck, and face,
I could not bear to see the place.

Poor little girl! and don't you know
The shocking trick that made her so?
'Twas all because she went and did
A thing her mother had forbid.

For once, when nobody was by her,
This silly child would play with fire,
And long before her mother came,
Her pin-afore was all in flame.

In vain she tried to put it out,
Till all her clothes were burnt about,
And then she suffer'd ten times more,
All over with a dreadful sore.

For many months before 'twas cur'd,
Most shocking torments she endur'd;
And even now, in passing by her,
You see what 'tis to play with fire.
                              [A. T.]

The Field Daisy.

I'm a pretty little thing,
Always coming with the spring,
In the meadows green I'm found,
Peeping just above the ground.
And my stalk is cover'd flat,
With a white and yellow hat.

Little lady, when you pass
Lightly o'er the tender grass,
Skip about, but do not tread
On my meek and healthy head,

For I always seem to say,
"Surly Winter's gone away."   [A. T.]

The Michaelmas Daisy.

I am very pale and dim,
With my faint and bluish rim;
Standing on my narrow stalk,
By the litter'd gravel walk,
And the wither'd leaves aloft,
Fall upon me very oft.

But I show my lonely head,
When the other flow'rs are dead,
And you're even glad to spy
Such a homely thing as I;
For I seem to smile, and say,
"Summer is not quite away."   [A. T.]

Dutiful Jem.

There was a poor widow, she liv'd
    in a cot,
She scarcely a blanket to warm her had
    got,
Her windows were broken, her walls
    were all bare,
And the cold winter-wind often
    whistled in there.

Poor Susan was old and too feeble
    to spin,
Her forehead was wrinkled, her hands
    they were thin;
And she must have starv'd, as so many
    have done,
If she had not been bless'd with a good
    little son.

But he lov'd her well, like a dutiful
　　lad,
He thought her the very best friend
　　that he had.
And now to neglect or forsake her,
　　he knew,
Was the most wicked thing he could
　　possibly do.

For he was quite healthy, and active,
　　and stout,
While his poor mother hardly could
　　hobble about,
And he thought it his duty and great-
　　est delight,
To work for her living from morning
　　to night.

So he went ev'ry morning, as gay as a
　　lark,
And work'd all day long in the fields
　　till 'twas dark,
Then came home again to his dear
　　mother's cot,
And joyfully gave her the wages he got.

And oh, how she lov'd him! how great
　　was her joy,
To think her dear Jem was a dutiful
　　boy:
Her arm round his neck she would
　　tenderly cast,
And kiss his red cheek, while the tears
　　trickled fast.

O then, was not little Jem happier far,
Than naughty, and idle, and wicked
　　boys are?
For, as long as he liv'd, 'twas his com-
　　fort and joy,
To think he'd not been an undutiful
　　boy.　　　　　　　　　　[J. T.]

The Ant's Nest.

IT is such a beautiful day,
　　And the sun shines so bright and so
　　　warm,
That the little ants, busy and gay,
　　Are come from their holes in a
　　　swarm.

All winter together they sleep,
　　Or in underground passages run.
Not one of them daring to peep,
　　To see the bright face of the sun.

But the snow is now melted away,
　　And the trees are all cover'd with
　　　green,
And the little ants, busy and gay,
　　Creeping out from their houses are
　　　seen.

They've left us no room to go by,
　　So we'll step aside on to the grass,
For a hundred poor insects might die,
　　Under your little feet as they pass.
　　　　　　　　　　　　　　[J. T.]

Sleepy Harry.

I do not like to go to bed,
Sleepy little Harry said,
So, naughty Betty, go away,
I will not come at all, I say.

O, what a silly little fellow,
I should be quite asham'd to tell her;
Then Betty, you must come and carry
This very foolish little Harry.

The little birds are better taught,
They go to roosting when they ought;

And all the ducks and fowls, you know,
They went to bed an hour ago.

The little beggar in the street,
Who wanders with his naked feet,
And has not where to lay his head,
O, he'd be *glad* to go to bed.   [J. T.]

Going to Bed.

Down upon my pillow warm,
  I do lay my little head,
And the rain, and wind, and storm,
  Cannot come a-nigh my bed.

Many little children poor,
  Have not any where to go,
And sad hardships they endure,
  Such as I did never know.

Dear mamma, I'll thank you oft
  For this comfortable bed,
And this pretty pillow soft,
  Where I rest my little head.

I shall sleep till morning light,
  On a bed so nice as this;
So, my dear mamma, good night,
  Give your little girl a kiss.   [J. T.]

Idle Mary.

O, MARY, this will never do!
  This work is sadly done, my dear,
And such a little of it too!
  You have not taken pains, I fear.

O! no, your work has been forgotten,
  Indeed you've hardly thought of
    that,

I saw you roll your ball of cotton
  About the floor, to please the cat.

See, here are stitches straggling wide,
  And others reaching down so far;
I'm very sure you have not tried
  At all to-day to please mamma.

The little girl who will not sew,
  Should neither be allow'd to play;
But then I hope, my love, that you
  Will take more pains another day.
                                    [J. T.]

One little Boy.

I'M a little gentleman,
Play, and ride, and dance I can;
Very handsome clothes I wear,
And I live on dainty fare:
And whenever out I ride,
I've a servant by my side.

And I never, all the day,
Need do any thing but play,
Nor even soil my little hand,
Because I am so very grand;
O! I'm very glad, I'm sure,
I need not labour, like the poor.

For I think I could not bear
Such old shabby clothes to wear;
To lie upon so hard a bed,
And only live on barley bread;
And what is worse, too, ev'ry day
To have to work as hard as they.
                                    [J. T.]

Another little Boy.

I'M a little husbandman,
Work and labour hard I can:

I'm as happy all the day
At my work, as if 'twere play;
Tho' I've nothing fine to wear,
Yet for that I do not care.

When to work I go along,
Singing loud my morning song,
With my wallet at my back,
Or my waggon whip to smack;
O, I am as happy then,
As the idle gentlemen.

I've a hearty appetite,
And I soundly sleep at night,
Down I lie content, and say,
"I've been useful all the day:
I'd rather be a plough-boy, than
A useless little gentleman."　　[J. T.]

The little Child.

I'M a very little child,
　Only just have learn'd to speak;
So I should be very mild,
　Very tractable and meek.

If my dear mamma were gone,
　I should perish soon, and die,
When she left me all alone,
　Such a little thing as I!

O, what service can I do,
　To repay her for her care?
For I cannot even sew,
　Nor make any thing I wear.

O, then, I will always try
　To be very good and mild;
Never now be cross and cry,
　Like a little fretful child.

For I often cry and fret,
　And my dear mamma I tease;
Often vex her, while I sit
　Dandled pretty on her knees.

O, how can I serve her so,
　Such a good mamma as this!
Round her neck my arms I'll throw,
　And her gentle cheek I'll kiss.

Then I'll tell her, that I will
　Try not any more to fret her;
And as I grow older still,
　I hope that I shall serve her better.
　　　　　　　　　　　　[J. T.]

The undutiful Boy.

LITTLE HARRY, come along,
And mama will sing a song,
All about a naughty lad,
Tho' a mother kind he had.

He never minded what she said,
But only laugh'd at her instead;
And then did just the same, I've heard,
As if she had not said a word.

He would not learn to read his book,
But wisdom's pleasant way forsook,
With wicked boys he took delight,
And learnt to quarrel and to fight.

And when he saw his mother cry,
And heard her heave a bitter sigh,
To think she'd such a wicked son,
He never car'd for what he'd done.

I hope my little Harry will
Mind all I say, and love me still;
For 'tis his mother's greatest joy,
To think he's not a wicked boy. [J. T.]

The old Beggar Man.

I SEE an old man sitting there;
His wither'd limbs are almost bare,
And very hoary is his hair.

Old man, why are you sitting so?
For very cold the wind doth blow,
Why don't you to your cottage go?

Ah, master, in the world so wide,
I have no home wherein to hide,
No comfortable fire-side!

When I, like you, was young and gay,
I'll tell you what I us'd to say,
That I would nothing do but play.

And so, instead of being taught
Some useful bus'ness, as I ought,
To play about was all I sought.

And now that I am old and grey,
I wander on my lonely way,
And beg my bread from day to day.

But oft I shake my hoary head,
And many a bitter tear I shed,
To think the useless life I've led!

[J. T.]

The little Coward.

W HY, here's a foolish little man,
Laugh at him, Donkey, if you can,
And cat, and dog, and cow, and calf,
Come, ev'ry one of you, and laugh:

For only think, he runs away,
If honest Donkey does but bray!
And when the bull begins to bellow,
He's like a crazy little fellow!

Poor Brindle cow can hardly pass
Along the hedge, to nip the grass,
Or wag her tail to lash the flies,
But off the little booby hies!

And when old Tray comes running too,
With bow, wow, wow, for how d'ye do,
And means it all for civil play,
'Tis sure to make him run away!

But all the while you're thinking, may
    be,
"Ah! well, but this must be a baby."
O! cat, and dog, and cow, and calf,
I'm not surpris'd to see you laugh,
He's five years old, and almost half.

[A. T.]

The Sheep.

L AZY sheep, pray tell me why
In the pleasant fields you lie,
Eating grass and daisies white,
From the morning till the night?
Every thing can something do,
But what kind of use are you?

Nay, my little master, nay,
Do not serve me so, I pray;
Don't you see the wool that grows
On my back, to make you clothes?
Cold, and very cold you'd get,
If I did not give you it.

True, it seems a pleasant thing,
To nip the daisies in the spring;
But many chilly nights I pass
On the cold and dewy grass,
Or pick a scanty dinner, where
All the common's brown and bare.

Then the farmer comes at last,
When the merry spring is past,
And cuts my woolly coat away,
To warm you in the winter's day:
Little master, this is why
In the pleasant fields I lie. [A. T.]

The sick little Boy.

Ah! why's my poor fellow so pale?
    And why do the little tears fall?
Come, tell me, love, what do you ail,
    And mother shall cure him of all.
There, lay your white cheek on my lap,
    With your pin-afore over your head,
And perhaps when you've taken a nap,
    Again your white cheek may be red.

O! no, don't be kind to me yet,
    I do not deserve to be kiss'd;
Some goosb'ries and currants I eat,
    For I thought that they would not
        be miss'd;
And so, when you left me alone,
    I took them, although they were
        green!
But is it not better to own
    What a sad naughty boy I have
        been?

O! yes, I am sorry to hear
    The thing that my Richard has
        done;
But as you have own'd it, my dear,
    You have not made two faults of
        one:
Be sure that you never again
    Forget that God watches your way,
And patiently bear with the pain
That does but your folly repay. [A. T.]

To a little Girl that liked to look in the Glass.

Why is my silly girl so vain?
Looking in the glass again;
For the meekest flow'r of spring,
Is a gayer little thing.

Is your merry eye so blue
As the violet, wet with dew?
Yet, it loves the best to hide
By the hedge's shady side.

Is your bosom half so fair
As the modest lilies are?
Yet their little bells are hung,
Broad and shady leaves among.

When your cheek the warmest glows,
Is it redder than the rose?
But its sweetest buds are seen
Almost hid with moss and green.

Little flow'rs that open gay,
Peeping forth at break of day,
In the garden, hedge, or plain,
Have more reason to be vain. [A. T.]

The cruel Boy and the Kittens.

What! go to see the kittens
        drown'd,
    On purpose, in the yard!
I did not think there could be found
    A little heart so hard.

Poor kittens! no more pretty play
    With pussy's wagging tail:

Oh! I'd go far enough away
  Before I'd see the pail.

No mother kind, nor pleasant bed,
  Nor merry games again!
But there to struggle till you're dead,
  And mew with bitter pain.

Poor things! the little child that can
  Be pleas'd to look and see,
Most likely, when he grows a man,
  A cruel man will be.

And many a wicked thing he'll do,
  Because his heart is hard;
A great deal worse than killing you,
  Poor kittens, in the yard.   [A. T.]

The Workbag.

COME here, I've got a piece of rag,
To make you quite a pretty bag;
Not make believe,—no, no, you'll see
The clever bag that it shall be.

And when 'tis done, I'll show you what
A handsome present I have got;
A needle-book, and scissors too,
Right earnest ones, and all for you.

And then, you know, you'll keep them
    in it,
So that you need not lose a minute,
In hunting up and down to say,
"Where can my scissors be to-day?

"Pray, somebody, do try and look,
To find my thread and needle-book;"
No, no,—but "I know where they are;
"They're in my little work-bag there."
                          [A. T.]

The best way to be happy.

I THINK I should like to be happy
    to-day,
If I could but tell which was the
    easiest way:
But then, I don't know any pretty
    new play:

And as to the old ones,—why, which is
    the best?
There's fine hot boil'd beans, whoop
    and hide, and the rest;
Or make-believe tea-time, with all my
    dolls drest.

But no,—let me see,—now I've thought
    of a way,
That really I think will be better than
    play,
I'll try to be good, if I can, the *whole
    day.*

No passion, no pouting, no crying; no,
    no,
They make me unhappy wherever I go,
And it *would* be a pity to spoil a day
    so.

I don't choose to be such a baby, not
    I,
To quarrel, and sulk, and be naughty,
    and cry,
So now I'll begin, for at least I can
    try.   [A. T.]

The frolicsome Kitten.

DEAR kitten, do lie still, I say,
  For much I want you to be quiet,

Instead of scampering away,
And always making such a riot!

There, only see, you've torn my frock,
And poor mamma must put a patch
in;
I'll give you a right earnest knock,
To cure you of this trick of scratch-
ing.

——Nay, do not scold your little cat,
She does not know what 'tis you're
saying;
And ev'ry time you give a pat,
She thinks you mean it all for
playing.

But if your pussy understood
The lesson that you want to teach
her,
And did not *choose* to be so good,
She'd be, indeed, a naughty crea-
ture.   [A. T.]

A fine Thing.

W HO am I with noble face,
Shining in a clear blue place?
If to look at me you try,
I shall blind your little eye.

When my noble face I shew,
Over yonder mountain blue,
All the clouds away do ride,
And the dusky night beside.

Then the clear wet dews I dry,
With the look of my bright eye;
And the little birds awake,
Many a merry tune to make.

Cowslips then, and hare-bells blue,
And lily-cups their leaves undo,

For they shut themselves up tight,
All the dark and foggy night.

Then the busy people go,
Every one his work unto;
Little girl, when yours is done,
Guess, if I am not the sun.   [A. T.]

A pretty Thing.

W HO am I that shine so bright,
With my pretty yellow light;
Peeping through your curtains grey!
Tell me, little girl, I pray.

When the sun is gone, I rise
In the very silent skies;
And a cloud or two doth skim
Round about my silver rim.

All the little stars do seem
Hidden by my brighter beam;
And among them I do ride,
Like a queen in all her pride.

Then the reaper goes along,
Singing forth a merry song;
While I light the shaking leaves,
And the yellow harvest sheaves.

Little girl, consider well,
Who this simple tale doth tell;
And I think you'll guess it soon,
For I only am the moon.   [A. T.]

Little Birds and cruel Boys.

A LITTLE bird built a warm nest in a
tree,
And laid some blue eggs in it, one, two
and three,

And then very glad and delighted was
   she.

So, after a while, but how long I can't
   tell,
The little ones crept, one by one, from
   the shell;
And their mother was pleas'd, and she
   loved them well.

She spread her soft wings on them all
   the day long,
To warm and to guard them, her love
   was so strong;
And her mate sat beside her, and sung
   her a song.

One day the young birds were all crying for food,
So off flew their mother away from
   her brood;
And up came some boys who were
   wicked and rude.

So they pull'd the warm nest down
   away from the tree;
And the little ones cried, but they
   could not get free;
So at last they all died away, one, two,
   and three:

But when back again the poor mother
   did fly,
O then she set up a most pitiful cry!
So she mourn'd a long while, and then
   lay down to die!   [J. T.]

The Snowdrop.

Now the spring is coming on,
Now the snow and ice are gone,
Come, my little snow-drop root,
Will you not begin to shoot?

Ah! I see your little head,
Peeping on my flower-bed,
Looking all so green and gay,
On this fine and pleasant day.

For the mild south wind doth blow,
And hath melted all the snow,
And the sun shines out so warm,
You need not fear another storm.

So your pretty flower shew,
And your leaves of white undo,
Then you'll hang your modest head,
Down upon my flower-bed.   [J. T.]

Romping.

Why now, my dear boys, this is
   always the way,
You can't be contented with innocent
   play,
But this sort of romping, so noisy
   and high,
Is never left off, till it ends in a cry.

What! are there no games you can
   take a delight in,
But kicking, and knocking, and box-
   ing, and fighting?
It is a sad thing to be forc'd to conclude,
That boys can't be merry, without
   being rude.

Now what is the reason you never
   can play,
Without snatching each other's playthings away?
Would it be any hardship to let them
   alone,
When ev'ry one of you has toys of
   his own?

I often have told you before, my dear
    boys,
That I do not object to your making
    a noise:
Or running and jumping about any
    how,
But fighting and mischief I cannot
    allow.

So, if any more of these quarrels are
    heard,
I tell you this once, and I'll keep to
    my word,
I'll take every marble, and spintop,
    and ball,
And not let you play with each other
    at all.   [J. T.]

Working.

WELL, now I will sit down, and
    work very fast,
And try if I can't be a good girl at
    last:
'Tis better than being so sulky and
    haughty,
I'm really quite tired of being so
    naughty.

For as mamma says, when my bus'ness
    is done,
There's plenty of time left to play and
    to run;
But when 'tis my work-time, I ought to
    sit still,
I know that I *ought*, and I certainly
    will.

But for fear, after all, I should get at
    my play,
I'll put my wax-doll in the closet away;
And I'll not look to see what the
    kitten is doing,

Nor yet think of any thing but my
    sewing.

I'm sorry I've idled so often before,
But I hope I shall never do so any
    more:
Mamma *will* be pleas'd when she sees
    how I mend,
And have done this long seam from be-
    ginning to end!   [J. T.]

The selfish Snails.

IT happen'd that a little snail
Came crawling with his slimy tail,
    Upon a cabbage-stalk;
But two more little snails were there,
Both feasting on this dainty fare,
    Engag'd in friendly talk.

"No, no, you shall not dine with us,
How dare you interrupt us thus,"
    The greedy snails declare;
So their poor brother they discard,
Who really thinks it very hard,
    He may not have his share.

But selfish folks are sure to know,
They get no good by being so,
    In earnest or in play;
Which these two snails confess'd, no
    doubt,
When soon the gardener spied them
    out,
    And threw them both away.   [J. T.]

Good Dobbin.

O THANK you, good Dobbin, you've
    been a long track,
And have carried papa all the way on
    your back;

You shall have some nice oats, faithful
    Dobbin, indeed,
For you've brought papa home to his
    darling with speed.

The howling wind blew, and the pelt-
    ing rain beat,
And the thick mud has cover'd his legs
    and his feet,
But yet on he gallop'd, in spite of the
    rain,
And has brought papa home to his
    darling again.

The sun it was setting a long while
    ago,
And papa could not see the road where
    he should go,
But Dobbin kept on through the
    desolate wild,
And has brought papa home again safe
    to his child.

Now go to the stable, the night is so
    raw,
Go, Dobbin, and rest your old bones on
    the straw;
Don't stand any longer out here in the
    rain,
For you've brought papa home to his
    darling again.   [J. T.]

Sulking.

Why is Mary standing there?
Leaning down upon a chair,
With pouting lip, and frowning brow:
I wonder what's the matter now?

Come here, my dear, and tell me true,
Is it because I scolded you,
For doing work so bad and slow,
That you are standing sulking so?

Why then, indeed, I'm griev'd to see,
That you can so ill-temper'd be:
You make your fault a great deal
    worse,
By being angry and perverse.

O, how much better it appears
To see you melting into tears,
And then to hear you humbly say,
"I'll not do so another day."

But when you stand and sulk about,
And look so cross, and cry and pout,
Why that, my little girl, you know,
Is *worse* than working bad and slow.
    [J. T.]

Time to go to Bed.

The sun at evening sets, and then
The lion leaves his gloomy den;
He roars along the forest wide,
And all who hear are terrified;
There he prowls at evening hour,
Seeking something to devour.

When the sun is in the west,
The white owl leaves his darksome
    nest;
Wide he opes his staring eyes,
And screams, as round and round he
    flies:
For he hates the cheerful light,
He sleeps by day, and wakes at night.

When the lion cometh out,
When the white owl flies about,
I must lay my sleepy head
Down upon my pleasant bed;
There all night I'll lay me still,
While the owl is screaming shrill. [J. T.]

Time to rise.

THE cock, who soundly sleeps at
    night,
Rises with the morning light,
Very loud and shrill he crows;
Then the sleeping ploughman knows,
He must leave his bed also,
To his morning work to go.

And the little lark does fly
To the middle of the sky;
You may hear his merry tune,
In the morning very soon;
For he does not like to rest,
Idle, in his downy nest.

While the cock is crowing shrill,
Leave my little bed I will,
And I'll rise to hear the lark,
For it is no longer dark;
'Twould be a pity there to stay,
When 'tis bright and pleasant day.
                     [J. T.]

The poor Fly.

So, so, you are running away, Mr.
    Fly,
But I'll come at you now, if you don't
    go too high;
There, there, I have caught you,—you
    can't get away:
Never mind, my old fellow, I'm only
    in play.

O Charles! cruel Charles! you have
    kill'd the poor fly,
You have pinch'd him so hard, he is
    going to die,
His legs are all broken, and he cannot
    stand;
There, now he has fallen down dead
    in your hand!

I hope you are sorry for what you have
    done,
You may *kill* many flies, but you can-
    not *make* one.
No,—you can't set it up—as I told you
    before,
It is dead—and it never will stand any
    more.

Poor thing! as it buzz'd up and down
    on the glass,
How little it thought what was coming
    to pass!
For it could not have guess'd, as it
    frisk'd in the sun,
That a child would destroy it for
    nothing but fun.

The spider, who weaves his fine cob-
    web so neat,
Might have caught him, indeed, for he
    wants him to eat;
But the poor flies must learn to keep
    out of *your* way,
As you kill them for nothing at all but
    your play.   [J. T.]

Tumble up.

TUMBLE down, tumble up, never
    mind it, my sweet,
  No, no, never beat the poor floor:
'Twas your fault, that could not stand
    straight on your feet,
  Beat yourself, if you beat any more.

O dear! what a noise: will a noise make
    it well?
  Will crying wash bruises away?
Suppose that it should bleed a little
    and swell,
  'Twill all be gone down in a day.

That's right, be a man, love, and dry
    up your tears,

Come,—smile, and I'll give you a
    kiss;
If you live in the world but a very
    few years,
    You must bear greater troubles than
    this.

Ah! there's the last tear dropping down
    from your cheek!
    All the dimples are coming again;
And your round little face looks as
    ruddy and meek,
    As a rose that's been wash'd in the
    rain.   [A. T.]

The little Fish that would
not do as it was bid.

DEAR mother, said a little fish,
    Pray, is not that a fly?
I'm very hungry, and I wish
    You'd let me go and try.

Sweet innocent, the mother cried,
    And started from her nook,
That horrid fly is put to hide
    The sharpness of the hook!

Now, as I've heard, this little trout
    Was young and foolish too,
And so he thought he'd venture out,
    To see if it were true.

And round about the hook he play'd,
    With many a longing look,
And—"Dear me," to himself he said,
    "I'm sure that's not a *hook*."

"I can but give one little pluck:
    Let's see, and so I will."
So on he went, and lo! it stuck
    Quite through his little gill.

And as he faint and fainter grew,

With hollow voice he cried,
  "Dear mother, had I minded you,
    I need not now have died."   [A. T.]

The two Babies.

WHAT is this pretty little thing,
That nurse so carefully doth bring,
And round its head her apron fling?
           A baby!

O! dear, how very soft its cheek,
Why nurse, I cannot make it speak,
And it can't walk, it is so weak,
           Poor baby.

Here, take a bit, you little dear,
I've got some cake and sweetmeats
    here:
'Tis very nice, you need not fear,
           You baby.

O! I'm afraid that it will die,
Why can't it eat as well as I,
And jump and talk? do let it try,
           Poor baby.

Why, you were once a baby too,
And could not jump as now you do,
But good mamma took care of you,
           Like baby.

And then she taught your pretty feet,
To pat along the carpet neat,
And call'd papa to come and meet
           His baby.

O! good mamma, to take such care,
And no kind pains and trouble spare,
To feed and nurse you, when you were
           A baby. [A. T.]

What came of firing a Gun.

Ah! there it falls, and now 'tis dead,
The shot went through its pretty head,
  And broke its shining wing!
How dull and dim its closing eyes!
How cold, and stiff, and still it lies!
  Poor harmless little thing!

It was a lark, and in the sky,
In mornings fine it mounted high,
  To sing a merry song;
Cutting the fresh and healthy air,
It whistled out its music there,
  As light it skimm'd along.

How little thought its pretty breast,
This morning, when it left its nest,
  (Hid in the springing corn,
To find some victuals for its young,
And pipe away its morning song,)
  It never should return.

Those pretty wings shall never more
Its callow nestlings cover o'er,
  Or bring them dainties rare:
But long their gaping beaks will cry,
And then with pinching hunger die,
  All in the bitter air.

Poor little bird!—if people knew
The sorrows little birds go through,
  I think that even boys
Would never call it sport and fun,
To stand and fire a frightful gun,
  For nothing but the noise.   [A. T.]

The little Negro.

Ah! the poor little blackamoor,
  see there he goes,
And the blood gushes out from his
  half frozen toes,

And his legs are so thin you may
  almost see the bones,
As he goes shiver, shiver, all along
  on the stones.

He was once a negro boy, and a
  merry boy was he,
Playing outlandish plays, by the tall
  palm-tree,
Or bathing in the river like a brisk
  water-rat,
And at night sleeping sound on a little
  piece of mat.

But there came some wicked people,
  and they stole him far way,
And then good-bye to palm-tree tall,
  and merry, merry play;
For they took him from his house and
  home, and ev'ry body dear,
And now, poor little negro boy, he's
  come a begging here.

And fie upon the wicked folks who did
  this cruel thing!
I wish some mighty nobleman would
  go and tell the king:
For to steal him from his house and
  home must be a crying sin,
Though he was a little negro boy,
  and had a sooty skin.   [A. T.]

Poor Donkey.

Poor Donkey, I'll give him a handful of grass,
I'm sure he's a good-natur'd, honest
  old ass;
He trots to the market to carry the
  sack,
And lets me ride all the way home on
  his back;
And only just stops by the ditch for a
  minute,

To see if there's any fresh grass for him
    in it.

'Tis true, now and then, he has got a
    bad trick
Of standing stock still, tho' he never
    will kick;
And then, poor old fellow, you know
    he can't tell
That standing stock still is not using
    me well;
For it never comes into his head,
    I dare say,
To do his work first, and then
    afterwards play.

No, no, my good Donkey, I'll give you
    some grass,
For *you* know no better, because you're
    an ass;
But what little Donkies some children
    must look,
Who stand, very like you, stock still
    at their book,
And waste ev'ry moment of time as
    it passes,
A great deal more stupid and silly
    than asses.   [A. T.]

The Spring Nosegay.

Come, my love, 'tis pleasant spring,
  Let us make a posy gay;
Ev'ry pretty flow'r we'll bring,
  Daisy white, and prickly May:
Then along the hedge we'll go,
Where the purple violets blow.

After that the primrose fair,
  Looking very pale and dim;
And we'll search the meadows, where
  Cowslips grow, with yellow rim;
With a buttercup or two,
Holding little drops of dew.

Then the snow-drop, hanging low
  On its green and narrow stalk;
And the crocuses, that blow
  Up and down the garden walk;
All these pretty flow'rs we'll bring,
To make a posy for the spring. [A. T.]

The Summer Nosegay.

Now the yellow cowslips fade,
  All along the woody walk;
And the primrose hangs her head,
  Faintly, on her tiny stalk;
Let us to the garden go,
Where the flow'rs of summer grow.

Come, and make a nosegay there,
  Plucking ev'ry flow'r that blows;
Brier sweet, and lily fair,
  That along the valley grows;
With a honeysuckle red,
Round the shady arbour led.

Then a budding rose or two,
  Half in mossy leaves enroll'd,
With the larkspur, red and blue,
  Streaky pink, and marygold:
These shall make our posy gay,
In the cheerful summer day. [A. T.]

The Autumn Nosegay.

Now the fog has risen high,
  Through the chilly morning air;
And the blue and cheerful sky
  Peeps upon us, here and there:
Once again we'll gather sweet,
Every pretty flow'r we meet.

Ah! the yellow leaves are now
  Over all the garden spread,
Scatter'd from the naked bough
  On the lonely flower-bed;
Where the autumn daisy blue
Opens, wet with chilly dew.

Lavender, of darksome green,
  Shows its purple blossoms near;
And the golden rod is seen,
  Shooting up his yellow spear:
These are all that we can find
In our posy gay to bind.   [A. T.]

The Winter Nosegay.

N ow the winds of winter blow,
  Fiercely through the chilly air;
Now the fields are white with snow,
  Can we find a posy there?
No, there cannot, all around,
A single blade of grass be found.

Nothing but the holly bright,
  Spotted with its berries gay;
Lauristinus, red and white;
  Or the ivy's crooked spray;
With a sloe of darksome blue,
Where the ragged blackthorn grew.

Or the hip of shining red,
  Where the wild rose us'd to grow;
Peeping out its scarlet head,
  From beneath a cap of snow:
These are all that dare to stay
Through the cutting winter's day.
     [A. T.]

The little Lark.

I HEAR a pretty bird, but hark!
  I cannot see it any where.

O! it is a little lark,
  Singing in the morning air.
Little lark, do tell me why
You are singing in the sky.

Other little birds at rest,
  Have not yet begun to sing;
Every one is in its nest,
  With its head behind its wing;
Little lark, then, tell me why
You sing so early in the sky.

You look no bigger than a bee,
  In the middle of the blue:
Up above the poplar tree;
  I can hardly look at you:
Come, little lark, and tell me why
You are mounted up so high.

'Tis to watch the silver star,
  Sinking slowly in the skies;
And beyond the mountain far,
  To see the glorious sun arise:
Little lady, this is why
I am mounted up so high.

'Tis to sing a merry song,
  To the pleasant morning light:
Why linger in my nest so long,
  When the sun is shining bright?
Little lady, this is why
I sing so early in the sky.

To the little birds below,
  I do sing a merry tune;
And I let the ploughman know,
  He must come to labour soon.
Little lady, this is why
I am singing in the sky.   [J. T.]

The quarrelsome Dogs.

O LD Tray and rough Growler are
    having a fight,

So let us get out of their way;
They snarl, and they growl, and they
    bark, and they bite!
    O dear, what a terrible fray.

Why, what foolish fellows!—now is it
    not hard
They can't live together in quiet?
There's plenty of room for them both
    in the yard,
    And always a plenty of diet.

But who ever said to old Growler
    and Tray,
    It was naughty to quarrel and fight?
They think 'tis as pretty to fight as to
    play;
    Nor know they the wrong from the
    right.

But when little children, who *know* it
    is wrong,
    Are angrily fighting away,
A great deal more blame unto them
    must belong,
    Than to quarrelsome Growler and
    Tray.   [J. T.]

The honest Ploughman.

POOR Tom is a husbandman, healthy
    and strong,
He follows his plough as it hobbles
    along,
And as he plods after it, sings him a
    song.

He's up in the morning before the
    cock crows,
For he should not be idle, he very well
    knows,
Tho' folks who *are* idle know that, I
    suppose.

And when the sun sets, and his work
    is done soon,
He finds his way home by the light of
    the moon:
She shines in his face, and he whistles
    a tune.

So when he gets home, (and he never
    delays,)
And sees his neat cot, and the cheerful
    wood blaze,
His heart glows within him with
    pleasure and praise.

'Tis those who won't work, that mayn't
    eat, it is said;
But Tom, with good appetite, takes his
    brown bread,
And cheerful and happy he goes to
    his bed.   [J. T.]

The great Lord.

A VERY great lord lives near
    Thomas's cot,
Who servants, and coaches, and horses
    has got;
And yet his poor neighbour Tom
    envies him not.

For coaches, and horses, and delicate
    food,
Can't make people happy, unless they
    are good;
But then he is idle, and wicked, and
    rude.

He never does any thing all the day
    long,
Altho' he is able, and healthy, and
    strong:
He does nothing right, but he often
    does wrong.

An then he's as vain as he ever can be,
He wears gaudy clothes, that poor
   people may see,
And laughs at good folks who are
   better than he.

And, tho' he's so rich, and so great,
   and so high,
He does no more good than a worm
   or a fly;
And no one would miss him, if he
   were to die.

I think 'tis much better, for all that I
   see,
A poor honest ploughman, like
   Thomas, to be,
Than a fine wealthy lord, but as
   useless as he.   [J. T.]

The little Beggar Girl.

THERE's a poor beggar going by,
  I see her looking in,
She's just about as big as I,
  Only so very thin.

She has no shoes upon her feet,
  She is so very poor;
And hardly any thing to eat;
  I pity her, I'm sure!

But I have got nice clothes, you know,
  And meat, and bread, and fire;
And you, mamma, that love me so,
  And all that I desire.

If I were forc'd to stroll so far,
  O dear, what should I do!
I wish she had a dear mamma,
  Just such a one as you.

Here, little girl, come back again,
  And hold your ragged hat,
For I will put a penny in;
  So buy some bread with that.
          [J. T.]

Poor Puss.

O HARRY! my dear, do not kick the
   poor cat,
For pussy, I'm sure, will not thank you
   for that;
She was doing no harm as she sat on
   the mat.

Suppose some great giant, amazingly
   strong,
Were often to kick you, and drive you
   along;
Now, would you not think it
   exceedingly wrong?

And Harry, I think, you're as greatly
   to blame,
When *you* serve poor pussy exactly
   the same,
For she's very gentle, and quiet, and
   tame.

She is under the table, quite out of
   your way,
But why should you tease her and
   drive her away?
She takes it in earnest, if you think
   it play.

There, now go and call her, and stroke
   her again,
And never, my love, give poor animals
   pain,
For, you know, when you hurt them,
   they cannot complain.   [J. T.]

The little Ants.

A LITTLE black ant found a large
    grain of wheat,
    Too heavy to lift or to roll;
So he begg'd of a neighbour he
    happen'd to meet,
    To help it down into his hole.

I've got my own work to see after,
    said he,
    You may shift for yourself, if you
    please;
So he crawl'd off, as selfish and cross
    as could be,
    And lay down to sleep at his ease.

Just then a black brother was passing
    the road,
    And seeing his neighbour in want,
Came up and assisted him in with his
    load;
    For he was a good-natur'd ant.

Let all who this story may happen to
    hear,
    Endeavour to profit by it;
For often it happens that children
    appear
    As cross as the ant, ev'ry bit.

And the good-natur'd ant, who assisted
    his brother,
    May teach those who choose to be
    taught,
That if little insects are kind to each
    other,
    Then children most certainly ought.

[J. T.]

Second Thoughts are best.

I HATE being scolded, and having a
    rout,
I've a good mind to stand in the corner
    and pout;
And if mamma calls me, I will not
    come out.

Yes, yes, here I'll keep, I'm resolv'd on
    it quite,
With my face to the wall, and my back
    to the light,
And I'll not speak a word, if I stand
    here all night.

And yet mamma says, when I'm
    naughty and cry,
She scolds me to make me grow good
    by and by,
And that, all the time, she's as sorry
    as I.

And she says, when I'm naughty and
    will not obey,
If she were to let me go on in that way,
I should grow up exceedingly wicked,
    one day.

O then, what a very sad girl I should
    be,
To be sulky and cross when she
    punishes me,
And grieve such a very kind mother
    as she.

Well, then I'll go to her directly, and
    say,
Forgive me this once, my dear mother,
    I pray;
For that will be better than sulking
    all day.   [J. T.]

The Meadows.

WE'LL go to the meadows, where
   cowslips do grow,
   And buttercups, looking as yellow
      as gold;
And daisies and violets, beginning to
      blow;
   For it is a most beautiful sight to
      behold.

The little bee humming about them
      is seen,
   The butterfly merrily dances along;
The grasshopper chirps in the hedges
      so green,
   And the linnet is singing his liveliest
      song.

The birds and the insects are happy
      and gay,
   The beasts of the field they are glad
      and rejoice,
And we will be thankful to God ev'ry
      day,
   And praise his great name in a
      loftier voice.

He made the green meadows, he
      planted the flow'rs,
   He sent his bright sun in the heavens
      to blaze;
He created these wonderful bodies of
      ours,
   And as long as we live we will sing
      of his praise.   [J. T.]

A Wasp and a Bee.

A WASP met a bee that was just
   buzzing by,
And he said, little cousin, can you
   tell me why

You are lov'd so much better by people
   than I?

My back shines as bright and as yellow
      as gold,
And my shape is most elegant too,
      to behold;
Yet nobody likes me for that, I am
      told.

Ah! cousin, the bee said, 'tis all very
      true.
But if I were half as much mischief
      to do,
Indeed they would love me no better
      than you.

You have a fine shape, and a delicate
      wing,
They own you are handsome, but then
      there's one thing
They cannot put up with, and that is
      your sting.

My coat is quite homely and plain,
      as you see,
Yet nobody ever is angry with me,
Because I'm a humble and innocent
      bee.

From this little story let people beware,
Because, like the wasp, if ill-natur'd
      they are,
They will never be lov'd, if they're
      ever so fair.   [J. T.]

Passion and Penitence.

HERE'S morning again, and a good
      fire-side,
   And a breakfast so nice, in a basin
      so full;
How good, dear mamma, for my wants
      to provide,

I ought to be good too—but sure
you are dull.

You don't smile to meet me, nor call
me your dear;
Nor place your arms round me so
kind on your knee;
Nor give the sweet kiss as I climb up
your chair:
Nay, sure that's a frown; are you
angry with me?

Oh! now I remember,—quite naughty
last night,
I left you in passion, nor came for
a kiss;
I bounc'd from the room in vexation
and spite:
Indeed, 'twas ungrateful, I did act
amiss.

My fretful ill-temper, so naughty and
rude,
To you was unkind, before God it
was wrong!
I'm asham'd to come near, when I
know I'm not good:
You ought not to kiss me for ever
so long.

Yet, indeed I do love you, and stoutly
will try
To subdue ev'ry passion that moves
me amiss:
I'll pray God to pardon my sin, lest
I die:
When you see my repentance, I
know you will kiss.   [J. T.]

The Dunce of a Kitten.

COME, pussy, will you learn to read?
I've got a pretty book:

Nay, turn this way, you must indeed:
Fie, there's a sulky look.

Here is a pretty picture, see,
An apple, and great A:
How stupid you will ever be,
If you do nought but play.

Come, A, B, C, an easy task,
What any fool can do:
I will do any thing you ask,
For dearly I love you.

Now, how I'm vex'd, you are so dull,
You have not learnt it half:
You will grow up a downright fool,
And make all people laugh.

Mamma told me so, I declare,
And made me quite asham'd;
So I resolv'd no pains to spare,
Nor like a dunce be blam'd.

Well, get along, you naughty kit,
And after mice go look;
I'm glad that I have got more wit,
I love my pretty book.   [J. T.]

A very sorrowful Story.

I'LL tell you a story, come, sit on
my knee;
A true and a pitiful one it shall be,
About an old man, and a poor man
was he.

He'd a fine merry boy, (such another
as you,)
And he did for him all that a father
could do;
For he was a kind father as ever I
knew.

So he hop'd, that one day, when his
darling should grow

A fine hearty man, he'd remember,
    you know,
To thank his old father for loving
    him so.

But what do you think came of all
    this at last?
Why, after a great many years had
    gone past,
And the good-natur'd father grew old
    very fast:

Instead of remembering how kind he
    had been,
This boy did not care for his father
    a pin,
But bade him be gone, for he should
    not come in!

So he wander'd about in the frost and
    the snow!
For he had not a place in the world
    where to go:
And you'd almost have cried to have
    heard the wind blow.

And the tears, poor old man, oh! how
    fast they did pour!
As he shiver'd with cold at his wicked
    child's door.
Did you ever now hear such a story
    before?   [A. T.]

THE END.

The Butterfly's Ball
and
The Peacock at Home

By WILLIAM ROSCOE

FRONTISPIECE.

"Come take up your hats & away let us haste." p. 2
Pub. Jan. 15. 1808. by J. Harris, corner St. Pauls Church Yd.

THE

BUTTERFLY's BALL,

AND THE

GRASSHOPPER's FEAST.

By Mr. ROSCOE.

———

LONDON:
PRINTED FOR J. HARRIS, SUCCESSOR TO E. NEWBERY,
AT THE ORIGINAL JUVENILE LIBRARY, CORNER
OF ST. PAUL'S CHURCH-YARD.

1808.

Frontispiece.

The Peacock addressing his Mates. P. 4.
Pub. Sep. 1. 1807. by J. Harris, corner St. Pauls Church Yd.

THE

PEACOCK *"AT HOME:"*

A

SEQUEL

TO THE

BUTTERFLY'S BALL,

WRITTEN

BY A LADY.

AND

ILLUSTRATED WITH ELEGANT ENGRAVINGS.

LONDON:
PRINTED FOR J. HARRIS, SUCCESSOR TO E. NEWBERY, AT THE
ORIGINAL JUVENILE LIBRARY, THE CORNER OF
ST. PAUL'S CHURCH-YARD.

1807.

WILLIAM ROSCOE's The Butterfly's Ball, and the Grasshopper's Feast *(1807) was the most famous production of John Harris, successor to Elizabeth Newbery. Since John Newbery, it seems, published everything for children except volumes of original poetry, it is noteworthy that the publishing firm he founded was ultimately responsible for the first successful nonsense verse. William Roscoe (1753– 1831), a botanist, banker, and member of Parliament for Liverpool, originally wrote the verses for his young son Robert and first published them in 1806 in the* Gentleman's Magazine.

The Butterfly's Ball *had phenomenal success. The publishers estimated that they sold forty thousand copies in the first year of publication of Roscoe's book and its sister publication,* The Peacock at Home *(1807) by Catherine Ann Dorset (1750–1817?). Dorset's verses, in the same style as Roscoe's, were preferred by some early reviewers. As Roscoe and Dorset are both reproduced here, the modern reader can judge for himself which is the better comic verse.*

The Peacock at Home *reached twenty-eight editions in its first ten years of publication. Certainly the copperplate engravings after William Mulready added to the total charm of the books, as did their pleasing size and shape, approximately four inches square. The text and illustrations seem unified in these sixteen-page rhyme books.*

Other verses in the same vein were The Lion's Masquerade *(1807), which may also be by Mrs. Dorset,* The Lion's Parliament *(1807),* The Elephant's Ball and Grand Fête Champêtre *(1807), and* The Wedding among the Flowers *(1808)) by Ann Taylor Gilbert. Note how soon the imitations came out. In some of the imitations the human figures disappear entirely.*

The Lion's Masquerade *shows some erosion of the light spirit of Roscoe's original. The animals vow to be as harmonious as birds:*

> In the feather'd *race here an example we find,*
> *Far better than that which is set by* Mankind.
> *How oft have their gala's a tragical end,*
> *One loses a mistress, another a friend—*

The clever couplets are still there, but The Butterfly's Ball *was written for sheer fun, not for a satiric point. There was no moralizing: the animals in Roscoe and Dorset simply had a ball, and so did the reader.*

The Butterfly's Ball *and its sequel,* The Peacock at Home, *are reproduced from 1883 facsimiles (London: Griffith and Farran) based on the 1807 editions. The text pages have been reduced, but the illustrations are the same size as the originals.*

THE

BUTTERFLY's BALL.

COME take up your Hats, and away let us
haste
To the *Butterfly's* Ball, and the *Grasshopper's*
Feast.
The Trumpeter, *Gad-fly*, has summon'd the
Crew,
And the Revels are now only waiting for
you.

4

So said little Robert, and pacing along,
His merry Companions came forth in a
Throng.
And on the smooth Grass, by the side of a
Wood,
Beneath a broad Oak that for Ages had
stood,

Saw the Children of Earth, and the Tenants
of Air,
For an Evening's Amusement together repair.

"Saw the children of earth & the tenants of air." p.4

5

And there came the *Beetle*, so blind and so
    black,
Who carried the *Emmet*, his Friend, on his
    Back.

And there was the *Gnat* and the *Dragon-fly*
    too,
With all their Relations, Green, Orange,
    and Blue.
And there came the *Moth*, with his Plu-
    mage of Down,
And the *Hornet* in Jacket of Yellow and
    Brown ;

6

Who with him the *Wasp*, his Companion, did
    bring,
But they promis'd, that Evening, to lay by
    their Sting.
And the sly little *Dormouse* crept out of
    his Hole,
And brought to the Feast his blind Brother,
    the *Mole*.

And the *Snail*, with his Horns peeping out
    of his Shell,
Came from a great Distance, the Length of
    an Ell.

"*And the sly little dormouse, crept out of his hole.*" p. 6

7

A Mushroom their Table, and on it was laid
A Water-dock Leaf, which a Table-cloth made.

The Viands were various, to each of their Taste,
And the *Bee* brought her Honey to crown the Repast.
Then close on his Haunches, so solemn and wise,
The *Frog* from a Corner, look'd up to the Skies.

8

And the *Squirrel* well pleas'd such Diversions to see,
Mounted high over Head, and look'd down from a Tree.
Then out came the *Spider*, with Finger so fine,
To shew his Dexterity on the tight Line.

From one Branch to another, his Cobwebs he slung,
Then quick as an Arrow he darted along,

"And the *Bee* brought her honey" &c.   *p.* 7

9

But just in the Middle,—Oh! shocking to
  tell,
From his Rope, in an Instant, poor Harlequin fell.

Yet he touch'd not the Ground, but with
  Talons outspread,
Hung suspended in Air, at the End of a
  Thread.
Then the *Grasshopper* came with a Jerk and
  a Spring,
Very long was his Leg, though but short was
  his Wing ;

"*Hung suspended in air.*" &c.   *p. 9*

10

He took but three Leaps, and was soon out
of Sight,
Then chirp'd his own Praises the rest of the
Night.
With Step so majestic the *Snail* did ad-
vance,
And promis'd the Gazers a Minuet to
dance.

But they all laugh'd so loud that he pull'd
in his Head,
And went in his own little Chamber to
Bed.

"With step so Majestic the snail did advance." p. 10

11

Then, as Evening gave Way to the Shadows
of Night,
Their Watchman, the *Glow-worm*, came out
with a Light.

Then Home let us hasten, while yet we
can see,
For no Watchman is waiting for you and
for me.
So said little Robert, and pacing along,
His merry Companions returned in a
Throng.

END OF THE BUTTERFLY'S BALL.

"So said little Robert, & pacing along." &c.

THE

PEACOCK "*AT HOME*."

THE Butterfly's Ball, and the Grasshopper's Feasts,
Excited the spleen of the Birds and the Beasts:
For their mirth and good cheer—of the Bee was the theme,
And the Gnat blew his horn, as he danc'd in the beam.
'Twas humm'd by the Beetle, 'twas buzz'd by the Fly,
And sung by the myriads that sport 'neath the sky.

4

The Quadrupeds listen'd with sullen displeasure,
But the Tenants of Air were enrag'd beyond measure.
The PEACOCK display'd his bright plumes to the Sun,
And, addressing his Mates, thus indignant begun:
"Shall we, like domestic, inelegant Fowls,
"As unpolish'd as Geese, and as stupid as Owls,
"Sit tamely at home, hum drum, with our Spouses,
"While Crickets, and Butterflies, open their houses?
"Shall such mean little Insects pretend to the fashion?
"Cousin Turkey-cock, well may you be in a passion!
"If I suffer such insolent airs to prevail,
"May Juno pluck out all the eyes in my tail;

Frontispiece.

"The Peacock addressing his Mates.
P. 4.

5

"So a Fete I will give, and my taste I'll display,

"And send out my cards for Saint Valentine's Day."

—This determin'd, six fleet Carrier-Pigeons went out,

To invite all the Birds to Sir Argus's Rout.

The nest-loving TURTLE-DOVE sent an excuse;

DAME PARTLET lay in, as did good Mrs GOOSE.

The TURKEY, poor soul! was confin'd to the rip:

For all her young Brood had just fail'd with the pip.

And the PARTRIDGE was ask'd; but a Neighbour hard by,

Had engag'd a snug party to meet in a Pye;

The WHEAT-EAR declin'd, recollecting her Cousins,

Last year, to a Feast were invited by dozens.

6

But alas! they return'd not; and she had no taste

To appear in a costume of vine-leaves or paste.

The WOODCOCK prefer'd his lone haunt on the moor;

And the Traveller, SWALLOW, was still on his tour.

The CUCKOO, who should have been one of the guests,

Was rambling on visits to other Bird's Nests.

But the rest, all accepted the kind invitation,

And much bustle it caus'd in the plumed creation:

Such ruffling of feathers, such pruning of coats

Such chirping, such whistling, such clearing of throats,

Such polishing bills, and such oiling of pinions!

Had never been known in the biped dominions.

"Such ruffling of feathers, such pruning of coats". &c.

P. 5.

7

The TAYLOR BIRD offer'd to make up new clothes;

For all the young Birdlings, who wish'd to be Beaux:

He made for the ROBIN a doublet of red,

And a new velvet cap for the GOLDFINCH's head;

He added a plume to the WREN's golden crest,

And spangled with silver the GUINEA-FOWL's breast;

While the HALCYON bent over the streamlet to view,

How pretty she look'd in her boddice of blue!

Thus adorn'd, they set off for the Peacock's abode,

With the Guide INDICATOR,* who shew'd them the road:

> * Cuculus Indicator, a Bird of Cuckow kind, found in the interior parts of Africa; it has a shrill note, which the Natives answer by a soft whistle; and the Birds repeating the note, the Natives are thereby conducted to the wild Bee-hives, which this Bird frequents.

8

From all points of the compass, came Birds of all feather;

And the PARROT can tell who and who were together.

There came Lord CASSOWARY and General FLAMINGO,

And Don PEROQUETO, escap'd from Domingo;

From his high rock-built eyrie the EAGLE came forth,

And the Duchess of PTARMIGAN flew from the North.

The GREBE and the EIDER DUCK came up by water,

With the SWAN, who brought out the young CYGNET, her daughter.

From his woodland abode came the PHEASANT, to meet

Two kindred, arriv'd by the last India fleet:

The one, like a Nabob, in habit most splendid,

Where gold with each hue of the Rainbow was blended:

9

In silver and black, like a fair pensive Maid,
Who mourns for her love! was the other array'd.
The CHOUGH came from Cornwall, and brought up his Wife;
The GROUSE travell'd south, from his Lairdship in Fife;
The BUNTING forsook her soft nest in the reeds;
And the WIDOW-BIRD came, though she still wore her weeds;
Sir John HERON, of the Lakes, strutted in a *grand pas*,
But no card had been sent to the pilfering DAW,
As the Peacock kept up his progenitors' quarrel,
Which Æsop relates, about cast-off apparel;
For Birds are like Men in their contests together,
And, in questions of right, can dispute for a feather.

10

The PEACOCK, Imperial, the pride of his race,
Receiv'd all his guests with an infinite grace,
Wav'd high his blue neck, and his train he display'd,
Embroider'd with gold, and with em'ralds inlaid.
Then with all the gay troop to the shrubb'ry repair'd,
Where the musical Birds had a concert prepar'd;
A holly bush form'd the Orchestra, and in it
Sat the Black-bird, the Thrush, the Lark, and the Linnet;
A BULL-FINCH, a captive! almost from the nest,
Now escap'd from his cage, and, with liberty blest,
In a sweet mellow tone, join'd the lessons of art
With the accents of nature, which flow'd from his heart.

"A Holly bush form'd the Orchestra, and in it &c.

11

The CANARY, a much-admir'd foreign musician,

Condescended to sing to the Fowls of condition.

While the NIGHTINGALE warbled, and quaver'd so fine,

That they all clapp'd their wings, and pronounc'd it divine !

The SKY LARK, in extacy, sang from a cloud,

And CHANTICLEER crow'd, and the YAFFIL laugh'd loud.

The dancing began, when the singing was over ;

A DOTTEREL first open'd the ball with the PLOVER ;

Baron STORK, in a waltz, was allow'd to excel,

With his beautiful partner, the fair DEMOISELLE.*

* The Numidian Crane, or Demoiselle, from the elegance of its appearance, and its singular carriage, is called the Demoiselle, which means the
young Lady ; for this Bird walks very gracefully, and sometimes skips and
leaps, as though it were trying to dance.

"Baron Stork in a Waltz was allow'd to excel." &c.

P.11.

12

And a newly-fledg'd GOSLING, so spruce and genteel,

A minuet swam with young Mr TEAL.

A London-bred SPARROW—a pert forward Cit;

Danc'd a reel with Miss WAGTAIL, and little TOM-TIT.

And the Sieur GUILLEMOT next perform'd a *pas seul*,

While the elderly Bipeds were playing a Pool.

The Dowager Lady TOUCAN first cut in,

With old Doctor BUZZARD, and Adm'ral PENGUIN,

From Ivy-bush Tow'r came Dame OWLET the Wise,

And Counsellor CROSSBILL sat by to advise.

The Birds past their prime, o'er whose *heads* it was fated,

Should pass many St. Valentines—yet be unmated,

"The Dowager Lady Toucan first cut in." &c.

P. 12.

13

Look'd on, and remark'd, that the prudent and sage,

Were quite overlook'd in this frivolous age,

When Birds, scarce pen-feather'd, were brought to a rout,

Forward Chits! from the egg-shell but newly come out;

That in their youthful days, they ne'er witness'd such frisking,

And how wrong! in the GREENFINCH to flirt with the SISKIN.

So thought Lady MACKAW, and her Friend COCKATOO,

And the RAVEN foretold that "no good could ensue!"

They censur'd the BANTAM for strutting and crowing,

In those vile pantaloons, which he fancied look'd knowing.

And a want of decorum caus'd many demurs,

Against the GAME CHICKEN, for coming in spurs.

14

Old Alderman CORM'RANT, for supper impatient,

At the Eating-room door, for an hour had been station'd,

Till a MAGPIE, at length, the banquet announcing,

Gave the signal, long wish'd for, of clamouring and pouncing.

At the well-furnish'd board all were eager to perch;

But the little Miss CREEPERS were left in the lurch.

Description must fail; and the pen is unable

To describe all the lux'ries which cover'd the table.

Each delicate viand that taste could denote,

Wasps *a la sauce piquante*, and Flies *en compôte;*

Worms and Frogs *en friture*, for the web-footed Fowl,

And a barebecued Mouse was prepar'd for the Owl;

15

Nuts, grains, fruit, and fish, to regale ev'ry palate,

And groundsel and chick-weed serv'd up in a sallad.

The Razor-Bill carv'd for the famishing group,

And the Spoon-Bill obligingly ladled the soup ;

So they fill'd all their crops with the dainties before 'em,

And the tables were clear'd with the utmost decorum.

When they gaily had caroll'd till peep of the dawn,

The Lark gently hinted, 'twas time to be gone ;

And his clarion, so shrill, gave the company warning,

That Chanticleer scented the gales of the morning.

So they chirp'd, in full chorus, a friendly adieu ;

And, with hearts quite as light as the plumage that grew

On their merry-thought bosoms, away they all flew......

16

Then long live the Peacock, in splendour unmatch'd,

Whose Ball shall be talk'd of, by Birds yet unhatch'd ;

His praise let the Trumpeter* loudly proclaim,

And the Goose lend her quill to transmit it to Fame.

* The Agami, or Trumpeter, a native of America, remarkable for
a singular noise, resembling the instrument from which it takes its name.

THE END.

"The Razor-bill care'd for the famishing group." &c.

P 15

Mrs. Leicester's School: or, The History of Several Young Ladies

By CHARLES and MARY LAMB

FRONTISPIECE

*In this manner, the epitaph on my mother's
tomb being my primer and my spelling-book,
I learned to read.___Page 9.*

MRS. LEICESTER'S SCHOOL:

OR,

THE HISTORY

OF

SEVERAL YOUNG LADIES,

RELATED BY THEMSELVES.

London:

PRINTED FOR M. J. GODWIN, AT THE JUVENILE
LIBRARY, NO. 41, SKINNER-STREET.

1809.

A SCHOOL STORY LIKE *Sarah Fielding's* The Governess; or, Little Female Academy *is* Mrs. Leicester's School; or, The History of Several Young Ladies, Related by Themselves *(1809) by Mary Lamb (1764–1847) and Charles Lamb (1775–1834). Although the book was published anonymously, Mary Lamb was responsible for seven of the ten tales, Charles for the others: the stories of Maria Howe ("The Witch Aunt"), Susan Yates ("First Going to Church") and Arabella Hardy ("Sea Voyage"). There were ten English editions by 1836 and a French version,* Les Jeunes Pensionnaires, ou Histoires de plusieurs jeunes Demoiselles racontes par elles-memes *(2d ed., 1834). Landor judged the Elinor Forester tale (with the exception of* The Bride of Lammermoor*) "the most beautiful tale in prose composition in any language, ancient or modern."*

While Coleridge was certain Mrs. Leicester's School *would be a permanent jewel in English literature, that distinction properly goes to another Mary and Charles Lamb cooperative venture,* Tales from Shakespeare *(1807). The twenty prose paraphrases of Shakespeare's plays were also split: one-third by Charles (six plays) and two-thirds by Mary (fourteen plays). This, their most successful book for children, is still in print in many editions.*

The last joint Lamb production for children was Poetry for Children Entirely Original by the Author of Mrs. Leicester's School *(1809), which contains some pleasant verse plus some muted interest in natural science. Here's a sample from "Breakfast," a poem which describes how sleepy Robert likes*

> *To sit and watch the vent'rous fly*
> *Where the sugar's piled high,*
> *Clambering o'er the lumps so white,*
> *Rocky Cliffs of sweet delight.*

There was evidently a fly fixation in eighteenth-century books for children. While the poems of the Lambs were said to sell quickly, Charles Lamb forgot to retain a copy for himself, and William Godwin and his wife never put out another edition, although there was one in America in 1812. In 1877 Swinburne, taken with the selections of the spinster and bachelor, tried to revive interest in the poems, which never were as popular as those of the Taylor sisters.

Mrs. Leicester's School is reprinted from volume three of The Works of Charles Lamb: The Works for Children *(London: Methuen and Company Ltd., 1912), edited by E. V. Lucas and based on the 1809 second edition of the original book.*

DEDICATION
To
The Young Ladies at Amwell School

My dear young friends,

Though released from the business of the school, the absence of your governess confines me to Amwell during the vacation. I cannot better employ my leisure hours than in contributing to the amusement of you my kind pupils, who, by your affectionate attentions to my instructions, have rendered a life of labour pleasant to me.

On your return to school I hope to have a fair copy ready to present to each of you of your own biographical conversations last winter.

Accept my thanks for the approbation you were pleased to express when I offered to become your *amanuensis*. I hope you will find I have executed the office with a tolerably faithful pen, as you know I took notes each day during those conversations, and arranged my materials after you were retired to rest.

I begin from the day our school commenced. It was opened by your governess for the first time, on the ——day of February. I pass over your several arrivals on the morning of that day. Your governess received you from your friends in her own parlour.

Every carriage that drove from the door I knew had left a sad heart behind.—Your eyes were red with weeping, when your governess introduced me to you as the teacher she had engaged to instruct you. She next desired me to show you into the room which we now call the play-room. "The ladies," said she, "may play, and amuse themselves, and be as happy as they please this evening, that they may be well acquainted with each other before they enter the school-room to-morrow morning."

The traces of tears were on every cheek, and I also was sad; for I, like you, had parted from my friends, and the duties of my profession were new to me, yet I felt that it was improper to give way to my own melancholy thoughts. I knew that it was my first duty to divert the solitary young strangers: for I considered that this was very unlike the entrance to an old established school, where there is always some good-natured girl who will shew attentions to a new scholar, and take pleasure in initiating her into the customs and amusements of the place. These, thought I, have their own amusements to invent; their own customs to establish. How unlike too is this forlorn meeting to old school-fellows returning after the holidays, when mutual greetings soon lighten the memory of parting sorrow!

I invited you to draw near a bright fire which blazed in the chimney, and looked the only cheerful thing in the room.

During our first solemn silence, which, you may remember, was only broken by my repeated requests that you would make a smaller, and still smaller circle, till I saw the fireplace fairly inclosed round, the idea came into my mind, which has since been a source of amusement to you in the recollection, and to myself in particular has been of essential benefit, as it enabled me to form a just estimate of the dispositions of you my young pupils, and assisted me to adapt my plan of future instructions to each individual temper.

An introduction to a point we wish to carry, we always feel to be an aukward affair, and generally execute it in an aukward manner; so I believe I did then: for when I imparted this idea to you, I think I prefaced it rather too formally for such young auditors, for I began with telling you, that I had read in old authors, that it was not unfrequent in former times, when strangers were assembled together, as we might be, for them to amuse themselves with telling stories, either of their own lives, or the adventures of others. "Will you allow me, ladies," I continued, "to persuade you to amuse yourselves in this way? you will not then look so unsociably upon each other: for we find that these strangers of whom we read, were as well acquainted before the conclusion of the first story, as if they had known each other many years. Let me prevail upon you to relate some little anecdotes of your own lives. Fictitious tales we can read in books, and [*they*] were therefore better adapted to conversation in those times when books of amusement were more scarce than they are at present."

After many objections of not knowing what to say, or how to begin, which I overcame by assuring you how easy it would be, for that every person is naturally eloquent when they are the hero or heroine of their own tale, the *Who should begin* was next in question.

I proposed to draw lots, which formed a little amusement of itself. Miss Manners, who till then had been the saddest of the sad, began to brighten up, and said it was just like drawing king and queen, and began to tell us where she passed last twelfth day; but as her narration must have interfered with the more important business of the lottery, I advised her to postpone it, till it came to her turn to favour us with the history of her life, when it would appear in its proper order. The first number fell to the share of miss Villiers, whose joy at drawing what we called the *first prize*, was tempered with shame at appearing as the first historian in the company. She wished she had not been the very first:—she had passed all her life in a retired village, and had nothing to relate of herself that could give the least entertainment:—she had not the least idea in the world where to begin.

"Begin," said I, "with your name, for that at present is unknown to us. Tell us the first thing you can remember; relate whatever happened to make a great impression on you when you were very young, and if you find you can connect your story till your arrival here to-day, I am sure we shall listen to you with pleasure; and if you like to break off, and only treat us with a part of your history, we will excuse you, with many thanks for the amusement which you have afforded us; and the lady who has drawn the second number will, I hope, take her turn with the same indulgence, to relate either all, or any part of the events of her life, as best pleases her own fancy, or as she finds she can manage it with the most ease to herself."—Encouraged by this offer of indulgence, miss Villiers began.

If in my report of her story, or in any which follow, I shall appear to make her or you speak an older language than it seems probable that you should use, speaking in your own words, it must be remembered, that what is very proper and becoming when spoken, requires to be arranged with some little difference before it can be set down in writing. Little inaccuracies must be pared away, and the whole must assume a more formal and correct appearance. My own way of thinking, I am sensible, will too often intrude itself, but I have endeavoured to preserve, as exactly as I could, your own words, and your own peculiarities of style and manner, and to approve myself

Your faithful historiographer, as well as true friend,

M. B.

I

ELIZABETH VILLIERS

(By Mary Lamb)

MY FATHER IS THE CURATE of a village church, about five miles from Amwell. I was born in the parsonage-house, which joins the church-yard. The first thing I can remember was my father teaching me the alphabet from the letters on a tombstone that stood at the head of my mother's grave. I used to tap at my father's study-door; I think I now hear him say, "Who is there?—What do you want, little girl?" "Go and see mamma. Go and learn pretty letters." Many times in the day would my father lay aside his books and his papers to lead me to this spot, and make me point to the letters, and then set me to spell syllables and words: in this manner, the epitaph on my mother's tomb being my primmer and my spelling-book, I learned to read.

I was one day sitting on a step placed across the church-yard stile, when a gentleman passing by, heard me distinctly repeat the letters which formed my mother's name, and then say, *Elizabeth Villiers*, with a firm tone, as if I had performed some great matter. This gentleman was my uncle James, my mother's brother: he was a lieutenant in the navy, and had left England a few weeks after the marriage of my father and mother, and now, returned home from a long sea-voyage, he was coming to visit my mother; no tidings of her decease having reached him, though she had been dead more than a twelvemonth.

When my uncle saw me sitting on the stile, and heard me pronounce my mother's name, he looked earnestly in my face, and began to fancy a resemblance to his sister, and to think I might be her child. I was too intent on my employment to observe him, and went spelling on. "Who has taught you to spell so prettily, my little maid?" said my uncle. "Mamma," I replied; for I had an idea that the words on the tombstone were somehow a part of mamma, and that she had taught me. "And who is mamma?" asked my uncle. "Elizabeth Villiers," I replied; and then my uncle called me his dear little niece, and said he would go with me to mamma: he took hold of my hand, intending to lead me home, delighted that he had found out who I was, because he imagined it would be such a pleasant surprise to his sister to see her little daughter bringing home her long lost sailor uncle.

I agreed to take him to mamma, but we had a dispute about the way thither. My uncle was for going along the road which led directly up to our house; I pointed to the church-yard, and said, that was the way to mamma. Though impatient of any delay, he was not willing to contest the point with his new relation, therefore he lifted me over the stile, and was then going to take me along the path to a gate he knew was at the end of our garden; but no, I would not go that way neither: letting go his hand, I said, "You do not know the way—I will shew you:" and making what haste I could among the long grass and thistles, and jumping over the low graves, he said, as he followed what he called my *wayward steps*, "What a positive soul this little niece of mine is! I knew the way to your mother's house before you were born, child." At last I stopped at my mother's grave, and, pointing to the tombstone, said, "Here is mamma," in a voice of exultation, as if I had now convinced him that I knew the way best: I looked up in his face to see him acknowledge his mistake; but Oh, what a face of sorrow did I see! I was so frightened, that I have but an imperfect recollection of what followed. I remember I pulled his coat, and cried "Sir, sir," and tried to move him. I knew not what to do; my mind was in a strange confusion; I thought I had done something wrong in bringing the gentleman to mamma to make him cry so sadly; but what it was I could not tell. This grave had always been a scene of delight to me. In the house my father would often be weary of my prattle, and send me from him; but here he was all my own. I might say anything and be as frolicsome as I pleased here; all was chearfulness and good humour in our visits to mamma, as we called it. My father would tell me how quietly mamma slept there, and that he and his little Betsy would one day sleep beside mamma in that grave; and when I went to bed, as I laid my little head on the pillow, I used to wish I was sleeping in the grave with my papa and mamma; and in my childish dreams I used to fancy myself there, and it was a place within the ground, all smooth, and soft, and green. I never made out any figure of mamma, but still it was the tombstone, and papa, and the smooth green grass, and my head resting upon the elbow of my father.

How long my uncle remained in this agony of grief I know not; to me it seemed a very long time: at last he took me in his arms, and held me so tight, that I began to cry, and ran home to my father, and told him, that a gentleman was crying about mamma's pretty letters.

No doubt it was a very affecting meeting between my father and my uncle. I remember that it was the first day I ever saw my father weep: that I was in sad trouble, and went into the kitchen and told Susan, our servant, that papa was crying; and she wanted to keep me with her that I might not disturb the conversation; but I would go back to the parlour to *poor papa*, and I went in softly, and crept between my father's knees. My uncle offered to take me in his arms, but I turned sullenly from him, and clung closer to my father, having conceived a dislike to my uncle because he had made my father cry.

Now I first learned that my mother's death was a heavy affliction; for I heard my father tell a melancholy story of her long illness, her death, and what he had suffered from her loss. My uncle said, what a sad thing it was for my father to be left with such a young child; but my father replied, his little Betsy was all his comfort, and that, but for me, he should have died with grief. How I could be any comfort to my father, struck me with wonder. I knew I was pleased when he played and talked with me; but I thought that was all goodness and favour done to me, and I had no notion how I could make any part of his happiness. The sorrow I now heard he had suffered, was as new and strange to me. I had no idea that he had ever been unhappy; his voice was always kind and cheerful; I had never before seen him weep, or shew any such signs of grief as those in which I used to express my little troubles. My thoughts on these subjects were confused and childish; but from that time I never ceased pondering on the sad story of my dead mamma.

The next day I went by mere habit to the study door, to call papa to the beloved grave; my mind misgave me, and I could not tap at the door. I went backwards and forwards between the kitchen and the study, and what to do with myself I did not know. My uncle met me in the passage, and said, "Betsy, will you come and walk with me in the garden?" This I refused, for this was not what I wanted, but the old amusement of sitting on the grave, and talking to papa. My uncle tried to persuade me, but still I said, "No, no," and ran crying into the kitchen. As he followed me in there, Susan said, "This child is so fretful to-day, I do not know what to do with her." "Aye," said my uncle, "I suppose my poor brother spoils her, having but one." This reflection on my papa made me quite in a little passion of anger, for I had not forgot that with this new uncle sorrow had first come into our dwelling: I screamed loudly, till my father came out to know what it was all about. He sent my uncle into the parlour, and said, he would manage the little wrangler by himself. When my uncle was gone I ceased crying; my father forgot to lecture me for my ill humour, or to enquire into the cause, and we were soon seated by the side of the tombstone. No lesson went on that day; no talking of pretty mamma sleeping in the green grave; no jumping from the tombstone to the ground; no merry jokes or pleasant stories. I sate upon my father's knee, looking up in his face, and thinking, *"How sorry papa looks,"* till, having been fatigued with crying, and now oppressed with thought, I fell fast asleep.

My uncle soon learned from Susan that this place was our constant haunt; she told him she did verily believe her master would never get the better of the death of her mistress, while he continued to teach the child to read at the tombstone; for, though it might sooth his grief, it kept it for ever fresh in his memory. The sight of his sister's grave had been such a shock to my uncle, that he readily entered into Susan's apprehensions; and concluding, that if I were set to study by some other means there would no longer be a pretence for these visits to the grave, away my kind uncle hastened to the nearest market-town to buy me some books.

I heard the conference between my uncle and Susan, and I did not approve of his interfering in our pleasures. I saw him take his hat and walk out, and I secretly hoped he was gone *beyond seas* again, from whence Susan had told me he had come. Where *beyond seas* was I could not tell; but I concluded it was somewhere a great way off. I took my seat on the church-yard stile, and kept looking down the road, and saying, "I hope I shall not see my uncle again. I hope my uncle will not come from *beyond seas* any more;" but I said this very softly, and had a kind of notion that I was in a perverse ill-humoured fit. Here I sate till my uncle returned from the market-town with his new purchases. I saw him come walking very fast with a parcel under his arm. I was very sorry to see him, and I frowned, and tried to look very cross. He untied his parcel, and said, "Betsy, I have brought you a pretty book." I turned my head away, and said, "I don't want a book;" but I could not help peeping again to look at it. In the hurry of opening the parcel he had scattered all the books upon the ground, and there I saw fine gilt covers and gay pictures all fluttering about. What a fine sight!—All my resentment vanished, and I held up my face to kiss him, that being my way of thanking my father for any extraordinary favour.

My uncle had brought himself into rather a troublesome office; he had heard me spell so well, that he thought there was nothing to do but to put books into my hand, and I should read; yet, notwithstanding I spelt tolerably well, the letters in my new library were so much smaller than I had been accustomed to, they were like Greek characters to me; I could make nothing at all of them. The honest sailor was not to be discouraged by this difficulty; though unused to play the schoolmaster, he taught me to read the small print, with unwearied diligence and patience; and whenever he saw my father and me look as if we wanted to resume our visits to the grave, he would propose some pleasant walk; and if my father said it was too far for the child to walk, he would set me on his shoulder, and say, "Then Betsy shall ride;" and in this manner has he carried me many many miles.

In these pleasant excursions my uncle seldom forgot to make Susan furnish him with a luncheon which, though it generally happened every day, made a constant surprise to my papa and me, when, seated under some shady tree, he pulled it out of his pocket, and began to distribute his little store; and then I used to peep into the other pocket to see if there were not some currant wine there and the little bottle of water for me; if, perchance, the water was forgot, then it made another joke,—that poor Betsy must be forced to drink a little drop of wine. These are childish things to tell of, and instead of my own silly history, I wish I could remember the entertaining stories my uncle used to relate of his voyages and travels, while we sate under the shady trees, eating our noon-tide meal.

The long visit my uncle made us was such an important event in my life, that I fear I shall tire your patience with talking of him; but when he is gone, the remainder of my story will be but short.

The summer months passed away, but not swiftly;—the pleasant walks, and the charming stories of my uncle's adventures, made them seem like years to me; I remember the approach of winter by the warm great coat he bought for me, and how proud I was when I first put it on, and that he called me Little Red Riding Hood, and bade me beware of wolves, and that I laughed and said there were no such things now; then he told me how many wolves, and bears, and tygers, and lions he had met with in uninhabited lands, that were like Robinson Crusoe's Island. O these were happy days!

In the winter our walks were shorter and less frequent. My books were now my chief amusement, though my studies were often interrupted by a game of romps with my uncle, which too often ended in a quarrel because he played so roughly; yet long before this I dearly loved my uncle, and the improvement I made while he was with us was very great indeed. I could now read very well, and the continual habit of listening to the conversation of my father and my uncle made me a little woman in understanding; so that my father said to him, "James, you have made my child quite a companionable little being."

My father often left me alone with my uncle: sometimes to write his sermons; sometimes to visit the sick, or give counsel to his poor neighbours: then my uncle used to hold long conversations with me, telling me how I should strive to make my father happy, and endeavour to improve myself when he was gone:—now I began justly to understand why he had taken such pains to keep my father from visiting my mother's grave, that grave which I often stole privately to look at; but now never without awe and reverence, for my uncle used to tell me what an excellent lady my mother was, and I now thought of her as having been a real mamma, which before seemed an ideal something, no way connected with life. And he told me that the ladies from the Manor-House, who sate in the best pew in the church, were not so graceful, and the best women in the village were not so good, as was my sweet mamma; and that if she had lived, I should not have been forced to pick up a little knowledge from him, a rough sailor, or to learn to knit and sew of Susan, but that she would have taught me all lady-like fine works and delicate behaviour and perfect manners, and would have selected for me proper books, such as were most fit to instruct my mind, and of which he nothing knew. If ever in my life I shall have any proper sense of what is excellent or becoming in the womanly character, I owe it to these lessons of my rough unpolished uncle; for, in telling me what my mother would have made me, he taught me what to wish to be; and when, soon after my uncle left us, I was introduced to the ladies at the Manor-House, instead of hanging down my head with shame, as I should have done before my uncle came, like a little village rustic, I tried to speak distinctly, with ease, and a modest gentleness, as my uncle had said my mother used to do; instead of hanging down my head abashed, I looked upon them, and thought what a pretty sight a fine lady was, and thought how well my mother must have appeared, since she was so much more graceful than these ladies were; and when I heard them compliment my father on the admirable behaviour of his child, and say how well he had brought me up, I thought to myself, "Papa does not much mind my manners, if I am but a good girl; but it was my uncle that taught me to behave like mamma."—I cannot now think my uncle was so rough and unpolished as he said he was, for his lessons were so good and so impressive that I shall never forget them, and I hope they will be of use to me as long as I live: he would explain to me the meaning of all the words he used, such as grace and elegance, modest diffidence and affectation, pointing out instances of what he meant by those words, in the manners of the ladies and their young daughters who came to our church; for, besides the ladies of the Manor-House, many of the neighbouring families came to our church because my father preached so well.

It must have been early in the spring when my uncle went away, for the crocuses were just blown in the garden, and the primroses had begun to peep from under the young budding hedge-rows.—I cried as if my heart would break, when I had the last sight of him through a little opening among the trees, as he went down the road. My father accompanied him to the market-town, from whence he was to proceed in the stage-coach to London. How tedious I thought all Susan's endeavours to comfort me were. The stile where I first saw my uncle, came into my mind, and I thought I would go and sit there, and think about that day; but I was no sooner seated there, than I remembered how I had frightened him by taking him so foolishly to my mother's grave, and then again how naughty I had been when I sate muttering to myself at this same stile, wishing that he, who had gone so far to buy me books, might never come back any more: all my little quarrels with my uncle came into my mind, now that I could never play with him again, and it almost broke my heart. I was forced to run into the house to Susan for that consolation I had just before despised.

Some days after this, as I was sitting by the fire with my father, after it was dark, and before the candles were lighted, I gave him an account of my troubled conscience at the church-stile, when I remembered how unkind I had been to my uncle when he first came, and how sorry I still was whenever I thought of the many quarrels I had had with him.

My father smiled, and took hold of my hand, saying, "I will tell you all about this, my little penitent. This is the sort of way in which we all feel, when those we love are taken from us.—When our dear friends are with us, we go on enjoying their society, without much thought or consideration of the blessing we are possessed of, nor do we too nicely weigh the measure of our daily actions;—we let them freely share our kind or our discontented moods; and, if any little bickerings disturb our friendship, it does but the more endear us to each other when we are in a happier temper. But these things come over us like grievous faults when the object of our affection is gone for ever. Your dear mamma and I had no quarrels; yet in the first days of my lonely sorrow, how many things came into my mind that I might have done to have made her happier. It is so with you, my child. You did all a child could do to please your uncle, and dearly did he love you; and these little things which now disturb your tender mind, were remembered with delight by your uncle; he was telling me in our last walk, just perhaps as you were thinking about it with sorrow, of the difficulty he had in getting into your good graces when he first came; he will think of these things with pleasure when he is far away. Put away from you this unfounded grief; only let it be a lesson to you to be as kind as possible to those you love; and remember, when they are gone from you, you will never think you had been kind enough. Such feelings as you have now described are the lot of humanity. So you will feel when I am no more, and so will your children feel when you are dead. But your uncle will come back again, Betsy, and we will now think of where we are to get the cage to keep the talking parrot in, he is to bring home; and go and tell Susan to bring the candles, and ask her if the nice cake is almost baked, that she promised to give us for our tea."

At this point, my dear miss Villiers, you thought fit to break off your story, and the wet eyes of your young auditors, seemed to confess that you had succeeded in moving their feelings with your pretty narrative. It now fell by lot to the turn of miss Manners to relate her story, and we were all sufficiently curious to know what so very young an historian had to tell of herself.—I shall continue the narratives for the future in the order in which they followed, without mentioning any of the interruptions which occurred from the asking of questions, or from any other cause, unless materially connected with the stories. I shall also leave out the apologies with which you severally thought fit to preface your stories of yourselves, though they were very seasonable in their place, and proceeded from a proper diffidence, because I must not swell my work to too large a size.

II

LOUISA MANNERS

(By Mary Lamb)

MY NAME IS LOUISA MANNERS; I was seven years of age last birthday, which was on the first of May. I remember only four birthdays. The day I was four years old is the first that I recollect. On the morning of that day, as soon as I awoke, I crept into mamma's bed, and said, "Open your eyes, mamma, for it is my birthday. Open your eyes, and look at me!" Then mamma told me I should ride in a post chaise, and see my grandmamma and my sister Sarah. Grandmamma lived at a farm-house in the country, and I had never in all my life been out of London; no, nor had I ever seen a bit of green grass, except in the Drapers' garden, which is near my papa's house in Broad-street; nor had I ever rode in a carriage before that happy birthday.

I ran about the house talking of where I was going, and rejoicing so that it was my birthday, that when I got into the chaise I was tired and fell asleep.

When I awoke, I saw the green fields on both sides of the chaise and the fields were full, quite full, of bright shining yellow flowers, and sheep and young lambs were feeding in them. I jumped, and clapped my hands together for joy, and I cried out This is

"Abroad in the meadows to see the young lambs,"

for I knew many of Watts's hymns by heart.

The trees and hedges seemed to fly swiftly by us, and one field, and the sheep, and the young lambs, passed away; and then another field came, and that was full of cows; and then another field, and all the pretty sheep returned, and there was no end of these charming sights till we came quite to grandmamma's house, which stood all alone by itself, no house to be seen at all near it.

Grandmamma was very glad to see me, and she was very sorry that I did not remember her, though I had been so fond of her when she was in town but a few months before. I was quite ashamed of my bad memory. My sister Sarah shewed me all the beautiful places about grandmamma's house. She first took me into the farm-yard, and I peeped into the barn; there I saw a man thrashing, and as he beat the corn with his flail, he made such a dreadful noise that I was frightened and ran away: my sister persuaded me to return; she said Will Tasker was very good-natured: then I went back, and peeped at him again; but as I could not reconcile myself to the sound of his flail, or the sight of his black beard, we proceeded to see the rest of the farm-yard.

There was no end to the curiosities that Sarah had to shew me. There was the pond where the ducks were swimming, and the little wooden houses where the hens slept at night. The hens were feeding all over the yard, and the prettiest little chickens, they were feeding too, and little yellow ducklings that had a hen for their mamma. She was so frightened if they went near the water. Grandmamma says a hen is not esteemed a very wise bird.

We went out of the farm-yard into the orchard. O what a sweet place grandmamma's orchard is! There were pear-trees, and apple-trees, and cherry-trees, all in blossom. These blossoms were the prettiest flowers that ever were seen, and among the grass under the trees there grew butter-cups, and cowslips, and daffodils, and blue-bells. Sarah told me all their names, and she said I might pick as many of them as ever I pleased.

I filled my lap with flowers, I filled my bosom with flowers, and I carried as many flowers as I could in both my hands; but as I was going into the parlour to shew them to my mamma, I stumbled over a threshold which was placed across the parlour, and down I fell with all my treasure.

Nothing could have so well pacified me for the misfortune of my fallen flowers, as the sight of a delicious syllabub which happened at that moment to be brought in.

Grandmamma said it was a present from the red cow to me because it was my birthday; and then because it was the first of May, she ordered the syllabub to be placed under the May-bush that grew before the parlour door, and when we were seated on the grass round it, she helped me the very first to a large glass full of the syllabub, and wished me many happy returns of that day, and then she said I was myself the sweetest little May-blossom in the orchard.

After the syllabub there was the garden to see, and a most beautiful garden it was;— long and narrow, a straight gravel walk down the middle of it, at the end of the gravel walk there was a green arbour with a bench under it.

There were rows of cabbages and radishes, and peas and beans. I was delighted to see them, for I never saw so much as a cabbage growing out of the ground before.

On one side of this charming garden there were a great many bee-hives, and the bees sung so prettily.

Mamma said, "Have you nothing to say to these pretty bees, Louisa?" Then I said to them,

> "How doth the little busy bee improve each shining hour,
> And gather honey all the day from every opening flower."

They had a most beautiful flower-bed to gather it from, quite close under the hives.

I was going to catch one bee, till Sarah told me about their stings, which made me afraid for a long time to go too near their hives; but I went a little nearer, and a little nearer, every day, and, before I came away from grandmamma's, I grew so bold, I let Will Tasker hold me over the glass windows at the top of the hives, to see them make honey in their own homes.

After seeing the garden, I saw the cows milked, and that was the last sight I saw that day; for while I was telling mamma about the cows, I fell fast asleep, and I suppose I was then put to bed.

The next morning my papa and mamma were gone. I cried sadly, but was a little comforted at hearing they would return in a month or two, and fetch me home. I was a foolish little thing then, and did not know how long a month was. Grandmamma gave me a little basket to gather my flowers in. I went into the orchard, and before I had half filled my basket, I forgot all my troubles.

The time I passed at my grandmamma's is always in my mind. Sometimes I think of the good-natured pied cow, that would let me stroke her, while the dairy-maid was milking her. Then I fancy myself running after the dairy-maid into the nice clean dairy, and see the pans full of milk and cream. Then I remember the wood-house; it had once been a large barn, but being grown old, the wood was kept there. My sister and I used to peep about among the faggots to find the eggs the hens sometimes left there. Birds' nests we might not look for. Grandmamma was very angry once, when Will Tasker brought home a bird's nest, full of pretty speckled eggs, for me. She sent him back to the hedge with it again. She said, the little birds would not sing any more, if their eggs were taken away from them.

A hen, she said, was a hospitable bird, and always laid more eggs than she wanted, on purpose to give her mistress to make puddings and custards with.

I do not know which pleased grandmamma best, when we carried her home a lap-full of eggs, or a few violets; for she was particularly fond of violets.

Violets were very scarce; we used to search very carefully for them every morning, round by the orchard hedge, and Sarah used to carry a stick in her hand to beat away the nettles; for very frequently the hens left their eggs among the nettles. If we could find eggs and violets too, what happy children we were!

Every day I used to fill my basket with flowers, and for a long time I liked one pretty flower as well as another pretty flower, but Sarah was much wiser than me, and she taught me which to prefer.

Grandmamma's violets were certainly best of all, but they never went in the basket, being carried home, almost flower by flower, as soon as they were found; therefore blue-bells might be said to be the best, for the cowslips were all withered and gone, before I learned the true value of flowers. The best blue-bells were those tinged with red; some were so very red, that we called them red blue-bells, and these Sarah prized very highly indeed. Daffodils were so very plentiful, they were not thought worth gathering, unless they were double ones, and butter-cups I found were very poor flowers indeed, yet I would pick one now and then, because I knew they were the very same flowers that had delighted me so in the journey; for my papa had told me they were.

I was very careful to love best the flowers which Sarah praised most, yet sometimes, I confess, I have even picked a daisy, though I knew it was the very worst flower of all, because it reminded me of London, and the Drapers' garden; for, happy as I was at grandmamma's, I could not help sometimes thinking of my papa and mamma, and then I used to tell my sister all about London; how the houses stood all close to each other; what a pretty noise the coaches made; and what a many people there were in the streets. After we had been talking on these subjects, we generally used to go into the old wood-house, and play at being in London. We used to set up bits of wood for houses; our two dolls we called papa and mamma; in one corner we made a little garden with grass and daisies, and that was to be the Drapers' garden. I would not have any other flowers here than daisies, because no other grew among the grass in the real Drapers' garden. Before the time of hay-making came, it was very much talked of. Sarah told me what a merry time it would be, for she remembered every thing which had happened for a year or more. She told me how nicely we should throw the hay about. I was very desirous indeed to see the hay made.

To be sure nothing could be more pleasant than the day the orchard was mowed: the hay smelled so sweet, and we might toss it about as much as ever we pleased; but, dear me, we often wish for things that do not prove so happy as we expected; the hay, which was at first so green, and smelled so sweet, became yellow and dry, and was carried away in a cart to feed the horses; and then, when it was all gone, and there was no more to play with, I looked upon the naked ground, and perceived what we had lost in these few merry days. Ladies, would you believe it, every flower, blue-bells, daffodils, butter-cups, daisies, all were cut off by the cruel scythe of the mower. No flower was to be seen at all, except here and there a short solitary daisy, that a week before one would not have looked at.

It was a grief, indeed, to me, to lose all my pretty flowers; yet, when we are in great distress, there is always, I think, something which happens to comfort us, and so it happened now, that gooseberries and currants were almost ripe, which was certainly a very pleasant prospect. Some of them began to turn red, and, as we never disobeyed grandmamma, we used often to consult together, if it was likely she would permit us to eat them yet, then we would pick a few that looked the ripest, and run to ask her if she thought they were ripe enough to eat, and the uncertainty what her opinion would be, made them doubly sweet if she gave us leave to eat them.

When the currants and gooseberries were quite ripe, grandmamma had a sheep-shearing.

All the sheep stood under the trees to be sheared. They were brought out of the field by old Spot, the shepherd. I stood at the orchard-gate, and saw him drive them all in. When they had cropped off all their wool, they looked very clean, and white, and pretty; but, poor things, they ran shivering about with cold, so that it was a pity to see them. Great preparations were making all day for the sheep-shearing supper. Sarah said, a sheep-shearing was not to be compared to a harvest-home, *that* was so much better, for that then the oven was quite full of plum-pudding, and the kitchen was very hot indeed with roasting beef; yet I can assure you there was no want at all of either roast beef or plum-pudding at the sheep-shearing.

My sister and I were permitted to sit up till it was almost dark, to see the company at supper. They sate at a long oak table, which was finely carved, and as bright as a looking-glass.

I obtained a great deal of praise that day, because I replied so prettily when I was spoken to. My sister was more shy than me; never having lived in London was the reason of that. After the happiest day bedtime will come! We sate up late; but at last grandmamma sent us to bed: yet though we went to bed we heard many charming songs sung: to be sure we could not distinguish the words, which was a pity, but the sound of their voices was very loud and very fine indeed.

The common supper that we had every night was very cheerful. Just before the men came out of the field, a large faggot was flung on the fire; the wood used to crackle and blaze, and smell delightfully: and then the crickets, for they loved the fire, they used to sing, and old Spot, the shepherd, who loved the fire as well as the crickets did, he used to take his place in the chimney corner; after the hottest day in summer, there old Spot used to sit. It was a seat within the fire-place, quite under the chimney, and over his head the bacon hung.

When old Spot was seated, the milk was hung in a skillet over the fire, and then the men used to come and sit down at the long white table.

Pardon me, my dear Louisa, that I interrupted you here. You are a little woman now to what you were then; and I may say to you, that though I loved to hear you prattle of your early recollections, I thought I perceived some ladies present were rather weary of hearing so much of the visit to grandmamma. You may remember I asked you some questions concerning your papa and your mamma, which led you to speak of your journey home: but your little town-bred head was so full of the pleasures of a country life, that you first made many apologies that you were unable to tell what happened during the harvest, as unfortunately you were fetched home the very day before it began.

III

ANN WITHERS

(By Mary Lamb)

My NAME YOU KNOW is Withers, but as I once thought I was the daughter of sir Edward and lady Harriot Lesley, I shall speak of myself as miss Lesley, and call sir Edward and lady Harriot my father and mother during the period I supposed them entitled to those beloved names. When I was a little girl, it was the perpetual subject of my contemplation, that I was an heiress, and the daughter of a baronet; that my mother was the honourable lady Harriot; that we had a nobler mansion, infinitely finer pleasure-grounds, and equipages more splendid than any of the neighbouring families. Indeed, my good friends, having observed nothing of this error of mine in either of the lives which have hitherto been related, I am ashamed to confess what a proud child I once was. How it happened I cannot tell, for my father was esteemed the best bred man in the county, and the condescension and affability of my mother were universally spoken of.

"Oh my dear friend," said miss — —, "it was very natural indeed, if you supposed you possessed these advantages. We make no comparative figure in the county, and my father was originally a man of no consideration at all; and yet I can assure you, both he and mamma had a prodigious deal of trouble to break me of this infirmity, when I was very young." "And do reflect for a moment," said miss Villiers, "from whence could proceed any pride in me—a poor curate's daughter;—at least any pride worth speaking of; for the difficulty my father had to make me feel myself on an equality with a miller's little daughter who visited me, did not seem an anecdote worth relating. My father, from his profession, is accustomed to look into these things, and whenever he has observed any tendency to this fault in me, and has made me sensible of my error, I, who am rather a weak-spirited girl, have been so much distressed at his reproofs, that to restore me to my own good opinion, he would make me sensible that pride is a defect inseparable from human nature; shewing me, in our visits to the poorest labourers, how pride would, as he expressed it, "prettily peep out from under their ragged garbs."—My father dearly loved the poor. In persons of a rank superior to our own humble one, I wanted not much assistance from my father's nice discernment to know that it existed there; and for these latter he would always claim that toleration from me, which he said he observed I was less willing to allow than to the former instances. "We are told in holy writ," he would say, "that it is easier for a camel to go through the eye of a needle, than for a rich man to enter into the kingdom of heaven." Surely this is not meant alone to warn the affluent: it must also be understood as an expressive illustration, to instruct the lowly-fortuned man that he should bear with those imperfections, inseparable from that dangerous prosperity from which he is happily exempt."—But we sadly interrupt your story.—

"You are very kind, ladies, to speak with so much indulgence of my foible," said

Miss Withers, and was going to proceed, when little Louisa Manners asked, "Pray, are not equipages carriages?" "Yes, miss Manners, an equipage is a carriage." "Then I am sure if my papa had but one equipage I should be very proud; for once when my papa talked of keeping a one-horse chaise, I never was so proud of any thing in my life: I used to dream of riding in it, and imagine I saw my playfellows walking past me in the streets."

"Oh, my dear miss Manners," replied miss Withers, "your young head might well run on a thing so new to you; but you have preached an useful lesson to me in your own pretty rambling story, which I shall not easily forget. When you were speaking with such delight of the pleasure the sight of a farm-yard, an orchard, and a narrow slip of kitchen-garden, gave you, and could for years preserve so lively the memory of one short ride, and that probably through a flat uninteresting country, I remembered how early I learned to disregard the face of Nature, unless she were decked in picturesque scenery; how wearisome our parks and grounds became to me, unless some improvements were going forward which I thought would attract notice: but those days are gone.—I will now proceed in my story, and bring you acquainted with my real parents.

Alas! I am a changeling, substituted by my mother for the heiress of the Lesley family: it was for my sake she did this naughty deed; yet, since the truth has been known, it seems to me as if I had been the only sufferer by it; remembering no time when I was not Harriot Lesley, it seems as if the change had taken from me my birthright.

Lady Harriot had intended to nurse her child herself; but being seized with a violent fever soon after its birth, she was not only unable to nurse it, but even to see it, for several weeks. At this time I was not quite a month old, when my mother was hired to be miss Lesley's nurse—she had once been a servant in the family—her husband was then at sea.

She had been nursing miss Lesley a few days, when a girl who had the care of me brought me into the nursery to see my mother. It happened that she wanted something from her own home, which she dispatched the girl to fetch, and desired her to leave me till her return. In her absence she changed our clothes: then keeping me to personate the child she was nursing, she sent away the daughter of sir Edward to be brought up in her own poor cottage.

When my mother sent away the girl, she affirmed she had not the least intention of committing this bad action; but after she was left alone with us, she looked on me, and then on the little lady-babe, and she wept over me to think she was obliged to leave me to the charge of a careless girl, debarred from my own natural food, while she was nursing another person's child.

The laced cap and the fine cambric robe of the little Harriot were lying on the table ready to be put on: in these she dressed me, only just to see how pretty her own dear baby would look in missy's fine clothes. When she saw me thus adorned, she said to me, "O, my dear Ann, you look as like missy as any thing can be. I am sure my lady herself, if she were well enough to see you, would not know the difference." She said these words aloud, and while she was speaking, a wicked thought came into her head—How easy it would be to change these children! On which she hastily dressed Harriot in my coarse raiment. She had no sooner finished the transformation of miss Lesley into the poor Ann Withers, than the girl returned, and carried her away, without the least suspicion that it was not the same infant that she had brought thither.

It was wonderful that no one discovered that I was not the same child. Every fresh face that came into the room, filled the nurse with terror. The servants still continued to pay their compliments to the baby in the same form as usual, saying, How like it is to its papa! Nor did sir Edward himself perceive the difference, his lady's illness probably engrossing all his attention at the time; though indeed gentlemen seldom take much notice of very young children.

When lady Harriot began to recover, and the nurse saw me in her arms caressed as her own child, all fears of detection were over; but the pangs of remorse then seized her: as the dear sick lady hung with tears of fondness over me, she thought she should have died with sorrow for having so cruelly deceived her.

When I was a year old Mrs. Withers was discharged; and because she had been observed to nurse me with uncommon care and affection, and was seen to shed many tears at parting from me; to reward her fidelity sir Edward settled a small pension on her, and she was allowed to come every Sunday to dine in the housekeeper's room, and see her little lady.

When she went home it might have been expected she would have neglected the child she had so wickedly stolen; instead of which she nursed it with the greatest tenderness, being very sorry for what she had done: all the ease she could ever find for her troubled conscience, was in her extreme care of this injured child; and in the weekly visits to its father's house she constantly brought it with her. At the time I have the earliest recollection of her, she was become a widow, and with the pension sir Edward allowed her, and some plain work she did for our family, she maintained herself and her supposed daughter. The doting fondness she shewed for her child was much talked of; it was said, she waited upon it more like a servant than a mother, and it was observed, its clothes were always made, as far as her slender means would permit, in the same fashion, and her hair cut and curled in the same form as mine. To this person, as having been my faithful nurse, and to her child, I was always taught to shew particular civility, and the little girl was always brought into the nursery to play with me. Ann was a little delicate thing, and remarkably well-behaved; for though so much indulged in every other respect, my mother was very attentive to her manners.

As the child grew older, my mother became very uneasy about her education. She was so very desirous of having her well-behaved, that she feared to send her to school, lest she should learn ill manners among the village children, with whom she never suffered her to play; and she was such a poor scholar herself, that she could teach her little or nothing. I heard her relate this her distress to my own maid, with tears in her eyes, and I formed a resolution to beg of my parents that I might have Ann for a companion, and that she might be allowed to take lessons with me of my governess.

My birth-day was then approaching, and on that day I was always indulged in the privilege of asking some peculiar favour.

"And what boon has my annual petitioner to beg to-day?" said my father, as he entered the breakfast-room on the morning of my birth-day. Then I told him of the great anxiety expressed by nurse Withers concerning her daughter; how much she wished it was in her power to give her an education, that would enable her to get her living without hard labour. I set the good qualities of Ann Withers in the best light I could, and in conclusion I begged she might be permitted to partake with me in education, and become my companion. "This is a very serious request indeed, Harriot," said sir Edward; "your mother and I must consult together on the subject." The result of this consultation was favourable to my wishes: in a few weeks my foster-sister was taken into the house, and placed under the tuition of my governess.

To me, who had hitherto lived without any companions of my own age except occasional visitors, the idea of a playfellow constantly to associate with, was very pleasant; and, after the first shyness of feeling her altered situation was over, Ann seemed as much at her ease as if she had always been brought up in our house. I became very fond of her, and took pleasure in shewing her all manner of attentions; which so far won on her affections, that she told me she had a secret intrusted to her by her mother, which she had promised never to reveal as long as her mother lived, but that she almost wished to confide it to me, because I was such a kind friend to her; yet, having promised never to tell it till the death of her mother, she was afraid to tell it to me. At first I assured her that I would never press her to the disclosure, for that promises of secrecy were to be held sacred; but whenever we fell into any confidential kind of conversation, this secret seemed always ready to come out. Whether she or I were most to blame I know not, though I own I could not help giving frequent hints how well I could keep a secret. At length she told me what I have before related, namely, that she was in truth the daughter of sir Edward and lady Lesley, and I the child of her supposed mother.

When I was first in possession of this wonderful secret, my heart burned to reveal it. I thought how praiseworthy it would be in me to restore to my friend the rights of her birth; yet I thought only of becoming her patroness, and raising her to her proper rank; it never occurred to me that my own degradation must necessarily follow. I endeavoured to persuade her to let me tell this important affair to my parents: this she positively refused. I expressed wonder that she should so faithfully keep this secret for an unworthy woman, who in her infancy had done her such an injury. "Oh," said she, "you do not know how much she loves me, or you would not wonder that I never resent that. I have seen her grieve and be so very sorry on my account, that I would not bring her into more trouble for any good that could happen to myself. She has often told me, that since the day she changed us, she has never known what it is to have a happy moment; and when she returned home from nursing you, finding me very thin and sickly, how her heart smote her for what she had done; and then she nursed and fed me with such anxious care, that she grew much fonder of me than if I had been her own; and that on the Sundays, when she used to bring me here, it was more pleasure to her to see me in my own father's house, than it was to her to see you her real child. The shyness you shewed towards her while you were very young, and the forced civility you seemed to affect as you grew older, always appeared like ingratitude towards her who had done so much for you. My mother has desired me to disclose this after her death, but I do not believe I shall ever mention it then, for I should be sorry to bring any reproach even on her memory."

In a few days after this important discovery, Ann was sent home to pass a few weeks with her mother, on the occasion of the expected arrival of some visitors to our house; they were to bring children with them, and these I was to consider as my own guests.

In the expected arrival of my young visitants, and in making preparations to entertain them, I had little leisure to deliberate on what conduct I should pursue with regard to my friend's secret. Something must be done I thought to make her amends for the injury she had sustained, and I resolved to consider the matter attentively on her return. Still my mind ran on conferring favours. I never considered myself as transformed into the dependant person. Indeed sir Edward at this time set me about a task which occupied the whole of my attention; he proposed that I should write a little interlude after the manner of the French Petites Pieces; and to try my ingenuity, no one was to see it before the representation except the performers, myself and my little friends, who as they were all younger than me, could not be expected to lend me much assistance. I have already told you what a proud girl I was. During the writing of this piece, the receiving of my young friends, and the instructing them in their several parts, I never felt myself of more importance. With Ann my pride had somewhat slumbered; the difference of our rank left no room for competition; all was complacency and good humour on my part, and affectionate gratitude, tempered with respect, on hers. But here I had full room to shew courtesy, to affect those graces—to imitate that elegance of manners practised by lady Harriot to their mothers. I was to be their instructress in action and in attitudes, and to receive their praises and their admiration of my theatrical genius. It was a new scene of triumph for me, and I might then be said to be in the very height of my glory.

If the plot of my piece, for the invention of which they so highly praised me, had been indeed my own, all would have been well; but unhappily I borrowed from a source which made my drama end far differently from what I intended it should. In the catastrophe I lost not only the name I personated in the piece, but with it my own name also; and all my rank and consequence in the world fled from me for ever.—My father presented me with a beautiful writing-desk for the use of my new authorship. My silver standish was placed upon it; a quire of gilt paper was before me. I took out a parcel of my best crow quills, and down I sate in the greatest form imaginable.

I conjecture I have no talent for invention; certain it is that when I sate down to compose my piece, no story would come into my head, but the story which Ann had so lately related to me. Many sheets were scrawled over in vain, I could think of nothing else; still the babies and the nurse were before me in all the minutiæ of description Ann had given them. The costly attire of the lady-babe,—the homely garb of the cottage-infant,—the affecting address of the fond mother to her own offspring;— then the charming equivoque in the change of the children: it all looked so dramatic:— it was a play ready made to my hands. The invalid mother would form the pathetic, the silly exclamations of the servants the ludicrous, and the nurse was nature itself. It is true I had a few scruples, that it might, should it come to the knowledge of Ann, be construed into something very like a breach of confidence. But she was at home, and might never happen to hear of the subject of my piece, and if she did, why it was only making some handsome apology.—To a dependant companion, to whom I had been so very great a friend, it was not necessary to be so very particular about such a trifle.

Thus I reasoned as I wrote my drama, beginning with the title, which I called "The Changeling," and ending with these words, *The curtain drops, while the lady clasps the baby in her arms, and the nurse sighs audibly.* I invented no new incident, I simply wrote the story as Ann had told it to me, in the best blank verse I was able to compose.

By the time it was finished the company had arrived. The casting the different parts was my next care. The honourable Augustus M————, a young gentleman of five years of age, undertook to play the father. He was only to come in and say, *How does my little darling do to-day?* The three miss ———'s were to be the servants, they too had only single lines to speak.

As these four were all very young performers, we made them rehearse many times over, that they might walk in and out with proper decorum; but the performance was stopped before their entrances and their exits arrived. I complimented lady Elizabeth, the sister of Augustus, who was the eldest of the young ladies, with the choice of the Lady Mother or the nurse. She fixed on the former; she was to recline on a sofa, and, affecting ill health, speak some eight or ten lines which began with, *O that I could my precious baby see!* To her cousin miss Emily ——— was given the girl who had the care of the nurse's child; two dolls were to personate the two children, and the principal character of the nurse, I had the pleasure to perform myself. It consisted of several speeches, and a very long soliloquy during the changing of the children's clothes.

The elder brother of Augustus, a gentleman of fifteen years of age, who refused to mix in our childish drama, yet condescended to paint the scenes, and our dresses were got up by my own maid.

When we thought ourselves quite perfect in our several parts, we announced it for representation. Sir Edward and lady Harriot, with their visitors, the parents of my young troop of comedians, honoured us with their presence. The servants were also permitted to go into a music gallery, which was at the end of a ball-room we had chosen for our theatre.

As author, and principal performer, standing before a noble audience, my mind was too much engaged with the arduous task I had undertaken, to glance my eyes towards the music gallery, or I might have seen two more spectators there than I expected. Nurse Withers and her daughter Ann were there; they had been invited by the housekeeper to be present at the representation of miss Lesley's first piece.

In the midst of the performance, as I, in the character of the nurse, was delivering the wrong child to the girl, there was an exclamation from the music gallery, of "Oh, it's all true! it's all true!" This was followed by a bustle among the servants, and screams as of a person in a hysteric fit. Sir Edward came forward to enquire what was the matter. He saw it was Mrs. Withers who had fallen into a fit. Ann was weeping over her, and crying out, "O miss Lesley, you have told all in the play!"

Mrs. Withers was brought out into the ball-room; there, with tears and in broken accents, with every sign of terror and remorse, she soon made a full confession of her so long concealed guilt.

The strangers assembled to see our childish mimicry of passion, were witness to a highly wrought dramatic scene in real life. I had intended they should see the curtain drop without any discovery of the deceit; unable to invent any new incident, I left the conclusion imperfect as I found it: but they saw a more strict poetical justice done; they saw the rightful child restored to its parents, and the nurse overwhelmed with shame, and threatened with the severest punishment.

"Take this woman," said sir Edward, "and lock her up, till she be delivered into the hands of justice."

Ann, on her knees, implored mercy for her mother.—Addressing the children who were gathered round her, "Dear ladies," said she, "help me, on your knees help me to beg forgiveness for my mother." Down the young ones all dropped—even lady Elizabeth bent her knee. "Sir Edward, pity her distress. Sir Edward, pardon her!" All joined in the petition, except one whose voice ought to have been loudest in the appeal. No word, no accent came from me. I hung over lady Harriot's chair, weeping as if my heart would break; but I wept for my own fallen fortunes, not for my mother's sorrow.

I thought within myself, if in the integrity of my heart, refusing to participate in this unjust secret, I had boldly ventured to publish the truth, I might have had some consolation in the praises which so generous an action would have merited: but it is through the vanity of being supposed to have written a pretty story, that I have meanly broken my faith with my friend, and unintentionally proclaimed the disgrace of my mother and myself. While thoughts like these were passing through my mind, Ann had obtained my mother's pardon. Instead of being sent away to confinement and the horrors of a prison, she was given by sir Edward into the care of the housekeeper, who had orders from lady Harriot to see her put to bed and properly attended to, for again this wretched woman had fallen into a fit.

Ann would have followed my mother, but sir Edward brought her back, telling her that she should see her when she was better. He then led Ann towards lady Harriot, desiring her to embrace her child; she did so, and I saw her, as I had phrased it in the play, *clasped in her mother's arms*.

This scene had greatly affected the spirits of lady Harriot; through the whole of it it was with difficulty she had been kept from fainting, and she was now led into the drawing-room by the ladies. The gentlemen followed, talking with sir Edward of the astonishing instance of filial affection they had just seen in the earnest pleadings of the child for her supposed mother.

Ann to went with them, and was conducted by her whom I had always considered as my own particular friend. Lady Elizabeth took hold of her hand, and said, "Miss Lesley, will you permit me to conduct you to the drawing-room?"

I was left weeping behind the chair where lady Harriot had sate, and, as I thought, quite alone. A something had before twitched my frock two or three times, so slightly I had scarcely noticed it; a little head now peeped round, and looking up in my face said, "She is not miss Lesley:" it was the young Augustus; he had been sitting at my feet, but I had not observed him. He then started up, and taking hold of my hand with one of his, with the other holding fast by my clothes, he led, or rather dragged me, into the midst of the company assembled in the drawing-room. The vehemence of his manner, his little face as red as fire, caught every eye. The ladies smiled, and one gentleman laughed in a most unfeeling manner. His elder brother pattted him on the head, and said, "You are a humane little fellow. Elizabeth, we might have thought of this."

Very kind words were now spoken to me by sir Edward, and he called me Harriot, precious name now grown to me. Lady Harriot kissed me, and said she would never forget how long she had loved me as her child. These were comfortable words; but I heard echoed round the room, "Poor thing, she cannot help it.—I am sure she is to be pitied.—Dear lady Harriot, how kind, how considerate you are!" Ah! what a deep sense of my altered condition did I then feel!

"Let the young ladies divert themselves in another room," said sir Edward; "and, Harriot, take your new sister with you, and help her to entertain your friends." Yes, he called me Harriot again, and afterwards invented new names for his daughter and me, and always called us by them, apparently in jest; yet I knew it was only because he would not hurt me with hearing our names reversed. When sir Edward desired us to shew the children into another room, Ann and I walked towards the door. A new sense of humiliation arose—how could I go out at the door before miss Lesley?—I stood irresolute; she drew back. The elder brother of my friend Augustus assisted me in this perplexity; pushing us all forward, as if in a playful mood, he drove us indiscriminately before him, saying, "I will make one among you to-day." He had never joined in our sports before.

My luckless Play, that sad instance of my duplicity, was never once mentioned to me afterwards, not even by any one of the children who had acted in it, and I must also tell you how considerate an old lady was at the time about our dresses. As soon as she perceived things growing very serious, she hastily stripped off the upper garments we wore to represent our different characters. I think I should have died with shame, if the child had led me into the drawing-room in the mummery I had worn to represent a nurse. This good lady was of another essential service to me; for perceiving an irresolution in every one how they should behave to us, which distressed me very much, she contrived to place miss Lesley above me at table, and called her miss Lesley, and me miss Withers; saying at the same time in a low voice, but as if she meant I should hear her, "It is better these things should be done at once, then they are over." My heart thanked her, for I felt the truth of what she said.

My poor mother continued very ill for many weeks: no medicine would remove the extreme dejection of spirits she laboured under. Sir Edward sent for the clergyman of the parish to give her religious consolation. Every day he came to visit her, and he would always take miss Lesley and me into the room with him. I think, miss Villiers, your father must be just such another man as Dr. Wheelding, our worthy rector; just so I think he would have soothed the troubled conscience of my repentant mother. How feelingly, how kindly he used to talk of mercy and forgiveness!

My heart was softened by my own misfortunes, and the sight of my penitent suffering mother. I felt that she was now my only parent; I strove, earnestly strove, to love her; yet ever when I looked in her face, she would seem to me to be the very identical person whom I should have once thought sufficiently honoured by a slight inclination of the head, and a civil How do you do, Mrs. Withers? One day, as miss Lesley was hanging over her, with her accustomed fondness, Dr. Wheelding reading in a prayer-book, and, as I thought, not at that moment regarding us, I threw myself on my knees and silently prayed that I too might be able to love my mother.

Dr. Wheelding had been observing me: he took me into the garden, and drew from me the subject of my petition. "Your prayers, my good young lady," said he, "I hope are heard; sure I am they have caused me to adopt a resolution, which, as it will enable you to see your mother frequently, will, I hope, greatly assist your pious wishes.

I will take your mother home with me to superintend my family. Under my roof doubtless sir Edward will often permit you to see her. Perform your duty towards her as well as you possibly can.—Affection is the growth of time. With such good wishes in your young heart, do not despair that in due time it will assuredly spring up."

With the approbation of sir Edward and lady Harriot, my mother was removed in a few days to Dr. Wheelding's house: there she soon recovered—there she at present resides. She tells me she loves me almost as well as she did when I was a baby, and we both wept at parting when I came to school.

Here perhaps I ought to conclude my story, which I fear has been a tedious one: permit me however to say a few words concerning the time which elapsed since the discovery of my birth until my arrival here.

It was on the fifth day of ———— that I was known to be Ann Withers, and the daughter of my supposed nurse. The company who were witness to my disgrace departed in a few days, and I felt relieved from some part of the mortification I hourly experienced. For every fresh instance even of kindness or attention I experienced went to my heart, that I should be forced to feel thankful for it.

Circumstanced as I was, surely I had nothing justly to complain of. The conduct of sir Edward and lady Harriot was kind in the extreme; still preserving every appearance of a parental tenderness for me, but ah! I might no longer call them by the dear names of father and mother.—Formerly when speaking of them, I used, proud of their titles, to delight to say, "Sir Edward or lady Harriot did this, or this;" now I would give worlds to say, "My father or my mother."

I should be perfectly unkind if I were to complain of miss Lesley—indeed, I have not the least cause of complaint against her. As my companion, her affection and her gratitude had been unbounded; and now that it was my turn to be the humble friend, she tried by every means in her power, to make me think she felt the same respectful gratitude, which in her dependant station she had so naturally displayed.

Only in a few rarely constituted minds, does that true attentive kindness spring up, that delicacy of feeling, which enters into every trivial thing, is ever awake and keeping watch lest it should offend. Myself, though educated with the extremest care, possessed but little of this virtue. Virtue I call it, though among men it is termed politeness, for since the days of my humiliating reverse of fortune I have learned its value.

I feel quite ashamed to give instances of any deficiency I observed, or thought I have observed, in miss Lesley. Now I am away from her, and dispassionately speaking of it, it seems as if my own soreness of temper had made me fancy things. I really believe now that I was mistaken; but miss Lesley had been so highly praised for her filial tenderness, I thought at last she seemed to make a parade about it, and used to run up to my mother, and affect to be more glad to see her than she really was after a time; and I think Dr. Wheelding thought so, by a little hint he once dropped. But he too might be mistaken, for he was very partial to me.

I am under the greatest obligation in the world to this good Dr. Wheelding. He has made my mother quite a respectable woman, and I am sure it is owing a great deal to him that she loves me as well as she does.

And here, though it may seem a little out of place, let me stop to assure you, that if I ever could have had any doubt of the sincerity of miss Lesley's affection towards me, her behaviour on the occasion of my coming here ought completely to efface it. She entreated with many tears, and almost the same energy with which she pleaded for forgiveness for my mother, that I might not be sent away.—But she was not alike successful in her supplications.

Miss Lesley had made some progress in reading and writing during the time she was my companion only, it was highly necessary that every exertion should be now made—the whole house was, as I may say, in requisition for her instruction. Sir Edward and lady Harriot devoted great part of the day to this purpose. A well educated young person was taken under our governess, to assist her in her labours, and to teach miss Lesley music. A drawing-master was engaged to reside in the house.

At this time I was not remarkably forward in my education. My governess being a native of France, I spoke French very correctly, and I had made some progress in Italian. I had only had the instruction of masters during the few months in the year we usually passed in London.

Music I never had the least ear for, I could scarcely be taught my notes. This defect in me was always particularly regretted by my mother, she being an excellent performer herself both on the piano and on the harp.

I think I have some taste for drawing; but as lady Harriot did not particularly excel in this, I lost so much time in the summer months, practising only under my governess, that I made no great proficiency even in this my favourite art. But miss Lesley with all these advantages which I have named, every body so eager to instruct her, she so willing to learn—every thing so new and delightful to her, how could it happen otherwise? she in a short time became a little prodigy. What best pleased lady Harriot was, after she had conquered the first difficulties, she discovered a wonderful talent for music. Here she was her mother's own girl indeed—she had the same sweet-toned voice—the same delicate finger.—Her musical governess had little now to do; for as soon as lady Harriot perceived this excellence in her, she gave up all company, and devoted her whole time to instructing her daughter in this science.

Nothing makes the heart ache with such a hopeless, heavy pain, as envy.

I had felt deeply before, but till now I could not be said to envy miss Lesley.—All day long the notes of the harp or the piano spoke sad sounds to me, of the loss of a loved mother's heart.

To have, in a manner, two mothers, and miss Lesley to engross them both, was too much indeed.

It was at this time that one day I had been wearied with hearing lady Harriot play one long piece of Haydn's music after another, to her enraptured daughter. We were to walk with our governess to Dr. Wheelding's that morning; and after lady Harriot had left the room, and we were quite ready for our walk, miss Lesley would not leave the instrument for I know not how long.

It was on that day that I thought she was not quite honest in her expressions of joy at the sight of my poor mother, who had been waiting at the garden-gate near two hours to see her arrive; yet she might be, for the music had put her in remarkably good spirits that morning.

O the music quite, quite won lady Harriot's heart! Till miss Lesley began to play so well, she often lamented the time it would take, before her daughter would have the air of a person of fashion's child. It was my part of the general instruction to give her lessons on this head. We used to make a kind of play of it, which we called lectures on fashionable manners: it was a pleasant amusement to me, a sort of keeping up the memory of past times. But now the music was always in the way. The last time it was talked of, lady Harriot said her daughter's time was too precious to be taken up with such trifling.

I must own that the music had that effect on miss Lesley as to render these lectures less necessary, which I will explain to you; but, first, let me assure you that lady Harriot was by no means in the habit of saying these kind of things. It was almost a solitary instance. I could give you a thousand instances the very reverse of this, in her as well as in sir Edward. How kindly, how frequently, would they remind me, that to me alone it was owing that they ever knew their child! calling the day on which I was a petitioner for the admittance of Ann into the house, the blessed birthday of their generous girl.

Neither dancing, nor any foolish lectures could do much for miss Lesley, she remained wanting in gracefulness of carriage; but all that is usually attributed to dancing, music effected. When she was sitting before the instrument, a resemblance to her mother became apparent to every eye. Her attitudes and the expression of her countenance were the very same. This soon followed her into every thing; all was ease and natural grace; for the music, and with it the idea of lady Harriot, was always in her thoughts. It was a pretty sight to see the daily improvement in her person, even to me, poor envious girl that I was.

Soon after lady Harriot had hurt me by calling my little efforts to improve her daughter trifling, she made me large amends in a very kind and most unreserved conversation that she held with me.

She told me all the struggles she had had at first to feel a maternal tenderness for her daughter; and she frankly confessed that she had now gained so much on her affections, that she feared she had too much neglected the solemn promise she had made me, *Never to forget how long she had loved me as her child.*

Encouraged by her returning kindness, I owned how much I had suffered, and ventured to express my fears, that I had hardly courage enough to bear the sight of my former friends, under a new designation, as I must now appear to them, on our removal to London, which was expected to take place in a short time.

A few days after this she told me in the gentlest manner possible, that sir Edward and herself were of opinion it would conduce to my happiness to pass a year or two at school.

I knew that this proposal was kindly intended to spare me the mortifications I so much dreaded; therefore I endeavoured to submit to my hard fate with cheerfulness, and prepared myself, not without reluctance, to quit a mansion which had been the scene of so many enjoyments, and latterly of such very different feelings.

I V

ELINOR FORESTER

(By Mary Lamb)

WHEN I WAS VERY YOUNG, I had the misfortune to lose my mother. My father very soon married again. In the morning of the day in which that event took place, my father set me on his knee, and, as he often used to do after the death of my mother, he called me his dear little orphaned Elinor, and then he asked me if I loved miss Saville. I replied "Yes." Then he said this dear lady was going to be so kind as to be married to him, and that she was to live with us, and be my mamma. My father told me this with such pleasure in his looks, that I thought it must be a very fine thing indeed to have a new mamma; and on his saying it was time for me to be dressed against his return from church, I ran in great spirits to tell the good news in the nursery. I found my maid and the house-maid looking out of the window to see my father get into his carriage, which was new painted; the servants had new liveries, and fine white ribbands in their hats; and then I perceived my father had left off his mourning. The maids were dressed in new coloured gowns and white ribbands. On the table I saw a new muslin frock, trimmed with fine lace ready for me to put on. I skipped about the room quite in an ecstasy.

When the carriage drove from the door, the housekeeper came in to bring the maids new white gloves. I repeated to her the words I had just heard, that that dear lady miss Saville was going to be married to papa, and that she was to live with us, and be my mamma.

The housekeeper shook her head, and said, "Poor thing! how soon children forget every thing!"

I could not imagine what she meant by my forgetting every thing, for I instantly recollected poor mamma used to say I had an excellent memory.

The women began to draw on their white gloves, and the seams rending in several places, Anne said, "This is just the way our gloves served us at my mistress's funeral." The other checked her, and said "Hush!" I was then thinking of some instances in which my mamma had praised my memory, and this reference to her funeral fixed her idea in my mind.

From the time of her death no one had ever spoken to me of my mamma, and I had apparently forgotten her; yet I had a habit which perhaps had not been observed, of taking my little stool, which had been mamma's footstool, and a doll, which my mamma had drest for me, while she was sitting in her elbow-chair, her head supported with pillows. With these in my hands, I used to go to the door of the room in which I had seen her in her last illness; and after trying to open it, and peeping through the keyhole, from whence I could just see a glimpse of the crimson curtains, I used to sit down on the stool before the door, and play with my doll, and sometimes sing to it mamma's pretty song, of "Balow my babe;" imitating as well as I could, the weak voice in which she used to sing it to me. My mamma had a very sweet voice. I remember now the gentle tone in which she used to say my prattle did not disturb her.

When I was drest in my new frock, I wished poor mamma was alive to see how fine I was on papa's wedding-day, and I ran to my favourite station at her bed-room door. There I sat thinking of my mamma, and trying to remember exactly how she used to look; because I foolishly imagined that miss Saville was to be changed into something like my own mother, whose pale and delicate appearance in her last illness was all that I retained of her remembrance.

When my father returned home with his bride, he walked up stairs to look for me, and my new mamma followed him. They found me at my mother's door, earnestly looking through the keyhole; I was thinking so intently on my mother, that when my father said, "Here is your new mamma, my Elinor," I turned round, and began to cry, for no other reason than because she had a very high colour, and I remembered my mamma was very pale; she had bright black eyes, my mother's were mild blue eyes; and that instead of the wrapping gown and close cap in which I remembered my mamma, she was drest in all her bridal decorations.

I said, "Miss Saville shall not be my mamma," and I cried till I was sent away in disgrace.

Every time I saw her for several days, the same notion came into my head, that she was not a bit more like mamma than when she was miss Saville. My father was very angry when he saw how shy I continued to look at her; but she always said, "Never mind. Elinor and I shall soon be better friends."

One day, when I was very naughty indeed, for I would not speak one word to either of them, my papa took his hat, and walked out quite in a passion. When he was gone, I looked up at my new mamma, expecting to see her very angry too; but she was smiling and looking very good-naturedly upon me; and she said, "Now we are alone together, my pretty little daughter, let us forget papa is angry with us; and tell me why you were peeping through that door the day your papa brought me home, and you cried so at the sight of me." "Because mamma used to be there," I replied. When she heard me say this, she fell a-crying very sadly indeed; and I was so very sorry to hear her cry so, that I forgot I did not love her, and I went up to her, and said, "Don't cry, I won't be naughty any more, I won't peep through the door any more."

Then she said I had a little kind heart, and I should not have any occasion, for she would take me into the room herself; and she rung the bell, and ordered the key of that room to be brought to her; and the housekeeper brought it, and tried to persuade her not to go. But she said, "I must have my own way in this;" and she carried me in her arms into my mother's room.

O I was so pleased to be taken into mamma's room! I pointed out to her all the things that I remembered to have belonged to mamma and she encouraged me to tell her all the little incidents which had dwelt on my memory concerning her. She told me, that she went to school with mamma when she was a little girl, and that I should come into this room with her every day when papa was gone out, and she would tell me stories of mamma when she was a little girl no bigger than me.

When my father came home, we were walking in a garden at the back of our house, and I was shewing her mamma's geraniums, and telling her what pretty flowers they had when mamma was alive.

My father was astonished; and he said, "Is this the sullen Elinor? what has worked this miracle?" "Ask no questions," she replied, "or you will disturb our new-born friendship. Elinor has promised to love me, and she says too that she will call me 'mamma.'" "Yes, I will, mamma, mamma, mamma," I replied, and hung about her with the greatest fondness.

After this she used to pass great part of the mornings with me in my mother's room, which was now made the repository of all my playthings, and also my school-room. Here my new mamma taught me to read. I was a sad little dunce, and scarcely knew my letters; my own mamma had often said, when she got better she would hear me read every day, but as she never got better it was not her fault. I now began to learn very fast, for when I said my lesson well, I was always rewarded with some pretty story of my mother's childhood; and these stories generally contained some little hints that were instructive to me, and which I greatly stood in want of; for, between improper indulgence and neglect, I had many faulty ways.

In this kind manner my mother-in-law has instructed and improved me, and I love her because she was my mother's friend when they were young. She has been my only instructress, for I never went to school till I came here. She would have continued to teach me, but she has not time, for she has a little baby of her own now, and that is the reason I came to school.

V

MARGARET GREEN

(By Mary Lamb)

M<small>Y</small> <small>FATHER</small> has been dead near three years. Soon after his death, my mother being left in reduced circumstances, she was induced to accept the offer of Mrs. Beresford, an elderly lady of large fortune, to live in her house as her companion, and the superintendent of her family. This lady was my godmother, and as I was my mother's only child, she very kindly permitted her to have me with her.

Mrs. Beresford lived in a large old family mansion; she kept no company, and never moved except from the breakfast-parlour to the eating-room, and from thence to the drawing-room to tea.

Every morning when she first saw me, she used to nod her head very kindly, and say, "How do you do, little Margaret?" But I do not recollect she ever spoke to me during the remainder of the day; except indeed after I had read the psalms and the chapters, which was my daily task; then she used constantly to observe, that I improved in my reading, and frequently added, "I never heard a child read so distinctly."

She had been remarkably fond of needle-work, and her conversation with my mother was generally the history of some pieces of work she had formerly done; the dates when they were begun, and when finished; what had retarded their progress, and what had hastened their completion. If occasionally any other events were spoken of, she had no other chronology to reckon by, than in the recollection of what carpet, what sofa-cover, what set of chairs, were in the frame at that time.

I believe my mother is not particularly fond of needle-work; for in my father's lifetime I never saw her amuse herself in this way; yet, to oblige her kind patroness, she undertook to finish a large carpet, which the old lady had just begun when her eye-sight failed her. All day long my mother used to sit at the frame, talking of the shades of the worsted, and the beauty of the colours;—Mrs. Beresford seated in a chair near her, and, though her eyes were so dim she could hardly distinguish one colour from another, watching through her spectacles the progress of the work.

When my daily portion of reading was over, I had a task of needle-work, which generally lasted half an hour. I was not allowed to pass more time in reading or work, because my eyes were very weak, for which reason I was always set to read in the large-print Family Bible. I was very fond of reading; and when I could unobserved steal a few minutes as they were intent on their work, I used to delight to read in the historical part of the Bible; but this, because of my eyes, was a forbidden pleasure; and the Bible never being removed out of the room, it was only for a short time together that I dared softly to lift up the leaves and peep into it.

As I was permitted to walk in the garden or wander about the house whenever I pleased, I used to leave the parlour for hours together, and make out my own solitary amusement as well as I could. My first visit was always to a very large hall, which, from being paved with marble, was called the marble hall. In this hall, while Mrs. Beresford's husband was living, the tenants used to be feasted at Christmas.

The heads of the twelve Cæsars were hung round the hall. Every day I mounted on the chairs to look at them, and to read the inscriptions underneath, till I became perfectly familiar with their names and features.

Hogarth's prints were below the Cæsars: I was very fond of looking at them, and endeavouring to make out their meaning.

An old broken battledore, and some shuttlecocks with most of the feathers missing, were on a marble slab in one corner of the hall, which constantly reminded me that there had once been younger inhabitants here than the old lady and her gray-headed servants. In another corner stood a marble figure of a satyr: every day I laid my hand on his shoulder to feel how cold he was.

This hall opened into a room full of family portraits. They were all in the dresses of former times: some were old men and women, and some were children. I used to long to have a fairy's power to call the children down from their frames to play with me. One little girl in particular, who hung by the side of a glass door which opened into the garden, I often invited to walk there with me, but she still kept her station— one arm round a little lamb's neck, and in her hand a large bunch of roses.

From this room I usually proceeded to the garden.

When I was weary of the garden I wandered over the rest of the house. The best suite of rooms I never saw by any other light than what glimmered through the tops of the window-shutters, which however served to shew the carved chimney-pieces, and the curious old ornaments about the rooms; but the worked furniture and carpets, of which I heard such constant praises, I could have but an imperfect sight of, peeping under the covers which were kept over them, by the dim light; for I constantly lifted up a corner of the envious cloth, that hid these highly-praised rarities from my view.

The bed-rooms were also regularly explored by me, as well to admire the antique furniture, as for the sake of contemplating the tapestry hangings, which were full of Bible history. The subject of the one which chiefly attracted my attention, was Hagar and her son Ishmael. Every day I admired the beauty of the youth, and pitied the forlorn state of him and his mother in the wilderness. At the end of the gallery into which these tapestry rooms opened, was one door, which having often in vain attempted to open, I concluded to be locked; and finding myself shut out, I was very desirous of seeing what it contained; and though still foiled in the attempt, I every day endeavoured to turn the lock, which whether by constantly trying I loosened, being probably a very old one, or that the door was not locked but fastened tight by time, I know not,— to my great joy, as I was one day trying the lock as usual, it gave way, and I found myself in this so long desired room.

It proved to be a very large library. This was indeed a precious discovery. I looked round on the books with the greatest delight. I thought I would read them every one. I now forsook all my favourite haunts, and passed all my time here. I took down first one book, then another.

If you never spent whole mornings alone in a large library, you cannot conceive the pleasure of taking down books in the constant hope of finding an entertaining book among them; yet, after many days, meeting with nothing but disappointment, it becomes less pleasant. All the books within my reach were folios of the gravest cast. I could understand very little that I read in them, and the old dark print and the length of the lines made my eyes ache.

When I had almost resolved to give up the search as fruitless, I perceived a volume lying in an obscure corner of the room. I opened it. It was a charming print; the letters were almost as large as the type of the Family Bible. In the first page I looked into I saw the name of my favourite Ishmael, whose face I knew so well from the tapestry, and whose history I had often read in the Bible.

I sate myself down to read this book with the greatest eagerness. The title of it was "Mahometism Explained." It was a very improper book, for it contained a false history of Abraham and his descendants.

I shall be quite ashamed to tell you the strange effect it had on me. I know it was very wrong to read any book without permission to do so. If my time were to come over again, I would go and tell my mamma that there was a library in the house, and ask her to permit me to read a little while every day in some book that she might think proper to select for me. But unfortunately I did not then recollect that I ought to do this: the reason of my strange forgetfulness might be that my mother, following the example of her patroness, had almost wholly discontinued talking to me. I scarcely ever heard a word addressed to me from morning to night. If it were not for the old servants saying "Good morning to you, miss Margaret," as they passed me in the long passages, I should have been the greatest part of the day in as perfect a solitude as Robinson Crusoe. It must have been because I was never spoken to at all, that I forgot what was right and what was wrong, for I do not believe that I ever remembered I was doing wrong all the time I was reading in the library. A great many of the leaves in "Mahometism Explained" were torn out, but enough remained to make me imagine that Ishmael was the true son of Abraham: I read here that the true descendants of Abraham were known by a light which streamed from the middle of their foreheads. It said, that Ishmael's father and mother first saw this light streaming from his forehead, as he was lying asleep in the cradle. I was very sorry so many of the leaves were torn out, for it was as entertaining as a fairy tale. I used to read the history of Ishmael, and then go and look at him in the tapestry, and then read his history again. When I had almost learned the history of Ishmael by heart, I read the rest of the book, and then I came to the history of Mahomet, who was there said to be the last descendant of Abraham.

If Ishmael had engaged so much of my thoughts, how much more so must Mahomet? His history was full of nothing but wonders from the beginning to the end. The book said, that those who believed all the wonderful stories which were related of Mahomet were called Mahometans, and true believers:—I concluded that I must be a Mahometan, for I believed every word I read.

At length I met with something which I also believed, though I trembled as I read it:— this was, that after we are dead, we are to pass over a narrow bridge, which crosses a bottomless gulf. The bridge was described to be no wider than a silken thread; and it said, that all who were not Mahometans would slip on one side of this bridge, and drop into the tremendous gulf that had no bottom. I considered myself as a Mahometan, yet

I was perfectly giddy whenever I thought of passing over this bridge.

One day, seeing the old lady totter across the room, a sudden terror seized me, for I thought, how would she ever be able to get over the bridge. Then too it was, that I first recollected that my mother would also be in imminent danger; for I imagined she had never heard the name of Mahomet, because I foolishly conjectured this book had been locked up for ages in the library, and was utterly unknown to the rest of the world.

All my desire was now to tell them the discovery I had made; for I thought, when they knew of the existence of "Mahometism Explained," they would read it, and become Mahometans, to ensure themselves a safe passage over the silken bridge. But it wanted more courage than I possessed, to break the matter to my intended converts; I must acknowledge that I had been reading without leave; and the habit of never speaking, or being spoken to, considerably increased the difficulty.

My anxiety on this subject threw me into a fever. I was so ill, that my mother thought it necessary to sleep in the same room with me. In the middle of the night I could not resist the strong desire I felt to tell her what preyed so much on my mind.

I awoke her out of a sound sleep, and begged she would be so kind as to be a Mahometan. She was very much alarmed, for she thought I was delirious, which I believe I was; for I tried to explain the reason of my request, but it was in such an incoherent manner that she could not at all comprehend what I was talking about.

The next day a physician was sent for, and he discovered, by several questions that he put to me, that I had read myself into a fever. He gave me medicines, and ordered me to be kept very quiet, and said, he hoped in a few days I should be very well; but as it was a new case to him, he never having attended a little Mahometan before, if any lowness continued after he had removed the fever, he would, with my mother's permission, take me home with him to study this extraordinary case at his leisure; and added, that he could then hold a consultation with his wife, who was often very useful to him in prescribing remedies for the maladies of his younger patients.

In a few days he fetched me away. His wife was in the carriage with him. Having heard what he said about her prescriptions, I expected, between the doctor and his lady, to undergo a severe course of medicine, especially as I heard him very formally ask her advice what was good for a Mahometan fever, the moment after he had handed me into the carriage. She studied a little while, and then she said, A ride to Harlow fair would not be amiss. He said he was entirely of her opinion, because it suited him to go there to buy a horse.

During the ride they entered into conversation with me, and in answer to their questions, I was relating to them the solitary manner in which I had passed my time; how I found out the library, and what I had read in the fatal book which had so heated my imagination,—when we arrived at the fair; and Ishmael, Mahomet, and the narrow bridge, vanished out of my head in an instant.

O what a cheerful sight it was to me, to see so many happy faces assembled together, walking up and down between the rows of booths that were full of showy things; ribbands, laces, toys, cakes, and sweetmeats! While the doctor was gone to buy his horse, his kind lady let me stand as long as I pleased at the booths, and gave me many things which she saw I particularly admired. My needle-case, my pin-cushion, indeed my work-basket, and all its contents, are presents which she purchased for me at this fair.

After we returned home, she played with me all the evening at a geographical game, which she also bought for me at this cheerful fair.

The next day she invited some young ladies of my own age, to spend the day with me. She had a swing put up in the garden for us, and a room cleared of the furniture that we might play at blindman's-buff. One of the liveliest of the girls, who had taken on herself the direction of our sports, she kept to be my companion all the time I staid with her, and every day contrived some new amusement for us.

Yet this good lady did not suffer all my time to pass in mirth and gaiety. Before I went home, she explained to me very seriously the error into which I had fallen. I found that so far from "Mahometism Explained" being a book concealed only in this library, it was well known to every person of the least information.

The Turks, she told me, were Mahometans, and that, if the leaves of my favourite book had not been torn out, I should have read that the author of it did not mean to give the fabulous stories here related as true, but only wrote it as giving a history of what the Turks, who are a very ignorant people, believe concerning the impostor Mahomet, who feigned himself to be a descendant of Ishmael. By the good offices of the physician and his lady, I was carried home at the end of a month, perfectly cured of the error into which I had fallen, and very much ashamed of having believed so many absurdities.

VI

EMILY BARTON

(By Mary Lamb)

WHEN I WAS a very young child, I remember residing with an uncle and aunt who lived in ———shire. I think I remained there near a twelvemonth. I am ignorant of the cause of my being so long left there by my parents, who, though they were remarkably fond of me, never came to see me during all that time. As I did not know I should ever have occasion to relate the occurrences of my life, I never thought of enquiring the reason.

I am just able to recollect, that when I first went there, I thought it was a fine thing to live in the country, and play with my little cousins in the garden all day long; and I also recollect, that I soon found that it was a very dull thing, to live in the country with little cousins who have a papa and mamma in the house, while my own dear papa and mamma were in London many miles away.

I have heard my papa observe, girls who are not well managed are a most quarrelsome race of little people. My cousins very often quarrelled with me, and then they always said, "I will go and tell my mamma, cousin Emily;" and then I used to be very disconsolate because I had no mamma to complain to of my grievances.

My aunt always took Sophia's part because she was so young; and she never suffered me to oppose Mary, or Elizabeth, because they were older than me.

The playthings were all the property of one or other of my cousins. The large dolls belonged to Mary and Elizabeth, and the pretty little wax dolls were dressed on purpose for Sophia, who always began to cry the instant I touched them. I had nothing that I could call my own but one pretty book of stories; and one day as Sophia was endeavouring to take it from me, and I was trying to keep it, it was all torn to pieces; and my aunt would not be angry with her. She only said, Sophia was a little baby and did not know any better. My uncle promised to buy me another book, but he never remembered it. Very often when he came home in the evening, he used to say, "I wonder what I have got in my pocket;" and then they all crowded round him, and I used to creep towards him, and think, May be it is my book that my uncle has got in his pocket. But, no; nothing ever came out for me. Yet the first sight of a plaything, even if it is not one's own, is always a cheerful thing, and a new toy would put them in a good humour for a while, and they would say, "Here, Emily, look what I have got. You may take it in your own hand and look at it." But the pleasure of examining it, was sure to be stopped in a short time by the old story of "Give that to me again; you know that is mine." Nobody could help, I think, being a little out of humour if they were always served so: but if I shewed any signs of discontent, my aunt always told my uncle I was a little peevish fretful thing, and gave her more trouble than all her own children put together. My aunt would often say, what a happy thing it was, to have such affectionate children as hers were. She was always praising my cousins because they were affectionate; that was sure to be her word. She said I had not one atom of affection in my disposition, for that no kindness ever made the least impression on me. And she would say all this with Sophia seated on her lap, and the two eldest perhaps hanging round their papa, while I was so dull to see them taken so much notice of, and so sorry that I was not affectionate, that I did not know what to do with myself.

Then there was another complaint against me; that I was so shy before strangers. Whenever any strangers spoke to me, before I had time to think what answer I should give, Mary or Elizabeth would say, "Emily is so shy, she will never speak." Then I, thinking I was very shy, would creep into a corner of the room, and be ashamed to look up while the company staid.

Though I often thought of my papa and mamma, by degrees the remembrance of their persons faded out of my mind. When I tried to think how they used to look, the faces of my cousins' papa and mamma only came into my mind.

One morning, my uncle and aunt went abroad before breakfast, and took my cousins with them. They very often went out for whole days together, and left me at home. Sometimes they said it was because they could not take so many children; and sometimes they said it was because I was so shy, it was no amusement to me to go abroad.

That morning I was very solitary indeed, for they had even taken the dog Sancho with them, and I was very fond of him. I went all about the house and garden to look for him. Nobody could tell me where Sancho was, and then I went into the front court and called, "Sancho, Sancho." An old man that worked in the garden was there, and he said Sancho was gone with his master. O how sorry I was! I began to cry, for Sancho and I used to amuse ourselves for hours together when every body was gone out. I cried till I heard the mail coachman's horn, and then I ran to the gate to see the mail-coach go past. It stopped before our gate, and a gentleman got out, and the moment he saw me he took me in his arms, and kissed me, and said I was Emily

Barton, and asked me why the tears were on my little pale cheeks; and I told him the cause of my distress. The old man asked him to walk into the house, and was going to call one of the servants; but the gentleman would not let him, and he said, "Go on with your work, I want to talk to this little girl before I go into the house." Then he sate down on a bench which was in the court, and asked me many questions; and I told him all my little troubles, for he was such a good-natured-looking gentleman that I prattled very freely to him. I told him all I have told you, and more, for the unkind treatment I met with was more fresh in my mind than it is now. Then he called to the old man and desired him to fetch a post-chaise, and gave him money that he should make haste, and I never saw the old man walk so fast before. When he had been gone a little while, the gentleman said, "Will you walk with me down the road to meet the chaise, and you shall ride in it a little way along with me." I had nothing on, not even my old straw bonnet that I used to wear in the garden; but I did not mind that, and I ran by his side a good way, till we met the chaise, and the old man riding with the driver. The gentleman said, "Get down and open the door," and then he lifted me in. The old man looked in a sad fright, and said, "O sir, I hope you are not going to take the child away." The gentleman threw out a small card, and bid him give that to his master, and calling to the post-boy to drive on, we lost sight of the old man in a minute.

The gentleman laughed very much, and said, "We have frightened the old man, he thinks I am going to run away with you;" and I laughed, and thought it a very good joke; and he said, "So you tell me you are very shy;" and I replied "Yes, sir, I am, before strangers:" he said, "So I perceive, you are," and then he laughed again, and I laughed, though I did not know why. We had such a merry ride, laughing all the way at one thing or another, till we came to a town where the chaise stopped, and he ordered some breakfast. When I got out I began to shiver a little; for it was the latter end of autumn, the leaves were falling off the trees, and the air blew very cold. Then he desired the waiter to go and order a straw-hat, and a little warm coat for me; and when the milliner came, he told her he had stolen a little heiress, and we were going to Gretna Green in such a hurry, that the young lady had no time to put on her bonnet before she came out. The milliner said I was a pretty little heiress, and she wished us a pleasant journey. When we had breakfasted, and I was equipped in my new coat and bonnet, I jumped into the chaise again, as warm and as lively as a little bird.

When it grew dark, we entered a large city; the chaise began to roll over the stones, and I saw the lamps ranged along London streets.

Though we had breakfasted and dined upon the road, and I had got out of one chaise into another many times, and was now riding on in the dark, I never once considered where I was, or where I was going to. I put my head out of the chaise window, and admired those beautiful lights. I was sorry when the chaise stopped, and I could no longer look at the brilliant rows of lighted lamps.

Taken away by a stranger under a pretence of a short ride, and brought quite to London, do you not expect some perilous end of this adventure? Ah! it was my papa himself, though I did not know who he was, till after he had put me into my mamma's arms, and told her how he had run away with his own little daughter. "It is your papa, my dear, that has brought you to your own home." "This is your mamma, my love," they both exclaimed at once. Mamma cried for joy to see me, and she wept again, when she heard my papa tell what a neglected child I had been at my uncle's. This he had found out, he said, by my own innocent prattle, and that he was so offended with his brother, my uncle, that he would not enter his house; and then he said what a little happy good child I had been all the way, and that when he found I did not know him, he would not tell me who he was, for the sake of the pleasant surprise it would be to me. It was a surprise and a happiness indeed, after living with unkind relations, all at once to know I was at home with my own dear papa and mamma.

My mamma ordered tea. Whenever I happen to like my tea very much, I always think of the delicious cup of tea mamma gave us after our journey. I think I see the urn smoking before me now, and papa wheeling the sopha round, that I might sit between them at the table.

Mamma called me Little Run-away, and said it was very well it was only papa. I told her how we frightened the old gardener, and opened my eyes to shew her how he stared, and how my papa made the milliner believe we were going to Gretna Green. Mamma looked grave, and said she was almost frightened to find I had been so fearless; but I promised her another time I would not go into a post-chaise with a gentleman, without asking him who he was; and then she laughed, and seemed very well satisfied.

Mamma, to my fancy, looked very handsome. She was very nicely dressed, quite like a fine lady. I held up my head, and felt very proud that I had such a papa and mamma. I thought to myself, "O dear, my cousins' papa and mamma are not to be compared to mine."

Papa said, "What makes you bridle and simper so, Emily?" Then I told him all that was in my mind. Papa asked if I did not think him as pretty as I did mamma. I could not say much for his beauty, but I told him he was a much finer gentleman than my uncle, and that I liked him the first moment I saw him, because he looked so good-natured. He said, "Well then, he must be content with that half-praise; but he had always thought himself very handsome." "O dear!" said I, and fell a-laughing, till I spilt my tea, and mamma called me Little aukward girl.

The next morning my papa was going to the Bank to receive some money, and he took mamma and me with him, that I might have a ride through London streets. Every one that has been in London must have seen the Bank, and therefore you may imagine what an effect the fine large rooms, and the bustle and confusion of people had on me; who was grown such a little wondering rustic, that the crowded streets and the fine shops, alone kept me in continual admiration.

As we were returning home down Cheapside, papa said, "Emily shall take home some little books.—Shall we order the coachman to the corner of St. Paul's church-yard, or shall we go to the Juvenile Library in Skinner-street?" Mamma said she would go to Skinner-street, for she wanted to look at the new buildings there. Papa bought me seven new books, and the lady in the shop persuaded him to take more, but mamma said that was quite enough at present.

We went home by Ludgate-hill, because mamma wanted to buy something there; and while she went into a shop, papa heard me read in one of my new books, and he said he was glad to find I could read so well; for I had forgot to tell him my aunt used to hear me read every day.

My papa stopped the coach opposite to St. Dunstan's church, that I might see the great iron figures strike upon the bell, to give notice that it was a quarter of an hour past two. We waited some time that I might see this sight, but just at the moment they were striking, I happened to be looking at a toy-shop that was on the other side of the way, and unluckily missed it. Papa said, "Never mind: we will go into the toy-shop, and I dare say we shall find something that will console you for your disappointment." "Do," said mamma, "for I knew miss Pearson, that keeps this shop, at Weymouth, when I was a little girl, not much older than Emily. Take notice of her;—she is a very intelligent old lady." Mamma made herself known to miss Pearson, and shewed me to her, but I did not much mind what they said; no more did papa;—for we were busy among the toys.

A large wax doll, a baby-house completely furnished, and several other beautiful toys, were bought for me. I sat and looked at them with an amazing deal of pleasure as we rode home—they quite filled up one side of the coach.

The joy I discovered at possessing things I could call my own, and the frequent repetition of the words, *My own, my own*, gave my mamma some uneasiness. She justly feared that the cold treatment I had experienced at my uncle's had made me selfish, and therefore she invited a little girl to spend a few days with me, to see, as she has since told me, if I should not be liable to fall into the same error from which I had suffered so much at my uncle's.

As my mamma had feared, so the event proved; for I quickly adopted my cousins' selfish ideas, and gave the young lady notice that they were my own playthings, and she must not amuse herself with them any longer than I permitted her. Then presently I took occasion to begin a little quarrel with her, and said, "I have got a mamma now, miss Frederica, as well as you, and I will go and tell her, and she will not let you play with my doll any longer than I please, because it is my own doll." And I very well remember I imitated as nearly as I could, the haughty tone in which my cousins used to speak to me.

"Oh, fie! Emily," said my mamma; "can you be the little girl, who used to be so distressed because your cousins would not let you play with their dolls? Do you not see you are doing the very same unkind thing to your play-fellow, that they did to you?" Then I saw as plain as could be what a naughty girl I was, and I promised not to do so any more.

A lady was sitting with mamma, and mamma said, "I believe I must pardon you this once, but I hope never to see such a thing again. This lady is miss Frederica's mamma, and I am quite ashamed that she should be witness to your inhospitality to her daughter, particularly as she was so kind to come on purpose to invite you to a share in her *own* private box at the theatre this evening. Her carriage is waiting at the door to take us, but how can we accept of the invitation after what has happened?" The lady begged it might all be forgotten; and mamma consented that I should go, and she said, "But I hope, my dear Emily, when you are sitting in the play-house, you will remember that pleasures are far more delightful when they are shared among numbers. If the whole theatre were your own, and you were sitting by yourself to see the performance, how dull it would seem, to what you will find it, with so many happy faces around us, all amused with the same thing!" I hardly knew what my mamma meant, for I had never seen a play; but when I got there, after the curtain drew up, I looked up towards the galleries, and down into the pit, and into all the boxes, and then I knew what a pretty sight it was to see a number of happy faces. I was very well convinced, that it would not have been half so cheerful if the theatre had been my own, to have sat there by myself.

From that time, whenever I felt inclined to be selfish, I used to remember the theatre, where the mamma of the young lady I had been so rude to, gave me a seat in her own box. There is nothing in the world so charming as going to a play. All the way there I was as dull and as silent as I used to be in ———shire, because I was so sorry mamma had been displeased with me. Just as the coach stopped, miss Frederica said, "Will you be friends with me, Emily?" and I replied, "Yes, if you please, Frederica;" and we went hand in hand together into the house. I did not speak any more till we entered the box, but after that I was as lively as if nothing at all had happened.

I shall never forget how delighted I was at the first sight of the house. My little friend and I were placed together in the front, while our mammas retired to the back part of the box to chat by themselves, for they had been so kind as to come very early that I might look about me before the performance began.

Frederica had been very often at a play. She was very useful in telling me what every thing was. She made me observe how the common people were coming bustling down the benches in the galleries, as if they were afraid they should lose their places. She told me what a crowd these poor people had to go through, before they got into the house. Then she shewed me how leisurely they all came into the pit, and looked about them, before they took their seats. She gave me a charming description of the king and queen at the play, and shewed me where they sate, and told me how the princesses were drest. It was a pretty sight to see the remainder of the candles lighted; and so it was to see the musicians come up from under the stage. I admired the music very much, and I asked if that was the play. Frederica laughed at my ignorance, and then she told me, when the play began, the green curtain would draw up to the sound of soft music, and I should hear a lady dressed in black say,

"Music hath charms to soothe a savage breast:"

and those were the very first words the actress, whose name was Almeria, spoke. When the curtain began to draw up, and I saw the bottom of her black petticoat, and heard the soft music, what an agitation I was in! But before that we had long to wait. Frederica told me we should wait till all the dress boxes were full, and then the lights would pop up under the orchestra; the second music would play, and then the play would begin.

This play was the Mourning Bride. It was a very moving tragedy; and after that when the curtain dropt, and I thought it was all over, I saw the most diverting pantomime that ever was seen. I made a strange blunder the next day, for I told papa that Almeria was married to Harlequin at last; but I assure you I meant to say Columbine, for I knew very well that Almeria was married to Alphonso; for she said she was in the first scene. She thought he was dead, but she found him again, just as I did my papa and mamma, when she least expected it.

VII

MARIA HOWE

(By Charles Lamb)

I WAS BROUGHT UP in the country. From my infancy I was always a weak and tender-spirited girl, subject to fears and depressions. My parents, and particularly my mother, were of a very different disposition. They were what is usually called gay: they loved pleasure, and parties, and visiting; but as they found the turn of my mind to be quite opposite, they gave themselves little trouble about me, but upon such occasions generally left me to my choice, which was much oftener to stay at home, and indulge myself in my solitude, than to join in their rambling visits. I was always fond of being alone, yet always in a manner afraid. There was a book-closet which led into my mother's dressing-room. Here I was eternally fond of being shut up by myself, to take down whatever volumes I pleased, and pore upon them, no matter whether they were fit for my years or no, or whether I understood them. Here, when the weather would not permit my going into the dark walk, *my walk*, as it was called, in the garden; here when my parents have been from home, I have stayed for hours together, till the loneliness which pleased me so at first, has at length become quite frightful, and I have rushed out of the closet into the inhabited parts of the house, and sought refuge in the lap of some one of the female servants, or of my aunt, who would say, seeing me look pale, that Hannah [Maria] had been frightening herself with some of those *nasty books:* so she used to call my favourite volumes, which I would not have parted with, no not with one of the least of them, if I had had the choice to be made a fine princess and to govern the world. But my aunt was no reader. She used to excuse herself, and say, that reading hurt her eyes. I have been naughty enough to think that this was only an excuse, for I found that my aunt's weak eyes did not prevent her from poring ten hours a day upon her prayer-book, or her favourite Thomas à Kempis. But this was always her excuse for not reading any of the books I recommended. My aunt was my father's sister. She had never been married. My father was a good deal older than my mother, and my aunt was ten years older than my father. As I was often left at home with her, and as my serious disposition so well agreed with hers, an intimacy grew up between the old lady and me, and she would often say, that she only loved one person in the world, and that was me. Not that she and my parents were on very bad terms; but the old lady did not feel herself respected enough. The attention and fondness which she shewed to me, conscious as I was that I was almost the only being she felt any thing like fondness to, made me love her, as it was natural; indeed I am ashamed to say that I fear I almost loved her better than both my parents put together. But there was an oddness, a silence about my aunt, which was never interrupted but by her occasional expressions of love to me, that made me stand in fear of her. An odd look from under her spectacles would sometimes scare me away, when I had been peering up in her face to make her kiss me. Then she had a way of muttering to herself, which, though it was good words and religious words that she was mumbling, somehow I did not like.

My weak spirits, and the fears I was subject to, always made me afraid of any personal singularity or oddness in any one. I am ashamed, ladies, to lay open so many particulars of our family; but, indeed it is necessary to the understanding of what I am going to tell you, of a very great weakness, if not wickedness, which I was guilty of towards my aunt. But I must return to my studies, and tell you what books I found in the closet, and what reading I chiefly admired. There was a great Book of Martyrs in which I used to read, or rather I used to spell out meanings; for I was too ignorant to make out many words; but there it was written all about those good men who chose to be burnt alive, rather than forsake their religion, and become naughty papists. Some words I could make out, some I could not; but I made out enough to fill my little head with vanity, and I used to think I was so courageous I could be burnt too, and I would put my hands upon the flames which were pictured in the pretty pictures which the book had, and feel them; but, you know, ladies, there is a great difference between the flames in a picture, and real fire, and I am now ashamed of the conceit which I had of my own courage, and think how poor a martyr I should have made in those days. Then there was a book not so big, but it had pictures in, it was called Culpepper's Herbal; it was full of pictures of plants and herbs, but I did not much care for that. Then there was Salmon's Modern History, out of which I picked a good deal. It had pictures of Chinese gods, and the great hooded serpent which ran strangely in my fancy. There were some law books too, but the old English frighted me from reading them. But above all, what I relished was Stackhouse's History of the Bible, where there was the picture of the Ark and all the beasts getting into it. This delighted me, because it puzzled me, and many an aching head have I got with poring into it, and contriving how it might be built, with such and such rooms, to hold all the world if there should be another flood, and sometimes settling what pretty beasts should be saved, and what should not, for I would have no ugly or deformed beast in my pretty ark. But this was only a piece of folly and vanity, that a little reflection might cure me of. Foolish girl that I was! to suppose that any creature is really ugly, that has all its limbs contrived with heavenly wisdom, and was doubtless formed to some beautiful end, though a child cannot comprehend it.— Doubtless a frog or a toad is not uglier in itself than a squirrel or a pretty green lizard; but we want understanding to see it.

Here I must remind you, my dear miss Howe, that one of the young ladies smiled, and two or three were seen to titter, at this part of your narration, and you seemed, I thought, a little too angry for a girl of your sense and reading; but you will remember, my dear, that young heads are not always able to bear strange and unusual assertions; and if some elder person possibly, or some book which you have found, had not put it into your head, you would hardly have discovered by your own reflection, that a frog or a toad was equal in real loveliness to a frisking squirrel, or a pretty green lizard, as you called it; not remembering that at this very time you gave the lizard the name of pretty, and left it out to the frog—so liable we all are to prejudices. But you went on with your story.

These fancies, ladies, were not so very foolish or naughty perhaps, but they may be forgiven in a child of six years old; but what I am going to tell I shall be ashamed of, and repent, I hope, as long as I live. It will teach me not to form rash judgements.

tions, I got out of bed, and crept softly to the adjoining room. My room was next to where my aunt usually sat when she was alone. Into her room I crept for relief from my fears. The old lady was not yet retired to rest, but was sitting with her eyes half open, half closed; her spectacles tottering upon her nose; her head nodding over her prayer-book; her lips mumbling the words as she read them, or half read them, in her dozing posture: her grotesque appearance; her old-fashioned dress, resembling what I had seen in that fatal picture in Stackhouse; all this, with the dead time of night, as it seemed to me, (for I had gone through my first sleep,) all joined to produce a wicked fancy in me, that the form which I had beheld was not my aunt but some witch. Her mumbling of her prayers confirmed me in this shocking idea. I had read in Glanvil of those wicked creatures reading their prayers *backwards*, and I thought that this was the operation which her lips were at this time employed about. Instead of flying to her friendly lap for that protection which I had so often experienced when I have been weak and timid, I shrunk back terrified and bewildered to my bed, where I lay in broken sleeps and miserable fancies, till the morning, which I had so much reason to wish for, came. My fancies a little wore away with the light, but an impression was fixed, which could not for a long time be done away. In the day-time, when my father and mother were about the house, when I saw them familiarly speak to my aunt, my fears all vanished; and when the good creature has taken me upon her knees, and shewn me any kindness more than ordinary, at such times I have melted into tears, and longed to tell her what naughty foolish fancies I had had of her. But when night returned, that figure which I had seen recurred;—the posture, the half-closed eyes, the mumbling and muttering which I had heard, a confusion was in my head, *who* it was I had seen that night:—it was my aunt, and it was not my aunt:—it was that good creature who loved me above all the world, engaged at her good task of devotions—perhaps praying for some good to me. Again, it was a witch,—a creature hateful to God and man, reading backwards the good prayers; who would perhaps destroy me. In these conflicts of mind I passed several weeks, till, by a revolution in my fate, I was removed to the house of a female relation of my mother's, in a distant part of the county, who had come on a visit to our house, and observing my lonely ways, and apprehensive of the ill effect of my mode of living upon my health, begged leave to take me home to her house to reside for a short time. I went, with some reluctance at leaving my closet, my dark walk, and even my aunt, who had been such a source of both love and terror to me. But I went, and soon found the good effects of a change of scene. Instead of melancholy closets, and lonely avenues of trees, I saw lightsome rooms and cheerful faces; I had companions of my own age; no books were allowed me but what were rational or sprightly; that gave me mirth, or gave me instruction. I soon learned to laugh at witch stories; and when I returned after three or four months absence to our own house, my good aunt appeared to me in the same light in which I had viewed her from my infancy, before that foolish fancy possessed me, or rather, I should say, more kind, more fond, more loving than before. It is impossible to say how much good that lady, the kind relation of my mother's that I spoke of, did to me by changing the scene. Quite a new turn of ideas was given to me. I became sociable and companionable: my parents soon discovered a change in me, and I have found a similar alteration in them. They have been plainly more fond of me since that change, as from that time I learned to conform myself more to their way of living. I have never since had that aversion to company, and going out with them, which used to make them regard me with less fondness than they would have wished to shew. I impute almost all that I had to complain of in their neglect, to my having been a little unsociable, uncompanionable mortal. I lived in this manner for a year or two, passing my time between our house, and the lady's who so kindly took me in hand, till by her advice, I was sent to this school; where I have told to you, ladies, what, for fear of ridicule, I never ventured to tell any person besides, the story of my foolish and naughty fancy.

VIII

CHARLOTTE WILMOT

(By Mary Lamb)

U NTIL I WAS ELEVEN years of age, my life was one continued series of indulgence and delight. My father was a merchant, and supposed to be in very opulent circumstances, at least I thought so, for at a very early age I perceived that we lived in a more expensive way than any of my father's friends did. It was not the pride of birth, of which, miss Withers, you once imagined you might justly boast, but the mere display of wealth that I was early taught to set an undue value on. My parents spared no cost for masters to instruct me; I had a French governess, and also a woman servant whose sole business it was to attend on me. My play-room was crowded with toys, and my dress was the admiration of all my youthful visitors, to whom I gave balls and entertainments as often as I pleased. I looked down on all my young companions as my inferiors; but I chiefly assumed airs of superiority over Maria Hartley, whose father was a clerk in my father's counting-house, and therefore I concluded she would regard the fine show I made with more envy and admiration than any other of my companions. In the days of my humiliation, which I too soon experienced, I was thrown on the bounty of her father for support. To be a dependent on the charity of her family, seemed the heaviest evil that could have befallen me; for I remembered how often I had displayed my finery and my expensive ornaments, on purpose to enjoy the triumph of my superior advantages; and with shame I now speak it, I have often glanced at her plain linen frock, when I shewed her my beautiful ball-dresses. Nay, I once gave her a hint, which she so well understood that she burst into tears, that I could not invite her to some of my parties, because her mamma once sent her on my birthday in a coloured frock. I cannot now think of my want of feeling without excessive pain; but one day I saw her highly amused with some curious toys, and on her expressing the pleasure the sight of them gave her, I said "Yes, they are very well for those who are not accustomed to these things; but for my part, I have so many, I am tired of them, and I am quite delighted to pass an hour in the empty closet your mamma allows you to receive your visitors in, because there is nothing there to interrupt the conversation."

Once, as I have said, Maria was betrayed into tears: now that I insulted her by calling her own small apartment an empty closet, she turned quick upon me, but not in anger, saying, "O, my dear miss Wilmot, how very sorry I am——" here she stopped; and though I knew not the meaning of her words, I felt it as a reproof. I hung down my head abashed; yet, perceiving that she was all that day more kind and obliging than ever, and being conscious of not having merited this kindness, I thought she was mean-spirited, and therefore I consoled myself with having discovered this fault in her, for I thought my arrogance was full as excusable as her meanness.

In a few days I knew my error; I learned why Maria had been so kind, and why she had said she was sorry. It was for me, proud disdainful girl that I was, that she was sorry; she knew, though I did not, that my father was on the brink of ruin; and it came to pass, as she had feared it would, that in a few days my play-room was as empty as Maria's closet, and all my grandeur was at an end.

My father had what is called an execution in the house; every thing was seized that we possessed. Our splendid furniture, and even our wearing apparel, all my beautiful ball-dresses, my trinkets, and my toys, were taken away by my father's merciless creditors. The week in which this happened was such a scene of hurry, confusion and misery, that I will not attempt to describe it.

At the end of a week I found that my father and mother had gone out very early in the morning. Mr. Hartley took me home to his own house, and I expected to find them there; but, oh, what anguish did I feel, when I heard him tell Mrs. Hartley they had quitted England, and that he had brought me home to live with them! In tears and sullen silence I passed the first day of my entrance into this despised house. Maria was from home. All the day I sate in a corner of the room, grieving for the departure of my parents; and if for a moment I forgot that sorrow, I tormented myself with imagining the many ways which Maria might invent, to make me feel in return the slights and airs of superiority which I had given myself over her. Her mother began the prelude to what I expected, for I heard her freely censure the imprudence of my parents. She spoke in whispers; yet, though I could not hear every word, I made out the tenor of her discourse. She was very anxious, lest her husband should be involved in the ruin of our house. He was the chief clerk in my father's counting-house; towards evening he came in and quieted her fears, by the welcome news that he had obtained a more lucrative situation than the one he had lost.

At eight in the evening Mrs. Hartley said to me, "Miss Wilmot, it is time for you to be in bed, my dear;" and ordered the servant to shew me up stairs, adding, that she supposed she must assist me to undress, but that when Maria came home, she must teach me to wait on myself. The apartment in which I was to sleep was at the top of the house. The walls were white-washed, and the roof was sloping. There was only one window in the room, a small casement, through which the bright moon shone, and it seemed to me the most melancholy sight I had ever beheld. In broken and disturbed slumbers I passed the night. When I awoke in the morning, she whom I most dreaded to see, Maria, who I supposed had envied my former state, and who I now felt certain would exult over my present mortifying reverse of fortune, stood by my bedside. She awakened me from a dream, in which I thought she was ordering me to fetch her something; and on my refusal, she said I must obey her, for I was now her servant. Far differently from what my dreams had pictured, did Maria address me! She said, in the gentlest tone imaginable, "My dear miss Wilmot, my mother begs you will come down to breakfast. Will you give me leave to dress you?" My proud heart would not suffer me to speak, and I began to attempt to put on my clothes; but never having been used to do any thing for myself, I was unable to perform it, and was obliged to accept of the assistance of Maria. She dressed me, washed my face, and combed my hair; and as she did these services for me, she said in the most respectful manner, "Is this the way you like to wear this, miss Wilmot?" or, "Is this the way you like this done?" and curtsied, as she gave me every fresh article to put on. The slights I expected to receive from Maria, would not have distressed me more, than the delicacy of her behaviour did. I hung down my head with shame and anguish.

In a few days Mrs. Hartley ordered her daughter to instruct me in such useful works and employments as Maria knew. Of every thing which she called useful I was most ignorant. My accomplishments I found were held in small estimation here, by all indeed except Maria. She taught me nothing without the kindest apologies for being obliged to teach me, who, she said, was so excellent in all elegant arts, and was for ever thanking me for the pleasure she had formerly received, from my skill in music and pretty fancy works. The distress I was in, made these complimentary speeches not flatteries, but sweet drops of comfort to my degraded heart, almost broken with misfortune and remorse.

I remained at Mr. Hartley's but two months, for at the end of that time my father inherited a considerable property by the death of a distant relation, which has enabled him to settle his affairs. He established himself again as a merchant; but as he wished to retrench his expences, and begin the world again on a plan of strict economy, he sent me to this school to finish my education.

IX

SUSAN YATES

(By Charles Lamb)

I WAS BORN and brought up, in a house in which my parents had all their lives resided, which stood in the midst of that lonely tract of land called the Lincolnshire fens. Few families besides our own lived near the spot, both because it was reckoned an unwholesome air, and because its distance from any town or market made it an inconvenient situation. My father was in no very affluent circumstances, and it was a sad necessity which he was put to, of having to go many miles to fetch any thing he wanted from the nearest village, which was full seven miles distant, through a sad miry way that at all times made it heavy walking, and after rain was almost impassable. But he had no horse or carriage of his own.

The church which belonged to the parish in which our house was situated, stood in this village; and its distance being, as I said before, seven miles from our house, made it quite an impossible thing for my mother or me to think of going to it. Sometimes indeed, on a fine dry Sunday, my father would rise early, and take a walk to the village, just to see how *goodness thrived*, as he used to say, but he would generally return tired, and the worse for his walk. It is scarcely possible to explain to any one who has not lived in the fens, what difficult and dangerous walking it is. A mile is as good as four, I have heard my father say, in those parts. My mother, who in the early part of her life had lived in a more civilised spot, and had been used to constant church-going, would often lament her situation. It was from her I early imbibed a great curiosity and anxiety to see that thing, which I had heard her call a church, and so often lament that she could never go to. I had seen houses of various structures, and had seen in pictures the shapes of ships and boats, and palaces and temples, but never rightly any thing that could be called a church, or that could satisfy me about its form. Sometimes I thought it must be like our house, and sometimes I fancied it must be more like the house of our neighbour, Mr. Sutton, which was bigger and handsomer than ours. Sometimes I thought it was a great hollow cave, such as I have heard my father say the first inhabitants of the earth dwelt in. Then I thought it was like a waggon, or a cart, and that it must be something moveable. The shape of it ran in my mind strangely, and one day I ventured to ask my mother, what was that foolish thing that she was always longing to go to, and which she called a church. Was it any thing to eat or drink, or was it only like a great huge play-thing, to be seen and stared at?—I was not quite five years of age when I made this inquiry.

This question, so oddly put, made my mother smile; but in a little time she put on a more grave look, and informed me, that a church was nothing that I had supposed it, but it was a great building, far greater than any house which I had seen, where men, and women, and children, came together, twice a-day, on Sundays, to hear the Bible read, and make good resolutions for the week to come. She told me, that the fine music which we sometimes heard in the air, came from the bells of St. Mary's church, and that we never heard it but when the wind was in a particular point. This raised my wonder more than all the rest; for I had somehow conceived that the noise which I heard, was occasioned by birds up in the air, or that it was made by the angels, whom (so ignorant I was till that time) I had always considered to be a sort of birds: for before this time I was totally ignorant of any thing like religion, it being a principle of my father, that young heads should not be told too many things at once, for fear they should get confused ideas, and no clear notions of any thing. We had always indeed so far observed Sundays, that no work was done upon that day, and upon that day I wore my best muslin frock, and was not allowed to sing, or to be noisy; but I never understood why that day should differ from any other. We had no public meetings:— indeed the few straggling houses which were near us, would have furnished but a slender congregation; and the loneliness of the place we lived in, instead of making us more sociable, and drawing us closer together, as my mother used to say it ought to have done, seemed to have the effect of making us more distant and averse to society than other people. One or two good neighbours indeed we had, but not in numbers to give me an idea of church attendance.

But now my mother thought it high time to give me some clearer instruction in the main points of religion, and my father came readily into her plan. I was now permitted to sit up half an hour later on a Sunday evening, that I might hear a portion of Scripture read, which had always been their custom, though by reason of my tender age, and my father's opinion on the impropriety of children being taught too young, I had never till now been an auditor. I was taught my prayers, and those things which you, ladies, I doubt not, had the benefit of being instructed in at a much earlier age.

The clearer my notions on these points became, they only made me more passionately long for the privilege of joining in that social service, from which it seemed that we alone, of all the inhabitants of the land, were debarred; and when the wind was in that point which favoured the sound of the distant bells of St. Mary's to be heard over the great moor which skirted our house, I have stood out in the air to catch the sounds which I almost devoured; and the tears have come in my eyes, when sometimes they seemed to speak to me almost in articulate sounds, to *come to church*, and because of the great moor which was between me and them I could not come; and the too tender apprehensions of these things have filled me with a religious melancholy. With thoughts like these I entered into my seventh year.

And now the time was come, when the great moor was no longer to separate me from the object of my wishes and of my curiosity. My father having some money left him by the will of a deceased relation, we ventured to set up a sort of a carriage—no very superb one, I assure you, ladies; but in that part of the world it was looked upon with some envy by our poorer neighbours. The first party of pleasure which my father proposed to take in it, was to the village where I had so often wished to go, and my mother and I were to accompany him; for it was very fit, my father observed, that little Susan should go to church, and learn how to behave herself, for we might some time or other have occasion to live in London, and not always be confined to that out of the way spot.

It was on a Sunday morning that we set out, my little heart beating with almost breathless expectation. The day was fine, and the roads as good as they ever are in those parts. I was so happy and so proud. I was lost in dreams of what I was going to see. At length the tall steeple of St. Mary's church came in view. It was pointed out to me by my father, as the place from which that music had come which I have heard over the moor, and had fancied to be angels singing. I was wound up to the highest pitch of delight at having visibly presented to me the spot from which had proceeded that unknown friendly music; and when it began to peal, just as we approached the village, it seemed to speak, *Susan is come*, as plainly as it used to invite me *to come*, when I heard it over the moor. I pass over our alighting at the house of a relation, and all that passed till I went with my father and mother to church.

St. Mary's church is a great church for such a small village as it stands in. My father said it was a cathedral, and that it had once belonged to a monastery, but the monks were all gone. Over the door there was stone work, representing saints and bishops, and here and there, along the sides of the church, there were figures of men's heads, made in a strange grotesque way: I have since seen the same sort of figures in the round tower of the Temple church in London. My father said they were very improper ornaments for such a place, and so I now think them; but it seems the people who built these great churches in old times, gave themselves more liberties than they do now; and I remember that when I first saw them, and before my father had made this observation, though they were so ugly and out of shape, and some of them seemed to be grinning and distorting their features with pain or with laughter, yet being placed upon a church, to which I had come with such serious thoughts, I could not help thinking they had some serious meaning; and I looked at them with wonder, but without any temptation to laugh. I somehow fancied they were the representation of wicked people set up as a warning.

When we got into the church, the service was not begun, and my father kindly took me round, to shew me the monuments and every thing else remarkable. I remember seeing one of a venerable figure, which my father said had been a judge. The figure was kneeling, as if it was alive, before a sort of desk, with a book, I suppose the Bible, lying on it. I somehow fancied the figure had a sort of life in it, it seemed so natural, or that the dead judge that it was done for, said his prayers at it still. This was a silly notion, but I was very young, and had passed my little life in a remote place, where I had never seen any thing nor knew any thing; and the awe which I felt at first being in a church, took from me all power but that of wondering. I did not reason about any thing, I was too young. Now I understand why monuments are put up for the dead, and why the figures which are upon them, are described as doing the actions which they did in their life-times, and that they are a sort of pictures set up for our instruction. But all was new and surprising to me on that day; the long windows with little panes, the pillars, the pews made of oak, the little hassocks for the people to kneel on, the form of the pulpit with the sounding-board over it, gracefully carved in flower work. To you, who have lived all your lives in populous places, and have been taken to church from the earliest time you can remember, my admiration of these things must appear strangely ignorant. But I was a lonely young creature, that had been brought up in remote places, where there was neither church nor church-going inhabitants. I have since lived in great towns, and seen the ways of churches and of worship, and I am old enough now to distinguish between what is essential in religion, and what is merely formal or ornamental.

When my father had done pointing out to me the things most worthy of notice about the church, the service was almost ready to begin; the parishioners had most of them entered, and taken their seats; and we were shewn into a pew where my mother was already seated. Soon after the clergyman entered, and the organ began to play what is called the voluntary. I had never seen so many people assembled before. At first I thought that all eyes were upon me, and that because I was a stranger. I was terribly ashamed and confused at first; but my mother helped me to find out the places in the Prayer-book, and being busy about that, took off some of my painful apprehensions. I was no stranger to the order of the service, having often read in a Prayer-book at home; but my thoughts being confused, it puzzled me a little to find out the responses and other things, which I thought I knew so well; but I went through it tolerably well. One thing which has often troubled me since, is, that I am afraid I was too full of myself, and of thinking how happy I was, and what a privilege it was for one that was so young, to join in the service with so many grown people, so that I did not attend enough to the instruction which I might have received. I remember, I foolishly applied every thing that was said to myself, so as it could mean nobody but myself, I was so full of my own thoughts. All that assembly of people, seemed to me as if they were come together only to shew me the way of a church. Not but I received some very affecting impressions from some things which I heard that day; but the standing up and the sitting down of the people; the organ; the singing;—the way of all these things took up more of my attention than was proper; or I thought it did. I believe I behaved better and was more serious when I went a second time, and a third time; for now we went as a regular thing every Sunday, and continued to do so, till, by a still further change for the better in my father's circumstances, we removed to London. Oh! it was a happy day for me my first going to St. Mary's church: before that day I used to feel like a little out-cast in the wilderness, like one that did not belong to the world of Christian people. I have never felt like a little outcast since. But I never can hear the sweet noise of bells, that I don't think of the angels singing, and what poor but pretty thoughts I had of angels in my uninstructed solitude.

X

ARABELLA HARDY
(By Charles Lamb)

I WAS BORN in the East Indies. I lost my father and mother young. At the age of five my relations thought it proper that I should be sent to England for my education. I was to be entrusted to the care of a young woman who had a character for great humanity and discretion: but just as I had taken leave of my friends, and we were about to take our passage, the young woman was taken suddenly ill, and could not go on board. In this unpleasant emergency, no one knew how to act. The ship was at the very point of sailing, and it was the last ship which was to sail that season. At last the captain, who was known to my friends, prevailed upon my relation who had come with us to see us embark, to leave the young woman on shore, and to let me embark separately. There was no possibility of getting any other female attendant for me, in the short time allotted for our preparation; and the opportunity of going by that ship was thought too valu-able to be lost. No other ladies happened to be going; so I was consigned to the care of the captain and his crew,—rough and unaccustomed attendants for a young creature, delicately brought up as I had been; but indeed they did their best to make me not feel the difference. The unpolished sailors were my nursery-maids and my waiting-women. Every thing was done by the captain and the men, to accommodate me, and make me easy. I had a little room made out of the cabin, which was to be considered as my room, and nobody might enter into it. The first mate had a great character for bravery, and all sailor-like accomplishments; but with all this he had a gentleness of manners, and a pale feminine cast of face, from ill health and a weakly constitution, which subjected him to some little ridicule from the officers, and caused him to be named Betsy. He did not much like the appellation, but he submitted to it the better, as he knew that those who gave him a woman's name, well knew that he had a man's heart, and that in the face of danger he would go as far as any man. To this young man, whose real name was Charles Atkinson, by a lucky thought of the captain, the care of me was especially entrusted. Betsy was proud of his charge, and, to do him justice, acquitted himself with great diligence and adroitness through the whole of the voyage. From the beginning I had somehow looked upon Betsy as a woman, hearing him so spoken of, and this reconciled me in some measure to the want of a maid, which I had been used to. But I was a manageable girl at all times, and gave nobody much trouble.

I have not knowledge enough to give an account of my voyage, or to remember the names of the seas we passed through, or the lands which we touched upon, in our course. The chief thing I can remember, for I do not remember the events of the voyage in any order, was Atkinson taking me up on deck, to see the great whales playing about in the sea. There was one great whale came bounding up out of the sea, and then he would dive into it again, and then would come up at a distance where nobody expected him, and another whale was following after him. Atkinson said they were at play, and that that lesser whale loved that bigger whale, and kept it company all through the wide seas: but I thought it strange play, and a frightful kind of love; for I every minute expected they would come up to our ship and toss it. But Atkinson said a whale was a gentle creature, and it was a sort of sea-elephant, and that the most powerful creatures in nature are always the least hurtful. And he told me how men went out to take these whales, and stuck long, pointed darts into them; and how the sea was discoloured with the blood of these poor whales for many miles distance: and I admired at the courage of the men, but I was sorry for the inoffensive whale. Many other pretty sights he used to shew me, when he was not on watch, or doing some duty for the ship. No one was more attentive to his duty than he; but at such times as he had leisure, he would shew me all pretty sea sights:—the dolphins and porpoises that came before a storm, and all the colours which the sea changed to; how sometimes it was a deep blue, and then a deep green, and sometimes it would seem all on fire: all these various appearances he would shew me, and attempt to explain the reason of them to me, as well as my young capacity would admit of. There was a lion and a tiger on board, going to England as a present to the king, and it was a great diversion to Atkinson and me, after I had got rid of my first terrors, to see the ways of these beasts in their dens, and how venturous the sailors were in putting their hands through the grates, and patting their rough coats. Some of the men had monkeys, which ran loose about, and the sport was for the men to lose them, and find them again. The monkeys would run up the shrouds, and pass from rope to rope, with ten times greater alacrity than the most experienced sailor could follow them; and sometimes they would hide themselves in the most unthought-of places, and when they were found, they would grin, and make mouths as if they had sense. Atkinson described to me the ways of these little animals in their native woods, for he had seen them. Oh, how many ways he thought of to amuse me in that long voyage!

Sometimes he would describe to me the odd shapes and varieties of fishes that were in the sea, and tell me tales of the sea-monsters that lay hid at the bottom, and were seldom seen by men; and what a glorious sight it would be, if our eyes could be sharpened to behold all the inhabitants of the sea at once, swimming in the great deeps, as plain as we see the gold and silver fish in a bowl of glass. With such notions he enlarged my infant capacity to take in many things.

When in foul weather I have been terrified at the motion of the vessel, as it rocked backwards and forwards, he would still my fears, and tell me that I used to be rocked so once in a cradle, and that the sea was God's bed, and the ship our cradle, and we were as safe in that greater motion, as when we felt that lesser one in our little wooden sleeping-places. When the wind was up, and sang through the sails, and disturbed me with its violent clamours, he would call it music, and bid me hark to the sea-organ, and with that name he quieted my tender apprehensions. When I have looked around with a mournful face at seeing all *men* about me, he would enter into my thoughts, and tell me pretty stories of his mother and his sisters, and a female cousin that he loved better than his sisters, whom he called Jenny, and say that when we got to England I should go and see them, and how fond Jenny would be of his little daughter, as he called me; and with these images of women and females which he raised in my fancy, he quieted me for a time. One time, and never but once, he told me that Jenny had promised to be his wife if ever he came to England, but that he had his doubts whether he should live to get home, for he was very sickly. This made me cry bitterly.

That I dwell so long upon the attentions of this Atkinson, is only because his death, which happened just before we got to England, affected me so much, that he alone of all the ship's crew has engrossed my mind ever since; though indeed the captain and all were singularly kind to me, and strove to make up for my uneasy and unnatural situation. The boat-swain would pipe for my diversion, and the sailor-boy would climb the dangerous mast for my sport. The rough foremast-man would never willingly appear before me, till he had combed his long black hair smooth and sleek, not to terrify me. The officers got up a sort of play for my amusement, and Atkinson, or, as they called him, Betsy, acted the heroine of the piece. All ways that could be contrived, were thought upon, to reconcile me to my lot. I was the universal favourite;—I do not know how deservedly; but I suppose it was because I was alone, and there was no female in the ship besides me. Had I come over with female relations or attendants, I should have excited no particular curiosity; I should have required no uncommon attentions. I was one little woman among a crew of men; and I believe the homage which I have read that men universally pay to women, was in this case directed to me, in the absence of all other woman-kind. I do not know how that might be, but I was a little princess among them, and I was not six years old.

I remember the first draw-back which happened to my comfort, was Atkinson's not appearing during the whole of one day. The captain tried to reconcile me to it, by saying that Mr. Atkinson was confined to his cabin;—that he was not quite well, but a day or two would restore him. I begged to be taken in to see him, but this was not granted. A day, and then another came, and another, and no Atkinson was visible, and I saw apparent solicitude in the faces of all the officers, who nevertheless strove to put on their best countenances before me, and to be more than usually kind to me. At length, by the desire of Atkinson himself, as I have since learned, I was permitted to go into his cabin and see him. He was sitting up, apparently in a state of great exhaustion, but his face lighted up when he saw me, and he kissed me, and told me that he was going a great voyage, far longer than that which we had passed together, and he should never come back; and though I was so young, I understood well enough that he meant this of his death, and I cried sadly; but he comforted me and told me, that I must be his little executrix, and perform his last will, and bear his last words to his mother and his sister, and to his cousin Jenny, whom I should see in a short time; and he gave me his blessing, as a father would bless his child, and he sent a last kiss by me to all his female relations, and he made me promise that I would go and see them when I got to England, and soon after this he died; but I was in another part of the ship when he died, and I was not told it till we got to shore, which was a few days after; but they kept telling me that he was better and better, and that I should soon see him, but that it disturbed him to talk with any one. Oh, what a grief it was, when I learned that I had lost my old ship-mate, that had made an irksome situation so bearable by his kind assiduities; and to think that he was gone, and I could never repay him for his kindness!

When I had been a year and a half in England, the captain, who had made another voyage to India and back, thinking that time had alleviated a little the sorrow of Atkinson's relations, prevailed upon my friends who had the care of me in England, to let him introduce me to Atkinson's mother and sister. Jenny was no more; she had died in the interval, and I never saw her. Grief for his death had brought on a consumption, of which she lingered about a twelvemonth, and then expired. But in the mother and the sisters of this excellent young man, I have found the most valuable friends which I possess on this side the great ocean. They received me from the captain as the little *protégée* of Atkinson, and from them I have learned passages of his former life, and this in particular, that the illness of which he died was brought on by a wound of which he never quite recovered, which he got in the desperate attempt, when he was quite a boy, to defend his captain against a superior force of the enemy which had boarded him, and which, by his premature valour inspiriting the men, they finally succeeded in repulsing. This was that Atkinson, who, from his pale and feminine appearance, was called Betsy. This was he whose womanly care of me got him the name of a woman, who, with more than female attention, condescended to play the hand-maid to a little unaccompanied orphan, that fortune had cast upon the care of a rough sea captain, and his rougher crew.

18

The Juvenile Spectator

By "ARABELLA ARGUS"

VOLUME ONE

'I cannot kiss you just now Grandmama,' said Susy, for I am writing to such a funny old Woman, about my wax Doll.'

Published June 7, 1810, by W. & T. Darton & Co. Holborn Hill, London.

THE

JUVENILE SPECTATOR;

BEING

OBSERVATIONS

ON THE

TEMPERS, MANNERS, AND FOIBLES

OF

VARIOUS YOUNG PERSONS,

INTERSPERSED

*With such lively Matter, as it is presumed will amuse
as well as instruct.*

By ARABELLA ARGUS.

" Teach me to feel another's woe,
To hide the fault I see ;
That mercy I to others show,
That mercy show to me."

LONDON :

PRINTED BY AND FOR W. AND T. DARTON,
58, HOLBORN-HILL,

1810.

ARABELLA ARGUS *was the pseudonym of a woman writer known for* The Adventures of a Donkey *(1815) and its sequel,* The Further Adventures of Jemmy Donkey *(1821),* Ostentation and Liberality *(1821), and* The Juvenile Spectator *(2 vols., 1810, 1812). In the last book cited, Argus, although she admits having "not quite so many" as a hundred eyes, reminds the reader of the clarity of her spectacles, which enable her to see children right through brick walls. This "very comical old woman," as she calls herself, lectures children on behavior like a Georgian advice columnist. Often grandmotherly and therefore kind, she admits her aim is not ". . . entirely to repress their [children's] little tastes." While her own grandchildren reform and learn to love "old spec," even William Mordaunt complains that "she seems very particular." A modern reader would agree, but there is some refreshing humor and irony in* The Juvenile Spectator. *Arabella Argus warns children not to pick on eccentric old ladies with long noses because they may not prove to be the real juvenile spectator. There is some mild satire of "Timothy Testy," who corresponds with Mrs. Argus, and Mr. Columbus the Peeper, another correspondent, is judged "a very successful discoverer." It is useless to complain, as does F. J. Harvey Darton, that Argus's lighter touches were not more freely used. The fact is that Arabella Argus wrote about real children, few of whom were goody-goody. Doggedly determined to improve them, she nonetheless wrote of them with tolerance, understanding and love.*

Volume I of The Juvenile Spectator *is reprinted from the first edition (1810).*

Volume One

The principles we imbibe, and the habits we contract in our early years, are not matters of small moment, but of the utmost consequence imaginable. They not only give a transient or superficial tincture to our first appearance in life, but most commonly stamp the form of our whole future conduct, and even of our eternal state.

ARISTOTLE.

PREFACE

I T IS NOT a *serious preface*, to which I invite my young readers to devote five minutes of their precious time; I understand the general characters of children: a preface is a part of a book, seldom perused by them; and, I am almost certain, that the *title* of this little volume, will, to many, appear very dull. "A Fairy Tale," "Amusing Stories," &c. &c. never fail to charm; and I have seen the eager eyes of many an amiable child, intent on the *marvellous* part of a story, while the *moral* of it, if it contained any, was wholly overlooked.

In order to make truths as pleasant as I can, permit me to tell my own story.

I am an old woman, but not an *old witch*, nor yet a *fairy*; yet, I will endeavour to prove to you, before I finish my book, that I am a very comical old woman, and the many *facts* that I shall relate, will, I am persuaded, make some of you think that I have wonderful powers. Such *secret* information as I shall set forth, under the terms of "*Nursery* anecdotes," "*Parlour* foibles," "*Garden* mischiefs," and "*Hyde Park* romps," will lead you to suppose, that I possess that wonderful *cap* of which you have all read, and am able to be in all places *unseen*.

But, as I am determined not to deceive you, I must, like an honest old woman, repeat,—my means are perfectly consistent with nature and truth. It is now twelve months since I was invited to eat my plumb-pudding with my grandchildren; I obeyed the summons with much delight, hoping to pass the Christmas season agreeably in their society. I was disappointed: I saw them all in health, and with every comfort around them; but their manners and dispositions were by no means suited to the happiness of their situation. My *spectacles*, which are remarkably clear, proved of great service to me on this visit. I had become an inmate of their house, to partake in the festivities of the holidays; of course I did not feel at liberty to interrupt what *they* called their days of pleasure: but my *reflections*, when I returned home, were given to the subjects of their errors and little contentions, and I resolved on committing my thoughts to paper. For this purpose, I imparted my intentions to a *few* friends, who have occasionally helped me with information from various families. One lady suggested, that if I would permit the epistles of children to be inserted, it would greatly assist my plan. I complied, and accordingly, many letters from young persons of both sexes will be found in this volume. I am *yet* in doubt how my book will succeed, and have, therefore, received *all* papers through the hands of my friendly agents, addressed to "*Mrs. Argus*," the name by which I choose to be known.

It will be highly gratifying to me, if they should prove as interesting to my young readers, as they were to me. I can assure them, I have *smiled* at many that will be found in these pages; have shed tears over a *few;* and, though I have been forced to *reject* one or two rather *intrusive* epistles, I yet hope I have retained sufficient matter, to engage the attention of a liberal *young* public, to whom I beg to subscribe myself,

their sincere friend and well-wisher,

ARABELLA ARGUS.

A PREFATORY CHAPTER

A Consultation.

MRS. BENTLY, who is my most intimate friend, and a woman whose judgment I reverence, was of opinion, that it was highly necessary she should announce me as a watchful observer of children. "Though unknown, I can transact a great part of your business," said my excellent friend, "and the children, when convinced that you are not an *imaginary* being, will be more sedulous and guarded in their conduct." I readily assented to her proposal, the result of which has more than answered my expectation; for my grandchildren, whose happiness I am most anxious to promote, are amongst my correspondents. I have no doubt that many of my young readers could testify to the tendernesses and indulgencies bestowed upon them by their grandmothers. I believe, nay I am assured, that I love mine most sincerely; but, as I wish them to be esteemed by every body, and know that they will not always remain under the eye of their parents,— that they will mix in the world, where a variety of characters and dispositions will contend for what each considers his right: I would wish them to cast aside all frowardness of temper, that selfishness which the fond circle called *home,* is often ill calculated to suppress.

A quarrel in a nursery, decided only by an indulgent and too partial nurse, will be no precedent for what the same child shall meet in a school. "Sugar-plumbs" and "kisses" are not the plaisters for a fall, or a rough blow among school-boys; they meet upon equal terms. And though I would not infer that happiness is not to be expected in schools as in other places, yet I am desirous of impressing on the minds of sensible children, that life, even from infancy, is subject to rebuffs, and that in fact these oppositions are highly serviceable to them. Which of you, but upon reflection, can remember to have heard your parents express some disappointment, some regret? And what are you that you should expect to pass through life exempt from them?

"To bear and forbear" is the duty of every person, whether young or old; but as I shall have occasion to speak at large on this subject, I will drop it for the present.

Mrs. Bently, in a very pleasant letter addressed to me some months since, expressed herself very sanguine in the good to be effected by my plan.

"I have been greatly amused, my dear Bella," said she; "all the little folks with whom I have spoken on the subject of the 'Juvenile Spectator,' are curious to know 'What sort of person you are?' 'Whether you are really an old woman?' 'Where you live?' 'If you walk the Park?' 'What dress you wear?' &c. to all which inquiries I am uniformly silent, only promising to transmit any letter or note to Mrs. Argus, which they choose to entrust to my care. I was present," continued my friend, "at a consultation in one family which amused me very much. Charles Osborn declared, that he knew Mrs. Argus. 'It is the old woman in the red cloak, who walked round the Serpentine last Thursday; don't you remember, Charlotte, she looked very cunningly at us, and told me that I was a thoughtless boy to walk so near the water?' Charlotte looked very wise, yet somewhat ashamed. 'I hope *she* is not the Spectator,' replied Charlotte Osborn, 'for I remember I laughed at her, and said you were big enough to take care of yourself.' 'I will stare at every old woman I meet,' said Charles, 'and if I see the same person again, I will take off my hat and say, 'How do you do Mrs. Argus?' I warned them not to make an attempt so rude," continued Mrs. Bently, "and after awakening their curiosity, and impressing them with respect for your character, took my leave. The next morning I received a letter from Charles Osborn, which I forward to you; your own discernment will lead you to a just under-standing of his disposition from the little I have said. I am a stranger to the contents of his address, and am now, as I shall continue to be, only my dear Arabella's agent in this her kind interest for the rising generation."

I own to you, my little friends, that I was rather curious to peruse this my first appeal, under my new title of Spectator. I broke the seal, and read as follows:

To Mrs. ARGUS.
A friend of my Mamma's says, that you are very clever at finding out the faults of children, pray tell me mine; for if you are as cunning as she says you are, I need not mention them to you.

I am certain I know you; don't you walk in the Park sometimes? I am sure you do though, and you have a very long nose; my sister Charlotte and I remarked it; you know when I mean, so you need not deny it. Mrs. Bently says you are very good-natured; do you ever make presents to the children you like? Charlotte and I hope you will answer this directly, for we are in a great hurry to be satisfied about you.

Your's,
CHARLES OSBORN.

I laid this letter on my writing table, and was musing on its contents, when my servant delivered a very neatly folded note, which I immediately unclosed. It ran thus:

To Mrs. ARGUS.
MADAM,
A lady, who is my godmother, assures me that you are very fond of children, and will give your advice to all such as address you on the subject. I have many questions to ask of you, but do not know how to begin; and, as I am twelve years of age, am afraid you should think me very childish in my inquiries. If you would be so good as to say what I *may* ask. I shall be much obliged to you. Till then, I remain,

Madam,
Your obedient Servant,
SOPHIA WILMOT.

The modesty and propriety of Miss Wilmot's note claimed my immediate notice. I took my pen, and addressed the following in reply:

Mrs. Argus will be happy to receive Miss Wilmot's communications on any subject which she shall think fit to communicate. To a young lady who expresses herself with so much becoming timidity, Mrs. Argus will have great pleasure in offering her advice; nor is it necessary that she should add, that the *age* of Miss Wilmot does not place her *above* childhood; as such, the inquiries which she hesitates to think proper, because childish, are perhaps the more essential to be made; as at all ages a love of inquiry leads to wisdom; and a habit of thinking correctly is only to be derived from forming our opinions on those principles which experience has sanctioned. Mrs. Argus will not think any question too trivial which shall help to establish the happiness of a young lady, whose well-written note, has impressed her with the most favourable opinion of the juvenile writer.

ARABELLA ARGUS.

I soon discovered that my character of Spectator was generally known, and rejoiced that my person was screened from notice. For on going to my daughter's one morning, I was compelled to smile internally, such a scene met my view; but I will describe it for the amusement of my readers. My four grandchildren were seated at a large book-table, each scribbling according to their abilities. "I cannot kiss you just now, grand-mamma," said Lucy, "for I am writing to such a funny old woman about my wax doll. Harriet wants me to let her nurse it sometimes, but I am determined she shall not; so I shall ask Mrs. Argus if I have not a right to do what I please with my own doll." I was on the point of replying, when Harriet overturned the ink-stand, which un-fortunately defaced the half-finished epistle of William, who, enraged at the accident, turned in great anger to his sister, and in reaching his hand to give her a slight chastisement, threw his elder sister, who was sitting on one corner of a chair, on the floor: in a moment all was confusion; my daughter, whose weak state of health, makes her incapable of that exertion so requisite in a young family, was so alarmed by Fanny's accident, as to be near fainting. I united with William in quieting her fears, and a small piece of gold-beater's skin being applied to Fanny's wounded elbow, tran-quillity was in a few minutes restored. The interference, which, at any other period, I should have considered necessary, would now have proved superfluous, as I purposed to reprove them under my fictitious character. Drawing their attention, therefore, to the blotted letter, I simply asked, "if they did not mean to prosecute their intention, and write to the Spectator?" William, who is an intelligent and clever boy, but rather thought-less, instantly took another sheet of paper, declaring he would tell the old woman the exact state of things, "that he had begun a letter to her, which was interrupted by the carelessness of Harriet." "Do not omit to name Fanny's custom of sitting on the corner of her chair;" said I, "nor yet your brotherly attempt to strike your sister." "Must I do all this," said he, pausing. "Certainly, my dear," I replied, "for as I suppose, you mean to ask the advice of this invisible old woman, it is impossible she can reply to you, unless you state facts exactly as they occur." "Then we will all join in the same letter," said Fanny, "and each of us speak of ourselves." This proposal meeting general assent, they proceeded with their epistle, and I entered into conversation with my daughter.

It had long been my wish that William should be sent to a public school; his mother had resisted my importunities, not equal to the idea of a second separation from her family; for I should apprize my readers, that Captain Mordaunt, my son-in-law, had attended his wife to the Continent, her health requiring a southern clime. They were absent nearly three years, in which time the children had been under the care of the captain's mother, who, from a mistaken tenderness to her grandchildren, had indulged them to an excess of weakness. William, whom she always pronounced a *hero*, was warm-hearted but self-willed. Fanny, gentle and affectionate, yet so inattentive as to appear indifferent to the wishes of her friends. Harriet, a lively little romp, always doing mischief from mere thoughtlessness. Lucy, a pet, with a strong inclination to selfishness. My own retired way of life, which until the return of Mrs. Mordaunt, had been uniformly passed in the country, made me an almost stranger to my grandchildren. I would willingly have received them into my care during the absence of their parents, but the captain's mother would not be refused; and being unwilling to interfere in a domestic arrangement, I yielded my right. I had good reasons for supposing that my daughter would have determined otherwise, but Captain Mordaunt was fondly attached to his mother, and had, besides, a strong prejudice in favour of the advantages of a metropolitan education. The children, however, had had little done for them in point of learning. Masters and instructresses *innumerable* had been engaged to attend them daily, but from their instructions, however well qualified to teach, it was impossible they could derive much, as a *sight* always superseded a lesson, the teachers often being dismissed, because the fatigue of an evening passed at Sadler's Wells, made the young votaries of pleasure incapable of *study* on the ensuing day. Thus, an immense sum of money had been expended to very little advantage.

The death of old Mrs. Mordaunt which happened immediately after my daughter's arrival, consigned the children to their disappointed mother. I had hastened to London to meet them *en famille*, and too soon perceived that their parents must experience much uneasiness before the effects of their unlimited indulgencies could be eradicated. I could not conform to the noise and continued dissentions of these little squabblers, and, therefore, provided myself with a small house contiguous to their dwelling. Even the few weeks which they termed holidays, because the masters were discontinued, were, as I have before related, so unpleasant to me as to cause me much uneasiness; and I had no sooner retired to my own peaceful dwelling, than my present plan of "Juvenile Spectator," occurred to me. After this, my family introduction, I presume my young readers will follow me through my miscellaneous subjects with more interest.

It really required some self-command on my part, when, after an hour spent in the composition of this letter by several hands, I heard the footman desired to go to Mrs. Bently's with it, and beg that she would send it as soon as possible. It would be impossible to describe all the varieties of disposition that were displayed during its composition. Fanny thought William said too much, and would not leave room for her; yet, when it was presented for her addition, she seemed wholly at a loss what to say, declaring that she did not know how to begin; she wished her mamma or grandmamma would just tell her the first sentence. Harriet wished her turn was come, for she had a great many thoughts in her head just at that moment; while Lucy said, she did not want a subject, as Harriet was always wanting her things, and she was sure the Spectator would agree with her, that "every body ought to be contented with their own."

As I entered my parlour, after a day of some fatigue and many regrets, I perceived two or three juvenile epistles waiting my arrival; their contents must make the subject of a new Chapter.

CHAPTER I

"For he that loveth not his brother, whom he hath seen, how can he love God, whom he hath not seen? And this commandment have we from him, that he who loveth God, loveth his brother also."

NEXT MORNING AT BREAKFAST I entered on my voluntary office of "Spectator." Though I could partly guess the purport of William Mordaunt's address, affection prompted me to read his letter first: I will transcribe it faithfully.

TO MRS. ARGUS.

I hear that you know Mrs. Bently; she is a very nice lady, and we, (that is, myself and my sisters) are very fond of her; yet she is rather particular, but then, she tells us very pleasant stories, which I believe she makes out of her own head, for they always make some of us blush, because they explain our faults. She told us the other day, that you would give us directions how to be good and happy, and I suppose you know that all children have faults. Pray what ought I to do? I am often very passionate and I cannot help it, for my sisters are so provoking. What ought I to do? I really love them very much, but just now Harriet turned the ink-stand over a letter I had almost finished, and meant to send to you. I was going to give her a thump of the head, and by accident threw Fanny off her seat; but, to be sure, she was only sitting upon the corner of her chair, and I was sorry afterwards, as it alarmed mamma, who is not well. Give me some directions, if you please, ma'am, and I shall be much obliged to you. I must leave off now, as Fanny wishes to say a few words to you.

WILLIAM MORDAUNT.

I am so stupid at writing letters, that I am afraid you will not have patience with me, madam. William has said enough to let you know that we do not agree so well as we ought. I have a habit of sitting on the corner of my chair, and though I am often told it is wrong, I always forget what is said. Yet, I can assure you, I love my mamma dearly, but grandmamma Mordaunt never used to notice it, so I did not know it was wrong. How shall I break myself of this custom. I am very desirous of pleasing my mamma: be so good as to tell me how I shall begin to correct this fault. I have many others, I believe, but this happened to frighten my mamma, who thought I was hurt by my fall, and it has convinced me that I ought to strive to get rid of it.

FANNY MORDAUNT.

Pray, madam, is there any harm in being a romp. I hope not, for I am such a giddy little thing, that I am always in mischief; the worst of it is, I am for ever getting tasks from my masters, and the governess who comes to hear us read, for I never have my lessons ready; so they give me more to do, though I have not time to learn what they set me. I used to get off with my other masters when grandmamma Mordaunt was alive, for she said I looked so pretty when I laughed, that it was worth a thousand lessons. But now, it is quite a different case: my mamma is not pleased if I don't please my teachers, and they are cross; and grandmamma Harley always looks so disappointed when I cannot give a good account of myself, that I am quite ashamed to meet her. She is such a nice old lady, and so wise, she can always tell by my looks if I have done well, that I should like to please her almost as well as mamma; but I really don't know how to begin, and I hope you will not say that I must give up play, for that is impossible; however, I will be sure to mind what you say—good bye.

HARRIET MORDAUNT.

None of them will let me see what they have written to you, Ma'am. I dare say it is all about me, but I don't care, for, as nurse Jenkins says—"one story is good till another is told." But Miss Harriet did not tell you that she is always undressing my doll, though it is my very own. She knows she broke hers the second day after she got it; and because she has given away all her pocket-money she wants me to let her have mine to give away too; but that I shall not do, for I have rubbed mine till they are so bright, they are quite like a looking glass, and I mean to keep up all I get till I am a woman, and then I shall be quite rich. Pray have not I a right to do as I please with my own things? I am sure you will say yes, and I hope you will write to us soon. I have nothing more to say at present.

LUCY MORDAUNT.

Had I been a stranger to my young correspondents, the preceding letters would fully have explained their dispositions, and I owned a very great degree of satisfaction in perceiving that their method of expressing themselves was so natural. There was evidently much to be done away, much improvement required, before they could either be a comfort to their parents or happy in themselves. For it is an invariable truth, "that to be good is to be happy." As my readers are acquainted with my consanguinity to these little folks, they will not wonder that their's was the first letter to which I replied this morning.

To Master WILLIAM MORDAUNT.

I lose no time in answering your ingenuous epistle. I should consider myself very culpable indeed if I suffered a day to elapse without writing to you, and this, simply from one word in your letter: you avow yourself passionate. It is a most dreadful and degrading trait of character—dreadful, because in one moment of passion we may forfeit the peace of our future days, and make ourselves unworthy of the protecting care of heaven: degrading, because passionate people are obliged to make concessions of the most humiliating sort. All human creatures are liable to err, and to confess our regret for a fault is at once noble, and must disarm the anger of those whom we have offended. But in cases of passion we have assumed a right inconsistent with our place in society. We are not to avenge even what we consider a wrong, much less become aggressors. I presume, that all those with whom I shall have the honour to correspond under the title of "Spectator," have made some advances in the best of all histories, "sacred history." As such let them reflect on the Son of God: his sufferings, the indignities to which he was subject, owning in himself all the virtue and purity of a saint, he submitted to insult, cruelty and pain: yet he, though reviled, "reviled not again." Reflection, that noble distinction between the human and animal creation, was bestowed upon us to be exercised. If you consider yourself offended, avow the same; let your language be moderate, and the *time* which your explanation will necessarily require, will subdue this unfortunate propensity, which is, in fact, a *temporary* madness.

That incident, to which your letter refers, appears trivial; but, had your sister fallen against a table, or any other piece of furniture having sharp corners, it might have occasioned instant death. *You* have no right to chastise the faults of your sisters. Represent what you feel to be offensive to you; and even this should be done with tenderness. You are of a sex born to protect females, and, as I doubt not that you wish to be thought *manly*, I must beg to tell you, there cannot be anything less like *courage* than an act of this sort. I hope you will consider this in a just point of view, and continue to give me your free communications. You may observe, that I address you as a boy of sense, and the *head* of a young family. You say, your mother was alarmed by your disagreement, let this likewise have its weight. Your remark, that "all children have faults," is in part just, perhaps; yet I hope, and indeed I have the pleasure to know some, who are very dutiful in every respect.

I will trouble you to acquaint your sisters, that I will answer their questions by tomorrow's post, having two or three *prior* favors, to which I must reply.

I remain,

Your sincere Friend,

ARABELLA ARGUS.

I dispatched this letter with all possible haste, and the hand-writing, or rather the *scrawl*, of Master Osborn, catching my eye, I felt it indispensible to give him a few lines. I took my pen, and wrote as follows:

To Master OSBORN.

SIR,

In my assumed character of "Spectator," I must necessarily *receive* all letters addressed to me; this avowal is by no means an acknowledgment that I shall *answer* all of them. Yours' happened to be the *first* epistle, and it is on this account I devote a little time to you.

I pretend to no particular *cunning*, the term is inelegant and offensive to me; I have no *personal* knowledge of you, or your sister Charlotte, nor am I conscious that my *nose* is remarkable in any way. With respect to presents, I have never considered that good children require rewards; the pleasure of doing our duty, in any situation, and at all periods of our lives, conveys more real delight to the heart, than all the treasures of the East could bestow; and excuse me, sir, when I add, that the manner and style of *your* letter would not, (if I had ever purposed to dispense rewards,) entitle *you* to such a distinction. I mention this to you with candour; nor do I wish to repress your inquiries, if, after this, you feel disposed to make any. On the contrary, you will rise in my opinion if you make the attempt. I have taken some time to consider your letter before I replied to it, and must ingenuously confess, that I have written to many of my young friends previously to my answering yours', and this, merely to prove to you that I do not attend to peremptory commands. Yet I am *your* sincere friend, and the friend of all children.

ARABELLA ARGUS.

My young readers will observe, that in addressing Charles Osborn I was careful to treat him with a *certain* respect; I was induced to this from my strong disapprobation of *his* very familiar and bold manner. It is a general fault in youth, and indeed in more mature age, to cast aside *decorum*, when they mean to be clever, witty, &c. These qualities are, in themselves, very unessential, if not detrimental to their possessors; and unfortunately, many persons esteem themselves brilliant in these points, who are in fact wholly destitute of such talents. But, as I am speaking of children, I cannot forbear observing, that it has often given me sincere concern when I have heard the smart answers, and wise sayings of children, related in their presence; it is a most injudicious mode of shewing our affection; a love of praise is a feeling predominant in the infant mind, and it is part of a parent's duty to bestow it, but it must be administered with caution, not lavished on slight occasions: the child who conquers a bad habit, or confesses an error, should meet all the encouragement which the *just* exercise of their reason demands. But, where an act, the simple effect of that affection which should ever bind us to our kindred,—where we have beheld the mere yielding of *one* to the comfort of *another*, I can see no reason in such a case for exalting the deed. Convince them that they have performed a *duty*, and that it will make the happiness of their future days certain; if in their youth they acquire the habit of considering their *duties* indispensible.

I am led to think more seriously on this subject, from having been present at a very unamiable contention some months since. I was making a morning visit to an old friend, whom I had not seen many years; she was surrounded by her family at my first entrance, and after a general introduction, the young folks withdrew to their respective amusements in different corners of the room. Mrs. Barlow and I had recurred to some serious circumstances, which wholly engrossed our attention, when a loud shriek startled us; I turned to discover from whence it came, and beheld a scene which astonished me,— the two elder girls were struggling for a book, which the younger of the two claimed as *her* property; and, in order to attain her object, she had twisted the wrist of her sister so violently, as to occasion the shriek which had alarmed us.

"How can you teize your sister, Helen," said Mrs. Barlow; "tell me, my love, what has she done to you?"

"I want that book which Eliza has been reading; it is my own, and I won't let any body have it."

"Why do you take your sister's books, Eliza?" said my friend; "you see how it vexes the child,—have you not books of your own?"

"Yes, mamma," replied Eliza Barlow, "but I have read all my own; and this happened to be upon the table, and Helen did not want it, for she did not know it was in the room, but as soon as she saw I was reading it, she said, she was *just* wishing for *that* book; and I only asked her to let me finish the story I was reading, and I would then give it to her; but she snatched it out of my hands, and hurt my wrist very much."——

"Well, I cannot take your part," said Mrs. Barlow, "you know I have bought each of you books for your own use, and if you will encroach upon your sister's property you must take the consequences."

I happened to think differently from my friend, and owned a wish to discover whether Helen really *wished* to read the book in question, or whether she asked for it merely to deprive her sister of it.

"Helen," said I, "what is the title of that book, of which you seem so fond?" Helen coloured, and glancing her eyes to the back of the volume, she replied, "O! I see, it is Cottage Tales."

"Then you did not know what book it was till now," said I, "and could you deprive your sister of a pleasure in your power to confer, and that without a reasonable excuse for such unkindness? Indeed I cannot consider this as the act of a sister. I see you are sorry, and I am glad of it."

Helen burst into tears, and giving the book to Eliza, begged she would read it through.

"There spoke my dear Helen;" said Mrs. Barlow, "she is a little hasty, and Eliza knows this, and should be cautious in her manner towards her; but my dear friend, you have no idea what strong feelings that child has; I am forced to encourage her when she shows any self-command. You are a very good girl," continued Mrs. Barlow, addressing her favourite, "I am very much pleased with you, and to-morrow I will get you some new book, which shall be entirely your own."

I believe I discovered my disapprobation of such misapplied praise by my countenance, for Mrs. Barlow looked disconcerted, and I soon after took leave; I had already commenced my career as a spectator, and in consequence gave a portion of the ensuing evening to reflections on the scene I had witnessed in the Barlow family.

It is absolutely necessary that I should here make a short digression.—If I am to be believed *sincere* in my wishes for the rising generation, it is a part of *my* duty to trace the *causes* of many of those errors which attach to children. And it is impossible to do this without throwing a *partial* censure on *some* parents; but here let me be understood.

Tenderness, mistaken indulgencies, and blindness to the faults of their children, are in themselves amiable weaknesses, as originating in that *natural* affection implanted in the human breast towards these immediate dependants on our care; and, though a thousand instances might be adduced to prove, that the happiness of children is not *increased* by such methods. The *motives* of parents yet remain in an amiable point of view; they are to be pitied in the disappointments they too frequently experience; and, at the same time, we may reasonably *lament*, that many very amiable mothers, from *excess* of tenderness, abridge their *own* happiness, and greatly diminish that of their children.

In the case before us, I trust all my young readers will perceive, that in bestowing praise upon Helen Barlow her mother was *injudicious;* but Helen was not only ungenerous, but ungrateful.

Helen Barlow, from infancy, had been delicate in her health; her mother had devoted herself to the comfort of this child with an assiduity highly praiseworthy. It pleased God to restore her to health, and at the period I name, Helen was ten years of age; consequently, an action so wholly inconsistent with kindness, so *unreasonable*, and destitute of good feeling, was very unpardonable.

In the first place, Eliza was her *elder* sister; the book in question had no charms for [Helen], for when she *contended* for its possession, she was unconscious of its *title*. What but a selfish, and ungenerous feeling could induce such conduct; and to a mother, who had provided these *rational* resources for her children, how *ungrateful* was that disposition, which converted her beneficence into a cause for dissention.

I have no doubt, but Helen would be greatly shocked to hear her conduct treated so seriously,—she would be hurt if I was to say, that she may have *learned* her catechism by *rote*, but that she is a stranger to its meaning. Let her repeat her "duty towards her neighbour." Let her dwell on that benevolent and *ever*-applicable sentence, "Do unto all men, &c." and then let her ask her heart, if *she* would choose that Eliza should retaliate her unkind treatment,—assuredly not. It was perfectly evident to me, that this selfish little girl knew her power over her mother; and, that in consequence of this knowledge she presumed. My friend's partiality for Helen at once grieved me, and excited my pity. But having since learned that this young lady's health is equal to all those indispensible exertions of *mind* and *body*, that are peculiarly requisite in youth, I have used the freedom of suggesting to her mother the propriety of calling them into action. She received my sincere professions on this head with all the warmth of real friendship; and I have reason to believe, that the Miss Barlow's will soon be my correspondents.

If it should happen, that the incident just related should apply to any of my young readers,—if they *recollect* having exerted an *authority* of such sort towards a brother, sister, or companion, though a *book* should not have been the bone of contention, but a toy, a pencil, or a *seat*, I entreat of them to reflect, to mark, how odious an act which took place in a moment of irritation, appears in description; and, that the most unfavorable conclusions might be drawn from such conduct, if witnessed by strangers. For my own part, the scene was not entirely new to me; I had more than once seen the Mordaunt's engaged in these *dumb* battles, and they had awakened in me the most uneasy sensations; for if actions of this kind occur amongst brothers and sisters, how very imperfectly they must comprehend the nature of their duties, and the commands of that God who has blessed them, in bestowing upon them the greatest of all comforts, *natural* relations.

I have always observed, that an only son, or daughter, laments the want of these endearing ties, while those who possess them, in *many* instances, seem deaf to the voice of nature.

The anguish that such dissentions must occasion parents, may be more easily imagined than described. And, that such conduct is contrary to the will of God, is obvious to the meanest capacity.

I refer my readers to the motto prefixed to this Chapter, and I beg them to give to it their serious consideration.

CHAPTER II

An Adventure.

Having promised to visit a friend in the neighbourhood of Kensington, next morning, I confined myself to answering the little Mordaunt's before my departure; and to convince my young friends that I am not partial, even where I may be *supposed* to feel an affectionate interest, I insert my letter.

To Miss Mordaunt.

I do not consider you so deficient in the art of writing a letter as you seem to consider yourself; you were perfectly right in suggesting, that your brother's address would apprize me, that you do not *agree* as brothers and sisters ought. This is, indeed, a cause of deep regret to me, and, if I did not hope that your confession was to be followed by a sincere desire to correct this unamiable conduct, I should not feel in the least disposed to class you amongst my correspondents.

The habit, to which you particularly refer, is certainly very ungraceful; it is more the manner of an infant than one of your age; and, as I conclude, that some expenses have been incurred in having you taught dancing, (which is more essential in the effect it produces in the manners, and straightness of the figure,) than in the *gestures* and agility of the science, I must, even in this point, consider you ungrateful. The most trivial expense into which a parent enters for the advantage of their children, calls upon them for a due exertion of their attention while learning, and a resolution to retain, as far as in their power, the instructions given.

Amongst the rules laid down in dancing, I do not remember such a *position* as that which you have acquired; to advise a girl of *your* age how to conquer such a foible, is simply to tell her that it is wrong,—that her parents must regret that their purposes are defeated by the *inattention* of their child, and that *all* habits of the sort are injurious in a great degree, as while children are growing they are liable to contract a stoop, if not a crookedness, which may remain during life.

I persuade myself, that though favored with your future correspondence, I shall have no occasion to revert to this subject again,—and as I cannot doubt your sincerity, that you *wish* to please your parents, I can assure you, that a desire to do well is usually followed by the power to effect the same; the tranquillity of your own mind, in an attempt so laudable, will fully compensate for any little difficulty that may at *first* appear formidable to you, for though all silly habits are easily acquired, they are not so immediately done away. God blesses the endeavours of all such as seriously apply themselves to wisdom, and that you may be worthy of the divine favour, is the wish of your sincere friend,

ARABELLA ARGUS.

P. S. Will you be so good as to tell your brother, that the word *thump*, which occurred in his letter, appears to me an expression unworthy of a well-educated child; but, as I trust the action will not be repeated, I have no doubt but that the *word* will become obsolete with him.

To Miss HARRIET MORDAUNT.

Though a romp, at *your* age, may be a very well-meaning little girl, it is by no means necessary to your happiness that your days should be devoted to play.

I regret that you are not *punctual* in learning your lessons, and am sorry that those who teach you have been so liberal as to consider you *wiser* than you really are. In fixing the length of your lessons, their *experience* led them to give you such portions as are usually given to children of *your* age. It appears they were mistaken in your capacity and I would advise you to shew them this letter, which may induce them to adopt a new plan, by placing you in a *lower* class of studies. Your love of *play* will be greatly indulged by these means, but I hope you have ingenuity sufficient to amuse yourself, for I should be sorry to hear, that at those hours devoted to business, you could find a *companion* in your own family.

The extreme indulgence of your grandmamma was most likely occasioned by the absence of your parents, (you see I know your family affairs,) she doubtless overlooked many of your little foibles on this account, but, as you are now under the protection of your mother, and express yourself anxious to please her, I know no method so likely to procure her approbation, as a regular performance of your duties. Your grandmamma Harley, will of course share in this satisfaction, as you seem to intimate that she takes much interest in your education; but if this attempt should appear difficult to you, I request you to adopt the following plan:

Give up *all* lessons for a *week*, and be careful to quit the room in which your brother and sisters are engaged in theirs. Devote yourself entirely to play, and give me your opinion freely, at the end of that time.

Be very particular in describing your feelings, and believe that I am interested in your happiness.

ARABELLA ARGUS.

P. S. Your *beauty*, (of which you seem to think much,) will be greatly encreased by a whole week of play; do not omit to name this, at the end of the term, which I have proposed to you.

To Miss LUCY MORDAUNT.

I hope that you are a *very* little girl; indeed, I should be glad to hear that you were an inattentive child; one who had not *sense* enough to listen to the voice of reason, or how shall I find a way to excuse the numberless faults which your letter exhibits.

But first let me observe, that the writing and spelling are excellent, and the sense clear; it is the sentiments which are objectionable. You are not, perhaps, conscious of the *character* you have given yourself.

I will explain it for you; you have avowed yourself *suspicious, ungenerous,* and *miserly*; and you justify these qualities, by vainly imagining that others will approve of them. Your nurse may be a good-natured and indulgent woman, but she is not retained to teach you how to express yourself. All sayings are vulgar, and, consequently, beneath the adoption of well-instructed children. I would always inculcate the necessity of kind and affectionate treatment towards the servants of your family, and indeed to all servants, but their language, is by no means an imitation desirable. If you suspect that all persons who write or speak in your presence make *you* their subject, you add *vanity* to suspicion, as if a child of your age, could be of such general consequence. When you refuse to a sister the trifling gratification of playing with your doll occasionally, your selfishness is evident, and this makes you unworthy of the future indulgence of your parents. In hoarding your money, you are guilty of a great fault, and are depriving yourself of the only blessing of riches, "the power of assisting the unfortunate." Are you *certain* that you shall *live* to spend all your bright money? and when you are rich, and a woman, to what purpose do you propose to apply this money? Be so good as to answer to these questions in your next, and likewise tell me if you have never read any book in which *charity* is named, as well-pleasing to God.

Your brother and sisters have received my sentiments already; I have spoken to them, with equal candour. I doubt not but they will shew you my letters; let me have the pleasure of discovering, in your next address, that you have compared *your* foibles with *theirs;* and then tell me, like an ingenuous little girl, that you perceive your errors, and will receive my advice and instructions for your future happiness. Until I am assured of this, it would be useless to say more, than that I am sincerely your friend,

ARABELLA ARGUS.

Dispatching these letters, I proceeded towards Kensington, when just as I had reached the garden-gate, I met William Mordaunt, walking with two of his sisters and their nursery maids. I thought I perceived William's colour heighten as I approached, and in a moment the cause was explained; for the nurses both expressed their pleasure at meeting me. "Master Mordaunt is so troublesome, ma'am," said Jenkins, "he runs away from us, and will go in the horse-ride, and is, besides, so thoughtless in throwing stones, that I am sure he will do somebody a mischief."

"How is this William," said I, "I thought you were the protector of your little sisters."

"I hate to walk with nurses," said William; "it is making quite a baby of me; I wish mamma would let me come out by myself."

"Yet you do not appear very fit to be trusted alone," said I; "but I will take this young rebel out of your charge for the present." I continued addressing myself to Jenkins, "Tell your mistress that Master Mordaunt will accompany me to Kensington, and that I will send him home early in the evening." William was delighted at the proposal, and the little girls, with a cheerfulness that was highly pleasing to me, took leave of us.

Being rather fatigued, I proposed resting in the gardens a little while, a rheumatic complaint to which I am subject, made me prefer one of the enclosed seats; we entered one, in which two children, a boy and girl, with a lady, were sitting. The usual courtesies having passed, I owned an unaffected surprise in hearing my grandson call the children, by the name of Osborn. "Here comes the old woman, Charlotte," said Master Osborn; "now see how I will quiz her." An elderly lady was walking slowly down the path. "Pray don't speak to her, Charles," said the little girl, "for if *she* really is the *Spectator*,

I should be quite afraid of her; she is such a cross impertinent thing." "Indeed, but I will," said Charles Osborn; and he ran across the path, to intercept the stranger.

"Your brother Charles is a rude child," said the young lady who had charge of Miss Osborn, "I well know that my word would not influence him to behave better, but he shall not walk with me again."—"But if my *mamma* says he may," returned Miss Osborn, with all the authority of a presuming little girl, "I suppose *you* will not say he shall not come."

"Do not trouble yourself to think upon the subject," said the governess of Miss Osborn; "you are too young to offer an opinion." "I will tell mamma, directly I go home," replied the arrogant little pet; "I wish I had my own good-natured nurse again."

The young person appeared much hurt by the manner of her ungracious pupil, and, looking towards me, she said, "This lady is a *Spectator*, Miss Osborn, and I think your manners will not fail to make an impression on her mind, not much to your advantage."

I felt myself inclined to humble the pride of this unamiable child, and, turning to her governess, I asked if her pupil could read. "Very indifferently;" was the reply. "I thought so," continued I, "for she appears to me, very uninformed;" "Pray what age is she?" "Miss Osborn is nine years old madam."—"Poor child," said I, "I pity her friends." The countenance of Miss Osborn, was instantly suffused by blushes, she looked at me for a moment; and, in the next, throwing her arms round the neck of her governess, she burst into tears. "Let us go," said she, in a half whisper, "and pray don't tell my papa that I have been rude to you."

"I will not name it, unless I am asked," said the young person. "I am persuaded," said I, extending my hand to the young culprit, "that this little girl, has not been long enough under your care to know the happiness and advantage of having a companion always ready to assist her pursuits, and encourage her when she really deserves it." "Miss Watson has only been with me a week," replied Charlotte Osborn. "You see I judged truly," I continued. "Little girls, who have not been used to a regular performance of lessons, and who have unfortunately been indulged by their nurses, are very unfit to judge for themselves; and, unless they feel their own ignorance, and are desirous, as well as willing, to gain knowledge, they will never find a governess, who will continue with them any time."

"You won't leave me?"—asked the child. "Certainly not, if you behave well, and are attentive," said Miss Watson. "Indeed, I will try," said the now-subdued Charlotte.— "And I am sure you will succeed," said I, at the same time offering one of my lozenges to my newly-acquired friend.

I was rising to look after my grandson, when I saw him advancing; he seemed heated and out of breath. "O, grandmamma," said William, "Charles Osborn has got into such a scrape;—but here he comes, and the lady with him. I knew she would, though he did not believe her when she said so." In a moment, the same venerable looking female who had passed some time before, approached the seat. "Does this young gentleman belong to you, madam?" said she, addressing me. I replied in the negative, and Miss Watson explained that he was under her care, and the son of General Osborn.

"I thank you, madam," said the stranger. "I have the honour of knowing his excellent father, who, I am well assured, would severely reprehend the impertinence of his son's conduct, if known." "Why, what have I done?" said Charles, in an humble tone of voice, "I did not think you knew my papa."

"O Grandmama," said William, "Charles
Osborn has got into such a scrape: – but
here he comes, and the Lady with him."

"And is this an apology?" said the lady; "or rather, does it not add cowardice to rudeness?—I see that you are alarmed, but I must remind you, sir, that this is not the first insult I have received from you; when I warned you, a week or two ago, that you were in danger of being drowned, by walking so near the water, you then evinced much vulgarity and ingratitude. I passed over this, because I considered that my caution clashing with that which you esteemed an amusement, might make you less guarded in your answers, than was consistent with good-breeding; but to-day there is no such excuse. I did not mean to recognise you when you boldly stopped me in my path, called me 'Old Spec long nose,' and 'Cross patch.' Even this was too vulgar to excite any other than silent contempt; but when you caught the walking-cane, which assists my lameness in a great degree, and were so insolent and cruel as to throw a stone at me, which has grazed my ancle, I felt that I should be equally criminal with yourself, if I concealed such disgraceful conduct from those who may be supposed to have some authority over you."

"Make my compliments to the general, madam," said the stranger, with a grave, but resolute countenance, turning to Miss Watson, "and have the goodness to say, that Lady Liston will do herself the honor of calling on him to-morrow-morning;" and, with a graceful curtsey, she retired.

I saw fear strongly depicted in the features of Charles Osborn. I took my leave of Charlotte and her governess, and as I proceeded on my way, was careful to discover if William had taken any part in the late disgraceful transaction.

"God forbid, grandmamma," said my little companion. "No, indeed I was ashamed of Charles Osborn, and begged him not to throw the stone at the lady; but he laughed at me, and said he hated old women, and he was so certain she was the old sly Spectator, that he was determined to vex her. The lady could not understand what he meant by 'Old Spec'" continued William, "but indeed, grandmamma, I do not wonder that Charles Osborn is mortified at the letter he has got from the Spectator, it is quite different to the one I received."

"I rejoice," cried I, "that there is a distinction in this particular, for I should certainly blush to own as a relation, a child who could bear the least resemblance to Master Osborn, and I doubt not but your manner of addressing this invisible friend, was as distinct as her reply. Lady Liston will, I trust, persevere in her resolution of waiting on General Osborn, who, from what I heard his little girl say, is too fond of his children not to reprove their faults. I have taken a fancy to Miss Osborn, who appears rather an indulged than an unamiable child; yet I hope you are not in the habit of visiting these little folks, for in their present characters, they are by no means desirable acquaintances." William assured me they were only *Park* friends, having met occasionally in their morning rambles.

I imagine that it is almost unnecessary for me to explain to my young readers, why my opinion of Charlotte Osborn on a sudden became so favourable, that I should avow I took an interest in the child. Lest I should be accused of whimsicality, I must simply state, that the real shame, so evident when I inquired her age and capacity of her governess, convinced me that she possessed feeling; and the earnestness with which she expressed her intention of *endeavouring* to act by the directions of Miss Watson, was a proof that she saw her errors; and I know no greater mark of wisdom, than that which a confession of our faults illustrates. No encouragement should be wanting where this disposition is observable, and I really regretted that I did not know the mother of this little girl, whose indulgence has, I fear, been the principal source of her childrens' very inelegant manners. I resolved, however, to use my pen in the service of Miss Osborn, at a period not very distant.

My grandson and I reached the house of my friend, where we passed a very agreeable day. There were no children to bear William company, but I was gratified by observing, that he seemed at no loss for amusement. The house was large, and a very fine garden, in high cultivation, was at once a new scene, and a great pleasure to a boy, accustomed only to see a few weakly plants arranged in a balcony during the spring season, and consequently an almost stranger to the thousand beauties that a living garden owns. So many *little* indecorums had met my eye, when mixing with the Mordaunt family, that I freely confess I was strict in observing the manner of William, when we first walked round the garden. I trembled lest he should, from thoughtlessness, destroy any of the flowers; I watched to see if he regarded the fruit with that sort of attention, which should compel my friend to offer some to his acceptance; and it was with infinite pleasure I remarked the propriety of his conduct in both these particulars. Few things could have been more painful to me, than to have had *occasion* to reprove him; in fact, there cannot be a more degrading thing, than that very erroneous, but general remark, "that it is *natural* for children to wish for fruit when they see it, and that it is impossible not to give them some." On this principle, I suppose, grown persons, who have outlived their *puerile* fancies, are to be gratified by attaining a house, carriage, or any thing which may happen to suit their taste; such a system would be equally proper, with that of indulging children in such points. I consider it of infinite advantage, that children should, at *times*, be present where such luxuries as are now in general use are admitted—that they should have forbearance sufficient to refrain from *asking* to partake of them; and that the limited portion which the judgment of their parents should deem it proper to allow them, should never be a *regular*, but an *occasional* indulgence. Of all indulgencies, that of the palate is most disgraceful to *reasonable* creatures; and to make nice fruit, tarts, or cakes, *rewards* to children who have performed their lessons well, is to level them with irrational animals. A very little reflection is necessary to establish my remark.

If a cat catches a mouse, (and the act is an important *accomplishment* in the *education* of a cat) we reward her by the dainty morsel; while to the dog, who sets up and begs, we throw the half-picked bone. The rewards are in these cases appropriate, for neither of the animals would understand us, if we expressed our approbation of their conduct, by *moderate* praises.

I intreat my little friends, however, not to imagine that I include Mother Hubbard's cat among the unenlightened of that species. I entertain the most perfect respect for *genius*, wherever it emanates; but, at the same time, must avow, that while I can hope to be serviceable to a higher class, in the persons of *children*, I shall never feel disposed to shew more favour to animals, than that which humanity dictates.

The behaviour of William Mordaunt, during our visit, was so well regulated, that in our ride to Town, I took occasion to express my approbation of his manners. My grandson seemed gratified by my praise. "Indeed, my dear boy," said I, as the coach drew up to the dwelling of my daughter, "if I had not heard you cast an indirect censure on your good mother, by disputing her right to send you out with female servants, I should have made a memorandum of this day in my *red* letter book. I shall say nothing of throwing stones; Master Osborn has given you an opportunity of judging that error, without my enlarging on the subject."—"My dear grandmother," said William, as he kissed my cheek, at parting, "I do think you would make the best *Spectator* in the world."—"God bless you, my child," said I, as he descended the steps, "it is for thy happiness, and that of thy dear family, that I have undertaken the arduous task; may the attempt prove successful, then may I proudly own, that I have not been an useless *Spectator*."

CHAPTER III

"O, let th' ungentle spirit learn from hence,
A small unkindness is a great offence."

O N ARRIVING AT HOME, I found three or four letters on my writing table. The first that engaged my attention was one, the superscription of which was ill written, and worse spelt; but on opening it, my surprise was superseded by the subject it contained; while, to the well-meaning writer, every allowance for the inaccuracy of its style was as instantly given. It ran thus:

TOO MISSUS HARGUS.

If you please Marm, I ope you wont be hangry with me for the liberty I take in riting to you. but Hi ham a nursery maid in a Gentelmuns fammerly, and hi likes my Missus very much. but the Yung Ladys, are not hover kind to me. you see they have comed from the hindies, and ad black slaves about um, and so they think we Engleish are slaves, they are so passernate, and want so many things at once, that hif I ad seven pair of ands I could not do hall they wish. hi ham very willing to please them, but I do not think they ave any rite to strike me, and call me creter, hand fool. Miss Louise run a pin hinto my fingers the other day, becaus hi did not ear when she ringed the Bell, and they say hi speak so bad, and make fun of me, but hif I dont know Grammur, that his not my faut, hi speaks has the peepel in my village do, hand has hi, never calls them names, but ham always sivil to um, I dont think they ave hany rite to treat me so—I hurd one of them say, she would rite to you about sumthing, so I thort you might praps be a survants frend has well has a Ladys. I ope you will hexcuse my bold-ness, and beleve me your

umble Sarvant
JENNY BENNET.

P. S. direct for Jenny Bennet hat Missus Murdock's Cavendish squere.

It was evident to me, that Jenny Bennet was in a situation for which she was not qualified; but this was no apology for the illiberality and cruelty of the Miss Murdocks'. I turned to the remaining letters, hoping that I should find one of them to be the production of Miss Murdock. I was not disappointed: a very ill-folded and irregularly written epistle came next under my consideration.

Mrs. ARGUS,

I know a young lady who has *writ* to you, and I have seen your answer; I mean Miss Wilmot. She is satisfied with what you say to her; but as I have quite different things to think of, I hope your answer to me will be very unlike what you *send* her. Mamma is very indulgent to us to be sure, but not quite so much as she used to be when we were *at* India; and indeed altogether the people here are not so respectful as what we met when we were *in* Bengal; and the servants in particular are monstrous impertinent, they do not obey us at all. We have got such an ignorant country girl in our nursery, that there is no beating any sense into her; she uses the *h* where it should not be sounded, and where it should be used, she is sure to leave it out. I don't think she ever heard of grammar in her life: now you know this is very provoking, as we have masters coming every day to us, and it makes me quite nervous to listen to her. And as to English servants being so active, it is quite a mistake; they are so slow, and so proud, if one calls them hastily, they seem ready to cry; and really when one is in a hurry, it is almost impossible to bear with them. Louisa happened to run a pin into our maid's hands, and if she had been a lady she could not have made more fuss about it, which is certainly very odd, for if we may not have some power over them, we might as well be without servants. Mamma is thinking of having a governess for us, but I hope she may not find one, for I am certain I should hate her, and indeed I know two or three young ladies, who tell me that it is the shockingest thing in the world to have a governess, and I am sure it is true, and I have no notion of there being thought so clever, for you know when you pay people, and keep them in the house, what are they but servants? We have told mamma about you, and she does not object to *my* writing to you; so any hint you choose to give about governesses would please us very much, as Miss Wilmot is such a favourite of mamma's, that she thinks you must be a proper person, because *she* speaks well of you. Pray write *against* governesses, for Louisa and *me* are quite dreading the thought of them.

> I remain your's,
> CAROLINE MURDOCK.

Cavendish Square.

The evening being far advanced, I confined myself to the perusal of the two remaining letters; and as I now glanced on the next in order, I felt an involuntary regret, that the address of my amiable little friend, Miss Wilmot, should have remained so long unnoticed. I broke the seal, and with an interest, suited to its artless contents, perused it more than once. But I submit it to my readers, many of whom will, I trust, share in my opinion of its merits.

To Mrs. ARGUS.

MADAM,

After having solicited your advice, and been obliged by your very kind answer to my letter, I fear you will think me rude in not having used the permission granted to me; I will endeavour to explain my reasons, and must trust to your goodness to excuse my seeming inattention.

My dear mamma has been dead nearly four years; she had suffered so much, that my papa taught me to thank God that she was released from her pain. Yet he always approves of my talking of her, and wearing her picture, and indeed we now frequently speak of the happy days when she used to be so cheerful, and so good in teaching me, for my papa is the best papa in the world.

Since that sad time to which I refer, I have been under the care of a governess, whom I love very much; she is almost like a mother to me, and my papa approves of her in all respects. It seems quite ungrateful in me to say that I am unhappy, for I know there must be many children who have not such friends as I possess; but indeed, madam, I hope I am not wicked in saying, that I cannot bear the thought of a new mamma; and I am told my papa is going to marry a lady, whom I used to think one of my best friends, but my nurse tells me, that she will make my papa forget me, and that I shall not make his breakfast, nor walk out with him as I do now. She says that all mothers-in-law are spiteful; indeed, she has frightened me so much by what she has said, that though I really like the lady, and used always to be glad when I was allowed to visit her, I now prefer remaining at home, rather than going to her house.

Nurse was very careful of me when I was a little girl, and my dear mamma, I remember, bade me to take care of her as I grew up. Of course I am careful to shew her every kindness in my power, yet I am very sorry she has explained so many sad things about mothers-in-law, for I am certain I should have loved Mrs. Dalton as a mamma, if she had not done so. But what really troubles me most is, that she has begged me not to name what she has told me to my governess. I never could tell why, but certainly nurse Jones does not like Mrs. Arnold, and I recollect that she used to say that I should find her very cross, which I am sure is wrong, for she is the kindest of friends. Pray, madam, give me your opinion; do you think Mrs. Dalton will be fond of me? And say if I ought to keep what nurse Jones has told me, a secret from my dear Mrs. Arnold? I am so used to tell her all my thoughts, that I find it very difficult to be reserved with her. She has found me crying once or twice, and was so affectionate in inquiring the cause, that nothing but my *promise* to Jones made me silent. And this morning, my papa, while we were walking together, observed my looks. "I thought," said my dear papa, "that my Sophia loved her father; indeed, I was going to treat her as a friend, but I find she does not wish that I should consider her so wise."—"O, my dear sir," said I, "I should be very happy if you"——And here, ma'am, I am afraid you will think me wrong, but I could not speak another word, my heart was so full; all I know is, that my papa pressed me in his arms, and declared he loved me as I deserved, and that I should ever find him the tenderest of fathers and of friends.

I am so unhappy since this, and feel so sure that I have acted wrong, that I am most anxious for your advice and opinion. I beg you, madam, to remember my *promise* to Jones, but hope you will give me some directions, that shall enable me to explain every thing to my papa, and Mrs. Arnold.

> I am, dear madam,
> Your respectful and obliged
> humble servant,
> SOPHIA WILMOT.

The remaining letter made me smile. The gentleman was a perfect stranger to me. He may, however, be known to some of my young friends, and should any of his remarks suit them, I hope they will endeavour to correct their foibles. Though there is certainly some asperity in the manner of my new correspondent, I must confess, that his censure is, for the most part, just.

MADAM,

Though I heartily wish you success in your laudable attempt, I can scarcely hope that you will attain it. The children of the present day are as distinct from those with whom my youth was passed, as boldness and modesty can make them. I beg your pardon for the force of my expression, but I am absolutely enraged at all I see and hear in families whose sense and respectability are unquestionable. I am an old batchelor, and have much delight in neatness, whether applied to the person, or the apartments in which I visit or reside. My acquaintance is extensive, and I have many invitations to dinner; but I really believe I must give up all ideas of society, for nothing can equal the inconveniences to which these dinner tickets subject me. Permit me to explain a few of those unseasonable introductions of which I complain. One, and not the least serious, of my vexations occurred about a week since, where a very interesting and rational conversation was interrupted by the lady of the house calling our united attention to a recitation, or rather what I should call a downright *murder*, of Cato's Soliloquy. We waited some time, while the boy grumbled out his "noes," and "indeeds," but all he could say, had no effect. His mother declared Jackey would be a second Pit[t]. I groaned internally at this presumptuous assertion. Jackey thumbed his buttons, scratched his head,

&c. &c. At length he set off; Gilpin himself did not travel with more expedition than our orator gabbled, and like that famous jockey, who, when he got to the calender's, turned about his horse and began his journey to London with equal speed: so Jackey, once put in motion, had no mercy on us. Speech succeeded to speech: the ladies declared he was quite a genius, while one or two men, in a voice scarcely intelligible, said something about "good memory." For my part, I was silent. The orator was introduced at the desert, and here, again, his genius was called forth. He was to construe a Latin sentence, which had been used by a very intelligent young man. The dictionary was exhibited, and we, one and all, were obliged to refer with Jackey in order to establish the fact of his amazing capacity. Madam, there is no man more willing to do justice to youthful talents; I honour them wherever I meet them, but I cannot bear to see children thus forced into notice; it is spoiling them and destroying the purposes of society: an applicable remark or correct reference that grows out of the present conversation is worthy of commendation, but, to the obtrusive interruptions of children, I can neither give my time nor my approbation.

Another source of unspeakable inconvenience to me, was the introduction of a very fine boy, a few evenings since, whom all the party denominated a *"Pickle."* I happened unfortunately to be the only man in the room who wore a queue. I was leaning back on a stuffed sofa, when my attention being suddenly called to observe a lady who was just rising to take a seat at the piano, I made a motion to follow and assist her in arranging the music-book, when I felt a shock inexpressible. Master "Pickle" had fastened my hair ribbon to the sofa-cover. I was not sufficiently master of myself to disguise my feelings, but in very plain language expressed my dislike of such jokes. The ladies, who love a little *innocent* mischief at the expense of an old bachelor, smiled amongst themselves, but to me it was no laughing matter. I really suffered much pain from this young gentleman's frolic. "Tell me, Ned," said the mother of 'little Pickle,' "why did you fix on Mr. Testy for a joke." "Because I thought his queue was false," said the boy. "I wish your conjecture had been just," said I, "it would have saved me much pain." I saw half a dozen highly frizzled heads in the company, who seemed amused at my disaster, and confess I was one who joined in a laugh which was general an hour or two after, when a wig a la Brutus was brought to the carpet by our young "Pickle," who had dared the gentleman to an unequal sparring contest, and when vanquished by the one hand of his enemy, took revenge on his wig.

I have already intruded on your time most unmercifully, but let me beg of you, my good Mrs. Argus, to represent the folly of these ridiculous introductions. I do not agree with the old adage, "that children should be seen but not heard." But I must condemn all forwardness: it is very unbecoming, and unless there is some reform in this particular, I shall be compelled to give up a great many friends whom I esteem, and henceforth take my meals at home and alone.

I am, Madam,
Your obedient servant,
TIMOTHY TESTY.

P. S. If I have not tired you let me know, and I will give a few more examples of my miseries.

This gentleman's complaints appeared to me too well founded to be disregarded; and I, in consequence, resolved on assuring him of my attention to his communications; but the night was now hastening to its close, and I, with the permission of my little friends, will here close my Chapter.

CHAPTER IV

*"Children, like tender osiers take the bow,
And as they first are fashioned, always grow."*

T HERE IS SCARCELY a more important step in the formation of the youthful character, than that of inculcating the necessity of order in all their undertakings. I am persuaded, that more of our happiness in advanced life depends upon this than on any other or more shining quality. The subject, however dull it may appear upon a cursory view, is capable of much enlargement; and among those observations which my present character has led me to make, I feel certain, that the greater part of the foibles, errors, and misapplication of talents, which I have so often deplored, proceeds, in a great degree, from a want of method,—from a total disregard of our most valuable, yet most fleeting possession, *time*.

The thousand dangers to which delay subjects us it were an endless task to enumerate. A few of those peculiar to children, who are in themselves free from intentional error, shall suffice in this place. What excuse can be made for a girl, who, after the age of eight, is not able to find those articles of dress called *walking things?* who must disturb the servants from their dinner, to help her to find her shoes, hat, and pelisse. How can it happen that such things are mislaid? The answer is simple. When the young lady comes in from her walk, she leaves her shoes in one place, her gloves in another; and how is it possible that *she* should seek into such matters. Does not her mamma keep servants to attend to such things, and what are they for? It is not in reason to expect that servants will be very anxious to administer to the comforts of such arbitrary little despots. A sense of their duty may lead them to a slovenly performance in some particulars, but these juvenile tyrants will certainly experience some mortifications. For instance, I was present a few days since, where a young lady was told to put on her pelisse, &c. and she should take an airing with her mother and myself. Mary Woodgate ran away "to get ready," as she said. I heard the nursery-bell ringing incessantly, but I was not sufficiently intimate to enquire into causes. The carriage arrived. Mrs. Woodgate and I were ready, and as we opened the drawing-room door to descend, my friend called to her daughter, saying, "she could not wait." "What an ill-natured thing you are," said a voice which I instantly discovered to be Miss Woodgate. "Indeed Miss Woodgate," said the servant, "you would make any body cross. Your mamma has repeatedly told me not to put away your gloves or bonnet, and as I always have your shoes ready, I know I have done my part." "Dear me, I have got odd gloves," said Mary. "Run Sally, look in my drawers or my box, and you will find one." We had reached the carriage and were seated. My friend, who is at once a tender and a judicious mother, leaned forward, and regarding her daughter who had now made her appearance—"My dear Mary," said Mrs. Wood-gate, "you have forfeited your airing this morning. I heard you speaking very intemperately to Sally. You look out of humour. Your cloaths are not put on with neatness, and your gloves are not suited; when you are careful to put these things in their proper places, you will always know where to find them. I could not think of introducing my daughter to a very old and esteemed friend, when so visibly unfitted for company." This gentle, yet praiseworthy reproof, had its full effect on the humbled Mary, who retired into the house, evidently much affected by her disappointment. I could not refrain from expressing my approbation of my friend's conduct. "My dear Mrs. Harley," said Mrs. Woodgate, "I am fully sensible of the bounty of Providence in making me the mother of a healthy little family; but as they are not *entirely mine*, as their happiness, in a great measure, will depend upon their self-government, I am most anxious to impress on their infant minds, the necessity of *humanity, activity,* and *obedience.* Mary possesses many excellent qualities, but a little thoughtlessness of character, at times, overshadows these good properties. I have so often expressed my wish, that she should regularly fold and put away certain articles of her cloaths which I have specified, that were I to overlook her inattention, she would consider that I had no motive for such an exaction; and as I never ask my children to perform any thing but from a strong conviction of its conducing to their happiness, I cannot submit to have my commands disputed. There are many persons who object to wounding the feelings of children; but where they evince intellect, I must consider it the most effectual method to address them through the medium of reason: to a child of weak capacity, a system more lenient should be observed; but really, my dear friend, when I reflect that all my care and assiduity, blessed by the protecting favour of heaven in their lengthened lives, is ultimately to fit them for situations that must remove them from my fostering arms, the necessity of making them amiable seems more than ever essential. If I can discover a speck, what would less tender arbiters discern? And has not it been enjoined us, to 'Train up a child in the way he should go.' Surely then, that system which religion dictates and nature and reason sanctifies, must be at once the model for parents, and the bliss of their offspring."

I left Mrs. Woodgate with increased respect and esteem. A contrast of the most striking sort presented itself in my next visit.

On calling at Sir George Astons, I entered the drawing-room at a moment of extraordinary confusion. A boy of twelve years old was crying in so loud a tone, that he nearly stunned me. Lady Aston was coaxing him to moderate his grief, while Sir George rang the bell, and ordered Mr. Spencer to be told that "he wanted him." "My dear Mrs. Harley," said Sir George, "I am ashamed you should have arrived at so unfortunate a season; but allow me a few moments for investigation, and I will then attend to friendship." I had scarcely acquiesced by a bow ere Mr. Spencer appeared. "Pray, sir," said Sir George, "why do you refuse Master Aston his half holiday." "For a very simple reason," replied Mr. Spencer, "he does not deserve one." "How is this, George," said the baronet, "did not you tell me that you had performed your duties to the satisfaction of your tutor." "No—yes;" said George, "but Mr. Spencer is so particular, and expected more of me to-day than usual, only because he knew I wanted to go to my cousin's as soon as possible."

I saw the countenance of Mr. Spencer crimson with honest indignation. "Sir George," said the offended tutor, "your son is so little advanced in his studies, that were he as zealous as boys of his age usually are, it would be many months before he could acquire the necessary spur to learning, *order*. He is seldom ready for me, and if any recreation is in view, his manner of saying his lessons is slovenly, and he presumes to compromise the matter by avowing, that he will do better to-morrow, but that to-day he is going out, or expects visitors. These frivolous excuses have been offered to me three times this week: when I express my disappointment, he accuses me of particularity, &c. The freedom is improper, as addressed to his teacher, and if he cannot make his business perfect before he takes his pleasure, he will never prove himself worthy of indulgence, or do credit to those who have the charge of him." "Very just," said Sir George, "your statement is exactly what I expected, nor should I have drawn you from your study but to gratify Lady Aston, who is unfortunately but little skilled in the modes proper to be used with boys." Mr. Spencer bowed cooly, and was retiring, when Lady Aston, with an imploring accent, begged Mr. Spencer would forgive George this once, and she would answer for his being a good boy to-morrow. "My power over this young gentleman is at an end, Madam," replied the tutor; "he has thought proper to arraign my motives; if I am capable of a meanness so contemptible, I am unfit for the charge reposed in me by Sir George; and permit me to add, that where I cannot excite esteem, I should consider my instructions lost;" and with a respectful bow he withdrew.

The baronet, whose vexation was evident, turned to his son, and with much acrimony arraigned his ignorance and stupidity, declaring, that he should not leave the house for a month; nay, it was very probable, he would seek some cheap school, at a distance from London, to which he would send him, until he had conquered his baby-like follies. Lady Aston now joined her tears with those of her pet: I was awkwardly situated; but while I was hesitating how to depart, Sir George bade his son go to his room for the remainder of the day. "Do advise with Aston," said her ladyship, "he loves the dear boy just as well as I do, but he has no fixed plan for him as yet."

"If this charge is just," said I, smiling, "I wonder what excuse ye *grown* babies have to offer for yourselves." "None," said the baronet, "we are the most mistaken pair in the kingdom; but it is *chiefly* Lady Aston's fault: if the boy remains a *whole* morning with his tutor, she takes fright at the pallidness of his looks when he makes his appearance in the drawing-room; and again, when she meets children, his junior by some years, who are intelligent, and do credit to their instructors, she is full of regrets."—"My dear Sir George," retorted her ladyship, "it is you who are impatient; have you not frightened the poor boy by telling him that he is to be a counsellor, and that you expect he will study morning, noon, and night, till he has got through all the books in your library; and between ourselves, Mr. Spencer is very harsh; George's nerves are delicate, he cannot bear contradiction."

"My dear madam," said I, "though the age and appearance of your son might justify the belief that he had made some proficiency in his learning, I am tempted to think that you have engaged a tutor for him somewhat too soon; unless you could reconcile yourself to yield your right in all that relates to the privileges of a tutor. When men of character and science undertake a task of this sort, they are *accountable* for the manner in which they acquit themselves; they are in the situation of an author, who gives a work to the world, which is to tarnish his name, or carry it down to posterity with honour. And, though some *few* instances might be adduced of pupils dishonouring the care of their early guardians, I trust, and believe, there are thousands who look back to this happy period of their lives, and these kind friends of their youth, with feelings that do them honour. But, if you are only *now* beginning the education of your son, forgive me, if I say, that much caution is required to make learning appear, what it ever should be, a pleasure. I am unacquainted with the causes that have delayed his improvement; and, though I would recommend every gentle incitement to be offered that can rouse a love of knowledge, and would recommend such books as exemplify the uses and advantages of emulation, I would by no means dismay, by the vastness and profundity of abstruse learning."

"All this is true," said Sir George, "we have delayed the matter too long; but his mother has always been so full of fears, he was too delicate to bear reproof; in short, she has suggested so many obstacles to all my plans with regard to our son, that I am at this moment wholly undetermined how to act by him,—what would you advise?"

"Dismiss the idea of sending your child from home," said I; "a school, though eminently calculated to inspire emulation in a *prepared* mind, would, in this case, prove the tomb of intellect. Humiliations innumerable would assail him in such a situation. Keep him under your eye, but consign the task of tuition to one in whom you have implicit confidence, and to that person give *discretionary* power of acting. It is by no means necessary that you should be restrained from interfering in every particular which relates to your son, but it is rarely, if ever, requisite, that *children* should be a party in any of the opinions, objections, or purposes, that may naturally result between parents and instructors. One of the most prominent traits in the infant character is that of *imitation;* and they are generally observed to shape *their* manners, and express their sentiments, by those of their parents; thus, the teacher, who, it is but natural and reasonable to suppose less esteemed by them, falls into disrepute on the most trivial expression of disapprobation that the parent shall utter. With Master Aston I should recommend very lenient and conciliating measures; his lessons should be short, but frequent; his rewards, uniformly your *moderate* approbation. Visiting, presents, or toys, would break in upon the application so necessary to his advancement and I must believe, that to confine the happiness of children to home, to that meed which it is always in the power of parents to bestow, is not only the most judicious method, but also the most effectual way of binding children to their parents, and teaching them to value their favour as it should be valued."

Sir George and his lady appeared to coincide in my sentiments, and before I took leave they had resolved on committing their son to the care of Mr. Spencer, with all the requisite privileges that could assist his education. In my drive home, my reflections fully established the remark used in the preceding part of this Chapter.—What, but want of *order* had produced the lamentable deficiencies of George Aston? want of health in infancy may and does frequently retard learning, but the earliest season of convalescence should be seized by the watchful parent, to make a good impression; however slow the progress, the seed should be sown, and the culture attended to with the nicest care. The intellects of children vary, one shoots out luxuriantly, almost spontaneously; another produces rare and superior fruit, by slow and progressive care; while a third starts prematurely into society, bearing, even with its blossoms, the rankling weed: of how much consequence, then, is an early attention to order, an uniform regard—to the time present. Yet even with some, who have imagined themselves actuated by this essential principle, there are many instances of vanity. I have heard children go through their regular business with all the order that had been suggested by their teachers, and have heard them exact some promised indulgence, when, in fact, their exertions have been of a sort to claim no such distinctions. To repeat a number of lessons, in a slovenly way, is to disgrace the understanding that it has pleased Heaven to bestow upon you; to hurry through those prayers which are appointed for your morning and evening devotion, is not what has been asked of you. I know that some of you will find excuses "you are sleepy" or "the night is cold," "you have sat up later than usual." why did you so?—you reply, you just wanted to finish some trifle, with which you were engaged.—Why not leave the trifle till to-morrow, and use the hour permitted to you in that service, which it is ungrateful to delay?

How frequently do these little subterfuges occur, and how often have I heard children entreat half an hour longer for their *amusement* in the drawing-room, who have, by their imperfect devotional exercises, convinced me that they deserved no indulgence of the sort.—We do not expect from children, either that reflection or forethought which experience alone can establish, but habits of order, may and should be inculcated, even in infancy. Order originates in duty to those who have charge of us. Delay is consequently a stranger to that child who is reared on this most amiable and virtuous principle.

In every important situation of our lives, the comfort derived from a just disposition, or division, of our time, is clearly demonstrated; and, in all the lesser objects that engage the attention, as applied to pleasure or convenience, its advantages are equally obvious: in the two instances, on which I have expatiated, it must be observed, that the little idlers met their disappointments. The reader may, perhaps, regard Miss Woodgate's deprivation inconsiderable,—but let me remind them, that to her mortification must be added, the temporary displeasure of her mother; a circumstance, in itself, truly painful to an amiable and well-disposed child; nor is it unimportant to reflect, that strangers may be led to form unfavourable opinions, in cases where the commands of parents have been neglected. Of George Aston, it would be ungenerous to say much: from mistaken indulgence, and irresolute plans, his parents have brought him through the plastic season of infancy, unimpressed with the value of this peace-making quality; for my own part, I feel assured, that education might commence, even from the cradle. The disposition and temper might be in a state of improvement while intellect was dormant; for, as a learned and truly amiable writer has observed; "The mind is originally an unsown field, prepared it may be for the reception of any crop; but, if those to whom the culture of it belongs, neglect to fill it with good grain, it will speedily and spontaneously be covered with weeds."

But, as *I* have avowed myself a friend to *order*, let my practice prove my sincerity. I have many letters to answer, I must hasten to the performance of my duty.

CHAPTER V

"If I am right, thy grace impart
Still in the right to stay:
If I am wrong, Oh teach my heart
To find that better way."

IN CONFORMITY to my avowed love of *order*, the letter of Jenny Bennet was the first to which I replied. It was not my wish to encourage servants in betraying the secrets of families, though I certainly did not regret that an opportunity had occurred, which, by touching on the manners of children towards these humble friends, gave me an opening for a few observations. But as I imparted my real sentiments on this subject, in my epistolary correspondence, I will submit them to my young friends *verbatim*.

To Mrs. JENNY BENNET.

I am very sorry to understand, by your letter, that your situation in the family of Mrs. Murdock is uncomfortable. You are mistaken, in supposing that the Miss Murdock's are hasty in their tempers, because they have lived in India. As amiable children come from that quarter of the world, as from any other. The cruelty of Miss Louisa is very disgraceful to her character, and, I have no doubt, but her mother will hear your complaint, and use proper means to prevent her repeating such a fault. I am very willing to believe that you are civil to the young ladies under your charge, and, as such, think you entitled to kind and considerate treatment from them. I am much ashamed of that very criminal sort of language they use towards you, and the weakness of ridiculing you[r] dialect betrays much ignorance. If a regular attention to the duties required from you, civil manners, and willingness to oblige, mark your conduct, they have no right to complain. Young women in your rank of life, are not expected to understand Grammar, and it is only thoughtless and inexperienced children who would remark your deficiency in this respect. I perceive, by your letter, that you are from Worcestershire; and as, in a nursery, it is desirable that the servants should speak in a clear and *usual* dialect, I would advise you to undertake some other office in the house, where you would be more likely to lose your present manner of speaking. And be spared the mortifications of which you now complain.

I am, very sincerely,
Your friend,
ARABELLA ARGUS.

To Miss MURDOCK.

Though I am honoured by the correspondence of many young ladies, I confess myself at a loss how to reply to the favour of Miss Murdock. Truth is too valuable to me to be yielded on any occasion, and a letter is, of all compositions, that which should speak the exact feelings. Will you, after this frank confession, forgive my candour, and receive my admonitions? I must believe that you will, for, however the fluctuations of the youthful mind may induce error or exhibit passion, I trust there are very few instances where they wholly reject advice, or doubt the sincerity of those who evince themselves anxious for their happiness. Though in your letter you name the indulgence of your mother, you seem to intimate that it is less now, than formerly; this is an indirect censure cast upon your parent, and, consequently, a breach of duty. You are not satisfied with the manners of your servants; ask your own heart, if your uniform conduct towards them deserves an attention more respectful than that which they shew you. That your nursery-maid should be ignorant of grammatical propriety is not in the least surprising; she speaks according to the custom of that county in which she was born, and, it is most probable, never received any rules for her language. Now *you* apprize me that masters attend you daily, and that your *nerves* are affected by the ignorance and manner of your servant's speech. I am really afraid, that you have been more solicitous to discover the defects of others than to acquire knowledge for yourself; or how shall we account for the many errors, not only in your orthography and etymology; where the tenses of the verbs are so obviously misapplied: for instance, writ for *written*; say for *said*; send for *sent*; *at* India, in place of *in* India; with many other improprieties inexcusable in a young lady, who is being taught daily, and who is likewise a critic: but I must not omit the application of the objective pronoun *me*, in lieu of the nominative *I*. For the little errors of children, in their first attempts at letter-writing, every allowance should be made, as to style, &c. but, for grammatical inaccuracies, their memories are to be blamed. Grammar being their first, and, next to the study of scriptural history, the most important, branch of education; for not to speak, and write your own language correctly, when you are so happy as to have the advantages of good instruction, argues much inattention, if not a weak mind.

You appear to entertain unreasonable objections towards governesses; I term them unreasonable, because you have evidently decided on their characters from the representation of a few children, who, perhaps like yourself are hasty in disposition, and consequently ill qualified to draw just conclusions. I should consider you as very fortunate if your mamma prosecutes her intention of engaging one to instruct her daughters. But should she do this, and pay her as is usual in such cases, I must beg to remind you that she will never be termed a *servant*, but by those who are unacquainted with the proper forms and distinctions used in society. All persons who become inmates in families, and are paid for their services are called dependants; but as their worth or talents generally cause them to be received in these capacities, they claim a portion of respect, perfectly distinct from that which is usually observed towards servants. I should be sorry to understand your remark, (that you should hate a governess) as true. The expression is contrary to every principle of Christianity; nay, I should hope, that a very little time, passed under the tuition of a competent friend of this description, would lead you to recant this assertion, and most happy should I be, if you favoured my prediction, by imparting your sentiments to me on this head.

I do not mean to restrict your addressing me whenever you think proper; but, as you are honoured by the acquaintance of Miss Wilmot, I would advise you to regard that young lady's manners as worthy of imitation; and I beg of you to apply to her respecting governesses; I think she will efface some of your erroneous opinions, and assist in establishing those of

Your
Very sincerely,
ARABELLA ARGUS.

To Miss WILMOT.

My dear little friend,

To your very ingenuous and natural epistle I feel much pleasure in replying, more especially, as I hope to disperse those imaginary fears which have caused you so much uneasiness. The sacredness of a promise is a very serious consideration; and it is this seriousness which should prevent our entering into obligations of the sort without due reflection. You have so fully explained to me, that you regret having assented to the mistaken zeal of your nurse, that I am persuaded you will in future avoid all such engagements. As you are now situated, it is strictly conformable to virtue and honour, that you should forbear to speak of your nurse's communication. But should she again attempt to weaken your confidence in the judgment of your father, or the kindness of Mrs. Arnold, do not suffer yourself to be misled by her perhaps affectionate, but certainly mistaken interference. It is in your power to reprove her, and evince your own duty to a good parent, by simply observing, that your father has a right to act for himself, and that you will always endeavour to love those whom he esteems;—reject all news which is communicated under the term of "a secret;" it rarely deserves the name, and frequently leads to much anguish of mind.

Those little domestic employments, which the tenderness of your good father has permitted you to exercise in his family, are in themselves highly advantageous to you as a female; for to study "household good," is an excellence in woman. Should the lady who you expect will be your mother, eventually fill that situation, remember, it is your place to yield, to resign those offices, which, as mistress of your father's house, will become her right. Yet, it is very probable, she may discover your capacity in these points, and have much pleasure in increasing your little privileges: much more will depend upon yourself than on her,—you acknowledge that you *did* like her, and I have too good an opinion of your understanding, to suppose that you could be prejudiced against an old friend, merely because your father has thought proper to distinguish her, as the woman with whom he could be happy. I would advise you to use an early opportunity, of talking on this subject with Mrs. Arnold; I imagine you may do so, without infringing your promise with Jones, as the event is, no doubt, generally expected in the family. Perhaps your governess wisely awaits your communication in this particular; confide in her, and I am persuaded you will not only relieve your mind, but acquire a certain portion of comfort, in looking forward to the protection of an amiable mother as you advance in life; and Mrs. Arnold appears, from your description, a friend, capable of directing your mind, to a just understanding of all that relates to your happiness.

When your father shall condescend to make you his friend, by apprising you of his intentions, do not hesitate to express your sorrow, at having exhibited such *visible,* though *silent,* opposition to his wishes—he will receive it as a proof, not only of duty, but good sense; and to the lady, observe an uniform and kind attention, which, I am fully persuaded, will lead to the happiest result;—continue to cherish the memory of your *own* mother, reflect on all her admonitions, and apply yourself to the practice of them with attention; what one good and amiable woman has suggested, can never prove objectionable to another.

On your nurse, continue to bestow those little marks of kindness which are her due, as the protector of your helpless infancy,—but do not, by any means, accustom yourself to habitual intimacy with any servant,—all that is kind, benevolent, and generous, may be performed towards these deserving and useful friends, without familiarity, which *usually* leads them into error, and *certainly* destroys our claim to their respect.

The unreasonable length of my letter, proceeds from the strong interest I take in your happiness, and it will give me sincere pleasure, if my advice assists in restoring your tranquillity. You were very right in observing, that "many children have more cause to repine than yourself;"—it must be so, for your's are *imaginary* troubles, and numberless little orphans might be found, whose sad and desolate fate, would cause you to blush at having anticipated sorrow. Consider, my dear child, that life is transient; and that to pass through our allotted term wholly exempted from trouble is impossible; that there is a season for all things; youth is the season of joy, embrace it while in your power; and let gratitude, for those blessings bestowed upon you, dispose your heart to cheerfulness, which is the handmaid of innocence. With perfect esteem for your character, and a firm reliance on your just claim to happiness, by endeavouring to deserve it,

I remain your very sincere,
and much interested friend,
ARABELLA ARGUS.

To TIMOTHY TESTY, Esquire.

SIR,

Though I have announced myself as the *professed* correspondent of *children*, your letter claims my thanks, as imparting some just matter for animadversion. You will excuse me if I add, that the obligation must be mine, as I cannot possibly find time for answering the letters of *grown* persons, though I shall be obliged by their communications. You must likewise forgive me, when I avow that I do not agree with you, as to the comparative manners of children now and in the days of our youth. Very few general rules are applicable; there will always be much to do for children, and there has certainly been much done for them; I *sometimes* think too much, for we have been seeking new methods, and new models, while the fundamental principles of all virtue, and all happiness, have ever been within our grasp, in the mild *precepts* and pure example of Christian revelation. No specific rule can possibly be recommended in the education of children, whose dispositions are as various as the flowers of the field; but there is not a defect or perfection in human nature for which the *God* of nature has not provided some *ensample* that *should* guard the erring; some *reward*, which should animate the virtuous. It is while we *neglect* this merciful mediation, between mortal and immortal judgment, that we betray our blindness, and, with wilful ignorance, seek a new path. I shall receive your further communications with pleasure, and am,

Very respectfully, sir,
Your obedient servant,
ARABELLA ARGUS.

Having dispatched my letters, I felt all that ease which results from performing our appointed duties. I was now at liberty to think, so true it is, that while the mind is clogged by obligations of any sort, it is impossible that our actions should be free and unrestrained. As this feeling is not individual, or peculiar to any season of life. It has often surprized me, when I have heard persons, whose independent situations in society have placed them at liberty to dispose of their time as they please;—to hear such persons, I repeat, lamenting that they are oppressed by the variety of their avocations, is truly ridiculous.

These imaginary inconveniences, even children affect, I have seen them surrounded by their books, pausing first on one, and then on another; and by the confusion which they are active in producing, destroying the necessary preliminary to study, *method*. And now that I am speaking of lessons, I cannot forbear to remark on the manner in which these portions are sometimes acquired: it is hardly necessary, to say how they should be learned, every child of sense gives a due proportion of time to the subject that is appointed for her attainment; not only because it is appointed for her, but that she aspires to excel, and would not be satisfied to perform any thing ill, which by a little application might be well performed. But I have seen children *rolling* the leaves of their books, while they pretended to be engaged by their lesson:—playing with the ribband which marks their places, and reckoning *every* repetition, as reducing the number of those readings, which they purpose to bestow on the lesson. Is it possible, that such tasks, can be well learned, where the thoughts and the actions are so much at variance? or, can a limited number of readings perfect *all* lessons? I grant, that the perception of some children is very acute, that they learn with much facility. Yet it sometimes happens, that they forget very easily, and when this is perceived, by those who instruct them, I can by no means accede to that petulance, which *sometimes* shews itself, at their memories being exercised frequently, and not on fixed days. It is very natural to suppose that those who *teach*, possess more knowledge than their pupils, and that their motives for exacting attention, in any point, would bear the strictest scrutiny; but it is not the part of the pupil to arraign or judge those motives nor yet to oppose the wishes of the instructress.

The task of rearing and teaching the infant mind has been defined a pleasing and delightful task. I *know* it is possible to make it such, but then a mutual esteem, and mutual assistance, must actuate the teacher and the scholar.

Quintilian observes on this subject,

"But let none imagine it possible to become learned by the labour of another."

This, from the comprehensive term *learned*, seems to apply to boys only; yet it may very properly be transferred to girls, as every advancement in knowledge is produced by learning, and the capability of the female mind cannot be doubted, while we can refer to the respected names of a Carter, a Talbot, or a Montague.* But that wisdom can be attained without exertion, is an idea which none but the weak, and the *idle* can possibly entertain. The very advantageous and happy domestic friendships which exist, more especially between girls and their instructresses, may certainly, by *mutual* attention, be made productive of lasting and most beneficial consequences. But, unless a child can *esteem*, as well as *respect* her governess, the happiness of each is destroyed. If lessons are considered *punishments*, though recommended for their usefulness; if an anxiety to do only an equal portion of business every day, supersedes that graceful and hopeful thirst for knowledge, inseparable from true genius, I repeat, where these defects are evident, the teachers task, not only becomes irksome, but altogether hopeless. Let it be remembered, that

---

* Mrs. Montague.

"Nothing is easy without previous toil."

That

"Ten thousand labours must concur to raise exalted excellence."

And that, unless we are as sincerely disposed to *learn*, as our instructors are to *teach*, our time is lost, and our improvement impossible. To arrive at excellence is not in the power of every one, but there are certain perfections, to which the attention of children should be more particularly directed. The first, is to a strict and uniform compliance with the commands of their parents, and from this will proceed that most useful and salutary characteristic of a good mind, "the *government of the temper;*" for children, who obey their parents, must necessarily learn to yield, in many points. The affection and judgment of parents directing them frequently to counteract and interpose, in numberless instances, where acquiescence would not only injure their children, but, by increasing their self-will, make them arbitrary and unmanageable. With amiable and well-disposed children, the wishes of a parent are as commands. Nothing is more painful to a parent, than to be forced to make duties appear difficult; yet there are cases, in which such appearances, must exist, and to some of the causes, which produce this ungraceful portrait of life, I shall dedicate a future Chapter. I cannot withhold one general remark; which is, that the child, who is dutiful and attentive to the wishes of her parents, always carries this beautiful humility into every action of her life; it influences her manner towards her inferiors; it leads her to respect the aged and consider their comforts; she is alive to the best impressions from good reading, because the best books always inculcate moral virtues; and she who begins by duty, will undoubtedly receive delight and improvement from the perusal of that which is calculated to exalt her mind. But, while I am anxious to impress the beauty and amiability of such a character on the minds of my readers, I wish it to be understood, that these perfections are not showy, that they are usually the possession of *retired* children; of children who are chearful without rudeness; studious without affectation; methodical without vanity or preciseness; in short, they are peculiar to children who, considering themselves less wise than their parents, submit to be directed, and consequently attain, not only the approbation of their delighted parents, but, what is infinitely superior, the favour of God. I cannot conclude more appropriately than in the words of the royal Psalmist, "Them that are meek shall he guide in judgment; and such as are gentle, them shall he learn his way."

CHAPTER VI

'Tis something to advance a little way.
HORACE.

A NOTE FROM MY DAUGHTER, which was laid on my breakfast-table next morning, awakened my maternal feelings very sensibly. She requested my presence as early as possible, intimating, that her "spirits were much depressed, at the idea of William's departure for ——school." I was pleased, that a determination so essential to the advancement of my grandson had been resolved upon; yet the ill health of his mother gave me real uneasiness, well knowing that her attachment to her children was more than ordinarily tender. I hastened to ——street, and found them, as I expected, deeply engaged in the concerns of the young adventurer. William seemed to regard his removal, as a matter which was to impress him with much consequence, he was giving orders and contradicting them in the next moment. He declared the girls were very teazing, and would not let any of his things alone; while all the dear little creatures were producing their treasures, and offering the so-long-valued bauble, as a keepsake to their brother. "Only think, grandmamma," said William, "even Lucy has given me this;" and he exhibited a dollar, in a high state of preservation. I saw the child blush, and a tear trembled in her eye. "Lucy is very right, in making you this present," said I, "but she does not mean it for a keepsake, she expects you will use it; and I beg that you will let Lucy and I know how you spend this dollar; we shall both learn something by the communication, I shall discover what degree of prudence attaches to my grandson, and Lucy will acquire a knowledge of some of the purposes to which money may be applied."

The sudden decision of my daughter, in favour of a public school, had taken rise in her observations, on the solid acquirements, and pleasing manners of some youths educated on the foundation; and a letter from Capt. Mordaunt, intimating his wish that William should be placed at school, arriving just after this favourable impression, she had immediately proceeded on the necessary arrangements, and only one day now remained ere he was to be removed to ——.

I was not so successful as I had hoped to be, in reconciling Mrs. Mordaunt to the separation; she was full of fears for his health, and very copious in her cautions and advice; to all of which, William was affectionately attentive, and as I perceived him ready to promise a great deal, I checked the intended obligations. "You are now entering on a new scene, my dear boy," said I, "and will engage in numberless avocations of which, at present, you are wholly ignorant. The first going to school, is an epoch in the life of boys to which too much consideration cannot be given. If your view of school-business conveys only the idea of liberty, an escape from certain restrictions, &c. you will find yourself deceived; you must earn that liberty so pleasant and, under due limitation, so advantageous to youth. I have never observed any very remarkable instances of disobedience in your character; some little irritability, and a few opinions contrary to those of your mother, have certainly fallen under my eye; I am willing to impute these to want of judgment, you must be sensible, that a parent has every claim to your duty and gratitude; I know you will be called upon to take part in sports and pastimes, quite contrary to your previous habits; to some of which, a degree of *danger* is very probably attached: do not, from a false idea of courage, attempt the performance of any thing beyond your powers; your failure will lead to certain *contempt*, while your success can produce no lasting advantage. There is a species of courage, to which, if a boy aspires, he must ultimately attain the desired good,—'*the knowledge of himself*:' for he who knows himself will not seek false honours. He will not be led to perform an act, on which he dares not reflect by all that the most *eloquent* of his associates can say in praise of things trifling, if not vicious; he will select for his companions, such boys, as are most worthy, who are always to be discovered, by their pursuits; for the *idle* are never found in the path which leads to wisdom; nor the *vicious*, in favour with those, whom learning delights. Reflect on your *home* with grateful and affectionate feelings; recur to the tenderness of your parents with delight; remember their injunctions, their advice; endeavour, and Heaven will favour your attempt, to unite those religious observances which have led you happily through infancy, in all the simplicity and innocence of childhood; unite these, I repeat, to your new and increasing studies; the task will be practicable, and the conscious peace, that so amiable a discharge of your duty will produce on your mind, will be a reward, to which nothing I could say on the subject would do justice."

William listened to me with silent and respectful attention, and I was delighted to observe his manner towards his mother, whose tears had claimed his notice; he had thrown his arm round her neck, and was kissing the tears from her cheek,—"My dear mother," said he, "shall I not be your son in every place; I am almost certain, that I shall think of you more often at school than I do now, and I will write to you every week, and tell you exactly what I do." "That will indeed be a comfort to me;" said his mother, "and my dear boy, never conceal even an error from *me*, I shall be willing to make every allowance for the foibles of youth, but I can accept no apology which estranges you from my heart."

I was forced to combat that softness which was actually stealing to my heart, lest we should depress the boy too much. "William will not forget this day," said I, with a smile; "he must indeed reflect on it with much satisfaction, and a little laudable vanity may justly mix in his recollection; we have certainly given him some idea of his own consequence by the value we have attached to his conduct, and the affection we have so unequivocally displayed; I trust, he will do credit to our anxious zeal, by respecting himself, and continuing to love those who love him so well."

"I am sure I am very sorry he is going," said Harriet, with a sigh. "I hope we are all sorry," replied Fanny; "but I dare say William will be very happy at school." I observed that these artless remarks made the child serious, and, proposing a walk to the little folks, we proceeded towards Hyde-Park. As we were walking across from Grovesnor-gate, Miss Osborn and her governess, Miss Watson, overtook us; the latter, courtesying to me, was passing on; but, perceiving in the countenance and manner of Miss Osborn, that diffidence so becoming in children, more especially girls, I held out my hand and enquired if she had forgotten me. "No ma'am," said the child, with a look of modest confusion, "indeed I have not." "Miss Osborn is growing a very amiable young lady, madam," said Miss Watson, who continued walking by my side. "I am now so happy in her society that I should be very sorry to quit her," I immediately introduced the children to each other, for the girls were unacquainted with the Osborns, and Miss Watson and I entered into conversation. She informed me, that the General had been so seriously displeased by the conduct of his son as to have confined him to his room for some days; that Lady Liston made her promised visit, and in the most lenient terms, made her just complaint against him; that the erring boy, first denied the charge, but, upon being closely questioned by his father, was brought to avow the truth. "I do not perceive that the modes used with Master Osborn have effected much improvement as yet," continued Miss Watson, "but he is going to ——school to-morrow, where, I hope he will acquire steadiness of character, at present his most predominant **defect.**"

I was really sorry to learn that Charles Osborn, was going to the same school as

William, yet a second thought dissipated the unpleasant feeling; there must ever be a
variety of dispositions, in all mixed societies; a school is a minor theatre, which is to fit
the boy for the larger and less virtuous scene of action, the *World*. If in this exercise
of his reason, he plays his part judiciously, by selecting from the few, a well-chosen
company, he can hardly fail to make a cautious arrangement, when his faculties are
improved and his knowledge of characters more comprehensive. Miss Watson, with an
amiable regard to her little charge, now acquainted me, that from the day of our meeting in Kensington Gardens, her pupil had expressed all those praiseworthy regrets
(natural to an ingenuous mind), at the impropriety of her conduct, both as regarding
her governess and the impression it must have made upon me. "I scarcely ever saw
shame so amiably evident," continued Miss Watson, "and so indefatigable has been the
desire of Miss Osborn, to attain my favour, that she almost anticipates my purposes by
the activity of her zeal." This eulogium was indeed most pleasing to me, and here my
general observation was truly applicable: while Charlotte Osborn was untaught, her
manners were bold and assuming; the moment she became sensible of the value of
learning, her deportment was timid and becoming. How just is that remark so often
quoted. "Modesty is one of the chief ornaments of youth; and has ever been esteemed
a presage of rising merit."

Convinced that my daughter would be anxious for our return, we bade adieu to Miss
Osborn and her governess, and turned towards home. "How very well behaved Miss
Osborn is to-day," said William, "she was not quite so polite when I saw her at Kensington." I agreed with my grandson in thinking her improved. "Lady Liston did go to
Charles Osborn's father," continued William, "his sister, has been telling me so." "Did
you enquire about it?" I asked. He replied in the affirmative, which proved satis-
factory to me; as few things could have lowered a child so much in my opinion, as that
of exposing the disgrace of her brother. From this unamiable trait of character, the little
Charlotte was fully exculpated; she had merely replied to the questions addressed to
her by William, and these not so copiously as to have increased his deserved humiliation.
"I cannot help thinking," rejoined William, after a serious pause, "how alarmed Charles
Osborn must have been when Lady Liston was announced; all his courage forsook him
I dare say." "There can be no doubt of that," I replied. "It was not courage, but insolence, which influenced his manner towards her ladyship. And that is a quality quite
distinct from courage, and one which always shrinks to insignificance, when openly
and dispassionately reproved." "How I rejoice," said William, "that I did not join with
him that day; he tried to advise me to do so." "I hope in this case," cried I, "that your
inclination was not in the least that way disposed, but I certainly approve of your firmness; always dare to think for yourself in such points; it argues much weakness of understanding, to be led into degrading situations, merely because an illiterate and captious
companion has pleasure in such scenes; nor does a disposition of this sort stop here; a
captious and insolent boy usually makes a presuming and quarrelsome man, and there
is not in society a more unamiable acquaintance or dangerous companion."

As I expected, we found Mrs. Mordaunt regarding our approach from the balcony.
I merely waited to deliver my dear little treasures into the hands of their mother, and
give my blessing to William, and then retired to my own house.

I have before expressed my disapprobation of presents, which, in fact, deserve another
name; they are bribes, consequently, my young friends will not be surprised that I

suffered my grandson to depart to school, without receiving one from me; yet, I thought that the dear boy seemed to expect such a mark of my esteem, for he had shown me all the various gifts of a very numerous acquaintance on this occasion, in a way which led me to conjecture, that my mite was wanting, but a remark of Lucy's would have deterred me from so doing, had I even projected it. "Ought William to cry, grand-mamma," said the child, "when he goes away to-morrow; only see what a great many presents he has got." "I hope he will cry," said I, "for I should be very sorry, my dear Lucy, that all his acquaintance had conspired to harden his heart." "My dear grand-mother," replied William, taking a seat by my side, "you have such a way of making trifles seem trifles, that I never know whether to value a thing till you have seen it." "What a flattering boy," said I, smiling; "I believe you will be writing to me soon, in-stead of the Spectator." "I will write to you certainly," rejoined my grandson, "but I must not forget old Spec.; I really like the old woman, though she took me to task a little; yet I must own there was a good deal of truth in what she said, but I must mind next time, and not use any words she can catch at, for she seems very particular." This recollection had been what I wished to produce, being very anxious to have his com-munications, when at a distance from his family; but I was fixed in my purpose, and, as I have before related, did not make my grandson any present. "I am very glad this cross old woman is not my grandmother" says one of my little readers. "I wonder what would be the use of doing one's best," says another; "to be sure she is vastly good, now, that she cannot eat sweet things *herself*," adds a third; "but really I think this Mrs. Argus a very troublesome old woman; perhaps some of our friends may think her plan a good one, and we shall be deprived of all the nice things which we used to get."

I am prepared, as you will perceive, to meet the disapprobation of a few; but I will not believe that I shall be left in the minority: it cannot be, for I am not writing to *babies*, but children, who have, I trust, been in the habit of exercising their reason; and would consequently, be offended, with the person who should address them, as though they were yet the inhabitants of the nursery.

I know it is so easy to acquire a taste for *"nice things,"* as they are called; and this taste, though apparently of no consequence in early youth, is so capable of deforming the human character, that I know not how to mark my disapprobation of this fault, in language sufficiently strong. I have witnessed the effects of this selfish principle, in many of its disfiguring and various stages. I have seen children so anxious to taste good things, that they descended to become thieves; in order to eat a spoonful of jelly, or pick a *corner* out of a cake. I have known them, with an indelicacy unpardonable, fix upon that dish at table of which there was the *least* in quantity. I have heard such exclamations of joy, when a nice dish, according to their idea, was placed upon the table, that I have been astonished how they could betray themselves so disgustingly; and, above all, I have seen these things pass unnoticed, by those who had a right to speak and to reprove this unfortunate tendency, for, that this quality, generates to consequences truly unfortunate, requires very little argument, to establish. The person who is devoted to the good things of this world is anxious for their attainment, and, to please his appetite, will yield his time, to his taste: an epicure is the most selfish of all animals; generosity is a stranger to his nature, and for what, is he thus *solicitous?* If he gratifies his palate, the pleasure is transient; but let him remember, that gluttony has been denounced an offence to God;—and, if this fails to reclaim him, let him be convinced, that the constitution is undermined by gross feeding, and that premature age, if not death, is the certain consequence of this odious vice.

You must know, for you are the peculiar favourites of God's mercy, who, in making you capable of reasoning, hath placed you above all the works of his hands;—you cannot be strangers to this mark of divine favour. Let me caution you, my little friends, against a vice so destructive as that of gluttony;—I trust it will be easy to persuade you, that it is a very unamiable indulgence, and under that term, more likely to fix your attention to the understanding of my meaning. We naturally attach to the characters and dispositions of youth, a softness, which seems natural to their age, and there is no epithet in the English language, which I should feel so much inclined to bestow upon children, as that of "amiable:"—it conveys a great deal of meaning;—I could imagine it to imply "gentleness," "humility," "modesty," "truth," and "intelligence." Now, let me ask, if these qualities could unite in an epicure, a glutton?—Impossible;—they are social virtues, the feelings natural to a generous mind; and a glutton lives only for himself, nor ever gives, but when satiety obliges him to become abstemious. And if a *laudable* ambition actuates your mind, if you wish to acquire knowledge, rest assured, that moderation in your diet, is a strong stimulus to learning, and not all the sweets that the storeroom of the housekeeper could produce, nor yet the nice cakes of your grandmothers or your godmothers, will ever compare with that delightful, and always attainable feast, a taste for learning. To that repast, observe how many great and virtuous characters invite you; it is true, they expect you to bring your ticket of admission, that is, *attention*; but, if you go into their society, thus prepared, your gleanings are certain. Sacred history offers to your expanding mind, the precepts for your guide through life, with such examples of divine mercy, as shall lead you to the practice of virtue, in order that you may "hope all things:"—while, in the less authentic pages of ancient and modern history, the ambition and discontent of mankind, will teach you the insufficiency of all worldly considerations. These are solid viands, from which a literary taste must make a wholesome *meal*. Geography, Natural History, and Poetry, make a *second* course, which I do not refuse to any who seek this sort of food;—nay, I will permit a *desert* to follow in these cases, because I think *such* epicures deserve a little indulgence. The best written and least marvellous fiction, should be given to these, my rational young friends, with one, and only one, restriction,—not to devour it too greedily, as there is very little nourishment in them, and consequently they will not be brought to table often.

CHAPTER VII

"Though I were perfect, yet would I not presume."

"To shun allurements is not hard,
"To minds resolved, forewarned, and well prepar'd."

THOUGH MISS WATSON had, with much leniency, denominated Charles Osborn's chief defect of character to be his want of steadiness, I was not disposed to coincide in this opinion, more especially, when I heard he had attempted to deny that he had been impertinent to Lady Liston.

I was glad he did not persevere in this most serious crime, but there really appeared to me so many shades of character in this boy, that I was led to consider the probable effects his occasional society might produce on my grandson. It is so essential to the virtue and happiness of children, that they should associate with those only who are well disposed; and it unfortunately happens, that some of the foibles of the vicious, are of a nature to raise a smile on the features of a youthful observer, while an experienced and reflecting *Spectator*, will discover the lurking mischief, and tremble for those who are exposed to the insidious deception. All these considerations, I repeat, pressed so on my mind, that I confess I was very anxious to hear from William Mordaunt. I was not, however, gratified in my *spectatoral* character: a few hasty lines, addressed to his mother, in which were some kind remembrances to myself, was all that I received for some days; but in the interim I was not idle, nor did some other of my correspondents neglect me.—The first letter which engaged my attention, was one from Mr. Testy; it deserves a place in this my miscellany, and it shall have one.

To Mrs. ARGUS.

More miseries, my dear madam; I shall certainly retire from society, unless I find that the publication of your intended volume has some effect upon these young tormentors. You are very right; all our searches after a new system of education, are superfluous:—what does the excellent Father Gerdil say on this subject?

"Suffer not, ye parents, the deceitful bait of a gaudy novelty to seduce you. Be cautious of trying on your children, the dangerous experiment of a method, not yet warranted by success. Let the holy maxims of our forefathers, maxims so venerable for their authority and antiquity, be always present before your eyes."

But I must not intrude upon your time: excuse me, madam, I fear I am prolix, but really I am greatly annoyed at this moment;—a lady, my cousin, with two little plagues, whom she calls "sweet, dear little cherubs," arrived two evenings since, at my house, and, *sans ceremonie*, declares she is come to spend a week with me. Now I really esteem my cousin, and, had she come alone, should have been sincerely glad to see her; indeed, had her children been tractable, I might have borne with them. My house is always kept in neat order, without that troublesome sort of nicety, sometimes to be seen in the houses of bachelors.

But my cousin is unfortunately the mother of two *geniuses*, and they must not be checked in any of their wild careers. I proposed, with my usual attention to comfort, that the little ones should make a nursery of the housekeeper's room. "No such thing; they are never to be in the company of a servant, and, if possible, to be brought up without a knowledge of these distinctions of persons." I stared: "What do you act the nurse, the tutoress, and mother?" said I. My cousin smiled with a look of self-importance, and declared she was. I own I was much surprised, as she is a young woman, and, till lately, accustomed to a London life. The next morning, at breakfast, I had some specimens of their genius which by no means suited my taste. The elder boy, on a sudden, uncovered the tea-urn to see what quantity of steam it contained. In vain I expostulated, and reminded him of the danger to which he exposed himself. He laughed at me, "What do you think I do not know that hot water will scald," said he. Now this might be very reasonable, but it was certainly rather rude. "I like the water to be kept boiling," said I. "You are not a philosopher, cousin," said my little reasoner. I own I was rather surprised at the forwardness of the boy, but before I could reply to him his mother exclaimed in an extasy, "Is he not a prodigy?" "I cannot tell yet," I replied, "the plan is new to me." Well, the breakfast was removed, and now a race, with my chairs turned down for horses, was projected by these young Nimrods. In vain I interposed, and requested that the trial might take place in some other apartment. They had set off, and nothing I said had the least effect. In turning one of these wooden horses, a jar of considerable value in my estimation, because it was my mother's, was forced from its quiet station under a card-table, hurled with eventful velocity into the middle of the room, and there, woeful to relate, it divided into three pieces. "I can mend it," said one of my young plagues, and he instantly rang the bell and ordered a saucepan full of milk, and some cotton or packthread to be brought to him. I positively counteracted this, and declared, that any experiment he chose to try, must be performed in Mrs. Bond's room. I thought my practical philosopher seemed to regard me with contempt, at which I felt a little indignant; but the boy retiring with my valet, I suppressed my feelings, and turning to my cousin, asked her, "what superior happiness she promised herself in *her* mode of education?" "Every thing is to be hoped," said she, "from a system in which reason takes the lead." "I cannot agree with you," I replied. "I am not quite certain that the reason of your children has not subjugated, if not wholly destroyed, all those lovely traits of character so essential to their happiness as social and dependent creatures. Where is that graceful and becoming quality, diffidence? That respect due to me as a stranger and their host? That modesty which makes them slow to speak and timid in answering?" "My dear friend," replied my cousin, "all these things were very well half a century ago, but this is the age of reason." "Poh, poh, Nancy," said I, "I do not believe that there ever was a period in my life in which I could not have told you that hot water was hot water, and that it would blister my skin and give me pain if I touched it incautiously; but I hope my reason would never have led me to the impertinence of arraigning the supposed ignorance of my elders, nor yet have prompted a boldness so conspicuous as that of deranging the furniture and destroying the property of those who entertained me. I do not see that men or women are more happy, more virtuous, nor yet more learned, by adopting any system which is to increase their vanity, for vanity is a great enemy to the attainment of sound reasoning." Whether I should have converted my cousin to my opinion is uncertain, for a loud and universal shriek now reached our ears, and a cry of fire echoed through the hall. I ran down, and with real alarm discovered that the *philosophers* had set Mrs. Bond's chimney on fire by having heaped an unnecessary quantity of fuel on the fire in order to expedite their chinamending business.

I turned these intruders from the apartment, and having seen the fire quenched, repaired to the drawing-room. "I have been telling the boys," says my cousin, "that you do not like experiments and persuading them to defer their attempts until we go home again." "I do not object to these things from any contempt of their utility," said I, "but I do not approve of such half-digested principles as those just exhibited. Could you suppose," I continued, addressing the elder boy, "that you were correct in your application of this process of mending china, when the vessel in which you placed the broken article was not sufficiently deep to guard it from the immense flames which played about the saucepan?" "I never thought of that," said the boy, "and indeed the fire frightened me so much that I did not take time to think." "I am pleased," continued I, "when I see children direct their attention to useful things; the attempt in question is in itself highly so; but I would advise every child who practises a thing of this sort to submit to be directed in his first essay. The loss of my jar I must regret, but the loss of my house would have been a serious evil." I saw that my cousin considered my remonstrance unkind, while the boys looked rather abashed, though certainly somewhat sullen. As this troublesome trio are yet my guests, it is very probable that some new illustrations of genius may fall under my observation; in which case, I shall not fail to trouble you; but, in the mean time, let me beg of you to take notice of these ebullitions of reason, which shoot out, and overwhelm modesty, respect and duty. I know it is usual to laugh at old bachelors, but, upon my word, madam, there is something vastly comfortable in the sound of that simple word, duty, and whether it is from the length of time to which I refer and recollect who claimed this feeling of me, or that I esteem it for its antiquity and divine institution, of this I am certain that no new word, theoretically or practically used, can supersede it, unless it bring along with it its amiable and becoming practice.

I am, dear madam,
Your obedient servant,
TIMOTHY TESTY.

The letter of Mr. Testy occasioned me some serious reflections; and, indeed, I so perfectly coincide in opinion with this gentleman, that I cannot resist delineating the feelings to which his letter gave rise.

I consider the present times as offering just cause for admiration in the many and ample elucidations of science and things, formerly hoarded only for the closet of the philosopher. But as vanity is an insidious, and almost inseparable foible of the inexperienced, too much care cannot be observed in the manner in which we introduce them to knowledge.

· It should be invariably inculcated, that wisdom is a store of which youth ought never to be prodigal; for with whatever facility they learn, however accurate their perceptions, they will discover in each revolving year, that they have yet much to learn, and that what they considered perfect, as their minds expand, will bear corrections if not revision. I do not by this wish to throw a damp on the lively and ardent spirits of the young. Chearfulness is a charm of character of which I am fully sensible, but there are few things more generally reprehended than forwardness of manner. It matters not how this quality shows itself; whether in vaunting its knowledge, in disrespect to elders, or in contempt for those whom we think less wise; in either case vanity is the primary cause of the failing, and a foundation more perishable cannot be imagined.

I have more than once witnessed the most humiliating consequences follow a disposition of this sort, and though I certainly took part in their feelings, and strove to lessen the portion of their shame by explaining the methods most likely to spare them a mortification of the kind in future, yet my memory, with a justice due to modest merit, was irresistibly impelled to revert to those families in which children, of an opposite character, had won my esteem and engaged my love.

Mr. Testy's habits in life, as is obvious, are very regular; consequently, he is more liable to be incommoded by any innovation than persons accustomed to children. Yet, I am persuaded that many people affect indifference to the intrusions of children who are actually well disposed to be offended: and I blame this sort of acquiescence; it is suffering errors to gain an established ascendancy, and ultimately rearing pragmatical men and presuming women.

There cannot possibly be a higher gratification, than that which we receive from the well arranged replies of children, of whom we seek inquiry. Every person is sensible of this, strangers as well as relatives; nor are *their* inquiries less interesting, when dictated by modesty, and preferred with an evident desire of gaining information: but I have heard children importunate to have an explanation, and wholly inattentive while that explanation was given. This is a sort of pomp, which betrays a very shallow understanding; besides which, the engaging a person to take the trouble of instructing you in the most trivial point, and not availing yourself of their kindness, is a strong mark of ill manners.

I am very much prepossessed in favour of those little experiments, so ably delineated by Miss Edgeworth, and other kind friends of the young. Every thing which tends to the usefulness of life, is highly worthy of our consideration;—but there is a boldness in bringing ourselves forward upon all occasions.

In the houses of your parents, in your fixed homes, the practical arcanum of childrens' philosophy, may be exemplified, not only with propriety, but much advantage to the attentive pupil. Wisdom of every kind is laudable, and they who begin to lay up treasures in youth, may hope, in advanced life, to reap the advantages, always to be derived from internal resources.

I had the happiness of knowing an amiable child, whom it pleased God to afflict with a most painful rheumatic complaint: the disposition of my dear little friend was naturally lively, and, in the intervals of her pain, she was always remarkably chearful; —but what chiefly leads to my speaking of her in this place is, to convince those for whom I write, that even in early life, it is possible to lay up resources in the mind, which shall teach patience under affliction, and qualify even a youthful sufferer, to comfort those most interested in her fate.

Anna C—— was always particularly attentive to her prayers, which she not only repeated with becoming seriousness, but had taken much trouble to comprehend. Her catechism was one of the duties, to which, all who heard her repetition, ever gave the most delighted approbation. Her manner was so mild and attentive, her enunciation so clear, and the punctuation (a most essential observance in this divine ordinance) so correct, that I may with truth assert, she incited many of her young companions, to give a more serious attention to this important duty, than all the previous instructions of their tutoress had been able to effect. I have seen her, when her younger sisters have been dancing, look on with all the admiration of a matured mind, that took pleasure in seeing the happiness of infancy. It is true, I have heard her say, she should like to have been able to join the group, but no vague regrets or pinings were her's. The affection of Anna's friends, led them to present her with numberless valuable toys and trinkets, which they imagined would cheer her sedentary life: she always received them with smiles, and expressed herself grateful for their attentions, but they could not engage her mind for any length of time.—"I ought to be grateful," said the dear girl, one day, "for every body is anxious to please and amuse me; but I have discovered, that sick people have only one comfort, one consolation; they must read the bible, where all that *they* suffer will appear as trifling, when compared with what is told us there." From this period, she had the scriptures laid on a table by her side, and when a more than ordinary pain shook her frame, she would turn to the book of Job, and read a chapter. There was no display in her manner, and it was only after a time, that her most intimate friends could discover, what reflections were produced from her study.—"In all my pains, I have friends about me," said the sweet child, one evening, "and that is indeed a great comfort; and when I *can* eat, I need only to express my wishes. How many are sick, and have none to assist them, nor yet the power of getting any thing they fancy." As her weakness increased, and the medical men seemed hopeless, she took upon herself the office of comforter to her parents. Frequently would a lively sally animate her intelligent countenance; and once she asked for a pencil, and sketched the scenery of her chamber, pourtraying her parents, as frightened at the length of the doctor's bill: this she shewed to the gentleman himself, who fully comprehended her intention, which was, in fact, to raise the spirits of her parents. At length she was removed from this world, dying, as she had lived, patient and resigned. I could not describe the deep regrets of her parents, who were long ere they regained their usual tranquillity; but I bring her forward as one proof, that the *really* amiable qualities of the mind, are not of a showy or intrusive nature: and I would likewise wish to impress on my young readers, the conviction, that religious knowledge is of equal importance to the young, as to those advanced in life; that its attainment is as perfectly consistent with cheerful dispositions as with the gloomy and retired character; and, above all, I invite them to reflect on the consolation that a parent must in *time* acquire, when they contemplate the virtues of such a child: "her pain and anguish has subsided," says the musing mother, "I have lost a child, but she is gone to a father, who loves all who trust in him; who have borne his will with humility, and, as far as earthly perfection extends, have been invariably strict to his laws." Such was Anna C——, a real character, one whom I loved, with the most sincere affection, and whose loss I as sincerely lamented.

I feel certain, that all who honour my book by a perusal, will readily enter into my opinion of the beauty of such a character; but it is not sufficient that we are capable of admiring and doing justice to virtue, we should indeavour to follow an example so amiable. I have amongst others, given appropriate praise to the child who applied any useful principle to its destined purpose; have been pleased with a correct specimen of music, a well executed drawing, &c. but, that neither or all of these combined are of equal moment, or will bear any comparison, with a mind that makes religion the basis of its happiness, and from the sacred volume of all that is good, and worthy of regard, draws guides for every action in life, a very little observation will confirm. The music lesson, the drawing, &c. live in the memory of the hearer during the visit; we may recollect the performer and the artist if we meet her, but an impression of early virtue is never effaced; we are interested for the child who has evinced an excellence of the kind, we regard it as a blissful promise, and are anxious not to lose sight of a mind which bears so fair a perspective.

Thus, it is obvious that what are termed accomplishments are, in themselves, very unessential qualities; though they may be graceful ornaments, yet their chief uses are that of occupying a vacant hour, and, by their variety, giving an elasticity to the mind highly serviceable, and suitable to the period of youth, which always requires relaxation, but it is on the solid acquirements that we pause. I record the character of my amiable little friend, as one that deserves remembrance, yet I might have added, that she possessed many superficial advantages; but I was speaking of her as a very superior child, and I did not feel that such trifles would have enhanced my sketch.

I do not pretend to hold the mirror to boys; their education usually places them beyond the sphere of women; yet it was not always so: mothers were formerly considered the best early tutors of boys, and such of my readers as have dipped into ancient history will no doubt recollect, that the decline of some states was dated from that period in which women resigned this important office. You will perceive, my little friends, that I am not disposed to be explicit, in any case in which your memories ought to elucidate facts. I would rather that I awakened your curiosity, than checked your pursuits. If I could write as those amiable matrons once taught, there is no doubt but I should grow eloquent upon the present occasion, and be tempted to contrast the analogy between philosophy and duty; for as morality is blended in the pursuits and attainments of the philosopher, we err deeply when we separate these natural and affectionate relatives.

I know you will enter into my feelings, and some of you will rejoice in the digression which circumstances here oblige me to make; a letter is presented to me, and I recognise the hand-writing of my beloved grandson. Dear boy, but I must insert his epistle.

To MRS. ARGUS.

Madam,

I hope this will be forwarded to you immediately, as I am really much in want of your advice. I am now, at — — school, and have been here above a week; I like it very much, and should be quite happy if it was not for one reason. The boys here think women such ridiculous creatures that they always speak of them with derision: now I love my mother and my grandmother dearly, and had promised to write to them often, but some of the boys have caught me, with my letter before me, just as I was beginning to write, and they quite laughed at me, and, when they saw the words "dear mother," or "dear grandmother," they asked me how I had been able to leave home, and one of them brought me a piece of packthread, which he recommended me to tie to my mothers apron, when next I saw her. I was so ashamed and vexed at this, that I put away my paper, and I am afraid my friends will be very uneasy at my silence.—But what can I do? a boy who came to school on the same day that I did, has told them that I am a sneak; because I would not join him in affronting a lady one day in Kensington Gardens. I told Charles Osborn, that I chose to act for myself, but he made out such a ridiculous story about it, that I confess I am at a loss what to say. I have got a chum, that is, a friend, already; he is a nice fellow, but not very happy, for he has neither father nor mother, and his guardian does not have him home at every holidays. He tells me, not to mind them, but to do as I feel proper. I believe he is right, yet I cannot bear to be laughed at. Charles Osborn is fag to a big boy, and he grumbles at it very much; but I can assure you he is forced to obey, and gets many a *thump*, I was going to say, but I remember you found fault with that word, but indeed I should not like the bruises he gets.

I am so lucky as to be on that form which does not fag, and, as I recollect that my mother has paid a great deal of money for masters to bring me forward in my learning, I am very unhappy, for fear she should think me undutiful. Do pray write to me directly, and if you say I ought to finish my letters, I will not mind the boys, and, though you are a woman, I shall be very much obliged to you, and will certainly go by your directions.

I remain, dear madam,
Your's, sincerely,
WILLIAM MORDAUNT.

P.S. I forgot to tell you, that I dream of my mother every night, and she looked so pale and unhappy, in my dream *last* night, that I am very impatient for your answer.

Need I say, that my paper was instantly folded, and my pen immersed in the ink, to answer this natural, and truly interesting epistle. I saw the dangers to which he was exposed with alarm, yet I owned much consolation in perceiving that he had paused, rather than consented to an erroneous and criminal imitation. My maternal heart was overcharged by its solicitude, and, while I ask the patience of my little friends to the epistle which follows, I will believe, that many of them possess in their own bosoms that tender affection for their relations, which shall lead them to peruse a *grandmother's* letter, not only with a leniency for its author, but an amiable interest in its purport.

To Master MORDAUNT.

Sir,

I embrace the earliest opportunity of replying to you, conceiving, that you are in danger of losing, or rather of sacrificing, the most amiable trait in the human character, *duty*, to a theory as wild as unsupported.

I rejoice that you have been so wise as to pause, ere you rendered yourself so weak and unhappy, nor need I expatiate on the many ill consequences that must attend a conduct so unfilial, as I perceive you are tenderly conscious, that you are not acting up to your character as a son. Understand, that between false and proper shame, there is a very distinct line; the former is the companion of the weak and cowardly mind, and leads to meanness, insolence, and falsehood, for though I perfectly comprehend, that those who recommend this system to you, appear very brave talkative sort of gentlemen, believe me, they could very easily be proved boys of the most contemptible dispositions, and uninformed minds. Common sense should dictate to every child in such a case. Can you suppose, that a few inexperienced boys, forming themselves into a society for the purpose of depreciating their earliest friends and most tender protectors, can find any just cause for this ridiculous sort of vaunting, and, if they presume to think it a manly resolution, how silly and blind they must be. Look around you, regard the conduct of your father, uncles, all your male connections, and you will invariably observe, that, towards females they are attentive, obliging and affectionate. Thus, you see, it is contrary to their characters as men to adopt so absurd a whim; they cannot support their affected principles, for they have no basis; their insolence is obvious in their attempt, and it is kindness to ascribe insincerity to their folly; for to believe they act from internal feeling, is to consider them lower in the scale of created beings than the most untaught savage.

It may require some courage in a boy of your age, to combat the opinions of these imperious directors, yet I am persuaded you have it in your power to come off victorious; and, though I am no friend to contention in any shape, I think the present deserves the title of an honourable battle: stand your ground, taking care to carry to the field of action a cool manner and respectful language; assure your opponents "that, as yet, you have every reason to consider women as amongst the best and kindest of your friends; declare, with as much *warmth* as your feelings dictate, that you love your mother and your grandmother, and that, until you can enter their society, like an honourable member, viz. fully believing in its rules and sentiments, you must decline the distinction."

Many, even of these boasters, will secretly applaud your courage; some will laugh at you; but if you are afraid of a laugh, yet not afraid to act the part of a hypocrite and deny your most virtuous feelings, you are the victim of false shame, and a total stranger to the only shame that a good mind should own—the shame of committing an action on which we dare not reflect. It is pleasing to perceive by your letter that your heart is at present properly attached to home. But you must be alert, nor make one sacrifice to these ill-judging blockheads. Finish your letters and continue to think for yourself in all matters that relate to your duty; while in those which belong to your studies be politely attentive to any information offered to your inexperience, and, in particular, I would advise you to shew a deference to your chum, who has evinced his good sense by his manner towards you. I dare say he would gladly own a claim to the kindness of some good woman, who should think of him while absent, and endeavour to make his vacations chearful. Make no friendship with Charles Osborn until he reforms his manners; but, at the same time, I would recommend you to live in peace with all your companions. Convince them that you are not to be shaken in your principles, and after that cultivate the good opinion of your schoolfellows as far as in your power.

I am persuaded your attention to my plan will restore you to that happiness which I am glad to discover you do not at present enjoy. The reflection that you have performed your duty will remove all doubt from your mind. That you should dream of your mother is not surprising. She has engaged your thoughts very much, and we usually dream of that which has most weight on our spirits. I trust that in future your conduct and your feelings will be so properly united, that your slumbers, like your mind, may be tranquil. The smiling period of youth has this delusive advantage over all other seasons of life. The world looks fair, and you believe all its promises. You have few cares and very little thought for yourselves. Alas! if ye have not some guardian, some kind friend to point out the shades in this seemingly perfect picture, you will add a tint to the ever-varying scene that shall finally overshadow you. I know you will forgive an old woman who is truly anxious for your happiness; one who would willingly guard your youth without blinding your judgment by gloomy prejudices.

I hope to hear from you again, and in that expectation subscribe myself,

Sincerely your's,

ARABELLA ARGUS.

Boys who have never quitted home, who, in the approbation of their parents and the delights of family intercourse, have been accustomed to own themselves happy, will hardly comprehend how it is possible for children to enter into a combination so un-natural. I am well assured, that this absurd custom which is most prevalent in public schools, loses its power over the minds of youth as reason usurps her throne, but that they should ever evince an ignorance so wilful, so truly unjustifiable, is certainly a matter of general concern to all who value the characters of youth.

CHAPTER VIII

To all those whom it may concern.

M Y DISPOSITION is naturally persevering, and from the moment in which I volunteered my services as a Spectator, my vigilance has been proportioned to my ardent interest for the happiness of children.

I know exactly what sort of writing pleases some children,—for instance, a story beginning—

"In a beautiful village in the north of England lived Mrs. Villars," &c. I see the eager eyes of a little story-loving dame glisten with delight at an opening so promising; while another, with equal pleasure reads the "Fairy Tale," and wishes, just to gratify her curiosity, that there were really such creatures as fairies. A third likes an opening of this sort—"Once upon a time there was an old woman," &c. It would be very hard upon the season of youth if we were entirely to repress their little tastes, or restrict them from the amusements suited to their age. But I am persuaded that an early course of light reading is very prejudicial to sound acquirement. I am, at the same time, convinced that many of the juvenile publications now in circulation are in themselves highly valuable, from the morality they have the power of inculcating, if their purport is comprehended by their readers; but I must believe that the scenery and decorations are the chief attractions with children. I wish I could impress upon my readers, that it is not the number of books which they peruse that will make them wise, but the application of the moral; the imitation of such amiable proofs of duty, good temper, and religious conduct, as is displayed in half a thousand of the little volumes which have fallen into my hands. For my own part, I am an avowed enemy to very extensive libraries for children. Give them a few books, and let them be of the best sort. If they really love reading they will not fail to go through them two or three times; there are few children who may not with propriety be termed superficial readers. Thus, the frequent perusal of a small, select library must consequently lay a good foundation for the watchful parent to improve; and though I am conscious there would be some difficulty in persuading children to think my plan agreeable, at first, I am so well assured of its utility, that I almost wish I had as many *tongues* to enforce my propo-sition as I have *eyes* to observe the many defects and foibles actually existing.

I presume that you have all heard of Argus who in mythological history is represented as having an hundred eyes; now I, as an old woman of the present times, can assure you I have not *quite* so many; yet I will prove to you that my eyes are very piercing. For instance, they penetrate through the thick brick wall of a certain nursery: what a scene presents itself! A battle between a young gentleman and the nurses. Let me be correct: oh! I perceive the women are holding the little tyrant's arms to prevent him from proving himself a coward, for none but cowards ever raise a hand to a female. Now let me state the cause of this confusion. Master Edward has asserted his right to the toy with which his brother is playing; one is an infant in arms, and is amused by the plaything, the other a boy of nine years of age. I almost doubted my sight in this case, and actually placed my spectacles on my nose to take a more accurate view. Alas! is it too true: the young rebel is kicking and squalling, while the dear little baby, quite unconscious of his offence, is laughing at the noise by which he is surrounded. Churlish, selfish, childish boy, I blush for you. Dry your tears and think for a moment: are you not a poor helpless dependent on the bounty of your parents? Regard the furniture that makes your home so comfortable, the bed on which you sleep, the bread you eat. Are you able of yourself to procure one of these conveniences of life? No: then how dare you presume to deprive a little innocent babe of a small share of those blessings you enjoy. Your brother has not the power to express his wishes yet; and if you use your reason to exhibit feelings so unamiable, you are both cruel and undutiful; cruel, because you neglect the opportunity of making your brother happy—and undutiful in forgetting that your parents have always considered you, and have in consequence a right to expect in return a strict attention to their happiness, which you cannot be so ignorant as to imagine you promote when you appear in a character so truly odious.

What would you say, when seated at the dinner-table, if your father was to enter the room and speak thus—"That mutton, those potatoes and pudding are mine; I see that Edward looks as though he could eat of each, but as he would like to do so I will deprive him of them." Yet your parents' right in this case is unanswerable; but they, being influenced by reason, are anxious to contribute to your comfort; you, as less endowed with reason, are not exactly capable of acting for yourself; but there are degrees of reason, and that of which all children are peculiarly sensible should be your guide, namely, that you would not like to be served thus yourself. Remember your catechism—"Do unto all men as I would they should do unto me." This liberal and just maxim applies to every stage of life, and if in childhood you regard it as you ought, you will be dutiful to your parents, affectionate to your brothers and sisters, and above all you will be doing the will of God who seeth all hearts, and hath tenderly recommended to us to love each other.

I turn my eye from this nursery fracas and behold a drawing-room cabal. Three or four children have been permitted to amuse themselves with drawing-books, maps, picture games, &c. upon certain terms, viz. that they replace each of these sources of present pleasure in their respective places. They have agreed to the proposal: but now that the games are over and the book ceases to amuse, they are quarrelling as to the share each is to take in this very essential and necessary duty, *order.*—Perhaps you are not exactly conscious of the extent of your errors in a case of this sort; let me enumerate them for you. First then, you break your word, which is a very serious fault: Secondly, you dispute the authority of your parents. I need not remind you where you are enjoined to "Honour your father and mother:" Thirdly you evince a very unamiable specimen of fraternal love when you argue and quarrel, where a little mutual exertion and good humour would not only make you acceptable to your parents, but encourage them to grant you any reasonable indulgence. I beg of you to reflect. You are now the happy inmates of one dwelling. Time, which is stealing from you imperceptibly, will, in the course of a few years, separate you. You will be called upon to take part in the active scenes of life, and when distance intervenes and you think of the dangers to which a brother is exposed, and remember with regret the many bickerings which occurred while ye were together, believe me, your happiness will be greatly diminished; and with girls whom school, distant friends, or any other contingence removes, the same feeling will certainly recur. Death, which has equal power over all the creatures of this world, may claim you for his own. Consider this, and make it your study to live together in "brotherly love." It is by ordering yourselves lowly and affectionately, that you acquire a fit temper of mind to mix in the world. A hasty word, or a blow given to a brother or sister frequently unknown to your parents and consequently unreproved, may establish from habit a violence of character which shall lead to most serious consequences. Strangers will not bear with your intemperance; they will chastise your presumption, and it is more than probable that the boy who in infancy tyrannizes over his juniors will fall a victim to false honour by becoming a duellist, the most guilty and criminal of characters. In girls a disposition of the kind has an effect equally deplorable; that gentleness of manner inseparable from a delicate mind is deformed; they are petulant, overbearing, unkind to their inferiors, and but lightly esteemed by their acquaintance. Friends are out of the question, for a tyrant has no friend. A female owning such a character is incapable of exercising the virtues which grace her sex. The voice of distress cannot reach her ear, for the desolate fear her scornful and impatient manner; thus she is a stranger to the delights of charity. Riches fail to make her respectable, for she knows not how to dispense them; or if she is led to confer a favour, the manner of her gift may add an additional pang to her heart-stricken applicant. Not one of ye but can discern the shades in these my unamiable portraits but do not, like the Pharisee, thank your God that you are not such. Your characters are not yet perfected; it is by adding foible to foible that they amount to errors, and errors will become vices. The word is too odious to bear reference to that class of beings for whom I am thus solicitous. But, as there is a progression in every pursuit and study in which you engage, so is there a progress in your faults; and if you suffer them to gain an ascendancy over you in early youth, it will be in vain that you look for happiness or honour in more advanced life.

I shall be greatly disappointed if I am considered rigid and severe as a spectator; yet I am certain that I cannot expect, or hope, to please *all* my young friends; but I candidly avow that whatever the decisions of my juvenile critics may be, I have not brought forward nor do I mean to exhibit a character, the likeness of which has not actually fallen under my observation.

I have before made some remarks on the manner in which *some* children repeat their lessons; it was *warm* weather when I wrote those pages, and I *now* beg to say something of *frosty morning* lessons. I believe we are all of us sensible of some degree of uncomfortableness on entering a cold room, early in the morning; but as those who *hear* a lesson, may be presumed to have the same feelings with those who *say* it, I cannot

understand the necessity of their interrupting their studies, by the extraordinary information, that "it is very cold," or, that "their voices are to be changed, from the clear
and smiling acquiescence, so graceful in youth, to the whine, if not the discord, of
sulkiness." Can a lazy posture, and a grumbling disapprobation of that, which it has
pleased God to order, either abridge your appointed business, or add to your amiability
of character?—Assuredly not: then why give way to such whims? Take into your consideration, how many aged people are exposed to the inclemency of the season! How
many must toil, ere they can procure a breakfast! How many children, younger than
yourself, are working in the various manufactories, which our happy island supports,
where they are excluded any material benefit from the comfort of a fire, and fare on
the most homely food, and that, perhaps, in limited proportions! There are very few
real troubles attached to childhood,—even those who are most unfortunately situated, by
which I mean children, who are orphans, who depend upon precarious friendships,
or are confined to sedentary employments;—even these find their hours of happiness,
and in play, a moderate recreation, or the approbation of their protectors, forget their
little sorrows. Nature has wisely in this, as in all her dispensations, given a sunshine to
the bosom of youth, which more than compensates for the light clouds which sometimes
gather over the pillow of infancy. If children, thus situated, are grateful and contented,
how unpardonable are those who make troubles and repine, when they ought to rejoice.
But I have really seen that, which was intended as a relaxation and kindness by a
parent, received with ill-humour and ingratitude by children: I mean the instructions of
masters;—for instance, the music master's lesson on one day, is the most delightful thing
in the world,—and the pupil performs *her* part correctly:—on another, she is not ready
for him,—she "hates the name of music;"—"she is sure the book is misprinted, and that
she knows best what the passage should be:" she wishes there was no such thing as
music. Now, if the cause of this distaste was sought into, it would be found to be as
ridiculous and ungrateful as folly could imagine. The young lady has some idea, that if
this had not been her music day, she should have been able to go out with her mamma
in the carriage, or have been at liberty to prosecute some more delightful because
newer occupation.

It is a very general error with children, to ridicule their masters: I know no foible
more reprehensible, or more likely to deprive them of the advantages to be derived
from their instructions.

As it is to be supposed, that parents always assure themselves of the capacity of the
persons whom they engage, it must be evident to these very *discerning* little judges,
that in that branch of science which they profess to teach, they must be superior to their
pupils. If your dancing master gives you the necessary rules for walking, attends to the
ease of your figure, and teaches you the steps usual and proper for a gentlewoman to
adopt, it is of no consequence to you, whether he speaks good English, dresses fashion-
ably, or has an odd looking countenance;—he does his part in attending to these
points, and, as *he* concludes he has been engaged to instruct the daughters of respectable families,—pray do not disappoint him, by forgetting yourselves. I might speak of
all masters, individually, but I shall confine myself to the unfortunate French master.
I see my readers smile,—boys, and well as girls. Each of you recollect a Monsieur somebody, who is the oddest creature in the world;—one remembers a long nosed Monsieur;
another, such a starved looking animal:—one boy recollects the good jokes he has put

upon an odious French usher;—another smiles at his stupid English, &c. &c. Can any thing be more contemptible, than conduct of this sort, when duly considered? The French language has become very general in this country since the Revolution, and the manner in which it is now spoken by the English, is very superior to our former acquirements in the language. This is to be imputed to the distresses and necessities, to which well educated Frenchmen and French women have been reduced;—and is that laudable spirit of industry, which has led them to exert their talents for their support, to make them the objects of our ridicule? I blush, while I put my hand to a record, so unworthy of a free and generous people; nor could any thing but my love of truth, induce me to pursue the subject further.

National prejudices, by which is understood a dislike to a person, merely because he is born in France, or in Ireland, or any other country, of which we entertain a mean opinion. When grown people exhibit a feeling of this sort, we are led to suppose, that they have some reasons for their conduct; but children, to whom I address myself, are very easily led to actions, truly unbecoming, without an idea of the consequences to which their folly may subject them; or any other motive for their prejudices, than the force of imitation. Many of you, if strictly questioned, "why you disliked a Frenchman," would appear very ridiculous in your replies. I remember once being present, where a boy had vented his excessive dislike to the French, when a lady asked him,—"What were his objections to them?" The young gentleman paused,—"Why they are so thin," said he.—"Have you no other accusation to bring?" retorted the lady.— "Yes; they talk so quick, and can eat any thing," rejoined the little critic.—"The form of their bodies does not depend upon themselves," observed the lady;—"The facility with which they speak, is no argument against them, but rather a characteristic of their country; they are lively and animated, and their language admits of a fluency, which our's does not. I do not agree with you, that they can eat any thing; they are less difficult in their food, and by no means so much addicted to gluttony as the English: and indeed this quality is much in their favour, in *my* opinion; while to *you*, who dislike them so much, it must be the cause of much satisfaction, that they will not interfere with the *good* things, of which we English think so much." The boy looked angry, and with some boldness, added,—"That they spoke such foolish English, that *he* could not help laughing, whenever a Frenchman pretended to think he understood it." —"Yet, I can assure you," continued the lady,—"that if you were in France, and expressed yourself inelegantly in *their* language, they would not be disposed to be rude; on the contrary, they would make judicious allowances for your *ignorance*, and, with much affability, assist you to understand whatever could conduce to your comfort."—"Then I hate them, because they are Frenchmen," said this little prejudiced mortal. The lady, smiling, dropped the argument, mildly adding,—"that such a decision was unanswerable, as neither reason nor humanity could convince a person, so unfortunately deficient in common sense." I saw the young gentleman looked very angry, but he did not venture any more remarks.

Yet, I fear, silly as this boy must appear, there are a *few* young reasoners, who could give no better explanation of their distaste to Frenchmen, than those I have exhibited. I would certainly recommend to the young of both sexes, the love of their country: in a boy, it leads to those researches in history, which must ultimately form the mind, and polish the manners; and in whatever situation of life he may chance to stand, a knowledge of that constitution he is born to support, is absolutely necessary to him as a man; —while girls, by contrasting the character of women, (in times, when their pursuits were very distinct to those of the present day,) may, by a just habit of thinking, acquire a knowledge of the capability and powers of the female mind, so amply illustrated in a Jane Grey, a Lady Russel, &c. &c. &c. But if our reading is to answer no other purpose, than to beguile the present hour, if we enter into society, with all the weak prejudices that are inseparable from the vain and the ignorant, we are indeed a very inferior people, and by no means an honour to our country.

I know that it would be almost impossible to convince a school-boy, who is turning over the pages of the Grecian and Roman Histories, that there was much to condemn in those characters, whose deeds of heroic valour, so completely captivate a young mind; yet a tyrant is a tyrant, in whatever clime he exerts his power.

It is highly criminal, to attach particular defects of character generally;—if we are at the trouble to understand the dispositions of those with whom we associate, it will rarely happen, that some trait of worth does not soften the human portrait, and it is the beauty of virtue to be seeking the good, rather than anticipating the errors, of a fellow-creature.

"What a dull Chapter," says one of my yawning readers:—"Dear, Mrs. Argus," says another,—"I really expected, from the opening of this Chapter, that you were going to tell us a story."

In pity to your exhausted patience, I will close this tedious paper, which, even to myself, appears rather desultory,—not much unlike to the frog, in the fable, who hopped about from "bank to bank." Yet, I cannot forbear one wish, which is, that my little friends, like the "steady snail," may always persevere in the path of duty, for duty is the basis of every virtue; a dutiful child must have an affectionate heart, for the best feelings of the mind are matured by the practice of duty. Thus generous friendships and liberal sentiments, are the natural blossoms of a well-regulated mind, which has too much pride to adopt an opinion, unsanctioned by observation and reflection; and too much humility to dare to "judge," when it has been enjoined us not to "judge, lest we be judged."

CHAPTER IX

"Be wise to-day, 'tis madness to defer."

I HAVE OFTEN, and with sincere pleasure, contemplated the features of children, when an expected happiness, or an agreeable surprise, has animated their countenances; but none of ye, however grateful, could look or feel more pleased than I did, when, on entering my breakfast-room, this morning, I discovered a letter, with the ———— post mark. I forgot my buttered toast;—the urn continued singing most sonorously:— I heeded neither, but clearing my spectacles, I broke the seal, and read as follows:

To Mrs. ARGUS.

My dear MADAM,

I have conquered, and gained two new friends into the bargain. Charles Osborn, brought five or six boys into my study last night, just as I had begun to write to my mother. They made a great row at first, and I could not make myself heard for some time; at last I told them, that I did not come there to be taught my duty by them;—that my study was my own, and I would do as I pleased in it;—that I loved my mother too well to make her unhappy, and would write to her and all my friends whenever I pleased. Charles Osborn made a snatch at my letter, but I soon got it from him, and gave him a hearty thrashing. He blubbered at first, and asked the boys to help him to give me a drubbing. I don't know whether they would have joined him, for just at that time my chum, Dennis O'Brien, with Lord George M———, came to the door, and inquired the cause of the row. I told them exactly how it was, and they both agreed that I was in the right: Dennis declared he would defend my cause against the whole school, and Lord George insisted upon it that I was a true Englishman, because I considered my study as my castle, and would not yield to intruders. While we were arguing the business, one of the masters came up, and Lord George explained the whole to him. He was very kind, and recommended me always to continue steady in my duty to my parents. He sent the others away, and this morning, while Osborn and his party were quizzing me, O'Brien and Lord George who heard it, came forward. My lord made such a good speech that I am sure he will be a great man in time; and Dennis spoke very clever; but I thanked them both, and told them I hoped they would always be my friends; but that I knew I could fight my own way in this business. They seemed to like me the better for this, and Mr. Wardon the master I mentioned, told me to day that he approved of my conduct. I hope you will think I have done right; I have seized the first moment to tell you these particulars, and

I remain, dear madam,
Your's, respectfully,
WILLIAM MORDAUNT.

P.S. I forget to say, that I have written to my grandmother as well as my mother; and will not fail to answer any letter you may be so kind as to send to me.

This letter, as my young friends will very readily believe, proved perfectly satisfactory to me, and I used an early opportunity to assure him of my approbation. When we reflect upon the advantages this child gained by an exertion of his reason, and see how completely insignificant the blustering prejudices of his antagonists appear, it must be obvious to every discerning mind, that none but weak and cowardly spirits yield up their opinions, without a due consideration of their subject. William Mordaunt stood upon a precipice, and had he not submitted to be directed, would have joined that thoughtless and unamiable band, whose object is to make others as unhappy as themselves; for that any person can be happy, who acts contrary to duty and humanity, is impossible.

My breakfast was scarcely removed, when my servant handed me a salver containing three letters. I will transcribe them in the order in which I perused them.

To Mrs. ARGUS.

MADAM,

I have waited much longer than I intended to do, because I was ashamed to address you till I had conquered my foolish habits, and I have now the pleasure of assuring you, that my mamma has not had occasion to reprove me for my manner of sitting for more than a week, so I hope I have got the better of this fault: indeed I have been so happy as to please her very much during the last fortnight, and she says it is not vanity in me to tell you so. I have always been particular in placing my chair *even* and sitting in the *centre* of it, and whenever I have found myself *leaning*, or *twisting* my ancles round each other, I have suddenly caught myself and remembered that I had said, "I *wished* to conquer the foible." We have been very much grieved at parting with our brother, who is gone to school, but he has written us word that he is quite happy, and the master has called upon my mamma, and speaks so well of him that we are quite delighted about it. My sisters mean to fill up the paper, so I must conclude.

I am, dear madam,

Your's, very respectfully,

FANNY MORDAUNT.

My dear MADAM,

Fanny did not explain to you how very much I have wished to write to you, but to be sure, I was a little ashamed how to begin, or else, I could have told you a fortnight ago, that I tried your method, and gave up all lessons for a week, but oh! how tired I was; I got all my bits of silk, and began to make pincushions; that would not do, for I had nobody to advise me about the shapes and the prettiest colours; well then, I took my playthings, and made a baby house, but I could not talk to the chairs, and my sisters were engaged with their masters; I had told my mamma, that I wished to have a whole week to myself and she gave me leave, and said she was certain it was the best plan, for she had read your letter. All my books and maps had been locked up at her desire; so I could not read, nor amuse myself with tracing the maps. I got so sleepy of an afternoon that I was forced to go to bed before six o'clock every evening; and you cannot think how vexed I was one morning, when I found that Miss Wilmot and Miss Woodgate had been at our house the evening before, and had danced reels with my sisters while my mamma played to them; was not this very vexatious? but though I tried to keep my eyes open the next night, I could not, and then I lost something, for my grandmamma came to tea, and I always love to be with her; but perhaps she would have found out that I had been idle, and would have talked to me about it. Now you see, madam, that I did as you desired, though I certainly did not understand your meaning then; it is quite plain to me now; you knew, that being idle, would tire me much more than my lessons could, and indeed you are right, for I have been very regular at my studies ever since, and am now very happy indeed, for my mamma is pleased with me, and I have had good tickets from my masters, almost every day. Please to tell me if you approve of my having a half holiday once a week; I shall be very much obliged to you; but pray do not order me to be idle again, for I never was so unhappy in my life. Lucy has a great deal to tell you, so I must bid you good bye.

> I am, dear madam,
> Your's, respectfully,
> HARRIET MORDAUNT.

Dear MADAM,

I wish I could write better, because what I have to tell you is much prettier than any story I ever read, for it is quite true. I never will keep my money bright any more, for indeed it is very useful. My mamma took us to a nursery ground one day last week; and while she was chusing some flowers, Harriet and I ran about the gardens. Well, do you know that we saw an old man with white hair, and two big girls, sitting upon the ground, eating cold potatoes; so I did not know what to think of it, and I stood looking at them. At last I said that "I thought potatoes were much nicer roasted," and I asked them why they eat them cold. The old man smiled, and said, "they were certainly much better hot, but that they were glad to get them any how." Are these all the dinner you will have to day? said Harriet. They said it was. So I asked them why they dined so soon for it was only twelve o'clock, and the poor old man told me, that he and his two daughters had been at work ever since four in the morning. "Had you no luncheon?" said I. They said, "No." "What will you have for tea and for supper?" said Harriet. Only think how shocking, madam! they told us that a draught of water and a slice of bread must serve for their tea, and a few warm potatoes, and perhaps a little beer for supper. Just then, my mamma came down the walk, and I whispered to her, how sorry I was that I had not my purse with me, but she said she would lend me whatever sum I wanted. So I borrowed a seven shilling piece, and asked the old man if he would accept of it. Oh! if you had but seen how thankful he was; I never knew, till then, that happiness could make people cry. Harriet and I could not help crying when we saw the tears run down the poor man's cheeks, and his daughters blessing us, and thanking us; yet I was not uncomfortable while I cried, which is very odd, for I always used to feel uneasy when I had occasion to cry. My mamma talked with the poor man, and we found that he had a wife at home, very lame with the rheumatism. So mamma got her direction, and we bade them good bye. Well, then the coach was ordered to go to the poor woman's house. You cannot think what a mean room it was in which she lived! she was quite surprised, when we all got out of the carriage, and went into the house. She could not rise out of her seat, on account of her lameness, but she talked very sensibly with my mamma. While we were looking about us, and thinking how shocking it was for her to be lame, and have nobody to take care of her, one of the young girls we had seen in the garden came running into the room. "My dear mother," says she, "I have brought you a bit of meat." But when she saw we were there, she stopped. Only think madam, the poor creature had not tasted meat for more than a week, and if you had seen how joyfully she looked at it I am sure you would have cried as we did. I cannot tell you all that my mamma said; but she gave the poor woman a one pound note and told her she would send our doctor to see her, and we are to go again next week. I paid my mamma the seven shilling piece when we got home, but I have got three crowns and seven half-crowns left, so I shall buy some flannel for the poor woman and a pair of strong shoes for the old man, and I will not forget to take my purse in my pocket when we go the next time. Money is indeed very useful; what you said about it is just like what my grandmamma said when William was going to school. Really, I think you are very much like my grandmamma. There was a great deal more happened that morning, but I cannot describe it. I hope you will excuse my writing such a long letter, but I thought you would like to know that I had found out some of the ways in which money may be used.

I am, dear madam,

Very respectfully, yours,

LUCY MORDAUNT.

I hope that I have in every respect proved myself an impartial spectator, and that I shall be forgiven when I declare that the letter of Lucy Mordaunt appeared to me highly interesting. There was a naturalness in her mode of expression, a simplicity so characteristic, that I actually shed tears over its artless contents; while the letters of her sisters, as exhibiting evident proofs of their sincere desire to correct their faults, were very gratifying to me. It must be obvious to my readers, that my grandchildren had perfectly comprehended the nature of my advice by the manner in which they had conducted themselves. There was one remark in the letter of Fanny on which I dwelt with much satisfaction; namely, that she recollected having said, that "she wished to conquer her bad habit of sitting." Trifling as this may appear to a superficial observer, it is, upon reflection, a very conclusive argument in favour of her principles as well as understanding. It is so easy to say a thousand things which bear a correct import without the least attention to their meaning, that I cannot forbear recommending to all my readers to pause on this subject a little. "I wish I could get the better of this foible," says a young lady whose mother had reproved her for a very inelegant custom of lolling on the dinner-table; "but I shall lose it as I grow older if you would let me dine with you every day, mamma; I am sure I should soon forget it." "With whom do you usually take your meals, Maria," said the lady. Maria blushed. "Why, indeed, mamma," said the unsteady Maria, "my governess does tease me so while I am at dinner with her, that she is quite a torment to me." "I dislike the expression, Maria," replied the lady, "and very much regret that you consider the good wishes and kind attentions of Miss Richards so lightly. So far from thinking your remark reasonable, or that you would conquer this foible by being admitted to my table, I should feel I did the greatest injustice to Miss Richards in complying with your request, and could never expect you to be attentive to my wishes while you dispute the capability and intentions of the person whom my approbation and esteem has appointed to take the immediate charge of my daughter. Nay, I should certainly disgrace you on every opportunity, by observing to all who noticed your awkwardness, that you were self-willed and above advice."

Now had Maria, like Fanny Mordaunt, been really desirous of obliging her friends, had she seriously set about reforming her manners, this just rebuke of her mother's had not reached her ear. That silly compliment which she had hoped would gain her point, like all unmeaning expressions, led to her humiliation; and did all mothers repel these little attempts at finesse with the same firmness, I am induced to believe that children would be more happy, and parents more generally obeyed. It is a most erroneous idea that youth may delay; are you acquainted with the number of your days? Hath providence unfolded to you how long you have to live? Assuredly not. Then consider this, ye who cavil with time; seize the moment in your power, and let duty grace all your actions. There is no fault too trivial not to deserve correction, nor any error of which we truly repent to which the God of mercy will not incline a willing ear.

I must not omit to make some comment on Harriet's epistle. How delighted I was to perceive that the little idler had discovered the value of time. I do not fear her relapsing into her former habits. for I believe it is almost impossible for those who have experienced that soothing consciousness which arises from the performance of our duties to forego its calm delights.

The next epistle which came under my consideration was from Miss Wilmot; and to use the language of the infant library, "see here it is:"

To Mrs. ARGUS.

My dear MADAM,

I can never thank you as I ought to do for your very kind advice. My papa very fortunately acquainted me a few days after I wrote to you, that he was going to marry Mrs. Dalton. I attended to all he said on the subject, and then explained to him how undutiful and prejudiced I had been; he was very kind to me, and took much trouble to make me sensible of the great danger of all prejudices. But he greatly surprized me by saying, that Mrs. Dalton had been much distressed by my manner towards her, that she understood my feelings perfectly, and was made very unhappy by the idea of becoming the mother of a child who appeared determined not to love her. This gave me much uneasiness, as I really had no reasons for my conduct but those which my nurse had represented to me. I did not mention Jones to my papa as I thought he would be displeased with her, and, indeed, I recollected my promise to her. I asked my papa if I might name what he had told me to Mrs. Arnold; he gave me leave, and the next morning after I had had a long conversation with my governess on the subject, I begged her to walk with me to Mrs. Dalton's house. I cannot explain all that passed. She listened to me with much kindness, and though I did not betray even to her who had been the cause of my very improper behaviour towards her, I am certain she attributed it to the right person. We parted on the best terms possible, and a few days afterwards she became my mamma. You cannot imagine, madam, how happy we are. I continue to make the breakfast as usual, and Mrs. Arnold is just of my opinion that there cannot be a more amiable woman than my mamma. Nurse Jones told me the other day not to fret, as I had a fortune of my own when I came of age, and could then live with whoever I chose. But I took that opportunity of explaining myself, and entreated of her never to name the subject again, as I was quite ashamed of ever having listened to it. She cried very much, and said she meant every thing for my good. But even Jones has changed her opinion now, and yesterday declared that she believed her mistress was a very good sort of woman. I hope she will continue to think so, for I should be much grieved to part with her as my own mamma requested she might always remain in the family. Mrs. Arnold expressed herself so much like yourself, madam, when I first told her my foolish prejudices, and, indeed, Mrs. Dalton's sentiments were very similar, that I now clearly perceive that all good people think alike on this fault. I shall in future be very cautious how I take dislikes, for I perceive it is very ungenerous; and though I certainly love Nurse Jones, I shall content myself in giving her proofs of my regard, but will never listen to her advice in matters which do not belong to her office. I thought you would like to hear that I had profited by your kindness, and must now only beg to add, that I am your greatly obliged and very obedient servant,

SOPHIA WILMOT.

I was much elated as I reflected on the uniform and happy improvement so visible in the mind and manners of my amiable correspondents. I was not so vain as to imagine that *my* advice alone had effected these happy consequences, as well might we expect a sandy desart to become spontaneously fruitful. No: I perceived with grateful delight that I had been employed in the culture of a favourable soil, engaged in assisting the blossoms of virtue to expand, to cast aside the noxious weeds which would in time have grown up and wholly destroyed the fair promises of original intellect.

And, again, I am obliged to enlarge upon the great danger of all sorts of prejudice. In the particular case of Miss Wilmot, this evil would inevitably have rendered her unhappy in herself, and unamiable to those whom providence has made her natural guardians. The motives of her nurse might very probably be well intended, but while I would recommend kindness and humanity to every domestic in your family, I would guard you against an implicit confidence or weak adoption of opinions, which neither the education nor observations of this class of persons qualifies them to offer. I am so well assured, that many thoughtless children have been led to conduct of the most undutiful kind, on reasons as unfounded as those which had nearly proved fatal to Miss Wilmot, that I cannot but offer this fact to the consideration of my readers as one very deserving of their serious attention.

The remaining letter was from Mr. Testy, and as I am tempted to believe that many of ye are more amused by them than by my lectures, I am not so ungenerous as to suppress what may give pleasure.

To Mrs. Argus.

Madam,

Being once more in possession of my house I embrace the earliest opportunity of submitting my recent grievances to your consideration. I had fully imagined, that my unequivocal disapprobation of my young visitors conduct, would have induced their mother to restrain them, in a degree, during the remainder of their visit.—I was mistaken. To all my hints she invariably replied—"Dear creatures, this is their season; let them enjoy the present moment." "They have no enjoyment," said I: "do not you perceive that they are constantly projecting some new plan, and never satisfied when they have effected it. Why not inculcate the necessity rather of using than abusing time?" "Cousin, cousin," said my kinswoman, "you quite forget your own youth; were you always consistent?" "I was like other boys, no doubt," said I, "often in the wrong, but I do not remember any period of my life, while blessed by the protection of my parents, that I disputed their commands, or had the vanity to speak and vaunt opinions that were presuming." There was a custom in my youth which seems now quite out of use—that of reproving a child for a fault. I do not think harsh measures justifiable, but if children are laughed at when they should be admonished, and petted when they should experience a temporary banishment from your presence, all sense of duty and respect must be effaced from their minds; and, indeed, I am persuaded, madam, that more mischief is done by laughing at the *wit* of children than people generally imagine. Nay, I have seen this mistaken applause lead them into the heinous crime of falsehood, in order to have a good saying ready for the company. The species of falsehood to which I refer is that of passing off as your own, what you have read in some of those silly compilations called 'Encyclopædias of Wit:' there cannot be a more contemptible sort of vanity, nor one more likely to lead the retailer into the most humiliating situations. I would remind the boy, (for I am positive this foible must be confined to the *masculine* gender) who is thus prone, to look into the Iliad of Homer, who says,—

"Nothing's so tedious as a twice told tale."

This is a feeling of which many are sensible, though politeness seals their lips.

Now my cousin's boys were wits, and they very courageously attempted to pass some of their counterfeit coin upon me.—"I am very sorry you have devoted your time to such light reading," said I, to a well-applied *jeu d'esprit* of one of them.—"*I* say so, cousin," said the boy,—"But the *book* said so before you," said I, and I placed the volume before him. He looked angrily at me, but his kind mother did away all my rebuke, by observing, that next to the actual saying of a good thing, its just application was the best proof of wit: thus the boy remains satisfied of his own talents, and of course considers me a very ill-natured, not to say very ignorant, old fellow.

But I feel that I am intruding upon your invaluable time, madam, and will only beg to subjoin a statement of the expenses to which my young visitors have put me. I am rather eccentric, I own, and as such, have inclosed an exact copy of what follows to my cousin, who will, I trust, see my motives in a just point of view, and give me the happiness, when she next introduces her sons to me, of making a ballance more in favour, and more congenial to my feelings, than that which I have recently dispatched to her.

Edward & Joseph B——— Drs.
To Timothy Testy.

	£.	s.	d.
To damaging the lid of a Tea-urn, by unnecessary pressures, &c.	0	3	6
To breaking 3 Chairs, in a poney race	0	15	6
To demolishing a China Jar, the gift of my dear mother	4	14	0
To expense of repairing Chimney, viz. Sweepers, Brooms, &c. not mentioning the alarm	1	5	0
To a new Looking-glass, shot at with a pea-shooter, Ned being a good marksman	7	10	0
To playing Cricket in the Hall, and thereby breaking the Hall Lamp, though expressly forbidden	3	3	0
Total	17	11	0
Memorandum, intended to have bought Ned a Poney,—prized one at Tattersall's—asked—deduct	14	14	0
Ballance due £	2	17	0

I have no doubt but my cousin will be very angry, when she receives my bill; but as I really have much esteem for her, and her boys will, in the course of time, become the inheritors of my property, I wish her to understand me, and shall be very happy if she takes the hint, and permits me to esteem those, whom it is sincerely my intention to serve. If my letter should not appear too tedious, you may perhaps take the trouble of inserting it in your purposed publication; it may be of service to rash philosophers, and would-be wits:—but I leave this to the discretion of Mrs. Argus, to whom I beg to subscribe myself, a very sincere friend, and well-wisher,

TIMOTHY TESTY.

I felt no hesitation in complying with the request of this gentleman, nor need I make any comment on the contents of his letter. Whimsical as Mr. Testy's manner may appear, I yet discover much justness of reasoning, and a very kind interest in the real happiness of his relations. Children, I believe, very rarely consider those persons their friends, whose candour leads them to tell them of their faults, and it is so usual for people to smile, and commend the follies of childhood, in the presence of their parents, that I certainly can make some allowance for the disappointment their little vanities experience, when a *real* friend ventures to speak the truth.

Edward and Joseph B—— are by this time apprized of their cousin's sentiments, and as a poney is an object of much consideration with boys, they are, perhaps, now vainly regretting their imbecile and babyish horsemanship in the drawing-room of Mr. Testy. I should be glad to hear that they profited by his humorous statement, and I have that opinion of the liberality of their relation, that should they attend to his advice, he will give me the pleasure of acquainting my little friends of a circumstance, always so grateful to my feelings. I dispatched my answers to each of the foregoing epistles, and being somewhat fatigued with writing, I walked to my daughter's. I found Mrs. Mordaunt descending from the drawing-room, in order to see the children dine, and accompanying her into the eating-room, I took my station near the table; there were two young ladies added to the family, whose names I did not immediately recollect, though their features appeared familiar to me. My daughter, however, introduced them as the Miss Barlows, and I now made my inquiries concerning their family. The dinner was simple, and in every respect suited to the little party; but, as I am an avowed *Spectator*, I must not omit to give my sentiments faithfully.

My granddaughter Fanny was seated at the head of the table, and carved the joint of meat placed before her, with much ease and delicacy, by which I mean, that she did not seem to consider it as a very fatiguing business, nor was she so awkward as to spill the gravy, &c. &c. I observed that the Miss Barlows ate very sparingly, and heard Helen, the younger of the two, whisper Harriet, and ask if *she* never ordered her own dinners. Harriet looked much surprised, and answered in the negative.—"Only think how droll," said my little unguarded Harriet,—"the Miss Barlows have what they like for dinner." "Because we are very delicate," said Miss Barlow,—"and do not like mutton." Mrs. Mordaunt immediately ordered some cold chicken to be brought to table for these young epicures, and I beheld with astonishment, that they devoured it, without an idea of the impropriety and great indelicacy of their behaviour; while, with real delight, I perceived on the countenances of the little Mordaunts timid blushes, and very comprehensive looks glanced at each other. These *delicate* young ladies gave us a very copious example of their powers in the eating way; for my own part, I was really afraid they would be injured by their excess, and as gluttony is in itself a most gross and degrading propensity, I was not in the least surprised at the accompanying inelegancies which marked the manners of the Barlows:—they talked loudly during the whole of the meal;—spoke with their mouths full;—handled the bones of the chicken;—and made so great a noise with their lips, that I was really pained at letting such glaring foibles pass unnoticed; but I committed each of them to memory, determined to enlarge on their very odious appearance, and serious tendency on their characters, as females. I must not omit to state, that the knife was more frequently used by these ladies, than the fork;—that they drank without wiping their mouths, and bit their bread, in place of breaking it. Besides which, they more than once remarked, during dinner, "how much they loved chicken, and curry, and asparagus," &c. &c.

The Mordaunts never appeared to such advantage, as on the present occasion. Fanny sat irresolute, and, after some hesitation, asked her visitors if they would eat a bit of rice-pudding? This, as may be supposed, was declined. I saw Mrs. Mordaunt was on the point of ordering something better; but I discouraged the intention by a glance, thinking she had already shewn too much deference to these bold girls.—"Well, I declare I am very glad that I like what my mamma orders for us," said Lucy, "for I suppose she knows best what is good for us." This remark was certainly rather impolite, but the Miss Barlows were not in the least discomposed by it, they continuing to express their liking, and dislike to various dishes, of which my grandchildren knew not even the names. The little party followed Mrs. Mordaunt and myself to the drawing-room, and, as I considered that these young ladies would elicit some other traits of character during their visit, I was very particular in observing them.

"How happy you must be," said Miss Barlow, to Fanny Mordaunt, "you have not a teazing governess to watch you, and tell tales of you." Before Fanny could arrange a reply, Helen added.—"Have you ever *writ* to that ugly old woman, the *Spectator?* I will always hate her; for do you know that Eliza and *me* writ her a letter, and told her how we hated governesses,—and she sent us such an impudent answer, all about charity and grammar, and such stuff;—but the worst of it is, she made mamma get us a governess, for she liked the letter, but she cannot make us like Mrs. Pattin; so Eliza and *me* often call her the old Spectator, and she don't know what we mean, and we make such fun of her."

Here the Mordaunts, as if actuated by one voice, interrupted the talkative and illiberal Helen:—but their praises and their gratitude were so flattering, that I dare not repeat them, lest my readers should consider me a *vain* Spectator;—yet I can assure you, that I felt my cheeks glow with blushes, as they thus added to my *spectatoral* laurels, and it was with some difficulty I refrained from embracing, and thanking them as *I* thought they deserved.

I rather imagine that these little tatlers observed my countenance, for the rest of their conversation was carried on in a loud whisper; but the Mordaunts invariably replied in a voice perfectly to be understood, indeed this was a point in which their mother had always been very particular. She, with myself, deeming the very usual habit of whispering amongst children, as a custom of the most vulgar sort.

Two or three attempts were made by Helen Barlow, to rouse the little Lucy to assert her right to some particular toy, with which the others were engaged. "If it is your own," said Helen, "say you want it,—I would if I was you." "We had better wait," replied

Lucy, "for I have been made quite ashamed of being selfish since Mrs. Argus has written to me." "How can you like that cross old woman?" rejoined Helen, "I declare I cannot bear her name. Why our nursery-maid Jenny Bennet, went away because she advised her to go; and was it not very impertinent of a *servant* to write to the Spectator?" "I am sure I don't know," said Lucy; "come what shall we play at?" Just at this moment Harriet joined them, and with all that liveliness which marks her character, proposed a number of plays, to none of which her visitor assented; "Pray what do you like?" asked the little madcap. "Why something new," said Miss Helen; "I am quite tired of all *them* you have named." "Then pray invent one," said Harriet; "and be quick, or all the day will be gone before we fix upon what we will do." I saw Miss Helen did not much like the playfulness of my granddaughter; whether it damped her powers of invention, or from what other cause I know not, but they never arrived at the happiness of a decision; and while Helen was yet debating on the subject, their carriage was announced; and, I, with secret satisfaction, saw the Miss Barlows depart.

Before I say more of the foibles of these children I will beg to make a general appeal to my readers. Have ye not all of you experienced the feeling I have recently described? viz. been so much at a loss to find an amusement, in which each takes mutual pleasure, that the moment for separation has arrived, before you have come to an agreement. I see the blushes and the looks of reflection, which agitate my little friends;—you are all *guilty* in part; but you remember that if it had not been for Miss M—— or Miss D—— it would have been decided very soon. Perhaps you are correct, and it is well, if your youthful memories do not bring it more home. And, you are spared the recollection that *you* were the dissentient voice. It might not be so easy to prove to you that these irresolute purposes and half-formed plans are lessons of wisdom in disguise, early lessons of the imperfection of all earthly enjoyments; and that they prove most forcibly to you that *we* are very incompetent to judge of what will make us happy, while they equally teach us not to waste the present moment in unmeaning argument, but by using them innocently, prove our gratitude to him who hath "numbered our days."

I am persuaded that I have very little occasion to recur to the subject of gluttony, so unfortunately conspicuous in the character of the Miss Barlows; but as I believe there may be *some* children who have a very favourable idea of *nice* dishes and good things, and that, perhaps, a few have been so imprudent as to interrupt their mother, while giving her orders to the cook, by an anxious desire for a very rich pudding; or the remains of some well-remembered luxury now dismissed from the first table. I beg them to pause on this very unamiable foible; not one of you but will readily perceive how improper the conduct of the Miss Barlows has appeared in this our Chapter. But though I am led to hope that there are very few children like them in all particulars; yet let us not forget the "beam in our own eye," while we are quick to discover "the mote in that of our brother."

That girls of their disposition should be insensible to the kindness of their mother, in engaging a governess to take charge of them, is not in the least surprising, or that they should continue to express themselves in language so ungrammatical is not extraordinary; they are ignorant and self-willed, and unfortunately are indulged by their mother in many points which tend to retard their improvement. Could they be convinced of their errors, and gently directed to that path in which certain success attends their journey, by which I mean, "the path of duty," they might yet become happy and worthy of regard.

If I had not been so fortunate as to have given a very pleasing contrast to these faulty characters in the beginning of this Chapter, I should really have owned much regret at the occasion which brought these little actresses upon our juvenile stage; but as I trust, equally to the humanity as to the liberality of my audience, I am convinced that they will pity the errors of ignorance, and be duly grateful that they possess friends who are watchful and diligent for them.

CHAPTER X

To learn easily, is naturally pleasant to all men.
ARISTOTLE.

AYE, AND TO ALL WOMEN TOO, not omitting to name girls and boys,—but how to learn easily? that is the question! Why really, my dear little friends, I am tempted to venture a very bold opinion, and say, that it is with a few exceptions a very easy matter. I grant that we must begin early and be very strict examiners of ourselves, never passing over a lesson with slovenly haste, nor receiving too much assistance from those who hear us; and the *temper* in mind in which we apply ourselves to any thing, generally illustrates itself in the manner of its performance; if we regard the appointed task as a great deal *too* long, and are rather anxious to count the lines than learn them, I prophecy that the lesson will be bad; if, with presumption, *sometimes* an accompaniment of youth, we are detecting the *author's* ignorances, when we should prove our wisdom by imbibing his sentiments; why here, it is impossible we can gain much, our vanity places us above the instructions of the writer, whose greatest degradation is his having fallen into the hands of a self-sufficient and half-learned critic. If fatigue oppresses us and we are forced to lean on the table, with our elbows spread and the fingers *sometimes* making a tour through the air, every person possessed of *feeling* will compassionate our situation, and take into their consideration that we have many things to do. But there are *some* people who think one can have no occasion for supports of this kind, and who will insist upon it that sitting upright, and even in one's chair gives a seriousness to the deportment that helps the lesson, now it is not possible to shew these ill-natured things, that one will not do *exactly* as they say—have none of you thought of an invention?—ah! I see you have, there are a great number of smiles bestowed upon this page, and I hope some few blushes; for I can develope your plans whether male or female reader. It is so easy to sit a little to the right, or a little to the left, and thus avoid the crime of obedience, and though you may take your elbow off the table you can continue just to touch it, never mind any little pain you may experience from the cramped position in which you hold your arm, the pleasure of proving to your teacher, that you have a will of your own, will amply repay you for any inconvenience of the kind; and a boy of courage, he, too, knows how to play his part: If his tutor dares to think he has not taken sufficient time to learn his lesson, he hesitates to receive the book; "is sure he knows it," &c. &c. If, at last, he is forced to take the book, he looks any where but into it, and with all a dunce's courage again offers himself to be heard; the result may be easily guessed, he says it incorrectly, stands twisting his buttons, or rubbing the table with his coat sleeve, and if his tutor is properly persevering, he not only gets his book again but his task doubled.

Seriously then, my little friends, you want the proper sort of courage when you look upon books as your enemies, and consider lessons as punishments: Quintilian, an ancient author, speaking of children, says, "there is no time of life which is less easily fatigued;" the remark is very just, whether applied to their personal or mental exertions: if the little journeys of children could be accurately calculated, I am persuaded that in the course of a day, it would be found that even very young children walk many miles; and with respect to the powers of the mind, they must be exercised in order to ascertain its capabilities; the earlier we begin the important task of education the more pleasant will the work appear, and though I would certainly recommend to all persons who instruct children, to make it as agreeable to them as possible; I do not entirely approve of a custom now very prevalent, that of making almost every branch of learning a play; with children of dull understandings, it may be necessary to adopt such plans, but I really think it is an offence to an intelligent child, to lead him by any than that sense of duty which should impel every creature to seek knowledge on whom God has bestowed reason; and that all who apply themselves to learning, may, in a degree, acquire that pleasure which is so fully expressed in the motto prefixed to this Chapter, is a truth which has been and is continually offering itself to our observation: how many persons born in obscurity, and reared in ignorance, have, on a sudden, become intense students, and ultimately arrived at excellence.

Yet, are the progressive footsteps to knowledge those from which we expect most,—how gratefully we look upon the flowers which bloom in the spring season; we reflect with conscious delight, that we have done our part in preparing the earth to receive them, and we anticipate the perfection of that *summer* whose early promise thus flatters our care, and from the mind which has been sedulously cultivated, the purest and most graceful blossoms of science may reasonably be expected. Yet, that late education has produced men of great talents, is an unquestionable fact, amongst others, the learned Joseph Scaliger, whose application was of the most extraordinary kind, it is recorded of him, that he learned all Homer by heart in twenty-one days, the Iliad containing 31,670 verses, and the Odyssey about the same number, and in a few months, most of the other Greek poets. As a contrast to him I will mention the great Erasmus, who when a boy had all Terence and Horace by heart.

There are few circumstances that retard the progress of children more effectually than that of pressing *too* much upon their memories in very early youth; yet the necessity of exercising this faculty of the mind, must be obvious to all my young friends; many of whom, I have no doubt, will agree with me, that the more frequently they exercise their memories the greater the facility with which they learn.

That which we acquire by labour is not easily lost, the impression it makes is deep and lasting; and while I would reject the idea of fatiguing or harassing the spirits of a child by very long lessons, I beg to make myself clearly understood. The pupil should submit to the decisions of the teacher, and use his or her exertions to attain the task appointed, and not reject it without a trial;—setting out upon a plan, in effect, resembling the following: viz. "that they are sure it is too much," "that they never had so much to learn before;" "that grown people have no consideration for children;" and "they would not like it if they were children," &c. &c. First prove to your instructors, that they were wrong in having estimated your abilities so highly, and there can be no doubt but *they* will, in future, adapt lessons more suited to the weakness of your capacities.

If I had purposed to swell this work to the extent of two or three volumes, I am much afraid that I could not fully express myself on one subject,—a subject so important to the capacities of the young, that I am really very solicitous to gain converts to my opinion: I mean a respect and affection for those who teach you; unless this actually exists, in a degree, neither happiness nor improvement can result from the association. It was a saying of the ancients, that "no adequate compensation can ever be made to our parents, and to our preceptors, for the benefits they confer upon us:" and in the New Testament it is written "I beseech you that you would take notice of them that take pains with you, and that admonish you; and that you would have them in singular love for their work's sake."

Much has been said, on the pleasure of teaching children, but I am tempted to observe, that the task is not always so pleasant: some of ye will, perhaps, understand me, when I point out a few more facts, which occasionally mix in the school-room exhibitions. Observe, I call that room in which lessons are done by this term, whether in a private family or not. Suppose a scholar is reminded, that to stand erect, and hold the book with both hands, is a graceful and proper custom; and suppose the young lady does not chuse to think it such; she need not use her tongue to express this, but she can throw all the weight of the body on one foot, place her elbow close to her side, and retain the book so slightly that it may fall to the ground once or twice during the lesson. All this may be done, without a word escaping the lips of the little oppositionist; yet she has the power of making her instructress truly unhappy by such conduct. Her simple order being disregarded, she is obliged, in her own defence, because it is her duty, to endeavour at making her pupil tractable, in order to make her happy. I repeat, she is forced to use authority, and restrict the child in some particular, or give her some additional lesson. Then the young rebel calls her ill-natured, and she is sure that no other child has so much to do, and she wishes *she* was any where, and she grumbles and pouts. To what is all this owing?—to want of duty. Children who have been in the practice of observing the commands of a parent will, in every circumstance of their lives, exhibit this graceful and lovely trait of character: they will conform to the wishes of an instructress, because their parent has engaged the person for their advantage: in fact, there is no quality of the human mind so extensive and blissful in its effects as duty: it is the foundation of every virtue; every imaginary hardship fades before this soothing and practicable effort of reason; and the only wonder is, that as nature dictates to every heart the necessity of its practice, that there can be any reasonable creature who wilfully acts contrary to its comfortable influence. When we read of the acts of criminals, and shudder at the enormity of their crimes, we are apt to trace their vices to some neglect of early education, or some natural disposition to evil; but, could we converse with these children of error, I am persuaded, that the real source of almost every species of guilt, originates in want of *duty*.

And though I know some of my little reasoners will find an exception, to this, my observation, and with much quickness remark, that there are children who have become orphans in their infancy, and consequently have never known a parent's care; I answer to this, that it would be difficult, if not wholly impossible, to find a child for whom Providence had not found some kind protector, either as a voluntary benefactor or by the liberal patronage of some public school; and to suppose that *duty* from a child thus benefitted, is not equally to be expected as though they were really bound by the tie of kindred, is to misunderstand the first and most important concern of our life— religion. Are we not told "to submit ourselves to all our governors, teachers, spiritual pastors and masters: to order ourselves lowly and reverently," and what are these commands, but an explicit exposition of our *duty*? not confined to any particular relation, but to all who have charge over us. I make every allowance for the superiority of a parent's claim to our regards; I am not unacquainted with its tender meaning, but I cannot yield my opinion, that *duty*, is the foundation of every virtue; no moral excellence can be attained, but by an early attention to those who guard your infancy; of yourselves, ye are the most helpless and pitiable objects in creation; nature has bountifully provided the animal world with instinct, which enables them to seek for support, and live independent; but the human race depend upon each other, nor can a more tender proof of God's mercy be adduced, than this his gracious ordination of the one great family of nature; we are all the creatures of his bounty, breathe the same air, are warmed by the same sun, and must all and equally return to that dust from which we sprang. Then let us, my dear, amiable young friends, bear in mind the great advantages of our rank in the scale of creation, and by conducting ourselves with humility, prove our sense of those gracious promises, which are in store for those who walk uprightly in the path of duty. Reflection, the grand distinction of our class, reflection being the offspring of *reason*, will, whether we confess it or not, silently admonish us of our errors. Let us not turn from the voice of our friend, but meet her warnings with a sincere and contrite heart; however trivial the lapse, it deserves and acquires correction, let us not add error to error, but remember, that "God is faithful and just to forgive us our sins, and to cleanse us from all unrighteousness."

I will not offer any apology for the seriousness of this my present address. I feel that I am not admonishing beings of an imperfect nature, but creatures whom God has endowed in the perfect image of himself; as such, their gratitude, and their moral pride, should lead them to contemplate their estate with appropriate reverence. "I am here to-day," says the reflecting being, "but I may to-morrow be called into the presence of my God. Am I fitted for a Judge so sublime? have I done my duty here? Lord thou knowest all the secrets of my heart; in thy sight all my actions stand clear and undisguised."

Consider this, ye, who yet in infancy fill a station so important, know, that you are the numbered atoms of an universal family; that your virtues, are the glory of that God, whose mercy is unbounded; and that your errors, however *trivial*, will incur the just displeasure of him, "in whose hands are all the corners of the earth."

It is by mistaking the motives of your instructors, that the foibles to which I have particularly alluded in this Chapter may justly be placed; can you seriously believe, that any thing but a wish to promote your happiness, actuates them; the more minute they are, in their observations on your habits, temper, &c. the greater your obligations to them; and though I have dwelt with a, perhaps, tedious strictness in many *existing* defects in the youthful character, I feel truly grateful, that my own knowledge of many amiable children, leaves me no doubt of that cordial and sincere affection, which should exist between persons situated in the relative characters of pupil and teacher; nay, I am sure, that one dear girl, for whom my warmest feelings are interested, could testify to the truth of my remark; she, like others, may have fallen into *little* errors, but her good sense never led her to *persist* in her foible, and I am persuaded, were she asked the question, that she would not only say she esteemed her governess, but that she loved her.

CHAPTER XI

"The wise and active conquer difficulties
By daring to attempt them: sloth and folly
Shiver and shrink at sight of toil and hazard,
And make th' impossibility they fear."

THOUGH my memory is certainly very correct, considering my age, I cannot trust the impression of the present moment to a future paper, and must therefore briefly state, that I am just returned from a morning ramble, in which such a variety of matter has forced itself upon my imagination, that I really am very anxious to impart my sentiments to my little friends.

My first purpose, on quitting home this morning, was to take a walk in Hyde Park; it is a recreation in which I frequently indulge, not more for the salubrity of its air, than the very extensive opportunity it gives me, of increasing my *spectatoral* knowledge. I have, as yet, been wholly silent on the subject of *walking;* yet it is one that will bear much analysis. I have observed the *trip;*—the *serpentine* scramble, where the ancles appear so distorted, and the figure so debilitated, as to give one a correct idea of a person in a state of inebriety. Next comes the masculine stride, with the arms swinging, and the pocket-handkerchief flaunting in the air. The hobble, with the toes most affectionately whispering each other; and the drawl, where the heels of the shoes are dropping at every step. There are many other methods of walking which might be described, but these shall suffice. If a preference could be given to any of those which I have named, it would certainly be to the trip, which, though somewhat affected, has one advantage,— that of appearing timid,—free from boldness. There were a great number of young persons in the Park, and, as I regarded the general inelegance of their walk, I could not but refer to the probable amount of all the money which had been expended upon dancing-masters for these children, and how completely it had failed in effecting a very simple, though certainly a very graceful, acquirement. My regrets were, perhaps, increased, at perceiving the dresses of many children short, even to impropriety; it made the awkward-ness of their manner more obvious, and I was tempted to think, that to a few it gave an additional air of boldness, perfectly distinct from that soft retiring modesty, at once the greatest beauty, and the peculiar charm of youth. It will appear to my readers, that I am a very particular person, one very difficult to please, when I add, that out of the many whom I saw this morning, I could not select one, whose manner of walking exactly pleased me. I am so fully persuaded, that walking is of more use than dancing, with very young children, that, for my own part, I would not permit a child (more especially a girl) to learn one step with a dancing-master, until she had acquired a firm and equal habit of walking. I know that all the good teachers of this art, begin by exercising their pupils in marching;—but this, either to please the children, or the parent, is too soon laid aside, and the consequences remain obvious, frequently through life. I should certainly lament to believe, that much time is dedicated to dancing, the uses of which are so unimportant to females in private life; nor do I ever hope to see greater knowledge in this art displayed, than that which tends to make children upright in their carriage, and easy in their walk: I do not mean to restrain them from the innocent, and very grateful recreation, of dancing occasionally; but, as I have some reason for thinking that these sort of meetings have a serious effect upon the minds of children; that they derange the regular system of education, and actually unfit them for their duties, I would certainly be very cautious in admitting them to interfere with those whom I loved. If, in your own family, you combine the requisites for a social ball, where neither dress, anticipation, nor late hours, lend their baneful influence, there cannot be a more innocent or healthy exercise.

But I have strayed from walking to dancing, even just as my little readers would feel inclined to do; but I must beg of them, to allow an old woman to walk by their side, yet a little longer. Let me ask of you one simple question;—Are you not anxious, in all your amusements, to make them as perfect as possible? Not one of you but could, with sincerity, reply in the affirmative:—then why neglect to make a duty, however trivial, perfect? It is probable that you may pass through life, having very few occasions to exert yourselves in dancing; but walking is indispensable to health, and is, of itself, a very great enjoyment:—rest assured, there is no acquirement, however simple, to which a certain degree of attention is not actually necessary; and, though the youthful idlers may not so readily admit this truth, the time will come, when they shall not only believe, but lament, their inattention. It would be impossible to enumerate all the various trifles, which appear as blemishes to an observing eye. We will drop the subject of walking, with a sincere wish, that some of my faulty pedestrians will take the hints given to them, and I will, by way of proving that trifles have an influence in deforming the appearance, and lessening the perfections, of the human character, illustrate my remark by a few facts.

I knew a lady, whose understanding was highly cultivated, and whose sentiments were consequently listened to with respect; yet, a very sensible pain was experienced by those to whom she addressed herself, by a habit she had of winking her eyes: the movement was so quick and incessant, that I have really felt my own eyes greatly weakened by looking at her, yet she appeared unconscious of it.

I have heard of an Englishman, of great talents, who was sent as ambassador to a foreign court, where his mind and manners were fully appreciated. It happened, that his qualifications were the subject of conversation amongst the courtiers one evening; each spoke of him as learned, affable, and polite. At length, a very polished and distinguished character, made this remark:—"I have observed him attentively, and am obliged to dissent from your eulogium in one particular; if he made less noise in *eating*, he would be all that you have said."

Another lady, for whom I have a sincere esteem, absolutely distracts the attention of those with whom she converses, by a waving motion of her body, if seated on a heavy chair; but, if the seat happens to be a light one, the chair takes the motion, and you are in expectation of her falling upon her face.

Neither of these inelegancies are acquired late in life; they are the unchecked or neglected foibles of youth, which have "grown with the growth, and strengthened with the strength," and I can very easily believe, are difficult to be eradicated.

Then how important does it make these trifles, with those who are yet under tuition! How evident must it be, even to the youngest of my readers, that they should listen to the voice of friendship, nor deem any habit too trivial to be corrected!

I have hitherto been silent upon the subject of personal vanity; indeed, excepting in the instance of Harriet Mordaunt's reference to her grandmamma's mention of her beauty, I had hoped to have no occasion to revert to this excessive folly:—but permit me here to add, that Harriet has been completely laughed out of her vanity, and has had the sense to allow, that duty and good-humour make the only beauty that is lasting, or worthy of esteem.

But I was going to observe, that we are never too *old* to learn: I, like an obstinate old woman, had not imagined that *personal* vanity was so general a foible; but alas! I find it exists under such a variety of characters, that I am compelled to devote a few pages, to corroborate my assertion.

One young lady avoids the fire in the morning, because it will catch her skin, and make her look coarse and heated;—but in the evening she leans on the fender, because a colour makes her look *pretty* at night.

Another tries on half a dozen necklaces, to discover which becomes her best; and will stand twenty minutes in the cold, to decide a matter so ridiculous, and, perhaps, grumbles at devoting half that time to her prayers, because "it is so cold."

A third is continually combing and brushing her hair,—the former sometimes in company; and while she is thus assiduous about external appearance, her mind remains rough and unpolished.

A fourth bites her lips, and simpers, and smiles, or laughs very heartily, in order to display her teeth, which have been denominated by some very *sincere* friend, "rows of pearl:" thus the laugh is always so ready, that the young lady passes for an idiot with the discerning observer, who deeply laments, that the child had not the sense to discern, that the subject was one which had claimed her sympathy, rather than her mirth.

A fifth has such *beautiful* little feet, that her shoes are of the greatest importance to all the family; no expense is too much to decorate the *pêtit pied*; and, of course, the young lady thinks her feet of more consequence than her head, or her heart.

How I pity these unfortunate children; and how sincerely do I wish, that if *any* one of the foibles I have here illustrated, attach to my readers, that they would take the trouble of reflecting upon it; it requires only common sense, to place *every* personal beauty in its just point of view. I remember reading a very descriptive and pleasing poem, entitled, the "Two Dolls," in which this perishable perfection is very justly delineated. In one part it says:

> "A fever's heat may spoil the grace,
> And quickly change the fairest face."

In another part:

> "Nor can the loveliest form dispense,
> With want of virtue, nor of sense."

And the moral of this (to me) valuable little poem, is particularly expressive:

> "Be uniformly good, perfection seek,
> And let the face a kindred mind bespeak."

I know that many of my young friends will pause upon these pages, and perhaps a few will refute my assertion, that personal beauty is of no consequence, because their memory helps them to the recollection of numberless compliments, addressed to them, on their entering the drawing-rooms of their mammas.—"I am sure" says Miss Patty Dazzle "that whenever *I* go into the drawing-room, every body calls me a lovely creature, and they say I shall be quite beautiful:"—while Cordelia Connelly, with equal truth, reverts to the many praises bestowed upon her person, under the appellations of—"a sweet little fairy,"—"an enchanting sylph," &c. &c.

Admitting that these things do actually occur, yet are they wholly unworthy of your regard, or remembrance: they are frequently uttered by persons who have scarcely looked at you, and are merely the common-place expressions of flatterers, who will not be at the trouble of discovering, whether you really possess qualities that deserve praise.

The graces of a cultivated mind, are the beauties which adorn the features of the young, a timid, yet chearful manner, a heart so practised in its duties, that a parent's displeasure would, but I will not say what should constitute the perfection of infant beauty, but relate my morning's perambulation faithfully, and leave the portrait for my readers to copy.

In my way from the Park, I called upon a friend in Brook Street. Mrs. Warren was instructing her daughter on my entrance. I apologized, fearing that I should interrupt the studies of Miss Warren, but my friend assuring me that her daughter would know how to dispose of her time, I took a seat, and entered into conversation with Mrs. Warren. I was not so much engrossed by the subject, but that I was at liberty to remark the manners of this child. I saw her take a dissected map and unite it with much facility. She then reached a book from the stand, and, retiring to a corner of the room, I perceived that she was acquiring some lesson, which I imagined to be poetry, by heart. This done, she resorted to her slate, which was clean, and to which a sponge was suspended—a custom which I sincerely wish was more general. Her calculation seemed quick, nor did I perceive that her finger played that sort of gamut, sometimes harmonized on the frame of the slate; on the contrary, her head appeared perfectly competent to the attempt, and as I saw her compare her sum with the assistant, and that a smile of expressive pleasure passed over her features, it was as satisfactory an answer to my enquiring look as her's was to the book from which she sought her information. All this passed so smoothly, with such an appearance of ease and method that I could not refrain from expressing my admiration of this amiable child to her mother. "Julia is a very good girl," said my friend. "She knows that I love her too well to require of her any thing beyond her capacity; and she is equally sensible that it is her duty to attend to my wishes." Now Julia Warren is by no means handsome, but I declare that as I gazed on this child, and beheld the modest blush which suffused her cheek at her mother's judicious praise, she appeared to me the handsomest child I had ever seen. Her eyes sparkled with animation, her countenance was open and expressive, and though she did not assume in consequence of her mother's approbation, it was very evident that she was gratified by it.

Julia soon after quitted the room, as I learned from my friend, to practise her music previous to the arrival of her music-master. It was then that I was fully gratified by the character of this amiable girl. Mrs. Warren spoke of her with freedom. She assured me that she could not call to mind *one* instance in which Julia had ever disputed her wishes; that her lessons were appointed for her, that she knew they were to be learned, and had a regular method of doing them. "If any friend favours me with a call," continued Mrs. Warren, "she avails herself of the immediate interruption, and turns to some other of her pursuits. I have never heard her express fatigue while at her lessons; in fact, she has never caused me a sigh since she was born, but when it pleased God to afflict my little treasure with those sicknesses incident to infancy."

Compliments, smiles, and praises, are, as I have illustrated, frequently applied to children; but, in this case, like a very odd old woman, as you will no doubt think I am, I could not repress a rising tear; the beauty of Julia Warren's mind claimed my delighted admiration, and as I looked forward, and anticipated her gradual advancement into life—her mind expanding, and her intellects gathering strength, I saw her an ornament to society, a comfort to her parents, and above all, when it should please God to call her hence, is she not of that class to whom the Omnipotent hath promised the "blessed hope of everlasting life," for "the pure in heart shall see God."

Much as I have said of Julia Warren, greatly as I admire her unaffected and amiable character, I am not so light an observer of causes and effects as to be insensible to the grand source of her present happiness. Her mother is at once the most gentle and discerning of women. She is a mother, with all a mother's tenderness, but none of those weaknesses which destroy the power of a parent; Julia has never been indulged, consequently she has no imaginary wants. And though she is not the companion of servants, she has been accustomed to administer to their comforts. She has been directed by her amiable mother to listen to the tale of domestic distress, to give the comfortable cloathing to the aged, to assist in making raiment for the helpless infant, to send coals to the shivering inhabitant of a chearless garret; to do all this without an idea of ostentation, but upon the firm basis of Christian principles, that they were needy, and Heaven had blessed her with the power to succour them in their distress.

I am so impressed with one species of vanity at this moment that I cannot forbear avowing it. I feel that I have engaged a number of admiring little friends for the amiable Julia. I hear you all, as with one voice, exclaiming, "What a delightful girl!" and a few, perhaps, are wishing that they had the power to act as Julia does. Here my vanity subsides and my regrets will interfere. Alas! are not many of ye blind to the advantages ye possess? Do not you expend your money in toys and trifles? Are not sweets very tempting? Charity does not consist in giving away that which you cannot use yourselves. Such an action is often performed by the most selfish and illiberal character, who from satiety and a love of novelty, gladly dispenses with that which is now valueless to them. Charity is the gentlest of all the virtues, the most retired, at the same moment that it is the most exalted, feeling of the human breast. It leads its amiable votaries to forego or abridge their own comforts in order to be serviceable to others. It is secret in its offerings, because it is conscious that even the most exalted deed that mortal can perform is poor, in comparison of those benefits which Providence has bestowed on thousands of happy beings; while that conscious peace which a duty so strictly in obedience to the commands of God incites, exalts its amiable dispensers, even in this life, to a rank to which no other application of the goods of fortune could raise them. They carry in their own bosoms, "that peace which the world cannot give." And, indeed, I would advise my readers to consider all the advantages of their various situations in life. From those who possess but little, little can be expected; but the purity of their intentions will enhance the gift, while such as own more extensive power, let them, with equal humility, make their offering.

I have another amiable and truly generous girl, to whom I will introduce my readers before I take my leave; but as I have already made this Chapter very diffuse, I must defer it for the present.

Though the particular manner in which I have specified the foibles of personal vanity are strictly conformable with truth, I have too much regard for the feelings of the parties to be more explicit. I am persuaded this volume will fall into the hands of one or two at whom I have glanced, and as the understanding always slumbers where Vanity erects her throne, I sincerely hope that my little friends will demolish the tottering fabric, and lay a foundation in their minds less liable to decay. Almost every person is capable of admiring a finished picture or a perfect character; but if we are contented to admire, nor seek into the requisite qualities which constitute the whole, we shall remain superficial and light observers through life. We must reform our defects, not shrinking from self-examination nor judging with partiality. We must not imagine that a day of repentance can eradicate the foibles which have been gaining upon us for months, perhaps years. Nor are we to be deterred from the attempt under the idea that the task is impracticable. Every thing is possible to a zealous heart; and the path of virtuous duty is so blooming and pleasant, Hope strews her blossoms so bounteously where duty and a sincere desire of improvement actuates the traveller, that I cannot conclude this Chapter without exhorting my little friends to commence their journey, and wishing them all the well-known happiness that ever results to travellers who take this road.

CHAPTER XII

"Time flies, oh how swiftly!"

THOUGH I DID once express an opinion, that the Miss Barlows would become my regular correspondents, I no sooner recognised them at my daughter's, and heard their conversation, than I dismissed the idea, well pleased to escape a task so hopeless as that of correcting girls so evidently ignorant and self-willed. Mrs. Mordaunt, like myself, disapproved of their manners, and, consequently, was sedulous in checking all intercourse between her family and the Miss Barlows. It is with sincere pleasure that I record this as the only correspondence from which I have receded. It is true, that Charles Osborn is prominent and giddy; yet one is more disappointed in finding a girl voluble and bold. No excuse can be made for females who act thus. After being admonished, had the young ladies in question evinced any symptoms of delicacy, I would gladly have volunteered my pen in their service. They have compelled me to leave them to their follies, and I much doubt if they will ever own a friend who will be at the trouble of directing them to the attainment of happiness.

It has often surprised me (even before I took upon me my present character) when I have of an evening reflected upon the unexpected variety which has chequered the day; but, really, since I have avowed myself a Spectator, it has appeared infinitely more obvious than ever; yet, perhaps, this is to be imputed to that watchful zeal with which I regard every thing which can possibly lead to my object.

But while I have been thus active for my little friends, Time has not been idle. He has closed one year, and brought me to the opening of another. I must not suffer this ceaseless traveller to pass unheeded; indeed, he has reminded me that a new year is not the most ineligible season for a present, and I am now almost regretting that I had not so arranged my plans, as to offer myself to your favour at the commencement of this year. It cannot be, and I must endeavour to flatter myself that you will be glad to see me, come when I may.

It is so impossible to form an exact idea of the reception I am to meet from my young patrons, that I really am growing very timid as I refer to the number of pages written, and feel the propriety of drawing towards a conclusion. Perhaps, you will receive me kindly, and encourage me to address you again; and it may so happen that my truths shall give offence, and you may reject me as a most impertinent old woman. I must await my fate, and, in the interim, as you have not the power to interdict my enjoyments, I shall continue to ramble in the Park, and make my circuits in certain squares; nay, it is very probable that I may jostle some of my young critics, for I am not an *imaginary* character. But let me ask of you that respect due to my age. Ah! do not wound my ears by your sarcasms. I am persuaded, that, like Charles Osborn, you will often *think* you have discovered the Spectator, yet I will venture to affirm, that you never will fix upon the right person. As such, be very cautious in your observations, and though each of you has sketched my figure in your own mind, do not let your fancies influence your judgment. To prove to you that I am prepared for the jibes and jeers of a youthful public, I am tempted to describe a few of those appearances, under which the "Juvenile Spectator" will be sought by the younger branches of the "Argus" family. In the first place, any elderly person who walks with a stick, and should chance to look about her, or who should take a seat upon one of the trees in the Park, or the benches in Kensington Gardens; if she appears thoughtful, or in the least observing, she will instantly be suspected. Again, a person of morose countenance, or whose nose should unfortunately happen to be rather longer than the generality of noses, she will certainly be a suspicious sort of person. Harriet Mordaunt, who is always ready with some lively remark, declared, the other day, that she believed the "Spectator" to be very much like "Mother Goose" in the pantomime of that name. I waited with some anxiety to observe the effect of this opinion. William, who was at home for a few days, and who was in fact the cause of their theatrical treat, expressed himself somewhat warmly in reply. "I am sure you are quite wrong, Harriet," said he, "for though I have no good reason for thinking so, I cannot help fancying that the 'Spectator' is like grandmamma, and I believe it is that which makes me like her so much." Fanny observed, that it was quite ridiculous to speak of "Mother Goose" and the "Spectator" at the same time, and she was very sorry that Harriet had done so. While Lucy, who often surprises me by the justness of her sentiments, asked Fanny why she was sorry about it. "Because," said Fanny, "I am afraid I shall in future always think of 'Mother Goose' when the 'Spectator' is named." "I wonder at you, Fanny," replied Lucy, "it seems quite strange to me. The 'Spectator' appears like a friend whom it would be very unkind to laugh at, but 'Mother Goose' is just the figure to make one laugh." "Just so," retorted William; "that is exactly what I mean. No one would expect 'Mother Goose' to give advice to children; and I am certain that the 'Spectator' is not a woman who could act the part of 'Mother Goose.'" I took part in the conversation at this juncture, and seized the passing moment to illustrate the absurdities into which a false association of ideas must necessarily lead such young reasoners. I brought them to coincide in my sentiments, and though the variety in their characters is striking, it was with unfeigned delight that I perceived each of them esteemed me under my assumed name. I could be as whimsical as the most lively of my readers, and go on describing myself under my probable appearances in public; but I must repress these juvenile feelings, for I hear a post-rap, and the well known creak of Michael's shoes assure me, that letters have been delivered for me.

My sagacity must already be so obvious to my friends, that I forbear expatiating on the subject. I was right;—four letters are now laying on my writing-table:—Mr. Testy's hand is now so familiar to me, that I instantly recognised it; and, as I am rather inclined to expect some pleasing consequences, from his whimsical proceedings with his young relations, I will give his letter precedence.

To Mrs. ARGUS.

MADAM,

I am sure you will rejoice with me on the success of my plan:—the rogues have paid my bill on demand, and written me such a receipt, that I actually believe I shall have it framed and glazed, and hung up in my drawing-room. I must be brief, as I have come to the resolution of going into ——shire to-morrow, in order to do away all my cousin's schemes. She, poor soul, is at last convinced of the necessity of curbing the lively spirits of her boys, and, like all people who have suffered their reason to slumber, she is now going into extremes, and has hinted, that she is about to place them at a school, fifty miles distance from their paternal home. This must not be: I will have the boys with me for a few months; they shall be trained into the habits usual with well-educated children. I will engage proper tutors for their instruction, and when they can, with safety to their characters as gentlemen, and emulative scholars, be presented at a public school, what pleasure I shall derive in the office! I inclose their epistle, which will be more satisfactory than any thing I could say, and beg to assure you, that I am, very respectfully,

Your obliged and obedient servant,

TIMOTHY TESTY.

(Inclosed in the foregoing.)

We are quite ashamed, dear cousin, yet we are determined to tell you the exact truth: we *did* think you very cross and particular; but, indeed, we now know that you are perfectly right. A brother of our dear papa's, has been here about a fortnight; he is a very good man, I believe, only he has lived many years in the West Indies, and he is hasty, and speaks so quick, that we are quite afraid of him. He does not advise us what to do, but scolds at us, and calls us block-heads, and tells my mother that she is a foolish woman. Now this we cannot bear, because all she does, is out of kindness and love for us, so Joe and I spoke out the other day, and told him so; but he would not listen to us, and gave poor Joe such a pinch of the ear, that he cried out with the pain. All this made us think of you; so we talked together, and thought how very ill we had behaved, when you used to explain to us what we ought to do. Well, soon after comes your letter; —oh! if you had but seen us:—why, what an expense! Joe declares, that the very first money he ever has of his own, he will buy all the things you name, quite new, and send them to you. I do not wish to see you again, till we are able to pay for the damages we have done. I dare say we should both think more about the poney, only, just now, we cannot help fretting about something;—but I suppose my mother has told you we are going to school:—perhaps it is best, but I am afraid we shall be expected to know more than we do. You may be certain we will pay you whenever we can;—till then, good bye.

EDWARD and JOE.

This letter was almost as acceptable to me, as it could be to Mr. Testy. There was much nature in the sentiments; all the proper shame of ingenuous minds; and these feelings did not grow out of the regrets they experienced from their cousin's statement of what they had lost by their follies, but had risen upon the most conclusive of all reasoning,—the comparative state of things. They evince, that they had discernment enough to distinguish between the tenderness of that advice, which friendship alone dictates, and the harsh mandates of discordant authority. They had drawn the line, I repeat, before the receipt of Mr. Testy's letter, and in this case, they had made one step towards improvement; for whoever looks back upon their foibles with *real* shame, and compares the happiness they have rejected, with their *present* imperfect portion of comfort, has proved, that they possess reasoning powers; and who, that is blessed with intellect, would continue the slave of bad habits? no one, and *I* will answer for the boys in question. I entertain the most favourable hopes of them, and most sincerely do I wish, that all mismanaged and spoiled children, had a relation who knew how to apply to their foibles, as Mr. Testy has done to his kinsmen.

The next letter, actually threw me into a tremor, nor will my young friends be surprised, when I explain that it was *written* by Dennis O'Brien, for my grandson William. I ran over it hastily, and my fears were appeased, but, as Mr. O'Brien's letter is well worth transcribing, I must not anticipate, but clear my spectacles, and endeavour to give it to my readers in the best way I can.

To Mrs. ARGUS.

MADAM,

My friend Mordaunt has requested me to write to you for him, he says he will dictate the letter, but to this I will not consent; as he has been ordered to be kept quiet, and not to talk, he agrees to my terms, and I will now begin.

You know Charles Osborn so well, that I need not describe him. Yesterday, Lord M———, Mordaunt, and I, were walking our limits, when just as we came by a stile, we saw an old woman, trying to lift a pail of water over the stile; Mordaunt ran forward and bade her stop, and he would assist her, he had got into the field, before we perceived that Osborn, and two of his cronies were behind the hedge. "You may well look

'He took the Pail and muttered something about he wished his Mother knew how ill he was used.'

ashamed," said the old woman, "you see though you thought fit to laugh at me, and throw stones into my pail, your betters will assist me;" we instantly made a ring round these young fellows, and desired the woman to state exactly how they had behaved to her; she did, and we found that they had abused and laughed at her, interrupted her in her work, and increased the weight of her pail, by throwing heavy stones into it. Osborn defended himself by saying, that he hated all women, especially those who were old. Lord M——, who is very keen, instantly proposed, that the pail should be carried by Osborn, to the brook in the adjoining field, that he should clean it from the dirt thrown into it, fill it afresh, and bring it to the stile for the woman. Osborn flounced at first, but Lord M——, is one of the monitors, and indeed, we generally carry our point, when once we have formed a resolution. He took the pail, and muttered something about he wished his mother knew how ill he was used; "Po'h," says I, "your mother is a woman, you know, and you hate all women;" "But she is a gentlewoman," said Charles. "And a pretty cub you are for the son of a gentlewoman," replied Lord M——; "go, sir, go directly;" and he followed Osborn to the brook, stood over him while he performed his task, and walked by his side to the stile again. Osborn's party were laughing in the hope that they should escape altogether, but we made two of them lift the pail over the stile, and carry it to the door of the old woman's cottage. Lord M—— told her, that if she ever found them troublesome again, she was to go up to the school and ask for him: the poor woman was much surprised when Mordaunt, and Lord M——, gave her some money; I was sorry I had none to give, but I am very much limited in my pocket-money, and do not get it regularly; I name this as an excuse, for I was really much ashamed at the time. Well, we all returned to school, and resolved not to take any further notice of the business, as we knew we had mortified these fellows properly: but in the evening, Mordaunt told me, he was certain that some plan was in agitation against the old woman; we kept a good look out, and about half an hour before the last bell, we ran down the village, and soon found our fears were right, for the glass of the casement, was almost entirely taken out of the window, and the cottage door, faced with mud and stones. While we were thinking how to act, Osborn with one of his chums, came round from the garden, each of them with a duck under his arm; if you had but seen them,—they let go the bills of the ducks, which instantly began quacking; we seized them by the arms, and the poor woman alarmed by the noise, opened the bed-room window, we explained matters to her, and cleared her door, then ordering our prisoners to march, and promising to call at the cottage next morning, we proceeded towards school. I believe Mordaunt and I laughed a little and I remember we called them deserters, which so enraged Osborn, that he turned round and spit in Mordaunt's face; Mordaunt could not bear this, so they fell to, and Osborn got it completely; I never saw a neater thing; he roared and cried all the way home; but poor Mordaunt sprained his shoulder, which however will not be of any consequence, as the doctor has assured us; this accounts for my writing to you. Mordaunt wants to know if he shall acquaint his mother with particulars, but he begs me to say he really does not feel ill, and thinks it would alarm her very much. I have made this a very long letter, but I was forced to be explicit, as Mordaunt would not be satisfied without it.

I am, madam,
Your obedient servant,
DENNIS O'BRIEN.

P. S. I should have told you that Osborn was much bruised and Lord M——, who came in to see how matters were going, made such a good placard about him, and placed it upon his bed-curtains,—for it was explaining, that the young woman-hater, had been indebted to the kindness of five women in less than an hour; which was true, for one woman bathed his ancle with vinegar, another put brown paper to his forehead, a third cut away the hair, which had got mixed with a little wound in the side of his head, a fourth made him some whey, and Mrs. Horton who is the nurse, sat by him great part of the night; so I think, he has very little reason to speak ill of the women.

Throughout this epistle, there appeared to me, a liberality and openness of character truly delightful. The accident under which my grandson was suffering, though treated lightly by his generous friend, yet awakened my fears; and I instantly addressed a note to my daughter, to inquire how they all were, assured, that if any serious consequence had ensued, she would have been apprized of it by the master, and indeed I did not feel that I could make all the inquiries necessary in a personal visit, at least it was more than probable, I should betray my fore-knowledge. Michael returned with a note which in a degree tranquillized my feelings; they were all well. The next letter was from a new correspondent, it ran thus.

To Mrs. ARGUS.

MADAM,

As a great variety of characters must necessarily have come under your consideration, during your present inquiry; I take the liberty of requesting your advice, as to what method you would recommend to a person situated as I am. I have lately undertaken the charge of a young lady, Miss Caroline Cavil; she is in her twelfth year, but certainly very unformed, both in mind and manners, yet, *she* never allows herself to be in the wrong, but *justifies* every foible, every mistake, with an address and volubility quite painful to those interested for her; if she misreads a sentence and receives a check from me, she instantly discovers, that it would be greatly improved by being corrected according to *her* reading; if a passage in her music is either beyond her capacity to perform, or that she *omits* some of the notes, the tune is ugly, or she *recollect*[s] that she played the *same* passage yesterday, exactly in the same way, and I did not find any fault, and she *sees* I am angry with her, and only find out occasion to oppose her; in short, Miss Cavil, in her own opinion, never is wrong. You may easily imagine how irksome my task must be; yet I am unwilling to resign this child, without giving her a longer trial, more especially as her parents are very amiable, and I do not shrink from difficulties; but, really, if I had not had some experience in the instruction of children, I should consider the present a hopeless case. The disposition of this young lady is entirely new to me. I have paid much attention to various and excellent writings on education, but am now more than ever certain, that a complete and practical system can never be generally applied: even in the same families, how different are the dispositions! and I have from sad experience proved, that in moving from one square to another, it is possible to find a difference as great as between the polished inhabitants of ancient Greece, and the scarcely rational native of Caffraria. I should be greatly obliged by your answer, madam, and I beg to subscribe myself,

Your obedient servant,
MARTHA MORRISON.

——street,
Portman square.

The fourth, and last letter was from Miss Wilmot. I feel that this young lady is a favourite with my readers, and I in consequence transcribe her epistle.

To Mrs. ARGUS.

Dear MADAM,

We are going into Wales, and shall remain there many months, but I could not leave town without acquainting you, that I am quite happy; my papa and mamma, are pleased to express themselves satisfied with my conduct, and my dear Mrs. Arnold does not find fault with me very often, and when she does, I know that she is perfectly right in all she says. I often think of my foolish prejudices, and can never be sufficiently grateful to all those kind friends, who were at the trouble of directing me how to conquer my faults. Nurse Jones really makes me smile sometimes, she praises my mamma so much, and declares that she feels she was very wicked in speaking ill of a lady who was quite a stranger to her; I hope I am now so well convinced of the danger of all prejudices, that I shall never in future forget myself. Mrs. Arnold begs me to offer her compliments to you, madam, and I trust you will believe, that I never shall forget your kindness to

Your most respectful,
and obedient servant,
SOPHIA WILMOT.

The complaint of Mrs. Morrison, was of a nature that required consideration: I entered into her feelings, and was truly sorry, that a girl of Miss Cavil's disposition should be introduced to my acquaintance at *this* period of my history, yet I resolved on answering her governess to-morrow. My best wishes attend the amiable Sophia, whose welfare through life will always be a point of much interest with me; and now, though I have more than once declared, that I do not yield to unnecessary fears in matters which relate to my grandchildren, I must be ingenuous, I shall not be happy, till I call in ——— street. I know that a note may be conveyed from the school by the carrier; and in fact there is a thousand ways in which news may be brought, and as all these ways will suggest themselves to my mind, I must even go and satisfy myself of particulars.

CHAPTER XIII

"What a goodly prospect spreads around."

As I approached my daughter's house, I saw a chaise drive off, and, with a palpitating heart, discovered as it passed me, that it belonged to ——— ——— but upon entering the hall, the servant quieted my fears, by assuring me that Master Mordaunt was not ill. I hastened into the drawing-room, and found the young visitor, surrounded by his family, while a fine tall boy was in the act of reciting that statement, which I have already given to my readers. Now I know you will all laugh at me, but I ask you to recollect, that I am an old woman, and a grandmother. Well, to proceed, I forgot my original wish of *concealment*, and turning to my grandson, "My dear William," said I, "why did you fight with that silly boy Osborn, you should have treated him with silent contempt." William was going to reply, when his friend declared it was impossible for any body to bear an insult like that, which Osborn had offered to him. "I must differ from you sir," said I, "the action was so beneath a gentleman, that I consider William to have degraded himself by resenting it;" the young champion shook his head, while William with a look of astonishment, asked how I had become acquainted with the circumstance. The question absolutely called blushes into my cheek; I paused for a moment, and then in a half whisper told him I would explain the particulars bye and bye. I was now apprised by my daughter, that she received a note early in the morning from William's master, saying, that he was a little indisposed, in consequence of having sprained his hand, and that, as a young gentleman, on whom he could depend, was going to town in a few hours, he should put Master Mordaunt under his care; he concluded by adding, that the season, had no such accident happened, would have entitled the pupils to a few days relaxation from study. I have often observed, that when once one has commenced by blundering a secret, we follow it up, by numberless

"Will you all continue to love your
Grandmother, when you hear her desire
that she is the Spectator."

trips of the tongue. Thus I addressed William's companion as Mr. O'Brien; I was right
in my conjecture, it was my amiable correspondent, and so interested was I in his plans,
that without considering how deeply I was plunging, I begged to know if he would not
remain with William during his short vacation: my daughter, who was equally pleased
with the manner and appearance of this youth, seconded my proposal with all the
eagerness of a mother; our efforts were unsuccessful, yet declined with that engaging
modesty, which yet more warmly interested us for him. He declared, he should be very
happy to accept our invitation, but that his guardian had called him to town suddenly,
and he was afraid he should not return to school again. "I am to go to India," continued
young O'Brien, "my parents had great interest there, and I hear it is the best that can
be done for me now." I thought there was an air of sadness in his countenance, while
giving this explanation, which seemed forcibly to express, that he did not like the
decision. We endeavoured to represent the many advantages which might result from
an eastern residence, and that the earlier he went out the better. But we could not
convert him to our opinion, and as William's lameness was not such as to affect his
spirits, we united in beguiling the time in as lively a way as possible. At length Mr.
O'Brien took leave, after having promised to engage his guardian's permission to dine
with the Mordaunts next day.

"Now, grandmamma," said William, as the door closed upon his friend, "now tell
me how you knew so well what had happened at ———. I have long had my suspicions
about you," continued the smiling boy. "I should be very unfit for that character which
I have assumed," I replied, "if I was to be disingenuous on any occasion; will you all
continue to love your grandmother, when you hear her declare that *she* is the *Spectator*."
"I thought so," says William, clapping his hands, "I knew it, it was so like your manner, and the hand-writing altogether, I have often said to myself that it must be you."
"Dear grandmamma," said Fanny, "I am quite happy to find that you are the Spectator."

"Why so, my love," said I. "Because," replied Fanny with a blush, "I would rather that you knew my faults than any body else in the world." "You know that I once told you in a letter, that I thought you like Grandmamma Harley," said Harriet; while Lucy declared, that she had most reason to rejoice, as her foibles had been much worse than any of her family's. "Upon comparison, my dear children," I interjoined, "your grandmother has much reason to be satisfied; I cannot term any of your little errors more than foibles; they had not amounted to faults, and I am so persuaded, that your own sense of right, and the certainty that nothing but my love for you actuated me to adopt the plan, which has so happily answered my expectations, that I shall resign my fictitious name, with the full conviction, that as children who love their parents, and creatures whom God has endowed with the power of reflection, you will henceforth act agreeably to reason. I admit, that it was not my *intention* to make myself known, your sagacity has defeated my plan, which is, in a degree, a disappointment, as Mrs. Bently, who has greatly assisted my views during my spectatoral inquiries, has been very anxious that I should publish the result. Will you agree to this?" I asked, turning to my little audience. "Oh! dear!" said the children in one voice, "why people would know us, and we should be quite ashamed to be seen." My daughter, who had really been as much surprized by my avowal as her family, now entered into the subject, and learning that I had actually arranged my papers so as to form a volume, she suggested, that, by changing the names of the parties, I might yet prosecute my intention. The children readily assented to this, and were soon brought to laugh in idea as they anticipated the publication of their letters.

I could not take leave of these dear creatures without making some observations on the general conduct of my grandson as a school-boy. I applauded his judicious choice in his friends. I commended his zeal in the service of the poor old woman. Each of these traits in his character evinced manliness and humanity, principles always synonymous; for the brave are uniformly generous and compassionate. His watchfulness in endeavouring to guard the cottager from the further cruelty of her petty agressor was commendable; but I could not understand the necessity of his fighting with an ill-bred coward, admitting that he received an insult. It should be remembered, that we are expressly forbidden to resent an injury; and that the most perfect being that ever wore the human form, was "persecuted, reviled, put to bodily pain, and finally to death;" yet he neither reviled again, nor was wrought to anger during any of the stages of his sufferings, and has left us in this, as in every record of his perfect life, a point for our admiration, and an example for our humble imitation.

It is by commanding our passions that we prove the strength of our reason. So many causes, trivial in themselves, have led to that most criminal of all contests, duelling, that I consider the government of the temper a matter of most serious consequence with boys in particular. Very few of the causes which induce boys to fight but would, upon reflection, appear in a very ridiculous and laughable point of view. Here William interrupted me. "What do you think, grandmamma, that to have a fellow, less than myself, spit in my face was a thing to be laughed at." "I think so, my dear," said I, "and for the very reason you have stated; he was less than you, and it was not only an ungentlemanlike action but a baby's revenge, and your contempt would have mortified him much more than your resentment; more especially as, according to that code of honour observed by school-boys, he gained some advantage over you." "Over me," said William, "not he indeed; I trounced him completely." "Yet, he contrived to lame you," continued I. "Not fairly," replied my grandson; "he tripped me up, as O'Brien and Lord M——both agree, and we all of us made Osborn confess that he had been beaten." "That was an ungenerous triumph, William, for these facts always speak for themselves." "Yes, with a fellow who has a spark of courage," rejoined William, "but we all know Osborn so well, that if he had been left to tell the story he would have turned it to his own advantage." "Here, again, your argument is weak, my child," I added. "So you compelled a coward who is in the habit of misstating things to declare, that you were able to conquer him. It is an advantage which any person might attain over a boy of such a character, who, to spare himself and avoid the difficulties of the present moment, would say any thing." William, at length, allowed that what I said appeared very right, but that it was not possible to do so at school. I fear he is right, but the reason is, old habits are not easily effaced, and it has been so long the custom to call brutality courage, that until we can find a better distinction for this inherent quality of the masculine mind, we must leave school-boys to fight their battles, even as they have done for centuries.

The Mordaunts now in the confidence of the mysterious Spectator, were impatient to know when I would give my papers into the hands of a bookseller. I promised them that I would be expeditious, as I easily foresaw that, like all children, they would reckon time by their own feelings.

On my return home I dedicated a few hours to putting names in those blanks which I had omitted until this period; but I beg it to be understood that my respect for all my correspondents led me to be equally scrupulous with them; not a name will appear in this volume which can be traced.

I was certainly very well pleased with the general success of my plan, yet must ingenuously confess, and I hope I shall be pardoned, when I declare that my chief source of satisfaction was derived from the general improvement of my grandchildren. My daughter had taken the opportunity of their casual absence to assure me, that Fanny was indefatigable in correcting her habit of sitting, speaking hastily to her sisters, &c. That Harriet was punctual in her lessons and quite satisfied with one half-holiday in a week; and Lucy not only generous to obje[c]ts who claimed her little power to be serviceable, but uniformly liberal in all her childish plays with her sisters. William had already expressed his honest shame at having ever raised his hand to a girl—adding, at the same time, his sincere wish that his father might never hear of it. "For I am certain he would be very angry, and perhaps prevent my wish of being a sailor," continued the penitent boy. I coincided in this opinion, for my son-in-law is an ornament of that profession to which he belongs.

I dedicated an hour next morning to writing in reply to Mrs. Morrison, but I must beg to insert this epistle, as I do not consider it of less importance than some others for which I have asked your patient attention.

MADAM,

The subject of your favour would have given me very serious uneasiness, had you not intimated that you were not hasty in your resolutions. I rejoice at this, as I trust that your perseverance and firmness of principle will eradicate those foibles which at present deform the character of your pupil.

We will not seek into the causes which have produced these unfortunate effects. There is no time to be lost. My advice, which you do me the honour of requiring, is simply this. If Miss Cavil remains insensible to gentle remonstrance, I would recommend that you should at all times insist upon her proving every argument that she advances, and this without regard to the situation in which she may at the moment be placed. I grant that her feelings may be very painfully wounded, as there can be no doubt of her ignorance by the manner in which she conducts herself. But as it is evident that she cannot be a respecter of the feelings of others by the rudeness with which she treats you, it is equitable in every point of view, that she should be taught that most useful of all lessons, to "do to others," &c. I have seen many instances in which a little personal humility has answered the best of purposes; and as I am persuaded that thoughtlessness of character is often classed under a term more offensive, I am willing to hope that Miss Cavil has been neglected in her education, and that your zeal and good management will efface these unpromising appearances. With sincere wishes that your task may become more pleasant, and that my advice may prove wholly superfluous, by your pupil's having exerted herself to acquire your esteem, I remain,

Madam,
Your obedient servant,
ARABELLA ARGUS.

I had almost forgotten to sketch the portrait of one of my favourites, which I half promised in a former Chapter. I hope that Julia Warren is yet in the remembrance of my young friends. I am now to speak of her cousin. Sophia Welmore is a girl who possesses some qualities rarely to be met with in those of her age. I have known her many years, and she is now in her thirteenth year. I have seen her parents present her with money, sometimes a guinea, at other times half that sum; and I have known her, uninfluenced by any advice whatever, devote it to the noblest purposes of humanity, in concert with a favourite nursery-maid, with whom she was never unbecomingly familiar. She has, on a Saturday evening, sent a crown to a poor family, with whose troubles she made herself acquainted. She was accustomed to calculate what would purchase a loaf and a joint of meat; to make and send a frock for one of the children. Even when the sickness of one of her pensioners was told to her, she had the thought to send and inquire what she could do for their comfort. I remember one instance in which a chair for the support of a very sick and distressed woman was required. I saw her obtain the permission of her amiable mother to send one to the invalid, and I shall never forget the pleasing animation of her countenance. I likewise heard from the excellent young woman, who was her agent in all these cases, how effectual the services of a child had proved to a family in circumstances of the deepest distress. I impute much of this amiable philanthropy to the good example she has in her mother. I wish I could impress upon my young friends how much they have it in their power to help their fellow-creatures. Sophia Welmore, to my knowledge, never expends a penny in any eatable whatever for herself. She has been taught to understand that the table prepared for her by the order of her parents is to suffice. Thus, she has none of those Epicurean longings after *good things* which so frequently disgrace children; and her happiness is consequently much encreased by this judicious plan, for how often does sickness succeed to these luxurious feasts. I could enumerate many instances of Sophia Welmore's liberality, but I am now so near the conclusion of my task that I must really curb my inclination which would certainly lead me to pursue a subject so grateful to my feelings; and what I wish particularly to recommend to the imitation of my readers is this—That as the happy circumstances of that class of children to whom I particularly address myself, exempts them from experiencing any of the real miseries of life, I advise them to consider all the advantages of their situation, and like my amiable Sophia, exert their little power in purposes so agreeable to the dictates of humanity.

I am now compelled to close this Chapter, as it is proper, before I take my final leave of you, that I should make one morning's perambulation in that circle from which I have drawn a great part of my spectatoral information. So, for the last time, imagine to yourselves, that you see Goody Argus setting off upon her tour of inquiry. But do not expect too much. Travellers are often very unfortunate in the hour which they choose for their departure; yet I am vain enough to imagine that as my road is one of my own planning, as I have never called in the assistance of any artist to aid my views, I repeat, that under all these circumstances, I presume to think that I have a right to expect some encouragement from the juvenile world. I do not aspire to a *royal* letter patent, but shall certainly feel much disappointed if I attain not that patent so much in your power to bestow, namely, your patience to my miscellaneous subjects, and your cordial belief that Arabella Argus is the sincere friend of children.

CHAPTER XIV

A Medley.

THE UNSETTLED SITUATION in which we left Master Aston some time since, made me resolve upon calling in —— square this morning. I did so; and, much to my regret, I found young Aston making preparations for his going to school. Lady Aston assured me, that it was entirely against her wishes, but that they had been so unfortunate in their tutors, that Sir George had lost his patience, and was now so determined, that she had lost all influence with him. She intreated me to exert myself in her interest; this I declined, considering it a matter of much delicacy, and indeed my respect for the feelings of the boy, (who appeared to enter but languidly into the arrangement) would have deterred me from an interference so unavailing.

The entrance of Sir George restrained the importunities of his lady.—"So you find we have decided at last," said the baronet; "our wrong-head is going to school." I bowed.—"You do not approve of the measure, I perceive," continued Sir George. I replied, with sincerity, "that I considered the parents, in these cases, ought to be the best judges." The baronet smiled, and telling his son to retire, he spoke unreservedly on the subject: but, when I heard that there had been six tutors engaged and dismissed, in the course of six months, I could not but imagine, that the mistaken tenderness of the parents, must have united with the whims of the boy, to occasion a change so frivolous, if not disgraceful; and I really considered, that the child must be benefited by being removed to a school, where, at least, he must acquire one beneficial lesson,—humility. In fact, there is scarcely a more dangerous sort of knowledge, than that which the too great indulgence of parents frequently induces;—I mean, that of letting children feel their importance, their power, over our hearts, if not our understandings. I know that it would be difficult to prove this to many parents; but the season may arrive, in which their own disappointment will corroborate my assertion.

That Sir George and Lady Aston will experience this, in a degree proportioned to their weak guardianship of their son, cannot be doubted. I left young Aston to his fate, and proceeded to the house of Mrs. Barlow. It cannot be supposed that I was influenced to this call by my esteem for these young ladies:—no; I must confess that a motive of curiosity led me thither. I saw Lady Liston alight from her carriage, and enter their house; and, as I had previously spoken to her ladyship, and been much pleased by her manners, I availed myself of the opportunity of again enjoying her conversation. I must candidly add, that I purposed, consistently with politeness, to make some inquiries after Miss Osborn, as I knew she was acquainted with the family. I found the Miss Barlows wholly unemployed, though it was *morning*; they appeared to me, as if waiting in the expectation of compliments from their Mother's visitors, for I observed that they were at some trouble to hold their heads very high, in fact, quite beyond what is graceful: and they were continually smoothing their hair with small pocket-combs,—a custom (setting aside the vanity of the action) highly indelicate. When Lady Liston addressed herself to either of them, they answered in a voice scarcely to be heard; while the courtesy that accompanied their reply, was the most fantastical movement I ever beheld;—such a slide, or rather a retrograde sweep.

I had not dismissed the singularity of this modern courtesy from my mind, when Lady Liston, turning to me, observed, "that even the fashion of courtesying, was greatly changed since our juvenile days." Mrs. Barlow interrupted my intended reply, by remarking, "that there had been much done in the science of dancing latterly; that all its branches had been greatly improved; and that the *carriage* of the females of the present day, was grace personified."

Lady Liston and I contended for old times: we agreed that a courtesy, *formerly*, was a serious movement, observed from a motive of respect, and performed with a mild and graceful deportment; that the present mode of salutation was highly affected, and in itself expressed, that it was made under an idea (though certainly a mistaken one) of *looking* very elegant. I saw that the young ladies had decided upon our sentiments, as those of two disagreeable old women; but we were indifferent as to their opinion. I took occasion to inquire of her ladyship, concerning Charlotte Osborn, and had the pleasure of hearing, that this amiable child continues to improve, under the good care of Miss Watson. Lady Liston further informed me, that Charles Osborn had come home for a short vacation, and been made the unconscious bearer of his own disgrace; for the letter which the master gave into his charge, acquainted his father of his irregular conduct, and quarrelsome disposition, and recommended to the general, to use his parental influence to check these faults, in order that the young offender might be spared the odium of public disgrace.

What a painful feeling must this excite in the bosom of a parent! Surely the child, who has *once* occasioned an anxiety of this kind, will "take heed to his ways, that he offend not again."

I endeavoured to gain some information of the Murdock family, but I learned that the young ladies had had a disagreement, and, to my utter astonishment, their young revilers declared, "they were the most disagreeable girls in the world;—that they could neither *dance*, play upon the piano, or sing;—that, in short, they were quite like Hotten-tots." "I hope not," said I, "for I trust that they can say their catechism and their prayers." "O, we never asked them *that*," said the Miss Barlows. "Yet, they are questions of much more importance, than those to which you allude," interjoined Lady Liston. "Why, to be sure, every body knows their catechism and their prayers," said Helen Barlow. "It is neces-sary to practice their tenets, as well as to repeat their form," said Lady Liston, "and, I imagine, that our duty to our neighbour does not inculcate malevolence; by which I mean, that it is contrary to the character of a good christian, to speak ill of any one: the term, neighbour, does not imply those only who live near us, but includes all those with whom we associate, or with whom we have dealings. Nature is supposed to direct our conduct towards those related to us; but that fellowship, or friendship, which com-mon humanity dictates, is not the least graceful ornament of the human character."

Mrs. Barlow reproved the volubility of her daughters, but, I am sorry to say, that the effect it produced was transient. Lady Liston and I took leave at the same time: on her ladyship's perceiving that I proposed to walk, she insisted upon putting me down; an offer I did not reject. Our conversation turned chiefly upon the education of children; but I will not repeat what passed, as I am unwilling to enlarge upon the subject at present. Our sentiments were so perfectly in unison, that we were quite old acquaintance before we reached my daughter's. As we drew up to Mrs. Mordaunt's my grandchild recognised Michael behind the coach.—"Here is grandmamma," was the exclamation from the balcony. Lady Liston regarded my beloved family with so much interest, and, having already intimated her wish, of furthering her acquaintance with me, I yielded to the impulse of the moment, and asked her to dispense with form, and permit me to intro-duce her to my daughter. To this her ladyship assented; and we entered the drawing-room of Mrs. Mordaunt together. The children who were prepared to receive me, with their usual and affectionate salute, retired respectfully as they perceived that I was not alone; but, after the introduction was over, they each claimed their privilege, and I saw, by the manner of Harriet, that she had some matter of moment to impart.—"Well, Harriet," said I, "is your communication of a nature to interest the present company?" "I think so," said the little fairy, "for it is about William's friend, O'Brien." "Then tell your story clearly, and in as few words as possible," I continued; "for though I am always disposed to attend to my dear children, I do not feel that it is proper to draw upon the time of others."

Lady Liston looked towards me, as if fearful of being considered averse to the habits of children; but I checked her purposed acquiescence, by observing, that there was much danger in suffering children to imagine, that they possess great powers to entertain: their wit may amuse, and their whims *sometimes* evince genius, but neither of these qualities are essential to their happiness; on the contrary, they frequently diminish it, by encour-aging the seeds of vanity to take root, which always leads to mortification, if not to contempt. Harriet Mordaunt, however, as if perfectly competent to distinguish between what *was* seasonable, and what was not, proceeded to explain, that Mr. O'Brien was then with William in the library, that her mamma had been questioning him, as to what profession he would prefer; "and only think, grandmamma," said the little orator, "O'Brien would like to be a sailor; so, you know, papa will be home soon, and he can take him on board of his ship, and when William is ready to go, they will be so glad to meet again." "This is a very delightful plan," said I, "if it can be effected; but I hope you have not told Mr. O'Brien of it, until his guardian's consent can be attained." My daughter now explained, that she purposed to inquire into the prospects of her young favourite; and, if she found that no pre-arranged plan would be destroyed by her proposition, to submit her wishes, and the power she possessed, to serve Mr. O'Brien, if his inclination really led him to prefer the navy. Lady Liston inquired to what family he belonged; and, as we could not satisfy her in this point, the young gentlemen were summoned from the library. "You are the son of Colonel O'Brien?" said her ladyship, rising, and taking the hand of the amiable Dennis, as he advanced towards a seat. "I am, madam," said the youth. "And your mother's name was Fanny Liston, before marriage?" "Yes, madam; and my name is Dennis Liston O'Brien." "How extraordinary!" continued her ladyship; "your mother was a cousin of my husband's: tell me, child, how have you been thus long a stranger to me?" Young O'Brien could not answer to this inquiry of her ladyship's; all he knew was, that he had been nursed in India, and sent home to Ireland, at the age of five years; that he had been apprised of his parent's death, before he was seven years old; and brought to England, three years previous to the present time; that he was informed that his patrimony was very small, and taught to believe, that India was the place in which he would be most likely to succeed. "Does the plan meet your wishes," asked her ladyship, "No madam," said O'Brien, "I wish to go into the navy:" "Your feelings shall be consulted," continued the amiable Lady Liston, "you must in future remember that you are my relation, and that I possess not only the inclination, but the power to serve you."

I am afraid, that had Charles Osborn, been present at this moment, he would have pronounced Mr. O'Brien, quite a sneak according to his usual language; yet, I am persuaded, that many of my young friends, will entertain an opinion of a very contrary nature, when I explain, that the kind words, and truly maternal manner of Lady Liston, so overpowered her newly discovered kinsman, as to occasion him to shed tears, nor did he endeavour to conceal them. Nay, I declare, we were all deeply affected by the scene, while William, with a warmth, which did him honour, assured her ladyship that she would love O'Brien better, the longer she knew him. As we took leave, Fanny whispered me, that she hoped I would not omit to mention all that related to this morning, in my intended publication, I assured her I had been too much gratified by the happy consequences of my introduction, to neglect a fact, so truly interesting. I was so intent upon concluding my career as a Spectator, that I withstood the united entreaties of the Mordaunt family to remain in —— street all day. I was conveyed to my own house by Lady Liston; in the course of our little ride, she gave me the heads of her history, but as they were irrelevant to the tastes of a juvenile reader, I suppress them, and will only add, that I felt very happy, in having been the cause of a meeting so apparently fortuitous; and sincerely hope that, under Providence, it may lead to consequences, honourable to both parties.

I had just inserted the foregoing statement, and was pausing upon my elbow, and half wishing that I had received *one* more communication from Mr. Testy, when behold, without the aid of the "emperor of the conjurors," in comes Michael, with the identical letter. I broke the seal, and read as follows.

To Mrs. ARGUS.

My dear MADAM,

You will do me the justice of believing me sincere, when I declare, that is it always most grateful to my feelings, to speak favourably of every body. I may have appeared rather irritable at times, but indeed my good madam, there are many real causes for regret, in the education of children, generally speaking.

I am now, however, so happily disappointed in those for whom I am more immediately interested, that I cannot forbear assuring you of it. My young cousins are at present, inmates of my house, they have masters who attend them daily; in those hours set apart for recreation, I am delighted to perceive their talents directed to laudable and rational pursuits. I am retreading my juvenile path, we are frequently play-fellows, and the young rogues are now so convinced of my affection for them, and so desirous of my approbation, that I am afraid they will reverse the business, and spoil me, for I am already beginning to count the weeks which remain, e're they are to be admitted at —— ——. But I must be firm, and I know, no more likely method; to re-assure me, that order and discipline are indispensible with boys; (I say nothing of girls) than a morning range, amongst the circle of dear kind-feeling mammas, who pet their over-grown babies, to the annoyance of all their acquaintance. I am persuaded you will partake in my present happiness, and beg to assure you, that

> I am, most
> respectfully your's,
> TIMOTHY TESTY.

I certainly was very well pleased to hear, that this gentleman had such good reason to be satisfied with his young relations; and have no doubt, but that his watchful zeal and affection, will in time perfect his hopes in them.

But I must now address myself to my readers, and as a *woman*, more especially to those of my own sex. I know it is very usual to say, that a young lady has *finished* her education; there cannot be a more erroneous assertion: we know, that a period in the lives of young people must arrive, in which the attendance of masters and governesses is discontinued. What then, are they to set down to *forget* what they have acquired, or are they to be contented with what they already know, and make no further enquiries.

Restraint is a feeling against which almost every disposition is inclined to contend; and the period of emancipation from regular business, and stated days for particular studies, appears to the emerging scholar the first and most desirable happiness: alas! how cruel do you consider the person, who attempts to throw shade into this smiling perspective; nor would any argument, though sanctioned by the most profound judgment and experience convince you that the season of youth is the happiest of your lives. I know *I* should lose even that little share of your favour, which I have (perhaps vainly) taken to myself, if I was to enlarge upon this theme; and I am too well convinced of the effect of an unfavorable impression, to hazard your displeasure in this stage of my work.

But with all those *eyes*, attributed to my *fictitious* name, I look into futurity, I read in the characters of a Sophia Wilmot, a Julia Warren, a Sophia Welmore, and, I trust, in *all* the Mordaunts, that amiability of disposition, and firmness of principle, which will lead *them* to seek knowledge at every period of their lives; that they will continue to be comforts to their parents, and an honour to human nature. I cannot resist transcribing in this place, a few lines from that admirable fable, "The Bee, the Ant, and the Sparrow." I take my quotation from that part where the Bee addresses the Ant.

"Ah! sister-labourer," says she,
"How very fortunate are we!
Who taught in infancy to know
The comforts which from labour flow;
Are independent of the great,
Nor know the wants of pride and state.
Why is our food so very sweet?
Because we earn, before we eat.
Why are our wants so very few?
Because we nature's calls pursue.
Whence our complacency of mind?
Because we act our parts assigned.
Have we incessant tasks to do?
Is not all nature busy too?
Doth not the sun with constant pace,
Persist to run his annual race?
Do not the stars which shine so bright,
Renew their courses every night?
Doth not the ox obedient bow,
His patient neck, and draw the plough?
Or when did e'er the generous steed,
Withhold his labour or his speed?
If you all nature's system scan,
The only idle thing is—man."

Every line of this applicable poem, conveys a moral lesson, and the most common observer is capable of discovering its justness. If the kind order of providence has placed the human class in a station differing in rank and power, it has never distinguished any one branch of the universal family as destined to live without toil. To those whom fortune has been bountiful, the cultivation of the *mind* becomes a duty as imperious as the manual exertion of the daily labourer; the mental knowledge of those who have *leisure* to learn, should be given in portions to the ignorant, appropriated to their capacities, and conveyed not in the language of vaunting superiority, but with all the humility that ever accompanies true wisdom.

Once more, my little friends, every thing is in your power,—embrace the present moment—impress upon your fertile minds, that you have a part to act, a character to sustain, and that you will finally be accountable for all, and the most trivial of your actions. These considerations are of equal moment with the young and happy, as with the more advanced in life. You can never be too good, for that state into which the just shall pass: and as the period for our summons, is withheld from mortal sight, oh! let it be the constant practice of your lives to render yourselves acceptable to that God "in whose hands are all the corners of the earth."

If I have pointed out an error, which shall speak home to any individual bosom, seize the moment of conviction and prove your heart. If, and I trust I have been so fortunate, if any of you possess those youthful virtues, on which I have dwelt with delight, do not fear to apply them, but be emulous, stop not here, let each new day, add strength to your good resolutions that the promises of your youth, may in riper years lead you nearer to perfection. In this wish you may have many dear friends, who are deeply interested, but not any whose sincerity is more worthy of your esteem, than, that of

ARABELLA ARGUS.

April 20, 1810.

Prince Dorus: or, Flattery Put Out of Countenance

By CHARLES LAMB

The Enchanted Cat.

PRINCE DORUS:

OR,

FLATTERY PUT OUT OF COUNTENANCE.

A POETICAL VERSION OF AN ANCIENT TALE.

ILLUSTRATED WITH A SERIES OF ELEGANT ENGRAVINGS.

LONDON:

PRINTED FOR M. J. GODWIN,

AT THE JUVENILE LIBRARY, NO. 41, SKINNER STREET;

AND TO BE HAD OF ALL BOOKSELLERS AND TOYMEN IN THE
UNITED KINGDOM.

1811.

PRINCE DORUS: Or, Flattery Put Out of Countenance. A Poetical Version of An Ancient Tale *(1811) was, like all of Charles Lamb's work for children, written for profit. Mary Jane Godwin, William's second wife, published this and all of Lamb's juvenile works, including* The Adventures of Ulysses *(1808). The latter was based somewhat on Chapman's translation of* The Odyssey *(1616). There were in addition English translations of Fénelon's* Télémaque *(1699), which may have inspired Lamb's Homeric book for children.* Prince Dorus *was somewhat derivative, as were all of Lamb's books for children. Lamb could have read about Prince Désir, a prototype of Prince Dorus, in Jeanne Marie Le Prince de Beaumont's* Young Misses Magazine *(1756) or in Edward Augustus Kendall's* Adventures of Musul *(1800), where the prince appears as "The Prince that had a Long Nose."*

Lamb's version, besides being in verse, is a fairy tale told for sheer fun which the illustrations after William Mulready accentuate:

> *And pray, Sir, while your hunger is supplied,*
> *Do lean your Nose a little on one side;*
> *The shadow, which it casts upon the meat,*
> *Darkens my plate, I see not what I eat—*

the fairy says to Prince Dorus. The verses had a second edition in 1818, but Lamb seems not to have fared well in his playful vein. When Henry Crabb Robinson suggested he versify Reynard the Fox, *Lamb replied tersely that society's "sense for humor is extinct."*

Earlier in The King and Queen of Hearts *(1805), the first piece for juveniles that Charles Lamb wrote, he had tried humor as well. The story was probably known to children earlier. Amplified as sheet music, it was adapted (ca. 1785) to a tune from Arne's* Artaxerxes, *the first play the young Charles Lamb ever saw. Lamb seems quite familiar with nursery rhymes, and in fact* The Oxford Dictionary of Nursery Rhymes *cites him on twelve separate nursery rhymes, some of which, like "Diddle, Diddle Dumpling," he even translated into Latin.*

Prince Dorus *is reproduced from the A. W. Tuer facsimile (London: Leadenhall Press, 1889) based on the 1811 edition.*

I N days of yore, as Ancient Stories tell,
A King in love with a great Princess fell.
Long at her feet submiss the Monarch sigh'd,
While she with stern repulse his suit denied.
Yet was he form'd by birth to please the fair,
Dress'd, danc'd, and courted with a Monarch's air;
But Magic Spells her frozen breast had steel'd
With stuborn pride, that knew not how to yield.

This to the King a courteous Fairy told,
And bade the Monarch in his suit be bold;
For he that would the charming Princess wed,
Had only on her cat's black tail to tread,
When straight the Spell would vanish into air,
And he enjoy for life the yielding fair.

He thank'd the Fairy for her kind advice.—
Thought he, "If this be all, I'll not be nice;
Rather than in my courtship I will fail,
I will to mince-meat tread Minon's black tail."

To the Princess's court repairing strait,
He sought the cat that must decide his fate;
But when he found her, how the creature stared!
How her back bristled, and her great eyes glared!
That, which he so fondly hop'd his prize,
Was swell'd by wrath to twice its usual size;
And all her cattish gestures plainly spoke,
She thought the affair he came upon, no joke.

With wary step the cautious King draws near,
And slyly means to attack her in her rear;
But when he thinks upon her tail to pounce,
Whisk—off she skips—three yards upon a bounce—
Again he tries, again his efforts fail—
Minon's a witch—the deuce is in her tail—

The anxious chase for weeks the Monarch tried,
Till courage fail'd, and hope within him died.
A desperate suit 'twas useless to prefer,
Or hope to catch a tail of quicksilver.—
When on a day, beyond his hopes, he found
Minon, his foe, asleep upon the ground;

Minon Asleep.

Her ample tail behind her lay outspread,
Full to the eye, and tempting to the tread.
The King with rapture the occasion bless'd,
And with quick foot the fatal part he press'd.
Loud squalls were heard, like howlings of a storm,
And sad he gazed on Minon's altered form,—
No more a cat, but chang'd into a man
Of giant size, who frown'd, and thus began:

"Rash King, that dared with impious design
To violate that tail, that once was mine;
What though the spell be broke, and burst the charms,
That kept the Princess from thy longing arms,—
Not unrevenged shalt thou my fury dare,
For by that violated tail I swear,
From your unhappy nuptials shall be born
A Prince, whose Nose shall be thy subjects' scorn.
Bless'd in his love thy son shall never be,
Till he his foul deformity shall see,
Till he with tears his blemish shall confess,
Discern its odious length, and wish it less!"

This said, he vanish'd; and the King awhile
Mused at his words, then answer'd with a smile,
"Give me a child in happy wedlock born,
And let his Nose be made like a French horn;

Prince Doras and his Maids.

His knowledge of the fact I ne'er can doubt,—
If he have eyes, or hands, he'll find it out."

So spake the King, self-flatter'd in his thought,
Then with impatient step the Princess sought
His urgent suit no longer she withstands,
But links with him in Hymen's knot her hands.

Almost as soon a widow as a bride,
Within a year the King her husband died;
And shortly after he was dead and gone,
She was deliver'd of a little son,
The prettiest babe, with lips as red as rose,
And eyes like little stars—but such a nose—
The tender Mother fondly took the boy
Into her arms, and would have kiss'd her joy;
His luckless nose forbade the fond embrace—
He thrust the hideous feature in her face.

Then all her Maids of Honour tried in turn,
And for a Prince's kiss in envy burn;
By sad experience taught, their hopes they miss'd,
And mourn'd a Prince that never could be kiss'd.

In silent tears the Queen confess'd her grief,
Till kindest Flattery came to her relief.
Her maids, as each one takes him in her arms,

Expatiate freely o'er his world of charms—
His eyes, lips, mouth—his forehead was divine—
And for his nose—they call'd it Aquiline—
Declared that Cæsar, who the world subdued,
Had such a one—just of that longitude—
That Kings like him compelled folks to adore them,
And drove the short-nos'd sons of men before them—
That length of nose portended length of days,
And was a great advantage many ways—
To mourn the gifts of Providence was wrong—
Besides, *the Nose was not so very long.*—

These arguments in part her grief redrest,
A mother's partial fondness did the rest;
And Time, that all things reconciles by use,
Did in her notions such a change produce,
That, as she views her babe, with favour blind
She thinks him handsomest of human kind.

Meantime in spite of his disfigured face,
Dorus (for so he's call'd) grew up apace;
In fair proportion all his features rose,
Save that most prominent of all—his Nose.
That Nose, which in the infant could annoy,
Was grown a perfect nuisance in the boy.
Whene'er he walk'd, his Handle went before,
Long as the snout of Ferret, or Wild Boar;
Or like the Staff, with which on holy day
The solemn Parish Beadle clears the way.

But from their cradle to their latest year,
How seldom Truth can reach a Prince's ear!
To keep th' unwelcome knowledge out of view,
His lesson well each flattering Courtier knew;
The hoary Tutor, and the wily Page,
Unmeet confederates! dupe his tender age.
They taught him that whate'er vain mortals boast—
Strength, Courage, Wisdom—all they value most—
Whate'er on human life distinction throws—
Was all comprised—in what?—a length of nose!
Ev'n Virtue's self (by some suppos'd chief merit)
In short-nosed folks was only want of spirit.

While doctrines such as these his guides instill'd,
His Palace was with long-nosed people fill'd;
At Court whoever ventured to appear
With a short nose, was treated with a sneer.

Each courtier's wife, that with a babe is blest,
Moulds its young nose betimes; and does her best,
By pulls, and hauls, and twists, and lugs and pinches,
To stretch it to the standard of the Prince's.

Dup'd by these arts, Dorus to manhood rose,
Nor dream'd of ought more comely than his Nose;
Till Love, whose pow'r ev'n Princes have confest,
Claim'd the soft empire o'er his youthful breast.
Fair Claribel was she who caused his care;
A neighb'ring Monarch's daughter, and sole heir.
For beauteous Claribel his bosom burn'd;
The beauteous Claribel his flame return'd;
Deign'd with kind words his passion to approve,
Met his soft vows, and yielded love for love.
If in her mind some female pangs arose
At sight (and who can blame her?) of his Nose,
Affection made her willing to be blind;
She loved him for the beauties of his mind;
And in his lustre, and his royal race,
Contented sunk—one feature of his face.

Blooming to sight, and lovely to behold,
Herself was cast in Beauty's richest mould;
Sweet female majesty her person deck'd—
Her face an angel's—save for one defect—
Wise Nature, who to Dorus over kind,
A length of nose too liberal had assign'd,
As if with us poor mortals to make sport,
Had giv'n to Claribel a nose too short:
But turned up with a sort of modest grace;
It took not much of beauty from her face;
And subtle Courtiers, who their Prince's mind
Still watch'd, and turned about with every wind,
Assur'd the Prince, that though man's beauty owes
Its charms to a majestic length of nose,
The excellence of Woman (softer creature)
Consisted in the shortness of that feature.
Few arguments were wanted to convince
The already more than half persuaded Prince;
Truths, which we hate, with slowness we receive,
But what we wish to credit, soon believe.

The Princess's affections being gain'd,
What but her Sire's approval now remain'd?
Ambassadors with solemn pomp are sent
To win the aged Monarch to consent

Claribel Carried off

(Seeing their States already were allied)
That Dorus might have Claribel to bride.
Her Royal Sire, who wisely understood
The match propos'd was for both kingdoms' good,
Gave his consent; and gentle Claribel
With weeping bids her Father's court farewell.

With gallant pomp, and numerous array,
Dorus went forth to meet her on her way;
But when the Princely pair of lovers met,
Their hearts on mutual gratulations set,
Sudden the Enchanter from the ground arose,
(The same who prophesied the Prince's nose)
And with rude grasp, unconscious of her charms,
Snatch'd up the lovely Princess in his arms,
Then bore her out of reach of human eyes,
Up in the pathless regions of the skies.

Bereft of her that was his only care,
Dorus resign'd his soul to wild despair;
Resolv'd to leave the land that gave him birth,
And seek fair Claribel throughout the earth.
Mounting his horse, he gives the beast the reins,
And wanders lonely through the desert plains;
With fearless heart the savage heath explores,
Where the wolf prowls, and where the tiger roars,
Nor wolf, nor tiger, dare his way oppose;

Visit to the Beneficent Fairy

The wildest creatures see, and shun, his NOSE.
Ev'n lions fear! the elephant alone
Surveys with pride a trunk so like his own.

At length he to a shady forest came,
Where in a cavern lived an aged dame;
A reverend Fairy, on whose silver head
A hundred years their downy snows had shed.
Here ent'ring in, the Mistress of the place
Bespoke him welcome with a cheerful grace
Fetch'd forth her dainties, spread her social board
With all the Store her dwelling could afford.
The Prince with toil and hunger sore opprest,
Gladly accepts, and deigns to be her guest.
But when the first civilities were paid,
The dishes rang'd, and Grace in order said;
The Fairy, who had leisure now to view
Her guest more closely, from her pocket drew
Her spectacles, and wip'd them from the dust,
Then on her nose endeavour'd to adjust;
With difficulty she could find a place
To hang them on in her unshapely face;
For if the Princess's was somewhat small,
This Fairy scarce had any nose at all.
But when by help of spectacles the Crone
Discern'd a Nose so different from her own,

Prince Dorus Offended.

What peals of laughter shook her aged sides!
While with sharp jests the Prince she thus derides.

FAIRY.
"Welcome great Prince of Noses, to my cell;
'Tis a poor place,— but thus we Fairies dwell.
Pray, let me ask you, if from far you come—
And don't you sometimes find it cumbersome?"

PRINCE.
"Find what?"

FAIRY.
"Your Nose—"

PRINCE.
"My Nose, Ma'am!"

FAIRY.
"No offence—
The King your Father was a man of sense,
A handsome man (but lived not to be old)
And had a Nose cast in the common mould.
Ev'n I myself, that now with age am grey,
Was thought to have some beauty in my day,
And am the Daughter of a King. Your sire
In this poor face saw something to admire—
And I to shew my gratitude made shift—
Have stood his friend—and help'd him at a lift—
'Twas I that, when his hopes began to fail,
Shew'd him the spell that lurk'd in Minon's tail—

Perhaps you have heard—but come, Sir, you don't eat—
That Nose of yours requires both wine and meat—
Fall to, and welcome, without more ado—
You see your fare—what shall I help you to?
This dish the tongues of nightingales contains;
This, eyes of peacocks; and that, linnets' brains;
That next you is a Bird of Paradise—
We fairies in our food are somewhat nice.—
And pray, Sir, while your hunger is supplied,
Do lean your Nose a little on one side;
The shadow, which it casts upon the meat,
Darkens my plate, I see not what I eat—"

The Prince on dainty after dainty feeding,
Felt inly shock'd at the old Fairy's breeding;
And held it want of manners in the Dame,
And did her country education blame.
One thing he only wonder'd at,—what she
So very comic in his nose could see.
Hers, it must be confest, was somewhat short,
And time and shrinking age, accounted for't;
But for his own, thank heaven, he could not tell
That it was ever thought remarkable;
A decent nose, of reasonable size,
And handsome thought, rather than otherwise.
But that which most of all his wonder paid,
Was to observe the Fairy's waiting Maid;
How at each word the aged Dame let fall;
She courtsied low, and smil'd assent to all;
But chiefly when the rev'rend Grannam told
Of conquests, which her beauty made of old.—
He smiled to see how Flattery sway'd the Dame,
Nor knew himself was open to the same!
He finds her raillery now increase so fast,
That making hasty end of his repast,
Glad to escape her tongue, he bids farewell
To the old Fairy, and her friendly cell.

But his kind Hostess, who had vainly tried
The force of ridicule to cure his pride,
Fertile in plans, a surer method chose,
To make him see the error of his nose;
For till he view'd that feature with remorse,
The Enchanter's direful spell must be in force.

Truth brought Home

Midway the road by which the Prince must pass,
She rais'd by magic art a House of Glass;
No mason's hand appear'd, nor work of wood;
Compact of glass the wondrous fabric stood.
Its stately pillars, glittering in the sun,
Conspicuous from afar, like silver, shone.
Here, snatch'd and rescued from th' Enchanter's might,
She placed the beauteous Claribel in sight.
The admiring Prince the chrystal dome survey'd,
And sought access unto his lovely Maid;
But, strange to tell, in all that mansion's bound,
Nor door, nor casement, was there to be found.
Enrag'd he took up massy stones, and flung
With such a force, that all the palace rung;
But made no more impression on the glass,
Than if the solid structure had been brass.
To comfort his despair, the lovely maid
Her snowy hand against her window laid;
But when with eager haste he thought to kiss,
His Nose stood out, and robb'd him of the bliss.
Thrice he essay'd th' impracticable feat;
The window and his lips can never meet.

The painful Truth, which Flattery long conceal'd,
Rush'd on his mind, and "O!" he cried, "I yield;

Self-Knowledge obtains its Reward.

Wisest of Fairies, thou wert right, I wrong—
I own, I own, I have a Nose too long."

The frank confession was no sooner spoke,
But into shivers all the palace broke,
His Nose of monstrous length, to his surprise
Shrunk to the limits of a common size;
And Claribel with joy her Lover view'd,
Now grown as beautiful as he was good.
The aged Fairy in their presence stands,
Confirms their mutual vows, and joins their hands.
The Prince with rapture hails the happy hour,
That rescued him from self-delusion's power;
And trains of blessings crown the future life
Of Dorus, and of Claribel, his wife.

THE END.

The History of
Little Henry and His Bearer

By MARTHA BUTT SHERWOOD

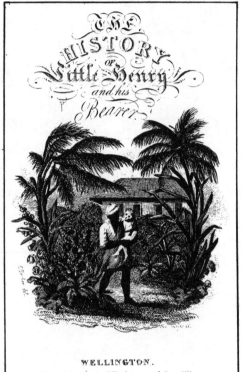

THE HISTORY OF Little Henry and his Bearer

WELLINGTON.

Printed by and for F. Houlston and Son 1814.

Entered at Stationer's Hall.

As a child *Martha Butt Sherwood (1775–1851) read* Robinson Crusoe, The Governess, *and Aesop's* Fables, *and acted in Hannah More's* Sacred Dramas. *In 1803 she married her cousin Captain Henry Sherwood. Leaving her first child, a daughter, in England, in April 1805 she sailed for India, where her husband was ordered. Here she notes in a commonplace book after she visited an English four-year old: "Is it not dreadful to leave children to such an age as this to the entire management not only of servants but of Pagans." This reflection was crystallized in* The History of Little Henry and His Bearer *(1814), which was written in India and finished in 1809. It is based somewhat on Sherwood's own son, who was born at Berhampore and given opium by his nurse. Her own child lived to be two; her fictional child died at eight. Little Henry was the idealized child her own child might have become. There are just enough references to "panjammahs" and "verandahs" to give the book an exotic flavor. The religious tone marks Sherwood's literary evangelical period.*

Called "the first missionary tale for children," Little Henry *was in twelve editions by 1818. A sequel,* The Last Days of Boosy, *recounting the conversion of Henry's servant, was published in 1842.*

Little Henry *pioneered the use of India as a setting for children's stories, employed later by Kipling and by Helen Bannerman in* Little Black Sambo *(1899). According to Kipling, Sherwood's book popularized India for Englishmen who ". . . came to an India . . . of palmyra-tree and rice, the India of the picture books, of 'Little Henry and His Bearer,' all dead and dry and baking heat."*

Sherwood's most famous extended work is The History of the Fairchild Family *(1818–1847). In a series of volumes, Lucy, Emily, and Henry are conducted through many religious and edifying experiences, none more grisly than the sight of a corpse. While the death scene was found in other nineteenth-century stories, Sherwood's version is the most graphic. The Fairchild Family was in print well into the twentieth century. A 1902 edition alone was in its eighth printing by 1931.*

It would be impossible to list all of Mrs. Sherwood's writings here. She wrote about four hundred separate articles, tracts and books. M. Nancy Cutt's Mrs. Sherwood and Her Books for Children *(London: Oxford University Press, 1974) includes a reprint of two stories by Mrs. Sherwood,* The Little Woodman and His Dog Caesar *and* Soffrona and Her Cat Muff.

Little Henry *is reprinted from an 1814 edition from the Special Collections of the Regenstein Library of the University of Chicago.*

H ENRY L——— was born at Dinapore in the East-Indies. His papa was an officer in the Company's service, and was killed in attacking a mud fort belonging to a *Zemeendar,** a few months after the birth of his son. His mamma also died before he was a year old. Thus little Henry was left an orphan when he was a very little baby: but his dying mother, when taking her last farewell of him, lifted up her eyes to heaven, and said, "O God, I leave my fatherless child with thee, claiming thy promise in all humility, yet in full confidence that my baby will never be left destitute; for in thee the fatherless find mercy." The promise to which she alluded is to be found in Jeremiah xlix. 11. *Leave thy fatherless children, I will preserve them alive; and let thy widows trust in me.*

As soon as Henry's mamma was dead, a lady, who lived at that time in a large *puckah*** house near the river between Patna and Dinapore, came and took little Henry, and gave him a room in her house, giving strict orders to her servants to provide him with every thing that he wanted. But as she was one of those fine ladies who will give their money (when they have any to spare) for the relief of distress, but have no idea how it is possible for any one to bestow all his goods to feed the poor, and yet want charity; she thought that when she had received the child, and given her orders to her servants, she had done all that was necessary for him. She would not afterwards suffer Henry to give her the least trouble, nor would she endure the smallest inconvenience on his account: and thus the poor child, being very young and unable to make known his wants, might have been cruelly neglected; had it not been for the attention of a *bearer,*† who had lived many years with his papa, and had taken care of Henry from the day that he was born.

When he was a very little baby, Boosy (for that was the *bearer's* name) attended him night and day, warmed his pap, rocked his cot, dressed and undressed and washed him, and did every thing for him as tenderly as if he had been his own child. The first word that little Henry tried to say was, Boosy; and when he was only ten months old he used to put his arms round his neck, and kiss him, or stroke his swarthy cheek with his delicate hand.

When Henry was carried to the lady's house, Boosy went with him; and for some years the little child had no other friend than his *bearer.* Boosy never left his *choota sahib,*†† except for two hours in the twenty-four when he went to get his *khauna.*▲ At night he slept on his mat at the foot of the child's cot; and whenever Henry called, he was up in a moment, and had milk or toast-and-water ready to give him to drink. Early in the morning, before sun-rise, he took him out in a little carriage which was provided for him, or carried him in his arms round the garden. When he brought him in, he bathed him and dressed him, and gave him his breakfast and put him in his cot to sleep: and all the day long he played with him; sometimes carrying him in his arms or on his back,

---

* A landholder.
** The meaning of *puckah* is ripe, or strong; it here means brick or stone.
† A servant, whose work is to carry a palanquin; but who is frequently employed to take care of children.
†† Little master.
▲ Food.

and sometimes letting him walk, or roll upon the carpet. Every body who came to the house noticed the kindness of Boosy to the child, and he got presents from many people for his goodness to Henry.

When Henry was two years old, he had a dreadful illness: so alarming indeed was it, that for many days it was thought he would die. He had another very severe illness when he was four years old, for he was never a very healthy child. During the height of these sicknesses, his *bearer* never left him; nor would he take any rest, even by the side of his bed, till he thought the danger was over.

These things considered, it cannot be a matter of wonder that this little boy as he grew older should love his *bearer* more than all the world besides; for his *bearer* was almost his only friend, no one else taking much thought about him. Henry could not speak English, but he could talk with Boosy in *his* language as fast as possible; and he knew every word, good or bad, which the natives spoke. He used to sit in the *verandah*,* between his *bearer's* knees, and chew *paun*,† and eat *bazar*‡ sweetmeats. He wore no shoes nor stockings; but was dressed in *panjammahs*,§ and had silver *bangles*‖ on his ancles. No one could have told by his behaviour or manner of speaking that he was not of Indian origin, but his delicate complexion, light hair, and blue eyes, at once shewed his parentage.

Thus his life passed till he was five years and a half old: for the lady in whose house he lived (although he was taught to call her mamma)· paid him no kind of attention; and it never occurred to her that it was right to give him any religious instructions. He used to see his *bearer* and the other natives performing *poojah*,** and carrying about their wooden and clay Gods; and he knew that his mamma sometimes went to church at Dinapore: so he believed that there were a great many Gods, and that the God to whom his mamma prayed at Dinapore was no better than the Gods of wood, and stone, and clay, which his *bearer* worshipped. He also believed that the River Ganges was a Goddess, and called Gunga; and that the water of the river could take away sins. He believed, too, that the Mussulmauns were as good as Christians, for his mamma's *khaunsaumaun*▲ had told him so. Henry was moreover taught by the servants many things, which a little boy should not know: but the servants, being Heathens, could not be expected to teach him any thing better; and therefore they were not so much to be blamed as the lady who had undertaken the charge of him, who might have been ashamed to leave the child of Christian parents under the care of such persons.

When Henry was five years old, a young lady, who was just arrived from England, came to reside for a while with his mamma. She was the daughter of a worthy clergyman in England, and had received from him a religious education. She had brought with

---

* An open gallery or passage.
† An intoxicating mixture of opium and sugar, &c.
‡ A market.
§ Trowsers.
‖ Ornaments generally worn round the wrists and ancles.
** Ceremony: Offering.
▲ A kind of house-steward.

her from home a box of Bibles, and some pretty children's books and pictures. When she saw poor little Henry sitting in the *verandah*, as his custom was, between his *bearer's* knees, with many other native servants surrounding him; she loved him, and was very sorry for him: for, indeed, it is a dreadful thing for little children to be left among people who know not God. So she took some of the prettiest coloured pictures she had, and spread them on the floor of the room, the door of which opened into the *verandah* near the place where the little boy usually sat. When Henry peeped in and saw the pictures, he was tempted by them to come into the room; but at first he would not venture in without his *bearer*. Afterwards, when he got more accustomed to the lady, he was contented that his *bearer* should sit at the door, while he went in. And at last he quite lost all fear, and would go in by himself: nay, he never was more happy than when he was with this lady; for she tried every means to gain his love, in order that she might lead him to receive such instructions as the time of her intended stay with his mamma would allow her to give him.

She was very sorry when she found that he could not speak English: however, she was resolved not to be checked by this difficulty. She taught him many English words by shewing him things represented in the coloured pictures, telling him their English names; so that in a short time he could ask for any thing he wanted in English. She then taught him his letters in one of the little books she had brought from home, and from his letters she proceeded to spelling: and so diligent was she, that before he was six years old he could spell any words, however difficult, and could speak English quite readily.

While this young lady was taking pains, from day to day, to teach little Henry to read, she endeavoured by word of mouth to make him acquainted with such parts of the Christian religion as even the youngest ought to know; and without the knowledge of which no man can be a Christian: and she did not like to wait until Henry could read his Bible, before she would instruct him in subjects of so much importance.

The first lesson of this kind which she strove to teach him, was, that there was only one true God, and that all things were made by him: namely, the glorious heaven, to which those persons go who have been made the children of God on earth; and the dreadful hell, prepared for those who die in their sins: the world and all things in it; the sun, the moon, the stars, and all the heavenly bodies. And she was going to teach him the following words from Colossians i. 16. *For by him were all things created, that are in heaven, and that are in earth*——but no sooner did little Henry understand that she meant to teach him that there is but *one* God, than he got very angry, and told her that she did not speak *a true word;* for his mamma had a God, and his *bearer* had a God, and there were a great many Gods besides: and he ran out into the *verandah*, and told his *bearer* what the *chootee bebee** had said; and down he sat between his *bearer's* knees, and would not come again to her that day, although she brought out her finest pictures and a new book on purpose to tempt him.

The young lady did not fail to pray very earnestly for little Henry that night, when she was withdrawn to her room, and her door shut. And her Father, on whom she called in secret, in the name of his beloved Son, heard her prayer: for the next day little Henry came smiling into her room, having quite forgotten his ill-humour; and she was now

---

* Young lady.

enabled to talk to him with advantage on the same subject. And she made him kneel down, and pray to God to give him sense to understand the truth. She had also provided herself with one of the Hindoo Gods made of baked earth; and she bid him look at it, and examine it well: she then threw it down upon the floor, and it was broken into a hundred pieces. Then she said, "Henry, what can this God do for you? it cannot help itself. Call to it, and ask it to get up. You see it cannot move."———And that day the little boy was convinced by her arguments.

The next discourse which the young lady had with Henry was upon the nature of God. She taught him that God is a Spirit: that he is every where; that he can do every thing; that he can see every thing; that he can hear every thing; that he knows even the inmost thoughts of our hearts; that he loves that which is good, and hates that which is evil; that he never had a beginning, and never will have an end. She also taught him, that in this one only and true God there are three Persons, namely, God the Father, God the Son, and God the Holy Ghost: and that these three Persons, although none is afore or after the other, perform different works or offices for man.

Henry now began to take pleasure in hearing of God, and asked many questions about him. He next learnt that God made the world in six days, and rested from his work on the seventh: and that he made man and woman innocent at first. He then was taught how our forefather Adam was tempted, with Eve his wife, to eat the forbidden fruit; and how by this means sin entering into the world, and the nature of Adam becoming sinful, all we his children, being born in his likeness, are sinful also.

Henry here asked what sin is?

"Sin, my child," answered the lady, "is whatever displeases God. If your mamma were to desire you to come into her room, or to do something for her, and you were to refuse, would she not have reason to be displeased with you?"

"Yes; I suppose so."

"Or, if you ask Boosy to fan you, or to carry you in your palanquin, and Boosy does something quite different; or if you desire him to carry you one way, and he carries you another: would he not do wrong?"

"Yes; to be sure."

"Well, then; whatever you do contrary to the commands of God, displeases him, and is sin."

But the lady still found great difficulty in making Henry understand the nature of sin: for he had been so neglected that he did not know right from wrong. He did not consider a lie as sinful; nor feel ashamed of stealing, unless it was found out. He thought, also, that if any body hurt him, it was right to hurt them in return. After several days, however, she made the subject clear to him; and then further explained how sin has corrupted all our hearts: and she made him repeat the following words till he could say them quite well: *The Lord looked down from heaven upon the children of men, to see if there were any that did understand, and seek God. They are all gone aside, they are altogether become filthy; there is none that doeth good, no, not one.* Psalm xiv. 2, 3.

She next made the little boy understand that eternal death, or everlasting punishment, is the consequence of sin: and he soon could repeat two or three verses to prove this; one was, *The unrighteous shall not inherit the kingdom of God.* 1 Corinthians vi. 9. and another, *They shall look upon the carcases of the men that have transgressed against me; for their worm shall not die, neither shall their fire be quenched; and they shall be an abhorring unto all flesh.* Isaiah lxvi. 24.

And now the lady had brought Henry to know that he and all the world were sinners, and that the punishment of sin is eternal death; and that it was not in his power to save himself, nor for any thing on the earth to wash him from his sins; and she had brought him several times to ask her with great earnestness what he must do to be saved, and how his sins could be forgiven, and his heart freed from evil tempers————her next lesson, therefore, was to explain to him what the Lord Jesus Christ had done for him: how *God was manifest in the flesh, justified in the Spirit, seen of angels, preached unto the Gentiles, believed on in the world, received up into glory;* 1 Timothy iii. 16. and how *we have redemption through his blood, he having made peace* for us *through the blood of his cross.* Colossians i. 14, 20.

Little Henry was particularly pleased whenever he heard of our Saviour: and, by divine grace, his heart seemed to be wonderfully filled with love for his Redeemer; and he was so afraid of offending him, that he became careful of every word he said, and of every thing he did; and he was always asking the young lady if this was right? and if that was right? and if God would be angry with him if he did this or that? so that in a short time his whole behaviour was altered. He never said a bad word, and was vexed when he heard any other person do it. He spoke mildly and civilly to every body. He would return the *salam** of the poorest *coolie†* in the *bazar.* If any body had given him a *rupee,‡* he would not spend it in sweetmeats or playthings; but he would change it into *pice,▲* and give it to the *fakeers||* who were blind or lame, or such as seemed to be in real distress, as far as it would go.

One day Henry came into the lady's room, and found her opening a box of books. "Come," said she, "Henry, help me to unpack these books, and to carry them to my bookcase." Now, while they were thus busy, and little Henry much pleased to think that he could make himself useful, the lady said, "These books have different kinds of covers, and some are larger than others, but they all contain the same words, and are the book of God. If you read this book, and, with God's help, keep the sayings written in it, it will bring you to heaven; it will bring you to where your beloved Redeemer is, to the throne of the Lamb of God, who was slain for your sins."

"O! I wish," said Henry, "that I had one of these books! I will give you all my play-things, ma'am, and my little carriage, for one of them."

The lady smiled, and said, "No, my dear, keep your play-things, and your little carriage, too: you shall have any one of these books you like best."

Henry thanked the lady with all his heart, and called Boosy in to give his advice whether he should choose a book with a purple morocco cover, or one with a red one. When he had fixed upon one, he begged a bit of silk of the lady, and carried it to the tailor to make him a bag for his new Bible; and that same evening he came to the lady to beg her to teach him to read it. So that day he began: and he was several days over

---

* Health: Salutation.
† A kind of low cast of men, who have no trade, but work at any kind of common employment.
‡ A silver coin of the value of half-a-crown.
▲ Pence.
|| Beggars: A religious order of men, something like monks or dervises.

the first chapter of Genesis; but the next chapter was easier, and the next easier still; till, very soon, he was able to read any part of the Bible without hesitation.

With what joy and gratitude to God did the young lady see the effect of her pious labours! She had, in the space of a year and a half, brought a little orphan from the grossest state of heathen darkness and ignorance to a competent knowledge of those doctrines of the Christian religion which are chiefly necessary to salvation. She had put into his hand the book of God, and had taught him to read it: and God had, in an especial manner, answered all her prayers for the dear child.

The time was now coming on very fast, when she must leave little Henry; and the thoughts of this parting was very painful to her. Some days before she set out on her journey, she called him into her room, and questioned him concerning the things which she had taught him; directing him, as often as he could, to give his answers from the Bible. Her first question was, "How many Gods are there?"

HENRY.

There is one God; and there is none other but he. Mark xii. 32.

LADY.

Do we not believe that there are three Persons in this one God?

HENRY.

There are three that bear record in heaven; the Father, the Word, and the Holy Ghost: and these three are one. 1 John v. 7.

LADY.

What do you mean by the Word?

HENRY.

The Word is the Lord Jesus Christ.

LADY.

Do you know that from the Bible?

HENRY.

Yes; for St. John says, in the first chapter of his Gospel, *In the beginning was the Word, and the Word was with God, and the Word was God. He was in the world, and the world was made by him, and the world knew him not.*

LADY.

Did God make man good at first?

HENRY.

Yes; for in the first chapter of the Bible, the last verse it is written, *God saw every thing that he had made, and, behold, it was very good.*

LADY.

Are men very good now? Can you find me one person who deserves to be called good?

HENRY.

I need not look into the Bible to answer that question. I need but just get into the *palanquin*, and go into the *bazar*, and shew you the people there: I am sure I could not find one good person in all the *bazar*.

LADY.

But I think, Henry, you might spare yourself the trouble of going into the *bazar* to see how bad human creatures are: could you not find proofs of that nearer home?

HENRY.

What, our servants you mean? Or, perhaps, the ladies who are in the hall with my mamma? they laughed at the Bible at breakfast; I knew what they meant, very well; and my mamma laughed too: I am sure nobody can say that they are good.

LADY.

No, my dear; those poor ladies are not good: it would be misleading you, to say that they are. But as we cannot make them better by speaking ill of them in their absence, it would be as well not to mention them at all, unless it were in prayer to God that he would turn their hearts. But to return to my question——You need not go so far as the hall for an answer to it. There is a little boy in this very room, called Henry: can he be said to be a good boy? A very few months ago, that little boy used to tell lies every day: and only yesterday I saw him in a passion, because the *sais** would not let him get on the back of one of the coach-horses; and I think, but I am not sure, that he gave the *sais* a blow.

HENRY.

I know it was very wicked: but I had no stick in my hand, and therefore I hope I did not hurt him. I hope God will give me grace never to do so again. I gave the *sais* all that I had left of my *rupee*, this morning; and I told him that I was very sorry.

LADY.

I mentioned it, my dear, that you might know where to look for an answer to my question.

HENRY.

Oh! I know that I am not good. I have done many, many naughty things, which nobody knows of; no, not even Boosy. And God only can know the naughtiness of my heart.

LADY.

Then you think yourself a sinner?

HENRY.

A very great one.

LADY.

Where do sinners go when they die?

HENRY.

The wicked shall be turned into hell, and all the nations that forget God. Psalm ix. 17.

LADY.

If all wicked people are turned into hell, how can you escape?

HENRY.

If I believe in the Lord Jesus Christ, I shall be saved. Stay one moment, and I will shew you the verse. *"Believe on the Lord Jesus Christ, and thou shalt be saved."* Acts xvi. 31.

LADY.

What! if you believe in the Lord Jesus Christ, shall you go to heaven with all your sins? Can sinful creatures be in heaven?

---

* A servant who has the charge of a horse.

HENRY.

No; to be sure not. God cannot live with sinners. He is *of purer eyes than to behold evil.* Habakkuk i. 13. But if I believe in the Lord Jesus Christ, he will take away my sin; for His *blood cleanseth from all sin:* 1 John i. 7. and he will give me a new heart, and make me a new creature, and I shall be purified as he is pure. 1 John iii. 3.

Now the Lady was pleased with little Henry's answers: and she thanked God in her heart for having so blessed her labours with the poor little boy. But she did not praise him, lest he should become proud: and she well knew that *God resisteth the proud, but giveth grace unto the humble.* James iv. 6. So she refrained from commending him; but she said, "What do you mean, my dear, by being made quite new again?"

HENRY.

Before I knew the Lord Jesus Christ, I used to think of nothing but naughty things. I loved myself more than any body else. I loved eating fruit and sweetmeats; and was so greedy of them, that I would have told a hundred lies, I do think, for one mouthful of them. Then I was passionate and proud. I used to be so pleased when any body bowed to me, and said, "*Sahib.*" And you cannot think how cruel I was to all kinds of little creatures I could get hold of, even the poor cock-roaches: I used to kill them just for my own pleasure. But now I do think my heart is beginning to change a little, I mean a very little, for I gave all my last sweetmeats to the *matre's** boy. But still I know that my heart is far from being clean yet; but God can make it white and clean when he pleases.

LADY.

You must pray every day, and oftentimes in the day, and in the night when you are awake, my dear child; that God will send his Holy Spirit into your heart, to make it clean and pure, and to lead and direct you in all you do. Blessed are those, my dear child, who love the Lord Jesus Christ: for unto them *the Spirit of truth* shall be revealed; and it *shall dwell with them, and be in them.* John xiv. 17.

She then shut the door of the room; and she and the little boy knelt down together, and prayed to God, that he would, for his dear Son's sake, *create a clean heart in the* child, *and renew a right spirit within* him. Psalm li. 10. When the young lady arose from her knees, she kissed little Henry, and told him, not without many tears, that she must soon go away from him.

When Henry heard this news, for some moments he could not speak; at length he cried out, "What shall I do, when you are gone! I shall have nobody to speak to but my *bearer,* for my mamma does not love me; and I shall spend all my time with the natives. I shall never more hear any body talk of God. Oh! I very much fear that I shall become wicked again."

"My poor child," said the lady, "do not doubt the power of God. When our Saviour was going to leave his disciples, he said, '*I will not leave you orphans;*** I will come to you.' John xiv. 18. And do you think, my child, that after the blessed Lord God has made himself known unto you, and adopted you as a dear son, that he will leave you comfortless? Think how good he was to call you from the paths of destruction, and

---

* A sweeper: a person of low cast, who eats every thing.
** The word is *orphans* in the original.

from the way of hell. You knew not so much as his holy name, and were living altogether among the Heathens. It was by his providence that I came here; that I remained here so long; that I loved you, and endeavoured to teach you; and that I had
a Bible to give you. *Faithful is he*, my beloved child, *who called you. He will preserve
your whole spirit and soul and body blameless unto the coming of the Lord Jesus.*"
1 Thess. v. 23, 24. She then sung a verse of a hymn to him; which he often repeated,
and would try to sing, when she was far away from him.

> Jesus sought me, when a stranger,
>   Wandering from the fold of God;
> He, to save my soul from danger,
>   Interpos'd his precious blood.*

   Now it would take more time than I have to spare, to repeat the several conversations which this young lady had with little Henry before she went away. He cried sadly
the day she went. He followed her down to the river-side; for she was going down to
Berhampore, where she was soon afterwards married to a very pious young man of the
name of Baron.
   Henry went on board the *budgerow,*** to take leave of her. She kissed him many times
before they parted; and gave Boosy, who was with him, four *rupees, buckshish*, that he
might continue to behave well to his little *sahib*. The last words almost that she said
to Henry were these, "You must try, my dear child, with the grace of God, to make
Boosy a Christian; that he may be no longer numbered among the Heathen, but may
be counted among the sons of God."
   When the *budgerow* was ready to sail, little Henry took his last leave of the lady, and
came on shore; where he stood under the shade of a Braminee fig-tree,† watching the
boat as it sailed down the broad stream of the Ganges, till it was hidden by the winding shore. Then Boosy, taking him up in his arms, brought him back to his mamma's
house: and from that time he was as much neglected as he had been before this good
young lady came; with this difference only, (and that indeed was a blessing for which I
doubt not he will thank God to all eternity,) that he was now able to read the book of
God; whereas, before, he knew not even God's holy name.
   Sometimes his mamma would let him eat his *tiffin*†† with her: but, as she always employed herself at table (when not actually eating) in smoking her *hookah*,▲ and as most
of her visitors did the same, the *tiffin*-time was very stupid to the little boy; for, instead of
pleasant and useful discourse, there was in general nothing to be heard at these meals
but the rattling of plates and knives-and-forks, the creaking of the *punkah*,|| and the

---

* Sung to the tune of the Sicilian Mariners' Hymn.
** A kind of barge.
† A tree, that takes root downward from its branches.
†† Luncheon.
▲ A kind of pipe, the smoke of which is drawn through water, and the motion of the air through
   the water causes a bubbling noise.
|| A large fan suspended from the ceiling.

guggling of the water in the *hookah;* except his mamma (which not unseldom happened) occasioned a little variety, by scolding the servants and calling them names in their own language.

So poor little Henry found no better companion than his *bearer;* and he never was more pleased than when he was sitting by him in the *verandah,* reading his Bible to himself.

And now the young lady's last words returned to his mind, namely, "You must try to make Boosy a Christian." But he did not know how to begin this work: it seemed to him, that the heart of poor Boosy could only be changed by the immediate interference of God; so fond was he of his wooden Gods and foolish ceremonies, and so much was he afraid of offending his *gooroo.** And in this respect Henry judged rightly; for no one can come to God without the help of God: yet he has pointed out the means by which we must endeavour to bring our fellow-creatures to him; and we must, in faith and humility, use these means, praying for the divine blessing to render them effectual.

The first step which Henry took towards this work, was to pray for Boosy. After some thought, he made a prayer, which was much to this purpose: "O, Lord God, hear the humble prayer of a poor little sinful child. Give me power, O God, for thy dear Son's sake, (who died for us upon the cross,) to turn the heart of my poor *bearer* from his wooden Gods, and to lead him to the cross of Jesus Christ." This prayer he never failed to repeat every night, and many times a day: and from time to time he used to talk to Boosy, and repeat to him many things which the young lady had taught him. But although Boosy heard him with good-humour, yet he did not seem to pay much heed to what the child said; for he would argue to this purpose: "There are many brooks and rivers of water, but they all run into the sea at last; so there are a great many religions, but they all lead to heaven: there is the Mussulmaun's way to heaven, and the Hindoo's way, and the Christian's way; and one way is as good as another." He asserted, also, that if he were to commit the greatest sin, and were to go immediately afterwards and wash in the Ganges, he should be quite innocent. And a great many other foolish things he had to say to the same purpose, so that he sometimes quite out-talked the child. But Henry was so earnest in the cause he had undertaken, that, although he might be silenced at one time, yet he would often (after having said his prayer and consulted his Bible) begin the attack again. He would some times get close to him, and look in his face, and say, "Poor Boosy! poor Boosy! you are going the wrong way, and will not let me set you right: there is but one way to heaven; our Saviour, the Lord Jesus Christ, is *the way* to heaven, and *no man cometh unto God but by him.*" John xiv. 6. Then he would try to explain who the Lord Jesus Christ is: how he came down to the earth; that he took man's nature upon him; suffered and died upon the cross for the sins of men; was buried, and arose again on the third day, and ascended into heaven; and is now sitting at the right hand of God, from whence he will come to judge the quick and the dead.

In this manner the little boy proceeded from day to day: but Boosy seemed to pay

---

* A religious teacher, or confessor.

him little or no attention; nay, he would sometimes laugh at him, and ask him why he was so earnest about a thing of so little consequence? However, to do Boosy justice, he never was ill-humoured or disrespectful to his little *sahib*.

Now it happened, about this time, that Henry's mamma had occasion to go to Calcutta; and, as she went by water, she took Henry and his *bearer* in the *budgerow* with her. Henry had not been well, and she thought the change of air might do him good. It was at the end of the rains; at that season of the year when India is most green and beautiful, although not most healthy. When the *budgerow* came to anchor in an evening, Henry used to take a walk with his *bearer;* and sometimes they would ramble among the fields and villages for more than a mile from the river. Henry had all his life been confined to one spot; so, you may be sure, he was well pleased to see so many different countries, and asked many questions about the things which he saw. And often, during these rambles, he used to have an argument with Boosy concerning the great Creator of all things: and Henry would say to his *bearer*, that the great God, who made all things, could not be like the Gods which he believed in, which, according to his accounts of them, were more wicked and foolish than the worst men.

Once, in particular; it was in one of those lovely places near the *Raja-mehal** hills; Henry and his *bearer* went to walk. Henry's mamma had during the day been very cross to him, and the poor little fellow did not feel well, although he did not complain; but he was glad when he got out of the boat. The sun was just setting, and a cool breeze blew over the water, with which the little boy being refreshed, climbed without difficulty to the top of a little hill where was a tomb. Here they sat down: and Henry could not but admire the beautiful prospect which was before them. On their left hand was the broad stream of the Ganges winding round the curved shore, till it was lost behind the *Raja-mehal* hills. The *budgerow*, gaily painted, was fastened to the shore just below them; and with it many lesser boats, with thatched and sloping roofs. The *dandies*** and native servants, having finished their day's work, were preparing their *khauna*, in distinct parties, according to their several *casts*, upon the banks of the river: some grinding their *mussala*,† some lighting their little fires, some washing their brass vessels, and others sitting in a circle upon the ground smoking their cocoa-nut *hookahs*. Before them, and on their right hand, was a beautiful country abounding with corn-fields, *topes* of trees, thatched cottages with their little bamboo porches, plantain and palm trees; beyond which the *Raja-mehal* hills were seen, some bare to their summits, and others covered with *jungle*,†† which even now afford a shelter to tigers, rhinoceroses, and wild hogs.

Henry sat silent a long time. At last he said, "Boosy, this is a good country: that is, it would be a very good country, if the people were Christians. Then they would not be so idle as they now are; and they would agree together, and clear the *jungles*, and build churches to worship God in. It will be pleasant to see the people, when they are Christians, all going on a Sunday morning to some fair church built among those hills,

---

* The hall of the rajah.
** Boatmen.
† A general name for spices, salt, medicine, &c.
†† Uncultivated waste land, overrun with brushwood or reeds.

and to see them in an evening sitting at the door of their houses reading the *shaster**—I do not mean your *shaster*, but our *shaster*, God's book."

Boosy answered, that he knew there would be a time when all the world would be of one religion, and when there would be no *cast*; but he did not know when that would be, and he was sure he should not live to see it.

"There is a country now," said Henry, "where there are no *casts*; and where we all shall be like dear brothers. It is a better country than this: there are no evil beasts; there is no more hunger, no more thirst; there the waters are sure; there the sun does not scorch by day, nor the moon smite by night. It is a country to which I sometimes think and hope I shall go very soon: I wish, Boosy, you would be persuaded either to go with me, or to follow me."

"What!" said Boosy, "is *sahib* going to *Willaet?***" And then he said, he hoped not; for he could never follow him through the black water, as the Hindoos call the seas.

Henry then explained to him, that he did not mean England, but heaven. "Sometimes I think," said he, "when I feel the pain which I did this morning, that I shall not live long: I think I shall die soon, Boosy. O, I wish! I wish I could persuade you to love the Lord Jesus Christ!" And then Henry, getting up, threw his arms round Boosy's neck, and begged him to be a Christian. "Dear Boosy," he said, "good Boosy, do try to be a Christian." But poor little Henry's attempts were yet quite ineffectual.

In little more than a month's time from their leaving Dinapore, they reached Calcutta, and were received into the house of a worthy gentleman of the name of Smith. When Henry's mamma was settled in Mr. Smith's house, she found less inclination, if possible, than ever, to pay any attention to Henry. According to the custom of India, she must pay the first visit to all her acquaintance in Calcutta. Her dresses, too, having all been made at Dinapore, did not agree with the last Europe fashions which were come out: these were all to be altered, and new ones bought; and it was a good deal of trouble to direct the tailor to do this properly. Her hair was not dressed in the fashion: and her *ayah*† was very stupid; it was many days before she could forget the old way, and learn the new one. So poor Henry was quite forgotten in all this bustle: and, although he was for several days very ill, and complained to his *bearer* that his side gave him great pain, yet his mamma never knew it.

Mr. and Mrs. Smith once or twice remarked, when they looked at Henry, that the child was very pale, and that his eyes were heavy: but his mamma answered, "O, this is nothing; the child is well enough; children in India, you know, have that look."

It happened one afternoon, as Mr. and Mrs. Smith and Henry's mamma were in the drawing-room after *tiffin*, while the ladies were giving their opinion upon a magazine, which contained an account of the last Europe fashion of carriages and dresses, &c. (for I am sorry to say, that Mrs. Smith, although she had the best example in her husband, had still to learn not to love the world,) Mr. Smith, half angry with them, and yet not knowing whether he should presume to give them a check, was walking up and down the room with rather a hasty step; when his eye, as he passed the door, caught

---

* The Hindoo religious books.
** Country: but generally applied to Europe.
† A waiting-maid.

little Henry sitting on the mat at the head of the stairs, between his *bearer's* knees, with his Bible in his hand. His back being turned towards the drawing-room door, Mr. Smith had an opportunity of observing what he was about without being seen; he accordingly stood still, and listened; and he heard the gentle voice of Henry, as he tried to interpret the sacred book to his *bearer* in the *bearer's* own language.

Mr. Smith at first could scarcely believe what he saw and heard: but, at last, being quite sure he was not dreaming, he turned hastily towards the ladies, exclaiming, "Twenty-five years have I been in India, and never have I seen any thing like this. Heaven be praised! truly is it written, '*Out of the mouth of babes and sucklings thou hast perfected praise.*' Matthew xxi. 16. For shame! for shame! Mrs. Smith, will you never lay aside your toys and gewgaws? Do give me that book, and I will let the cook have it to light his fire with.——Here are two persons, who have been nearly fifty years in the world, sitting together talking of their finery and painted toys; while a little creature, who eight years ago had not breathed the breath of life, is endeavouring to impart divine knowledge to the Heathen. *But God hath chosen the foolish things of the world, to confound the wise; and God hath chosen the weak things of the world, to confound the things which are mighty.*" 1 Corinthians i. 27.

"My dear," cried Mrs. Smith, "surely you forget yourself! What can you mean?—— Toys, and finery——my dear, my dear, you are very rude!"

"Rude!" said Henry's mamma, "rude indeed! Mr. Smith—and pray, sir, what do you mean by saying, 'Fifty years?' Do you suppose that I am fifty years old?——Extraordinary indeed!"

"I beg pardon," said Mr. Smith. "I did not mean to offend——but there is that little boy trying to explain the Bible to his *bearer*."

"But, surely," said Henry's mamma, "you do not think that I am fifty years of age?— you are mistaken by twenty years."

MRS. SMITH.

O! my dear madam, you must excuse my husband.——Whenever he is a little angry with me, he tells *me* that I am getting old. But I am so used to it, that I never mind it.

MR. SMITH.

Well, my dear; leave me, if you please, to speak for myself. I am not a man that disguises the truth. Whether I speak or not, time runs on, death and eternity approach. I do not see why it should be a matter of politeness to throw dust in each other's eyes ——But enough of this, and too much. I want to know the meaning of what I but now saw: a little English child of seven years of age endeavouring to explain the Bible to his *bearer*. I did not even know that the child could read.

"O," said Henry's mamma, "this matter is easily explained. I had a young lady in my house at Patna, some time since, who taught the child to read: for this I was obliged to her. But she was not satisfied with that alone: she made a methodist, a downright canting methodist, of the boy. I never knew it till it was too late."

MR. SMITH.

A methodist! What do you mean, madam?

"Indeed," said Henry's mamma, "the child has never been himself since. Captain D—— of the —— native infantry, when they were quartered at Dinapore, used to have such sport with him. He taught him, when he was but two years old, to call the dogs and the horses, and to swear at the servants in English——but I shall offend Mr. Smith again," she added; "I suspect him a little of being a methodist himself. Am I right, Mrs. Smith?" And she laughed at her own wit. But Mrs. Smith looked grave; and Mr. Smith lifted up his eyes to heaven, saying, "May God Almighty turn your heart!"

"O, Mr. Smith," said Henry's mamma, "you take the matter too seriously: I was only speaking in jest."

"I shall put that to the trial, madam," said Mr. Smith. "If you really feel no ill-will against religion, and people who call themselves religious, you will not refuse to let me consider Henry as my pupil while you remain in my house; which I hope will be as long as you can make it convenient. You have known me some years, (I will not say how many, lest you should be angry again,) and you will make allowances for my plain dealings."

"Well," said Henry's mamma, "we know you are an oddity: take your own way, and let me take mine." So she got up to dress for her evening airing on the course: and thus this strange conversation ended in good-humour; for she was not, upon the whole, an ill-tempered woman.

The same evening, his mamma being gone out, Mr. Smith called Henry into his own room; and learnt from him all that he could tell of his own history, and of the young lady who had taught him to read his Bible, and had advised him to try to make Boosy a Christian. I will relate to you the last part of this discourse which passed between Mr. Smith and Henry.

Mr. Smith.

Do you think that Boosy's heart is at all turned towards God?

Henry.

No, I do not think that it is; although for the last half year I have been constantly talking to him about God: but he still will have it, that his own idols are true Gods.

Mr. Smith.

It is almost dangerous, my dear little boy, for a child like you to dispute with an Heathen: for although you are in the right, and he in the wrong, yet Satan, who is the father of lies, may put words into his mouth which may puzzle you; so that your faith may be shaken, while his remains unchanged.

Henry.

Oh! sir; must I give up the hope of Boosy's being made a Christian? Poor Boosy! he has taken care of me ever since I was born.

Mr. Smith.

But suppose, my dear boy, that I could put you in a better way of converting Boosy: a safe way to yourself, and a better for him? Can Boosy read?

Henry.

Only a very little, I believe.

Mr. Smith.

Then you must learn to read for him.

Henry.

How, sir?

Mr. Smith.

If I could get for you some of the most important chapters in the Bible, such as the first chapters of Genesis, which speak of the creation of the world and the fall of man, with the first promise of the Saviour, and some parts of the Gospel, translated into Boosy's language, would you try to learn to read them to him? I will teach you the letters, or characters as they are called, in which they will be written.

HENRY.

O! I will learn them with joy.

MR. SMITH.

Well, my boy; come every morning into my study, and I will teach you the Persian characters; for those are what will be used in the copy of the chapters I shall put into your hands. Sometime or other, the whole Bible will be translated in this manner.

HENRY.

Will the words be Persian, sir? I know Boosy does not understand Persian.

MR. SMITH.

No, my dear; the words will be the same as those you speak every day with the natives. When you have as much of the Bible as I can get prepared for you in this manner, you must read it to your *bearer* every day; praying continually, that God will bless his holy word to him. And never fear, my dear, but that the word of God will do its work: "*For as the rain cometh down, and the snow, from heaven, and returneth not thither, but watereth the earth, and maketh it bring forth and bud, that it may give seed to the sower, and bread to the eater; so shall my word be that goeth forth out of my mouth: it shall not return unto me void; but it shall accomplish that which I please, and it shall prosper in the thing whereto I sent it.*" Isaiah lv. 10, 11. "But do not, my dear boy," added Mr. Smith, "argue and dispute with your *bearer* about religion; you are not yet able. Only read the Bible to him, and pray for him continually; leaving the rest with God."

But, not to make my story too long; while Henry's mamma remained at Calcutta, which was more than a year, Henry received a lesson every day from Mr. Smith in his study; and Mr. Smith taught him the Persian characters, and provided him with as many chapters in the Bible in Hindoostannee as he could get properly prepared in a short time: these he had bound together in red morocco, and presented them to Henry, not without asking the blessing of God upon them.

How delighted was Henry, when he received the book, and found that he could read it easily! He was in his place on the mat between Boosy's knees in a minute, and you might have heard him reading from one end of the house to the other, for he could not contain himself for joy. Nor was he contented with reading it himself, he must make Boosy learn to read it too. And this was brought about much sooner than you would have supposed it possible: for as Henry learnt the Persian letters from day to day of Mr. Smith, he had been accustomed afterwards to write them on a slate, and make Boosy copy them as they sat together; and so, by degrees, he had taught them all to his *bearer* before he was in possession of the Hindoostannee copy of the chapters.

"Now, my boy," said Mr. Smith, "you are in the safe way of giving instruction, in an *ancient path cast up* by God. Jeremiah xviii. 15. Do not trust to the words of your own wisdom, but to the word of God. Hold fast to the scripture, dear boy, and you will be safe. And be not impatient, if the seed you sow should not spring up immediately: something tells me that I shall see Boosy a Christian before I die; or if I do not see that day, he that outlives me will."

Now the time arrived, when Henry's mamma was to leave Calcutta. Indeed, she had stayed much longer there than she had at first proposed; but there were so many amusements going forward; so much gay company; so many fashionable dresses to purchase; that she could not find in her heart to leave them, although she was heartily tired of Mr. Smith's company. She respected him, indeed, as an old friend, and worthy man; but he had such particular ways, she said, that sometimes she had difficulty to put up with them.

She proposed, as she went up the country, to stop at Berhampore, to see Mrs. Baron. When Henry heard of this, he was greatly pleased; yet, when he came to take leave of Mr. Smith, he cried very much.

As they went up the river, Henry took every opportunity of reading his chapters to his *bearer*, when his mamma could not overhear him: and he had many opportunities early in the morning, and in the afternoon when his mamma was asleep, as she always slept for an hour after *tiffin*. He proceeded very well indeed, Boosy daily improving, at least, in his knowledge of the Bible: till the weather suddenly becoming excessively hot, Henry was seized with a return of violent pain in his side, and other very bad symptoms. He became paler and thinner, and could not eat. His mamma, having no company to divert her, soon took notice of the change in the child, and began to be frightened; and so was his *bearer*. So they made all the haste they could to Berhampore, that they might procure advice from the doctors there, and get into a cool house, for the boat was excessively hot: but, notwithstanding all the haste which they made, there was a great change in the poor little boy before they reached Berhampore.

When they were come within a day's journey of the place, they sent a servant forwards to Mrs. Baron's; so that, when the *budgerow* stopped the next day near the cantonments, Mrs. Baron herself was waiting on the shore with *palanquins* ready to carry them to her house. As soon as the board was fixed from the boat to the banks of the river, she jumped out of her *palanquin*, and was in the *budgerow* in a minute, with little Henry in her arms. "O, my dear, dear boy!" she said. "my dear, dear boy!" She could say no more, so great was her joy: but, when she looked at him, and saw how very ill he appeared, her joy was presently damped; and she said, in her haste, to his mamma, "Dear madam, what is the matter with Henry? he looks very ill."

"Yes," said his mamma, "I am sorry to say that he is very ill; we must lose no time in getting advice for him."

"Do not cry, dear Mrs. Baron," said little Henry, seeing the tears running down her cheeks; "we must all die, you know we must, and death is very sweet to those who love the Lord Jesus Christ."

"O, my child," said his mamma, "why do you talk of dying? you will live to be a judge yet, and we shall see you with seven silver sticks before your *palanquin*."

"I do not wish it, mamma," said Henry.

The more Mrs. Baron looked at Henry, the more she was affected. For some moments she could not speak, or command her feelings at all; but, after having drank a little water, she became more composed; and proposed, that they should all immediately remove to her house. And when she found herself shut up in her *palanquin*, she prayed earnestly to God, that whether the sweet baby lived or died, he might not be taken from her in his sickness; but that she might, with the help of God, administer holy nourishment to his immortal soul, and comfort to his little weak body.

When they were arrived at Mrs. Baron's house, she caused Henry to be laid on a sofa by day in the sitting room, and at night in a room close by her own. The chief surgeon of the station was immediately sent for, and every thing was done for little Henry that the tenderest love could suggest.

Berhampore happened at that time to be very full; and Henry's mamma, finding many of her old acquaintance there, was presently so deeply engaged in paying and receiving visits, that she seemed again almost entirely to forget Henry, and lost all her concern about him: comforting herself, when she was going to a great dinner or ball, that Mrs. Baron would be with him, and he would be well taken care of. But it is a poor excuse to make, for our neglect of duty, and one I fear that will not stand at the day of judgment, to say that there are others that will do it as well for us.

Notwithstanding all the surgeon could do, and all the care of Mrs. Baron, Henry's illness increased upon him; and every one had reason to think that the dear little fellow's time on earth would soon come to an end. Mr. and Mrs. Baron were by turns his almost constant attendants: when one left him, the other generally took the place by his couch. It was very interesting, and rather uncommon, to see a fine lively young man, like Mr. Baron, attending a little sick child; sometimes administering to him his food or medicine, and sometimes reading the Bible to him—but Mr. Baron feared God.

When Henry first came to Berhampore, he was able to take the air in an evening in a *palanquin*, and could walk about the house; and two or three times he read a chapter in the Hindoostannee Bible to Boosy: but he was soon too weak to read, and his airings became shorter and shorter; he was at last obliged to give them quite up, and to take entirely to his couch and bed, where he remained until his death.

When Boosy saw that his little *sahib's* end was drawing on, he was very sorrowful, and could hardly be persuaded to leave him night or day, even to get his *khauna*. He did every thing he could think of to please him, (and more, as he afterwards said, to please his dying master than his God:) he began to read his chapters with some diligence; and little Henry would lie on his couch, listening to Boosy as he read (imperfectly indeed) the word of God in Hindoostannee. Often he would stop him, to explain to him what he was reading; and very beautiful sometimes were the remarks which he made, and better suited to the understanding of his *bearer* than those of an older or more learned person would have been.

The last time that his *bearer* read to him, Mrs. Baron sitting by him, he suddenly stopped him, saying, "Ah, Boosy, if I had never read the Bible, and did not believe in it, what an unhappy creature should I now be! for in a very short time I shall *go down to the grave to come up no more;* Job vii. 9. that is, until my body is raised at the last day. When I was out last, I saw a very pretty burying ground with many trees about it. I knew that I should soon lie there; I mean, that my body would: but I was not afraid, because I love my Lord Jesus Christ, and I know that he will go down with me unto the grave; I shall sleep with him, and *I shall be satisfied, when I awake, with his likeness.*" Psalm xvii. 15. He then turned to Mrs. Baron, and said, "*I know that my Redeemer liveth, and that he shall stand at the latter day upon the earth: and though, after my skin, worms destroy this body, yet in my flesh I shall see God.*" Job xix. 25, 26. "O kind Mrs. Baron! who, when I was a poor sinful child, brought me to the knowledge of my dear Redeemer; anointing me with sweet ointment (even his precious blood) for my burial, which was so soon to follow."

"Dear child!" said Mrs. Baron, hardly able to preserve her composure, "dear child! give the glory to God."

"Yes, I will glorify him for ever and ever," cried the poor little boy; and he raised himself up in his couch, joining his small and taper fingers together: "yes, I will praise him, I will love him. I was a grievous sinner; every imagination of the thought of my heart was evil continually; I hated all good things; I hated even my Maker: but he sought me out; he washed me from my sins in his own blood; he gave me a new heart; he has clothed me with the garments of salvation, and hath put on me the robe of righteousness; he *hath abolished death, and brought life and immortality to light.*" 2 Timothy i. 10. Then turning to his *bearer,* he said, "O my poor *bearer!* what will become of you, *if you neglect so great salvation?*" Hebrews ii. 3. "O Lord Jesus Christ," he added, "turn the heart of my poor *bearer!*" This short prayer, which little Henry made in Hindoostannee, his *bearer* repeated, scarcely knowing what he was doing. And this, as Boosy afterwards told Mr. Smith, was the first prayer he had ever made to the true God —the first time he had ever called upon his holy name.

Having done speaking, little Henry laid his head down on his pillow, and closed his eyes. His spirit was full of joy, indeed, but his flesh was weak; and he lay some hours in a kind of slumber. When he awoke, he called Mrs. Baron, and begged her to sing the verse of the hymn he loved so much, "Jesus sought me, &c." which she had taught him at Dinapore. He smiled while she was singing, but did not speak.

That same evening, Boosy being left alone with his little master, and seeing that he was wakeful and inclined to talk, said, "*Sahib,* I have been thinking all day that I am a sinner, and always have been one; and I begin to believe that my sins are such as Gunga cannot wash away. I wish I could believe in the Lord Jesus Christ!"

When Henry heard this, he strove to raise himself up, but was unable, on account of his extreme weakness; yet his eyes sparkled with joy: he endeavoured to speak, but could not; and at last he burst into tears. He soon, however, became more composed, and pointing to his *bearer* to sit down on the floor by his couch, he said, "Boosy, what you have now said makes me very happy: I am very, very happy to hear you call yourself a sinner, and such a one as Gunga cannot make clean. It is the Spirit of God through Jesus Christ which has made this known to you: he has called you to come unto him. Faithful is he that calleth you. I shall yet see you, my poor *bearer,* in *the general assembly and church of the first-born.*" Hebrews xii. 23. "You were kind to me when my own father and mother were dead. The first thing I can remember, is being carried by you to the *Mangoe tope* near my mamma's house at Patna. Nobody loved me then but you: and could I depart in peace, and leave you behind me in the way to hell? I could not bear to think of it! Thank God! thank God! I knew he would hear my prayer: but I thought that, perhaps, you would not begin to become a Christian till I was gone. When I am dead, Boosy," added the little boy, "do you go to Mr. Smith at Calcutta. I cannot write to him, or else I would: but you shall take him one lock of my hair, (I will get Mrs. Baron to cut it off, and put it in paper,) and tell him that I sent it. You must say, that Henry L——, who died at Berhampore, sent it, with this request, that good Mr. Smith will take care of his poor *bearer* when he has lost *cast* for becoming a Christian." Boosy would have told Henry that he was not quite determined to be a Christian, and that he could not think of losing *cast;* but Henry, guessing what he was going to say, put his hand upon his mouth. "Stop! stop!" he said; "do not say words which will make God angry, and which you will be sorry for by and by: for I know you will die a Christian. God has begun a good work in you, and I am certain that he will finish it."

While Henry was talking to his *bearer*, Mrs. Baron had come into the room; but, not wishing to interrupt him, she had stood behind his couch; but now she came forward. As soon as he saw her, he begged her to take off his cap, and cut off some of his hair, as several of his friends wished for some. She thought that she would endeavour to comply with his request. But when she took off his cap, and his beautiful hair fell about his pale sweet face; when she considered how soon the time would be when the eye that had seen him should see him no more; she could not restrain her feelings; but, throwing down the scissars, and putting her arm round him, "O my child! my dear, dear child!" she said, "I cannot bear it! I cannot part with you yet!"

The poor little boy was affected: but he gently reproved her, saying, "*If you love me, you will rejoice, because I go to my Father.*" John xiv. 28.

There was a considerable change in the child during the night; and all the next day till evening he lay in a kind of slumber: and when he was roused to take his medicine or nourishment, he seemed not to know where he was, or who was with him. In the evening he suddenly revived, and asked for his mamma. He had seldom asked for her before. She was in the house: for she was not so hard-hearted (thoughtless as she was) as to go into gay company at this time, when the child's death might be hourly expected. She trembled much when she heard that he asked for her. She was conscious, perhaps, that she had not fulfilled her duty by him. He received her affectionately, when she went up to his bed-side, and begged that every body would go out of the room, saying, that he had something very particular to speak about to her. He talked to her for some time, but nobody knows the particulars of their conversation: though it is believed that the care of her immortal soul was the subject of the last discourse which this dear little boy held with her. She came out of his room with her eyes swelled with crying, and his little well-worn Bible in her hand, (which he had probably given to her, as it had hitherto always lain on his bed by him;) and shutting herself in her room, she remained, without seeing any one, till the news was brought that all was over. From that time she never gave her mind so entirely to the world as she had formerly done; but became a more serious character, and daily read little Henry's Bible.

But now to return to little Henry. As there are but few persons who love to meditate upon scenes of death, and too many are only able to view the gloomy side of them, instead of following, by the eye of faith, the glorious progress of the departing saint; I will hasten to the end of my story. The next day at twelve o'clock, being Sunday, he was delivered from this evil world, and received into glory. His passage was calm, although not without some mortal pangs. *May we die the death of the righteous, and may our last end be like his!* Numbers xxiii. 10.

Mr. and Mrs. Baron and his *bearer* attended him to the last moment, and Mr. Baron followed him to the grave.

Sometime after his death, his mamma caused a monument to be built over his grave, on which was inscribed his name, Henry L——, and his age, which at the time of his death was eight years and seven months. Underneath was a part of his favourite verse, from 1st. Thessalonians v. altering only one word. *"Faithful is he that called* me." And afterwards was added, by desire of Mr. Smith, this verse, from James v. 20. *"He which converteth the sinner from the error of his way, shall save a soul from death, and shall hide a multitude of sins."*

When I first visited Berhampore, I went to see little Henry's monument. It was then white and fair, and the inscription very plain: but I am told, that the damp of that climate has so defaced the inscription, and blackened the whole monument, that it cannot now be distinguished from the tombs which surround it. But this is of little consequence, as all who remember Henry L—— have long ago left Berhampore; and we are assured that this dear child has himself received *an inheritance that fadeth not away.* 1 Peter i. 4. *The world passeth away, and the lust thereof: but he that doeth the will of God abideth for ever.* 1 John ii. 17.

Every person who reads this story will, I think, be anxious to know what became of Boosy. Immediately after the funeral of his little *sahib,* having received his wages, with a handsome present; he carried the lock of hair, which Mrs. Baron sealed up carefully, with a letter from her to Mr. Smith. He was received into Mr. Smith's family, and removed with him to a distant part of India; where, shortly after, he renounced *cast,* and declared himself a Christian. After due examination, he was baptized; and continued till his death (which happened not very long after) a sincere Christian. It was on the occasion of the baptism of Boosy, to whom the Christian name of John was given, that the last verse was added to the monument of little Henry.

From Mrs. Baron and Mr. Smith I gathered most of the anecdotes relative to the history of Henry L——.

Little children in India, remember Henry L——, and *go and do likewise.* Luke x. 37. For *they that be wise shall shine as the brightness of the firmament; and they that turn many to righteousness, as the stars for ever and ever.* Daniel xii. 3.

FINIS.

A Select Bibliography of Secondary Works

The following bibliography omits some items referred to in the headnotes or in the introduction in Volume 3. It lists works particularly helpful to the student of children's books from Thomas Boreman to Charles Lamb, excluding many general histories. Emphasized are articles from periodicals, because they often escape cataloguing, and reprint editions, which often include valuable prefatory material and help make accessible the now-rare books of the period. The recent availability of such reprints suggests an awakening of interest in the first commercially successful secular literature for children in England and America.

Alderson, Brian. "Miniature Libraries for the Young." *The Private Library* 3d ser. 6, no. 1 (Spring 1983).

Andreae, Gesinea. *The Dawn of Juvenile Literature in England*. Amsterdam: J. J. Paris, 1925. Reprint. Detroit: Gale Research Co., 1975.

Arnold, Arnold, ed. *Pictures and Stories from Forgotten Children's Books*. New York: Dover Publications, 1969.

Avery, Gillian. *Childhood's Pattern: A Study of the Heroes and Heroines of Children's Fiction, 1770–1950*. London: Hodder & Stoughton, 1975.

_____. *Nineteenth Century Children: Heroes and Heroines in English Children's Stories, 1780–1900*. London: Hodder & Stoughton, 1965.

Bain, Iain, ed. *The Watercolours and Drawings of Thomas Bewick and His Workshop Apprentices*. 2 vols. London: Gordon Fraser, 1981.

Barchilon, Jacques. "Uses of the Fairy Tale in the Eighteenth Century." *Studies on Voltaire and the Eighteenth Century* 24 (1963):111–38.

Barchilon, Jacques, and Pettit, Henry, eds. *The Authentic Mother Goose Fairy Tales and Nursery Rhymes*. Denver: Allan Swallow, 1960.

Barnett, George L. "That Cursed Barbauld Crew, or Charles Lamb and Children's Literature." *The Charles Lamb Bulletin: The Journal of the Charles Lamb Society* n.s. 25 (June 1979).

Barry, Florence V. *A Century of Children's Books*. London: Methuen & Co., 1922. Reprint. Detroit: Singing Tree Press, 1968.

Bator, Robert. "Eighteenth-Century England versus the Fairy Tale." *Research Studies* 39 (March 1971):1–10.

_____. "Out of the Ordinary Road: Locke and English Juvenile Fiction in the Eighteenth Century." *Children's Literature* 1 (1972):46–53.

Berquin, Arnaud. *The Looking-Glass for the Mind; or, Intellectual Mirror.* London: E. Newbery, 1794. Reprint. New preface by Dana Herren. Early Children's Book Series, Toronto Public Library. New York: Johnson Reprint Corp., 1969.

Bingham, Jane, and Scholt, Grayce, eds. *Fifteen Centuries of Children's Literature: An Annotated Chronology of British and American Works in Historical Context.* Westport, Ct.: Greenwood Press, 1980.

Biography of a Spaniel: To Which Is Annexed The Idiot, a Tale. London: Minerva Press, 1804. Reprint. New preface by Judith St. John. Early Children's Book Series, Toronto Public Library. New York: Johnson Reprint Corp., 1969.

Blount, Margaret. *Animal Lore: The Creatures of Children's Fiction.* London: Hutchison & Co., 1974.

Botting, Roland B. "Christopher Smart and the *Lilliputian Magazine.*" *ELH* 9 (1942):286–87.

Cinderella; or, The Little Glass Slipper. London: Griffith & Farran, 186–. Facsimile reprint. London: Scolar Press, 1977.

Cotton, Nathaniel. *Visions in Verse.* 3d ed., rev. London: R. Dodsley, 1752. Reprint. New preface by Christine Buchanan. Children's Books from the Past Series, Toronto Public Library. Bern, Switzerland: Herbert Lang, 1973.

Cutt, Margaret N. "In Their Own Time: Footnotes to Social History." *Horn Book Magazine* 49 (Dec. 1973):617–23; 50 (Feb. 1974):24–31.

————. *Ministering Angels: A Study of Nineteenth-Century Evangelical Writing for Children.* Wormley, England: Five Owls Press, 1979.

Darton, F. J. Harvey. *Children's Books in England: Five Centuries of Social Life.* 3d ed., with corrections by Brian Alderson. Cambridge: At the University Press, 1982.

Delattre, F. "La littérature enfantine en Angleterre. " *Revue Pedagogique* n.s. 51 (Aug. 15, 1907):101–52.

DeMause, Lloyd. *The History of Childhood.* New York: Harper & Row, 1974.

Demers, Patricia, and Mayles, Gordon. *From Instruction to Delight: An Anthology of Children's Literature to 1850.* Toronto: Oxford University Press, 1982.

Develin, Christopher. *Poor Kit Smart.* London: Rupert Hart-Davis, 1961.

De Vries, Leonard, ed. *Flowers of Delight: An Agreeable Garland of Prose and Poetry.* New York: Pantheon, 1966.

Dundes, Alan, ed. *Cinderella: A Casebook.* New York: Wildman Press, 1983.

Early American Children's Books. Microfiche edition of A.S.W. Rosenbach Collection of the Free Library of Philadelphia. Millwood, N.Y.: KTO Microform, 1979.

Feaver, William. *When We Were Young: Two Centuries of Children's Book Illustration.* New York: Holt, Rinehart & Winston, 1977.

Feldmeier, Linda. "Where Skipping Lambkins Feed: Christopher Smart's *Hymns for the Amusement of Children.*" *Children's Literature* 4 (1975):64–69.

Fenn, Ellenor [Mrs. Teachwell]. *Fables in Monosyllables.* London: John Marshall, 1783. Reprint. New preface by Catherine Shakura. Early Children's Book Series, Toronto Public Library. New York: Johnson Reprint Corp., 1970.

Field, Carolyn W. *Special Collections in Children's Literature.* Chicago: American Library Association, 1982.

Field, Louise Frances. *The Child and His Book: Some Accounts of the History and Progress of Children's Literature in England.* 2d ed. London: Wells, Gardner, Darton, 1892. Reprint. Detroit: Singing Tree Press, 1968.

Gottlieb, Gerald. *Early Children's Books and Their Illustration.* Boston: David R. Godine for the Pierpont Morgan Library, 1975.

————. "Peculiar Difficulty: A Tale of the Eighteenth Century; Being an Account of Some Lamentable Lacks, Together with a Few Desperate Needs." In *Society and Children's Literature,* edited by James H. Fraser, pp. 121–36. Boston: David R. Godine in association with the American Library Association, 1978.

Green, Roger Lancelyn. *Tellers of Tales: Children's Books and Their Authors from 1800 to 1964.* Rev. ed. New York: Franklin Watts, 1965.

Grey, Jill E. "The *Lilliputian Magazine:* A Pioneering Periodical." *Journal of Librarianship,* April 2, 1970, pp. 107–15.

————. "Mrs. Teach'em—Children's Authors and Sarah Fielding." *The Junior Bookshelf* 32 (1968):285–88.

Grylls, David. *Guardians and Angels: Parents and Children in Nineteenth-Century Literature.* London and Boston: Faber & Faber, 1978.

Halsey, Rosalie V. *Forgotten Books of the American Nursery: A History of the Development of the American Story-Book.* Boston: Charles E. Goodspeed & Co., 1911. Reprint. Detroit: Gale Research Co., 1969.

Hammelman, H. A. "Miniature Libraries for Children." *Country Life* 122 (Dec. 26, 1957):1420–21.

Harden, O. Elizabeth McWhorter. *Maria Edgeworth's Art of Prose Fiction.* The Hague: Mouton, 1971.

Harwood, Dix. *Love for Animals and How It Developed in Great Britain.* New York: By the author, 1928.

Haviland, Virginia. *Children's Literature: A Guide to Reference Sources.* Washington, D.C.: Library of Congress, 1966. 1st supplement (with the assistance of Margaret N. Coughlan), 1972; 2d supplement, 1977.

Hawthorne, Julian. "Literature for Children." *North American Review* 138 (1884):383–96.

Hearn, M. P. "William Blake's Illustrations for Children's Books." *American Book Collector,* March–April 1981, pp. 33–43.

History of the Celebrated Nanny Goose, The. London: S. Hood, 1813. With *The History of the Prince Renard and the Lady Goosiana.* London: H. Fores, 1833. Reprint (2 vols. in l). Friends of the Osborne and Lillian H. Smith Collections, Toronto Public Library, 1973.

History of Little Fanny, The—Exemplified in a Series of Figures. 1st ed. London: Harris & Son, 1824. Facsimile reprint. London: Scolar Press, 1977.

History of Little Goody Two-Shoes, The. Reprint. Westport, Ct.: Redcoat Press, 1941.

History of Little Henry, The—Exemplified in a Series of Figures. 2d ed. London: S. & J. Fuller, 1810. Facsimile reprint. London: Scolar Press, 1977.

History of the Prince Renard and the Lady Goosiana, The. London: H. Fores, 1833. With *The History of the Celebrated Nanny Goose.* London: S. Hood, 1813. Reprint (2 vols. in l). Friends of the Osborne and Lillian H. Smith Collections, Toronto Public Library, 1973.

Hürlimann, Bettina. *Three Centuries of Children's Books in Europe.* Translated and edited by Brian W. Alderson. Cleveland and New York: World Publishing Co., 1968.

Hutchinson, Robert, comp. *1800 Woodcuts by Thomas Bewick and His School.* New York: Dover Publications, 1962.

Infant's Cabinet of Various Objects, The. 2 vols. London: John Marshall, 1801. Reprint Hertfordshire, England: Images Publishers, n.d.

Infant's Grammar, The; or, A Pic-Nic Party of the Parts of Speech. 1st ed. London: Harris & Son, 1824. Facsimile reprint. London: Scolar Press, 1977.

James, Philip. *Children's Books of Yesterday.* Edited by C. Geoffrey Holme. London and New York: Studio, 1933. Reprint. Detroit: Gale Research Co., 1976.

Johnson, Richard. *Juvenile Trials . . .* London: T. Carnan, 1786. Reprint. New preface by Kathryn Dixon. Children's Books from the Past Series, Toronto Public Library. Bern, Switzerland: Herbert Lang, 1973.

Kastner, Joseph. "Everyone Knows Her Rhyme, but Who Remembers Jane?" *Smithsonian* 14 (Oct. 1983):173–86.

Kendall, Guy. *Robert Raikes: A Critical Study.* London: Nicholson & Watson, 1939.

Kerby, W. M. *The Educational Ideas and Activities of Madame la Comtesse de Genlis.* Paris, 1926.

Kramnick, Isaac. "Children's Literature and Bourgeois Ideology: Observations on Culture and Industrial Capitalism in the Later Eighteenth Century." In *Culture and Politics from Puritanism to the Enlightenment,* edited by Perez Zagorin, pp. 203–40. Berkeley: University of California Press, 1980.

Kuhn, Reinhard Clifford. *Corruption in Paradise: The Child in Western Literature.* Hanover, N.H.: University Press of New England for Brown University Press, 1982.

Latham, Jean. *Happy Families: Growing Up in the Eighteenth and Nineteenth Centuries.* London: Adam & Charles Black, 1974.

Lawson, John, and Silver, Harold. *A Social History of Education in England.* London: Methuen, 1973.

Leader, Zachary. *Reading Blake's Songs.* Boston: Routledge & Kegan Paul, 1981.

Leif, Irving P. *Children's Literature: A Historical and Contemporary Bibliography.* Troy, N.Y.: Whitston Publishing Co., 1977.

Life and Death of an Apple Pie, The. London: D. Carvalho, 1825. Reprint. London: Scolar Press, 1978.

Little Rhymes for Little Folks. London: J. Harris, 1823(?). Facsimile reprint. London: Scolar Press, 1977.

Lorence, Bogna W. "Parents and Children in Eighteenth-Century Europe." *The History of Childhood Quarterly* 2 (1974–75):1–30.

Lucas, E. V., ed. *Forgotten Tales of Long Ago.* London: Wells, Gardner, Darton & Co.; New York: F. A. Stokes, 1906

————. *Old Fashioned Tales.* London: Wells, Gardner, Darton & Co., 1905.

Lurie, Alison, and Schiller, Justin G., eds. *Classics of Children's Literature, 1621–1932.* 73 vols. New York: Garland Publishing, 1976–78.

MacDonald, Ruth. *Literature for Children in England and America, 1659–1774.* Troy, N.Y.: Whitston Publishing Co., 1982.

Mahony, Bertha, and Latimer, Louise Payson. *Illustrators of Children's Books, 1744–1945.* Boston: Horn Book, 1947.

Maloney, Margaret Crawford, ed. *Facsimile Editions of Thirty-Five Early English Children's Books from the Osborne Collection, Toronto Public Library.* 35 vols. London: Bodley Head, 1981.

————. *English Illustrated Books for Children: A Descriptive Companion to a Selection from the Osborne Collection.* London: Bodley Head, 1981.

Moon, Marjorie, comp. *John Harris's Books for Youth, 1801–1843: A Check-list.* Cambridge, England: For the compiler in association with Five Owls Press, 1976. Supplement, 1983.

More, Hannah. *Sacred Dramas: Chiefly Intended for Young Persons; the Subjects Taken from the Bible.* London: T. Cadell, 1782. Reprint. New preface by Kathryn A. Howitt. Children's

Books from the Past Series, Toronto Public Library. Bern, Switzerland: Herbert Lang, 1973.

Mother Goose's Melodies. Facsimile edition of the Munroe and Francis "copyright 1833" version, with introduction and bibliographic note by E. F. Bleiler. New York: Dover Publications, 1970.

Mother Goose's Melodies. Facsimile reproduction of the earliest known edition, edited by W. F. Prideaux. London: A. H. Bullen, 1904.

Muir, Percy. *English Children's Books, 1600 to 1900.* London: Batsford, 1954. Reprint. New York: Praeger, 1969.

Mulherin, Jennifer. *Favourite Fairy Tales.* London: Granada, 1982.

_____. *Popular Nursery Rhymes: Mother Goose Rhymes with Explanations and Illustrations.* London: Granada, 1981.

Mure, Eleanor. *The Story of the Three Bears.* Facsimile of the 1831 edition in the Osborne Collection of Early Children's Books, Toronto Public Library. London: Oxford University Press, 1967.

Neuberg, Victor E. *The Penny Histories: A Study of Chapbooks for Young Readers over Two Centuries.* New York: Harcourt, Brace & World, 1968.

_____. *Popular Education in the Eighteenth Century.* London: Woburn Press, 1971.

Noel, Thomas. *Theories of the Fable in the Eighteenth Century.* New York: Columbia University Press, 1975.

Oliver, Grace A. *The Story of the Life of Anna Laetitia Barbauld.* 2d ed. Boston: Cupples, Upham & Co., 1886.

Opie, Iona, and Opie, Peter, eds. *The Classic Fairy Tales.* New York: Oxford University Press, 1974.

_____. *A Nursery Companion.* Oxford: Oxford University Press, 1980.

_____. *The Oxford Dictionary of Nursery Rhymes.* Oxford: Clarendon Press, 1952.

_____. *Three Centuries of Nursery Rhymes and Poetry for Children.* 2d ed., rev. and exp. Oxford: Oxford University Press, 1977.

Opie, Peter. "John Newbery and His Successors." *Book Collector* 24 (Summer 1975):259–69.

Original Mother Goose's Melody, The, as First Issued by John Newbery of London. Albany: Joel Munsell's Sons, 1889. Reprint. Detroit: Singing Tree Press, 1969.

Palmer, Melvin D. "Madame d'Aulnoy in England." *Comparative Literature* 27 (1975):237–53.

Palmer, Nancy, and Palmer, Melvin. "English Editions of the French *Contes de Fées* Attributed to Mme. d'Aulnoy." *Studies in Bibliography* 27 (1974):227–32.

Patterson, Sylvia. "Eighteenth-Century Children's Literature in England: A Mirror of Its Culture." *Journal of Popular Culture* 13 (Summer 1979):38–43.

_____. *Rousseau's Émile and Early Children's Literature.* Metuchen, N.J.: Scarecrow Press, 1971.

Pellowski, Anne. *The World of Children's Literature.* New York and London: R.R. Bowker Co., 1968.

Perrault, Charles. *Perrault's Tales of Mother Goose: The Dedication Manuscript of 1695.* Reproduced in colotype facsimile, with introduction and critical text by Jacques Barchilon. New York: Pierpont Morgan Library, 1956.

Pickering, Samuel, Jr. "Children's Books in Eighteenth-Century England." *AB Bookman's Weekly,* Nov. 16, 1981, pp. 3392–406.

_____. "Cozen'd into a Knowledge of the Letters: Eighteenth-Century Alphabetical Game Books." *Research Studies* 46 (Dec. 1978):223–36.

_____. "The Evolution of a Genre: Fictional Biographies for Children in the Eighteenth Century." *Journal of Narrative Technique* 7 (Winter 1977):1–23.

_____. *John Locke and Children's Books in Eighteenth-Century England.* Knoxville: University of Tennessee Press, 1981.

_____. "Mrs. Barbauld's *Hymns in Prose:* 'An Air-Blown Particle of Romanticism'?" *Southern Humanities Review,* Summer 1975, pp. 259–68.

_____. "Rousseau's Reputation in Britain." *Research Studies* 41 (1973):268–77.

Pitcher, E.W. "Anthologized Fiction for the Juvenile Reader, 1700–1800." *The Library, Transactions of the Bibliographic Society* (London) 6th ser. 3 (July 1981):132–41.

Plumb, J.H. "The New World of Children in Eighteenth-Century England." *Past and Present,* no. 67 (May 1975), pp. 64–93.

Polite Academy, The; or, School of Behaviour for Young Gentlemen and Ladies. London: R. Baldwin & B. Collins, 1765. Reprint. New preface by Linda Sibbald. Children's Books from the Past Series, Toronto Public Library. Bern, Switzerland: Herbert Lang, 1973.

Present for a Little Boy, A. London, 1797. Reprint. London: Norman-Stahli, 1969.

Present for a Little Girl, A. London, 1797. Reprint. London: Norman-Stahli, 1966.

Quayle, Eric. *The Collector's Book of Children's Books.* New York: Clarkson N. Potter, 1971.

Richardson, Selma K., ed. "The Study and Collecting of Historical Children's Books." *Library Trends* 27, no. 4 (Spring 1979).

Riehl, Joseph E. *Charles Lamb's Children's Literature.* Atlantic Highlands, N.J.: Humanities Press, 1980.

Roddier, Henri. *J.-J. Rousseau en Angleterre au xviii᷊ siècle: l'oeuvre et l'homme.* Paris: Boivin & Co., n.d.

Roscoe, S., and Brimmell, R. A. *James Lumsden and Son of Glasgow: Their Juvenile Books and Chapbooks.* Pinner, England: Private Libraries Association, 1981.

Rosenbach, A.S.W. *Early American Children's Books.* Portland, Me.: Southworth Press, 1933. Reprint. Gloucester, Mass.: Peter Smith, 1971.

St. John, Judith, comp. and ed. *The Osborne Collection of Early Children's Books: A Catalogue.* 2 vols. Toronto: University of Toronto Press, 1958, 1975.

Sale, Roger. *Fairy Tales and After: From Snow White to E. B. White.* Cambridge: Harvard University Press, 1978.

Salway, Lance. *A Peculiar Gift: Nineteenth-Century Writings on Books for Children.* Harmondsworth, England: Kestrel Books, 1976.

Sanders, Jean Butler. "Madame de Genlis and Juvenile Fiction in England." *Dissertation Abstracts* 26 (1965):3936.

Sangster, Paul. *Pity My Simplicity: The Evangelical Revival and the Religious Education of Children, 1738–1800.* London: Epworth Press, 1963.

Schiller, Justin G. "Artistic Awareness in Early Children's Books." *Children's Literature* 3 (1974):177–85.

_____. *Realms of Childhood: A Selection of 200 Important Historical Children's Books.* Catalogue 41. New York: Justin G. Schiller, 1983.

Slack, Mrs. Thomas, ed. *The Pleasing Instructor . . .* London: G. G. J. & J. Robinson, 1785. Reprint. New preface by Joanne Graham. Children's Books from the Past Series, Toronto Public Library. Bern, Switzerland: Herbert Lang, 1973.

Smith, Elva S. *The History of Children's Literature: A Syllabus with Selected Bibliographies.* Revised and enlarged by Margaret Hodges and Susan Steinfirst. Chicago: American Library Association, 1980.

Stewart, Christina Duff, ed. *Ann Taylor Gilbert's Album, with an Introduction and Biographical Notes.* New York and London: Garland Publishing, 1978.

Stone, Wilbur Macey. "The History of Little Goody Two-Shoes." *American Antiquarian Society Proceedings* 49 (Oct. 1939):333–70.

Stops, Mr. [pseud.]. *Punctuation Personified; or, Pointing Made Easy.* London: John Harris & Son, 1824. Reprint. London: Scolar Press, 1979.

Thwaite, Mary F. *From Primer to Pleasure in Reading.* 1st Amer. ed. Boston: Horn Book, 1972.

Todd, Janet. *Mary Wollstonecraft: An Annotated Bibliography.* New York: Garland Publishing, 1976.

Trigon, Jean de. *Histoire de la littérature enfantine de Ma Mère l'Oye au Roi Babar.* Paris: Libraire Hachette, 1950.

Tuer, Andrew White, ed. *Pages and Pictures from Forgotten Children's Books . . .* London: Leadenhall Press, 1898–99. Reprint. New York: Dover Publications, 1971.

———. *Stories from Old-Fashioned Children's Books.* London: Leadenhall Press, 1899–1900. Reprint. London: Evelyn, Adams & Mackay, 1969.

Walvin, James. *A Child's World: A Social History of English Childhood, 1800–1914.* Harmondsworth, England: Penguin Books, 1982.

Watts, Isaac. *Divine Songs Attempted in Easy Language for the Use of Children.* Facsimile reprint of the 1715 1st edition, with introduction and bibliography by J. H. P. Pafford. London: Oxford University Press, 1971.

Weedon, M. J. P. *Richard Johnson and the Successors to John Newbery.* London: Bibliographical Society, 1949.

Welch, d'Alté A. *A Bibliography of American Children's Books Printed Prior to 1821.* Worcester, Mass: American Antiquarian Society, 1972.

Welsh, Charles. *A Bookseller of the Last Century, Being Some Accounts of the Life of John Newbery.* London: Griffith, Farran, 1885. Reprint. Clifton, N.J.: Augustus M. Kelley Publishers, 1975.

West, Katharine. *Chapter of Governesses: A Study of the Governess in English Fiction, 1800–1949.* London: Cohen & West, 1949.

Whalley, Joyce Irene. *Cobwebs to Catch Flies: Illustrated Books for the Nursery and Schoolroom, 1700–1900.* Berkeley and Los Angeles: University of California Press, 1975.

Wollstonecraft, Mary. *Original Stories from Real Life.* London, 1788. New York: Folcroft Library Editions, 1972.